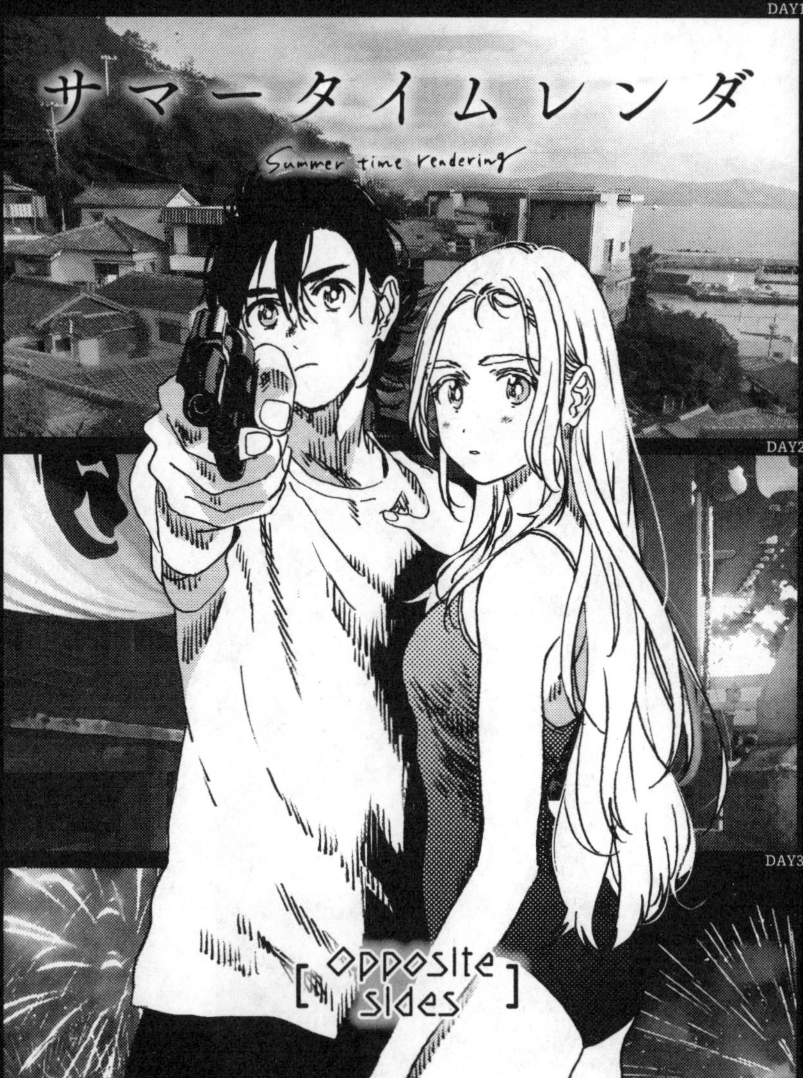
DAY1
サマータイムレンダ
Summer time rendering
DAY2
DAY3
[opposite sides]

田中靖規
TANAKA YASUKI

MEMO#016 TACHIBANA

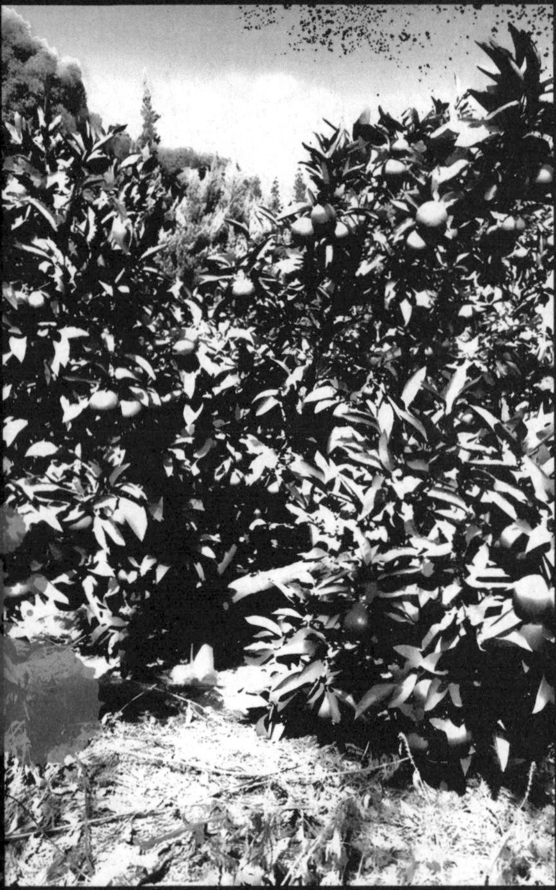

TACHIBANA (橘)

The tree that was planted in Hishigata Clinic's yard.

Tachibana is the original species of mandarin orange and they are native to Wakayama and commonly seen on Hitogashima.

According to the old folklore, the leaves of the tree are likened to eternity, and the fruits are useful as an eternal medicine which was called "tokijikunokagunokonomi" (非時香菓) for immortality.

The actual tachibana fruit is strongly acidic and it's not suitable for raw consumption. It's processed into jam and eaten that way.

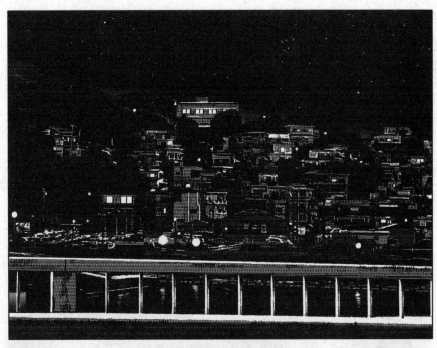

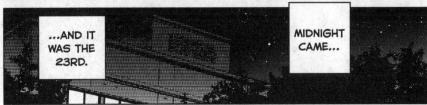

MIDNIGHT CAME...
...AND IT WAS THE 23RD.
JULY 23
BEEP
7/23 月
27.5 °C
60 %

*CLOCK = 7/23 MONDAY / TEMPERATURE: 27.5 DEGREES CELSIUS = 81.5 DEGREES FAHRENHEIT / HUMIDITY: 60%

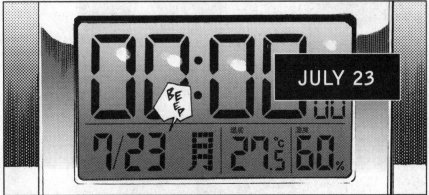

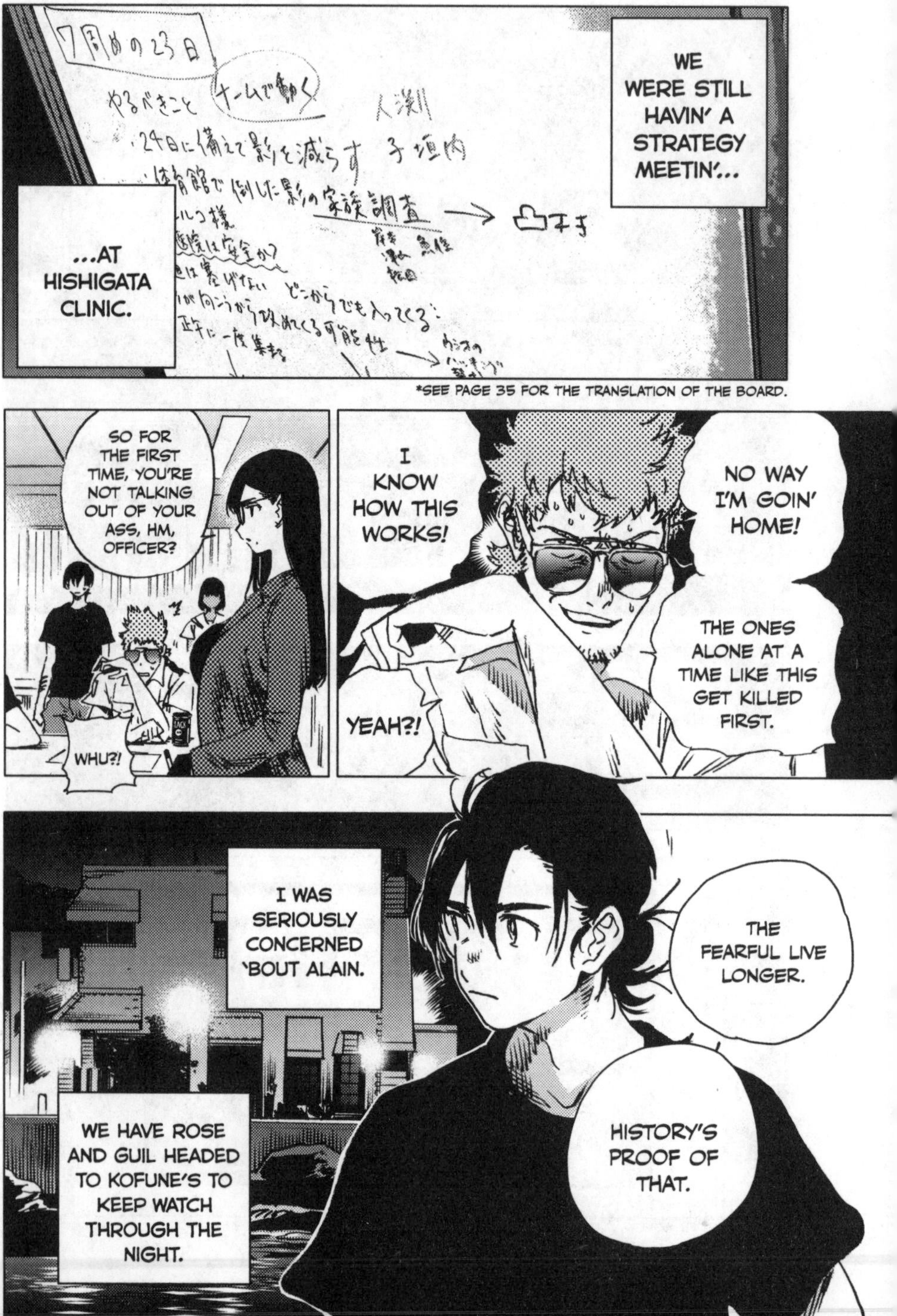
WE WERE STILL HAVIN' A STRATEGY MEETIN'...
...AT HISHIGATA CLINIC.
*SEE PAGE 35 FOR THE TRANSLATION OF THE BOARD.
NO WAY I'M GOIN' HOME!
I KNOW HOW THIS WORKS!
THE ONES ALONE AT A TIME LIKE THIS GET KILLED FIRST.
YEAH?!
SO FOR THE FIRST TIME, YOU'RE NOT TALKING OUT OF YOUR ASS, HM, OFFICER?
WHU?!
THE FEARFUL LIVE LONGER.
I WAS SERIOUSLY CONCERNED 'BOUT ALAIN.
HISTORY'S PROOF OF THAT.
WE HAVE ROSE AND GUIL HEADED TO KOFUNE'S TO KEEP WATCH THROUGH THE NIGHT.

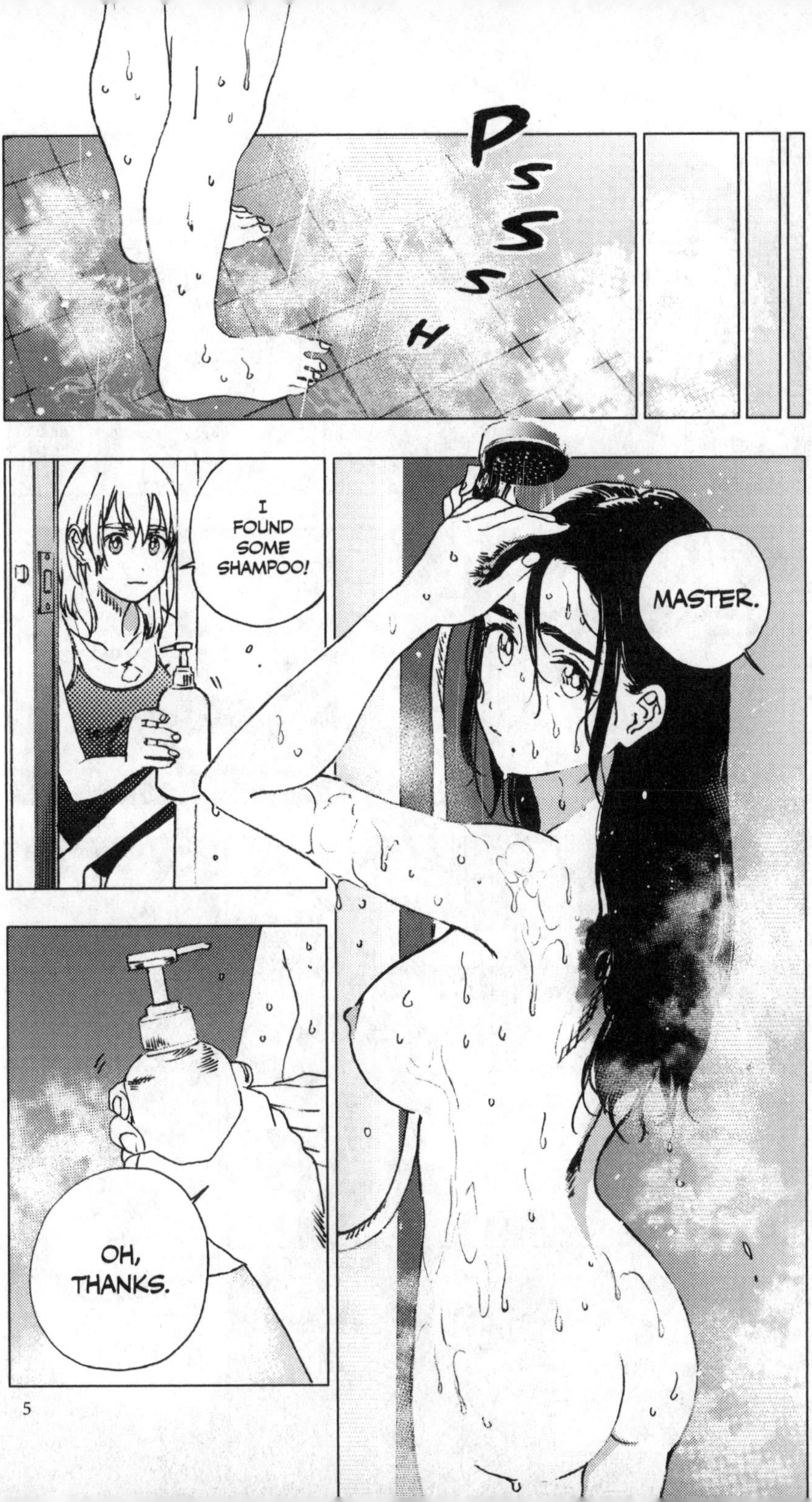
PSSSH
MASTER.
I FOUND SOME SHAMPOO!
OH, THANKS.

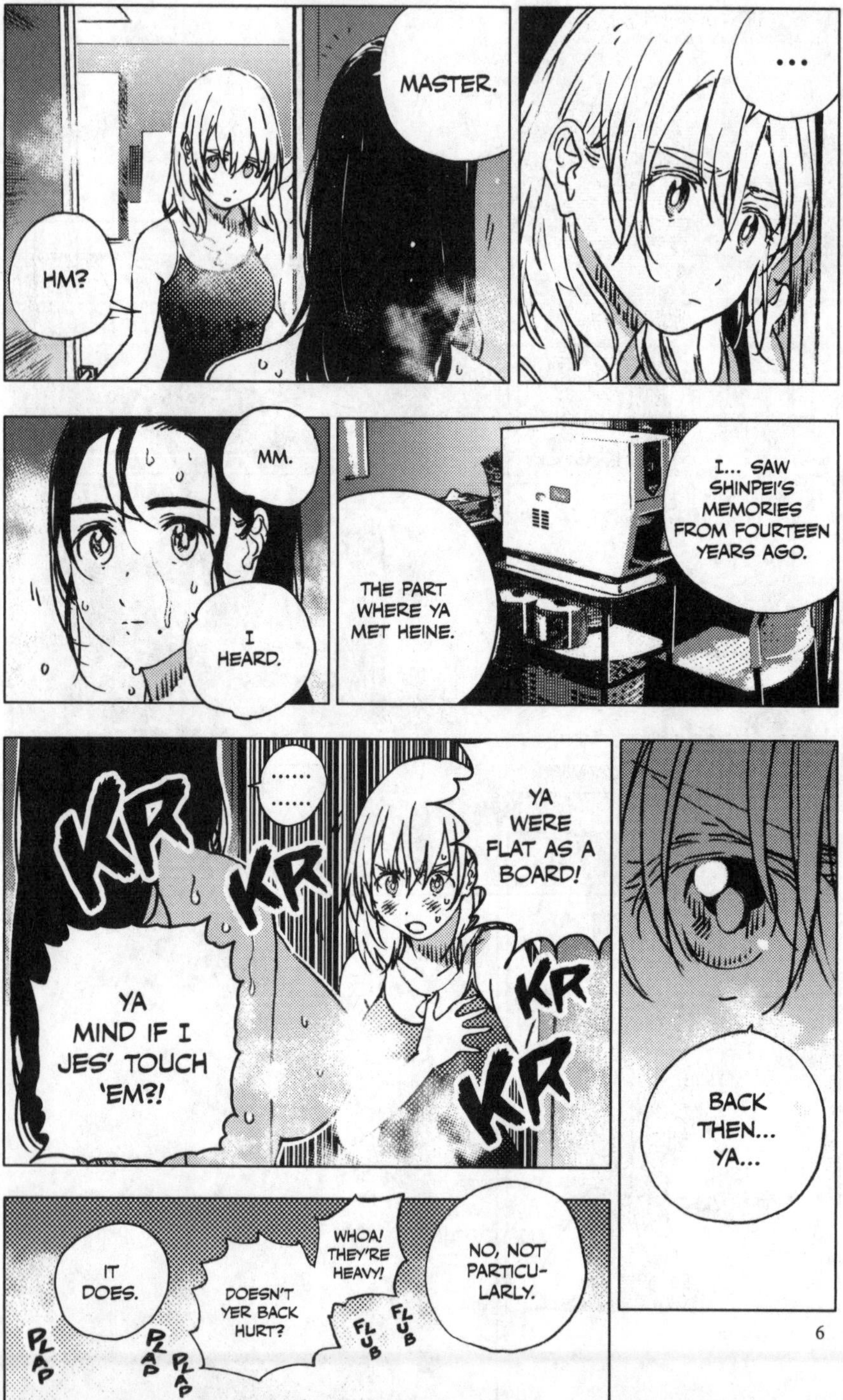
...
MASTER.
HM?
I... SAW SHINPEI'S MEMORIES FROM FOURTEEN YEARS AGO.
THE PART WHERE YA MET HEINE.
MM.
I HEARD.
BACK THEN... YA...
YA WERE FLAT AS A BOARD!
KR KR
KR KR
......
......
KR
KR
YA MIND IF I JES' TOUCH 'EM?!
NO, NOT PARTICU-LARLY.
FLUB FLUB
WHOA! THEY'RE HEAVY!
DOESN'T YER BACK HURT?
IT DOES.
PLAP PLAP PLAP

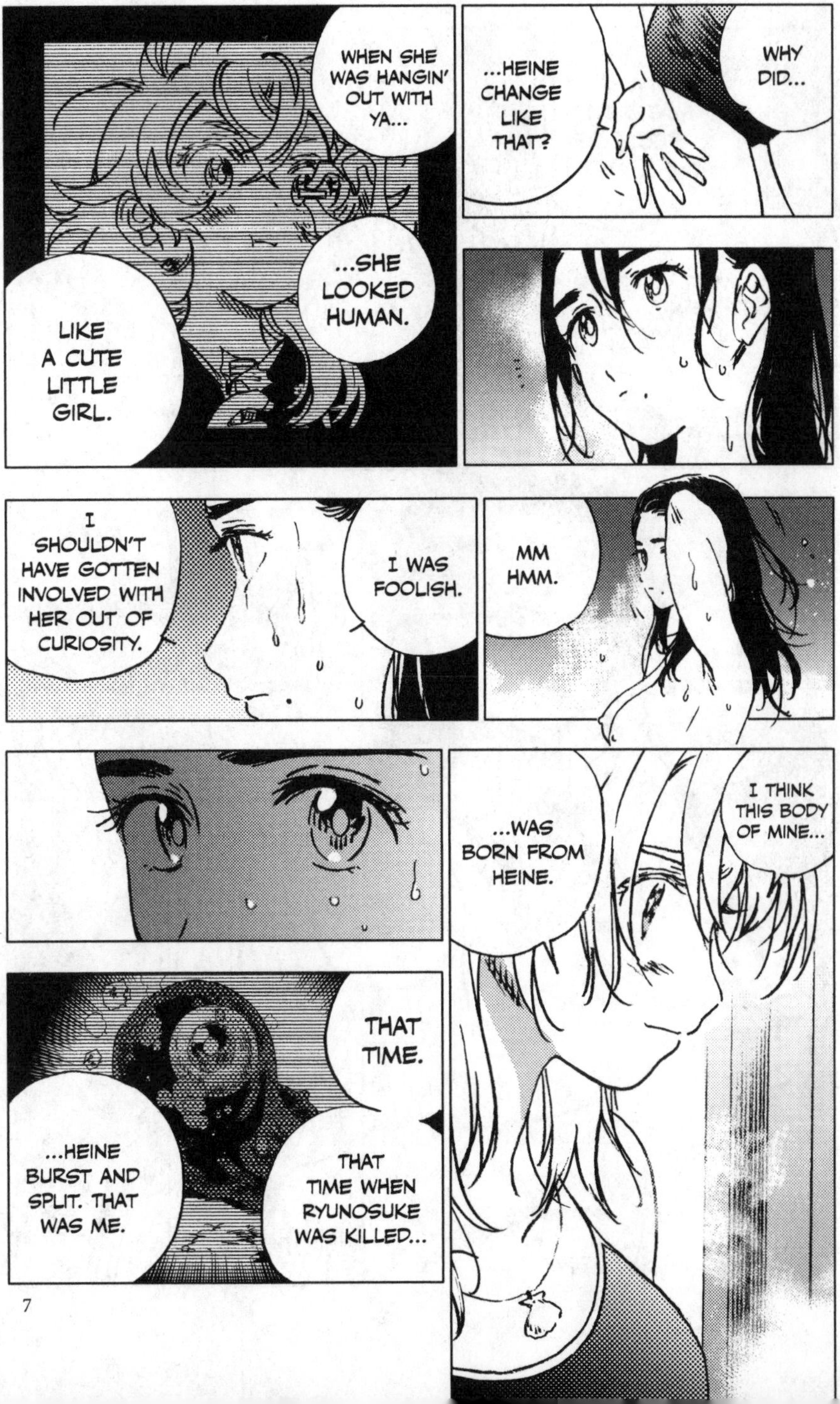
WHY DID...
...HEINE CHANGE LIKE THAT?
WHEN SHE WAS HANGIN' OUT WITH YA...
...SHE LOOKED HUMAN.
LIKE A CUTE LITTLE GIRL.
MM HMM.
I WAS FOOLISH.
I SHOULDN'T HAVE GOTTEN INVOLVED WITH HER OUT OF CURIOSITY.
I THINK THIS BODY OF MINE...
...WAS BORN FROM HEINE.
THAT TIME.
THAT TIME WHEN RYUNOSUKE WAS KILLED...
...HEINE BURST AND SPLIT. THAT WAS ME.

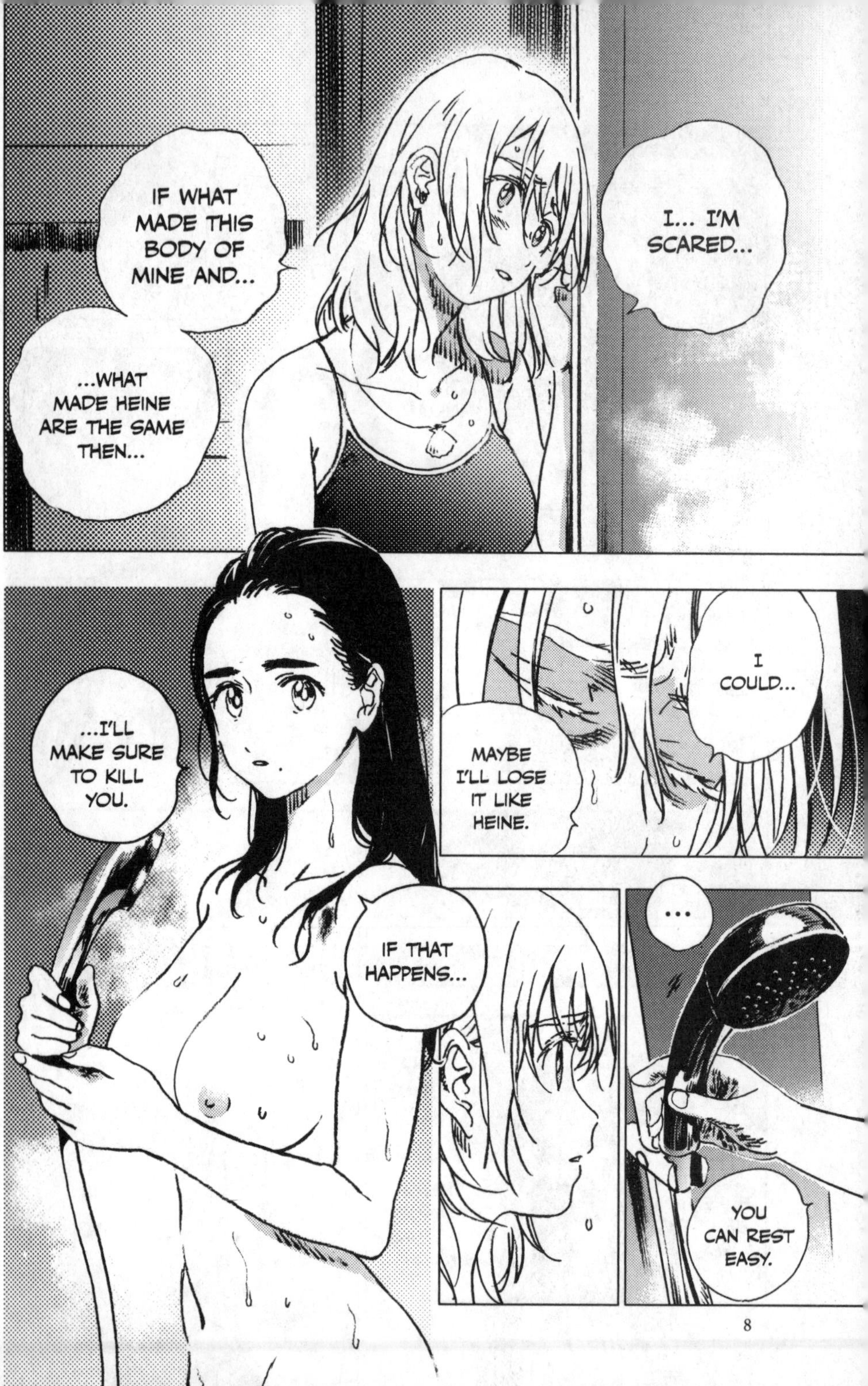
I... I'M SCARED...
IF WHAT MADE THIS BODY OF MINE AND...
...WHAT MADE HEINE ARE THE SAME THEN...
I COULD...
MAYBE I'LL LOSE IT LIKE HEINE.
...
YOU CAN REST EASY.
IF THAT HAPPENS...
...I'LL MAKE SURE TO KILL YOU.

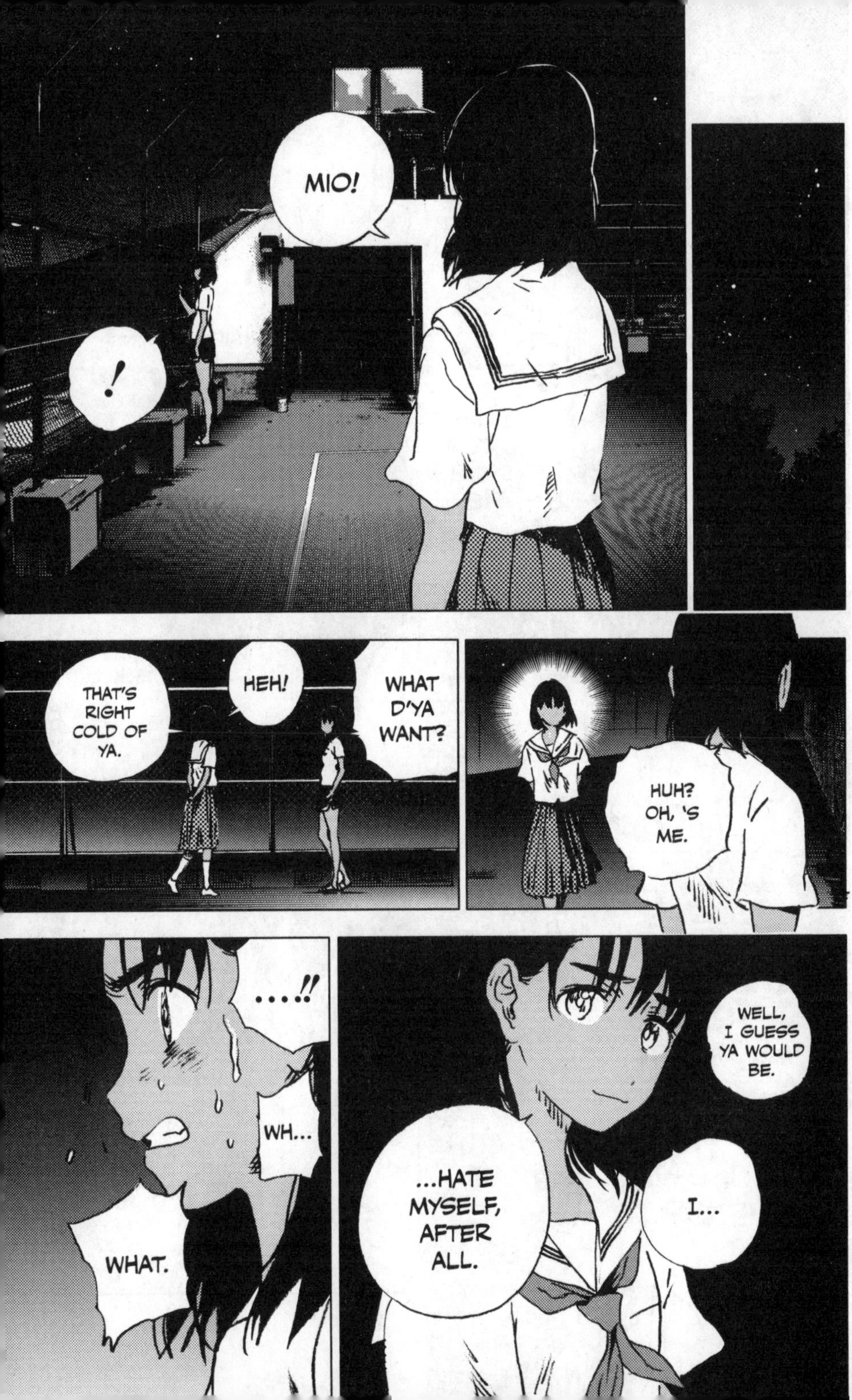
MIO!
!
HUH? OH, 'S ME.
WHAT D'YA WANT?
HEH!
THAT'S RIGHT COLD OF YA.
WELL, I GUESS YA WOULD BE.
I...
...HATE MYSELF, AFTER ALL.
....!!
WH...
WHAT.

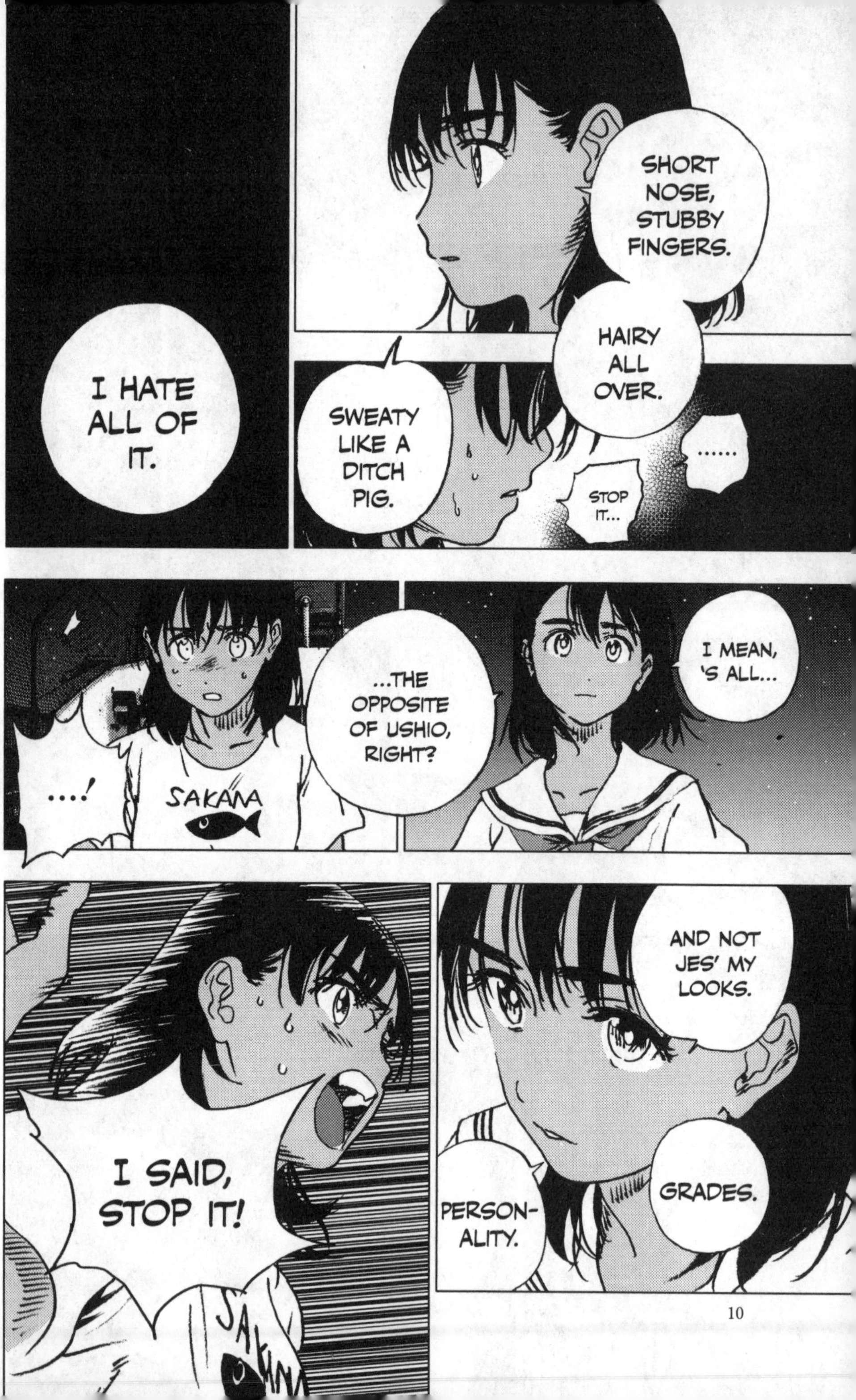
SHORT NOSE, STUBBY FINGERS.
HAIRY ALL OVER.
......
SWEATY LIKE A DITCH PIG.
STOP IT...
I HATE ALL OF IT.
I MEAN, 'S ALL...
...THE OPPOSITE OF USHIO, RIGHT?
...!
SAKANA
AND NOT JES' MY LOOKS.
GRADES.
PERSON-ALITY.
I SAID, STOP IT!

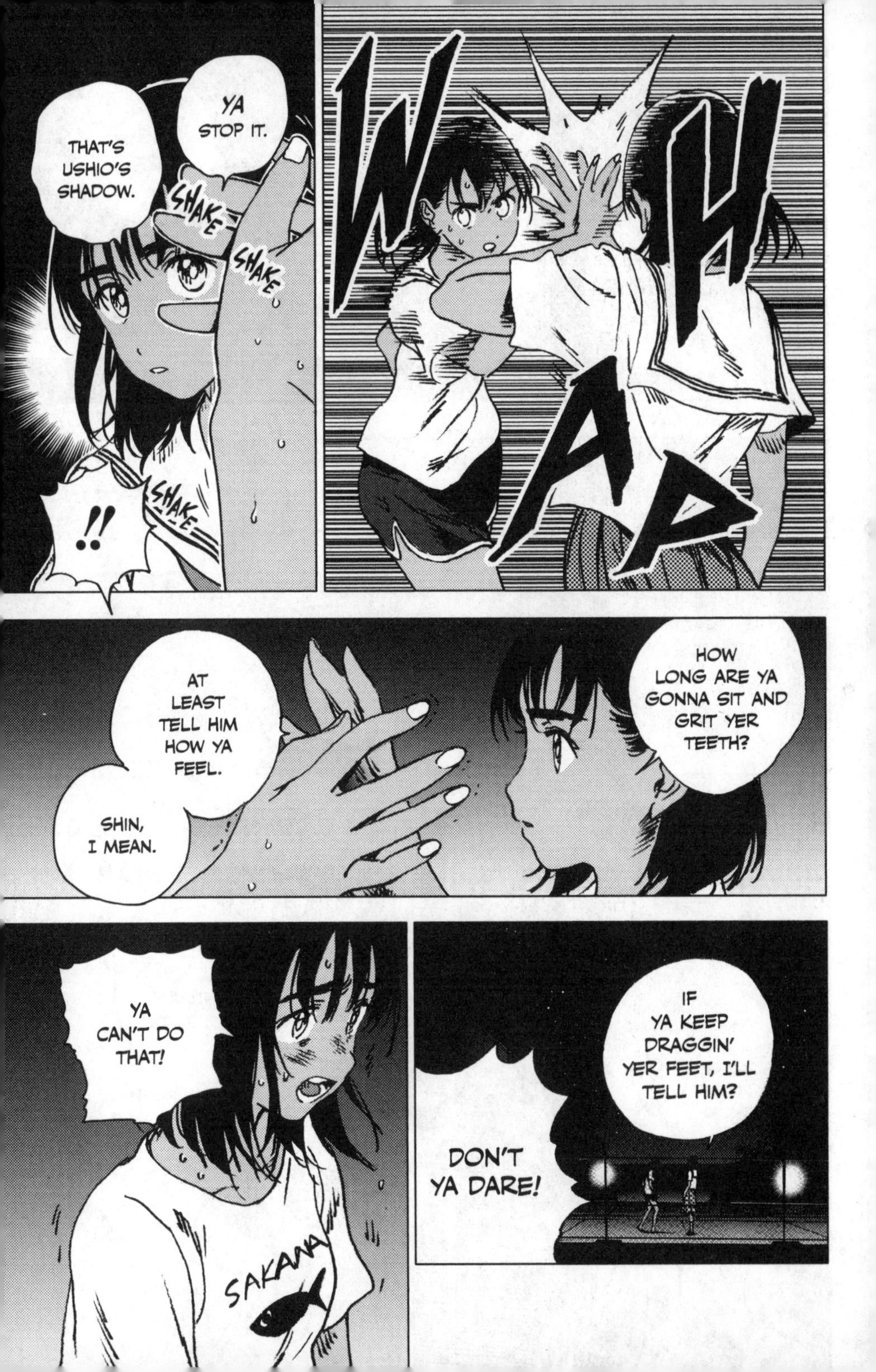
WHAP
YA STOP IT.
THAT'S USHIO'S SHADOW.
SHAKE
SHAKE
SHAKE
!!
HOW LONG ARE YA GONNA SIT AND GRIT YER TEETH?
AT LEAST TELL HIM HOW YA FEEL.
SHIN, I MEAN.
IF YA KEEP DRAGGIN' YER FEET, I'LL TELL HIM?
DON'T YA DARE!
YA CAN'T DO THAT!
SAKANA

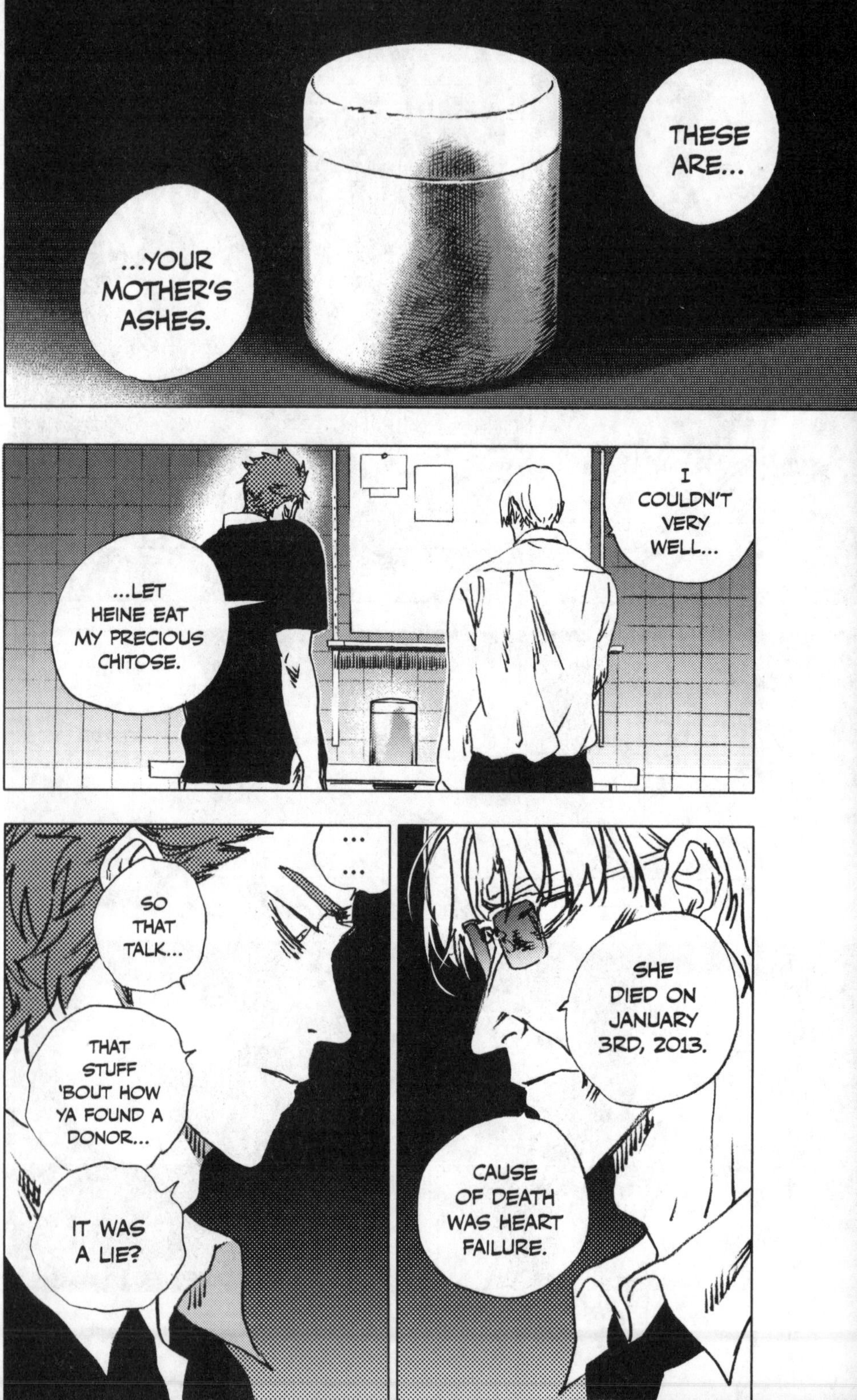
THESE ARE...
...YOUR MOTHER'S ASHES.
I COULDN'T VERY WELL...
...LET HEINE EAT MY PRECIOUS CHITOSE.
SHE DIED ON JANUARY 3RD, 2013.
CAUSE OF DEATH WAS HEART FAILURE.
...
...
SO THAT TALK...
THAT STUFF 'BOUT HOW YA FOUND A DONOR...
IT WAS A LIE?

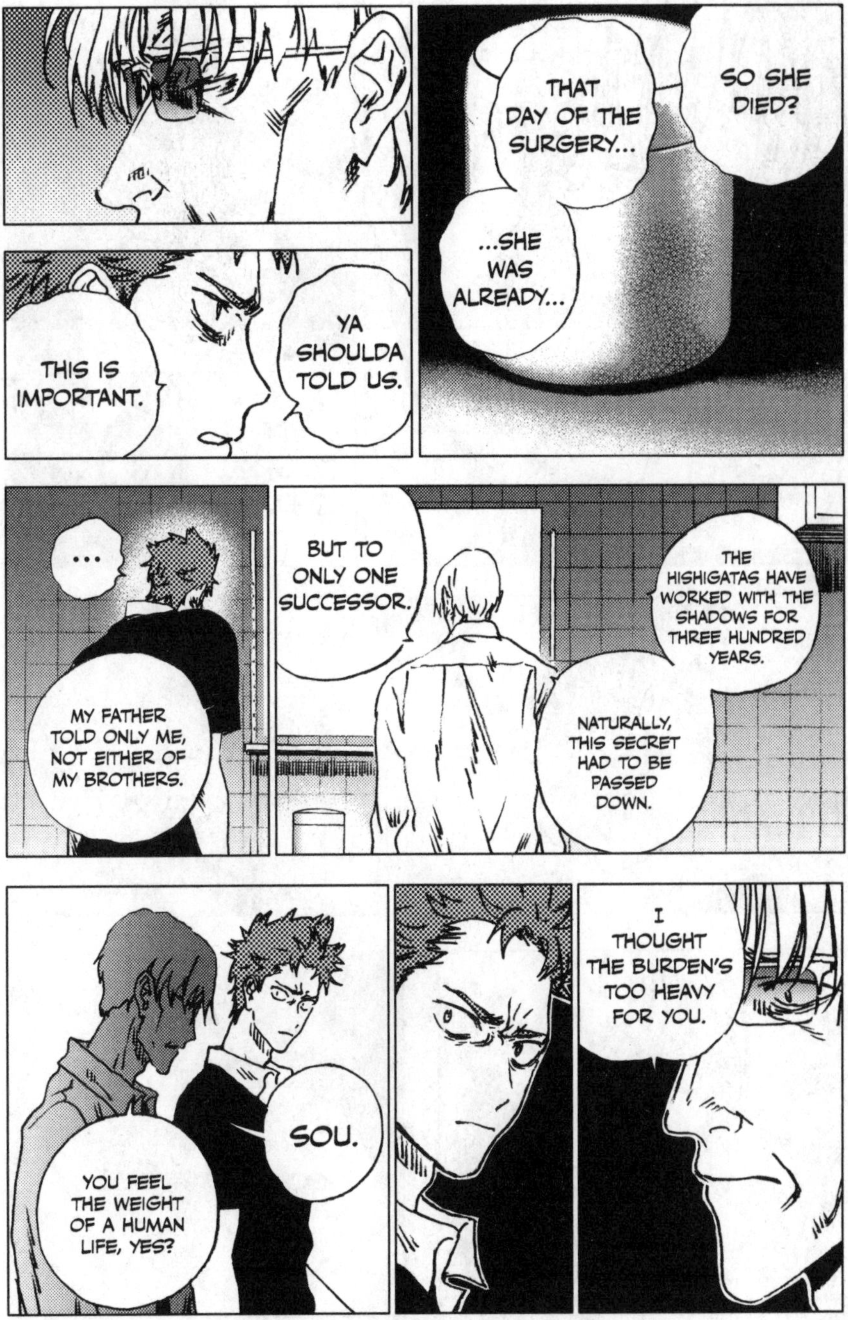
SO SHE DIED?
THAT DAY OF THE SURGERY...
...SHE WAS ALREADY...
YA SHOULDA TOLD US.
THIS IS IMPORTANT.
THE HISHIGATAS HAVE WORKED WITH THE SHADOWS FOR THREE HUNDRED YEARS.
NATURALLY, THIS SECRET HAD TO BE PASSED DOWN.
BUT TO ONLY ONE SUCCESSOR.
...
MY FATHER TOLD ONLY ME, NOT EITHER OF MY BROTHERS.
I THOUGHT THE BURDEN'S TOO HEAVY FOR YOU.
SOU.
YOU FEEL THE WEIGHT OF A HUMAN LIFE, YES?

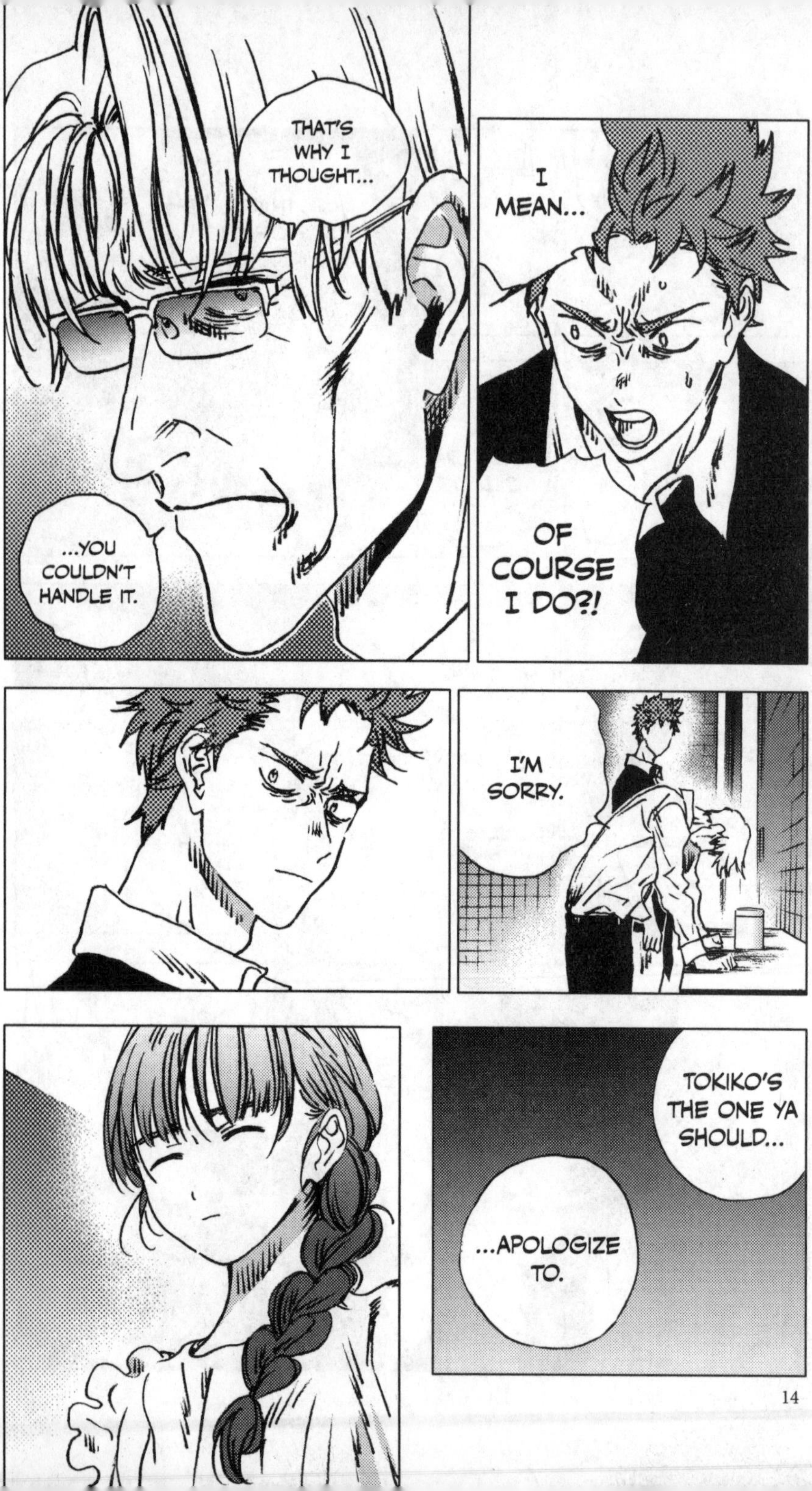
I MEAN...
OF COURSE I DO?!
THAT'S WHY I THOUGHT...
...YOU COULDN'T HANDLE IT.
I'M SORRY.
TOKIKO'S THE ONE YA SHOULD...
...APOLOGIZE TO.

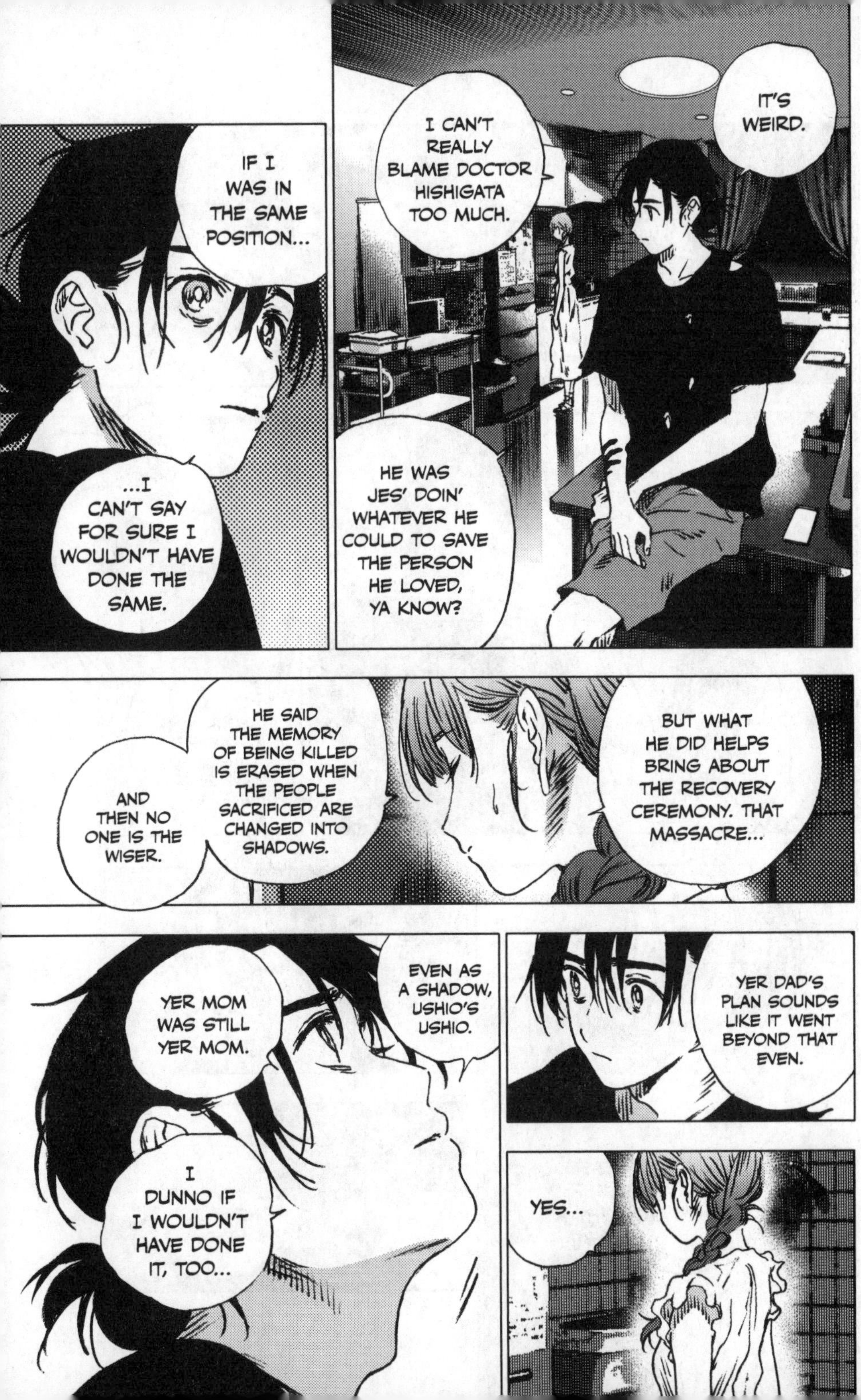
IT'S WEIRD.
I CAN'T REALLY BLAME DOCTOR HISHIGATA TOO MUCH.
HE WAS JES' DOIN' WHATEVER HE COULD TO SAVE THE PERSON HE LOVED, YA KNOW?
IF I WAS IN THE SAME POSITION...
...I CAN'T SAY FOR SURE I WOULDN'T HAVE DONE THE SAME.
BUT WHAT HE DID HELPS BRING ABOUT THE RECOVERY CEREMONY. THAT MASSACRE...
HE SAID THE MEMORY OF BEING KILLED IS ERASED WHEN THE PEOPLE SACRIFICED ARE CHANGED INTO SHADOWS.
AND THEN NO ONE IS THE WISER.
YER DAD'S PLAN SOUNDS LIKE IT WENT BEYOND THAT EVEN.
YES...
EVEN AS A SHADOW, USHIO'S USHIO.
YER MOM WAS STILL YER MOM.
I DUNNO IF I WOULDN'T HAVE DONE IT, TOO...

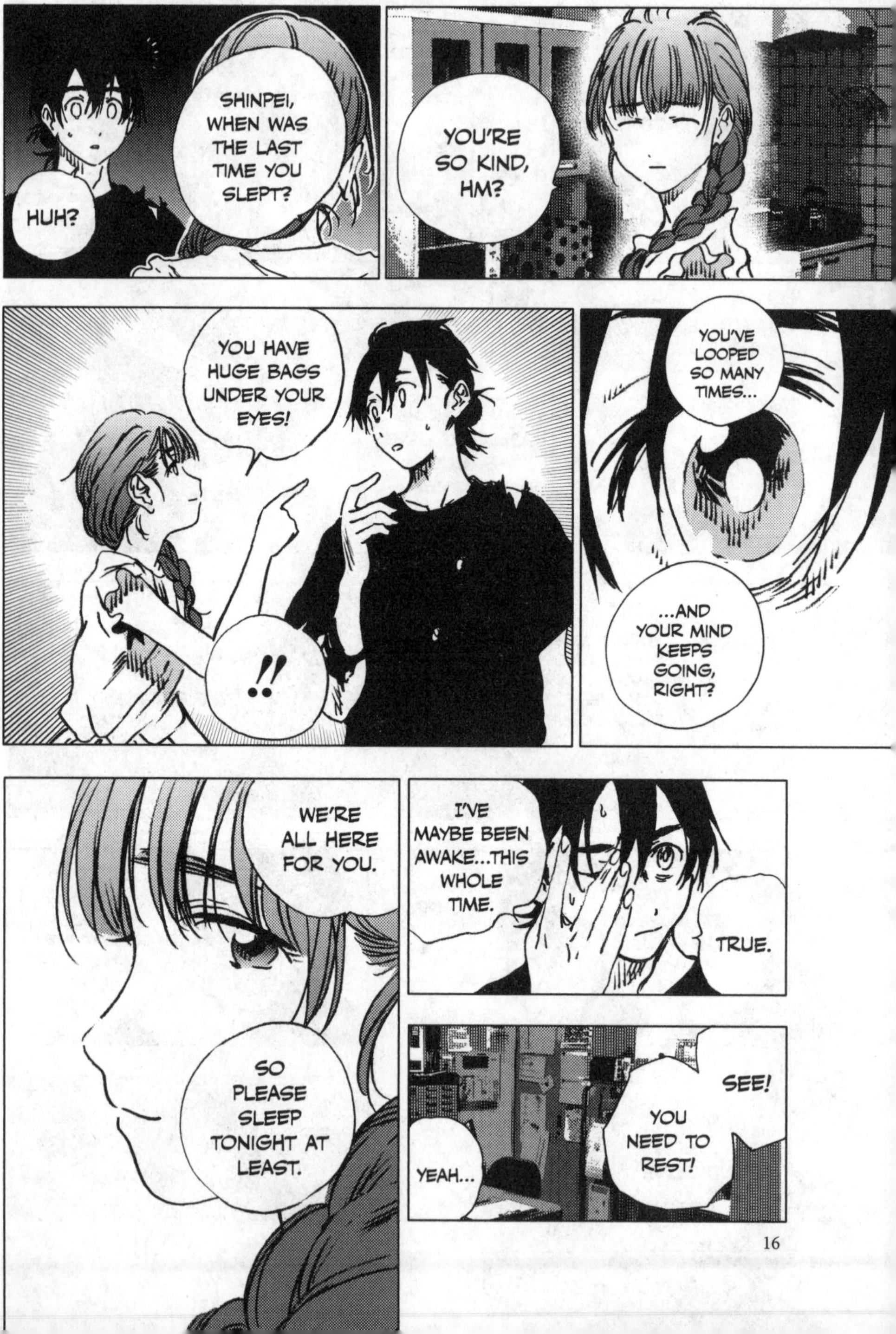
YOU'RE SO KIND, HM?
SHINPEI, WHEN WAS THE LAST TIME YOU SLEPT?
HUH?
YOU'VE LOOPED SO MANY TIMES...
...AND YOUR MIND KEEPS GOING, RIGHT?
YOU HAVE HUGE BAGS UNDER YOUR EYES!
!!
TRUE.
I'VE MAYBE BEEN AWAKE...THIS WHOLE TIME.
SEE!
YOU NEED TO REST!
YEAH...
WE'RE ALL HERE FOR YOU.
SO PLEASE SLEEP TONIGHT AT LEAST.

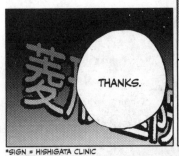

THANKS.

TOKI'S RIGHT.

THROB

THROB

I MIGHT NOT GET ANOTHER CHANCE TO REST.

SNRR

SNRR

MPH...

KYAK

SNAAR

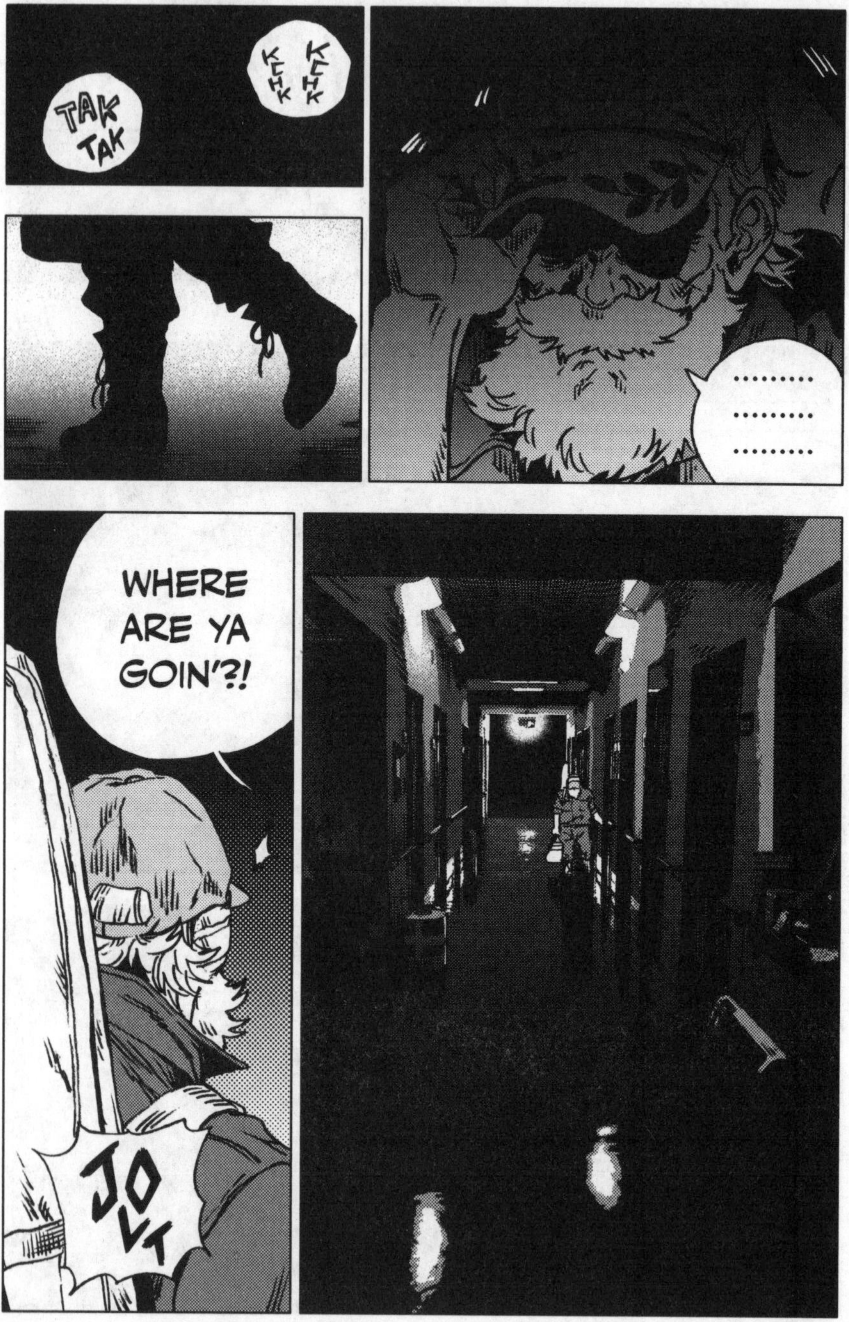
....
....
....
KCHK KCHK
TAK TAK
WHERE ARE YA GOIN'?!
JOLT

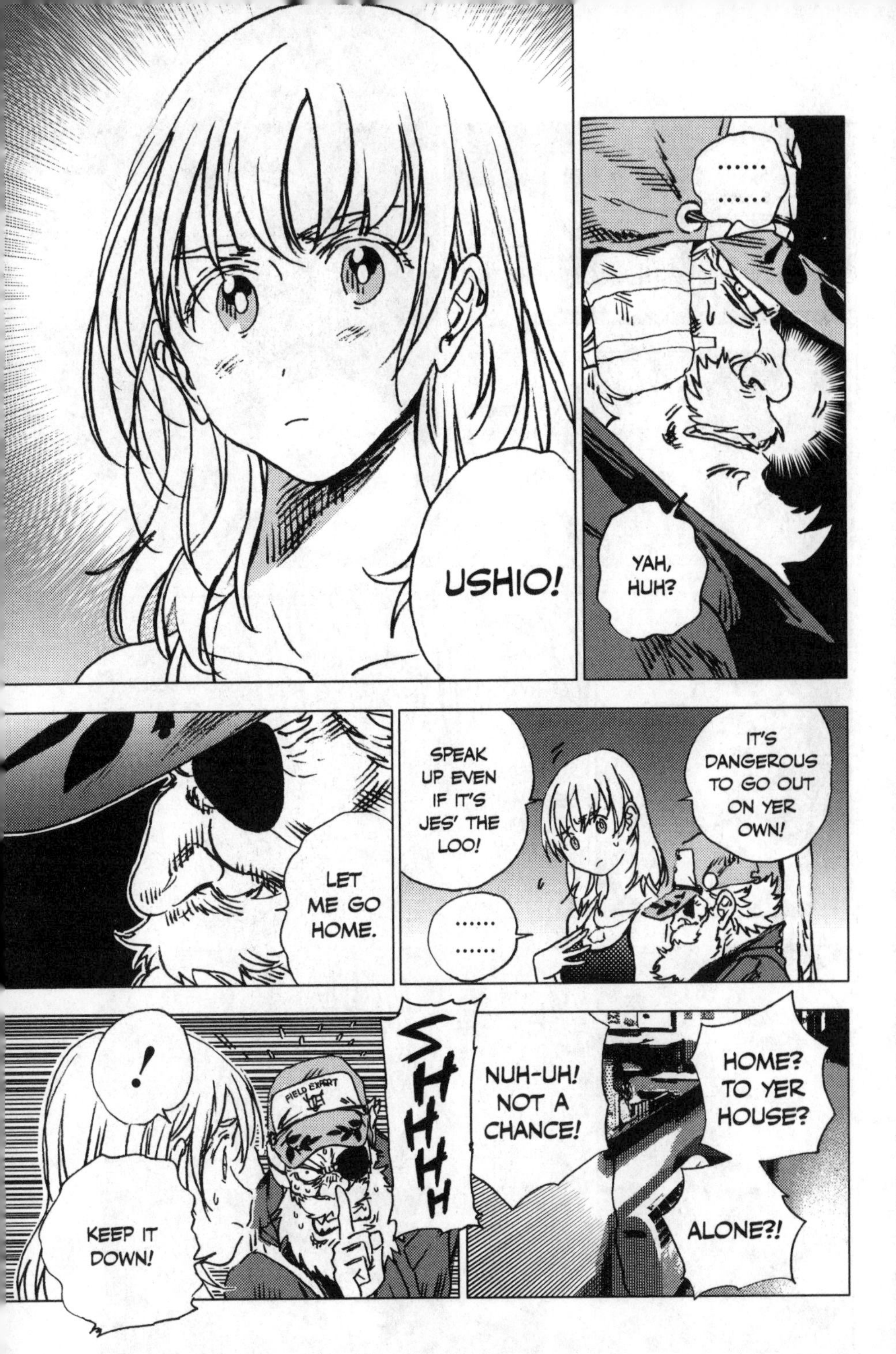

......
......
YAH, HUH?
USHIO!
IT'S DANGEROUS TO GO OUT ON YER OWN!
SPEAK UP EVEN IF IT'S JES' THE LOO!
......
......
LET ME GO HOME.
HOME? TO YER HOUSE?
ALONE?!
NUH-UH! NOT A CHANCE!
SHHHH
FIELD EXPERT
!
KEEP IT DOWN!

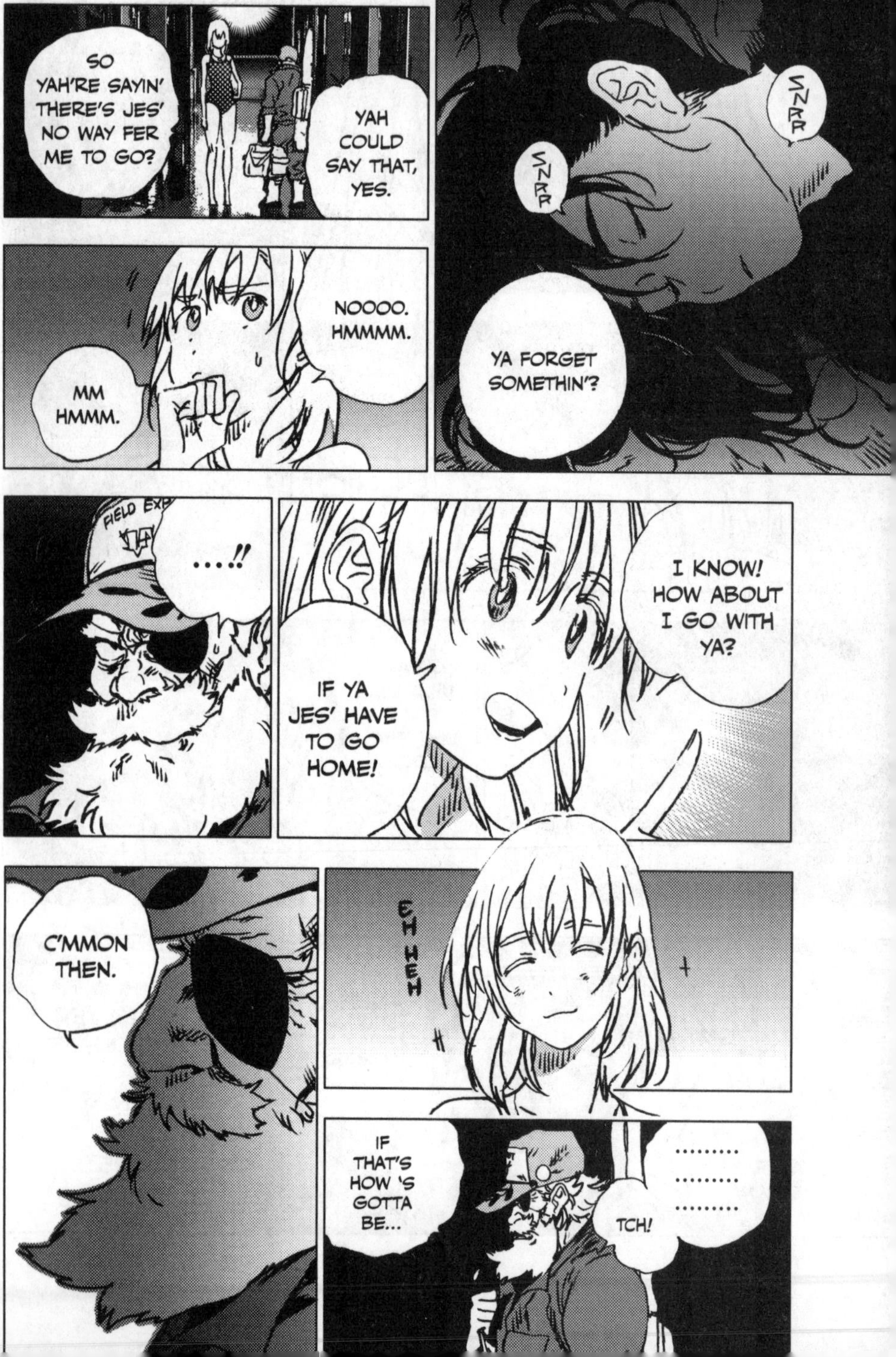
SNRR
SNRR
YA FORGET SOMETHIN'?
SO YAH'RE SAYIN' THERE'S JES' NO WAY FER ME TO GO?
YAH COULD SAY THAT, YES.
NOOOO. HMMMM.
MM HMMM.
I KNOW! HOW ABOUT I GO WITH YA?
IF YA JES' HAVE TO GO HOME!
....!!
EH HEH
....
....
....
TCH!
IF THAT'S HOW 'S GOTTA BE...
C'MMON THEN.

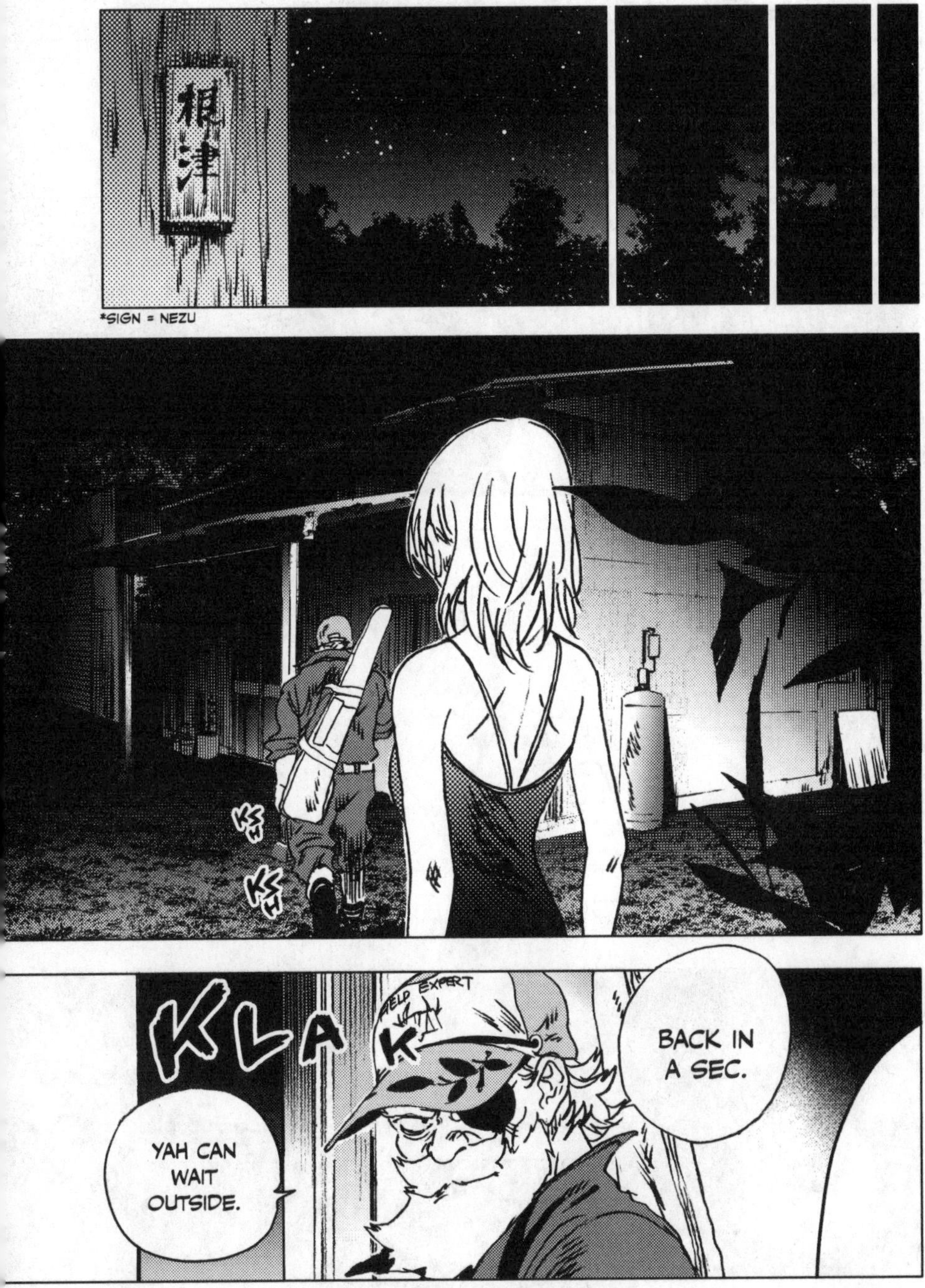
根津
*SIGN = NEZU
KSH
KSH
BACK IN A SEC.
KLAK
YAH CAN WAIT OUTSIDE.

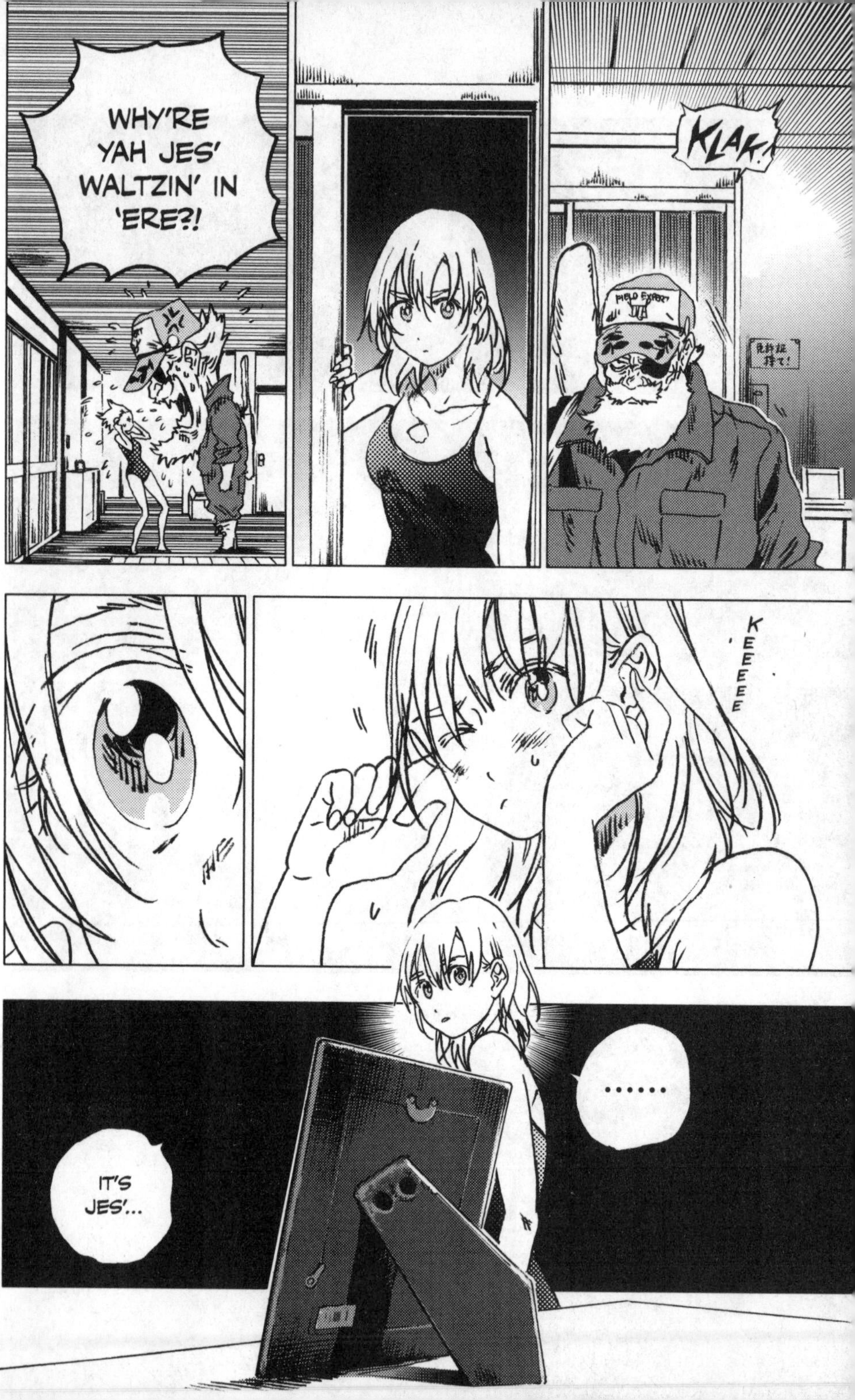
KLAK!
WHY'RE YAH JES' WALTZIN' IN 'ERE?!
KEEEEE
......
IT'S JES'...

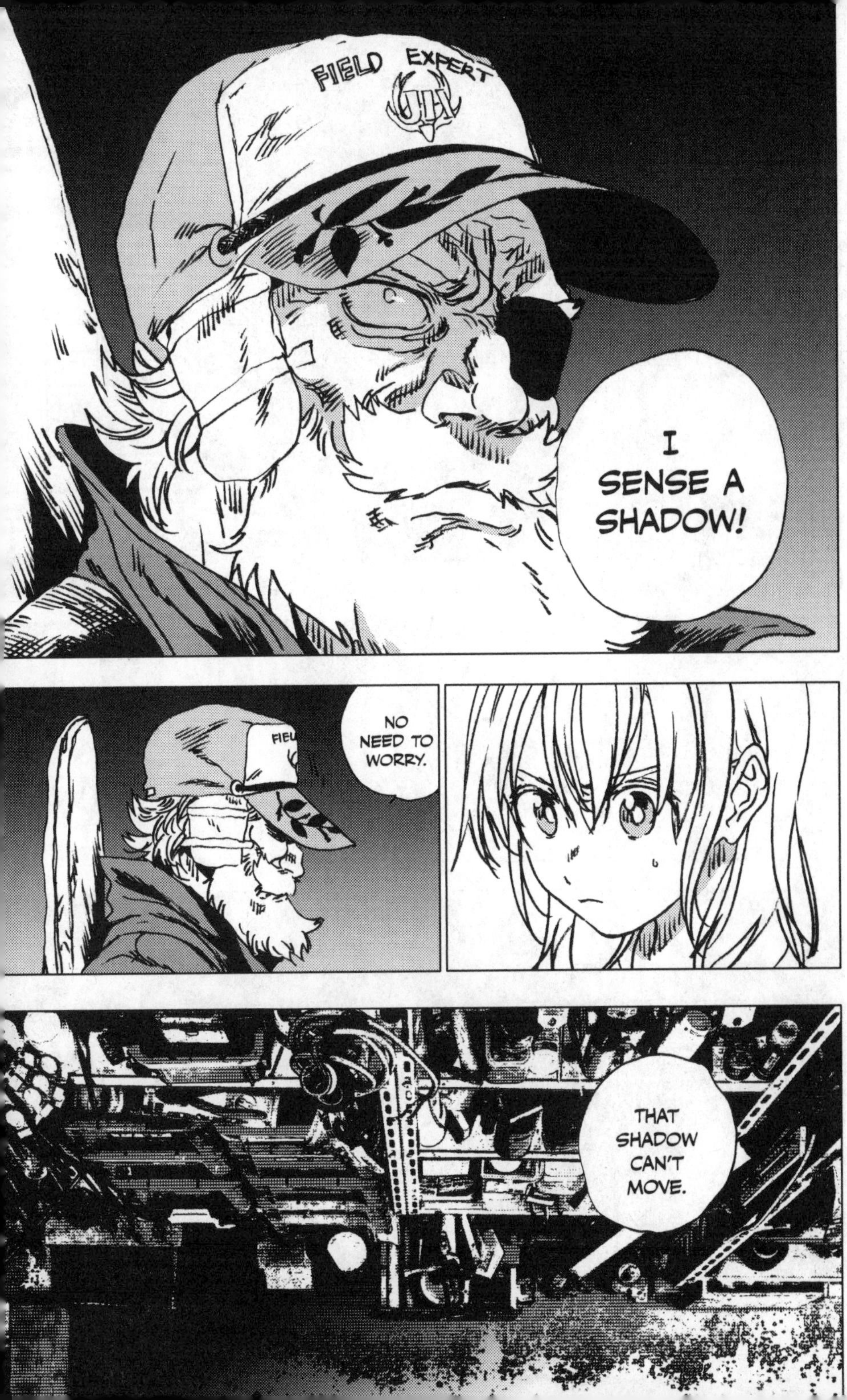
FIELD EXPERT
I SENSE A SHADOW!
NO NEED TO WORRY.
THAT SHADOW CAN'T MOVE.

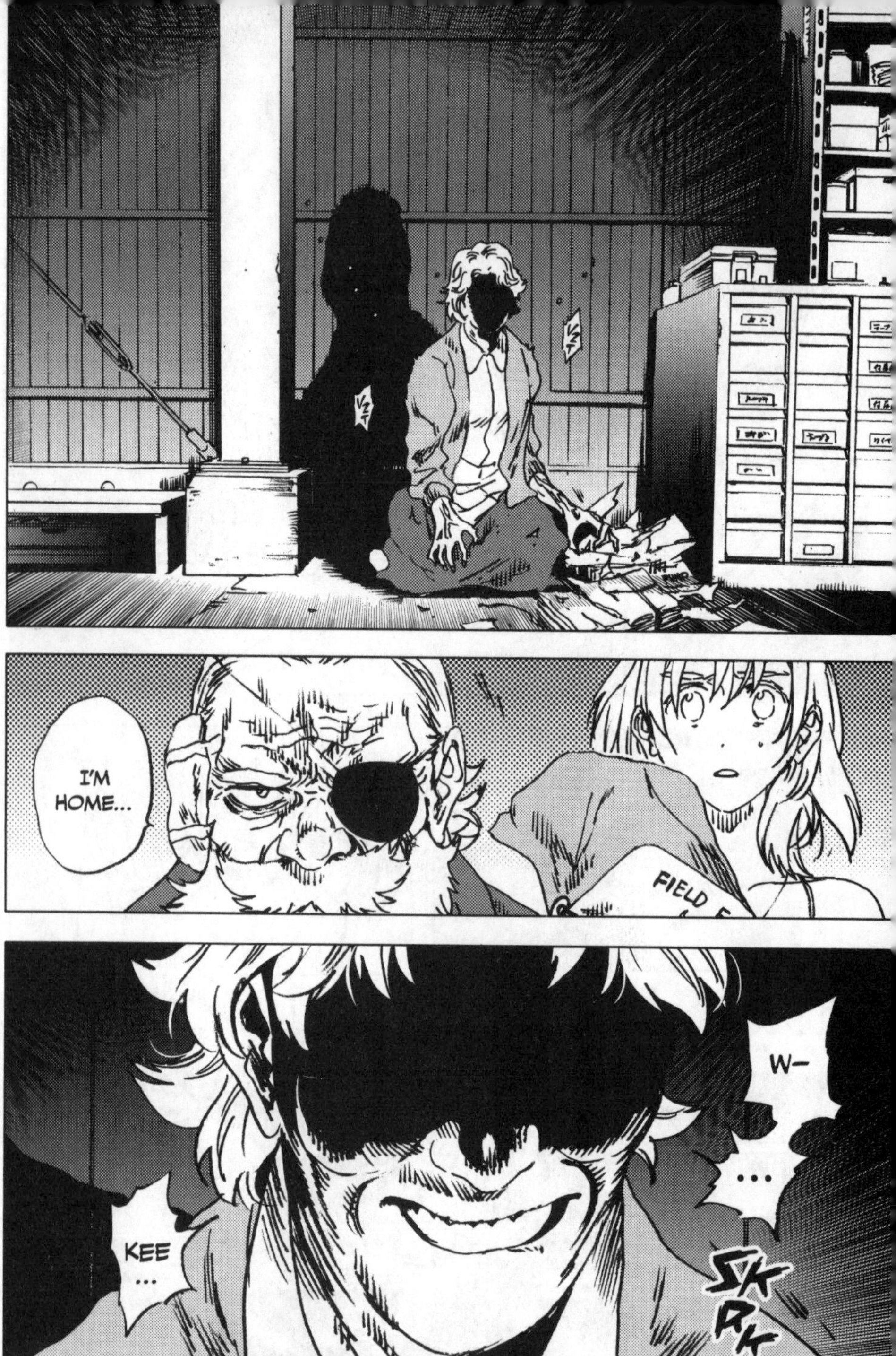
I'M HOME...
FIELD
W-
...
SKRK
KEE ...

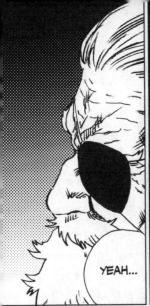

YEAH...

UM.

TH–

THIS ISN'T ACTUALLY YER...

KSH

A SHADOW.

MY WIFE'S...

SHE...

'ZACKTLY TWO MONTHS AGO.

SHE WAS OUT IN THE FIELDS 'LONE.

25

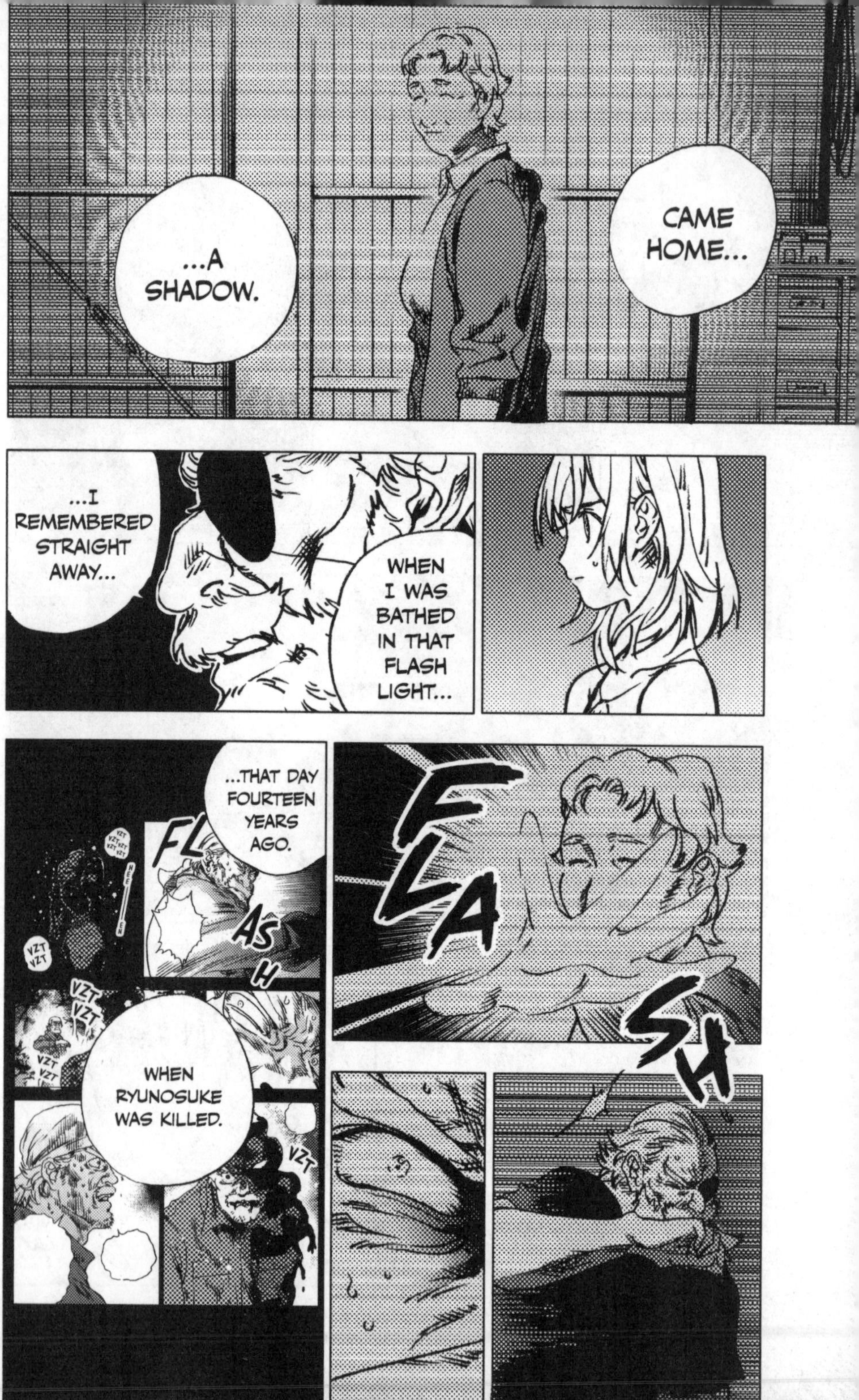
CAME HOME...
...A SHADOW.
WHEN I WAS BATHED IN THAT FLASH LIGHT...
...I REMEMBERED STRAIGHT AWAY...
FLASH
...THAT DAY FOURTEEN YEARS AGO.
FLASH
VZT VZT
VZT VZT
VZT VZT
WHEN RYUNOSUKE WAS KILLED.
VZT

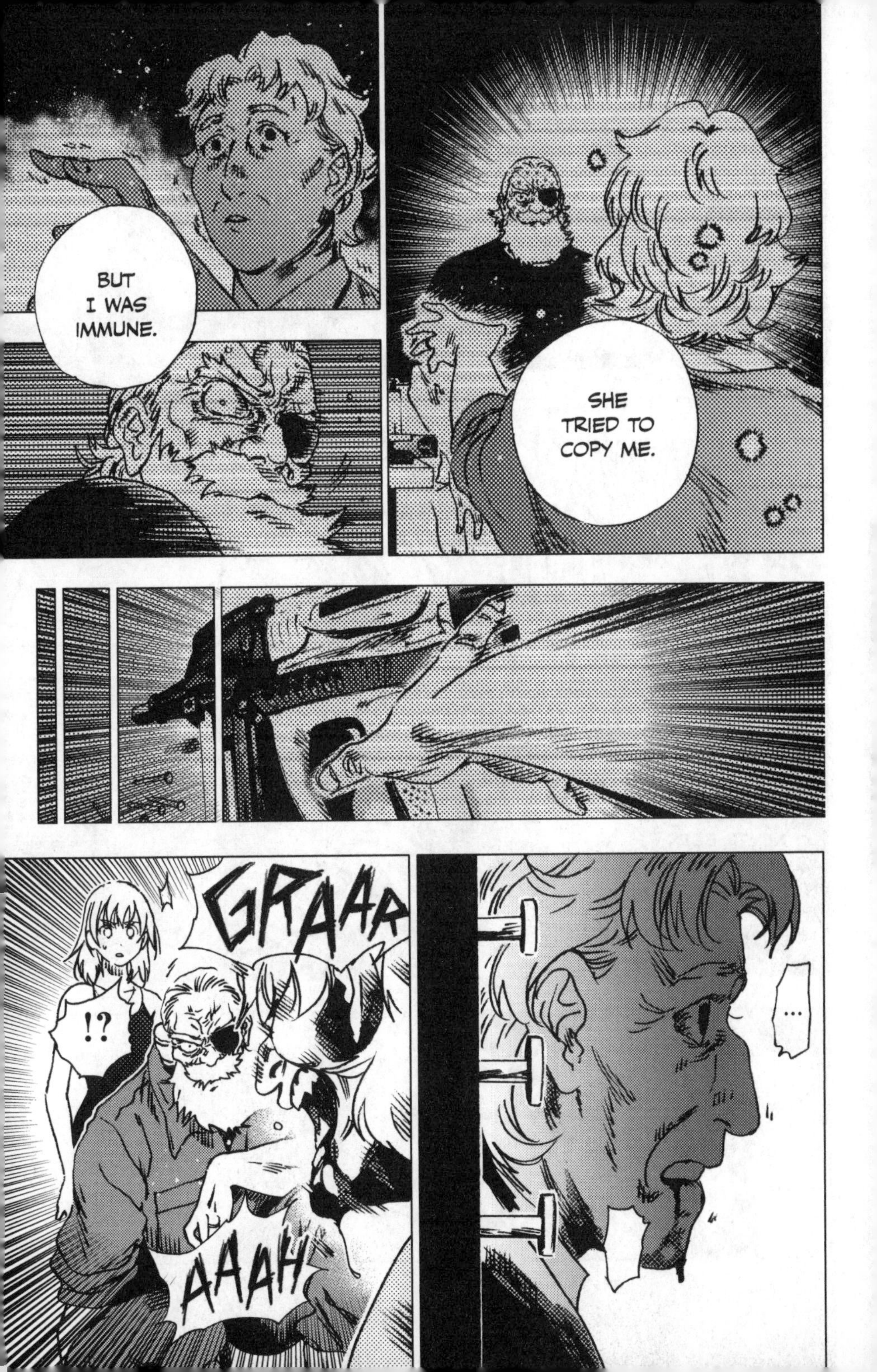
SHE TRIED TO COPY ME.
BUT I WAS IMMUNE.
...
GRAAR
!?
AAAH

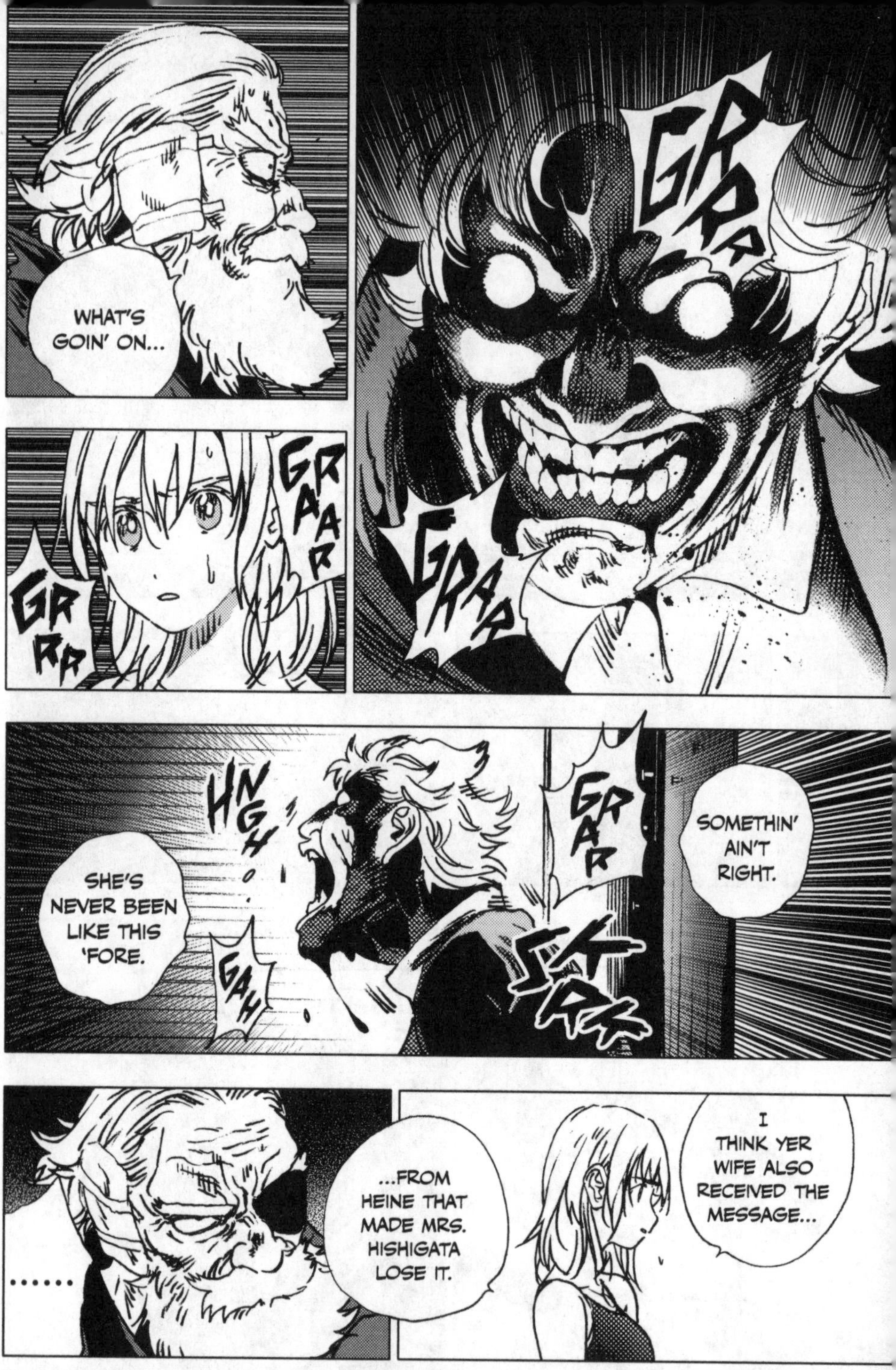
GRRR
GRAR
WHAT'S GOIN' ON...
GRAR
GRRR
SOMETHIN' AIN'T RIGHT.
GRAR
HNGH..
GAH
SHE'S NEVER BEEN LIKE THIS 'FORE.
I THINK YER WIFE ALSO RECEIVED THE MESSAGE...
...FROM HEINE THAT MADE MRS. HISHIGATA LOSE IT.
......

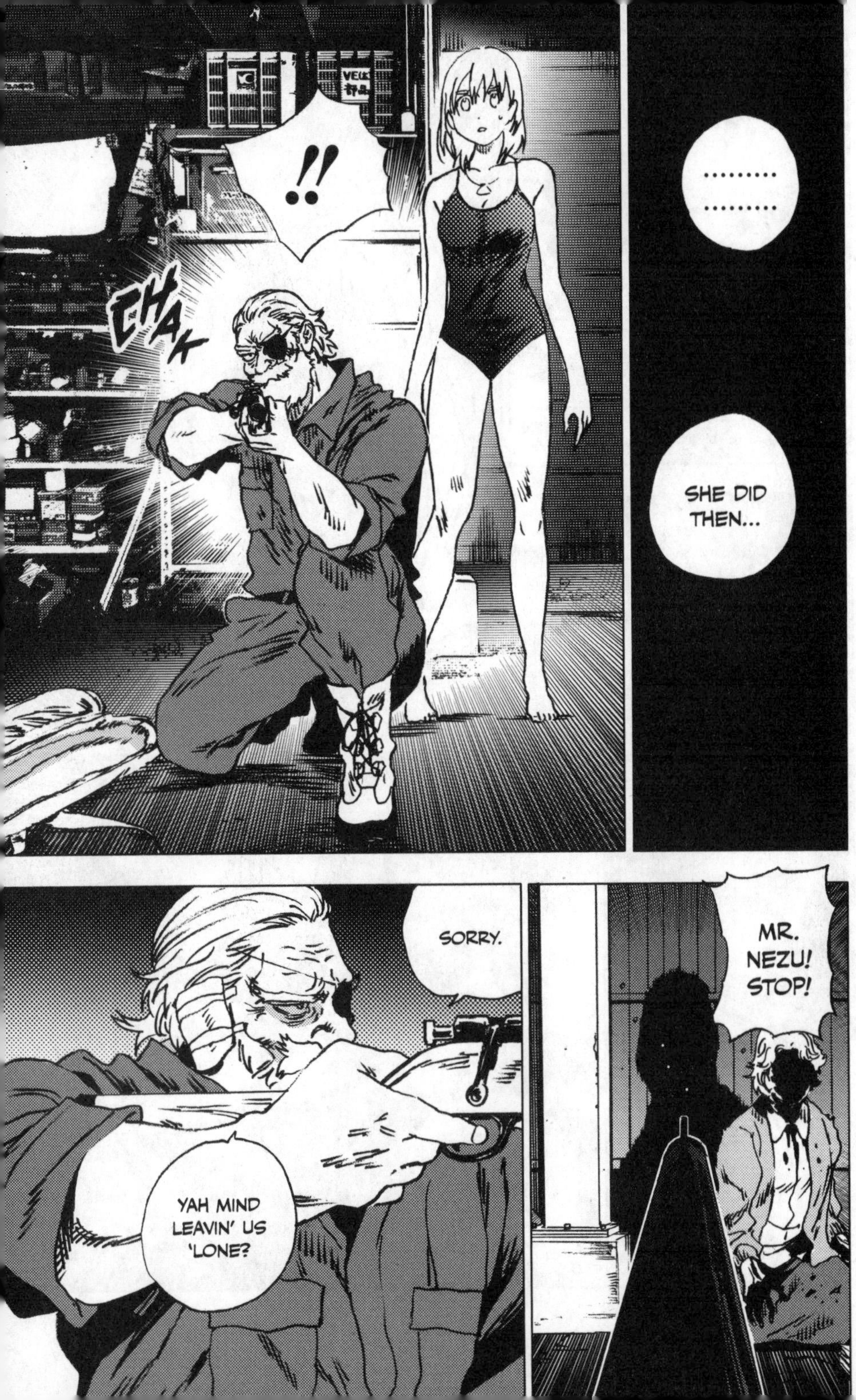

....
....
SHE DID THEN...
!!
CHAK
MR. NEZU! STOP!
SORRY.
YAH MIND LEAVIN' US 'LONE?

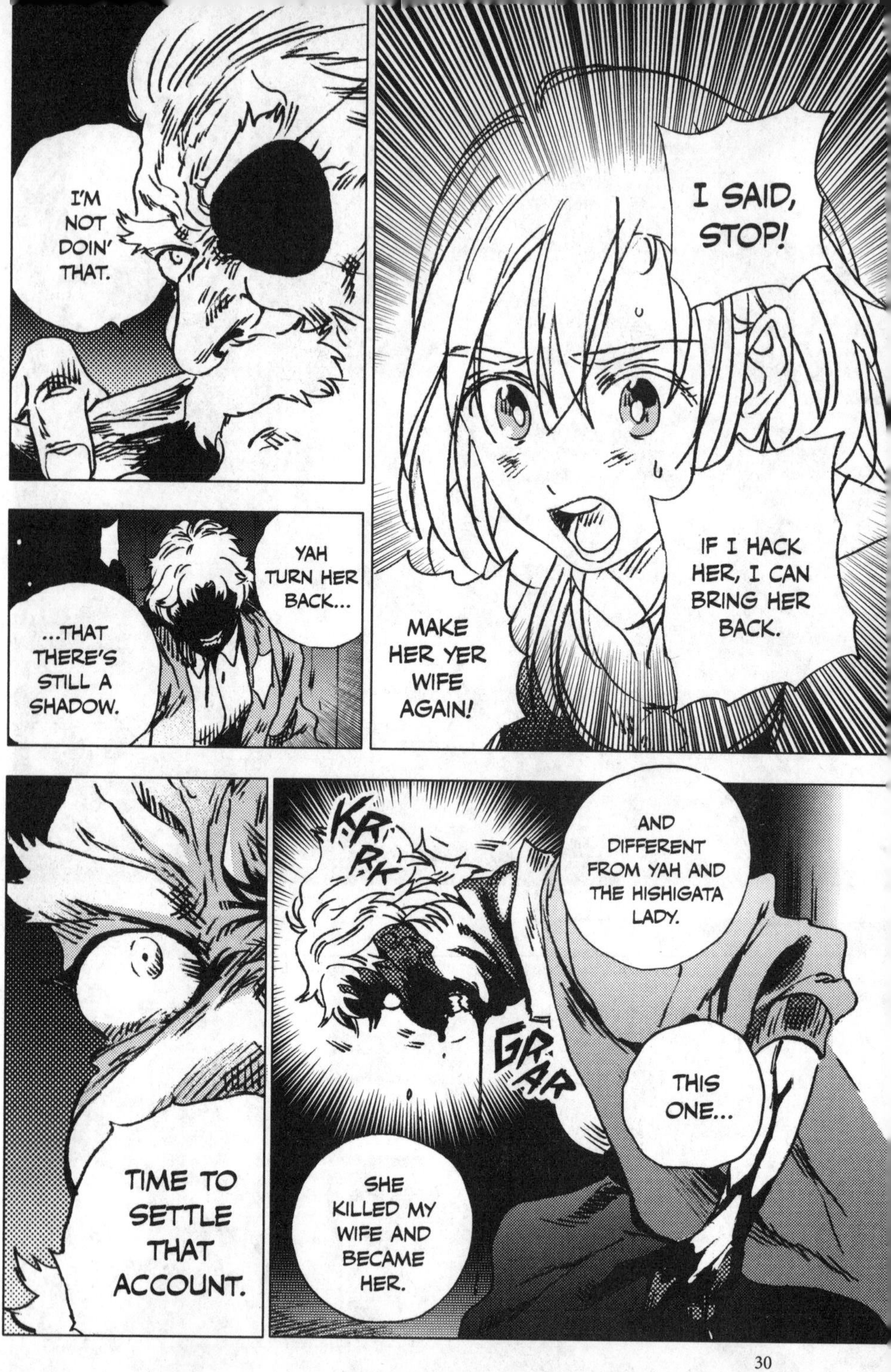
I SAID, STOP!
IF I HACK HER, I CAN BRING HER BACK.
MAKE HER YER WIFE AGAIN!
I'M NOT DOIN' THAT.
YAH TURN HER BACK...
...THAT THERE'S STILL A SHADOW.
AND DIFFERENT FROM YAH AND THE HISHIGATA LADY.
K-R-R-K
GRAR
THIS ONE...
SHE KILLED MY WIFE AND BECAME HER.
TIME TO SETTLE THAT ACCOUNT.

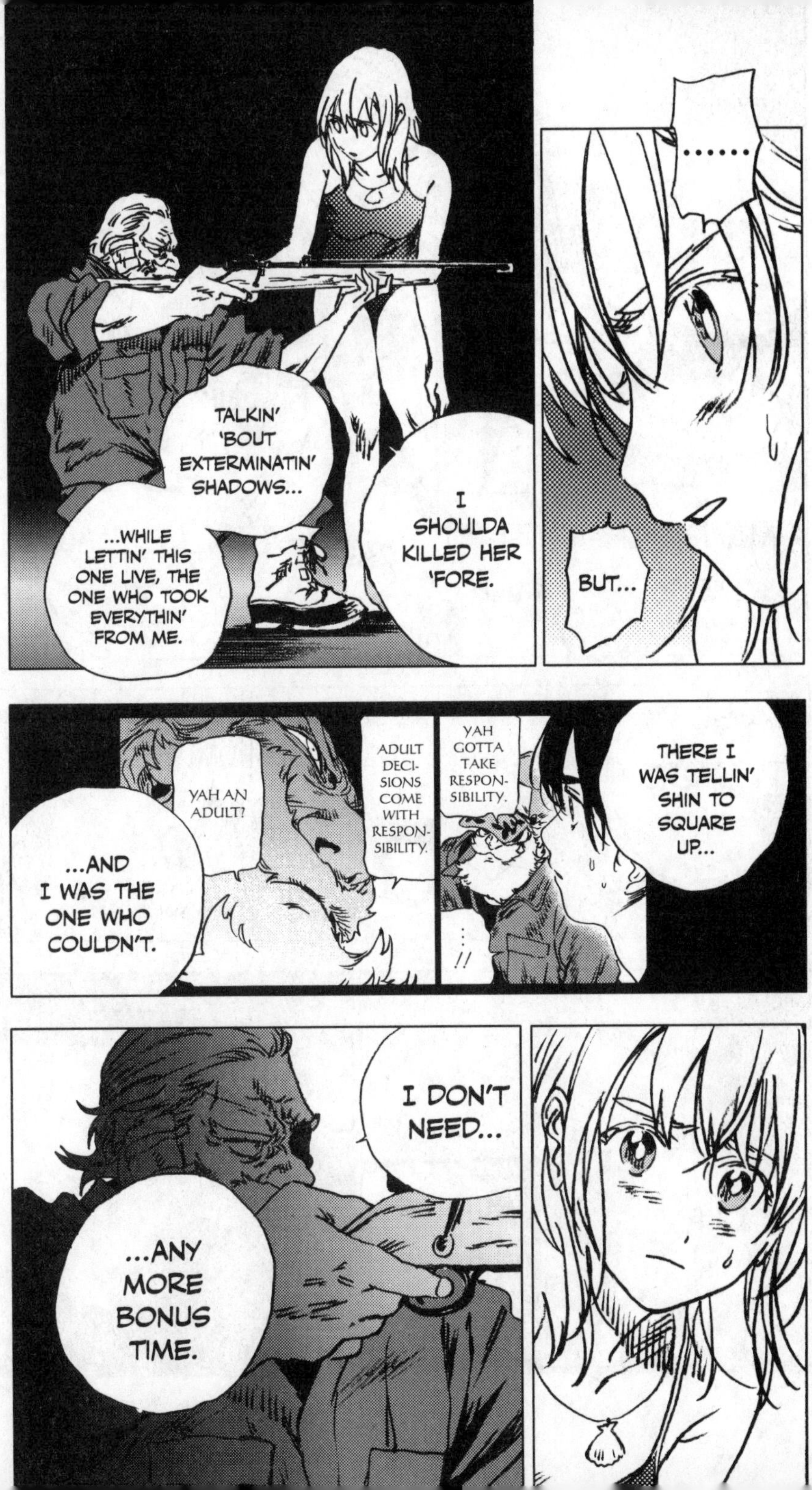
......
BUT...
I SHOULDA KILLED HER 'FORE.
TALKIN' 'BOUT EXTERMINATIN' SHADOWS...
...WHILE LETTIN' THIS ONE LIVE, THE ONE WHO TOOK EVERYTHIN' FROM ME.
THERE I WAS TELLIN' SHIN TO SQUARE UP...
YAH GOTTA TAKE RESPON-SIBILITY.
...!!
ADULT DECI-SIONS COME WITH RESPON-SIBILITY.
YAH AN ADULT?
...AND I WAS THE ONE WHO COULDN'T.
I DON'T NEED...
...ANY MORE BONUS TIME.

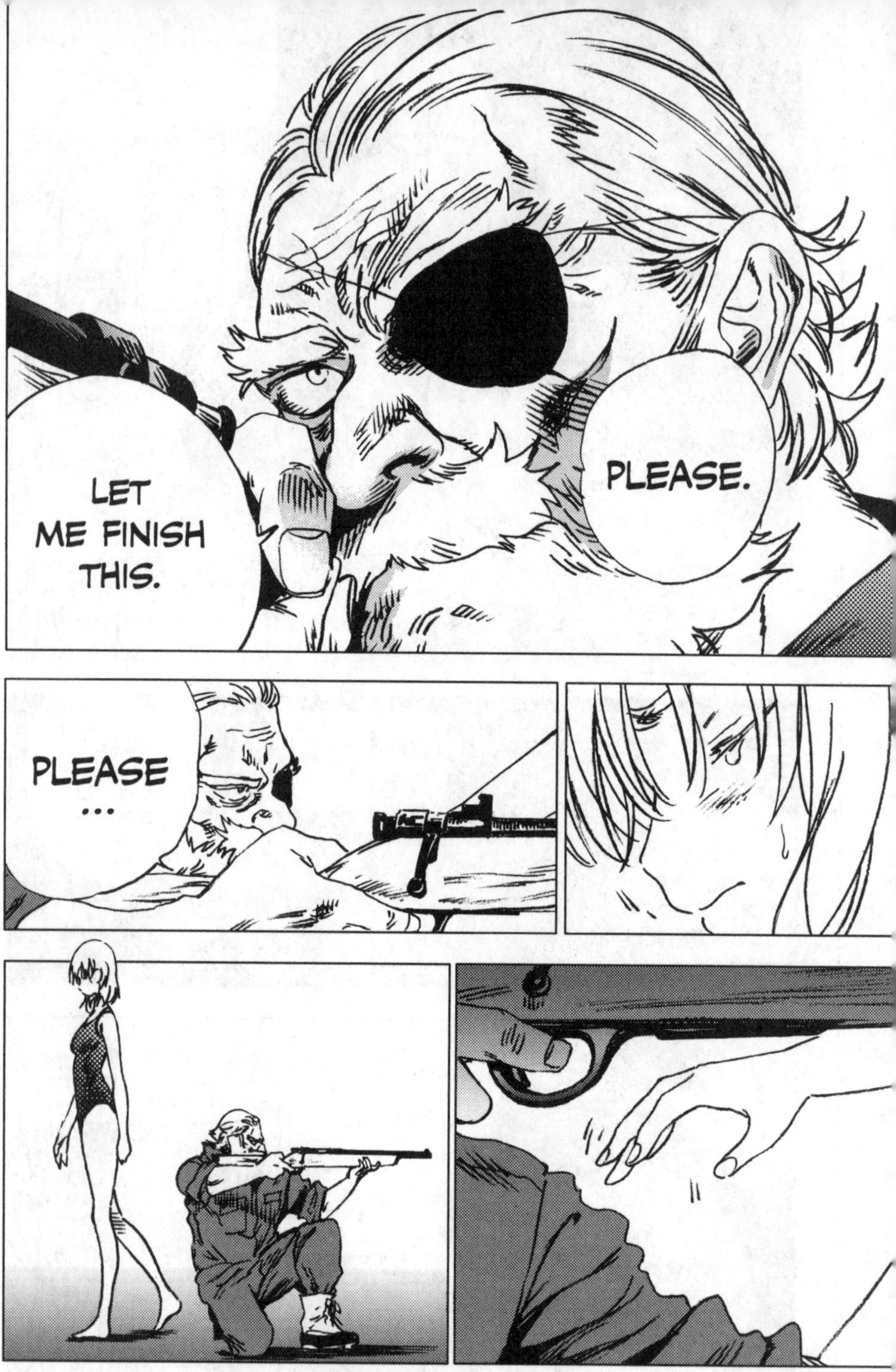
PLEASE.
LET ME FINISH THIS.
PLEASE ...

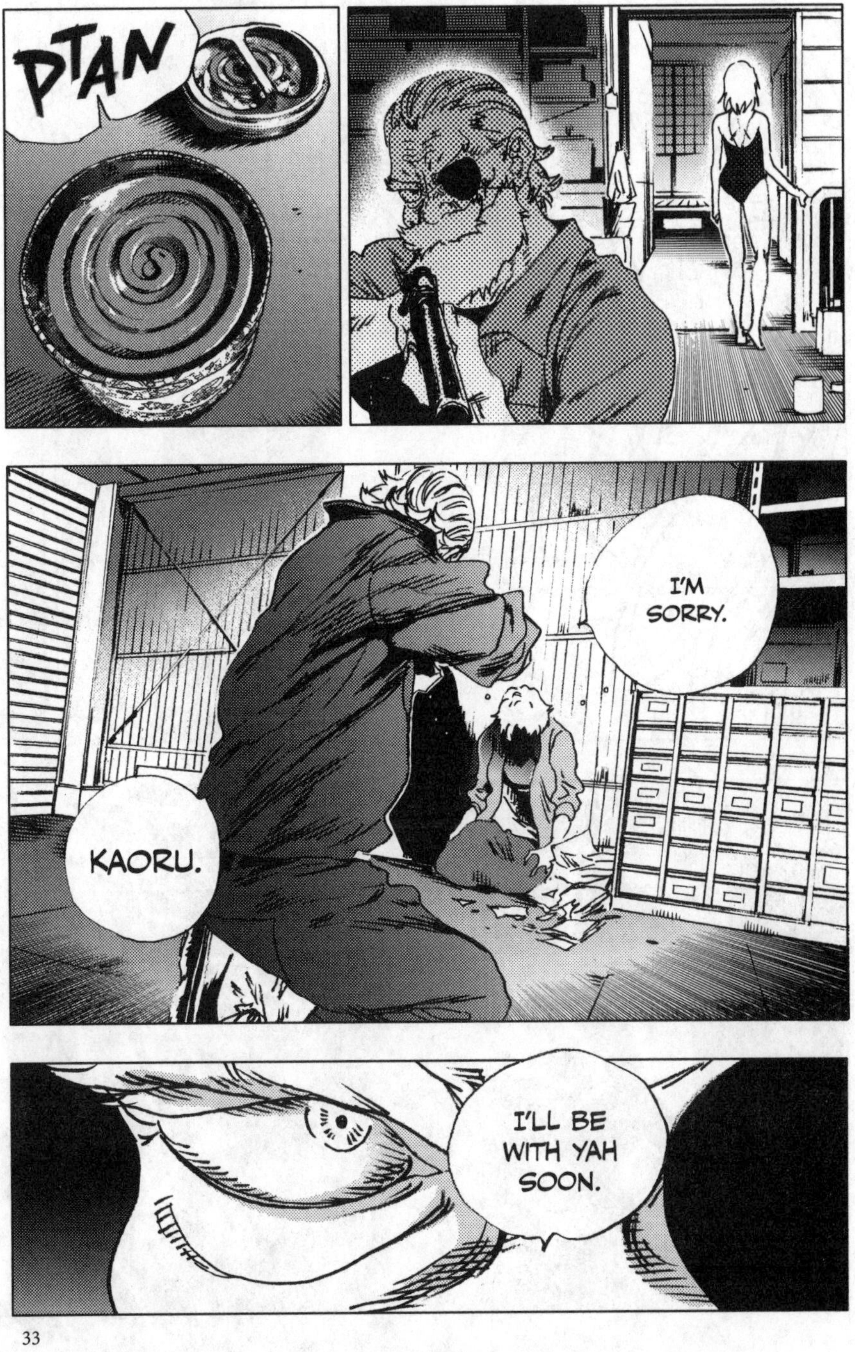
PTAN
I'M SORRY.
KAORU.
I'LL BE WITH YAH SOON.

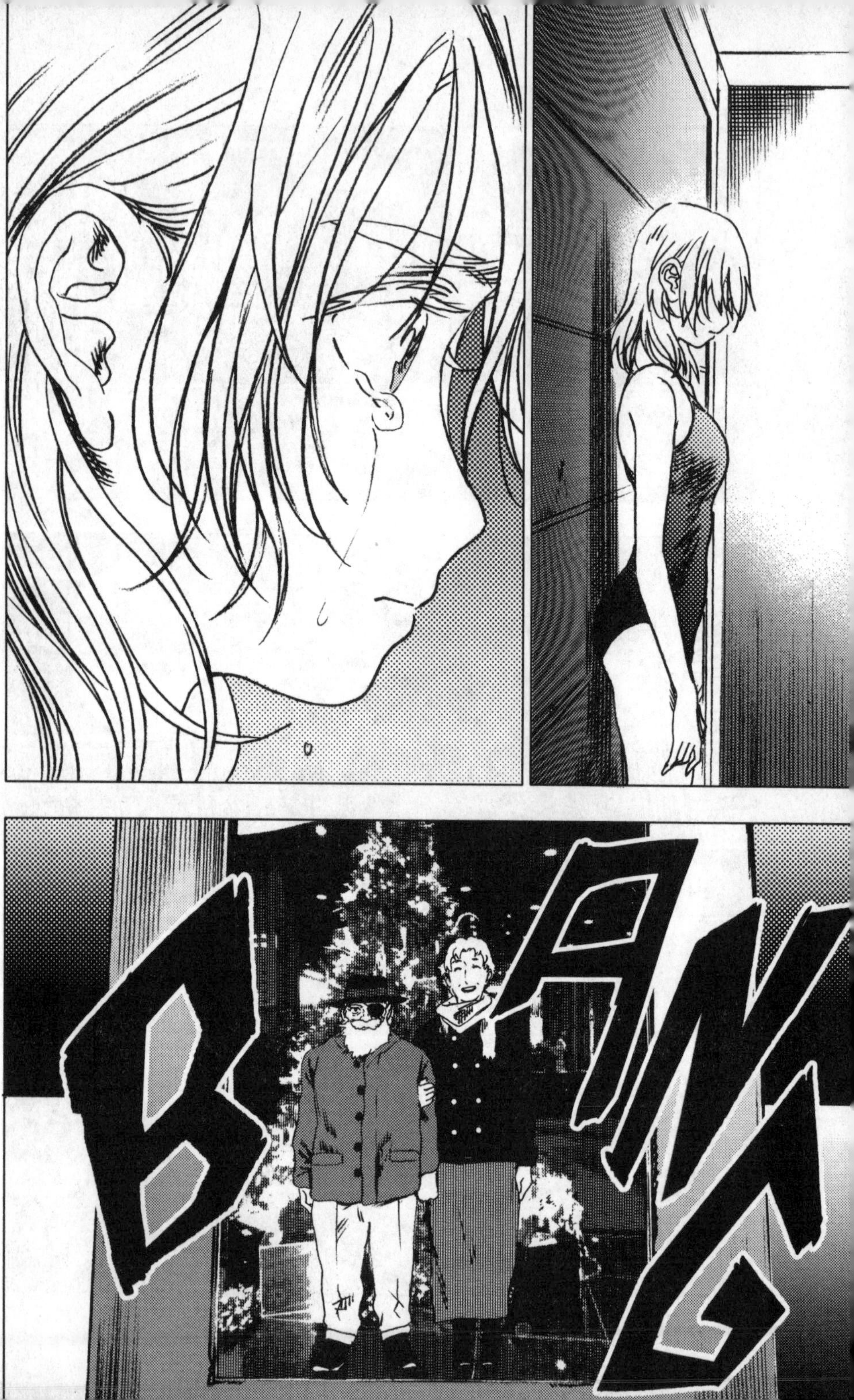
BANG

STRATEGY MEETING NOTES

NOTES WERE MADE ON THE WHITE BOARD
DURING THE MEETING AT HISHIGATA CLINIC
HELD AT MIDNIGHT ON JULY 23 OF THE SEVENTH LOOP.
(AS SEEN ON PAGE 4 OF THIS VOLUME)
HERE'S AN ENGLISH TRANSLATION
OF WHAT WAS WRITTEN ON THE BOARD.

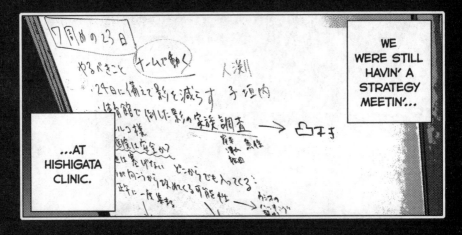

WE WERE STILL HAVIN' A STRATEGY MEETIN'...
...AT HISHIGATA CLINIC.

WE WERE STILL HAVIN' A STRATEGY MEETIN'...
23rd of the 7th Loop
Work as a team
What to do
Hitobuchi
Kogaito
Reduce number of shadows in prep for 24th.
Shadows killed in gym - check on those families.
Totsumura
Kishi
Tsuyama
Matsuda
Uozu
Great Hiruko
e Clinic safe?
an't be blocked. Can come in from anywhere.
ossibility they'll attack from the front.
Ushioh
Hacking
Meet up at noon
...AT HISHIGATA CLINIC.

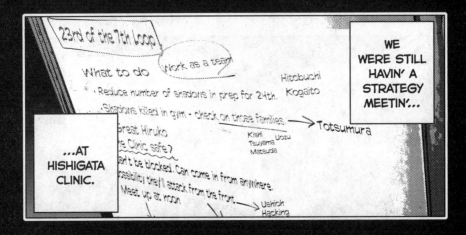

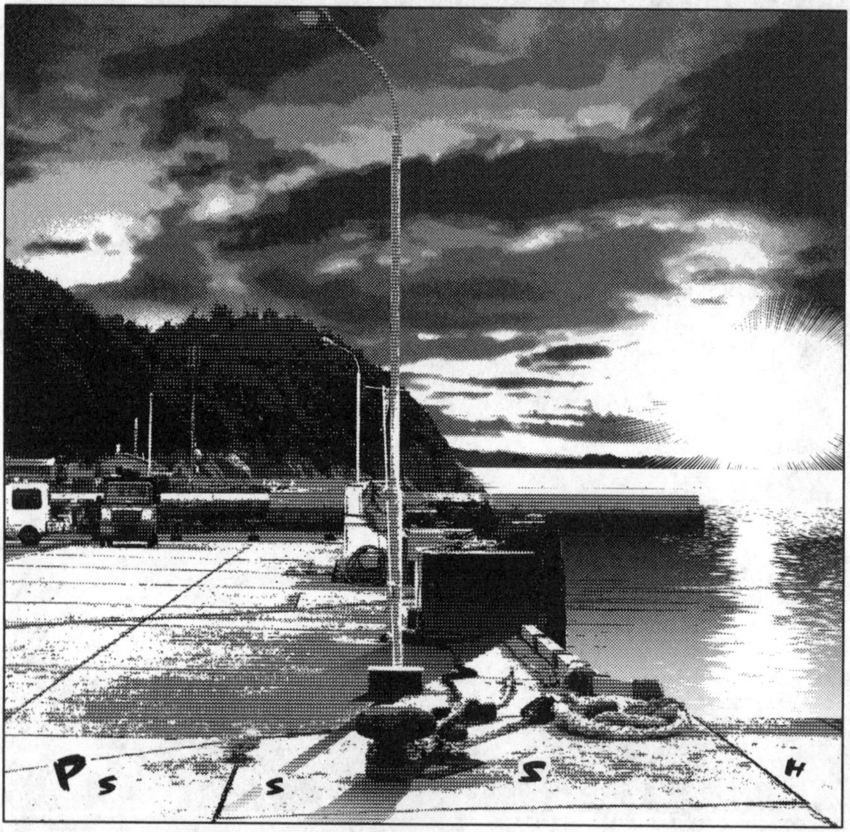
PSSSH

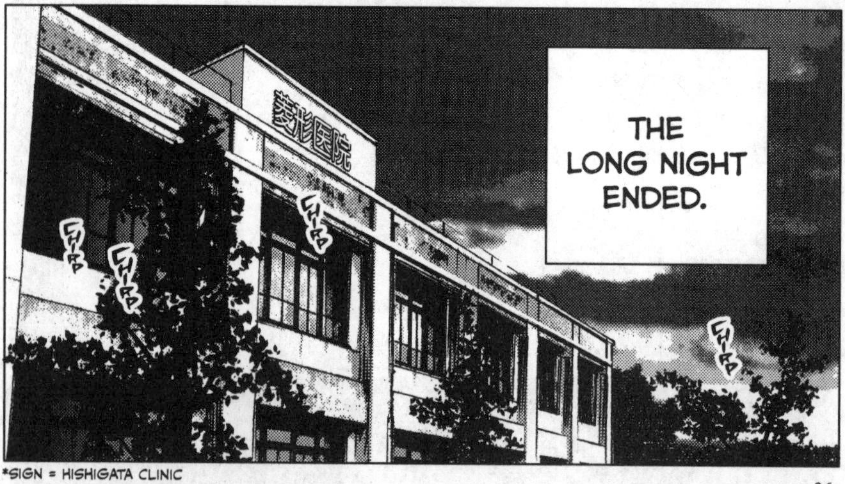
THE LONG NIGHT ENDED.
菱形医院
CHIRP
CHIRP
CHIRP
CHIRP

*SIGN = HISHIGATA CLINIC

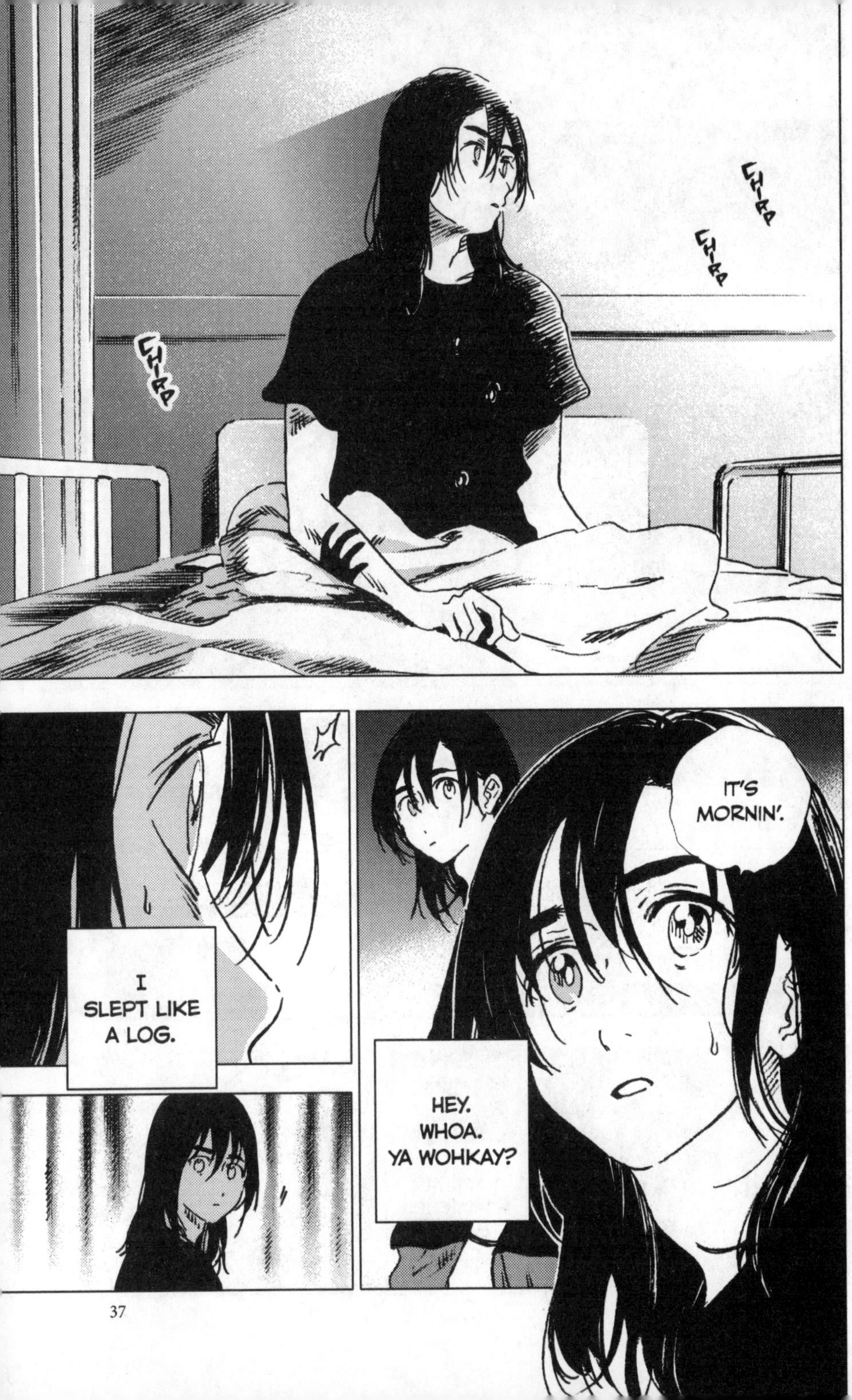
CHIRP
CHIRP
CHIRP
IT'S MORNIN'.
HEY. WHOA. YA WOHKAY?
I SLEPT LIKE A LOG.

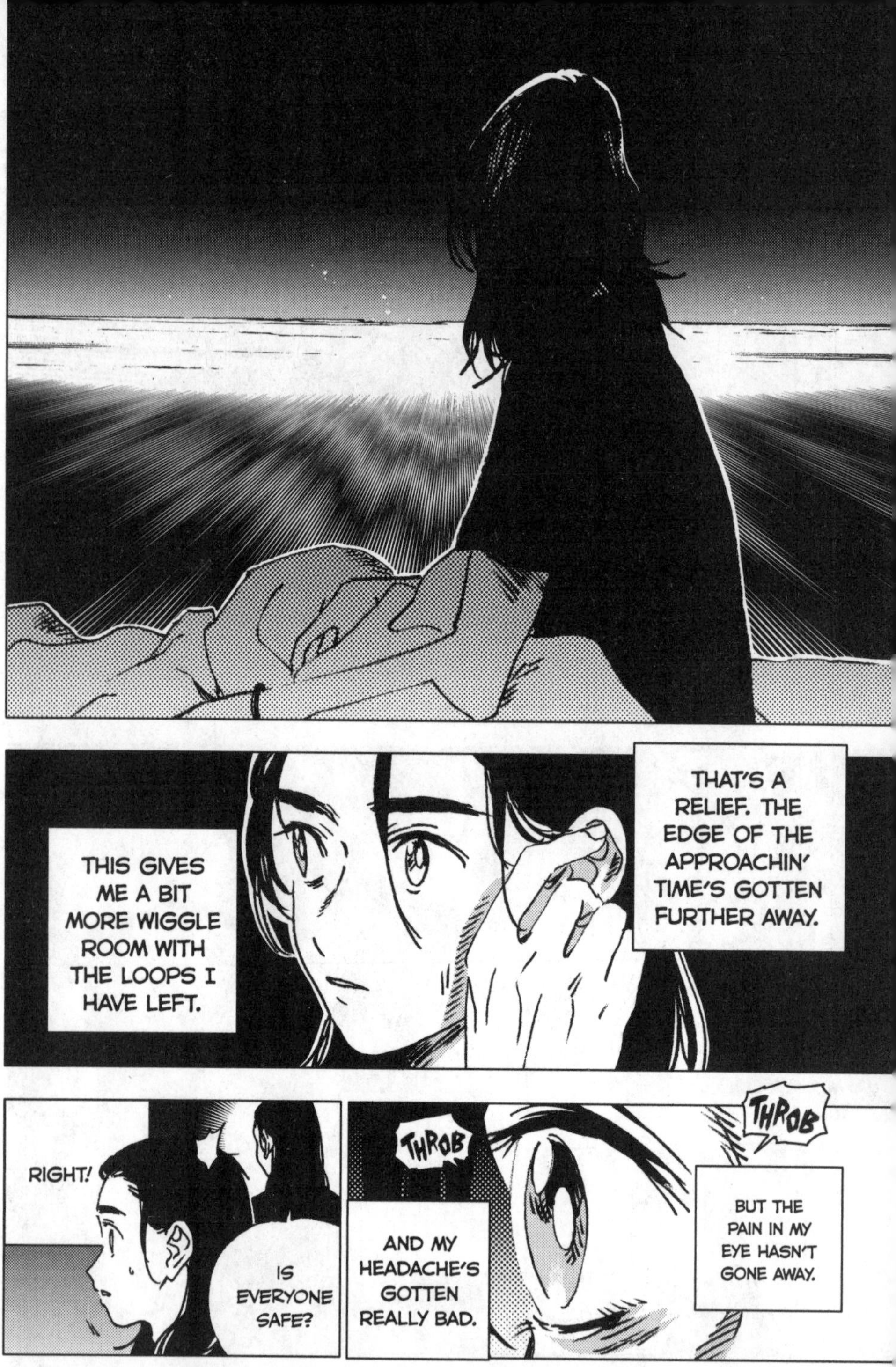
THAT'S A RELIEF. THE EDGE OF THE APPROACHIN' TIME'S GOTTEN FURTHER AWAY.
THIS GIVES ME A BIT MORE WIGGLE ROOM WITH THE LOOPS I HAVE LEFT.
THROB
BUT THE PAIN IN MY EYE HASN'T GONE AWAY.
THROB
AND MY HEADACHE'S GOTTEN REALLY BAD.
RIGHT!
IS EVERYONE SAFE?

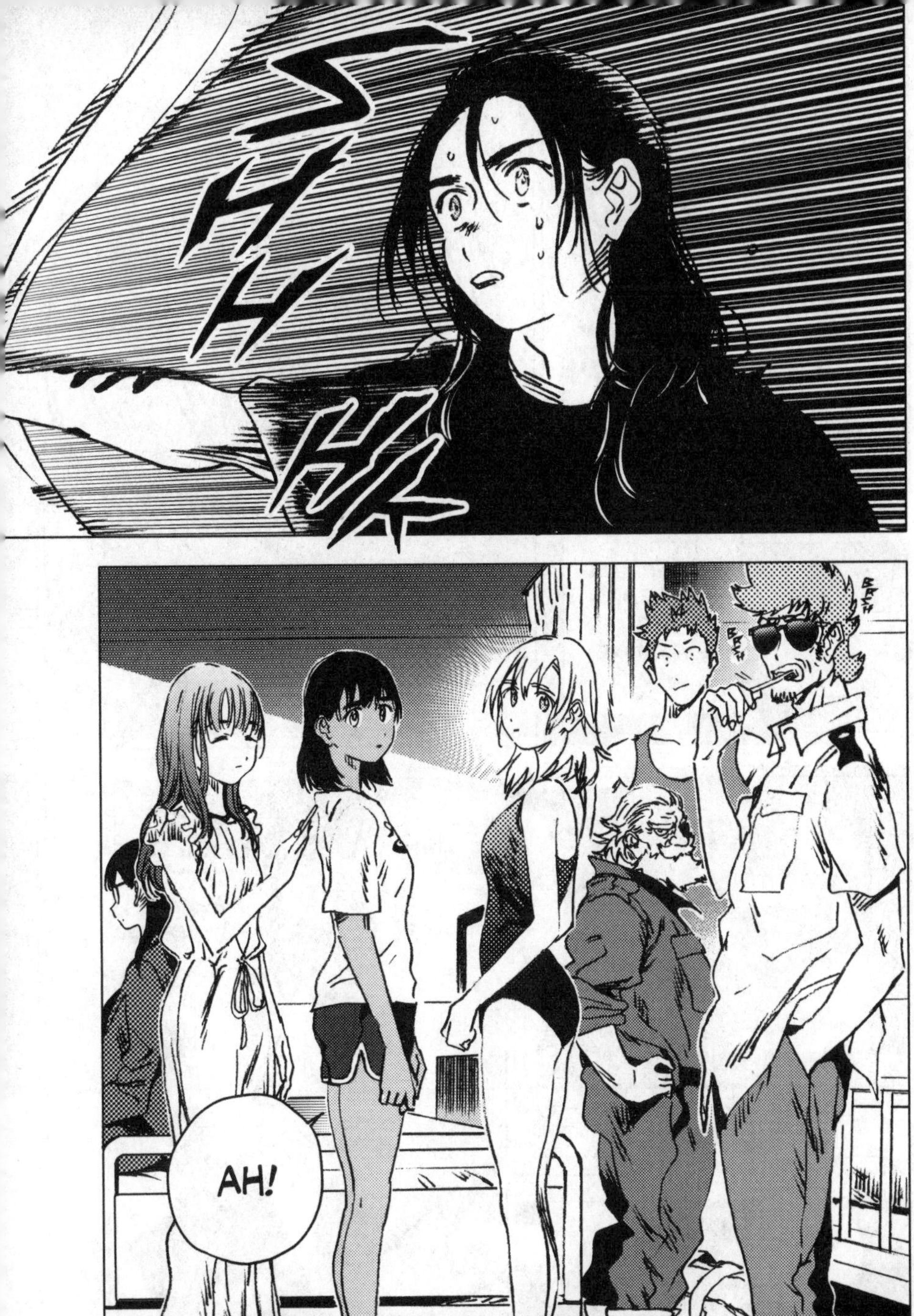
SHHHK
BRSH
BRSH
AH!

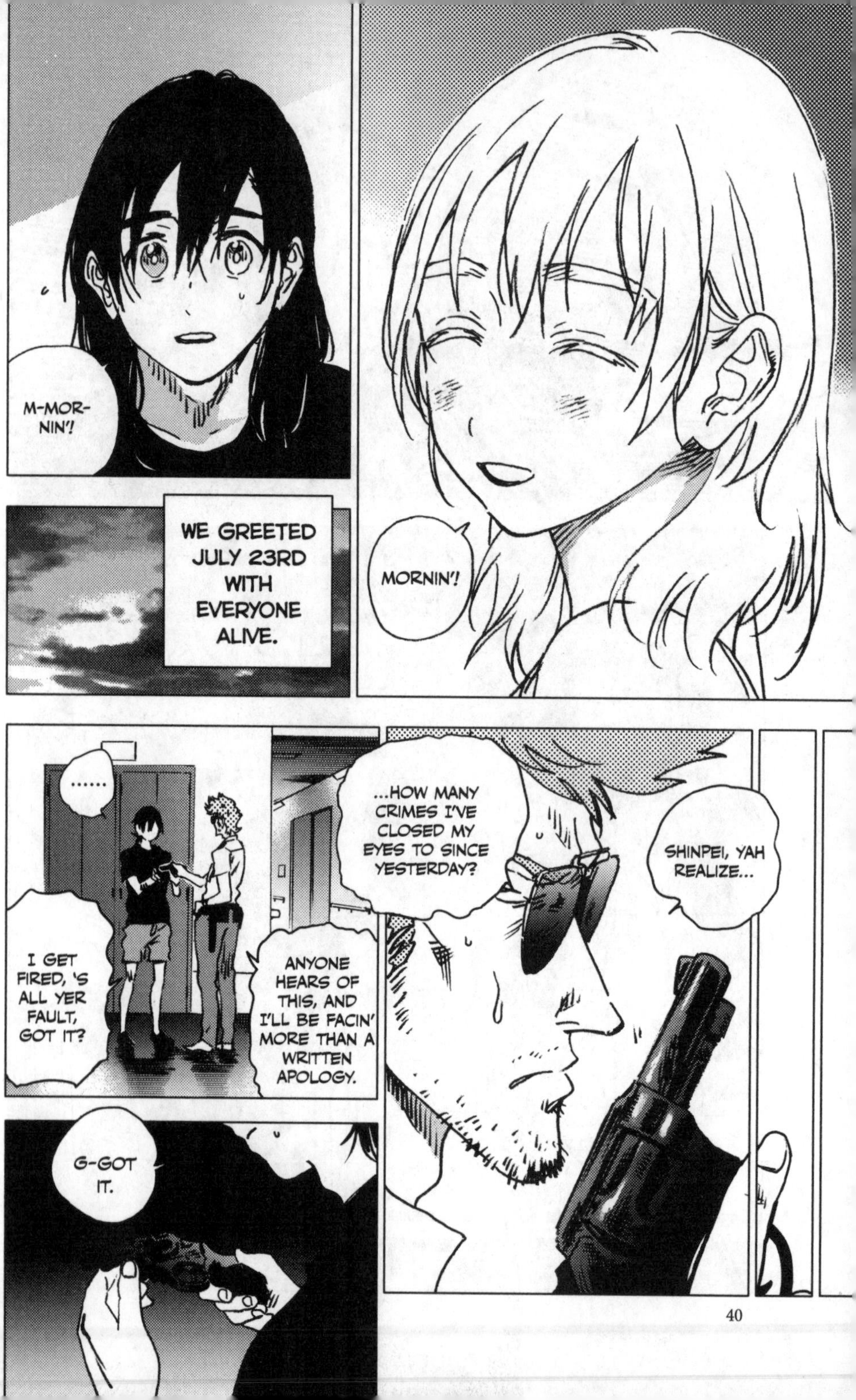
MORNIN'!
M-MOR-NIN'!
WE GREETED JULY 23RD WITH EVERYONE ALIVE.
SHINPEI, YAH REALIZE...
...HOW MANY CRIMES I'VE CLOSED MY EYES TO SINCE YESTERDAY?
ANYONE HEARS OF THIS, AND I'LL BE FACIN' MORE THAN A WRITTEN APOLOGY.
I GET FIRED, 'S ALL YER FAULT, GOT IT?
......
G-GOT IT.

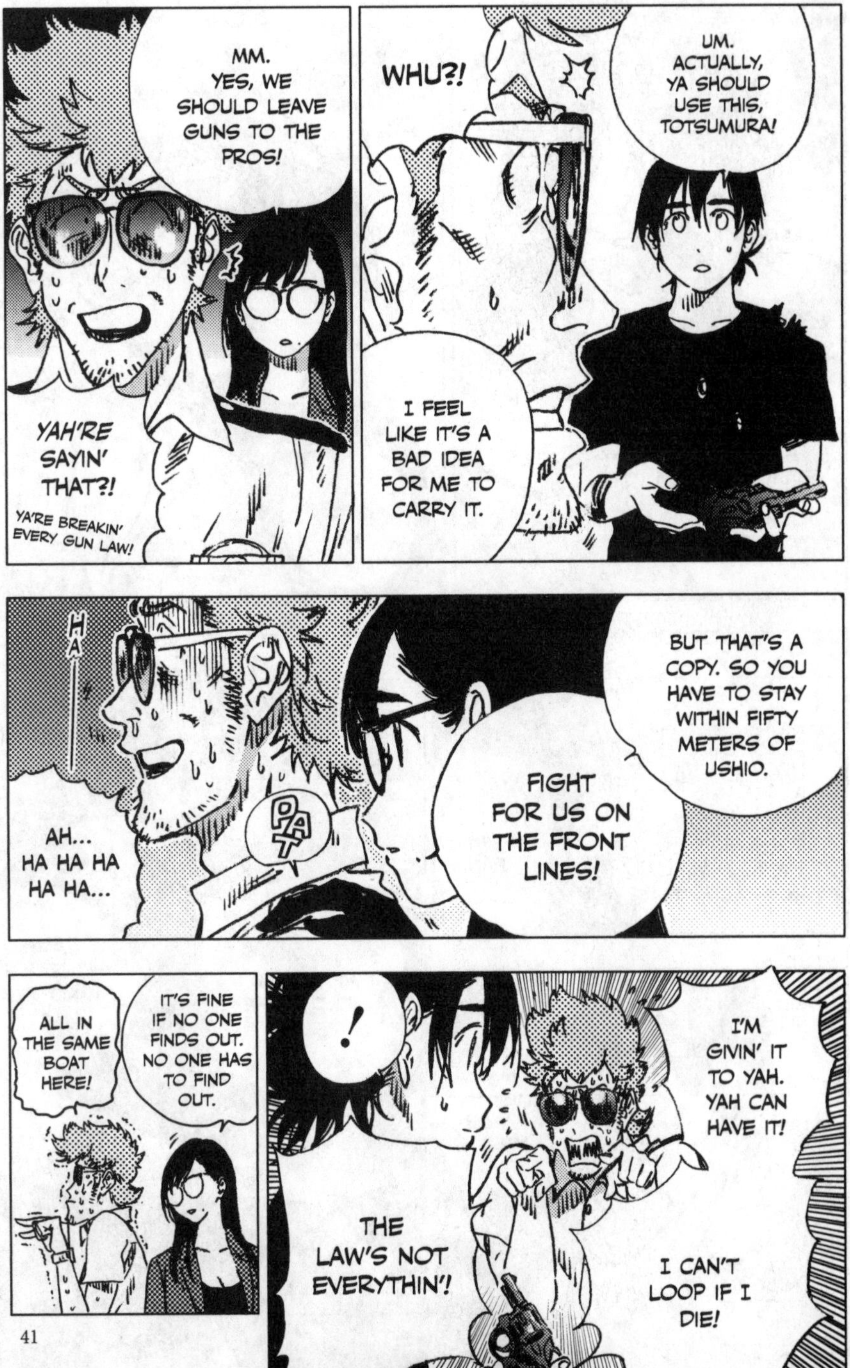
UM. ACTUALLY, YA SHOULD USE THIS, TOTSUMURA!
WHU?!
I FEEL LIKE IT'S A BAD IDEA FOR ME TO CARRY IT.
MM. YES, WE SHOULD LEAVE GUNS TO THE PROS!
YAH'RE SAYIN' THAT?!
YA'RE BREAKIN' EVERY GUN LAW!
BUT THAT'S A COPY. SO YOU HAVE TO STAY WITHIN FIFTY METERS OF USHIO.
FIGHT FOR US ON THE FRONT LINES!
PAT
HA
AH... HA HA HA HA HA...
I'M GIVIN' IT TO YAH. YAH CAN HAVE IT!
!
THE LAW'S NOT EVERYTHIN'!
I CAN'T LOOP IF I DIE!
IT'S FINE IF NO ONE FINDS OUT. NO ONE HAS TO FIND OUT.
ALL IN THE SAME BOAT HERE!

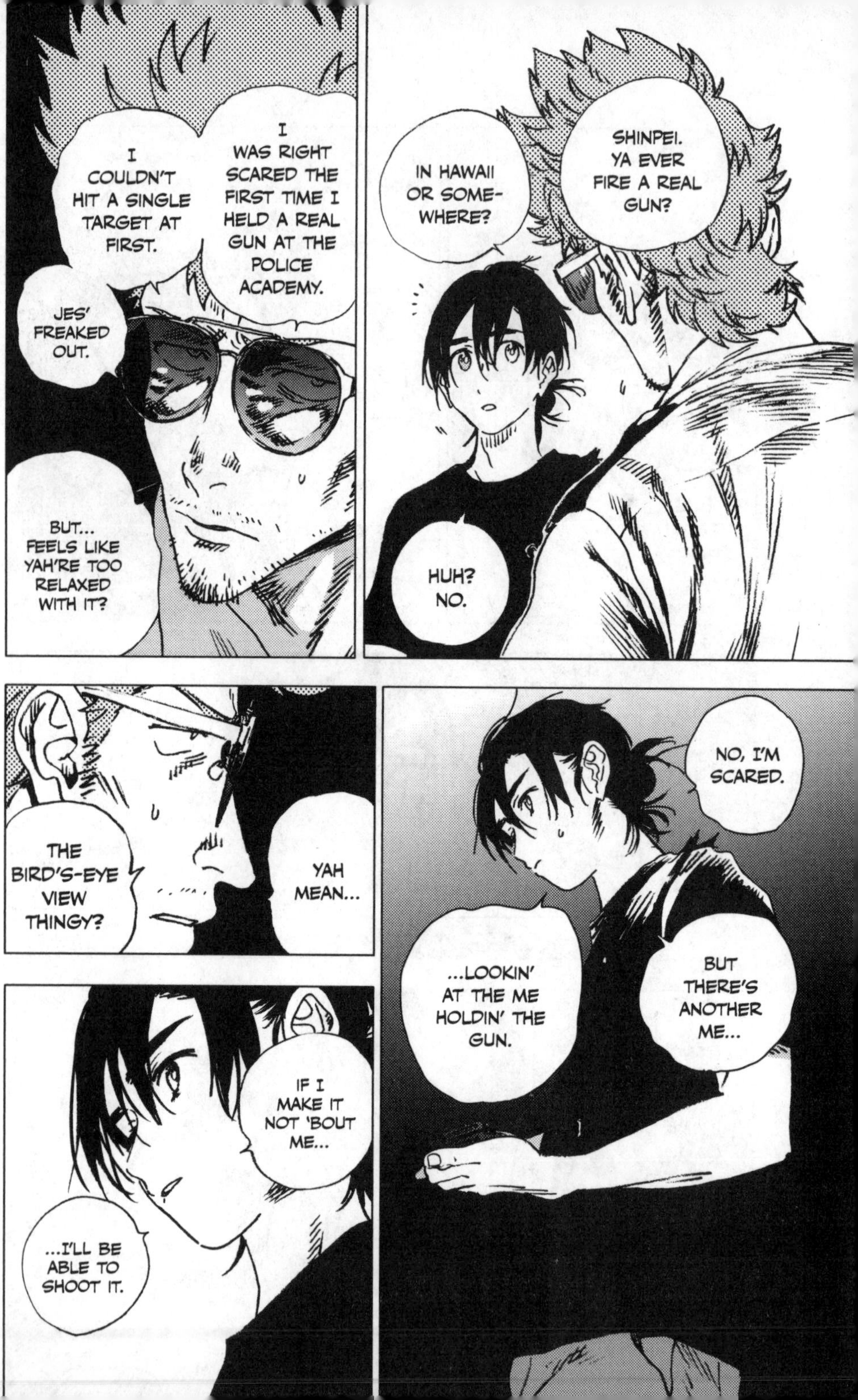
SHINPEI. YA EVER FIRE A REAL GUN?
IN HAWAII OR SOME-WHERE?
HUH? NO.
I WAS RIGHT SCARED THE FIRST TIME I HELD A REAL GUN AT THE POLICE ACADEMY.
I COULDN'T HIT A SINGLE TARGET AT FIRST.
JES' FREAKED OUT.
BUT... FEELS LIKE YAH'RE TOO RELAXED WITH IT?
NO, I'M SCARED.
BUT THERE'S ANOTHER ME...
...LOOKIN' AT THE ME HOLDIN' THE GUN.
YAH MEAN...
THE BIRD'S-EYE VIEW THINGY?
IF I MAKE IT NOT 'BOUT ME...
...I'LL BE ABLE TO SHOOT IT.

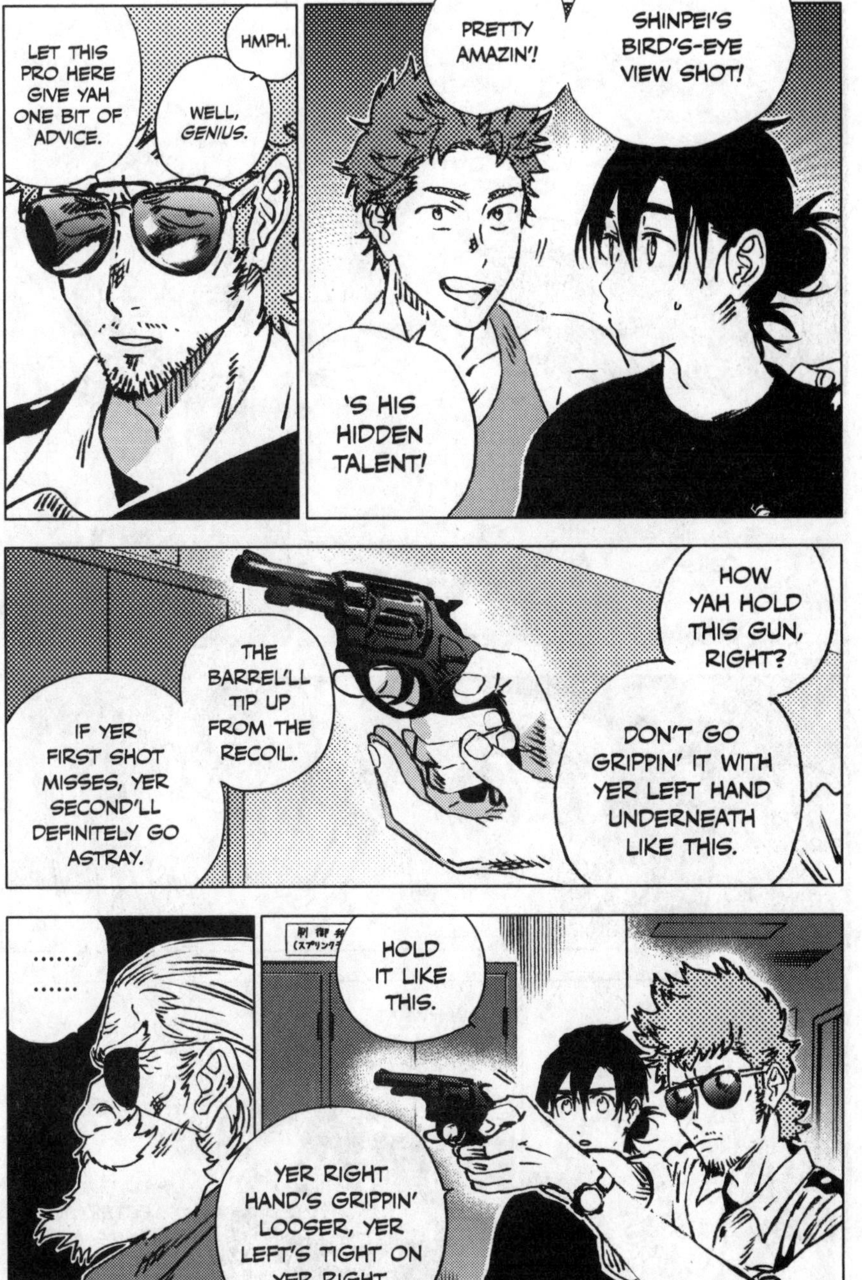
SHINPEI'S BIRD'S-EYE VIEW SHOT!
PRETTY AMAZIN'!
'S HIS HIDDEN TALENT!
HMPH.
WELL, GENIUS.
LET THIS PRO HERE GIVE YAH ONE BIT OF ADVICE.
HOW YAH HOLD THIS GUN, RIGHT?
DON'T GO GRIPPIN' IT WITH YER LEFT HAND UNDERNEATH LIKE THIS.
THE BARREL'LL TIP UP FROM THE RECOIL.
IF YER FIRST SHOT MISSES, YER SECOND'LL DEFINITELY GO ASTRAY.
HOLD IT LIKE THIS.
YER RIGHT HAND'S GRIPPIN' LOOSER, YER LEFT'S TIGHT ON YER RIGHT.
......
......

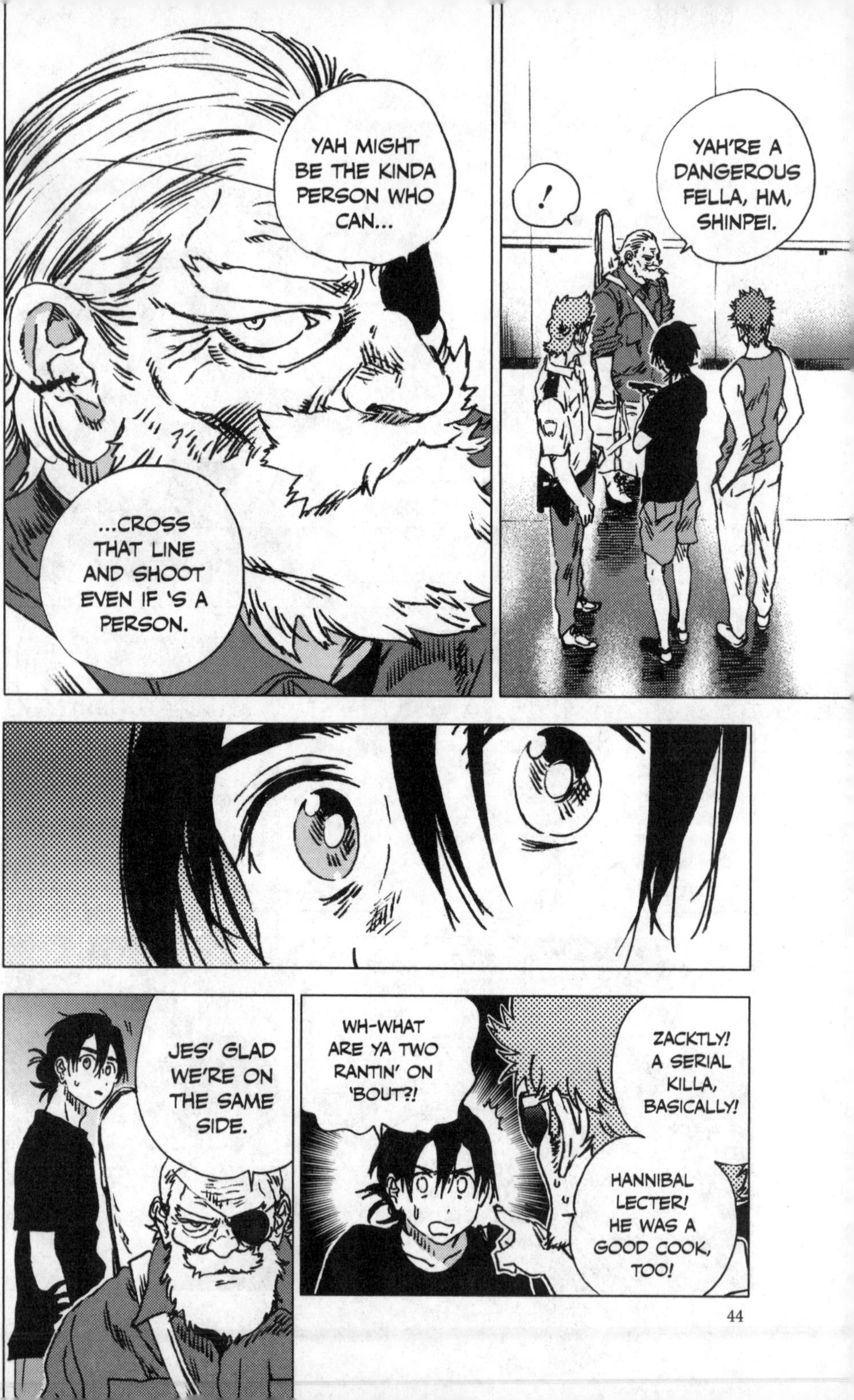
YAH'RE A DANGEROUS FELLA, HM, SHINPEI.
!
YAH MIGHT BE THE KINDA PERSON WHO CAN...
...CROSS THAT LINE AND SHOOT EVEN IF 'S A PERSON.
ZACKTLY! A SERIAL KILLA, BASICALLY!
WH-WHAT ARE YA TWO RANTIN' ON 'BOUT?!
HANNIBAL LECTER! HE WAS A GOOD COOK, TOO!
JES' GLAD WE'RE ON THE SAME SIDE.

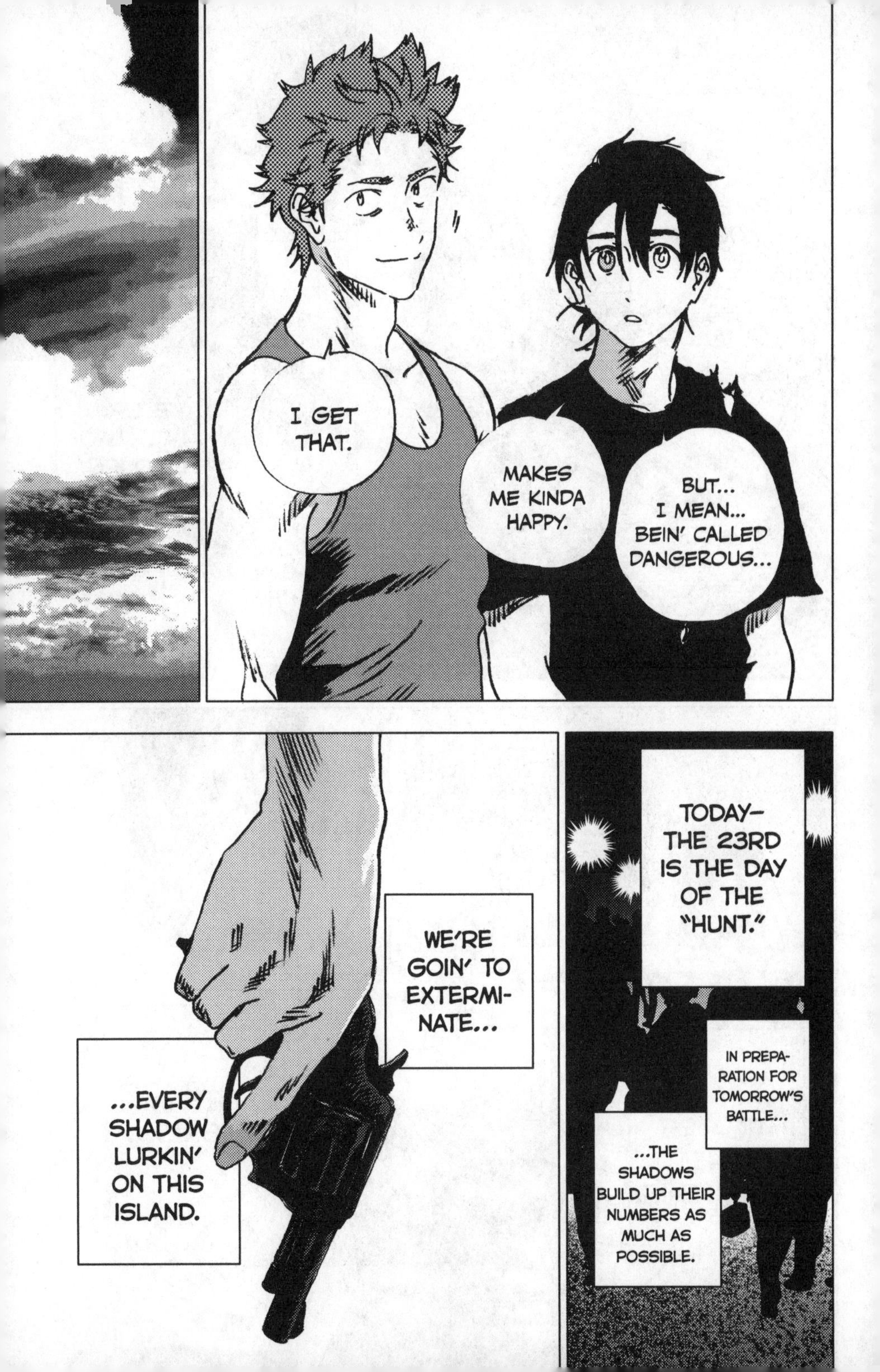
BUT... I MEAN... BEIN' CALLED DANGEROUS...
MAKES ME KINDA HAPPY.
I GET THAT.
TODAY— THE 23RD IS THE DAY OF THE "HUNT."
IN PREPARATION FOR TOMORROW'S BATTLE...
...THE SHADOWS BUILD UP THEIR NUMBERS AS MUCH AS POSSIBLE.
WE'RE GOIN' TO EXTERMINATE...
...EVERY SHADOW LURKIN' ON THIS ISLAND.

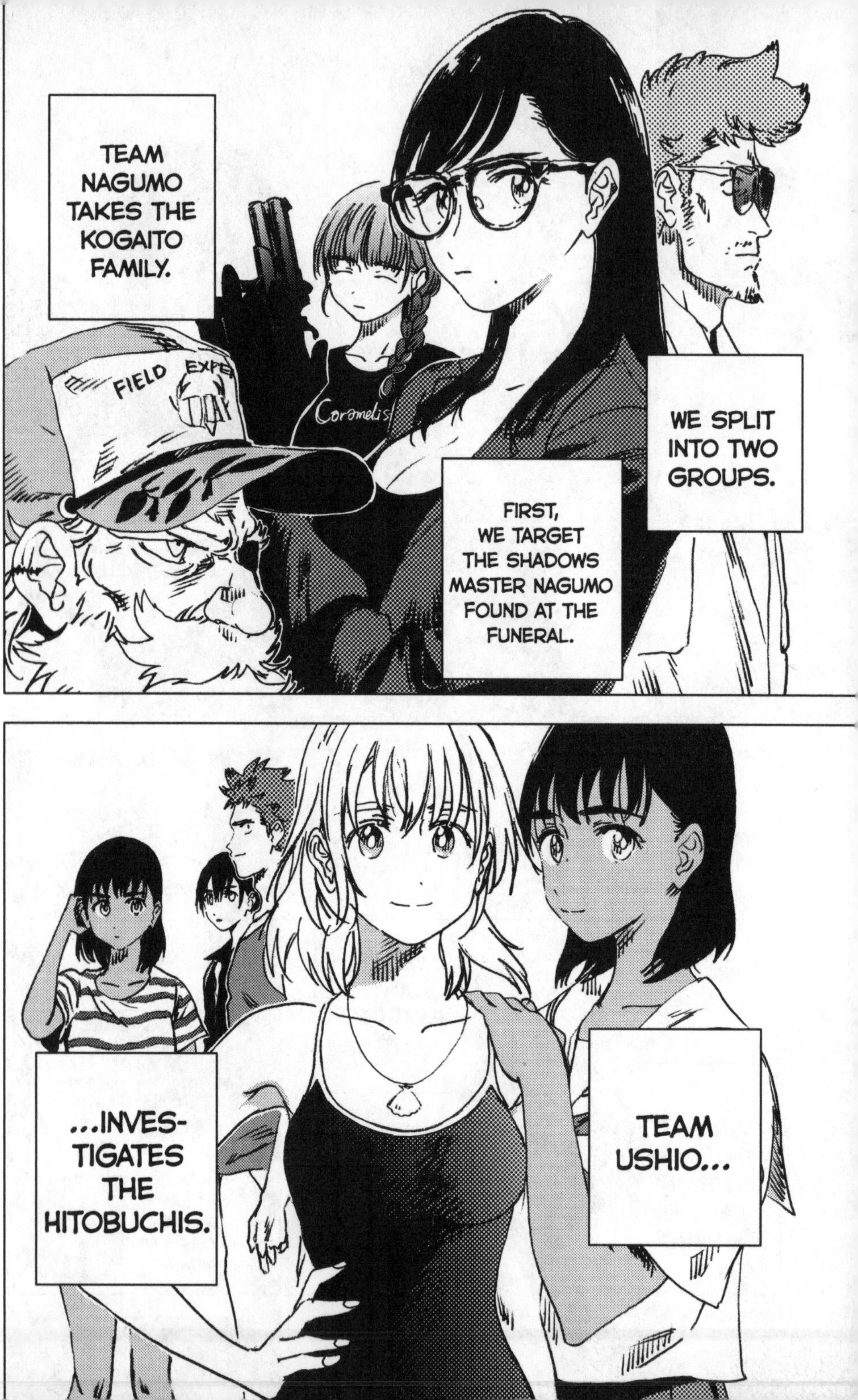
WE SPLIT INTO TWO GROUPS.
TEAM NAGUMO TAKES THE KOGAITO FAMILY.
FIRST, WE TARGET THE SHADOWS MASTER NAGUMO FOUND AT THE FUNERAL.
TEAM USHIO...
...INVES-TIGATES THE HITOBUCHIS.

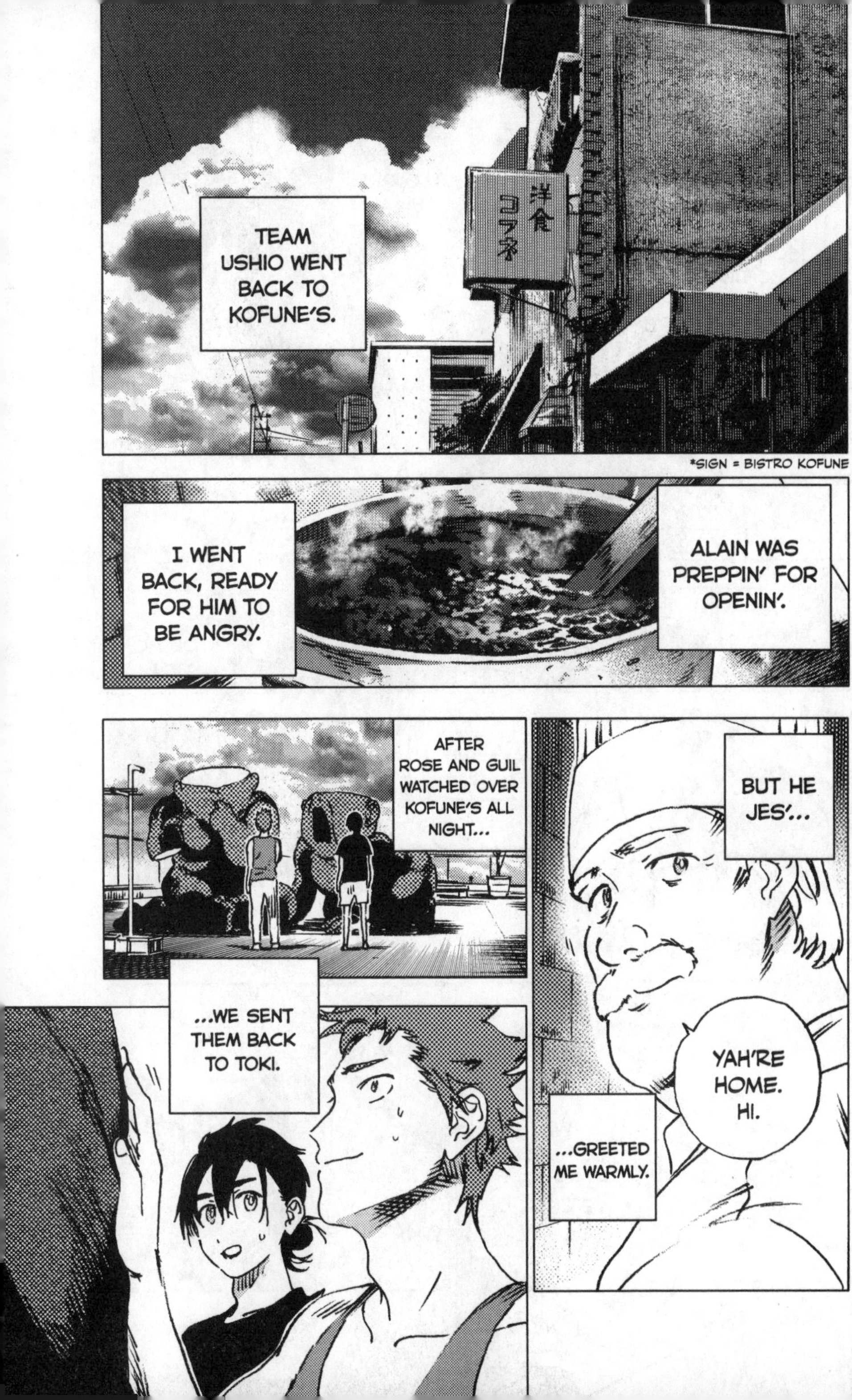
洋食
コフネ
TEAM USHIO WENT BACK TO KOFUNE'S.
*SIGN = BISTRO KOFUNE
ALAIN WAS PREPPIN' FOR OPENIN'.
I WENT BACK, READY FOR HIM TO BE ANGRY.
BUT HE JES'...
YAH'RE HOME. HI.
...GREETED ME WARMLY.
AFTER ROSE AND GUIL WATCHED OVER KOFUNE'S ALL NIGHT...
...WE SENT THEM BACK TO TOKI.

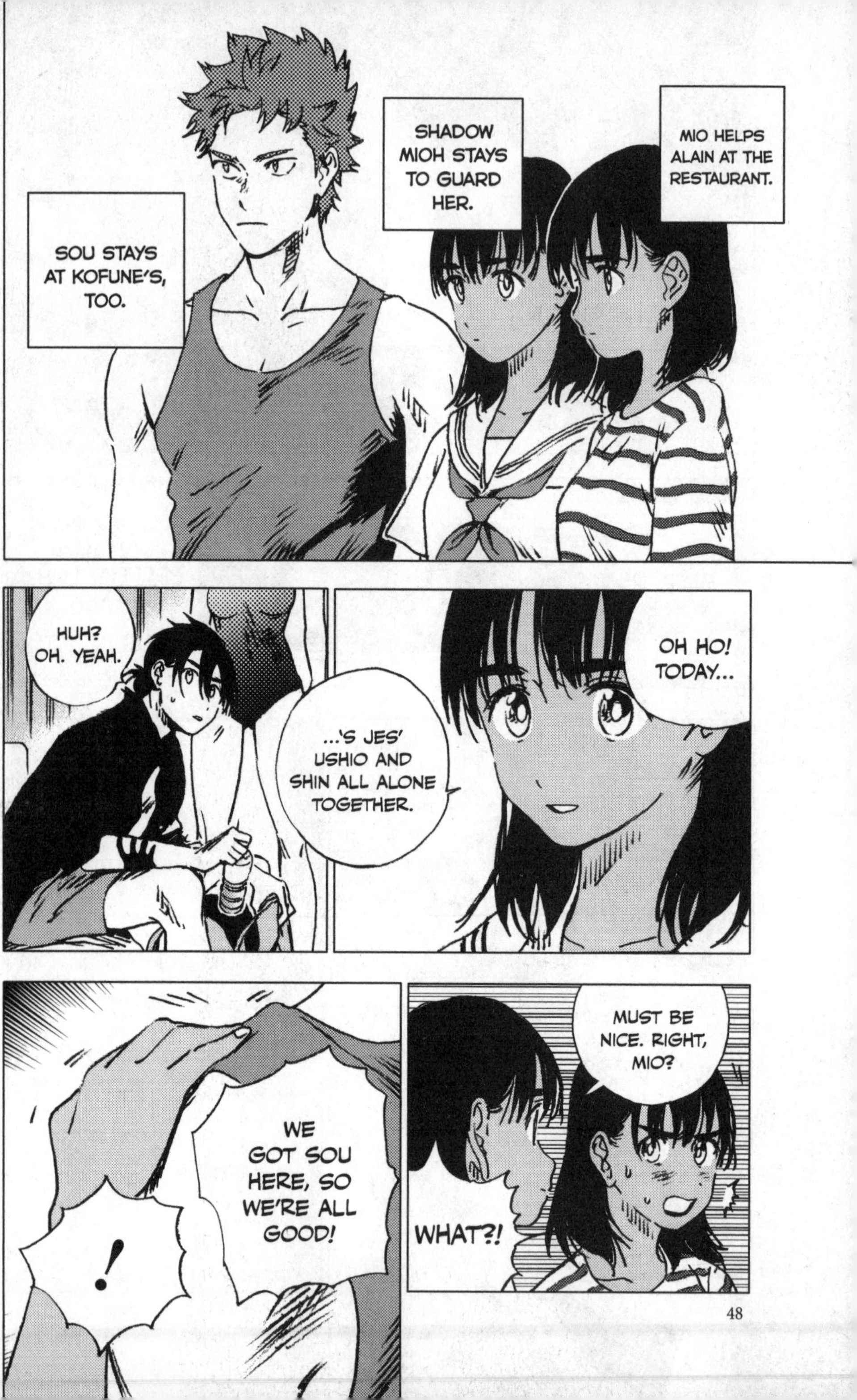
MIO HELPS ALAIN AT THE RESTAURANT.
SHADOW MIOH STAYS TO GUARD HER.
SOU STAYS AT KOFUNE'S, TOO.
OH HO! TODAY...
...'S JES' USHIO AND SHIN ALL ALONE TOGETHER.
HUH? OH. YEAH.
MUST BE NICE. RIGHT, MIO?
WHAT?!
WE GOT SOU HERE, SO WE'RE ALL GOOD!
!

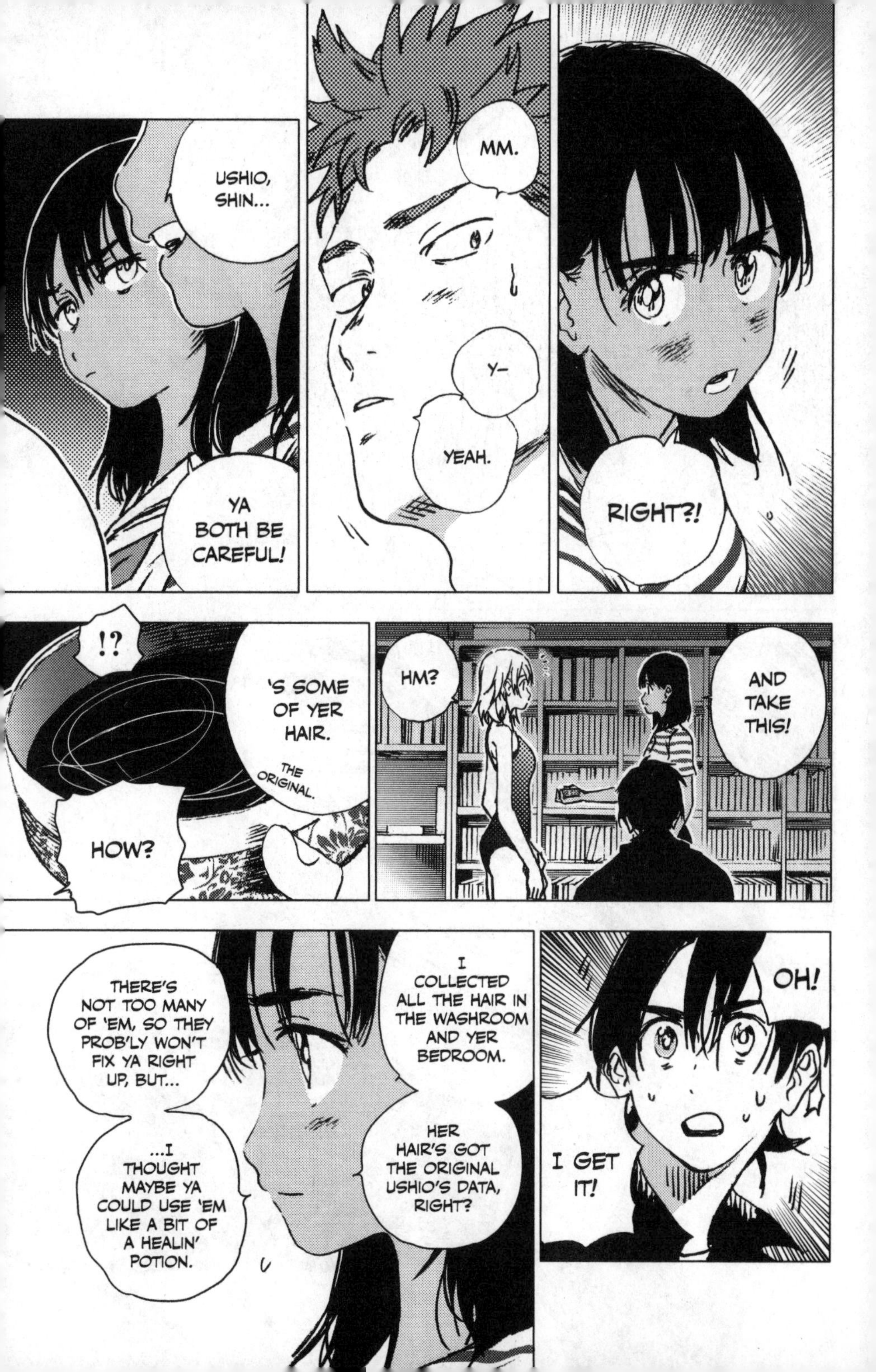
RIGHT?!
MM.
Y–
YEAH.
USHIO, SHIN...
YA BOTH BE CAREFUL!
AND TAKE THIS!
HM?
'S SOME OF YER HAIR.
THE ORIGINAL.
!?
HOW?
OH!
I GET IT!
I COLLECTED ALL THE HAIR IN THE WASHROOM AND YER BEDROOM.
THERE'S NOT TOO MANY OF 'EM, SO THEY PROB'LY WON'T FIX YA RIGHT UP, BUT...
HER HAIR'S GOT THE ORIGINAL USHIO'S DATA, RIGHT?
...I THOUGHT MAYBE YA COULD USE 'EM LIKE A BIT OF A HEALIN' POTION.

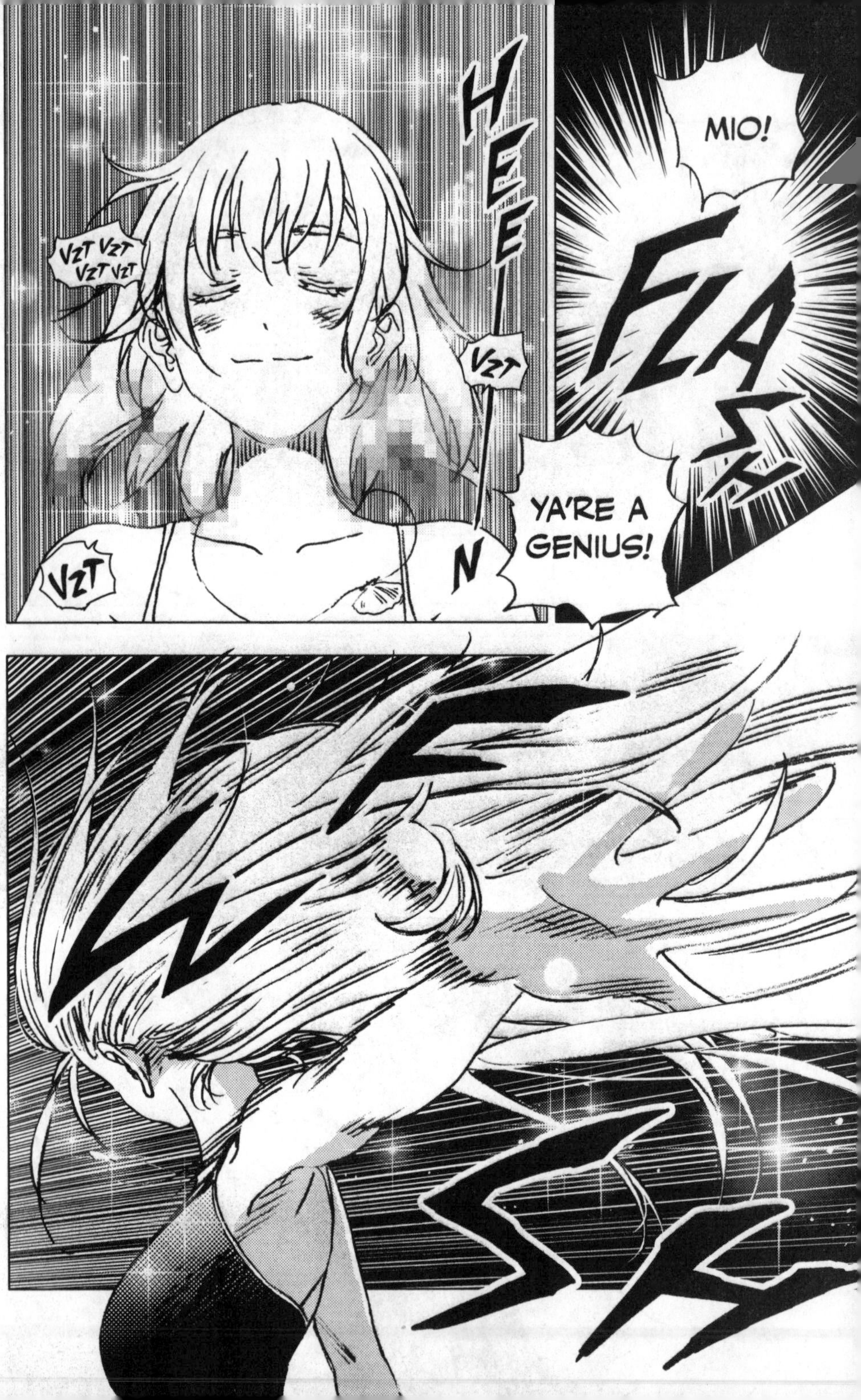
MIO!
YA'RE A GENIUS!
HEEEN
VZT VZT
VZT VZT
VZT
VZT

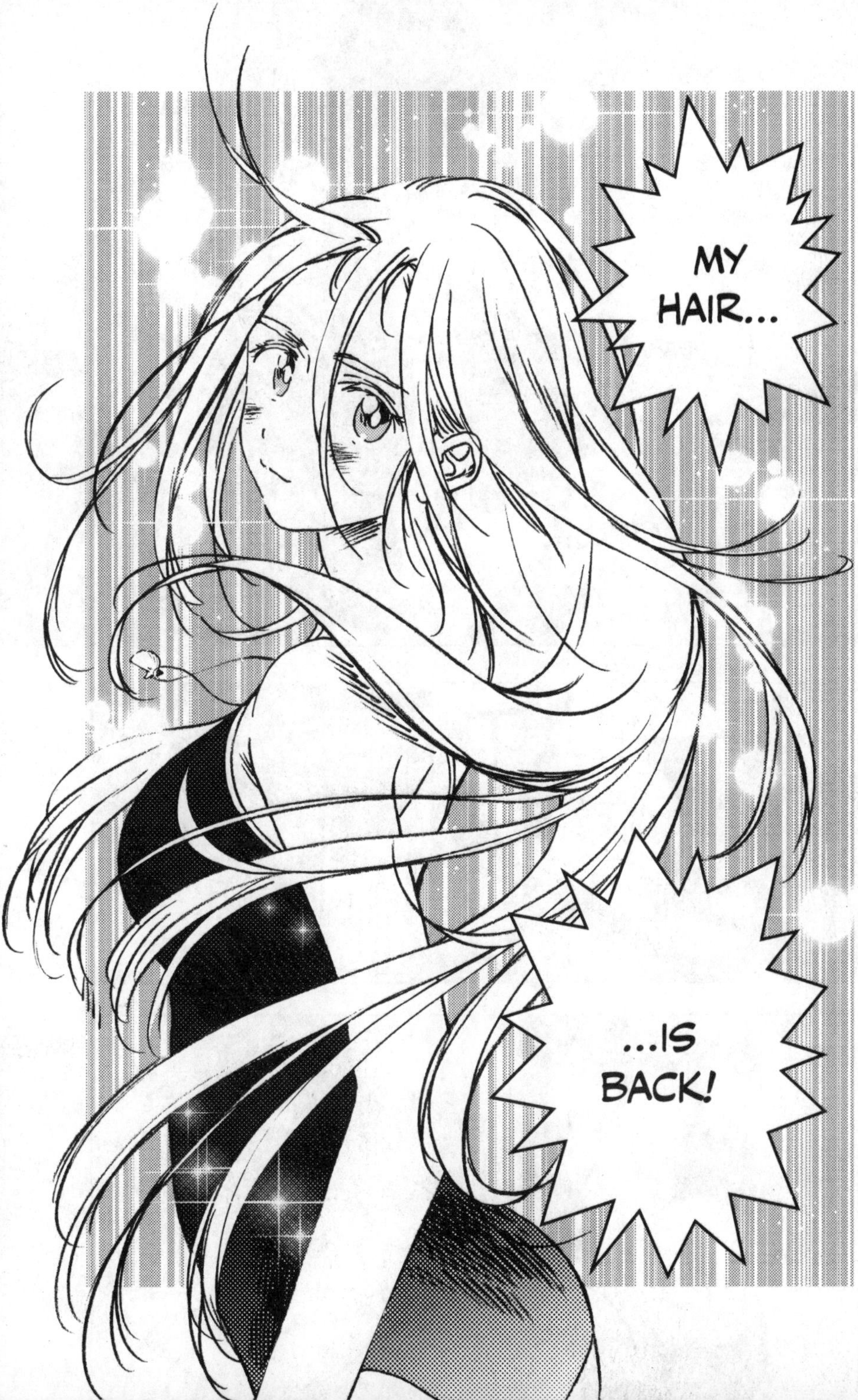
MY HAIR...
...IS BACK!

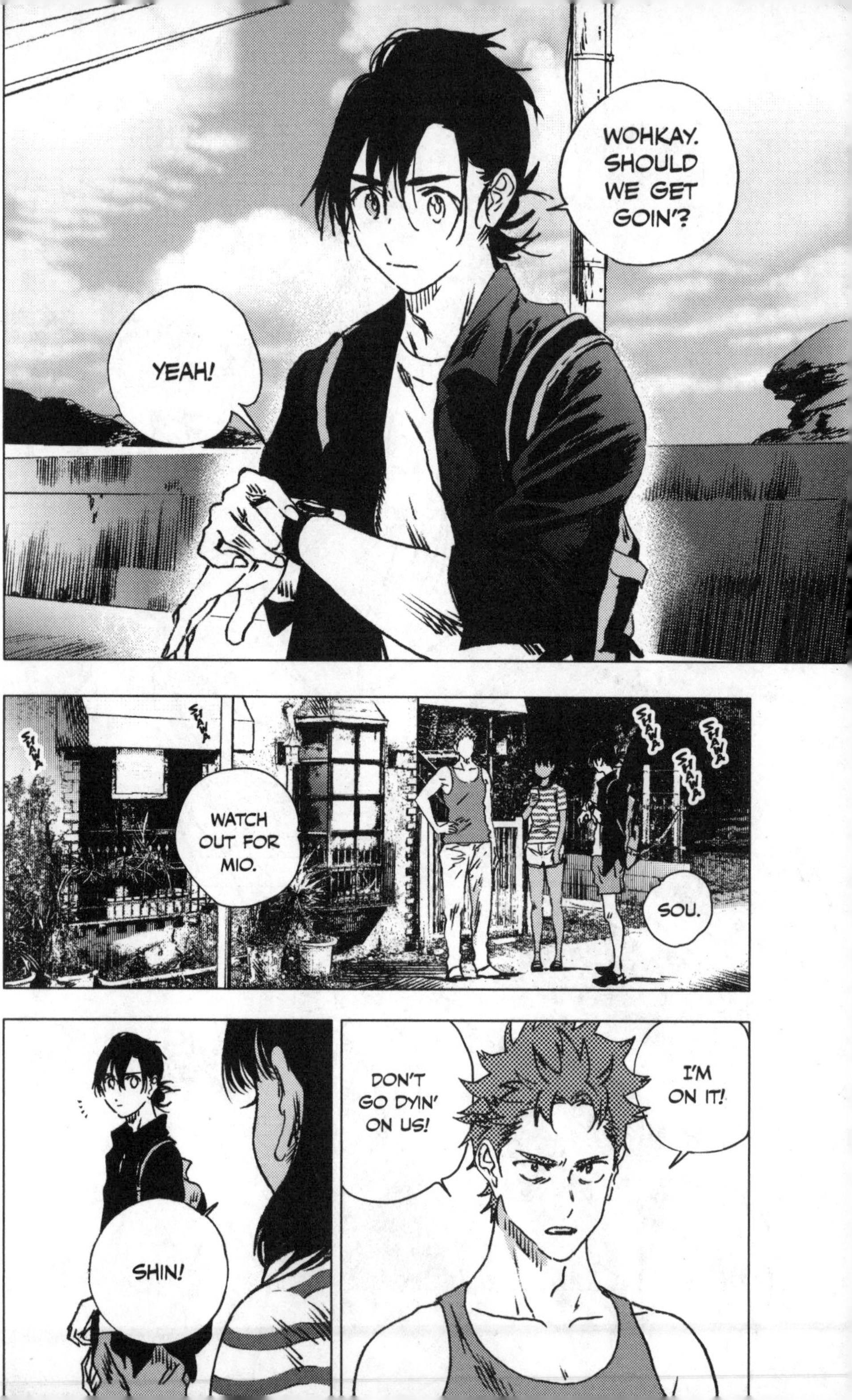
WOHKAY. SHOULD WE GET GOIN'?
YEAH!
SHAWA SHAWA
SHAWA SHAWA
SOU.
WATCH OUT FOR MIO.
SHAWA
SHAWA
I'M ON IT!
DON'T GO DYIN' ON US!
SHIN!

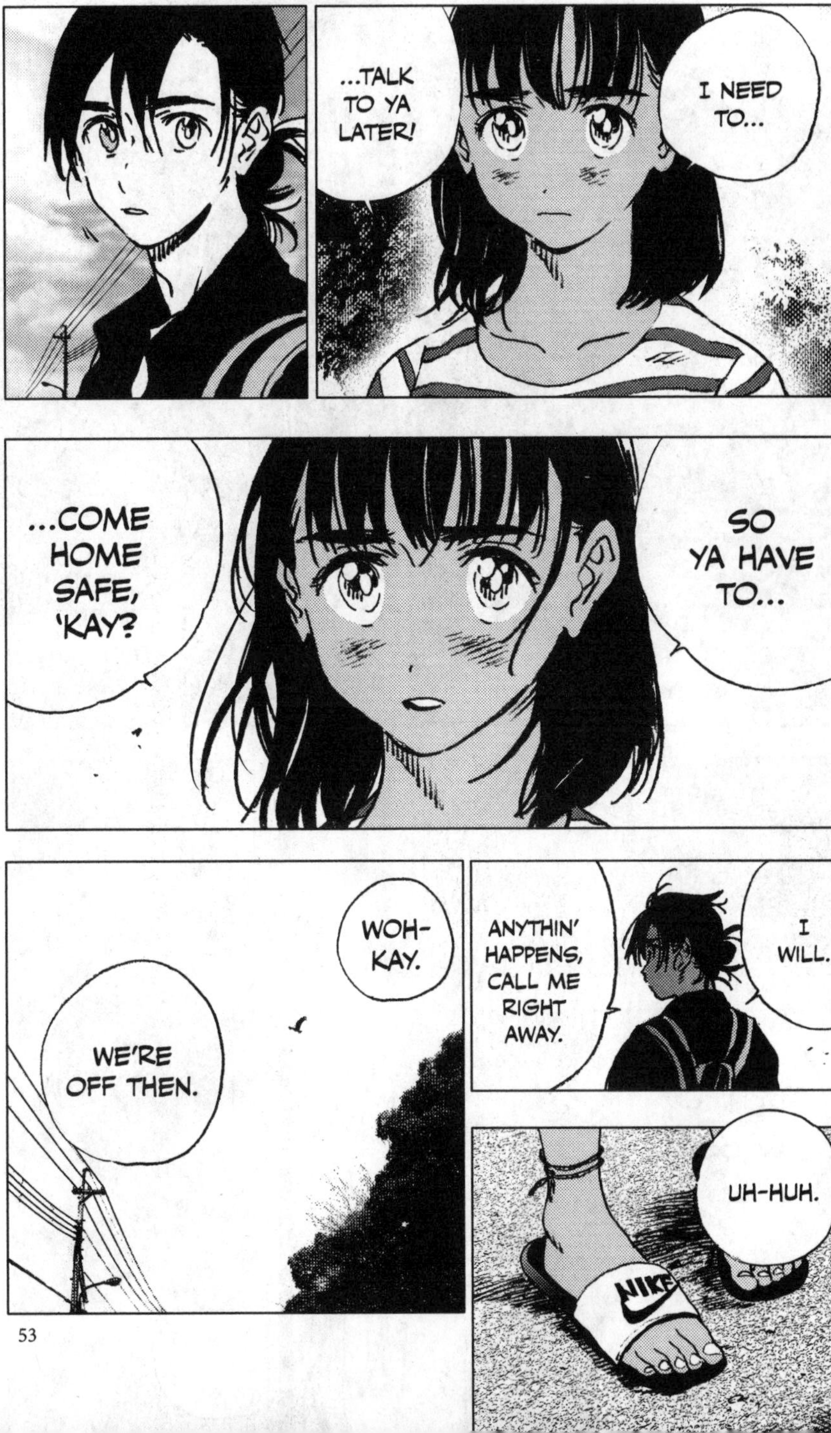
I NEED TO...
...TALK TO YA LATER!
SO YA HAVE TO...
...COME HOME SAFE, 'KAY?
I WILL.
ANYTHIN' HAPPENS, CALL ME RIGHT AWAY.
UH-HUH.
NIKE
WOH-KAY.
WE'RE OFF THEN.

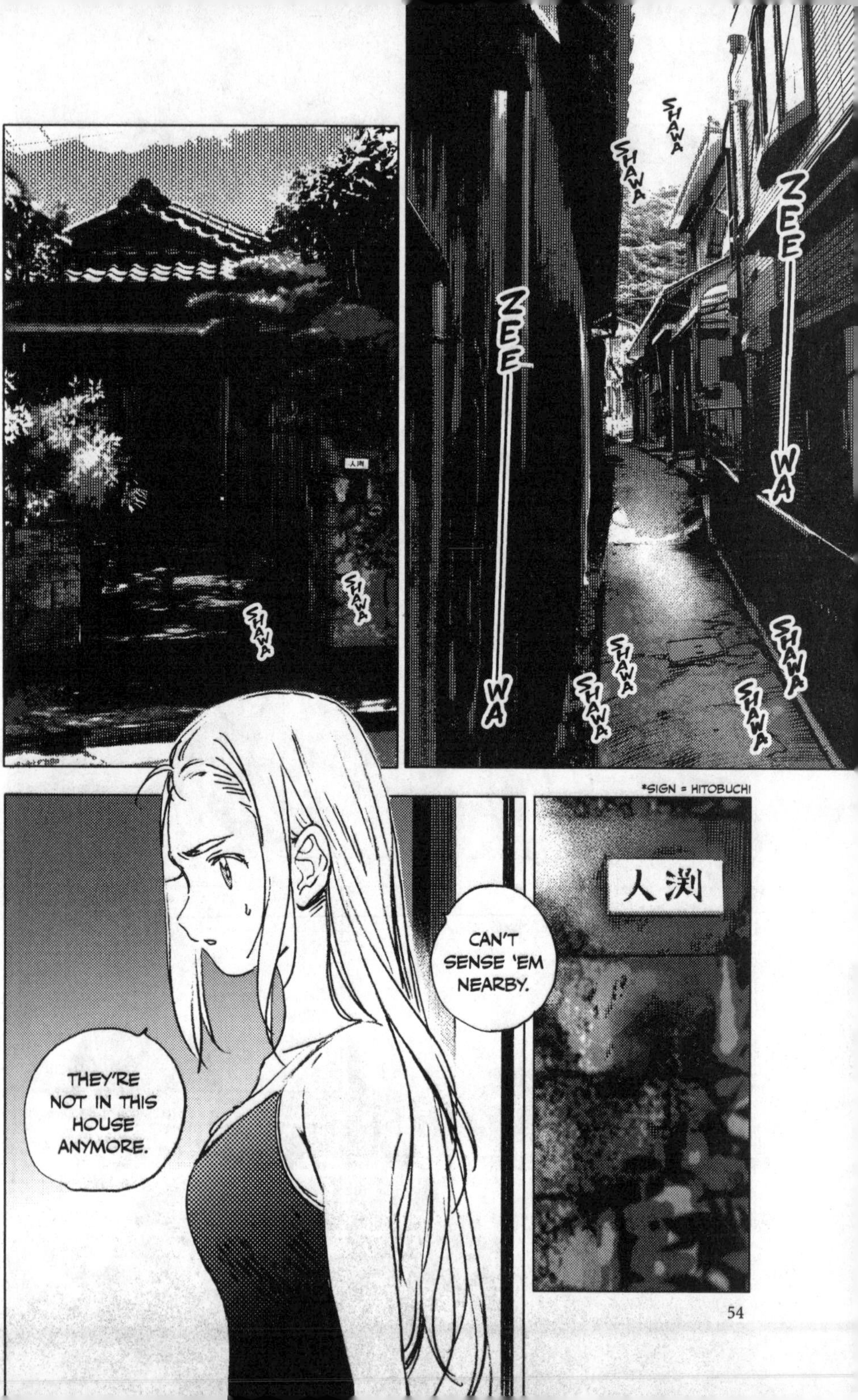
SHAWA
SHAWA
ZEE WA
ZEE WA
SHAWA
SHAWA
SHAWA
SHAWA
SHAWA
SHAWA
*SIGN = HITOBUCHI
人渕
CAN'T SENSE 'EM NEARBY.
THEY'RE NOT IN THIS HOUSE ANYMORE.

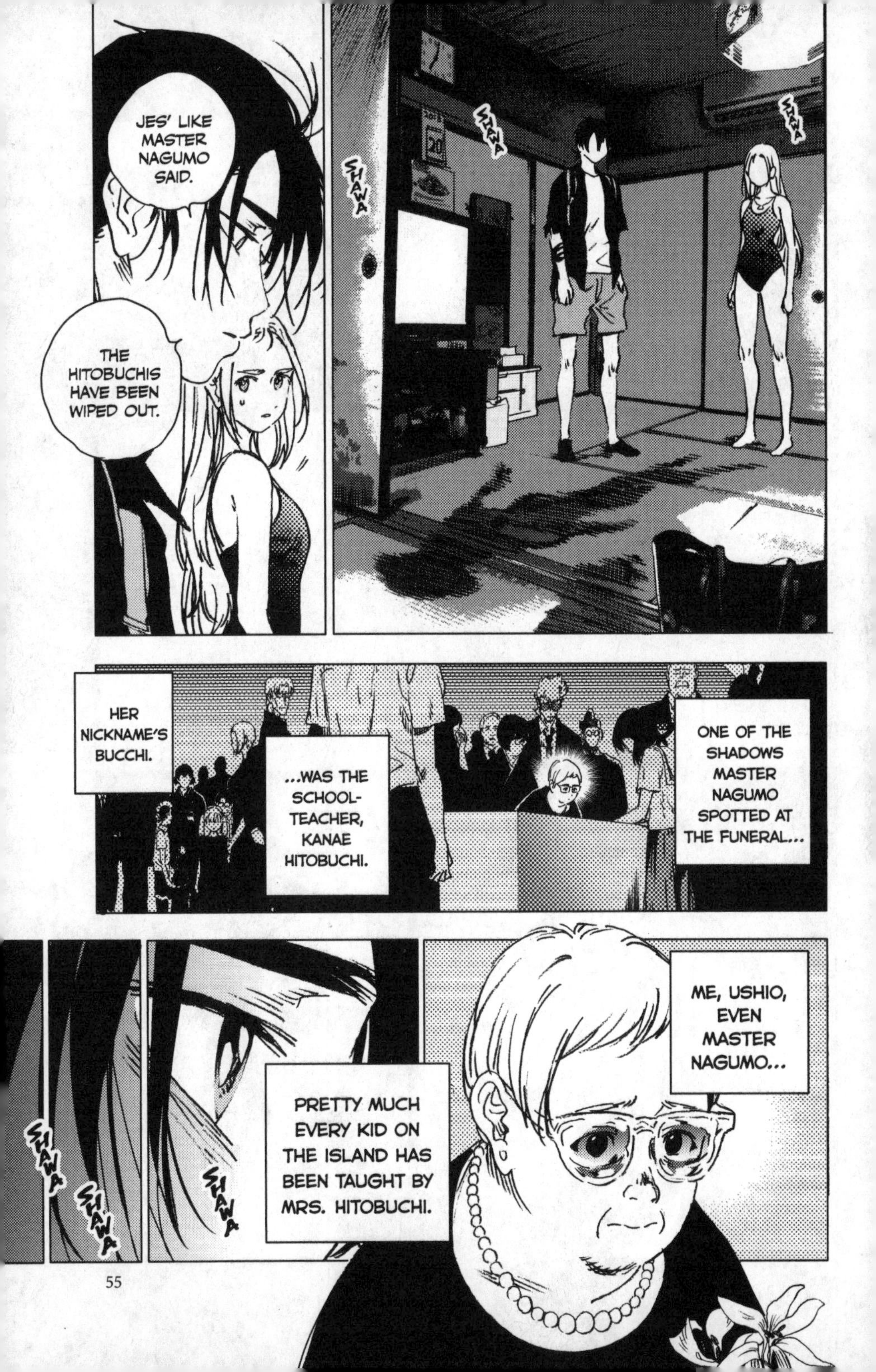
SHAWA
SHAWA
SHAWA
JES' LIKE MASTER NAGUMO SAID.
THE HITOBUCHIS HAVE BEEN WIPED OUT.
ONE OF THE SHADOWS MASTER NAGUMO SPOTTED AT THE FUNERAL...
...WAS THE SCHOOL-TEACHER, KANAE HITOBUCHI.
HER NICKNAME'S BUCCHI.
ME, USHIO, EVEN MASTER NAGUMO...
PRETTY MUCH EVERY KID ON THE ISLAND HAS BEEN TAUGHT BY MRS. HITOBUCHI.
SHAWA
SHAWA
SHAWA

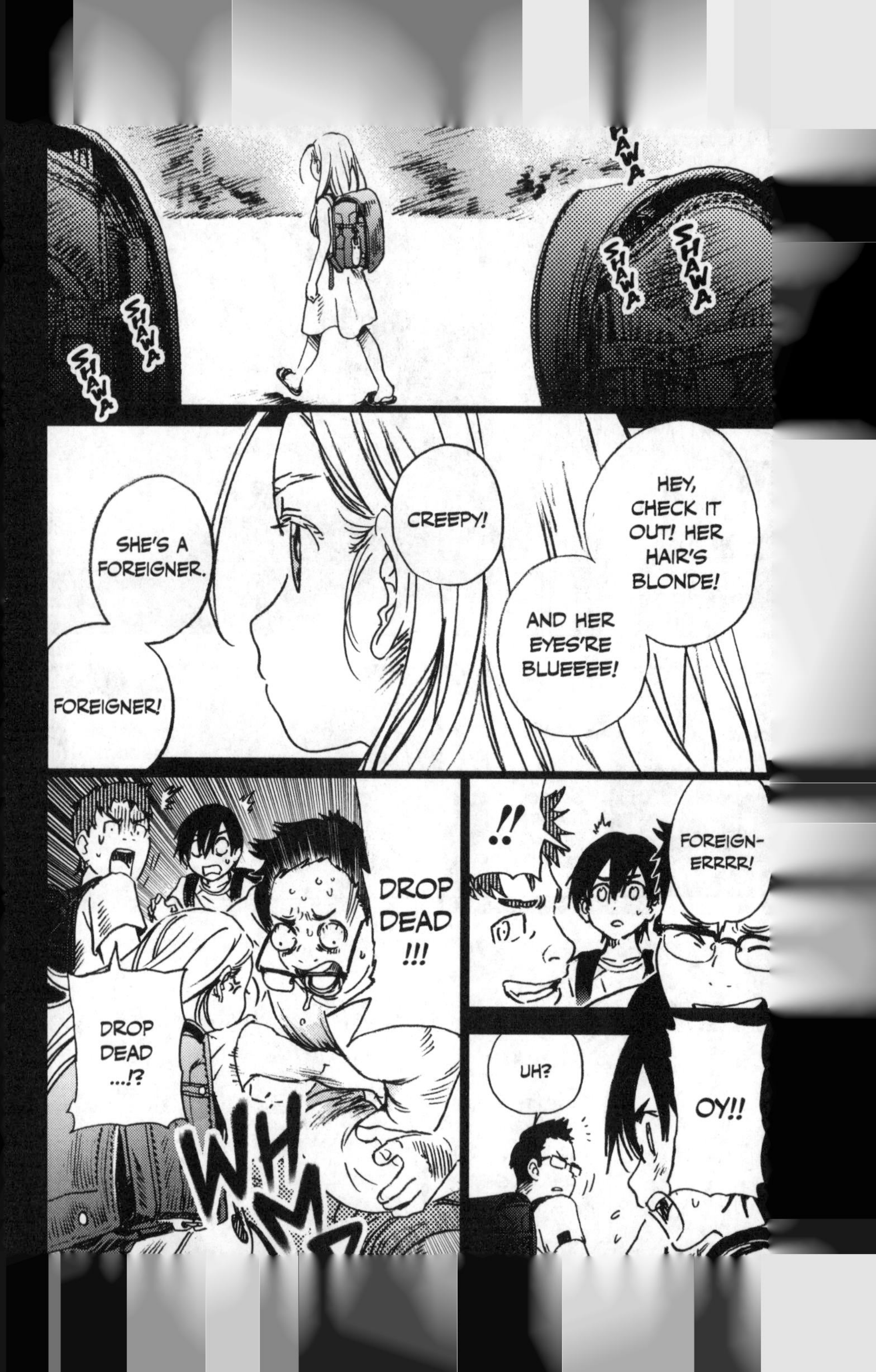
SHAWA
SHAWA
SHAWA
SHAWA
HEY, CHECK IT OUT! HER HAIR'S BLONDE!
AND HER EYES'RE BLUEEEEE!
CREEPY!
SHE'S A FOREIGNER.
FOREIGNER!
FOREIGN-ERRRR!
!!
OY!!
UH?
DROP DEAD !!!
DROP DEAD ...!?

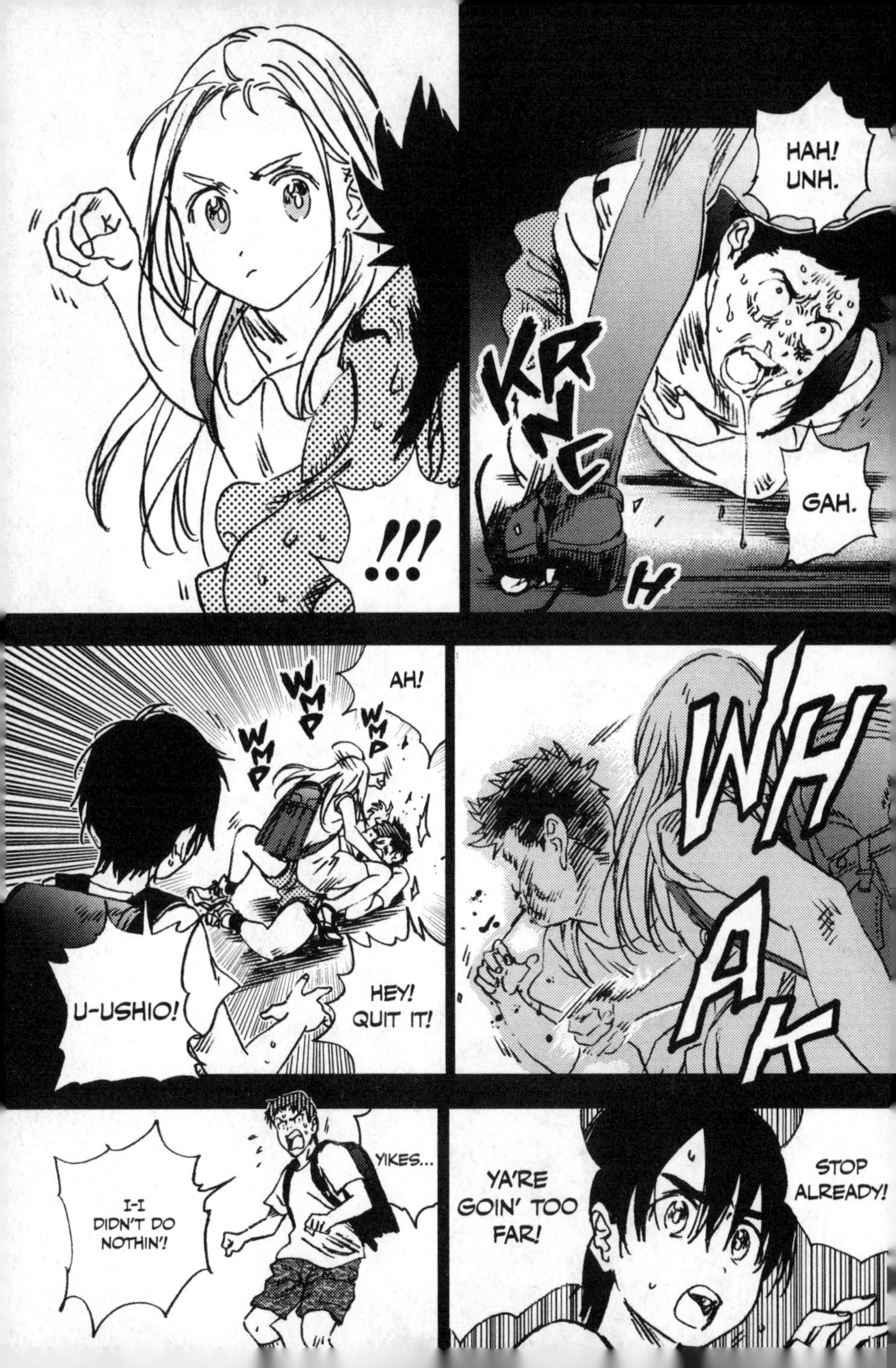
HAH! UNH.
KRNCH
GAH.
!!!
WHAK
AH!
WMP
WMP
WMP
HEY! QUIT IT!
U-USHIO!
STOP ALREADY!
YA'RE GOIN' TOO FAR!
YIKES...
I-I DIDN'T DO NOTHIN'!

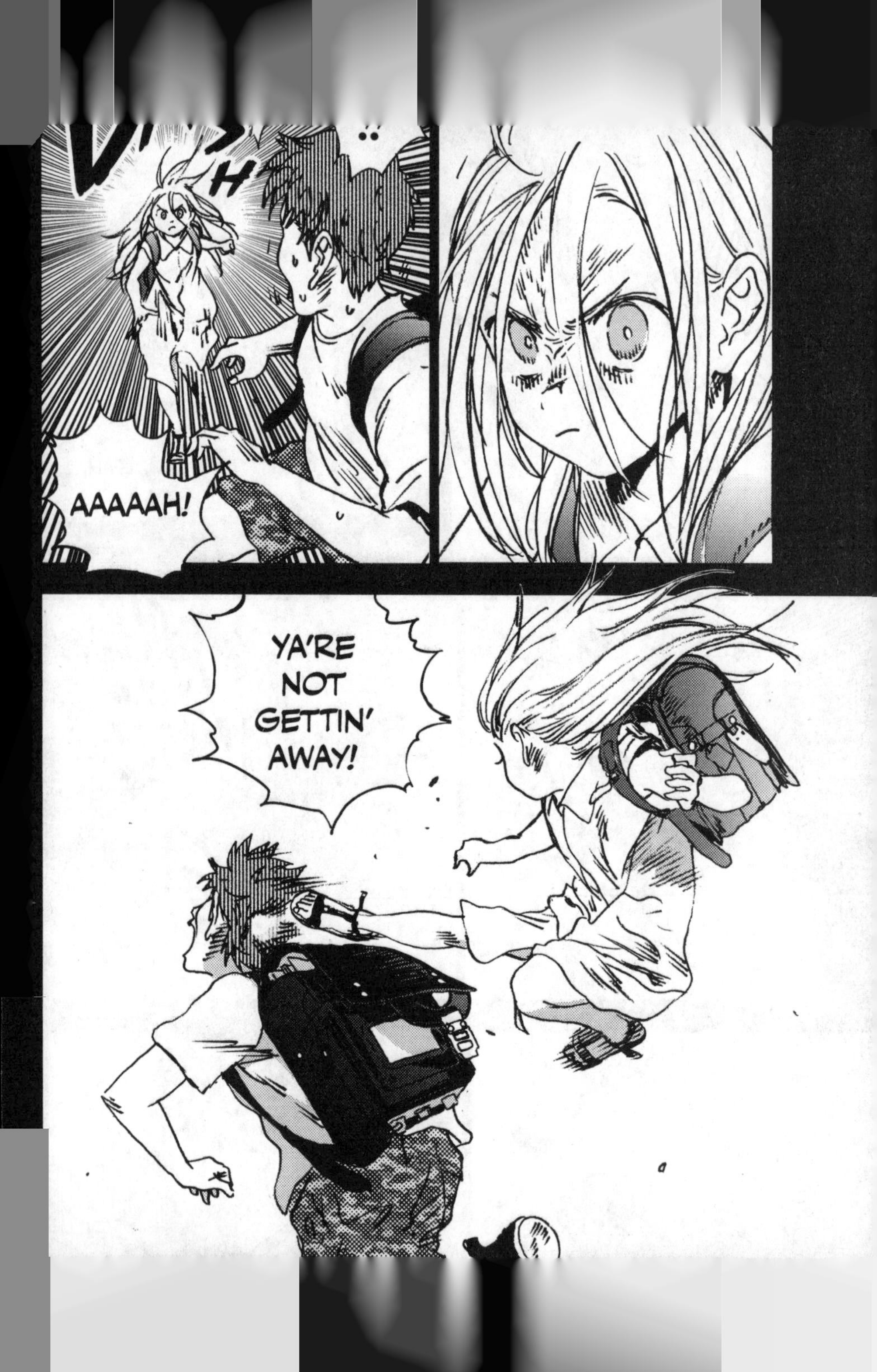
AAAAAH!
YA'RE NOT GETTIN' AWAY!

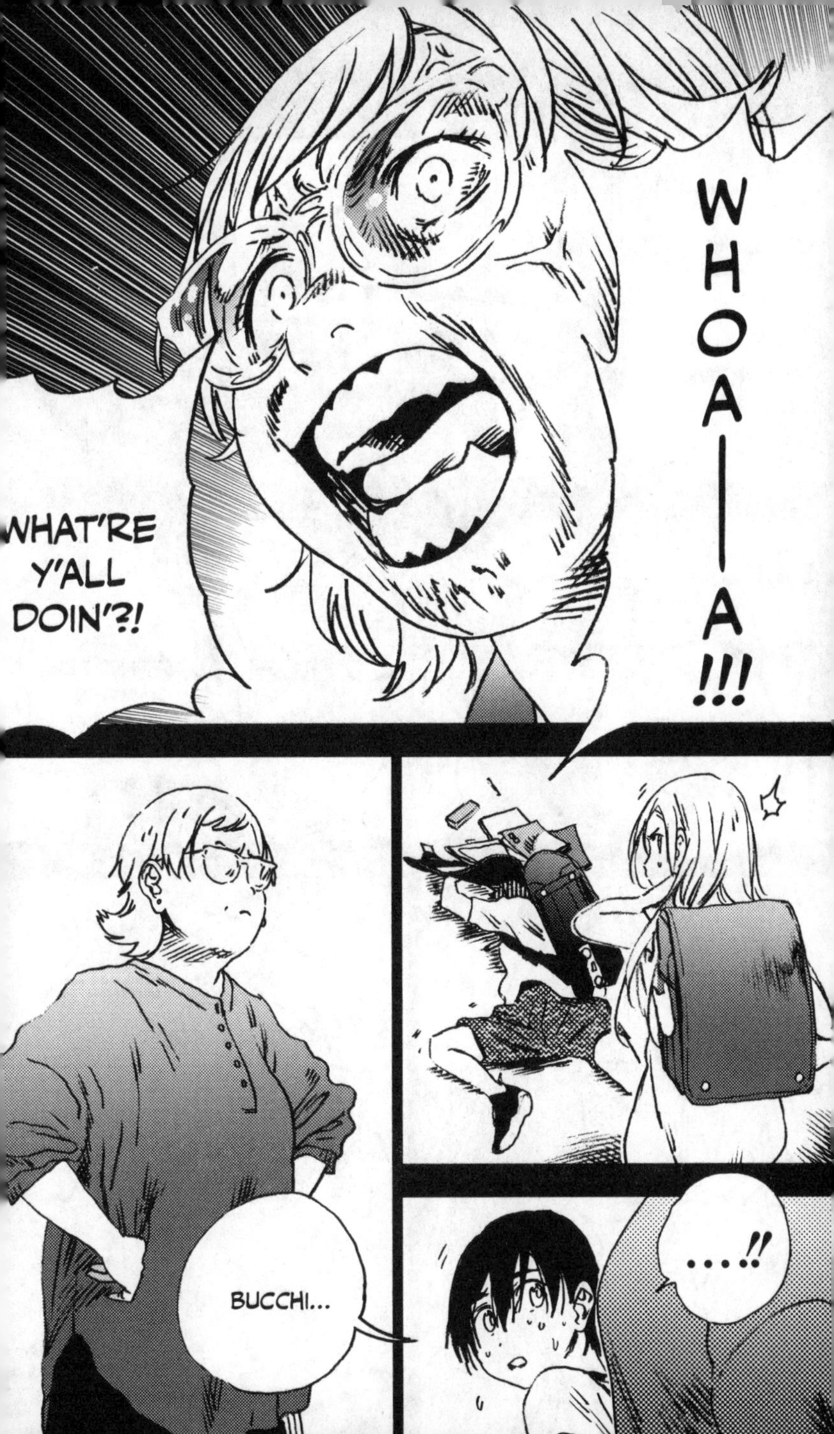
WHOA—A!!!
WHAT'RE Y'ALL DOIN'?!
....!!
BUCCHI...

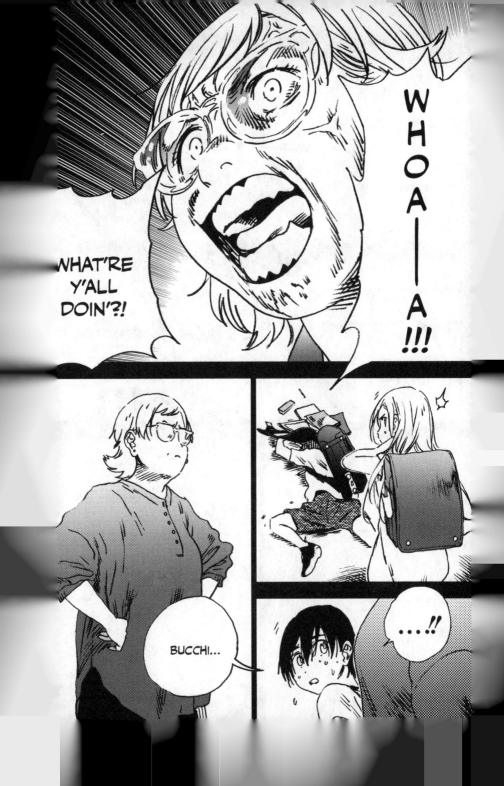

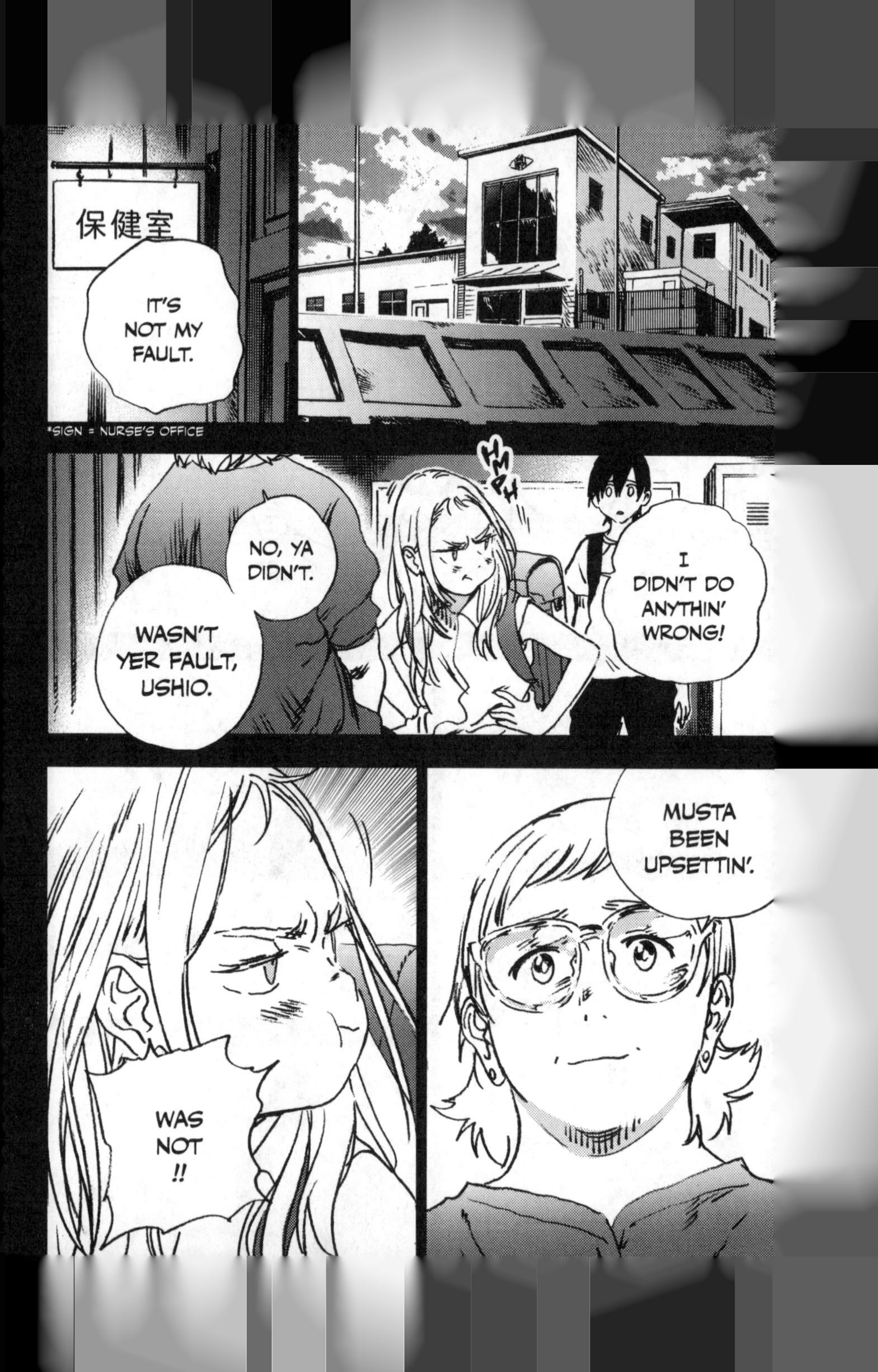
保健室
IT'S NOT MY FAULT.
HMPH
I DIDN'T DO ANYTHIN' WRONG!
NO, YA DIDN'T.
WASN'T YER FAULT, USHIO.
MUSTA BEEN UPSETTIN'.
WAS NOT !!

*SIGN = NURSE'S OFFICE

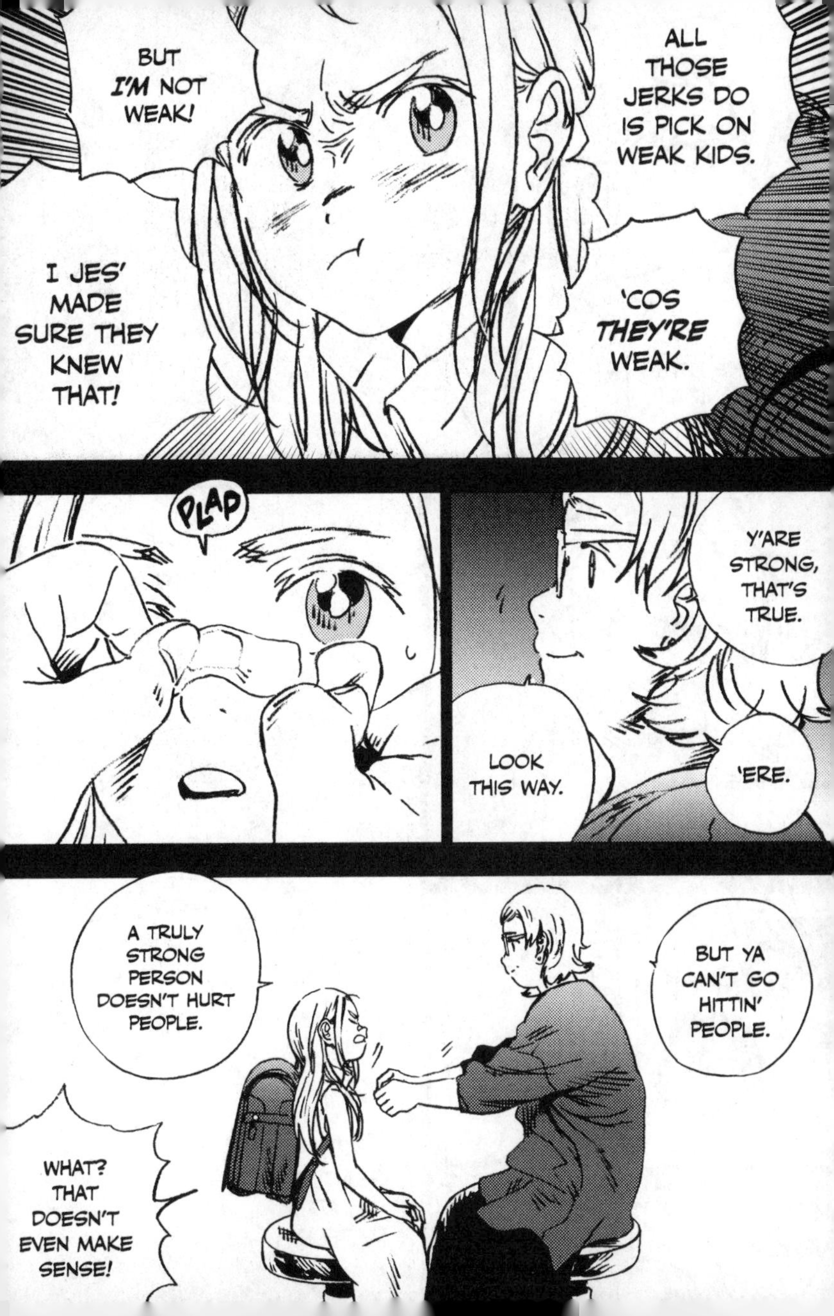
ALL THOSE JERKS DO IS PICK ON WEAK KIDS.
'COS *THEY'RE* WEAK.
BUT *I'M* NOT WEAK!
I JES' MADE SURE THEY KNEW THAT!
Y'ARE STRONG, THAT'S TRUE.
'ERE.
LOOK THIS WAY.
PLAP
BUT YA CAN'T GO HITTIN' PEOPLE.
A TRULY STRONG PERSON DOESN'T HURT PEOPLE.
WHAT? THAT DOESN'T EVEN MAKE SENSE!

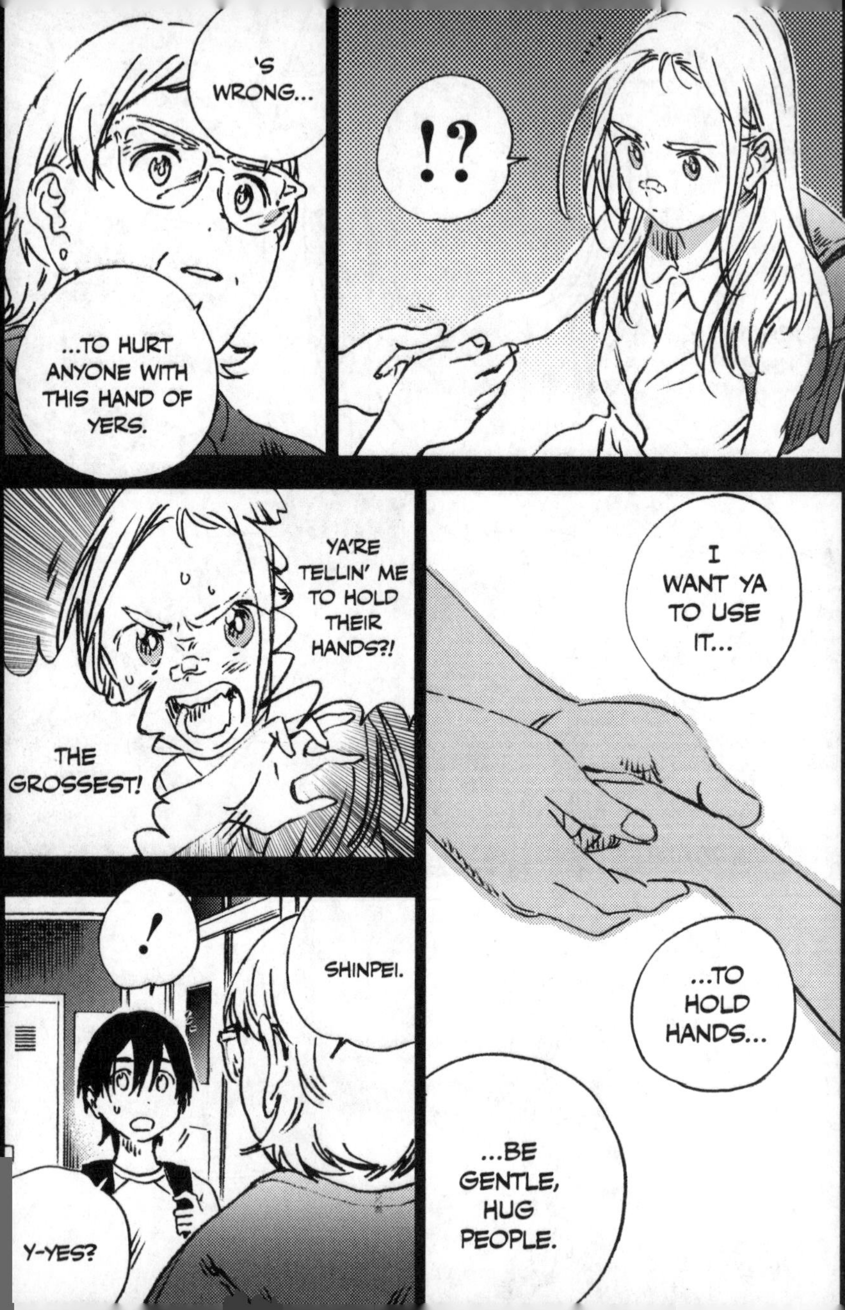
!?
'S WRONG...
...TO HURT ANYONE WITH THIS HAND OF YERS.
I WANT YA TO USE IT...
...TO HOLD HANDS...
...BE GENTLE, HUG PEOPLE.
YA'RE TELLIN' ME TO HOLD THEIR HANDS?!
THE GROSSEST!
SHINPEI.
!
Y-YES?

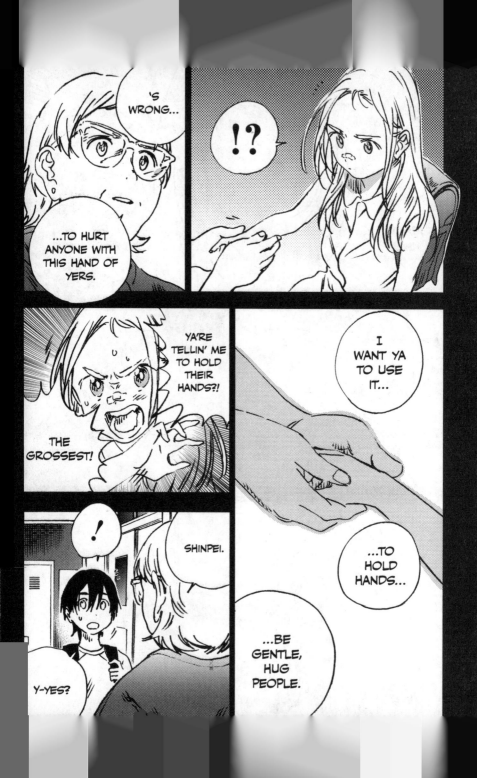

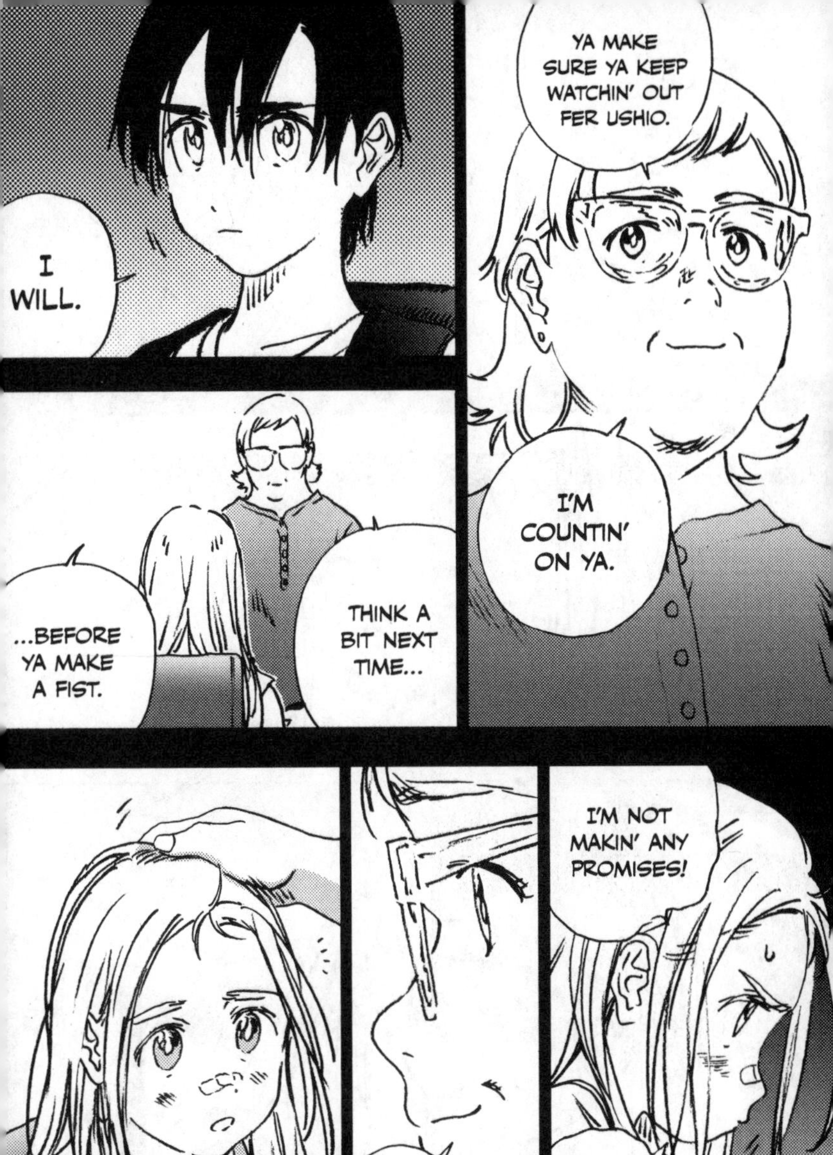
YA MAKE SURE YA KEEP WATCHIN' OUT FER USHIO.
I'M COUNTIN' ON YA.
I WILL.
THINK A BIT NEXT TIME...
...BEFORE YA MAKE A FIST.
I'M NOT MAKIN' ANY PROMISES!
THEY COME AT ME, I'M HITTIN' BACK!
OH?

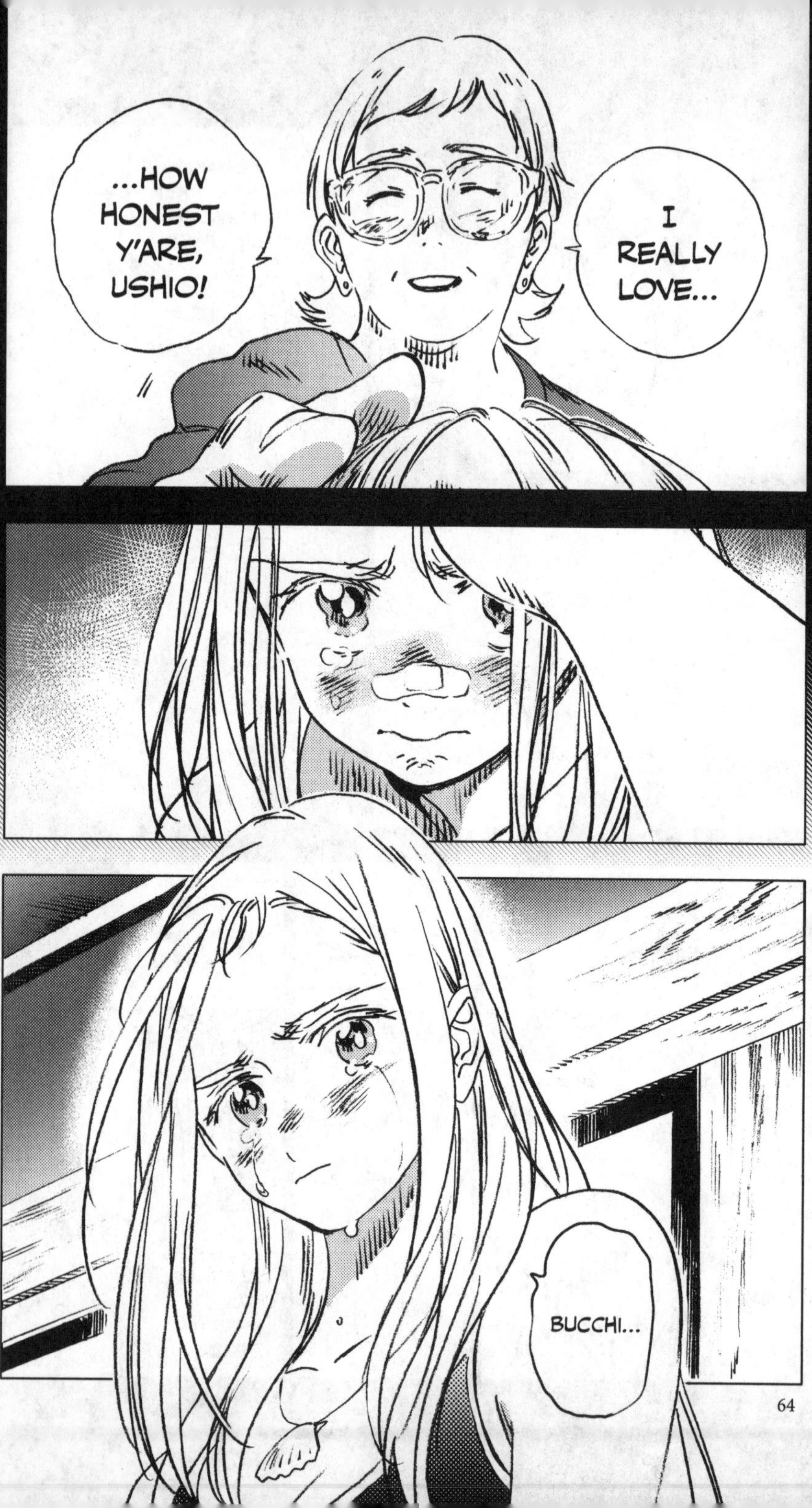
I REALLY LOVE...
...HOW HONEST Y'ARE, USHIO!
BUCCHI...

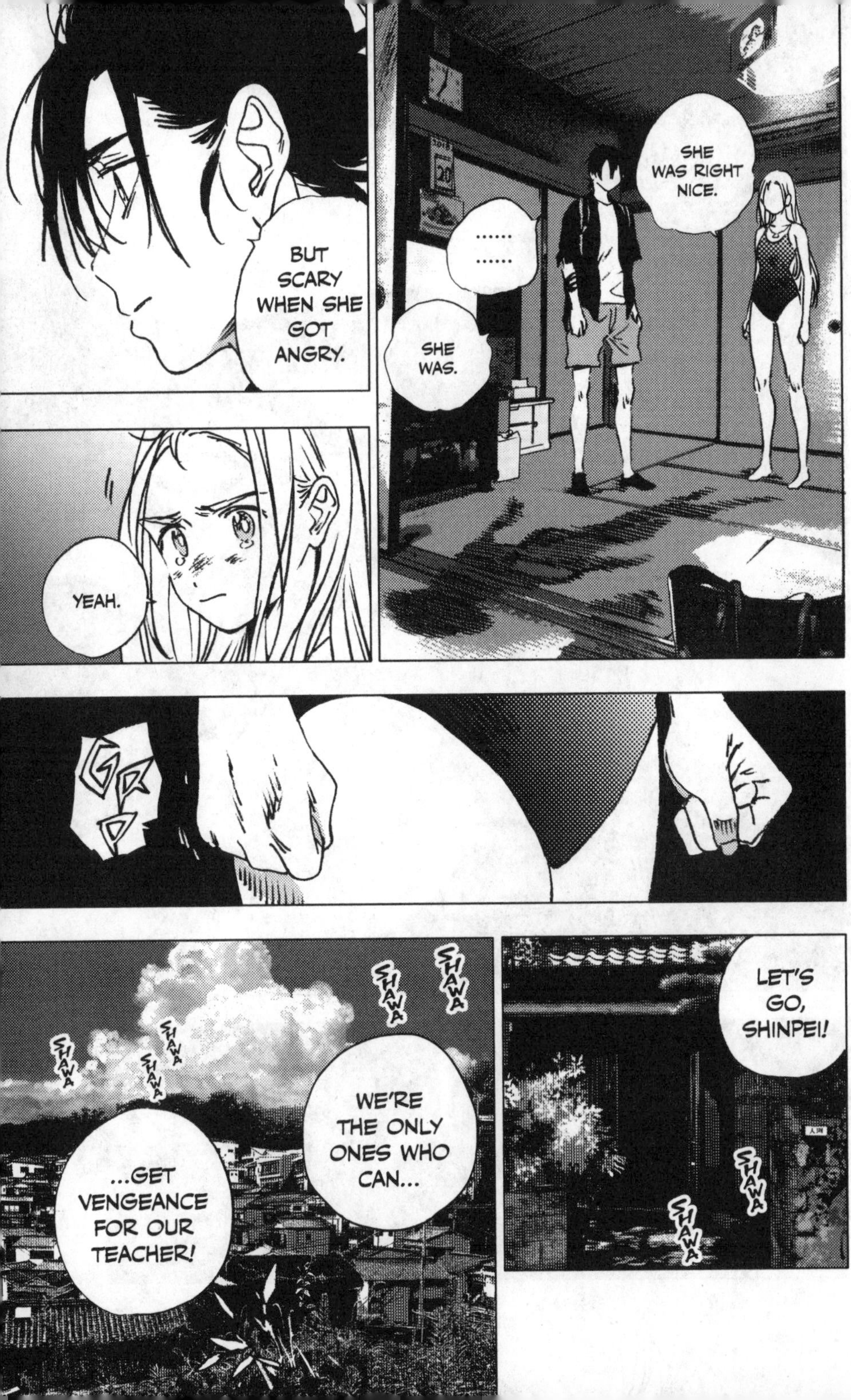
SHE WAS RIGHT NICE.
......
......
SHE WAS.
BUT SCARY WHEN SHE GOT ANGRY.
YEAH.
GRP
LET'S GO, SHINPEI!
SHAWA
SHAWA
SHAWA
SHAWA
SHAWA
SHAWA
WE'RE THE ONLY ONES WHO CAN...
...GET VENGEANCE FOR OUR TEACHER!

......
AS ALWAYS, NURSE NEGORO.
THE PERFECT TREATMENT.

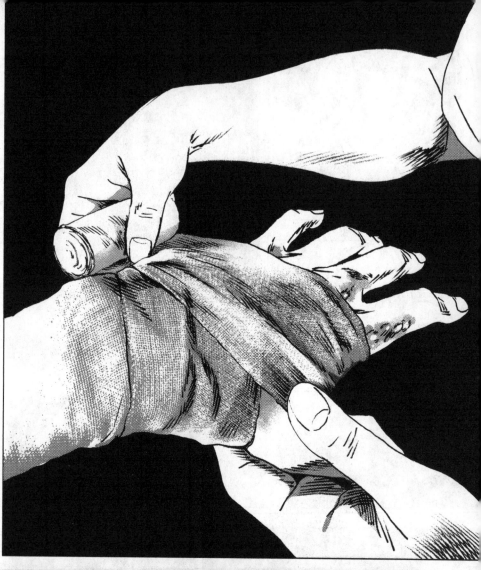

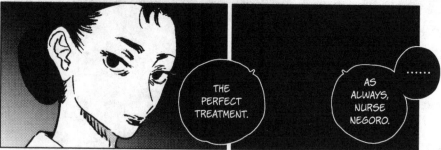

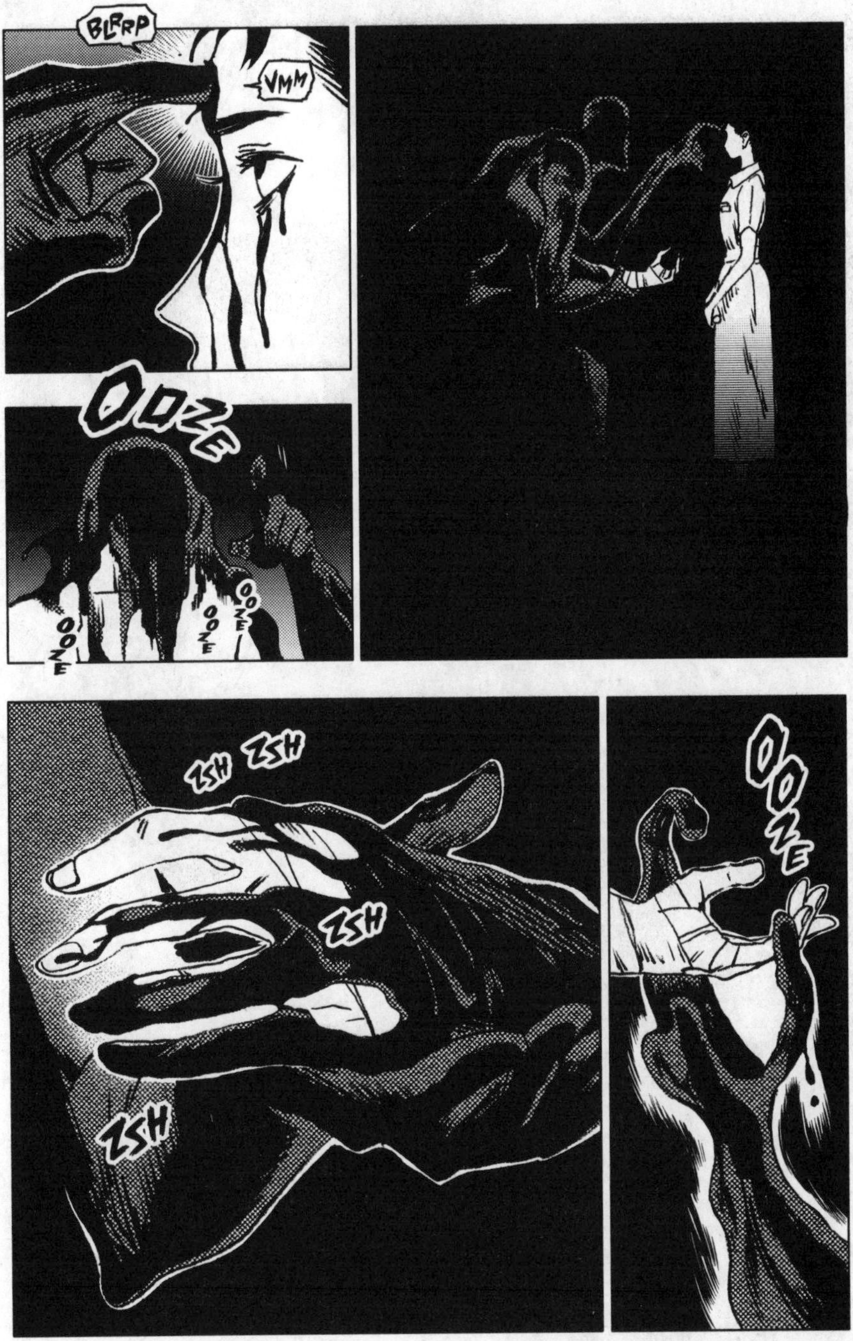
BLRRP
VMM
OOZE
OOZE
OOZE
OOZE
OOZE
ZSH ZSH
ZSH
ZSH

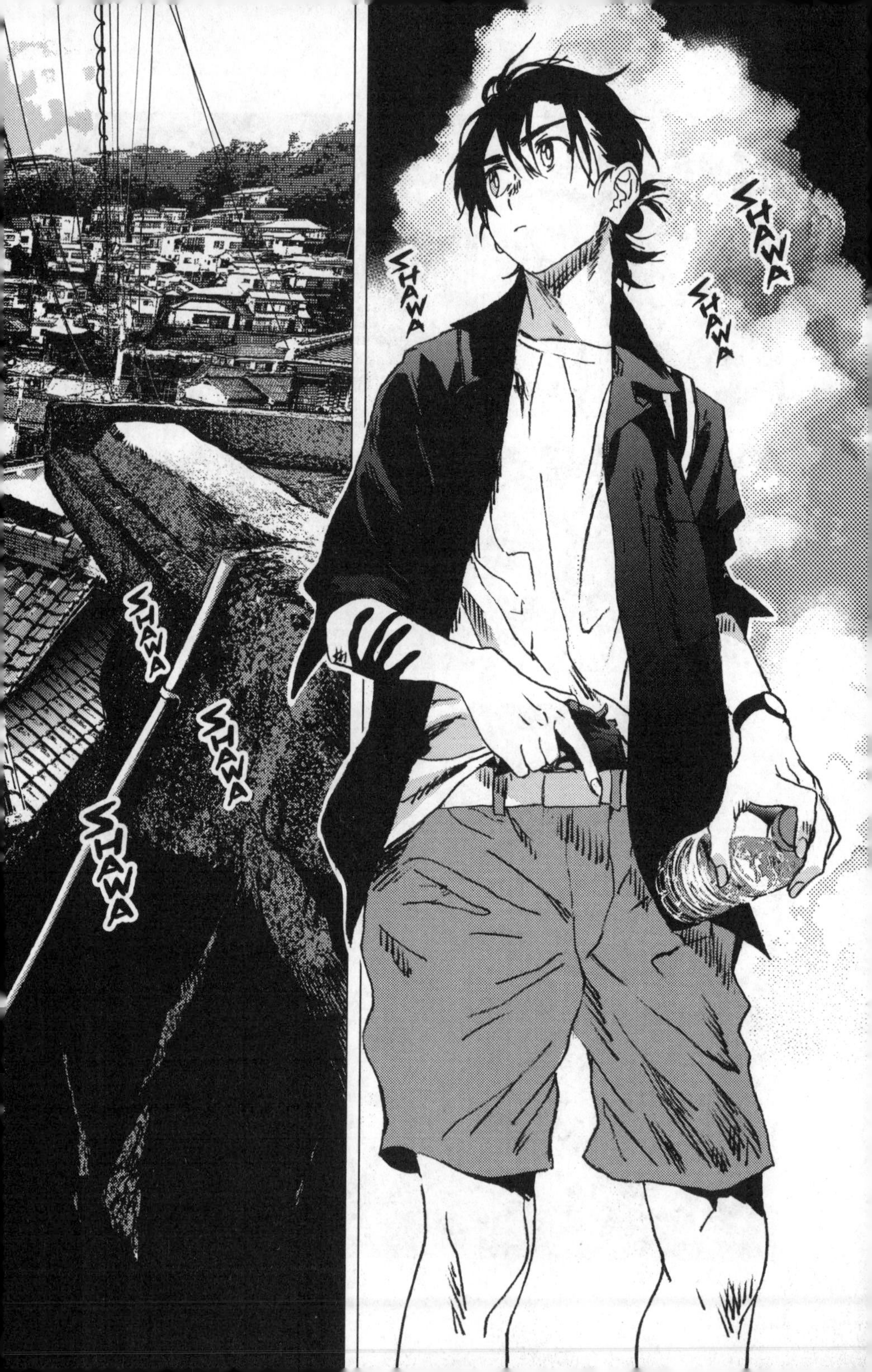
SHAWA
SHAWA
SHAWA
SHAWA
SHAWA
SHAWA

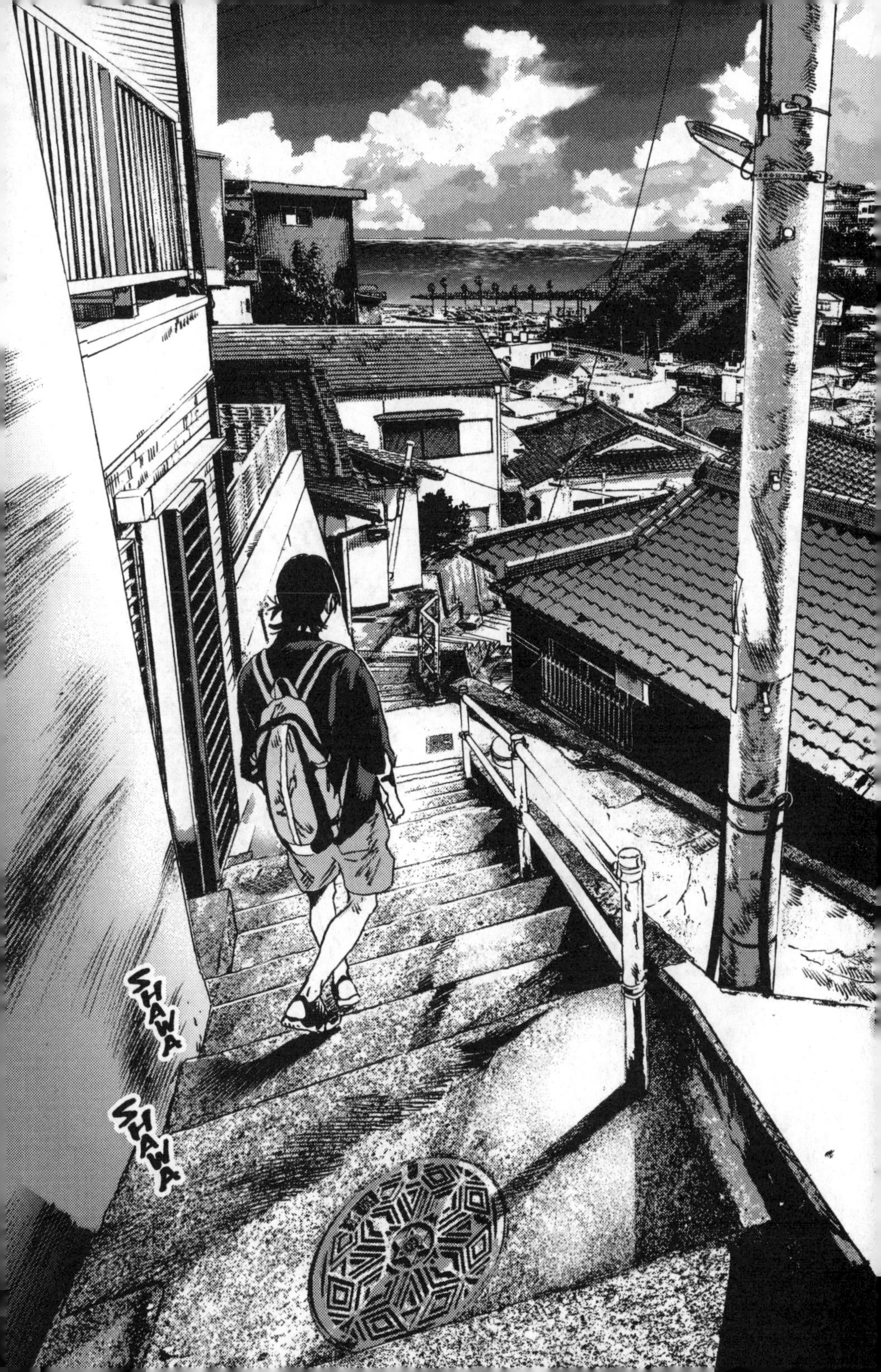
SHAWA
SHAWA

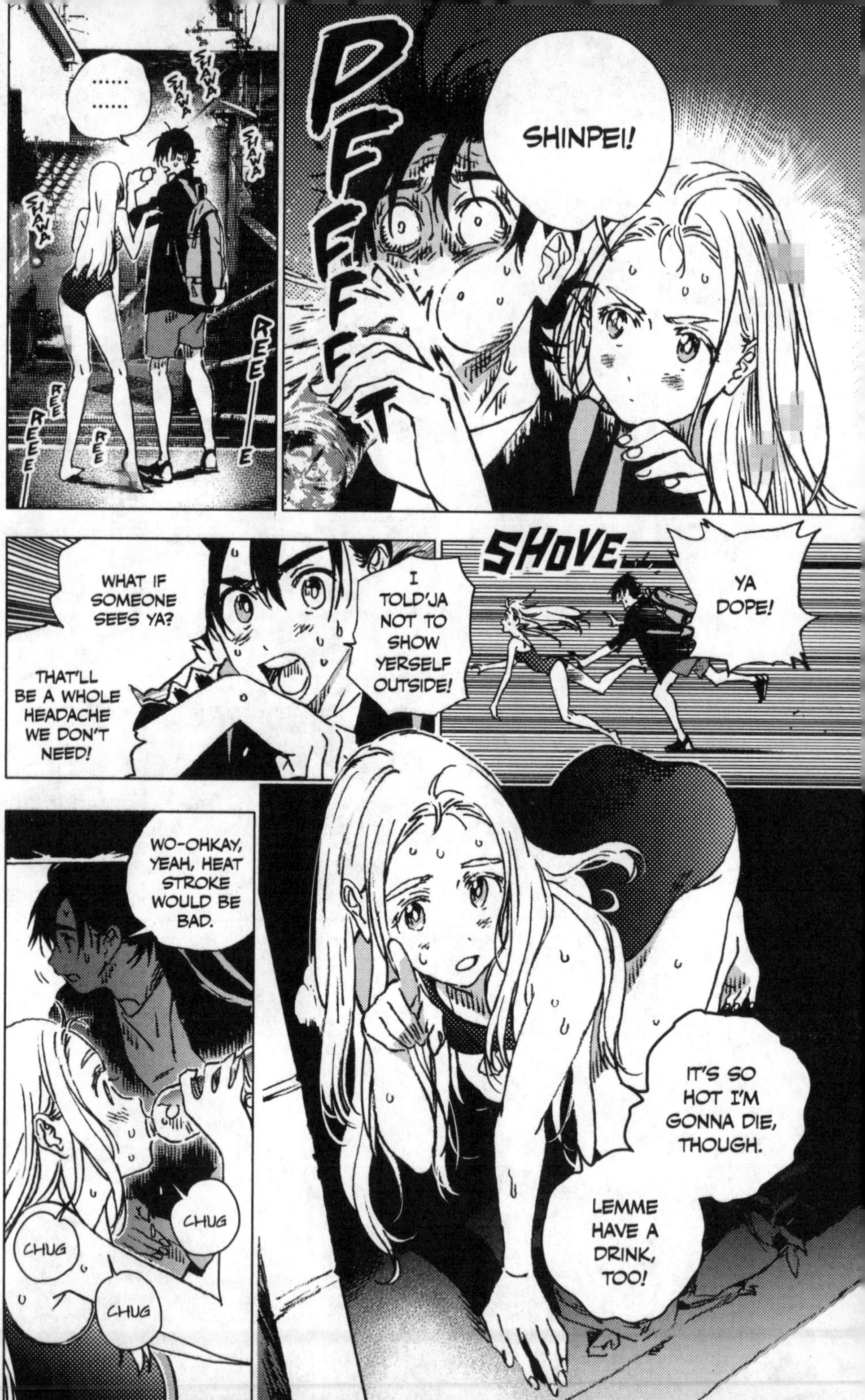
DFFFFFT
SHINPEI!
......
......
SHAWA
SHAWA
SHAWA
SHAWA
REE
E
REE
REE
REEE
SHOVE
YA DOPE!
I TOLD'JA NOT TO SHOW YERSELF OUTSIDE!
WHAT IF SOMEONE SEES YA?
THAT'LL BE A WHOLE HEADACHE WE DON'T NEED!
IT'S SO HOT I'M GONNA DIE, THOUGH.
LEMME HAVE A DRINK, TOO!
WO-OHKAY, YEAH, HEAT STROKE WOULD BE BAD.
CHUG
CHUG
CHUG

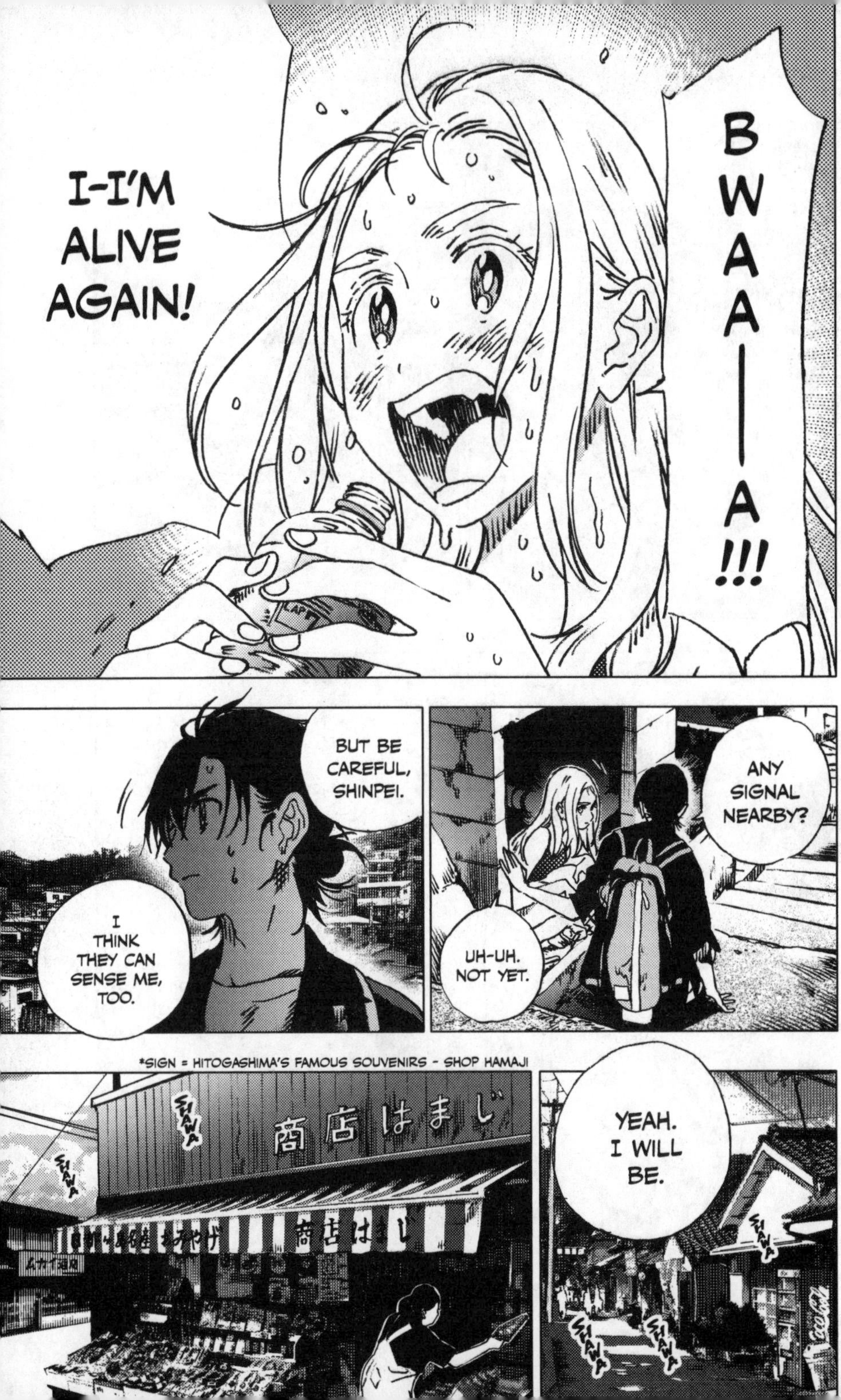
BWAA—A!!!
I-I'M ALIVE AGAIN!
ANY SIGNAL NEARBY?
UH-UH. NOT YET.
BUT BE CAREFUL, SHINPEI.
I THINK THEY CAN SENSE ME, TOO.
*SIGN = HITOGASHIMA'S FAMOUS SOUVENIRS - SHOP HAMAJI
YEAH. I WILL BE.
SHAWA
SHAWA
SHAWA
SHAWA
商店はまじ
SHAWA
SHAWA
商店はまじ

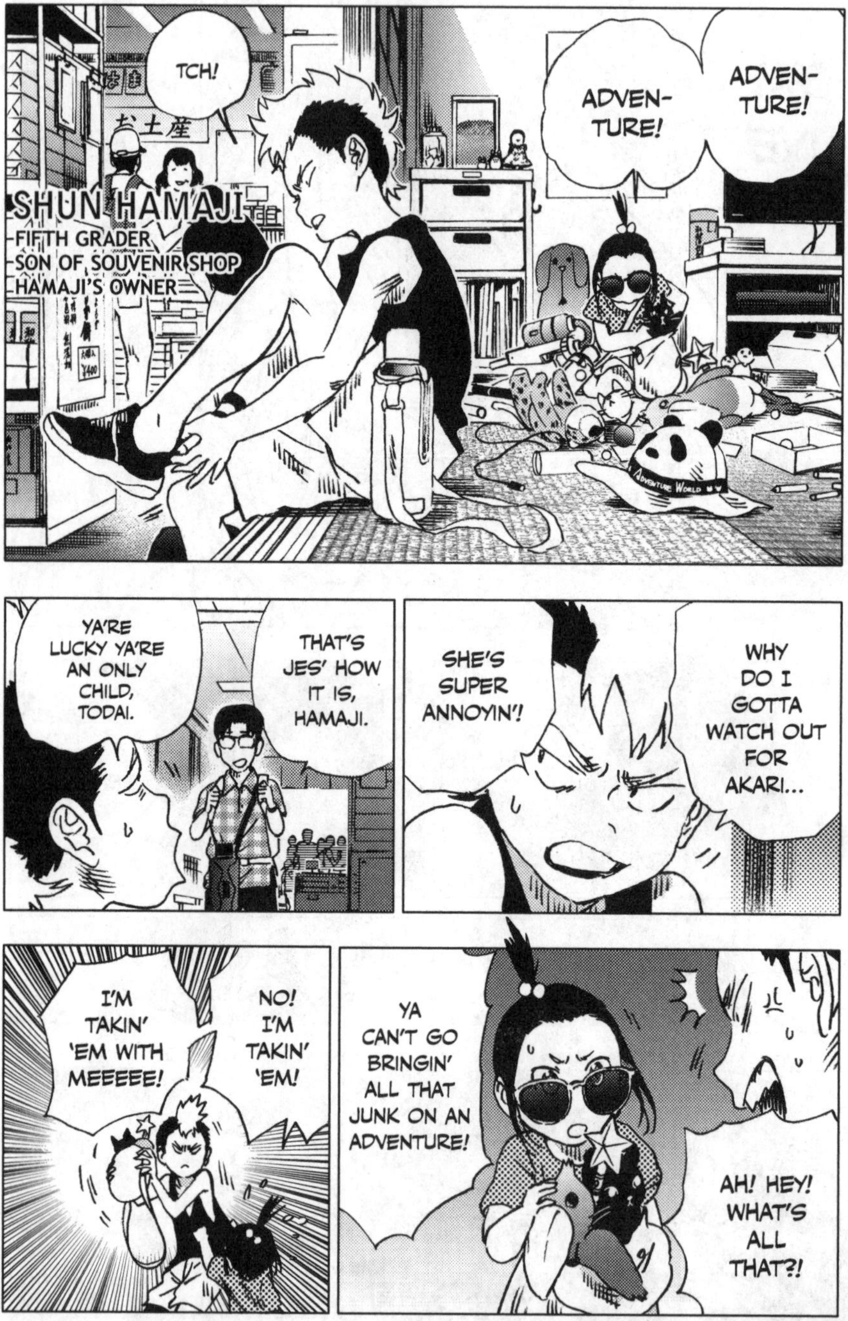
ADVEN-TURE!
ADVEN-TURE!
TCH!
お土産
SHUN HAMAJI
-FIFTH GRADER
-SON OF SOUVENIR SHOP HAMAJI'S OWNER
WHY DO I GOTTA WATCH OUT FOR AKARI...
SHE'S SUPER ANNOYIN'!
THAT'S JES' HOW IT IS, HAMAJI.
YA'RE LUCKY YA'RE AN ONLY CHILD, TODAI.
AH! HEY! WHAT'S ALL THAT?!
YA CAN'T GO BRINGIN' ALL THAT JUNK ON AN ADVENTURE!
NO! I'M TAKIN' 'EM!
I'M TAKIN' 'EM WITH MEEEEE!

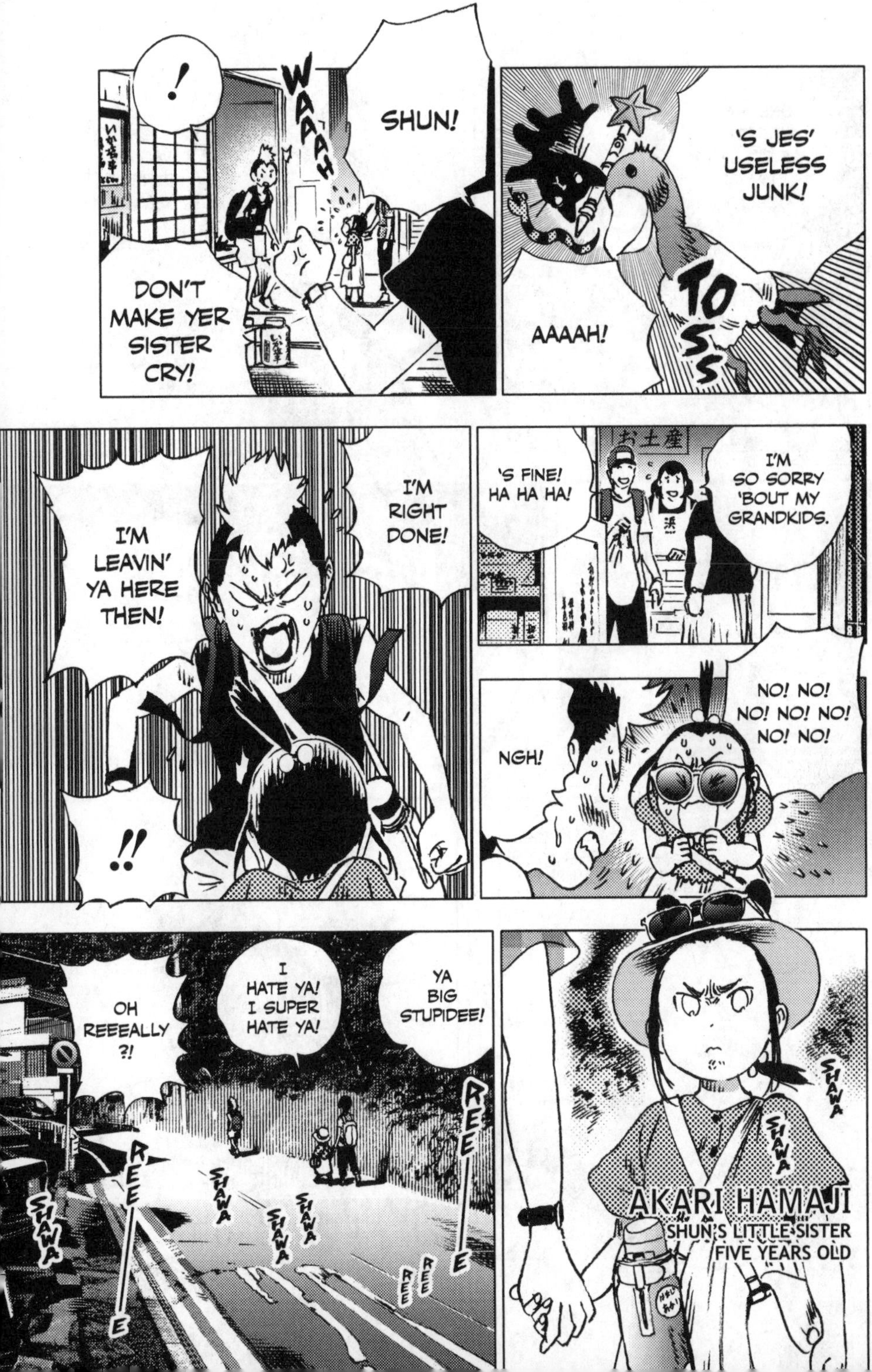
'S JES' USELESS JUNK!
TOSS
AAAAH!
SHUN!
WAAAAH
!
DON'T MAKE YER SISTER CRY!
I'M SO SORRY 'BOUT MY GRANDKIDS.
'S FINE! HA HA HA!
NO! NO! NO! NO! NO! NO! NO!
NGH!
I'M RIGHT DONE!
I'M LEAVIN' YA HERE THEN!
!!
SHAWA
SHAWA
AKARI HAMAJI
SHUN'S LITTLE SISTER
FIVE YEARS OLD
YA BIG STUPIDEE!
I HATE YA! I SUPER HATE YA!
OH REEEALLY ?!
REEE
REE
REE
SHAWA
SHAWA
SHAWA
REEE
SHAWA

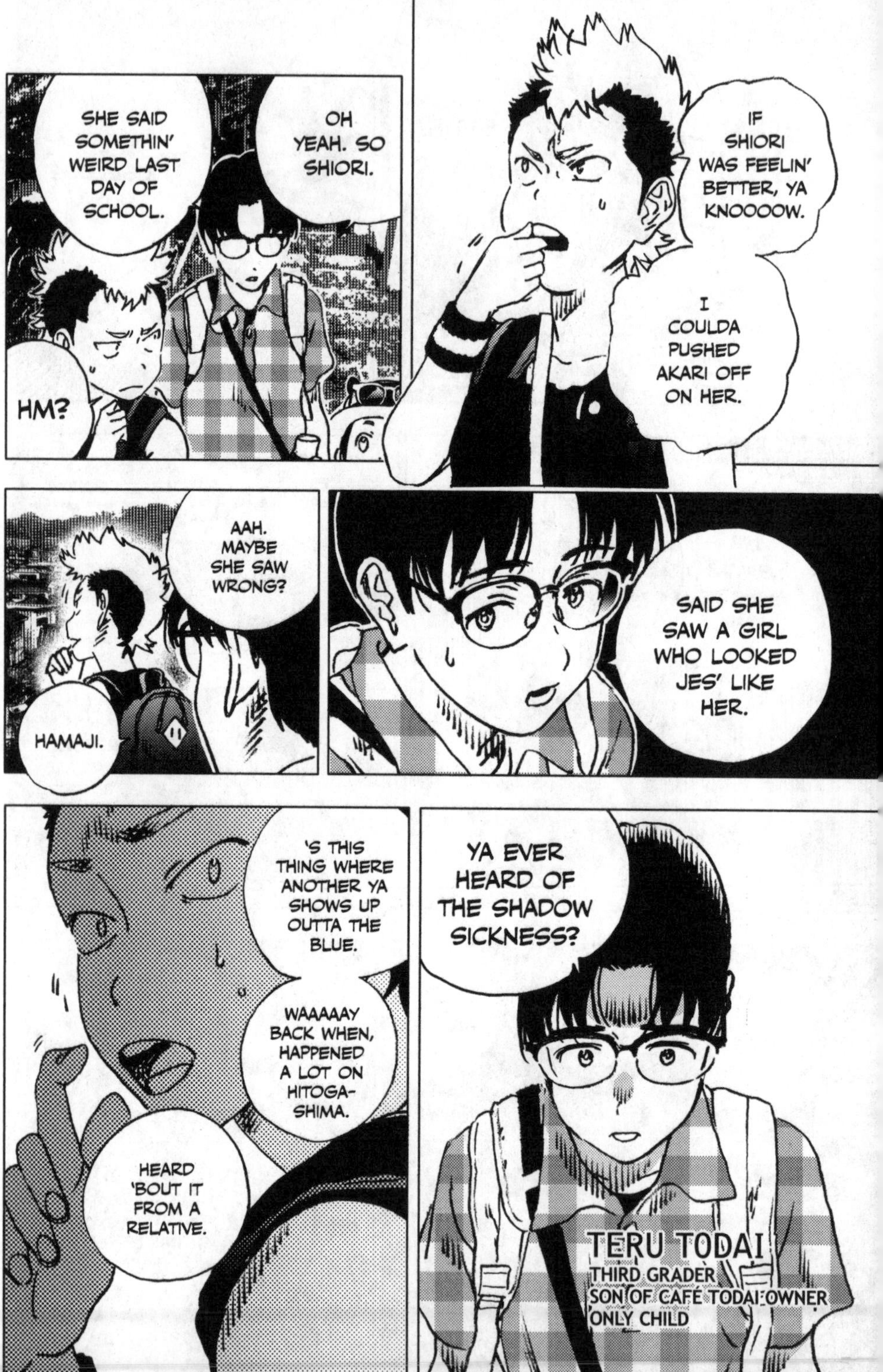
IF SHIORI WAS FEELIN' BETTER, YA KNOOOOW.
I COULDA PUSHED AKARI OFF ON HER.
OH YEAH. SO SHIORI.
SHE SAID SOMETHIN' WEIRD LAST DAY OF SCHOOL.
HM?
SAID SHE SAW A GIRL WHO LOOKED JES' LIKE HER.
AAH. MAYBE SHE SAW WRONG?
HAMAJI.
YA EVER HEARD OF THE SHADOW SICKNESS?
TERU TODAI
THIRD GRADER
SON OF CAFE TODAI OWNER
ONLY CHILD
'S THIS THING WHERE ANOTHER YA SHOWS UP OUTTA THE BLUE.
WAAAAAY BACK WHEN, HAPPENED A LOT ON HITOGA-SHIMA.
HEARD 'BOUT IT FROM A RELATIVE.

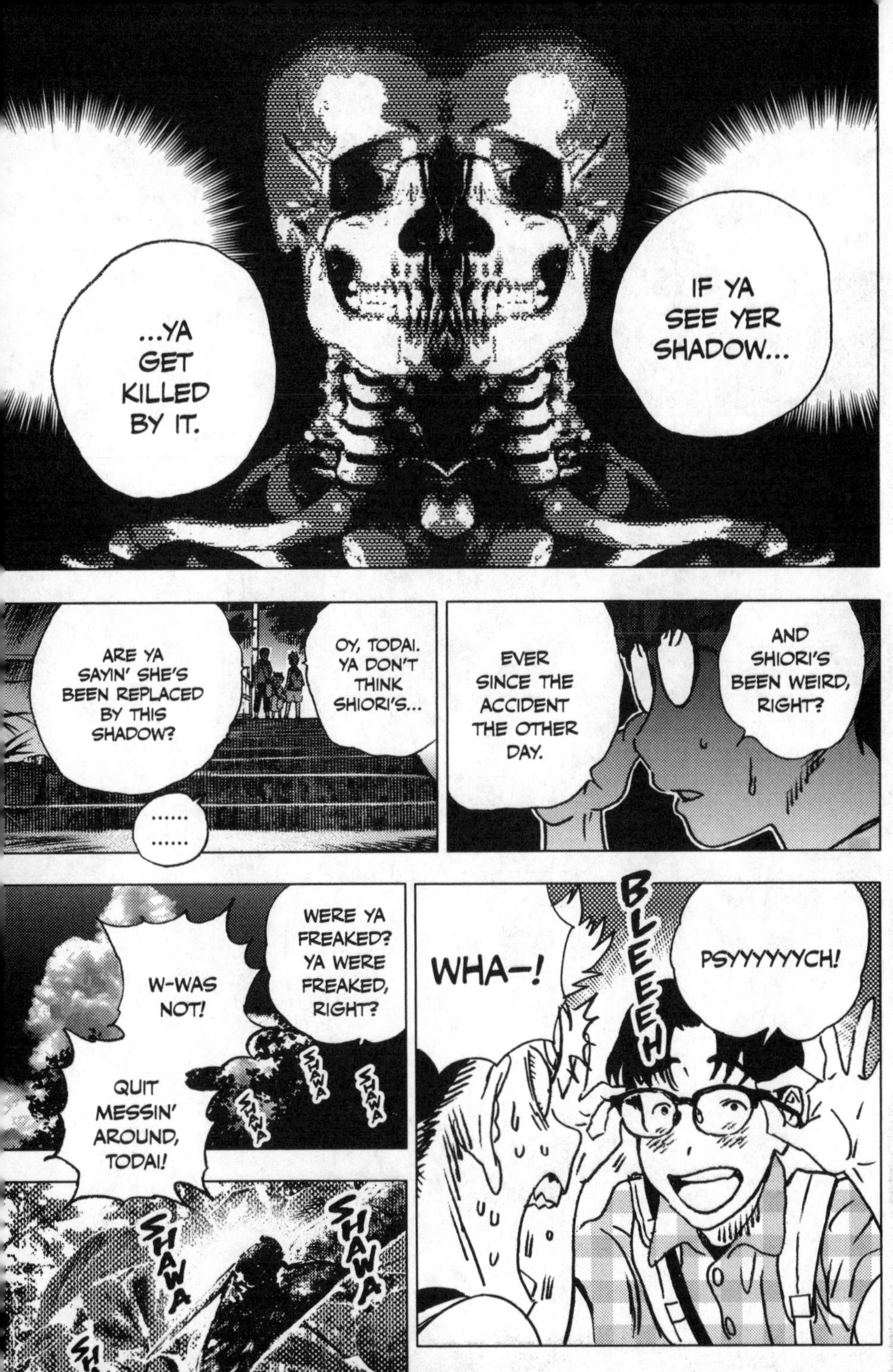
IF YA SEE YER SHADOW...
...YA GET KILLED BY IT.
AND SHIORI'S BEEN WEIRD, RIGHT?
EVER SINCE THE ACCIDENT THE OTHER DAY.
OY, TODAI. YA DON'T THINK SHIORI'S...
ARE YA SAYIN' SHE'S BEEN REPLACED BY THIS SHADOW?
....
PSYYYYYYCH!
BLEEEEH
WHA-!
WERE YA FREAKED? YA WERE FREAKED, RIGHT?
W-WAS NOT!
SHAWA
SHAWA
SHAWA
QUIT MESSIN' AROUND, TODAI!
SHAWA
SHAWA
SHAWA

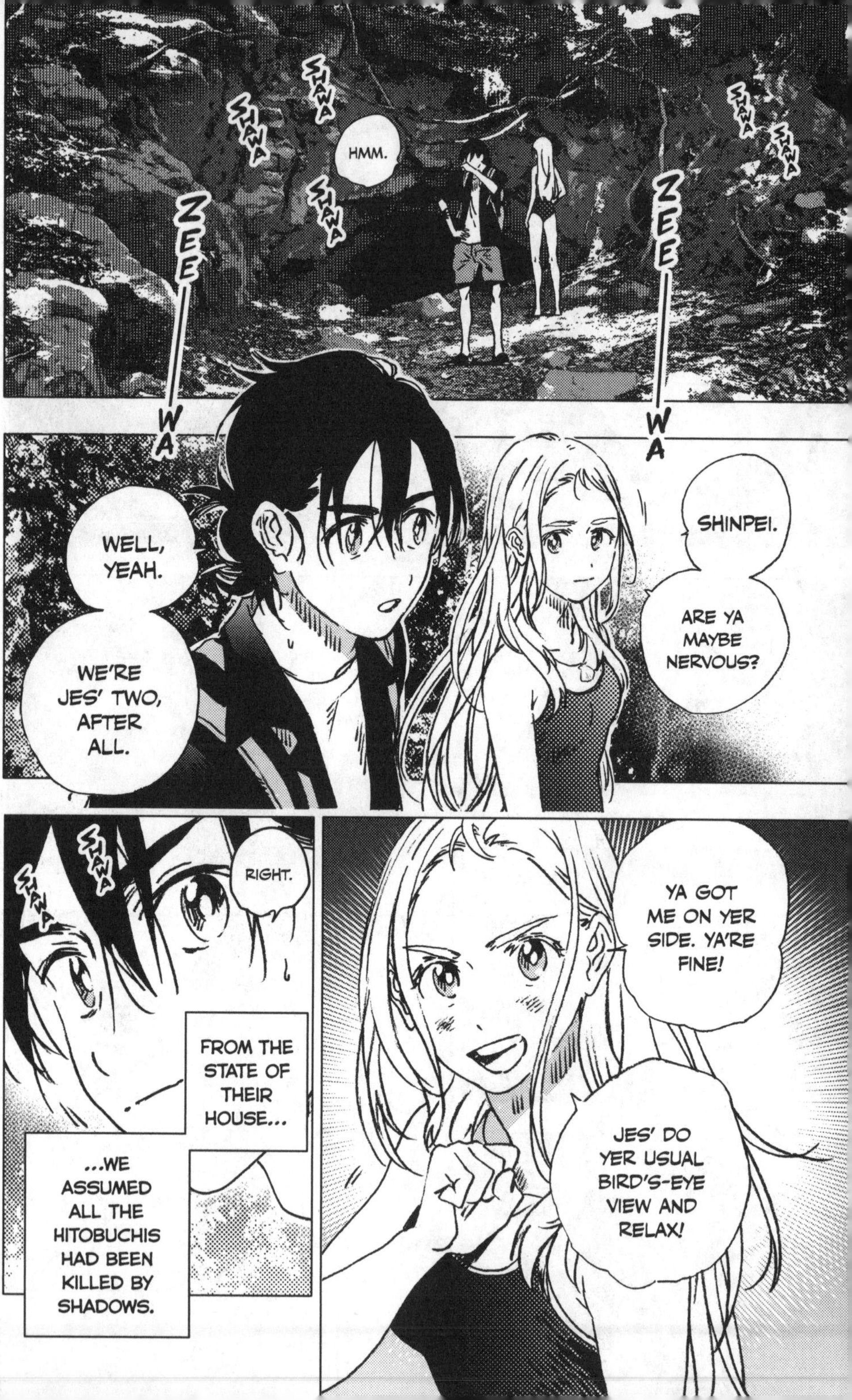
SHAWA
SHAWA
ZEE—WA
HMM.
SHAWA
SHAWA
ZEE—WA
SHINPEI.
ARE YA MAYBE NERVOUS?
WELL, YEAH.
WE'RE JES' TWO, AFTER ALL.
YA GOT ME ON YER SIDE. YA'RE FINE!
JES' DO YER USUAL BIRD'S-EYE VIEW AND RELAX!
RIGHT.
SHAWA
SHAWA
FROM THE STATE OF THEIR HOUSE...
...WE ASSUMED ALL THE HITOBUCHIS HAD BEEN KILLED BY SHADOWS.

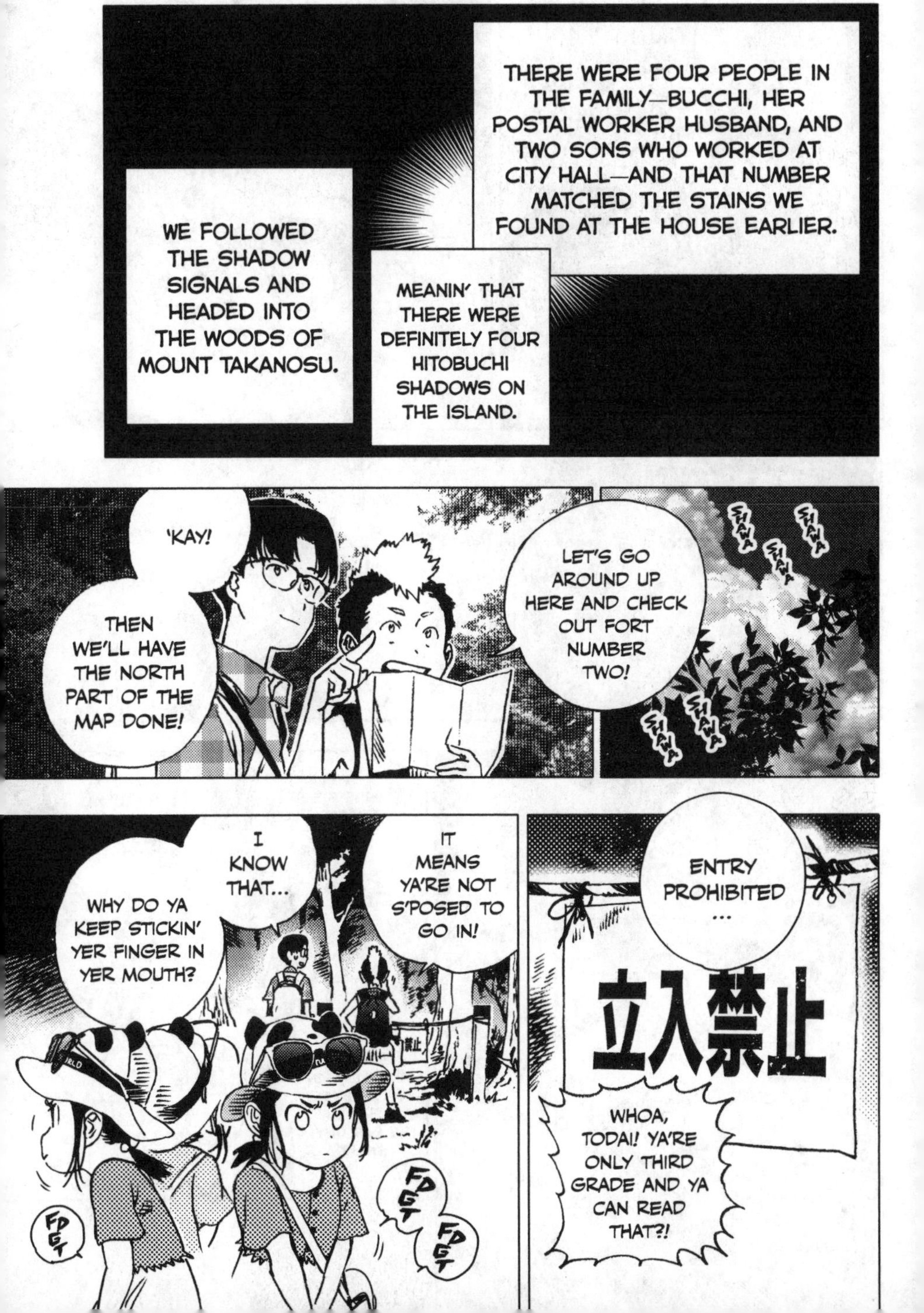
THERE WERE FOUR PEOPLE IN THE FAMILY—BUCCHI, HER POSTAL WORKER HUSBAND, AND TWO SONS WHO WORKED AT CITY HALL—AND THAT NUMBER MATCHED THE STAINS WE FOUND AT THE HOUSE EARLIER.
MEANIN' THAT THERE WERE DEFINITELY FOUR HITOBUCHI SHADOWS ON THE ISLAND.
WE FOLLOWED THE SHADOW SIGNALS AND HEADED INTO THE WOODS OF MOUNT TAKANOSU.
SHAWA
SHAWA
SHAWA
SHAWA
SHAWA
LET'S GO AROUND UP HERE AND CHECK OUT FORT NUMBER TWO!
'KAY!
THEN WE'LL HAVE THE NORTH PART OF THE MAP DONE!
ENTRY PROHIBITED ...
立入禁止
WHOA, TODAI! YA'RE ONLY THIRD GRADE AND YA CAN READ THAT?!
IT MEANS YA'RE NOT S'POSED TO GO IN!
I KNOW THAT...
WHY DO YA KEEP STICKIN' YER FINGER IN YER MOUTH?
FDGT
FDGT
FDGT

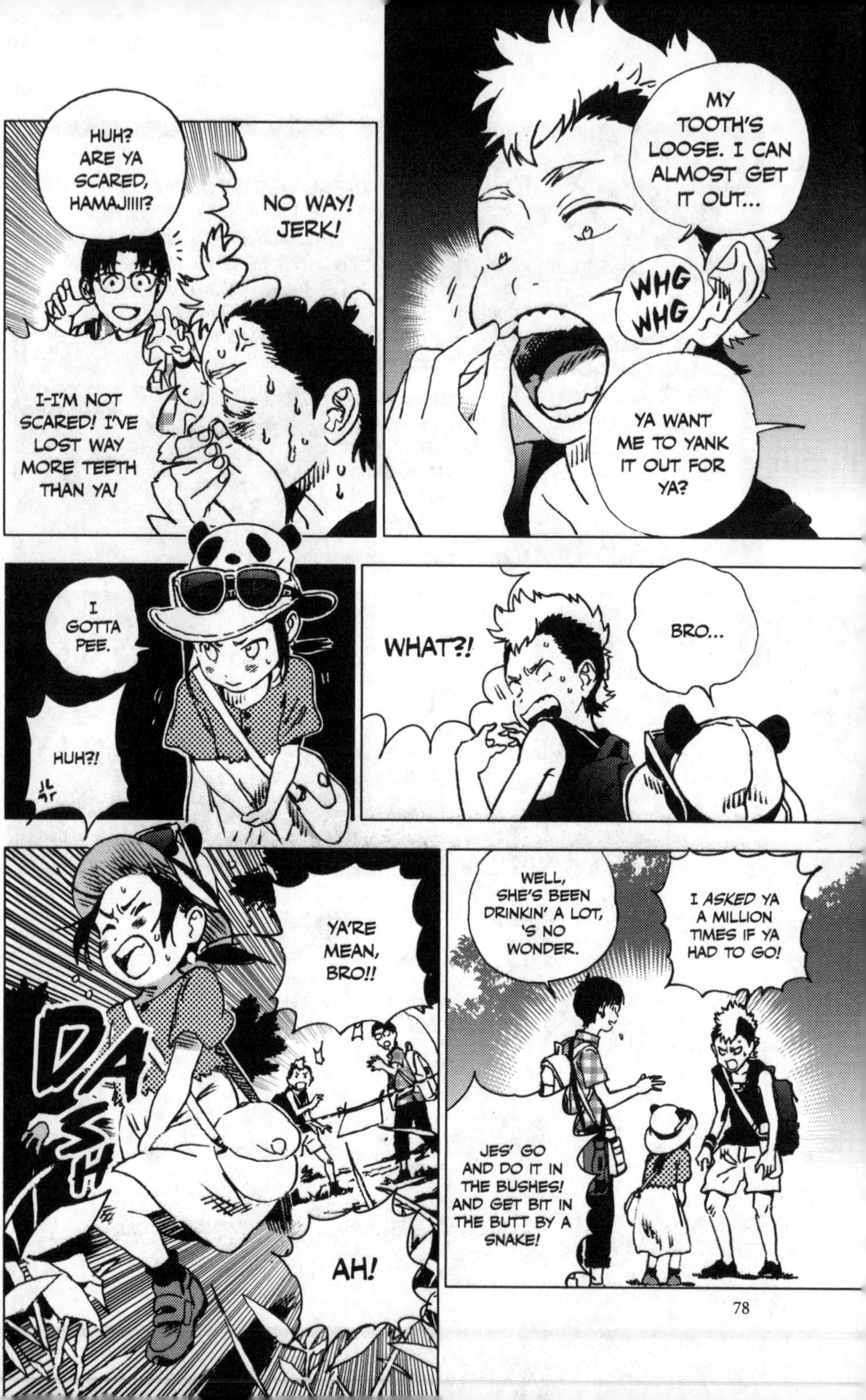
MY TOOTH'S LOOSE. I CAN ALMOST GET IT OUT...
WHG WHG
YA WANT ME TO YANK IT OUT FOR YA?
HUH? ARE YA SCARED, HAMAJIIII?
NO WAY! JERK!
I-I'M NOT SCARED! I'VE LOST WAY MORE TEETH THAN YA!
BRO...
WHAT?!
I GOTTA PEE.
HUH?!
I *ASKED* YA A MILLION TIMES IF YA HAD TO GO!
WELL, SHE'S BEEN DRINKIN' A LOT, 'S NO WONDER.
JES' GO AND DO IT IN THE BUSHES! AND GET BIT IN THE BUTT BY A SNAKE!
YA'RE MEAN, BRO!!
DASH
AH!

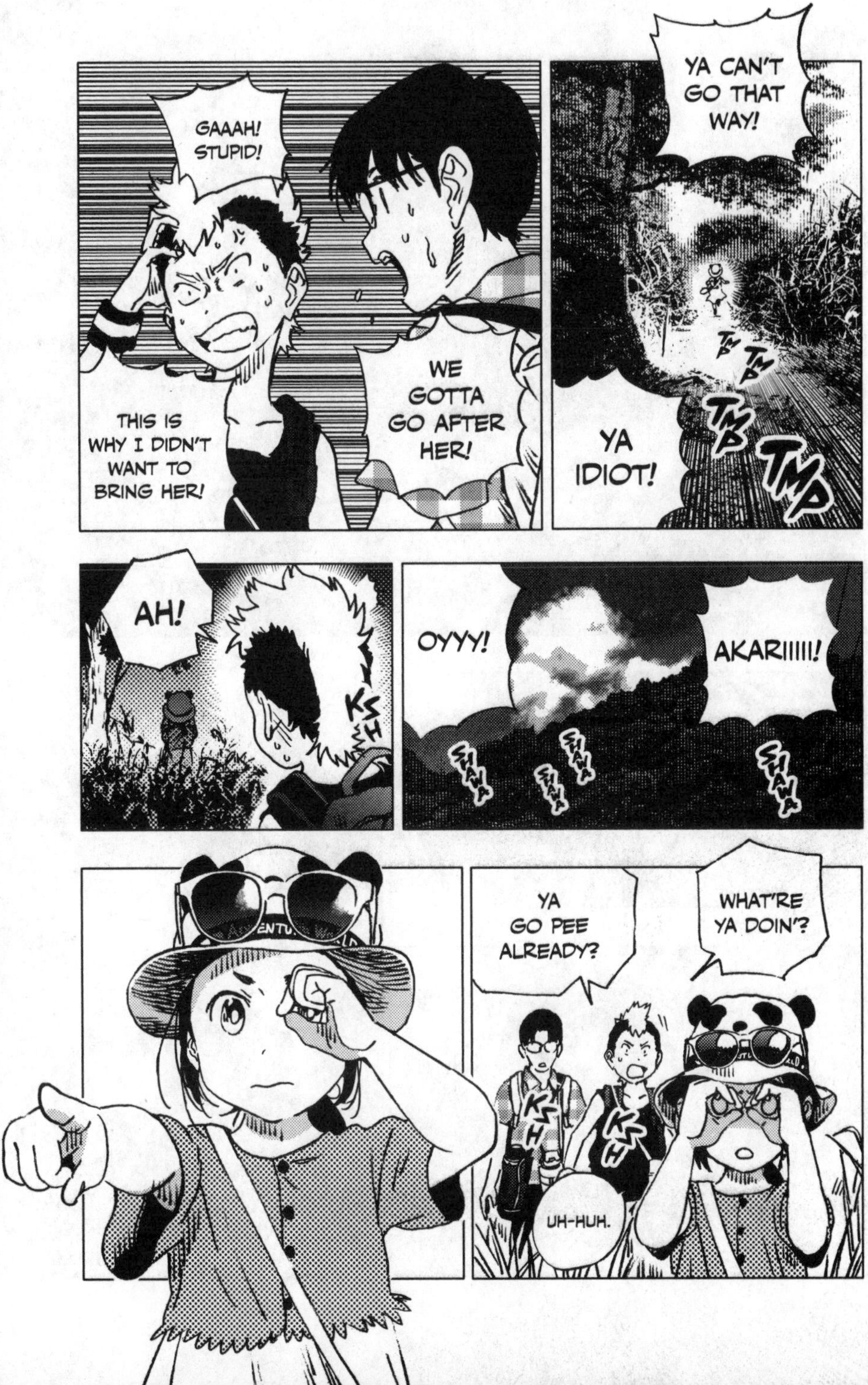
YA CAN'T GO THAT WAY!
TMP TMP
TMP TMP
YA IDIOT!
GAAAH! STUPID!
WE GOTTA GO AFTER HER!
THIS IS WHY I DIDN'T WANT TO BRING HER!
AKARIIIII!
OYYY!
SHAWA SHAWA SHAWA SHAWA
AH!
KSH
WHAT'RE YA DOIN'?
YA GO PEE ALREADY?
KSH KSH
UH-HUH.

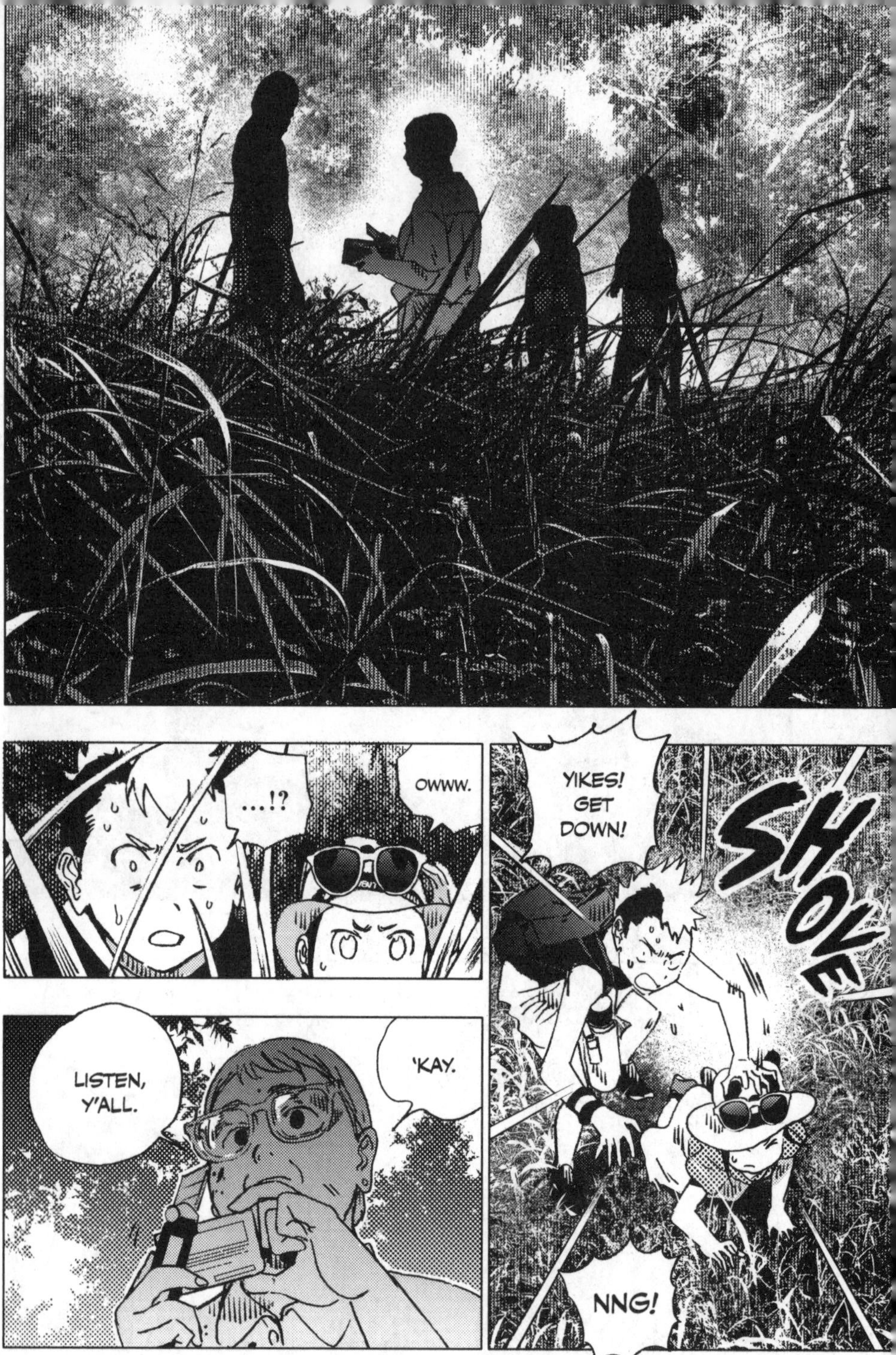

YIKES! GET DOWN!
SHOVE
NNG!
OWWW.
...!?
'KAY.
LISTEN, Y'ALL.

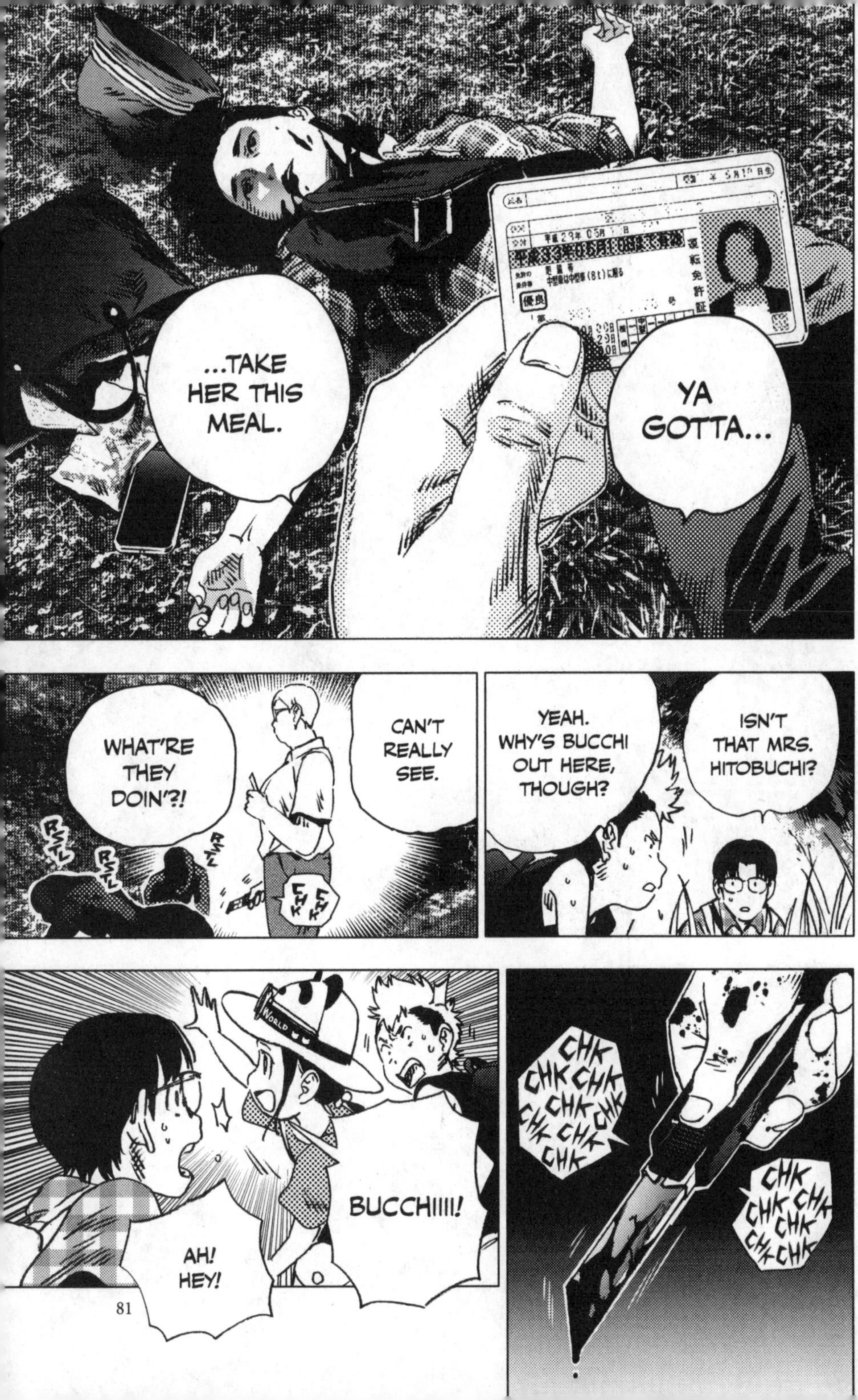
YA GOTTA...
...TAKE HER THIS MEAL.
ISN'T THAT MRS. HITOBUCHI?
YEAH. WHY'S BUCCHI OUT HERE, THOUGH?
CAN'T REALLY SEE.
WHAT'RE THEY DOIN'?!
RSTL
RSTL
RSTL
CHK CHK
CHK CHK CHK CHK CHK CHK
CHK CHK CHK CHK CHK CHK CHK CHK CHK CHK
BUCCHIIIII!
AH! HEY!

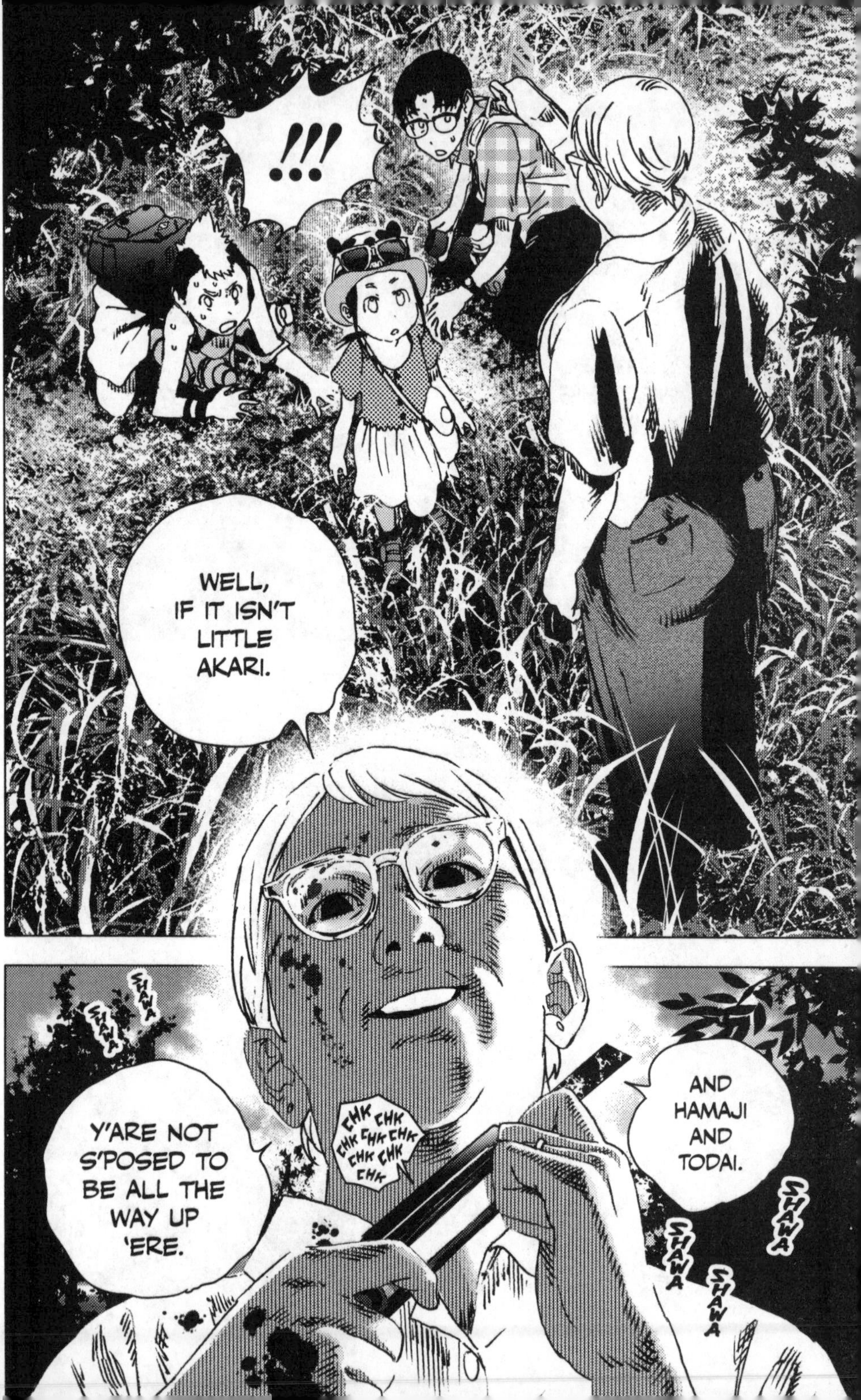
!!!
WELL, IF IT ISN'T LITTLE AKARI.
SHAWA SHAWA
AND HAMAJI AND TODAI.
CHK CHK CHK CHK CHK CHK CHK CHK CHK
Y'ARE NOT S'POSED TO BE ALL THE WAY UP 'ERE.
SHAWA SHAWA

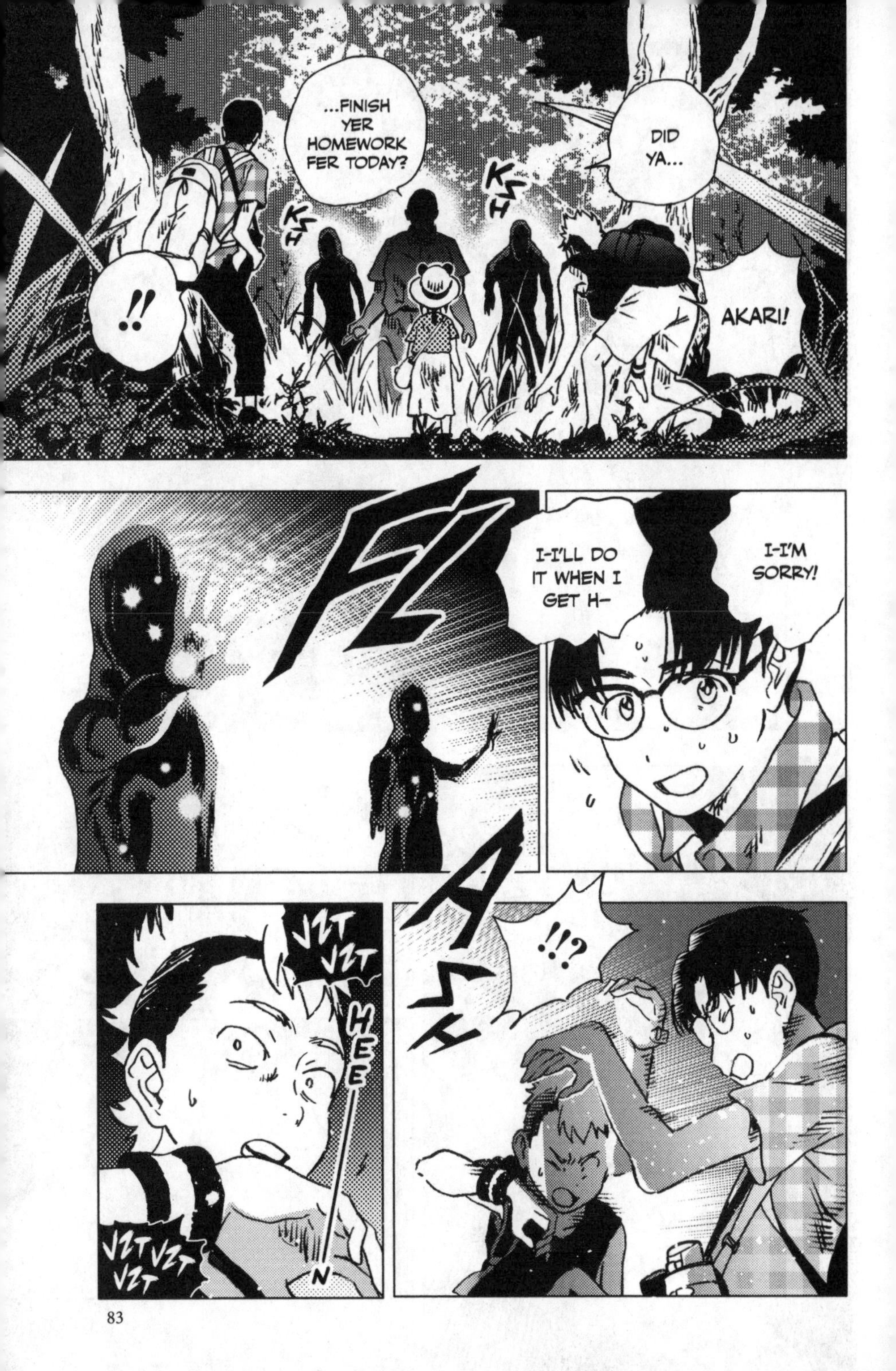
DID YA...
...FINISH YER HOMEWORK FER TODAY?
KSH
KSH
AKARI!
!!
I-I'M SORRY!
I-I'LL DO IT WHEN I GET H—
FZ
ASH
!!?
VZT VZT
HEEN
VZT VZT VZT

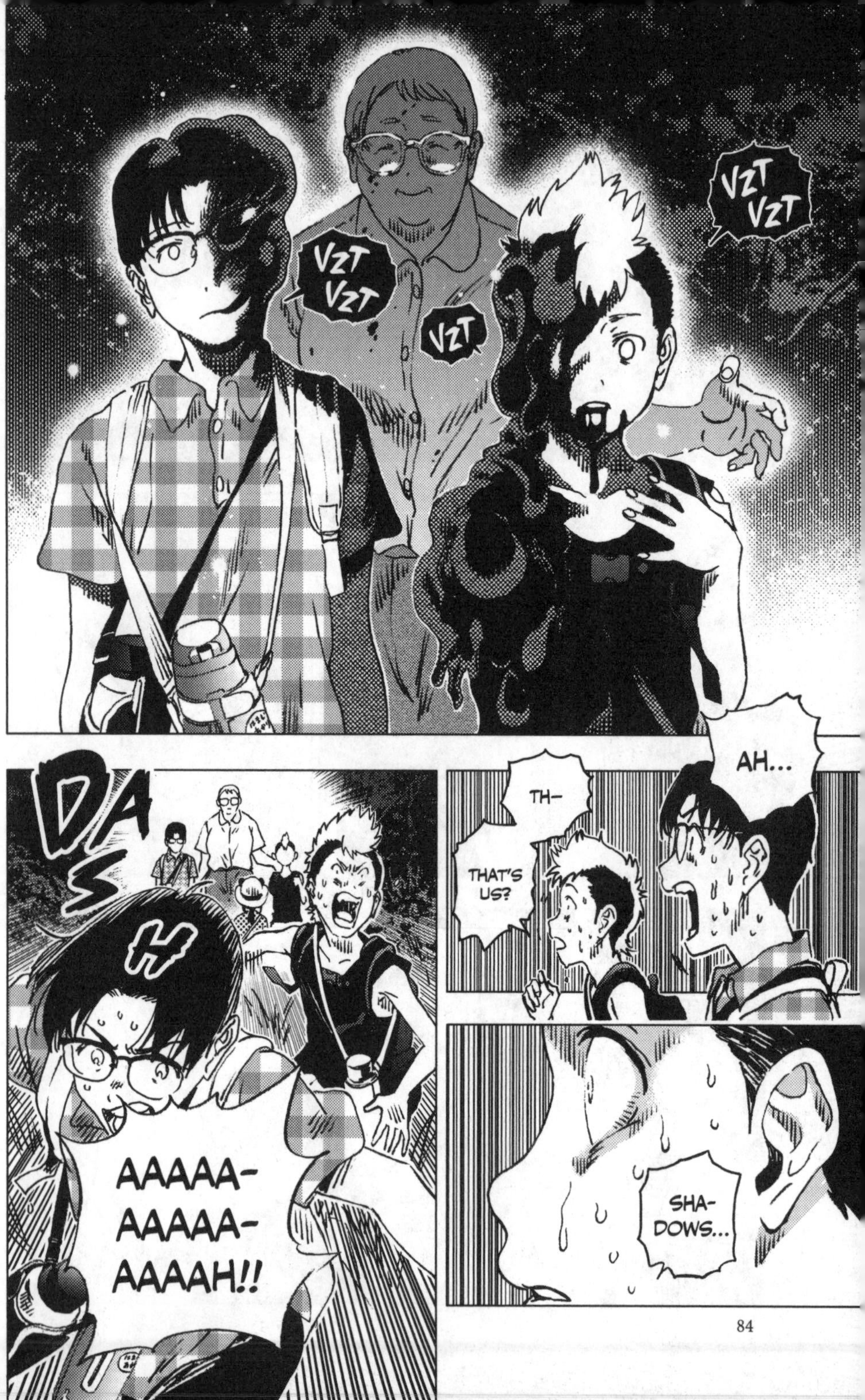

VZT VZT
VZT VZT
VZT
AH...
TH-
THAT'S US?
SHA-DOWS...
DASH
AAAAA-AAAAA-AAAAH!!

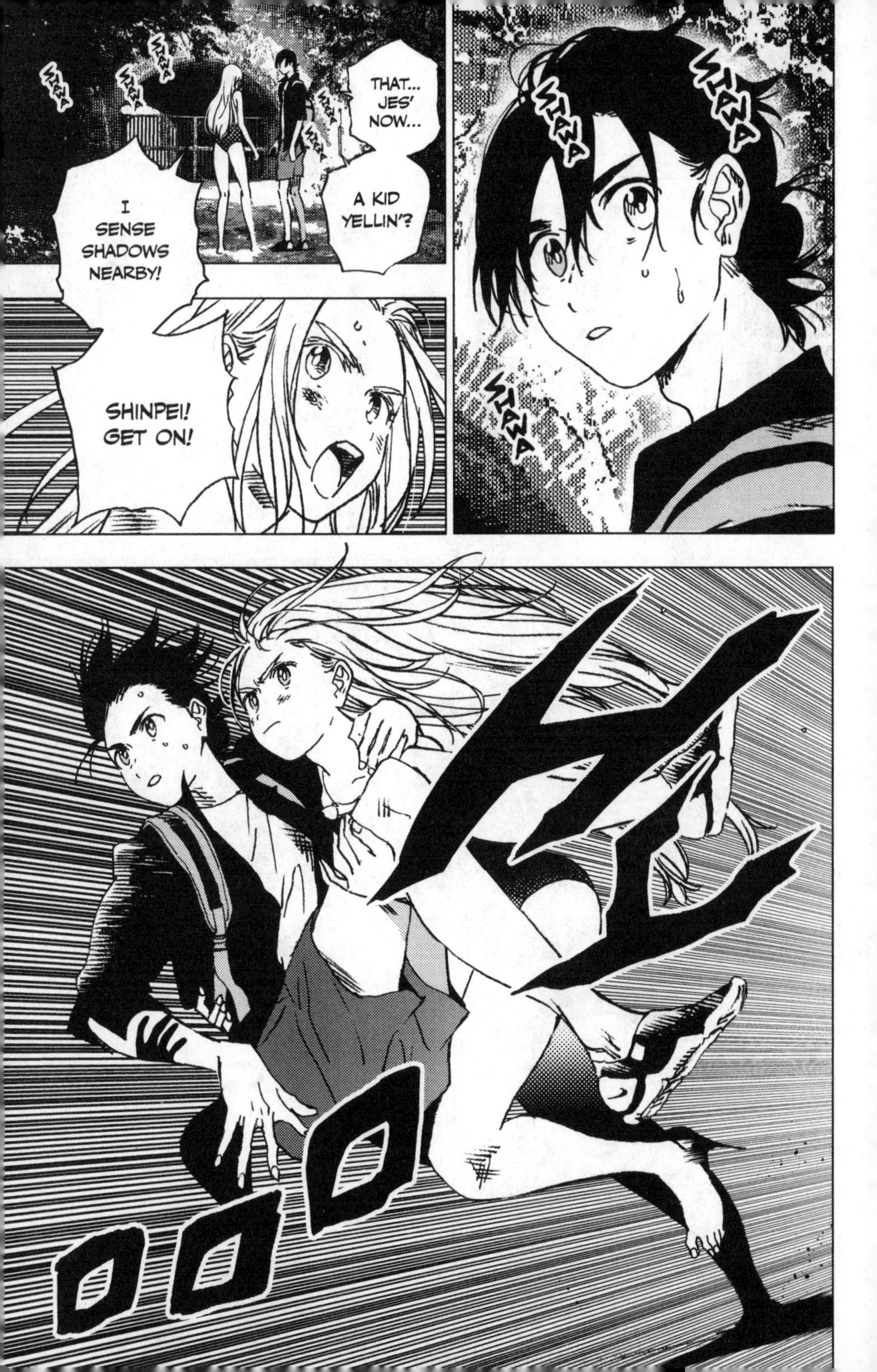
SHWA
SHWA
SHWA
THAT... JES' NOW...
A KID YELLIN'?
I SENSE SHADOWS NEARBY!
SHINPEI! GET ON!

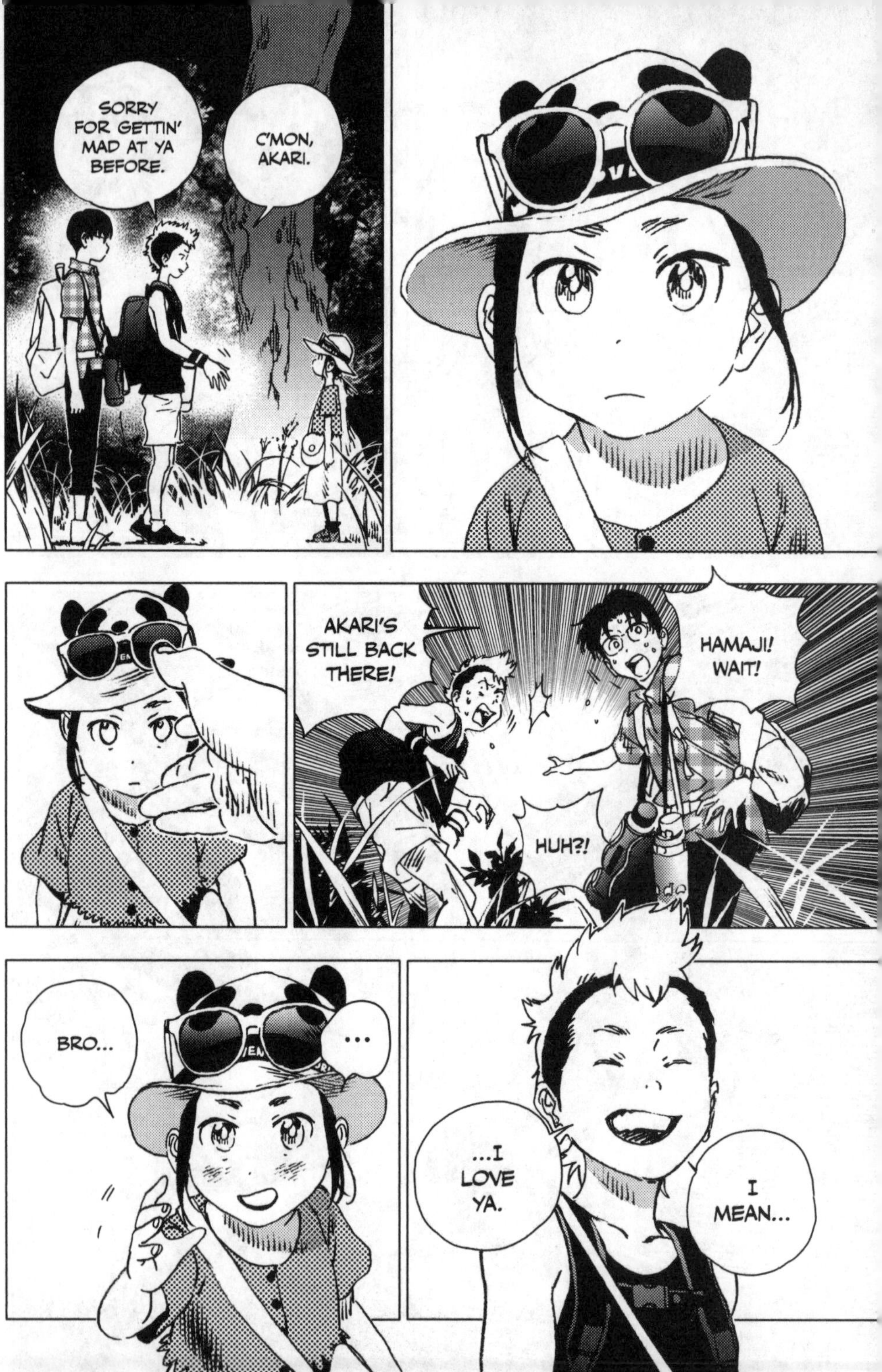
C'MON, AKARI.
SORRY FOR GETTIN' MAD AT YA BEFORE.
HAMAJI! WAIT!
AKARI'S STILL BACK THERE!
HUH?!
I MEAN...
...I LOVE YA.
...
BRO...

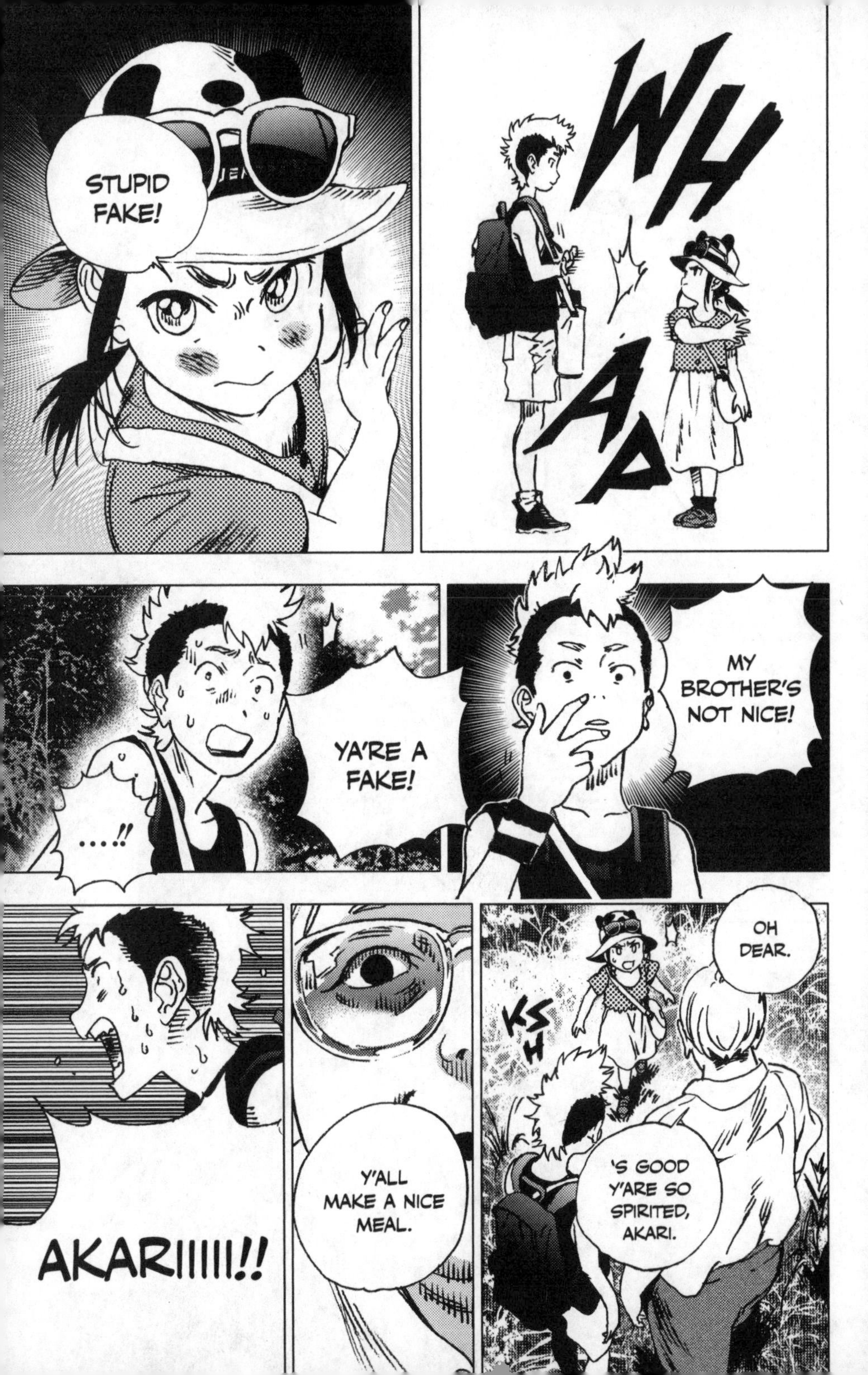
WHAA
STUPID FAKE!
MY BROTHER'S NOT NICE!
YA'RE A FAKE!
...!!
OH DEAR.
KSH
'S GOOD Y'ARE SO SPIRITED, AKARI.
Y'ALL MAKE A NICE MEAL.
AKARIIIIII!!

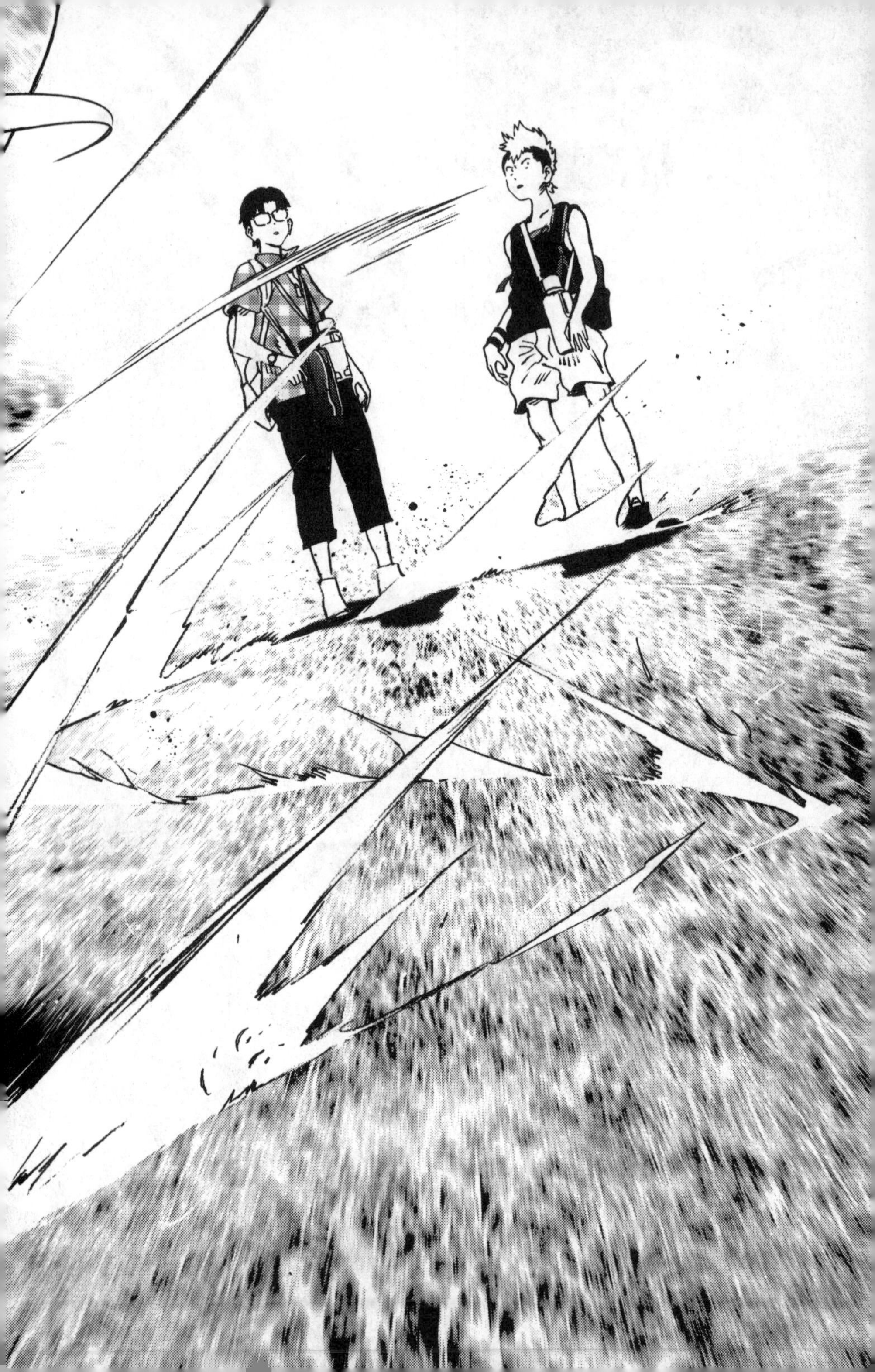

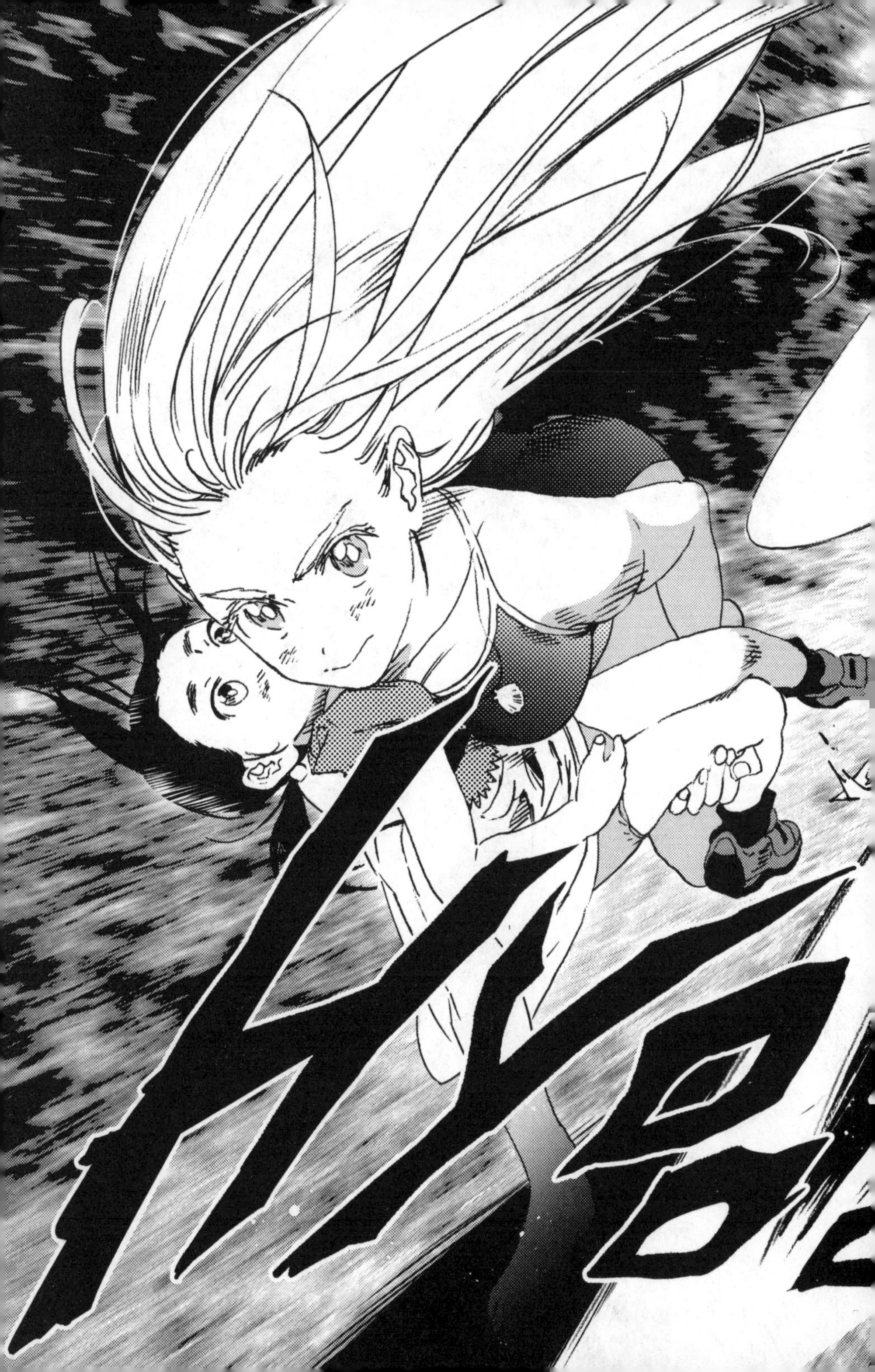

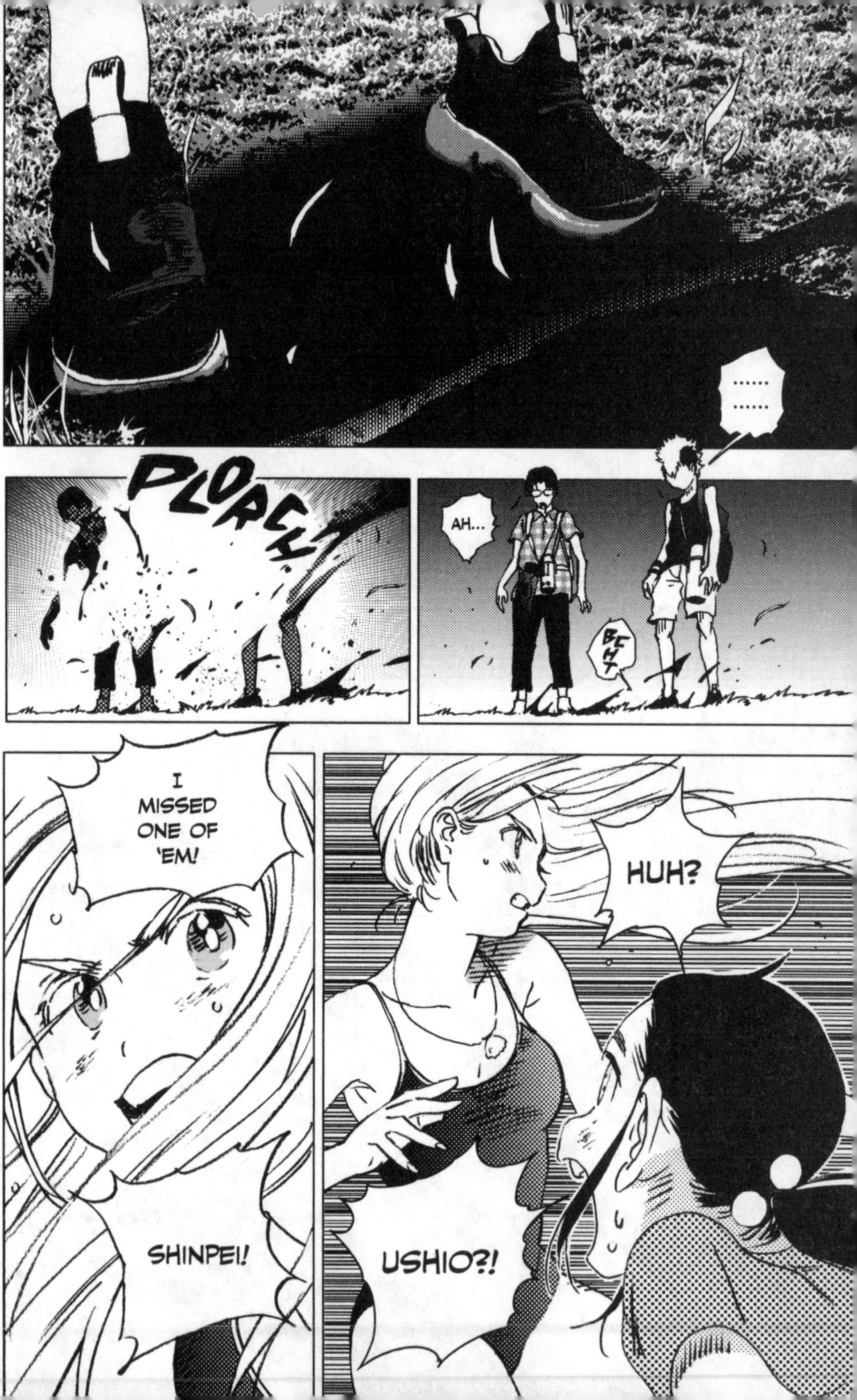
……
……
AH...
BCHT
PLORCH
HUH?
USHIO?!
I MISSED ONE OF 'EM!
SHINPEI!

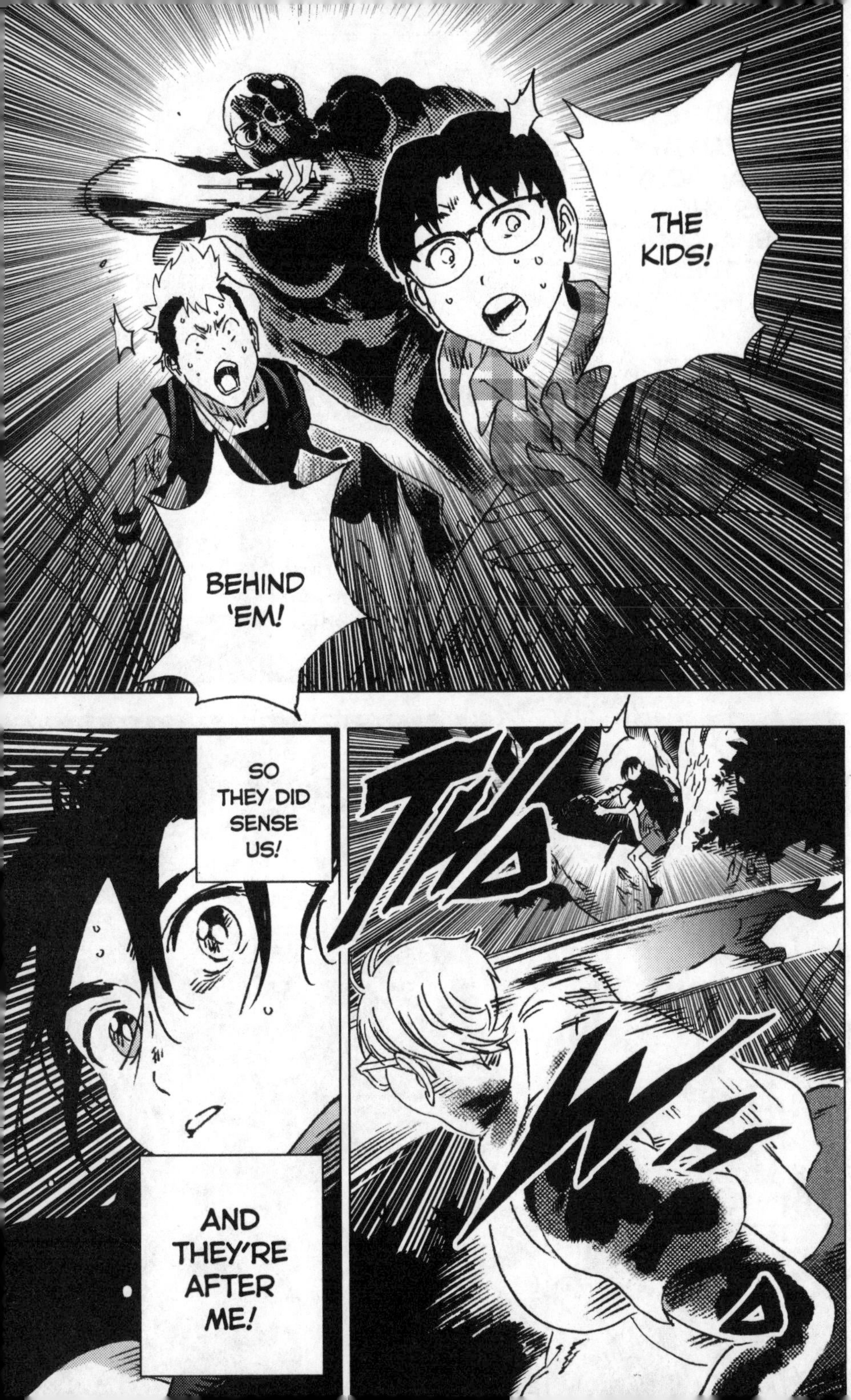
THE KIDS!
BEHIND 'EM!
SO THEY DID SENSE US!
AND THEY'RE AFTER ME!

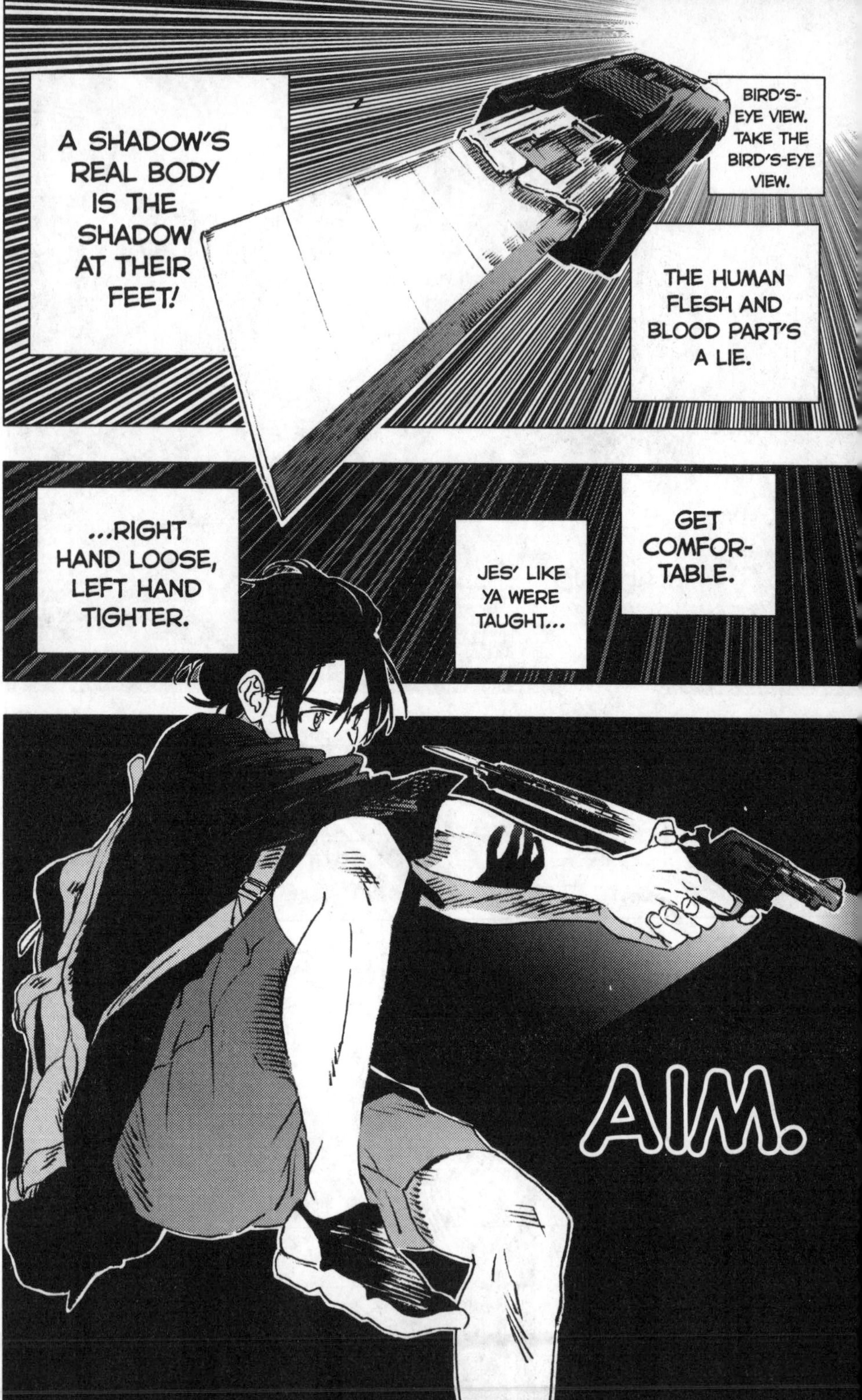
BIRD'S-EYE VIEW. TAKE THE BIRD'S-EYE VIEW.
THE HUMAN FLESH AND BLOOD PART'S A LIE.
A SHADOW'S REAL BODY IS THE SHADOW AT THEIR FEET!
GET COMFORTABLE.
JES' LIKE YA WERE TAUGHT...
...RIGHT HAND LOOSE, LEFT HAND TIGHTER.
AIM.

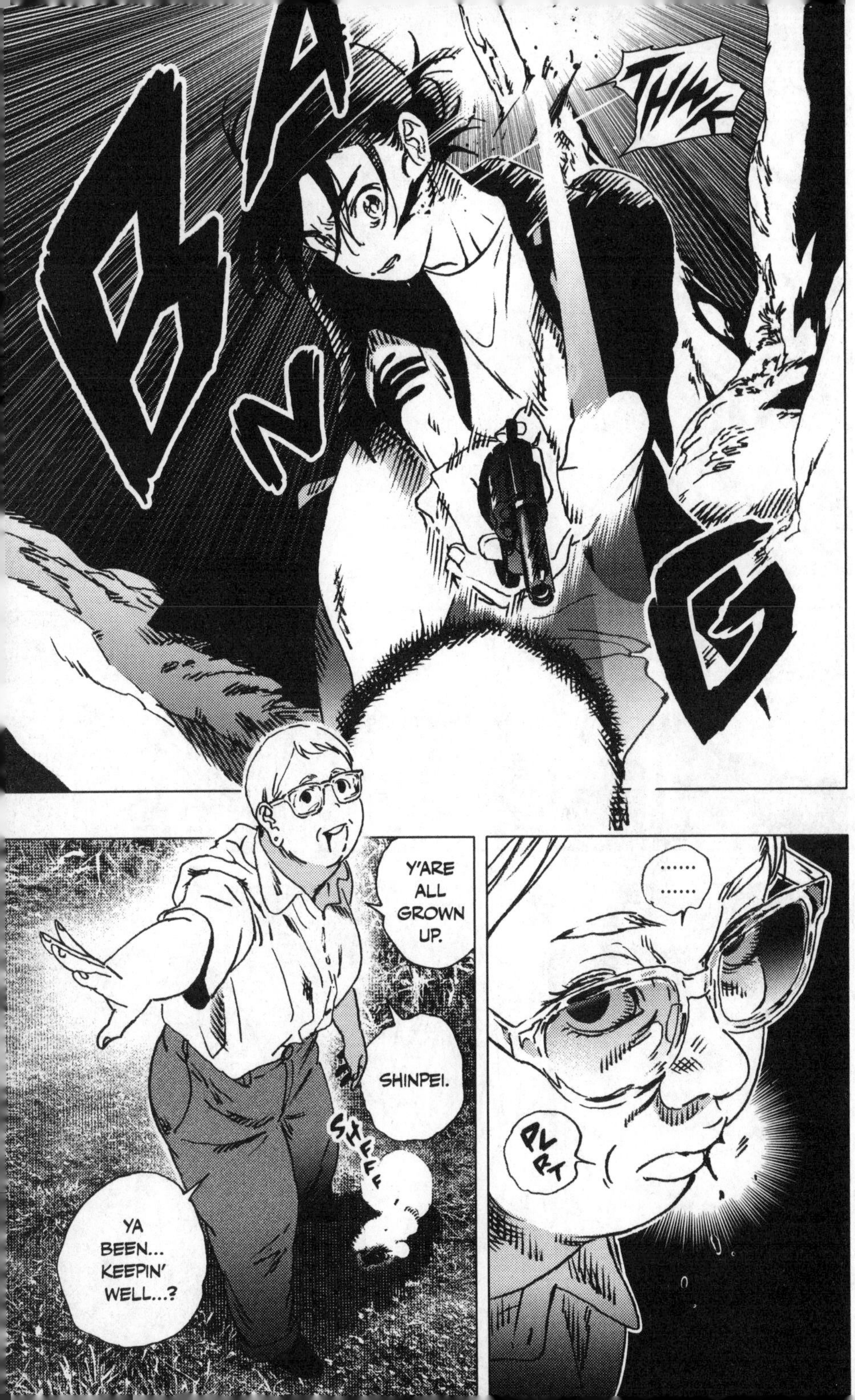
BANG
THWK
......
......
PLRT
Y'ARE ALL GROWN UP.
SHINPEI.
SHFFF
YA BEEN... KEEPIN' WELL...?

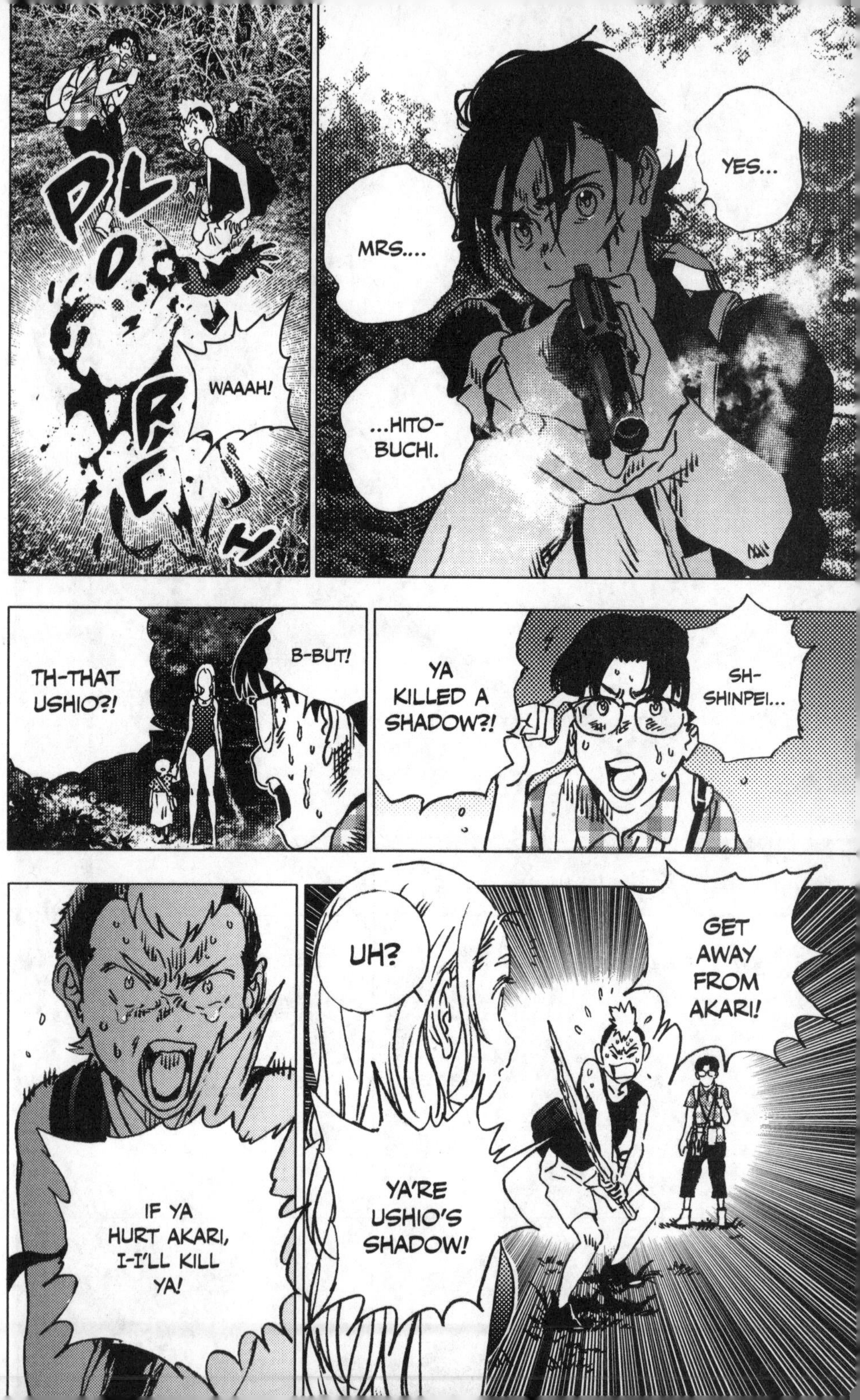
YES...
MRS....
...HITO-BUCHI.
WAAAH!
SH-SHINPEI...
YA KILLED A SHADOW?!
B-BUT!
TH-THAT USHIO?!
GET AWAY FROM AKARI!
UH?
YA'RE USHIO'S SHADOW!
IF YA HURT AKARI, I-I'LL KILL YA!

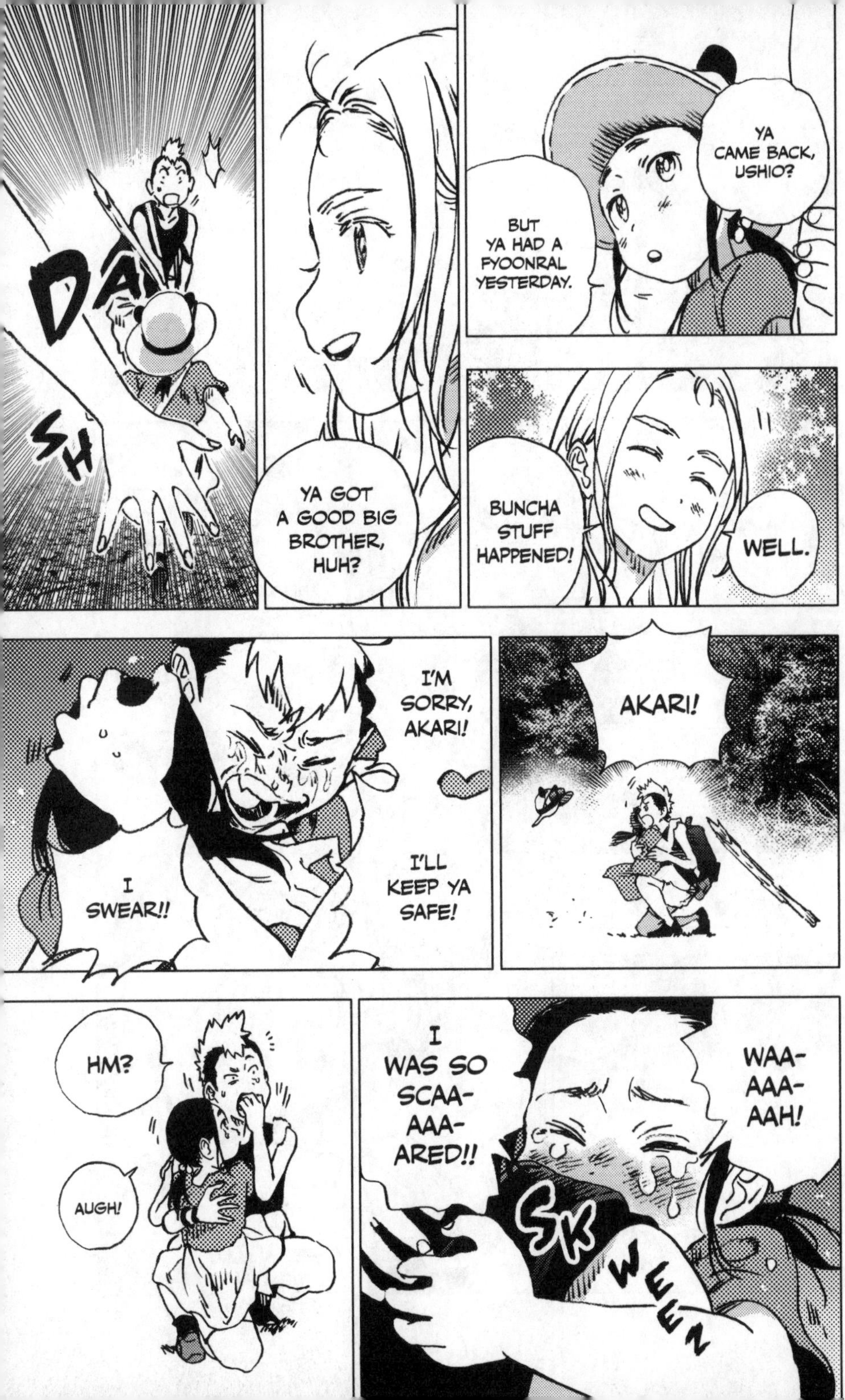
YA CAME BACK, USHIO?
BUT YA HAD A FYOONRAL YESTERDAY.
WELL.
BUNCHA STUFF HAPPENED!
YA GOT A GOOD BIG BROTHER, HUH?
DA
SH
AKARI!
I'M SORRY, AKARI!
I'LL KEEP YA SAFE!
I SWEAR!!
WAA-AAA-AAH!
I WAS SO SCAA-AAA-ARED!!
SK
WEEN
HM?
AUGH!

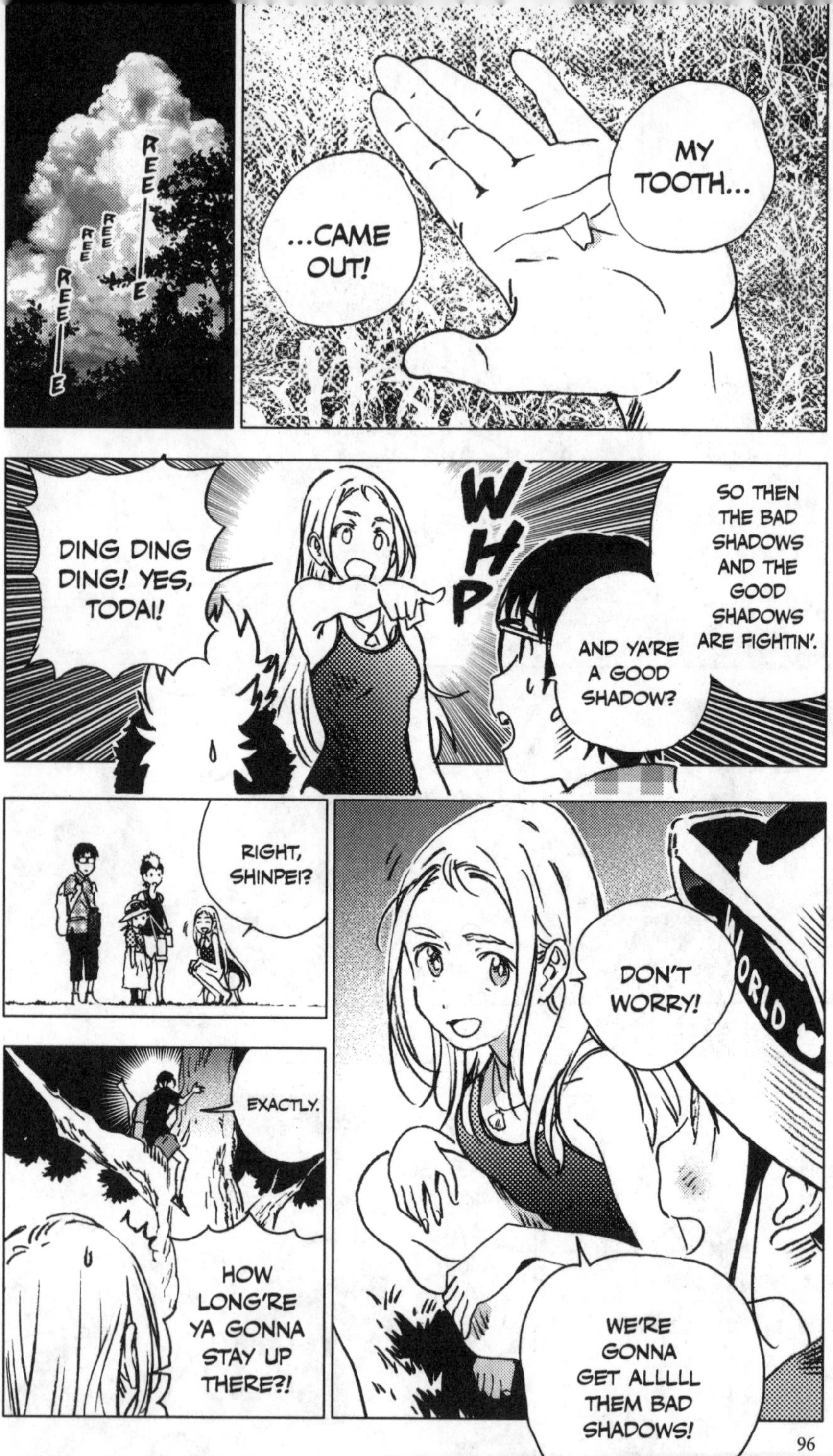
MY TOOTH...
...CAME OUT!
REE—E
REE
REE
REE—E
SO THEN THE BAD SHADOWS AND THE GOOD SHADOWS ARE FIGHTIN'.
AND YA'RE A GOOD SHADOW?
WHP
DING DING DING! YES, TODAI!
DON'T WORRY!
WORLD
WE'RE GONNA GET ALLLLL THEM BAD SHADOWS!
RIGHT, SHINPEI?
EXACTLY.
HOW LONG'RE YA GONNA STAY UP THERE?!

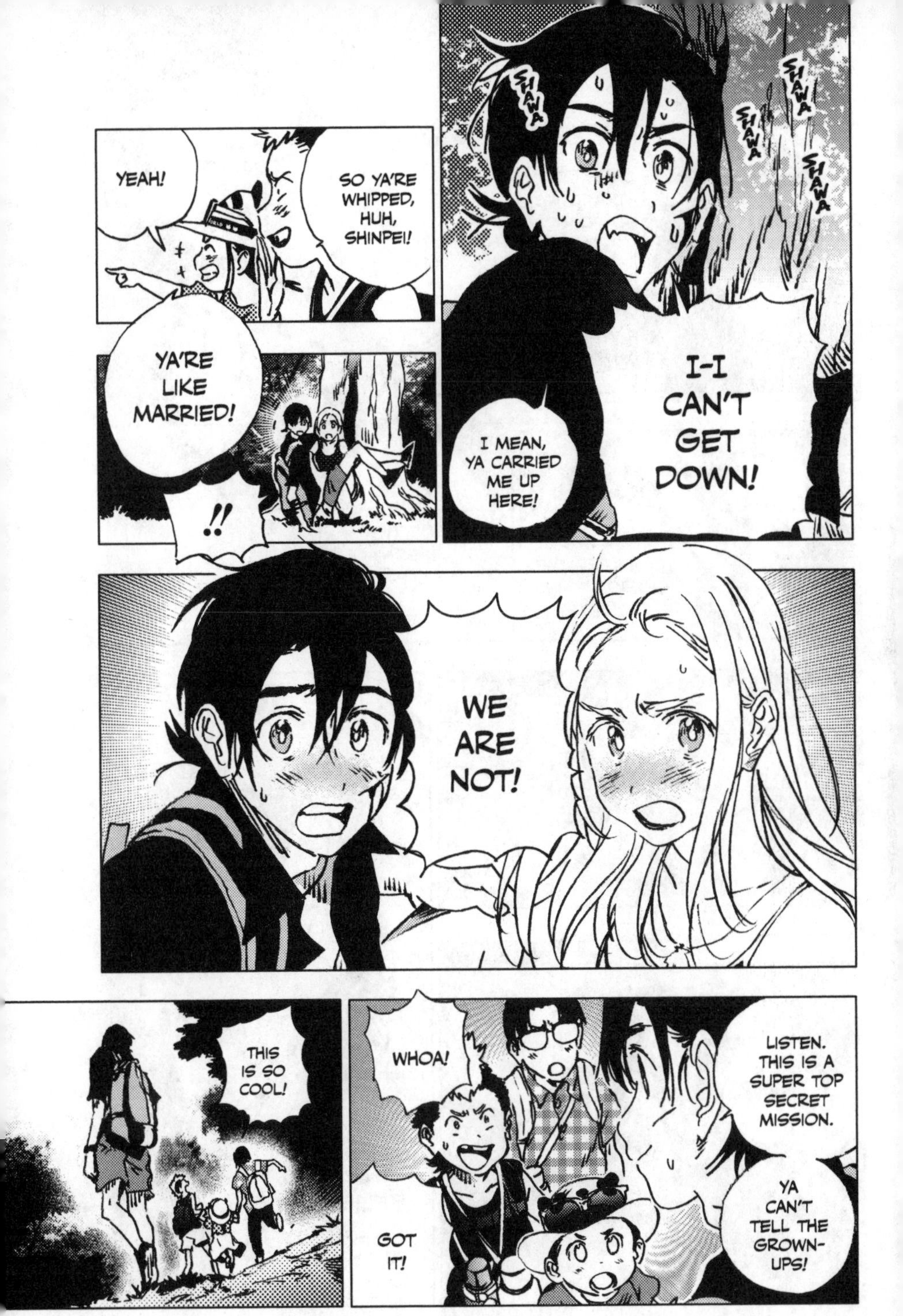

SHAWA
SHAWA
SHAWA
SHAWA
I-I CAN'T GET DOWN!
I MEAN, YA CARRIED ME UP HERE!
SO YA'RE WHIPPED, HUH, SHINPEI!
YEAH!
YA'RE LIKE MARRIED!
!!
WE ARE NOT!
LISTEN. THIS IS A SUPER TOP SECRET MISSION.
YA CAN'T TELL THE GROWN-UPS!
WHOA!
GOT IT!
THIS IS SO COOL!

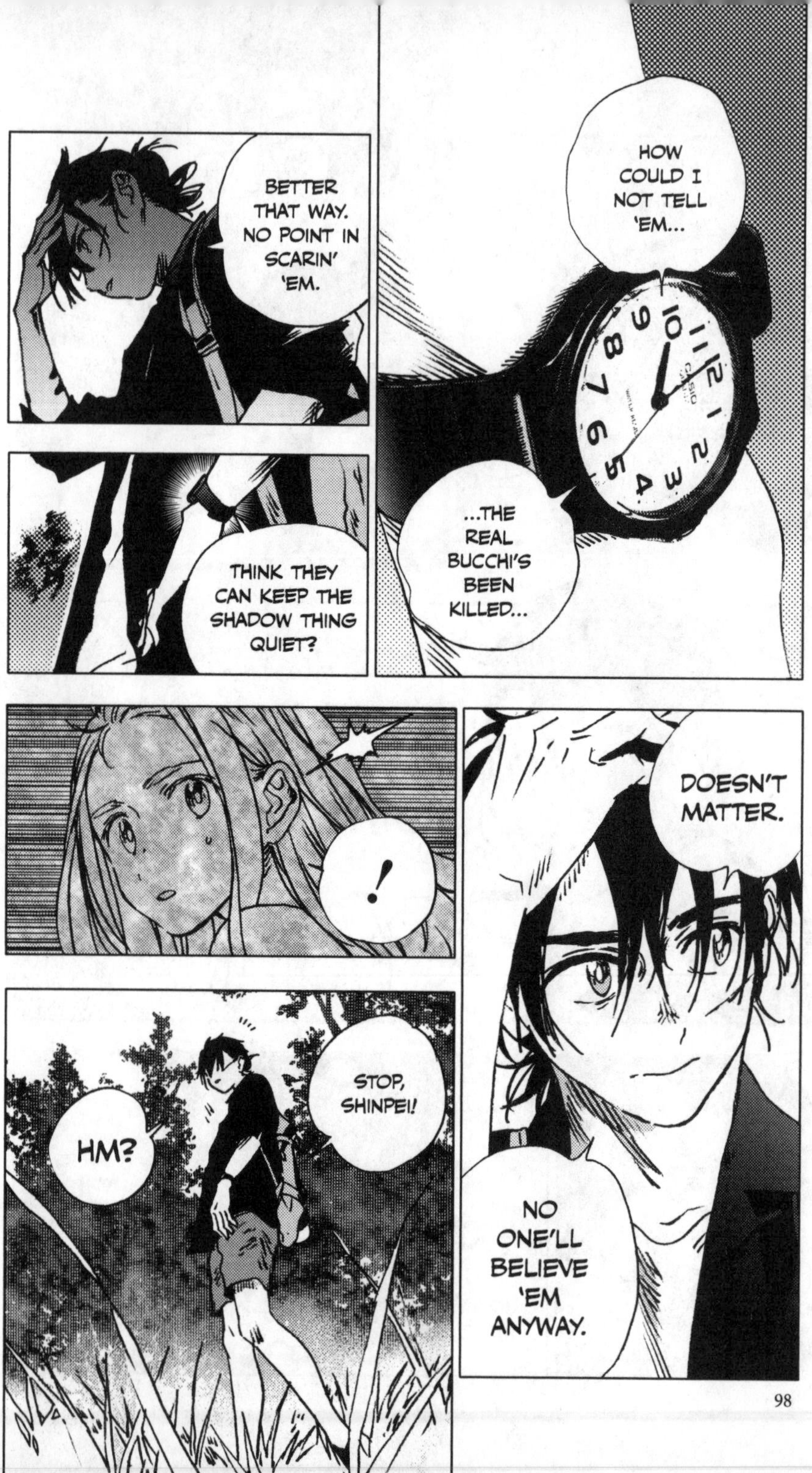
HOW COULD I NOT TELL 'EM...
...THE REAL BUCCHI'S BEEN KILLED...
BETTER THAT WAY. NO POINT IN SCARIN' 'EM.
THINK THEY CAN KEEP THE SHADOW THING QUIET?
DOESN'T MATTER.
NO ONE'LL BELIEVE 'EM ANYWAY.
!
STOP, SHINPEI!
HM?

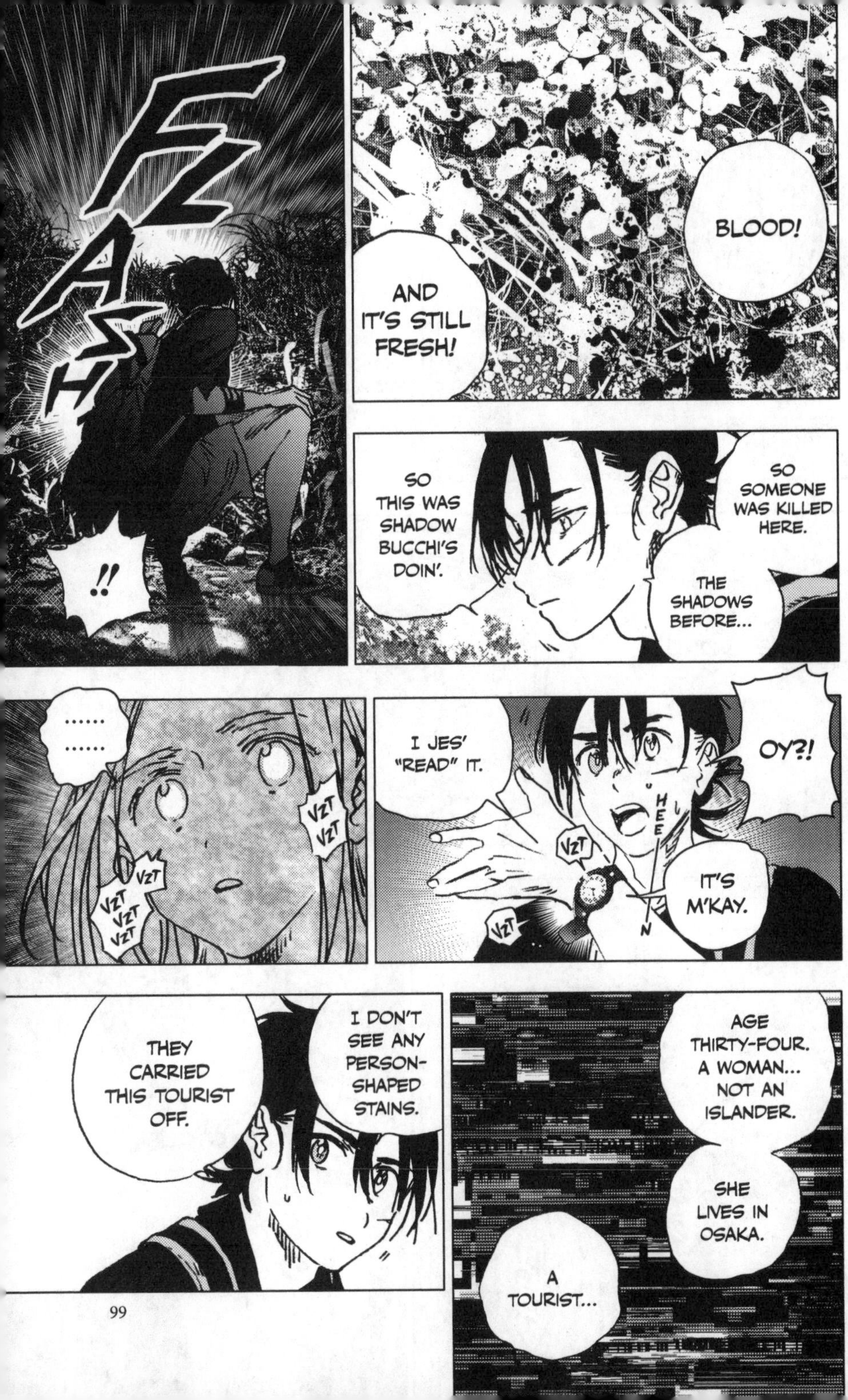
BLOOD!
AND IT'S STILL FRESH!
SO SOMEONE WAS KILLED HERE.
THE SHADOWS BEFORE...
SO THIS WAS SHADOW BUCCHI'S DOIN'.
FZASH
!!
OY?!
I JES' "READ" IT.
HEEEN
VZT
IT'S M'KAY.
VZT
......
......
VZT VZT
VZT
VZT VZT VZT
AGE THIRTY-FOUR. A WOMAN... NOT AN ISLANDER.
SHE LIVES IN OSAKA.
A TOURIST...
I DON'T SEE ANY PERSON-SHAPED STAINS.
THEY CARRIED THIS TOURIST OFF.

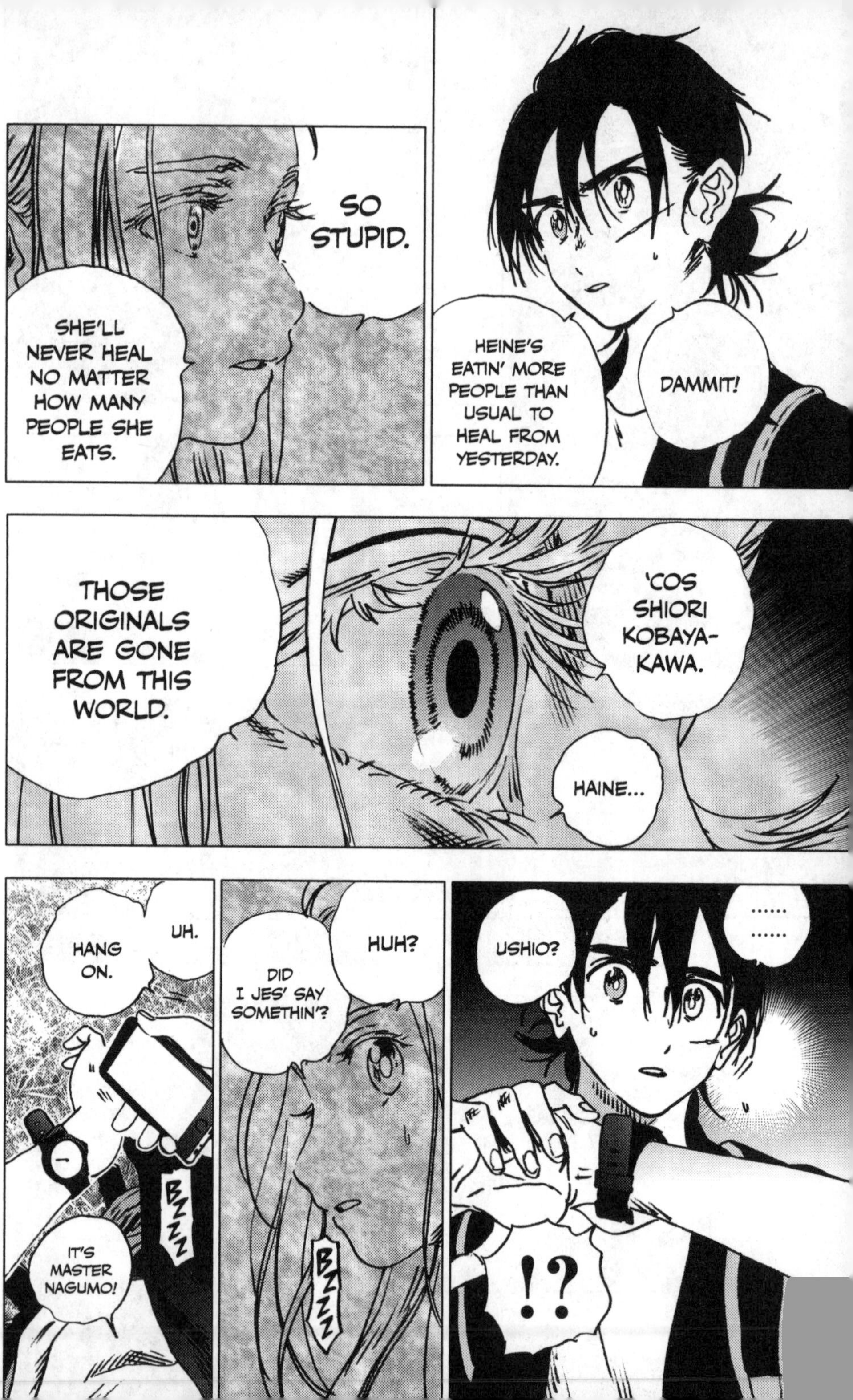
DAMMIT!
HEINE'S EATIN' MORE PEOPLE THAN USUAL TO HEAL FROM YESTERDAY.
SO STUPID.
SHE'LL NEVER HEAL NO MATTER HOW MANY PEOPLE SHE EATS.
'COS SHIORI KOBAYA-KAWA.
THOSE ORIGINALS ARE GONE FROM THIS WORLD.
HAINE...
......
......
USHIO?
!?
HUH?
DID I JES' SAY SOMETHIN'?
BZZZ
UH.
HANG ON.
BZZZ
IT'S MASTER NAGUMO!

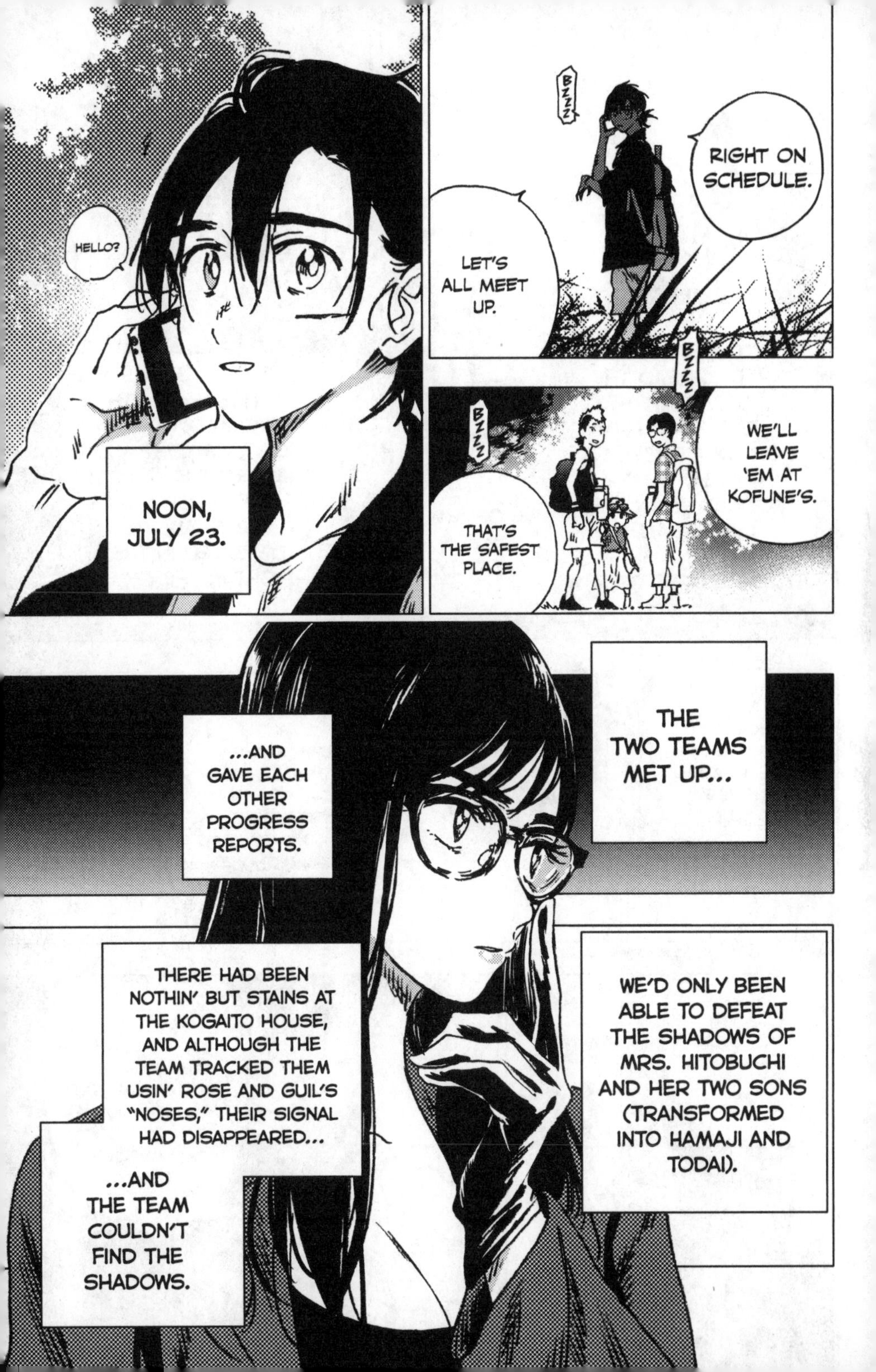
BZZZ
RIGHT ON SCHEDULE.
LET'S ALL MEET UP.
BZZZ
WE'LL LEAVE 'EM AT KOFUNE'S.
BZZZ
THAT'S THE SAFEST PLACE.
HELLO?
NOON, JULY 23.
THE TWO TEAMS MET UP...
...AND GAVE EACH OTHER PROGRESS REPORTS.
WE'D ONLY BEEN ABLE TO DEFEAT THE SHADOWS OF MRS. HITOBUCHI AND HER TWO SONS (TRANSFORMED INTO HAMAJI AND TODAI).
THERE HAD BEEN NOTHIN' BUT STAINS AT THE KOGAITO HOUSE, AND ALTHOUGH THE TEAM TRACKED THEM USIN' ROSE AND GUIL'S "NOSES," THEIR SIGNAL HAD DISAPPEARED...
...AND THE TEAM COULDN'T FIND THE SHADOWS.

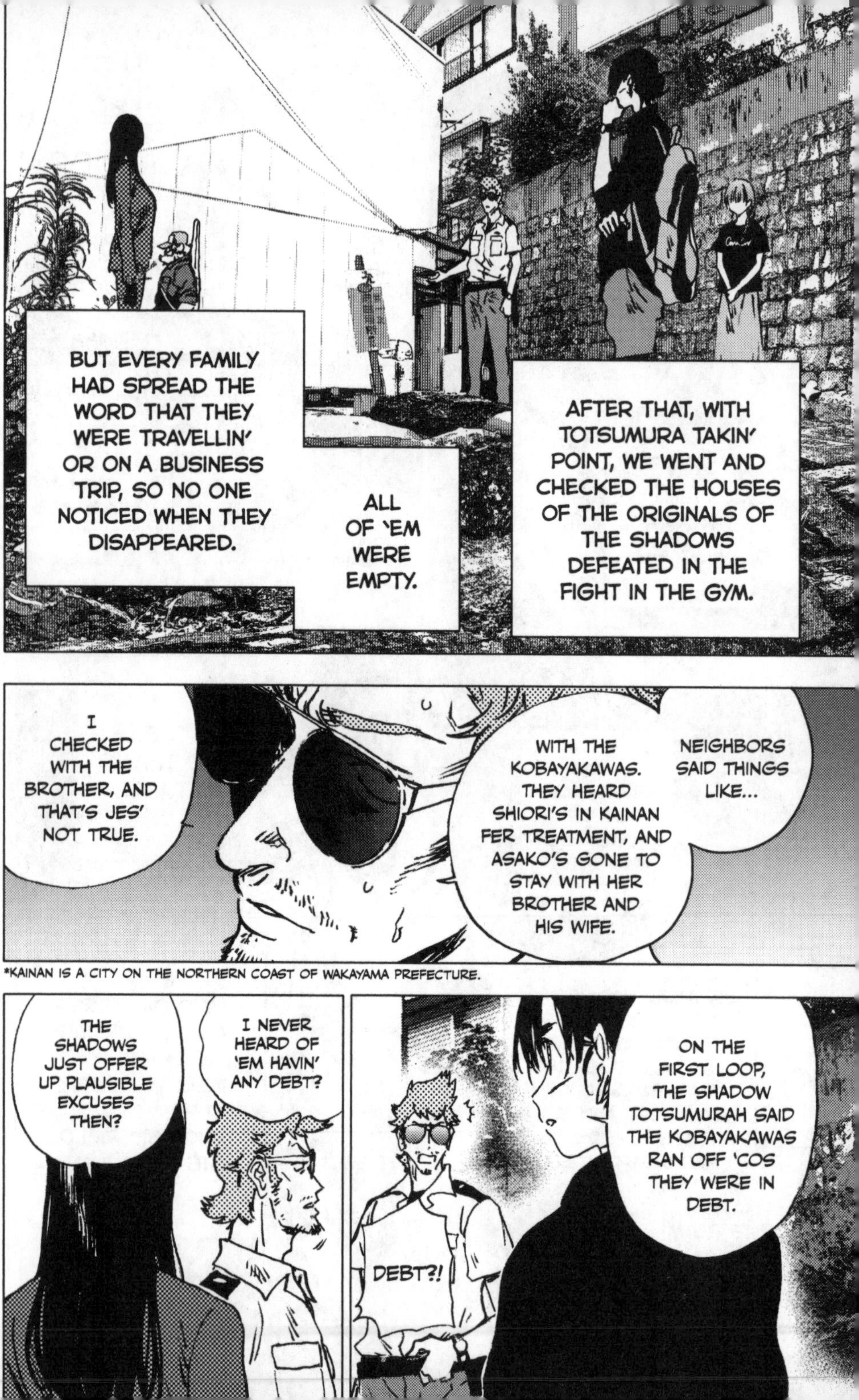
AFTER THAT, WITH TOTSUMURA TAKIN' POINT, WE WENT AND CHECKED THE HOUSES OF THE ORIGINALS OF THE SHADOWS DEFEATED IN THE FIGHT IN THE GYM.
ALL OF 'EM WERE EMPTY.
BUT EVERY FAMILY HAD SPREAD THE WORD THAT THEY WERE TRAVELLIN' OR ON A BUSINESS TRIP, SO NO ONE NOTICED WHEN THEY DISAPPEARED.
NEIGHBORS SAID THINGS LIKE...
WITH THE KOBAYAKAWAS. THEY HEARD SHIORI'S IN KAINAN FER TREATMENT, AND ASAKO'S GONE TO STAY WITH HER BROTHER AND HIS WIFE.
I CHECKED WITH THE BROTHER, AND THAT'S JES' NOT TRUE.
ON THE FIRST LOOP, THE SHADOW TOTSUMURAH SAID THE KOBAYAKAWAS RAN OFF 'COS THEY WERE IN DEBT.
DEBT?!
I NEVER HEARD OF 'EM HAVIN' ANY DEBT?
THE SHADOWS JUST OFFER UP PLAUSIBLE EXCUSES THEN?
*KAINAN IS A CITY ON THE NORTHERN COAST OF WAKAYAMA PREFECTURE.

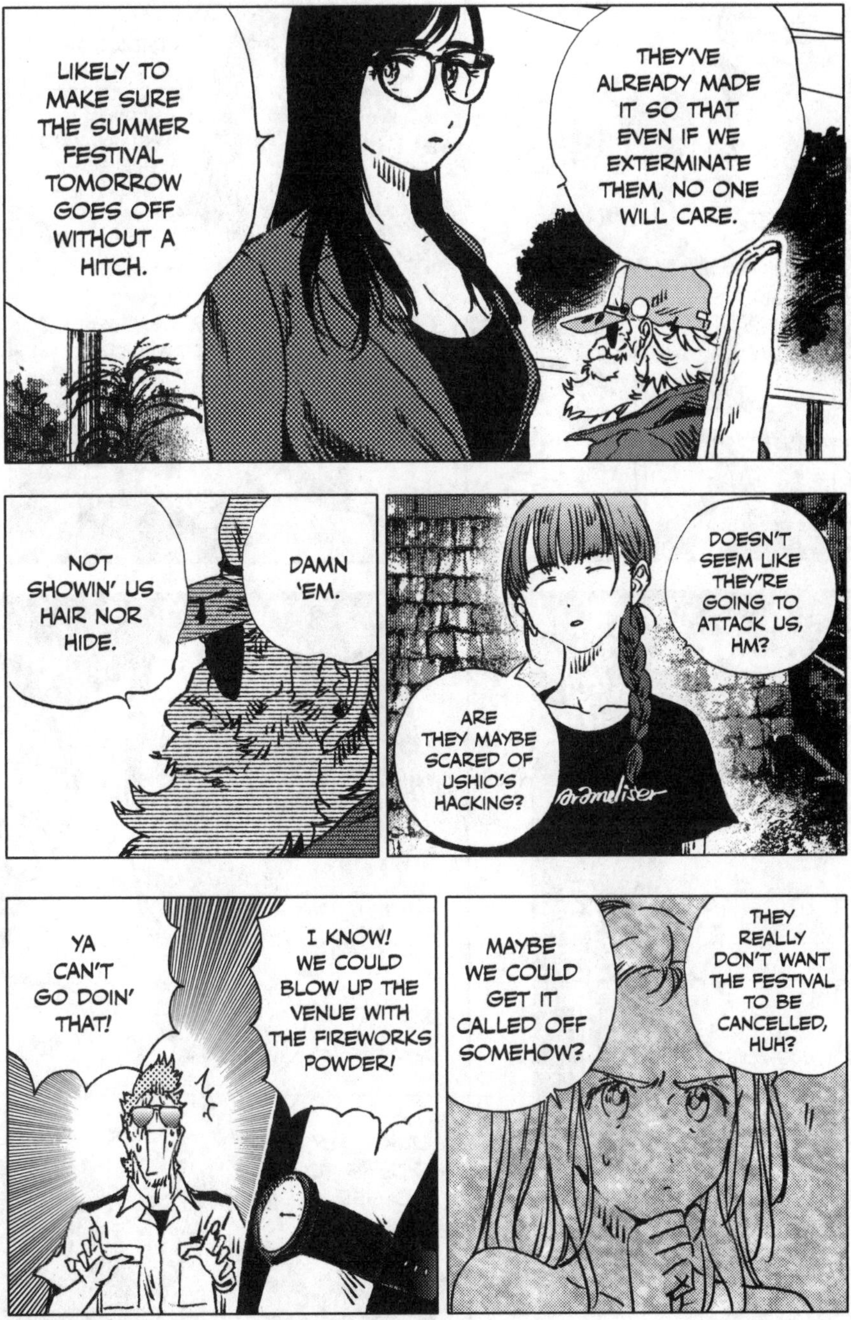
THEY'VE ALREADY MADE IT SO THAT EVEN IF WE EXTERMINATE THEM, NO ONE WILL CARE.
LIKELY TO MAKE SURE THE SUMMER FESTIVAL TOMORROW GOES OFF WITHOUT A HITCH.
DOESN'T SEEM LIKE THEY'RE GOING TO ATTACK US, HM?
ARE THEY MAYBE SCARED OF USHIO'S HACKING?
DAMN 'EM.
NOT SHOWIN' US HAIR NOR HIDE.
THEY REALLY DON'T WANT THE FESTIVAL TO BE CANCELLED, HUH?
MAYBE WE COULD GET IT CALLED OFF SOMEHOW?
I KNOW! WE COULD BLOW UP THE VENUE WITH THE FIREWORKS POWDER!
YA CAN'T GO DOIN' THAT!

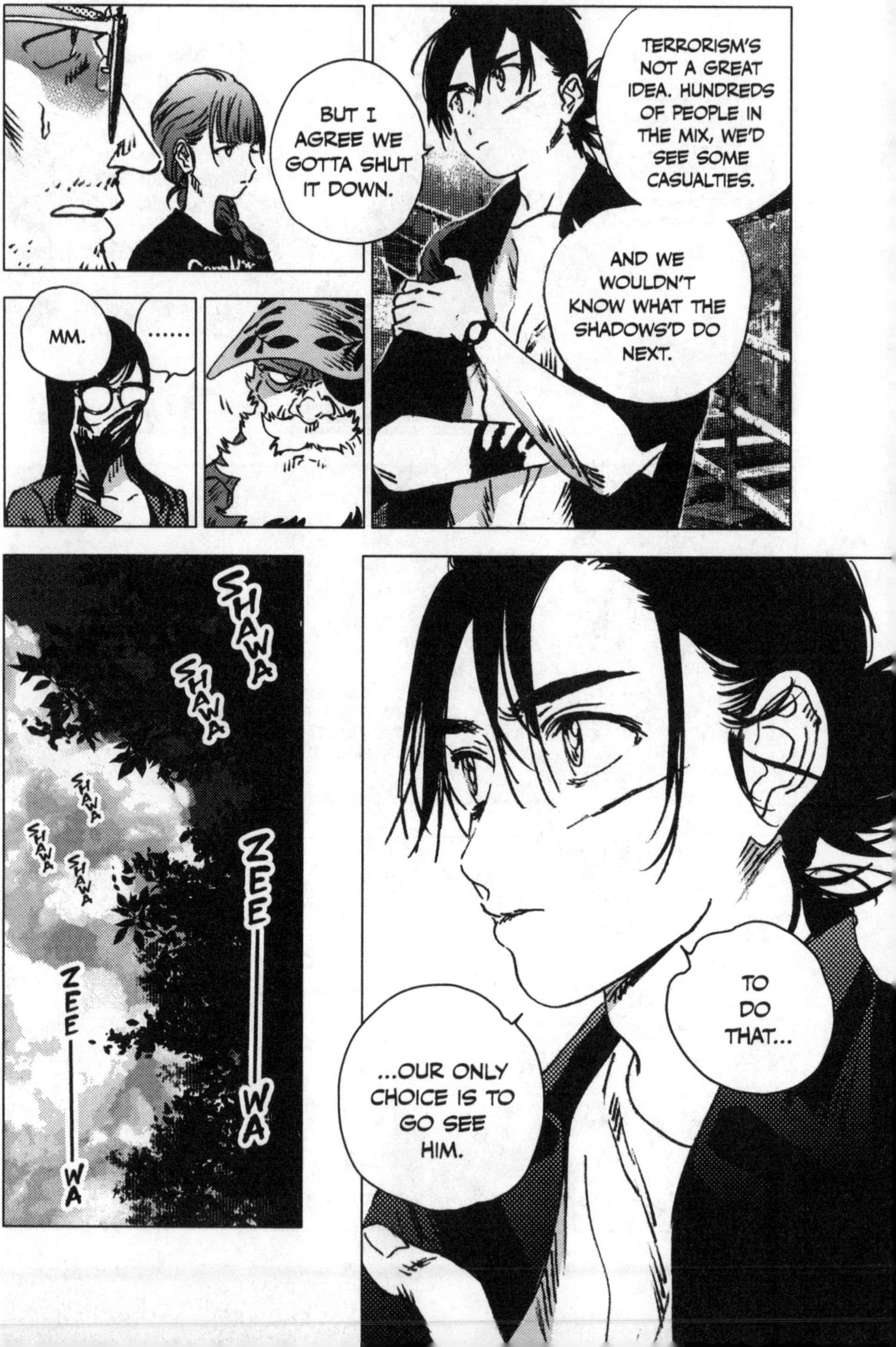
TERRORISM'S NOT A GREAT IDEA. HUNDREDS OF PEOPLE IN THE MIX, WE'D SEE SOME CASUALTIES.
AND WE WOULDN'T KNOW WHAT THE SHADOWS'D DO NEXT.
BUT I AGREE WE GOTTA SHUT IT DOWN.
......
MM.
TO DO THAT...
...OUR ONLY CHOICE IS TO GO SEE HIM.
SHAWA
SHAWA
ZEE—WA
SHAWA
SHAWA
SHAWA
ZEE—WA

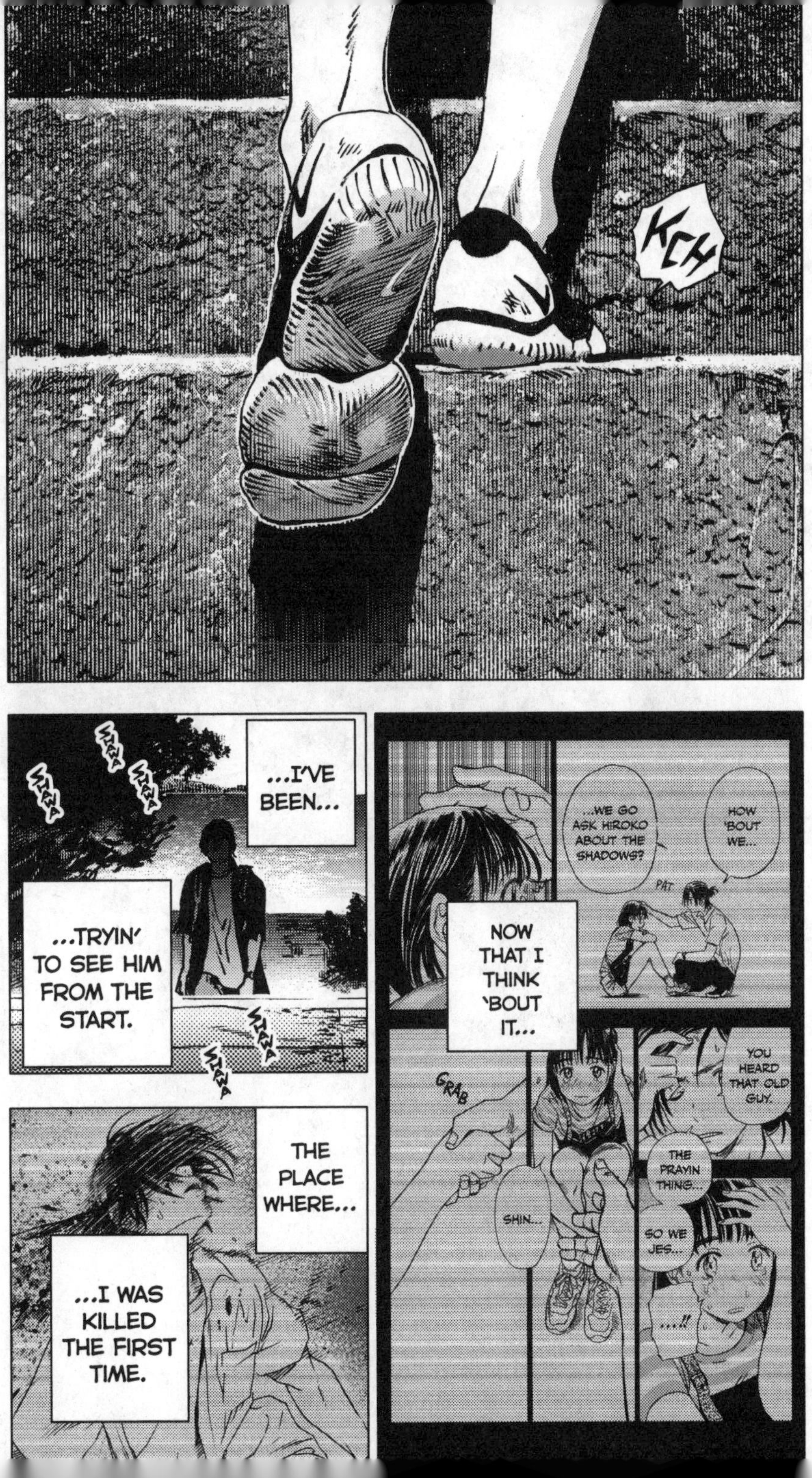
KCH
HOW 'BOUT WE...
...WE GO ASK HIROKO ABOUT THE SHADOWS?
PAT
NOW THAT I THINK 'BOUT IT...
YOU HEARD THAT OLD GUY.
THE PRAYIN THING...
SO WE JES...
...!!
SHIN...
GRAB
...I'VE BEEN...
SHWA SHWA SHWA
...TRYIN' TO SEE HIM FROM THE START.
SHWA SHWA
THE PLACE WHERE...
...I WAS KILLED THE FIRST TIME.

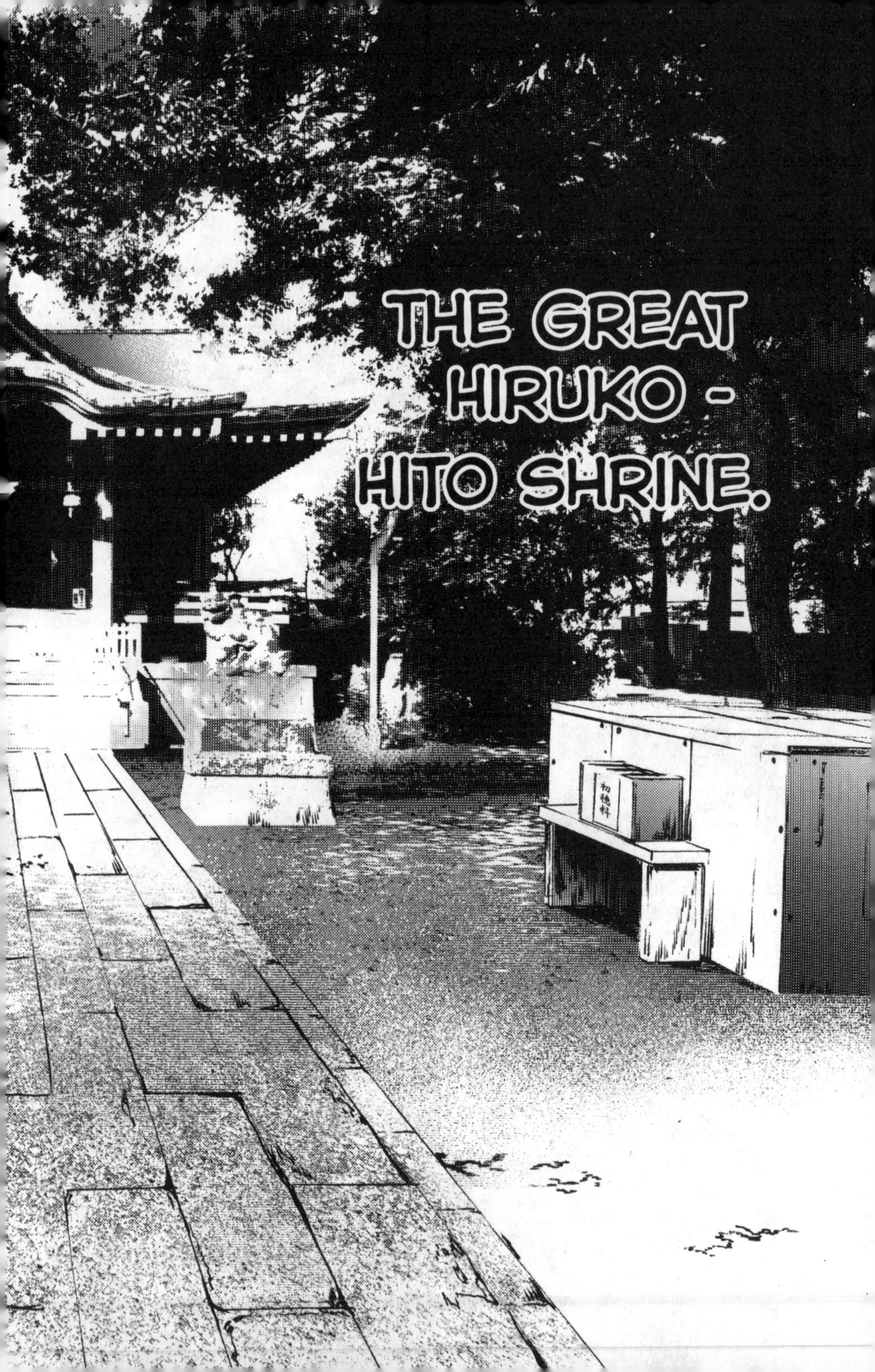
THE GREAT HIRUKO - HITO SHRINE.

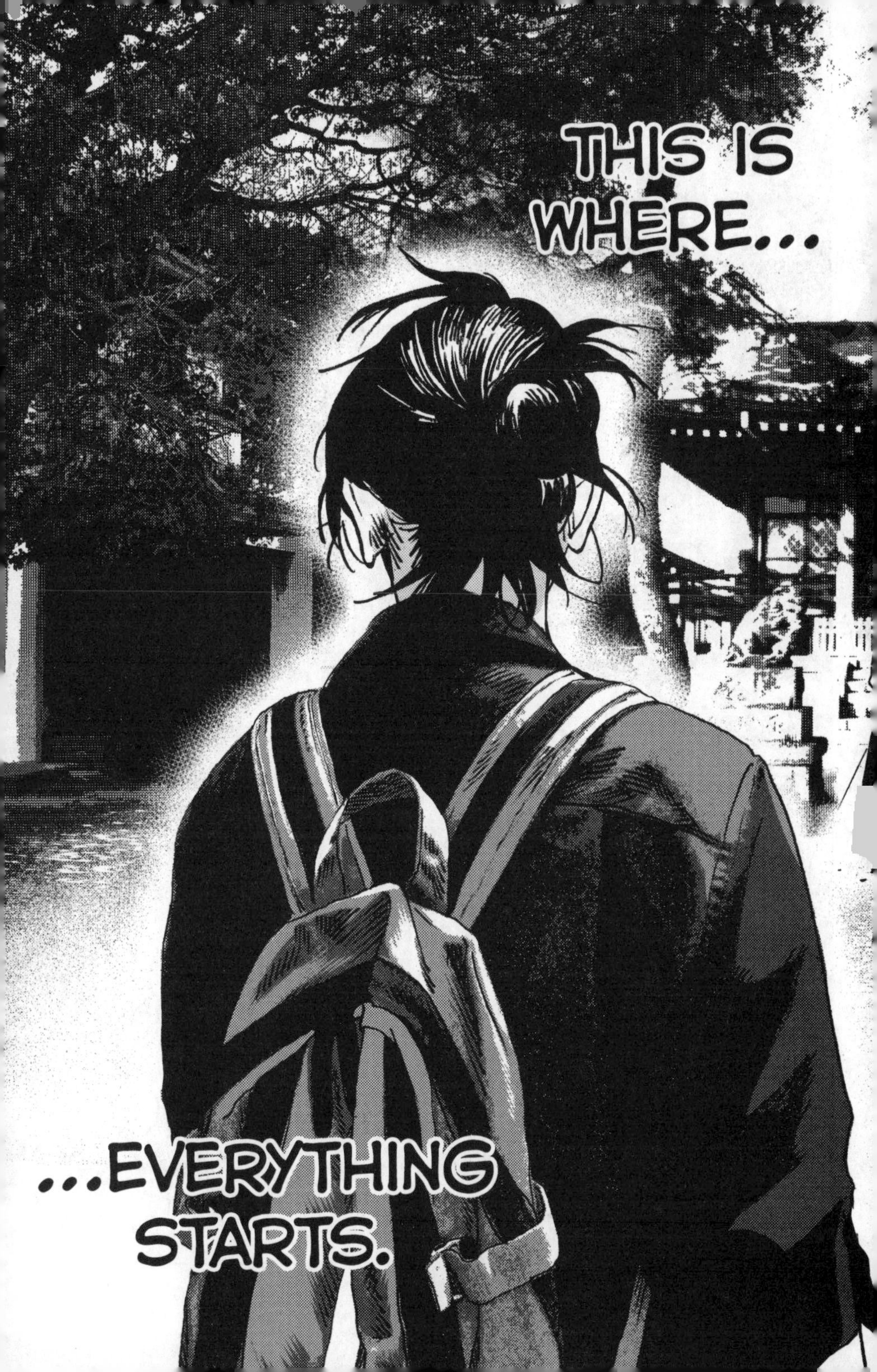
THIS IS WHERE...
...EVERYTHING STARTS.

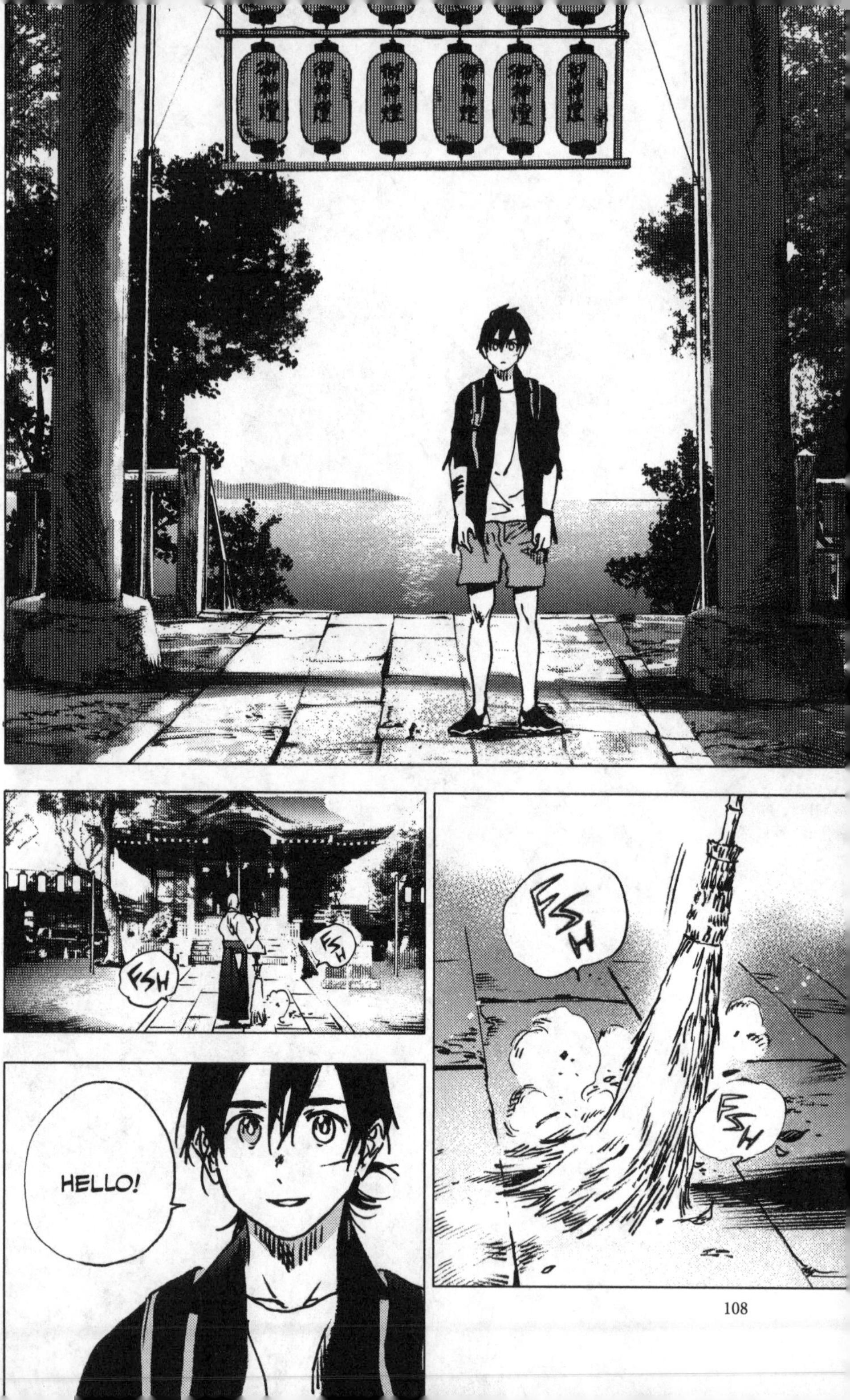
FSH
FSH
FSH
FSH
HELLO!

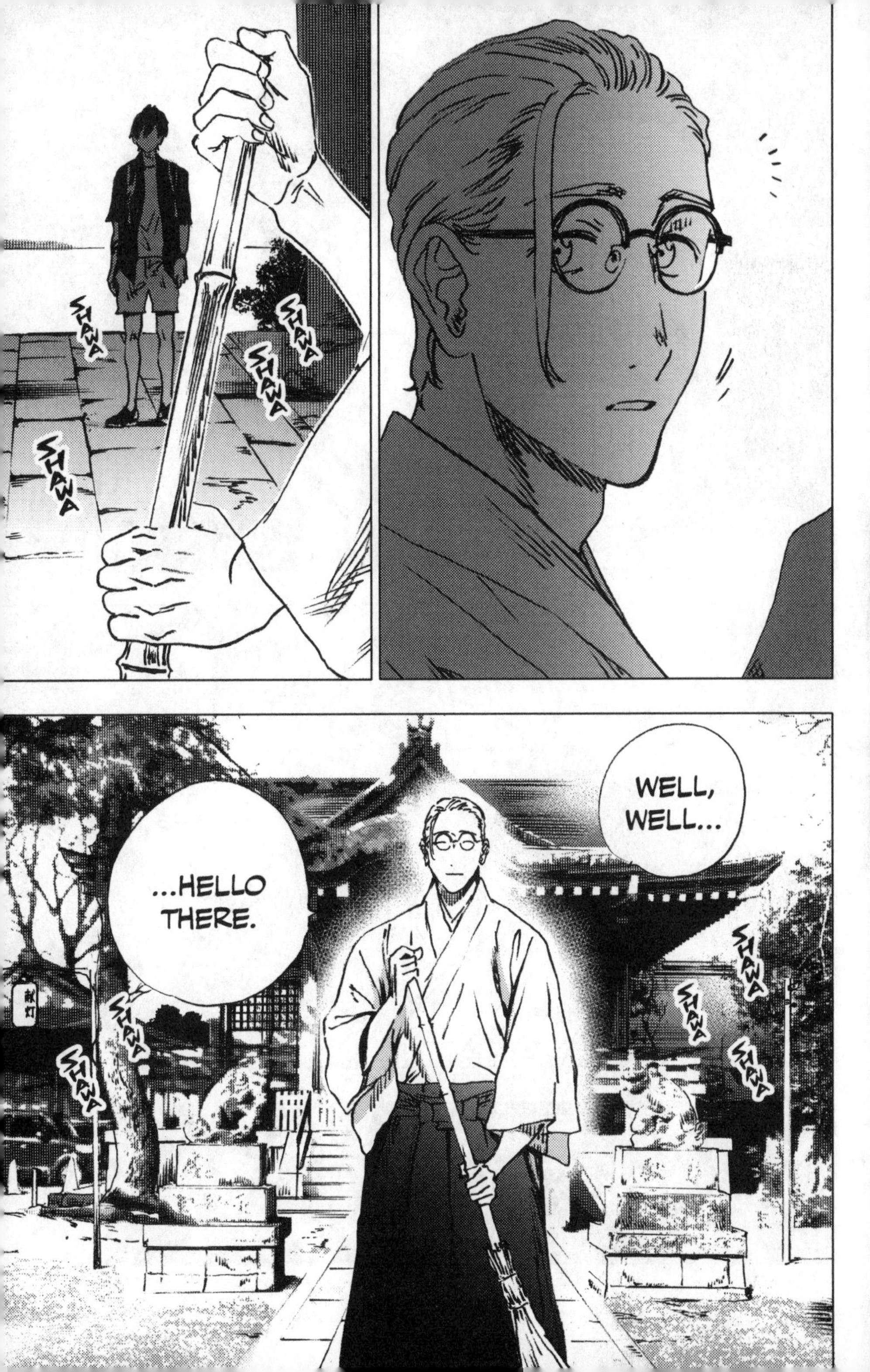
SHAWA
SHAWA
SHAWA
SHAWA
WELL, WELL...
...HELLO THERE.
SHAWA
SHAWA
SHAWA
SHAWA
SHAWA
献灯

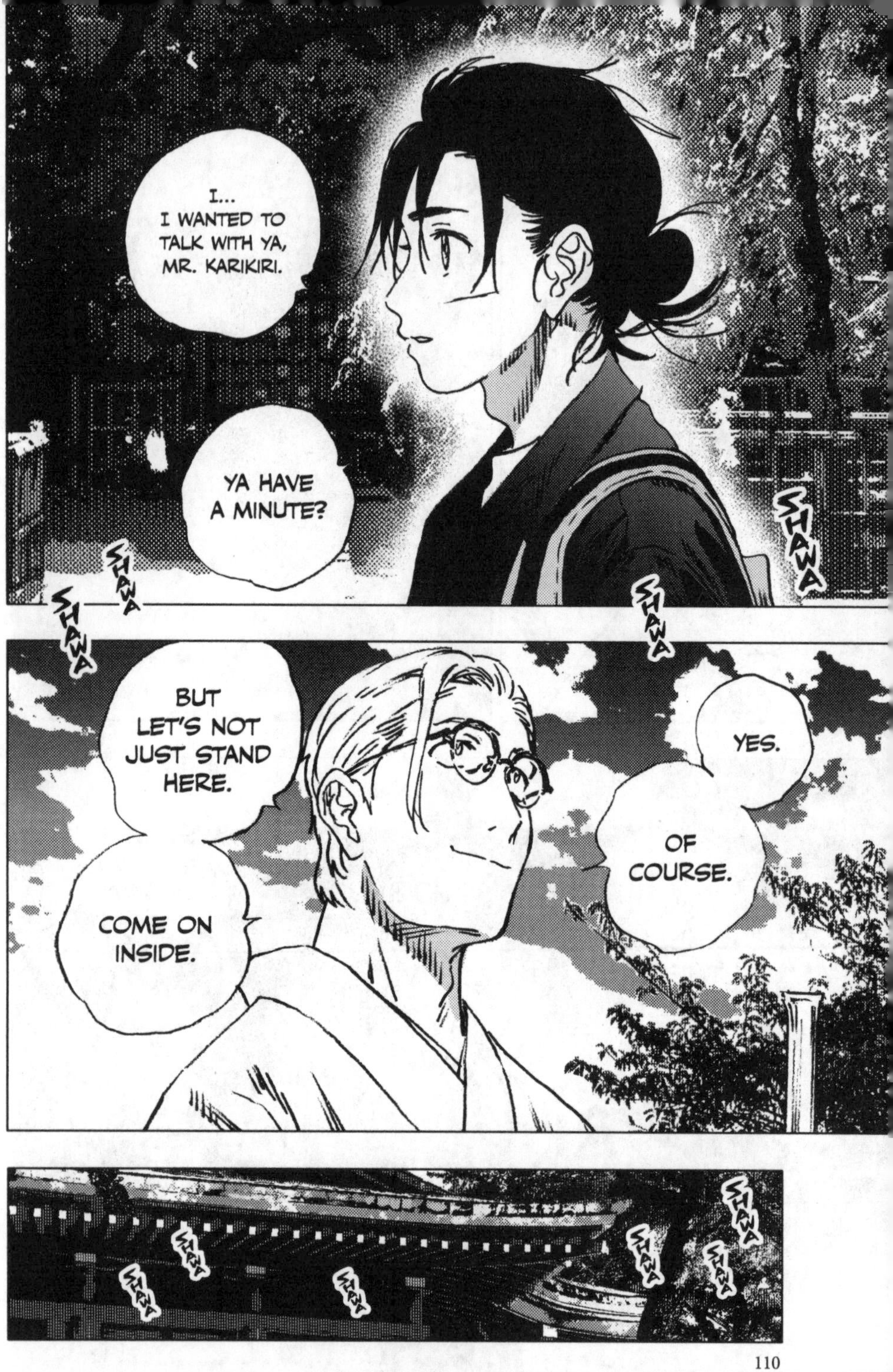
I... I WANTED TO TALK WITH YA, MR. KARIKIRI.
YA HAVE A MINUTE?
SHAWA
SHAWA
SHAWA
SHAWA
YES.
OF COURSE.
BUT LET'S NOT JUST STAND HERE.
COME ON INSIDE.
SHAWA
SHAWA
SHAWA
SHAWA
SHAWA
SHAWA

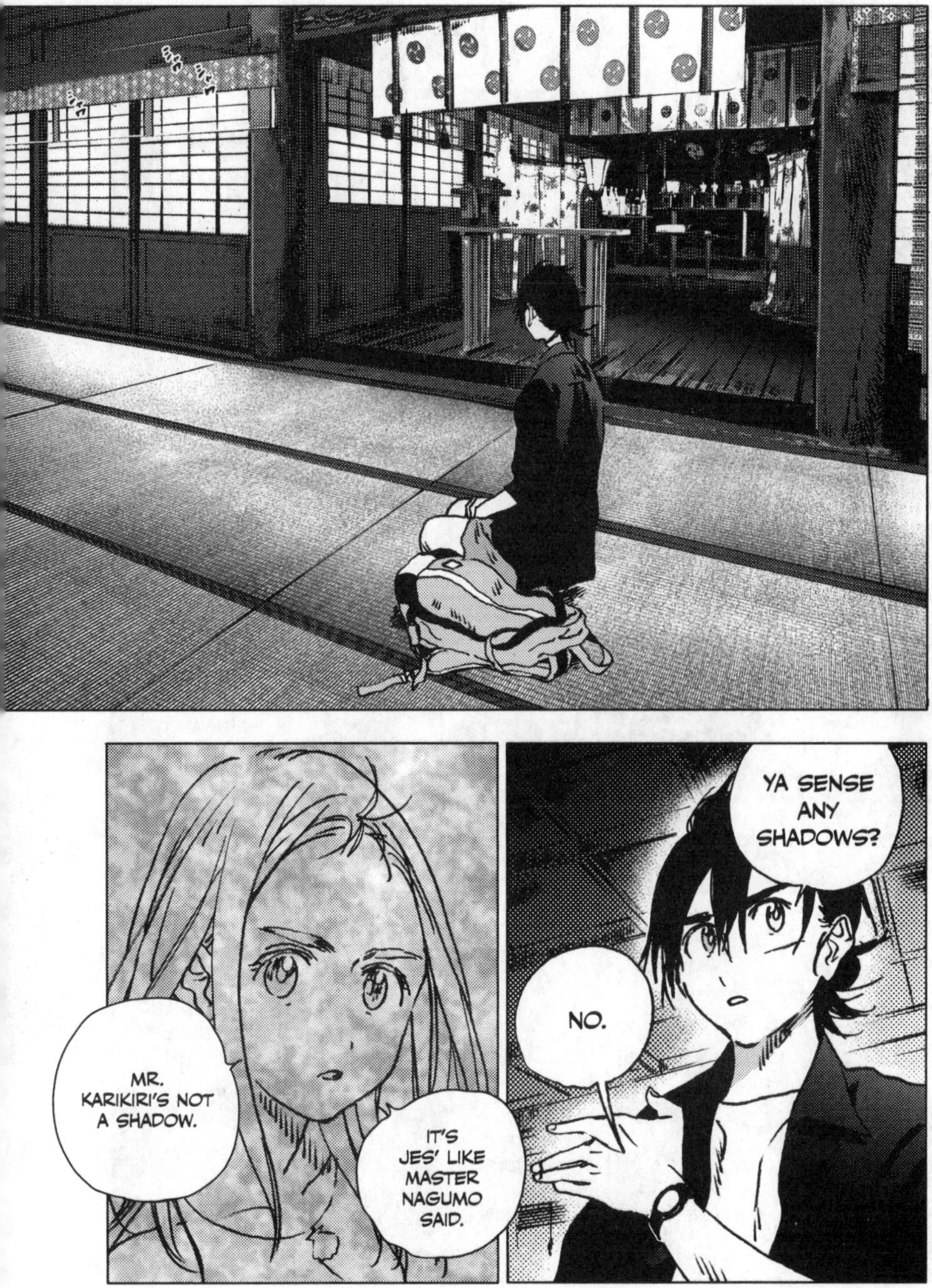
YA SENSE ANY SHADOWS?
NO.
MR. KARIKIRI'S NOT A SHADOW.
IT'S JES' LIKE MASTER NAGUMO SAID.

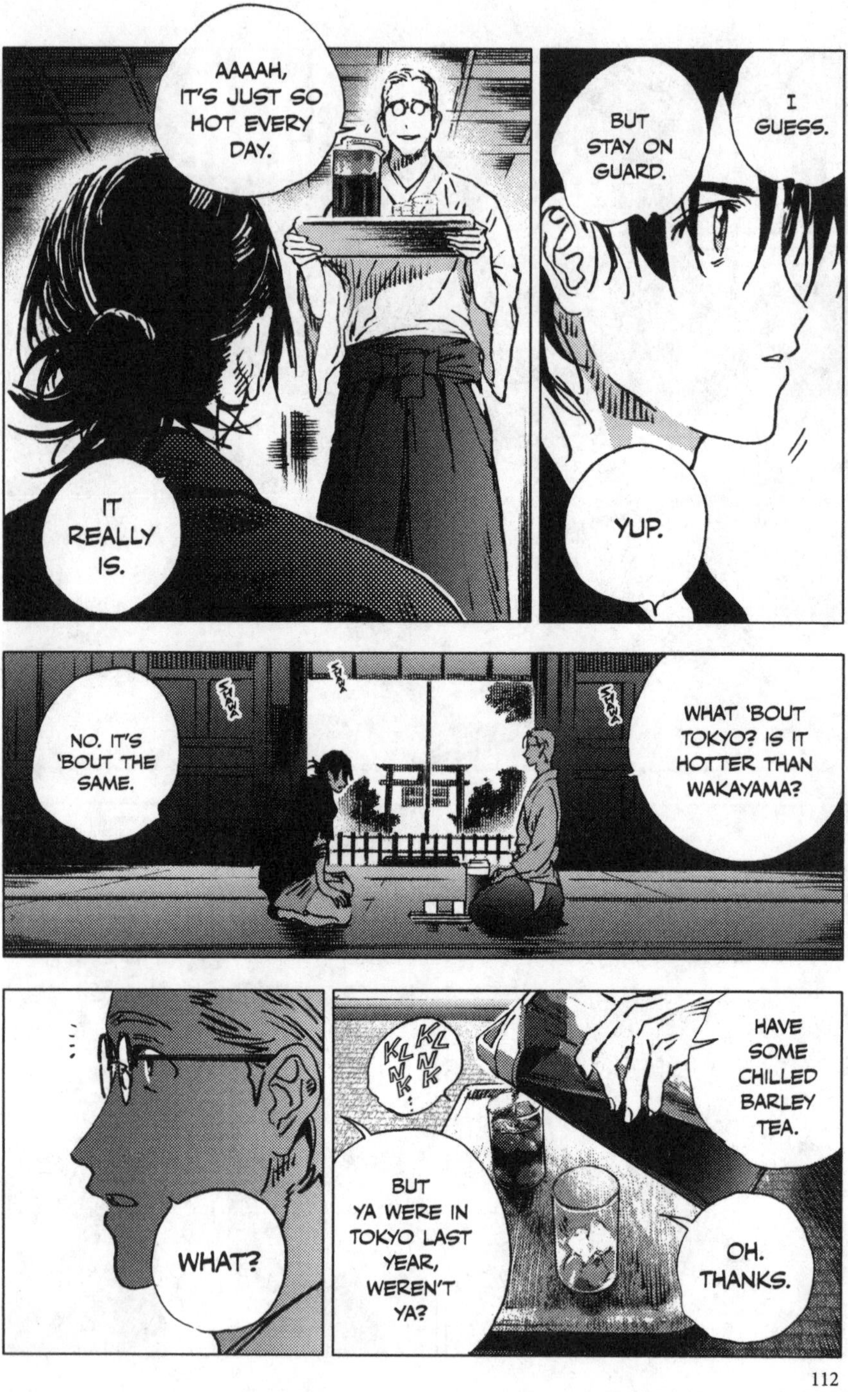
I GUESS.
BUT STAY ON GUARD.
YUP.
AAAAH, IT'S JUST SO HOT EVERY DAY.
IT REALLY IS.
WHAT 'BOUT TOKYO? IS IT HOTTER THAN WAKAYAMA?
NO. IT'S 'BOUT THE SAME.
HAVE SOME CHILLED BARLEY TEA.
KLNK KLNK...
OH. THANKS.
BUT YA WERE IN TOKYO LAST YEAR, WEREN'T YA?
WHAT?

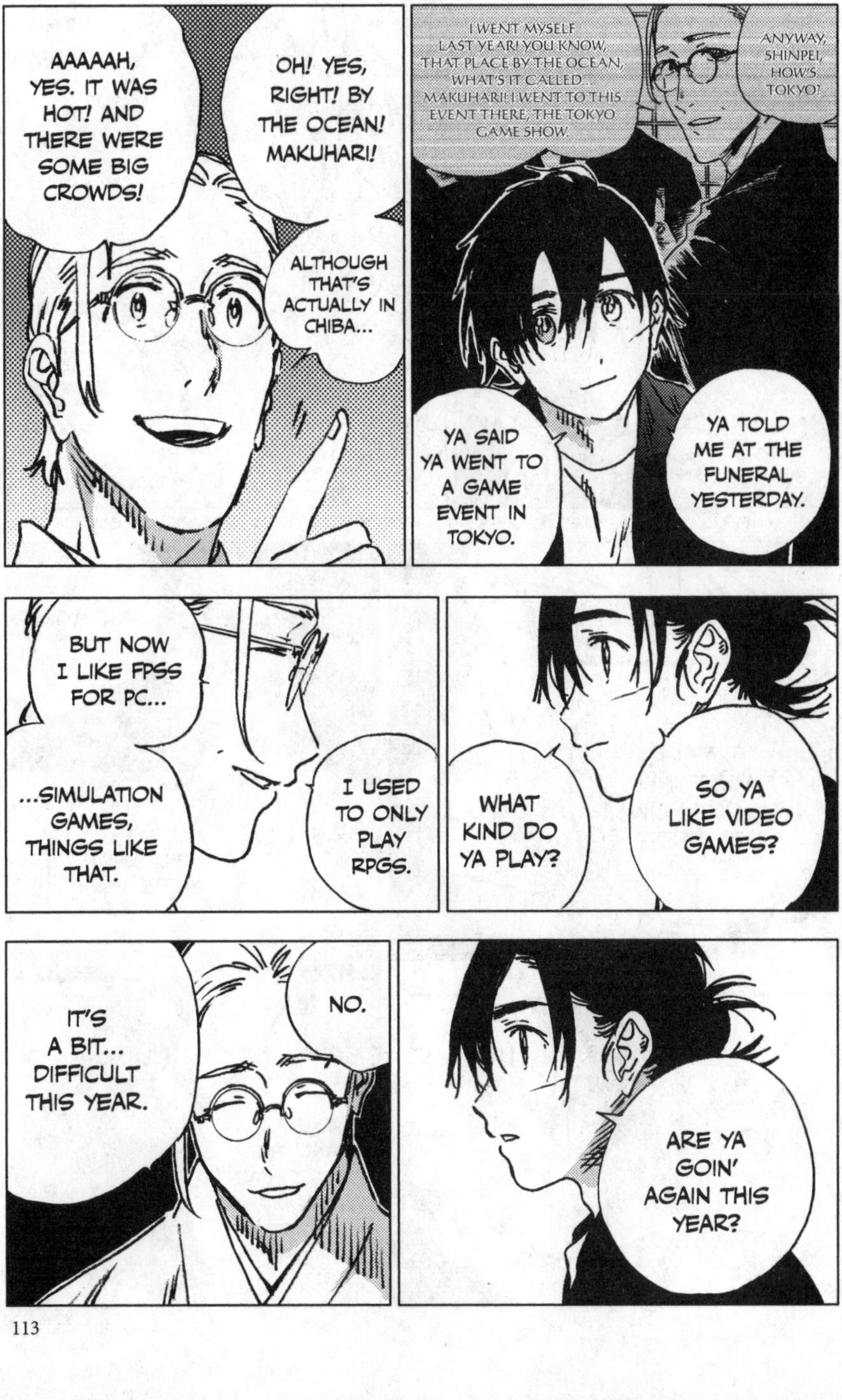
ANYWAY, SHINPEI, HOW'S TOKYO?
I WENT MYSELF LAST YEAR! YOU KNOW, THAT PLACE BY THE OCEAN, WHAT'S IT CALLED... MAKUHARI! I WENT TO THIS EVENT THERE, THE TOKYO GAME SHOW.
YA TOLD ME AT THE FUNERAL YESTERDAY.
YA SAID YA WENT TO A GAME EVENT IN TOKYO.
OH! YES, RIGHT! BY THE OCEAN! MAKUHARI!
AAAAAH, YES. IT WAS HOT! AND THERE WERE SOME BIG CROWDS!
ALTHOUGH THAT'S ACTUALLY IN CHIBA...
SO YA LIKE VIDEO GAMES?
WHAT KIND DO YA PLAY?
I USED TO ONLY PLAY RPGS.
BUT NOW I LIKE FPSS FOR PC...
...SIMULATION GAMES, THINGS LIKE THAT.
ARE YA GOIN' AGAIN THIS YEAR?
NO.
IT'S A BIT... DIFFICULT THIS YEAR.

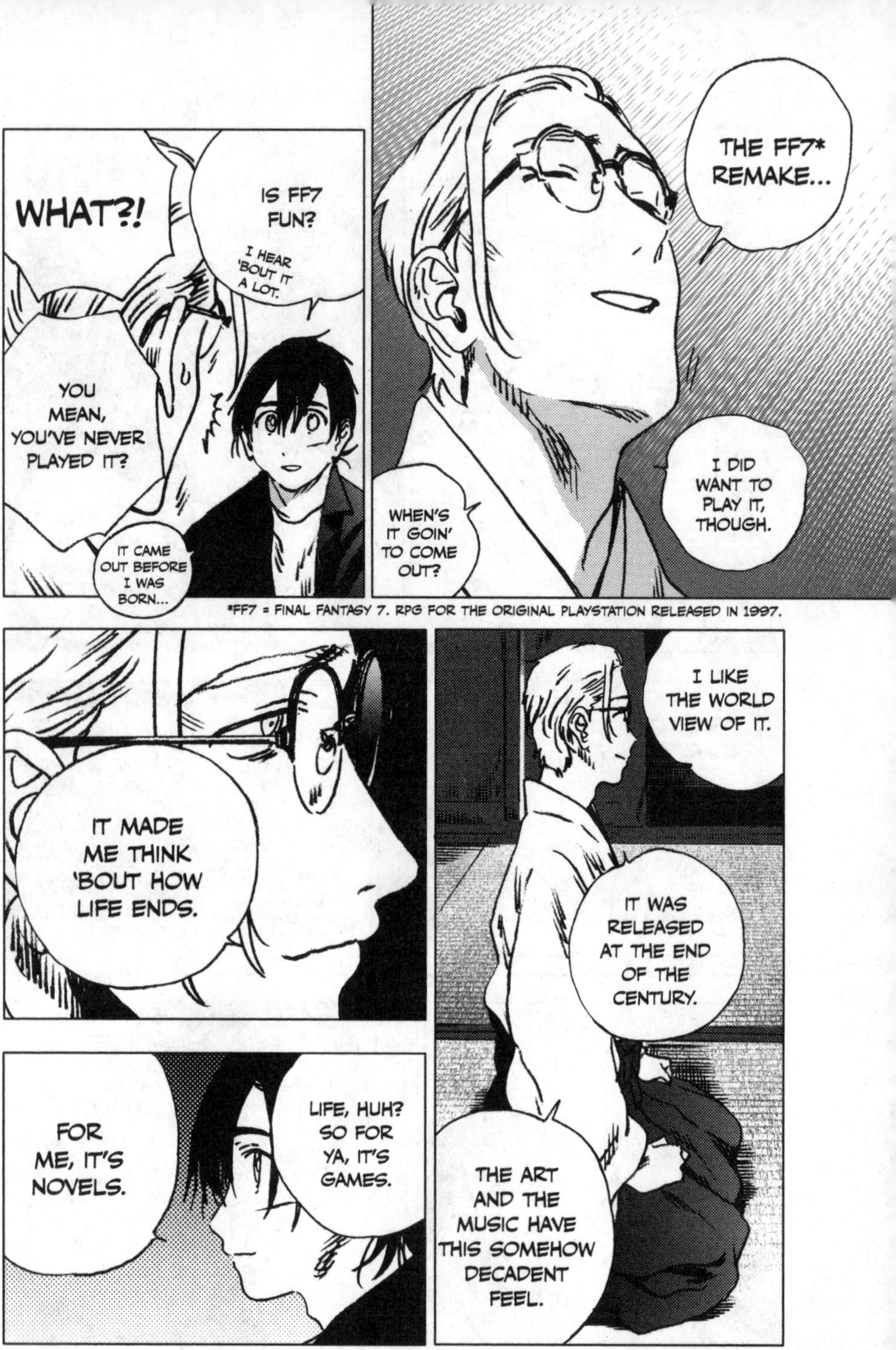
THE FF7* REMAKE...
I DID WANT TO PLAY IT, THOUGH.
WHEN'S IT GOIN' TO COME OUT?
IS FF7 FUN?
I HEAR 'BOUT IT A LOT.
WHAT?!
YOU MEAN, YOU'VE NEVER PLAYED IT?
IT CAME OUT BEFORE I WAS BORN...
I LIKE THE WORLD VIEW OF IT.
IT WAS RELEASED AT THE END OF THE CENTURY.
THE ART AND THE MUSIC HAVE THIS SOMEHOW DECADENT FEEL.
IT MADE ME THINK 'BOUT HOW LIFE ENDS.
LIFE, HUH? SO FOR YA, IT'S GAMES.
FOR ME, IT'S NOVELS.

*FF7 = FINAL FANTASY 7. RPG FOR THE ORIGINAL PLAYSTATION RELEASED IN 1997.

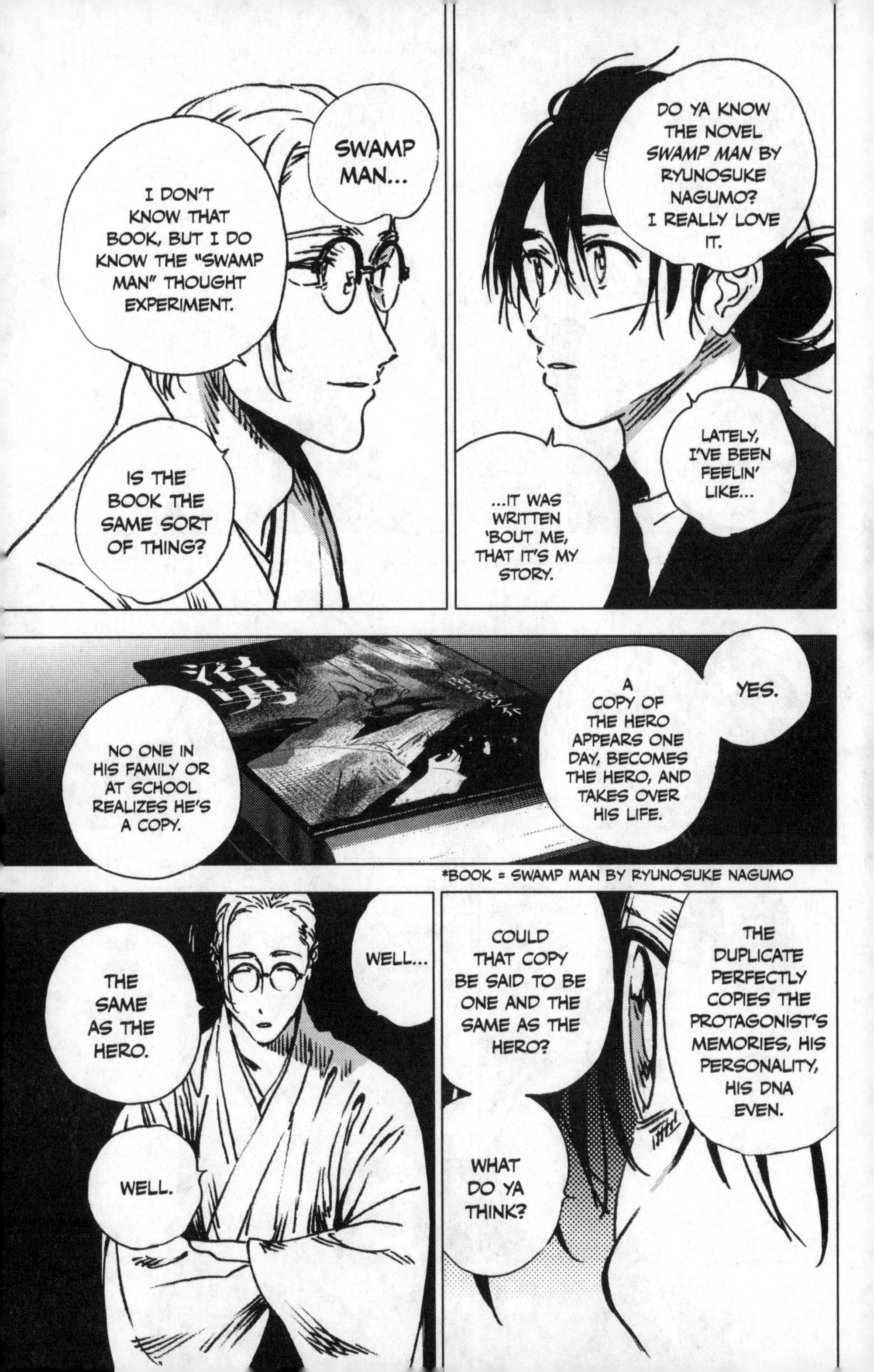
DO YA KNOW THE NOVEL *SWAMP MAN* BY RYUNOSUKE NAGUMO? I REALLY LOVE IT.
LATELY, I'VE BEEN FEELIN' LIKE...
...IT WAS WRITTEN 'BOUT ME, THAT IT'S MY STORY.
SWAMP MAN...
I DON'T KNOW THAT BOOK, BUT I DO KNOW THE "SWAMP MAN" THOUGHT EXPERIMENT.
IS THE BOOK THE SAME SORT OF THING?
YES.
A COPY OF THE HERO APPEARS ONE DAY, BECOMES THE HERO, AND TAKES OVER HIS LIFE.
NO ONE IN HIS FAMILY OR AT SCHOOL REALIZES HE'S A COPY.
*BOOK = SWAMP MAN BY RYUNOSUKE NAGUMO
THE DUPLICATE PERFECTLY COPIES THE PROTAGONIST'S MEMORIES, HIS PERSONALITY, HIS DNA EVEN.
COULD THAT COPY BE SAID TO BE ONE AND THE SAME AS THE HERO?
WHAT DO YA THINK?
WELL...
THE SAME AS THE HERO.
WELL.

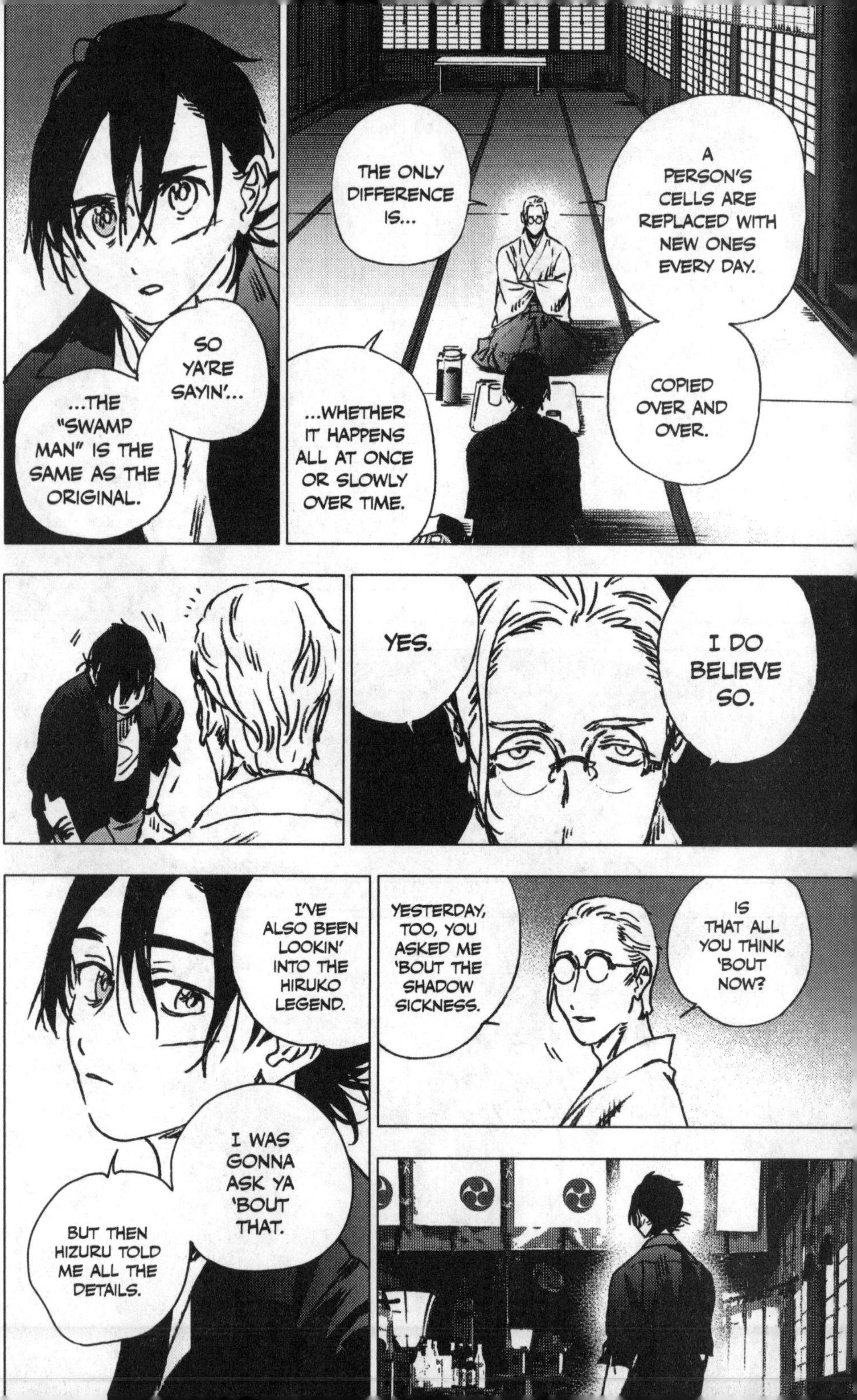
A PERSON'S CELLS ARE REPLACED WITH NEW ONES EVERY DAY.
COPIED OVER AND OVER.
THE ONLY DIFFERENCE IS...
...WHETHER IT HAPPENS ALL AT ONCE OR SLOWLY OVER TIME.
SO YA'RE SAYIN'...
...THE "SWAMP MAN" IS THE SAME AS THE ORIGINAL.
I DO BELIEVE SO.
YES.
IS THAT ALL YOU THINK 'BOUT NOW?
YESTERDAY, TOO, YOU ASKED ME 'BOUT THE SHADOW SICKNESS.
I'VE ALSO BEEN LOOKIN' INTO THE HIRUKO LEGEND.
I WAS GONNA ASK YA 'BOUT THAT.
BUT THEN HIZURU TOLD ME ALL THE DETAILS.

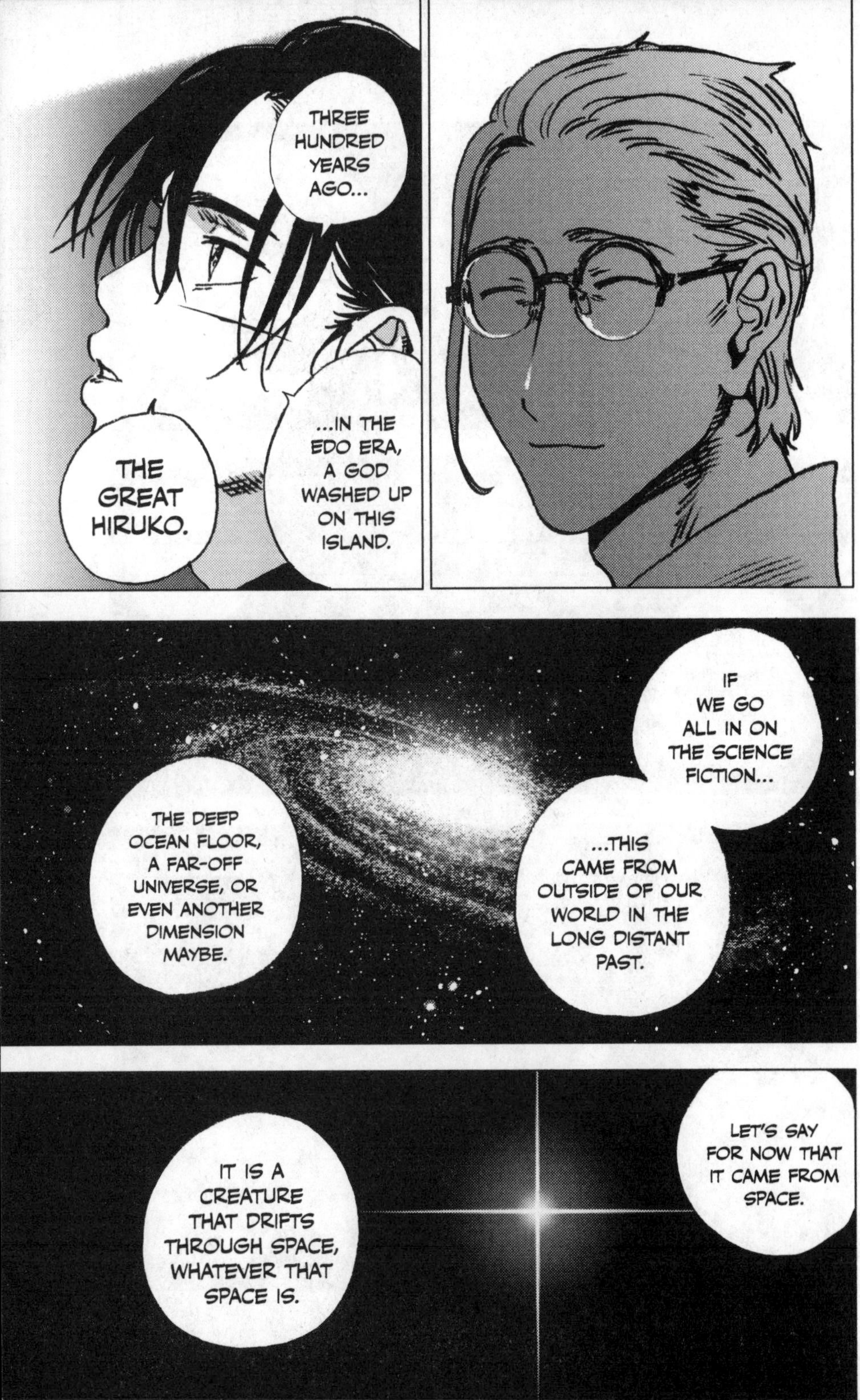
THREE HUNDRED YEARS AGO...
...IN THE EDO ERA, A GOD WASHED UP ON THIS ISLAND.
THE GREAT HIRUKO.
IF WE GO ALL IN ON THE SCIENCE FICTION...
...THIS CAME FROM OUTSIDE OF OUR WORLD IN THE LONG DISTANT PAST.
THE DEEP OCEAN FLOOR, A FAR-OFF UNIVERSE, OR EVEN ANOTHER DIMENSION MAYBE.
LET'S SAY FOR NOW THAT IT CAME FROM SPACE.
IT IS A CREATURE THAT DRIFTS THROUGH SPACE, WHATEVER THAT SPACE IS.

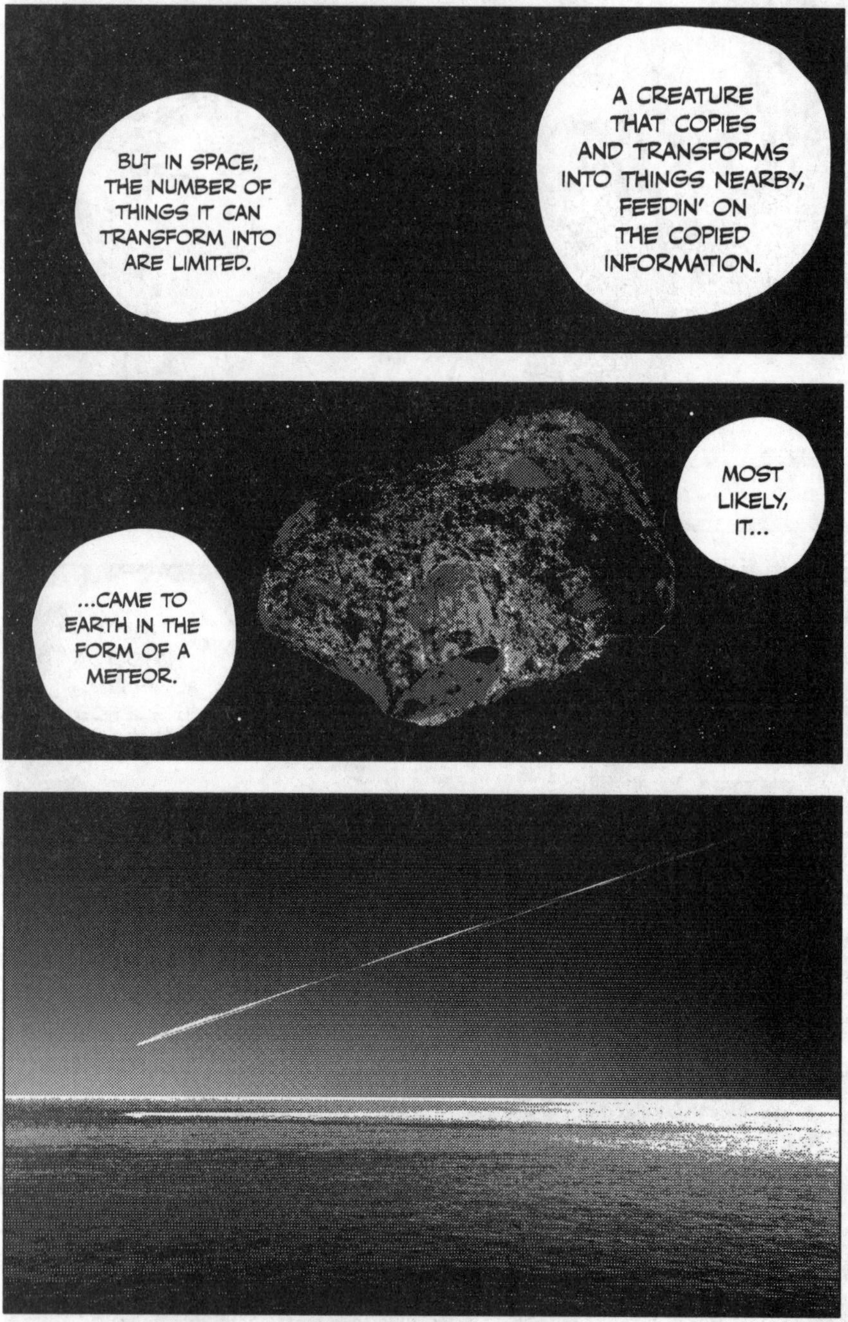
A CREATURE THAT COPIES AND TRANSFORMS INTO THINGS NEARBY, FEEDIN' ON THE COPIED INFORMATION.
BUT IN SPACE, THE NUMBER OF THINGS IT CAN TRANSFORM INTO ARE LIMITED.
MOST LIKELY, IT...
...CAME TO EARTH IN THE FORM OF A METEOR.

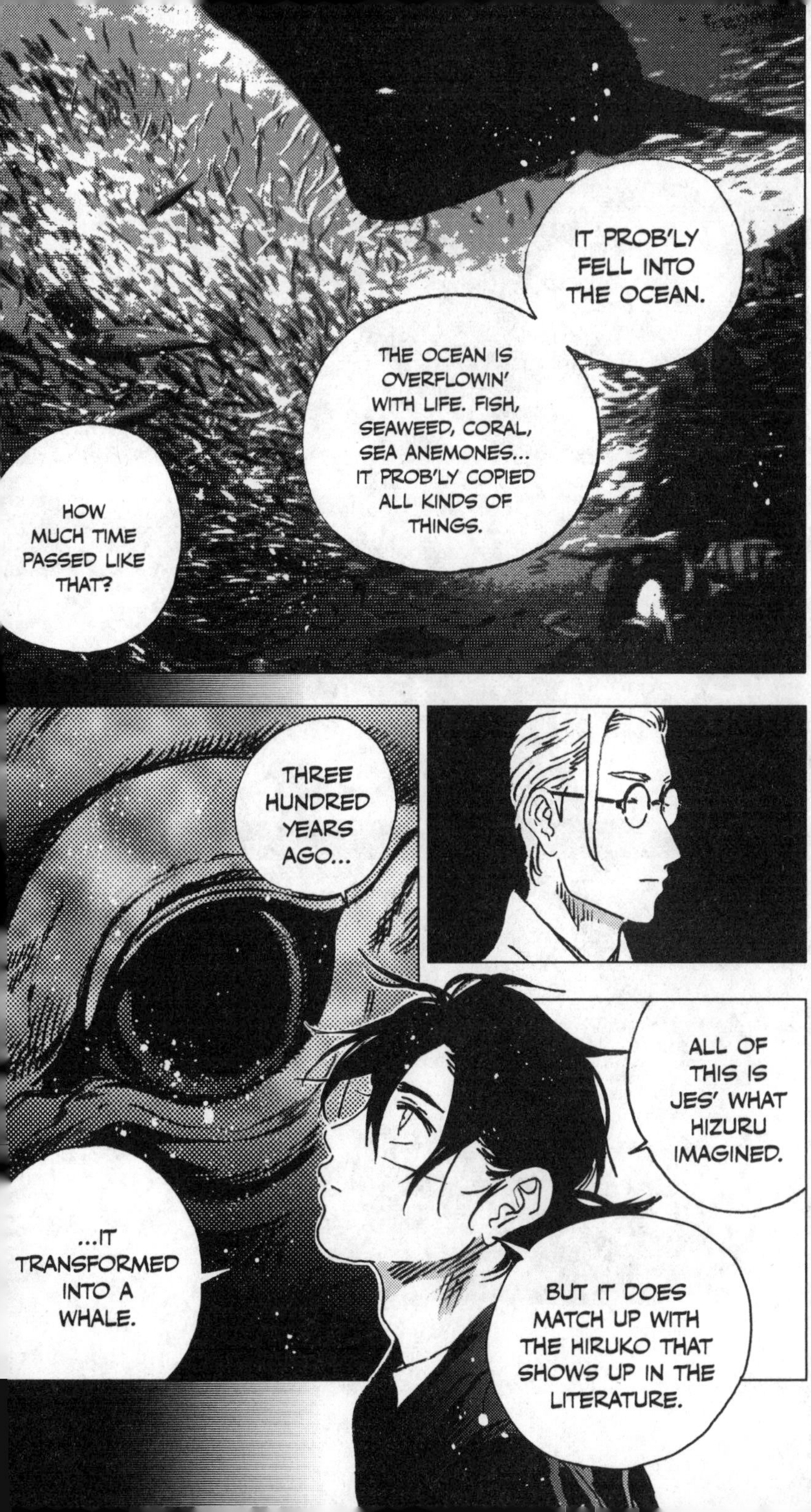
IT PROB'LY FELL INTO THE OCEAN.
THE OCEAN IS OVERFLOWIN' WITH LIFE. FISH, SEAWEED, CORAL, SEA ANEMONES... IT PROB'LY COPIED ALL KINDS OF THINGS.
HOW MUCH TIME PASSED LIKE THAT?
ALL OF THIS IS JES' WHAT HIZURU IMAGINED.
BUT IT DOES MATCH UP WITH THE HIRUKO THAT SHOWS UP IN THE LITERATURE.
THREE HUNDRED YEARS AGO...
...IT TRANSFORMED INTO A WHALE.

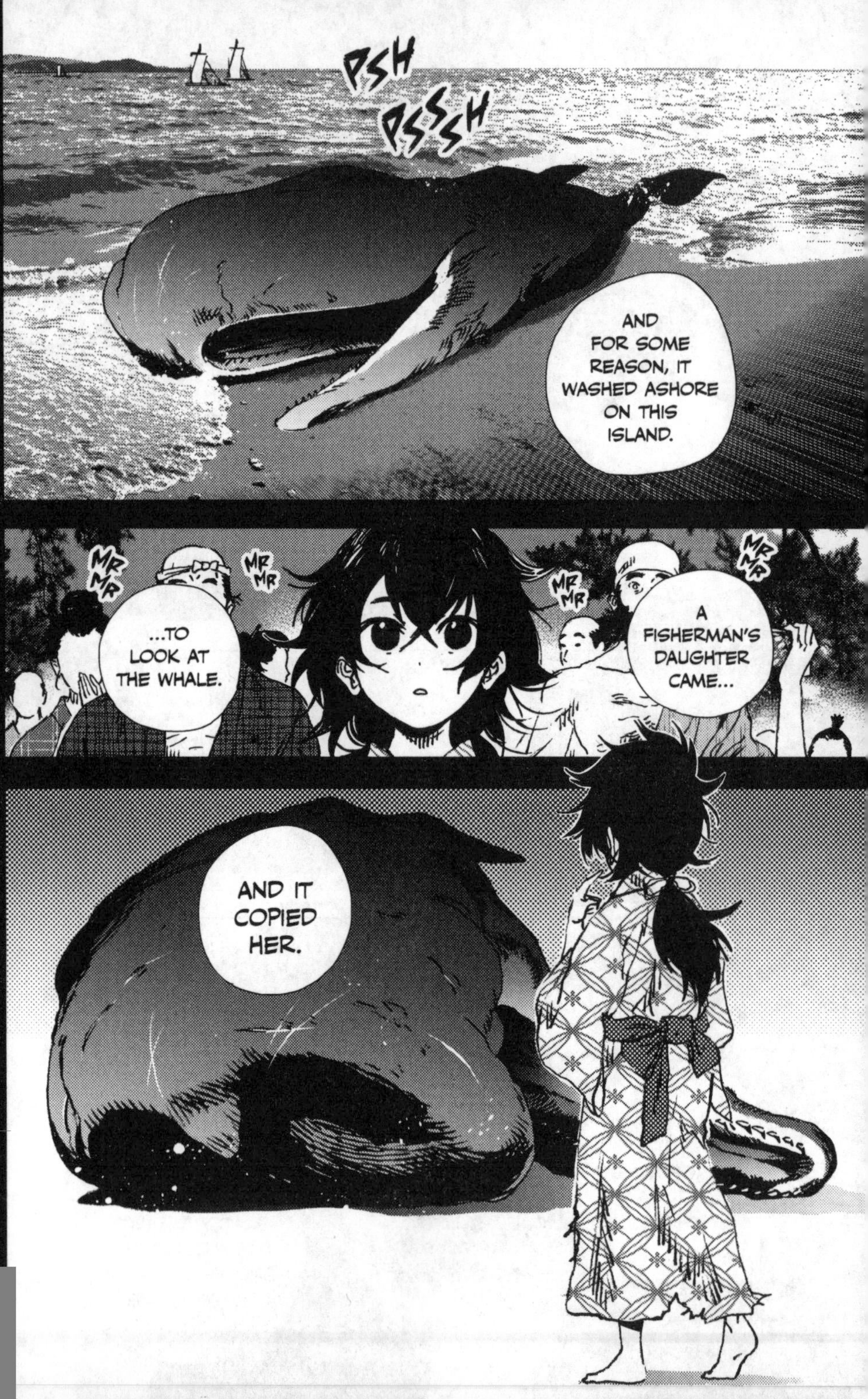
PSH
PSSSH
AND FOR SOME REASON, IT WASHED ASHORE ON THIS ISLAND.
MR MR
MR MR
A FISHERMAN'S DAUGHTER CAME...
MR MR
...TO LOOK AT THE WHALE.
MR MR
AND IT COPIED HER.

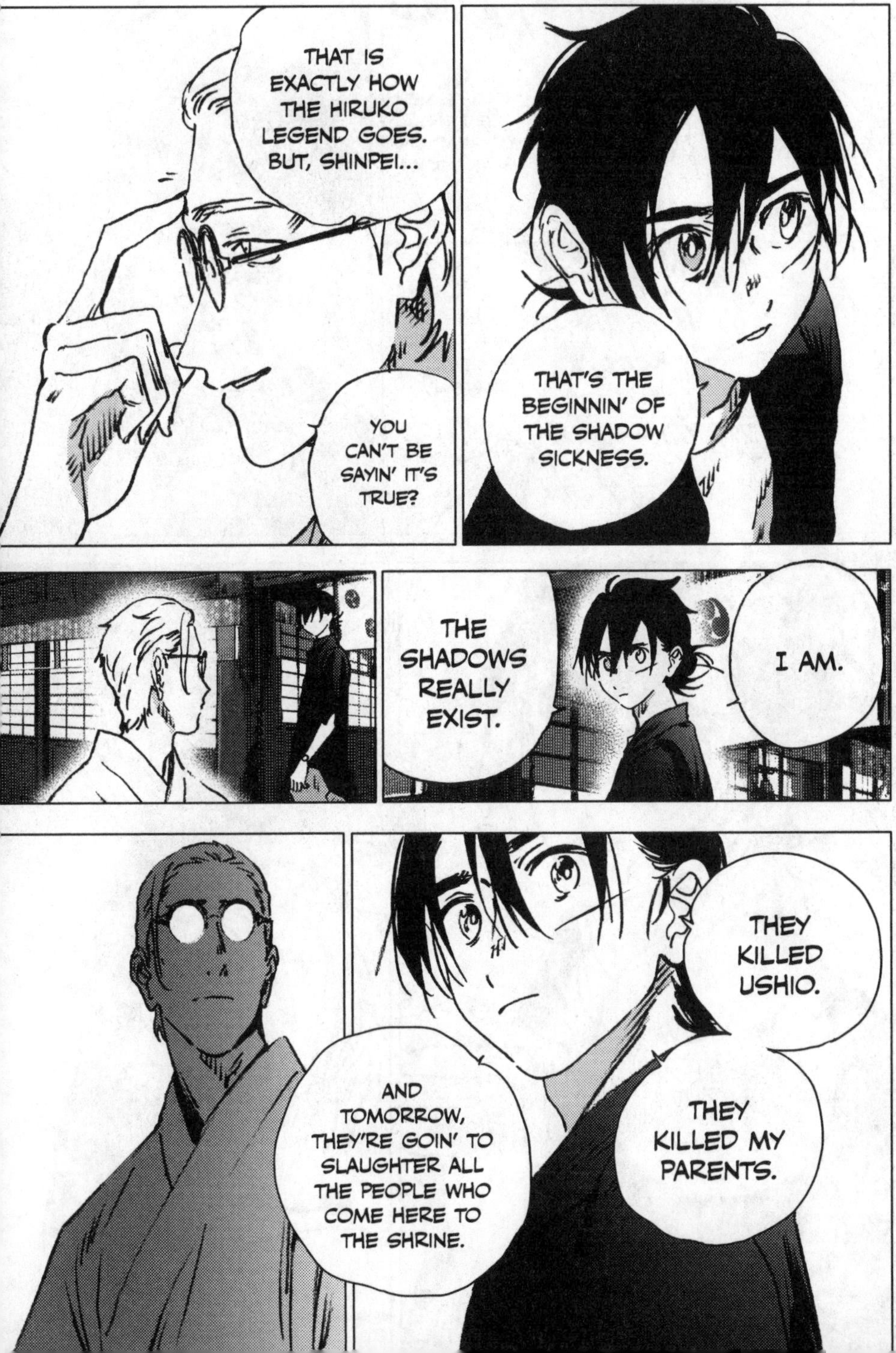
THAT'S THE BEGINNIN' OF THE SHADOW SICKNESS.
THAT IS EXACTLY HOW THE HIRUKO LEGEND GOES. BUT, SHINPEI...
YOU CAN'T BE SAYIN' IT'S TRUE?
I AM.
THE SHADOWS REALLY EXIST.
THEY KILLED USHIO.
THEY KILLED MY PARENTS.
AND TOMORROW, THEY'RE GOIN' TO SLAUGHTER ALL THE PEOPLE WHO COME HERE TO THE SHRINE.

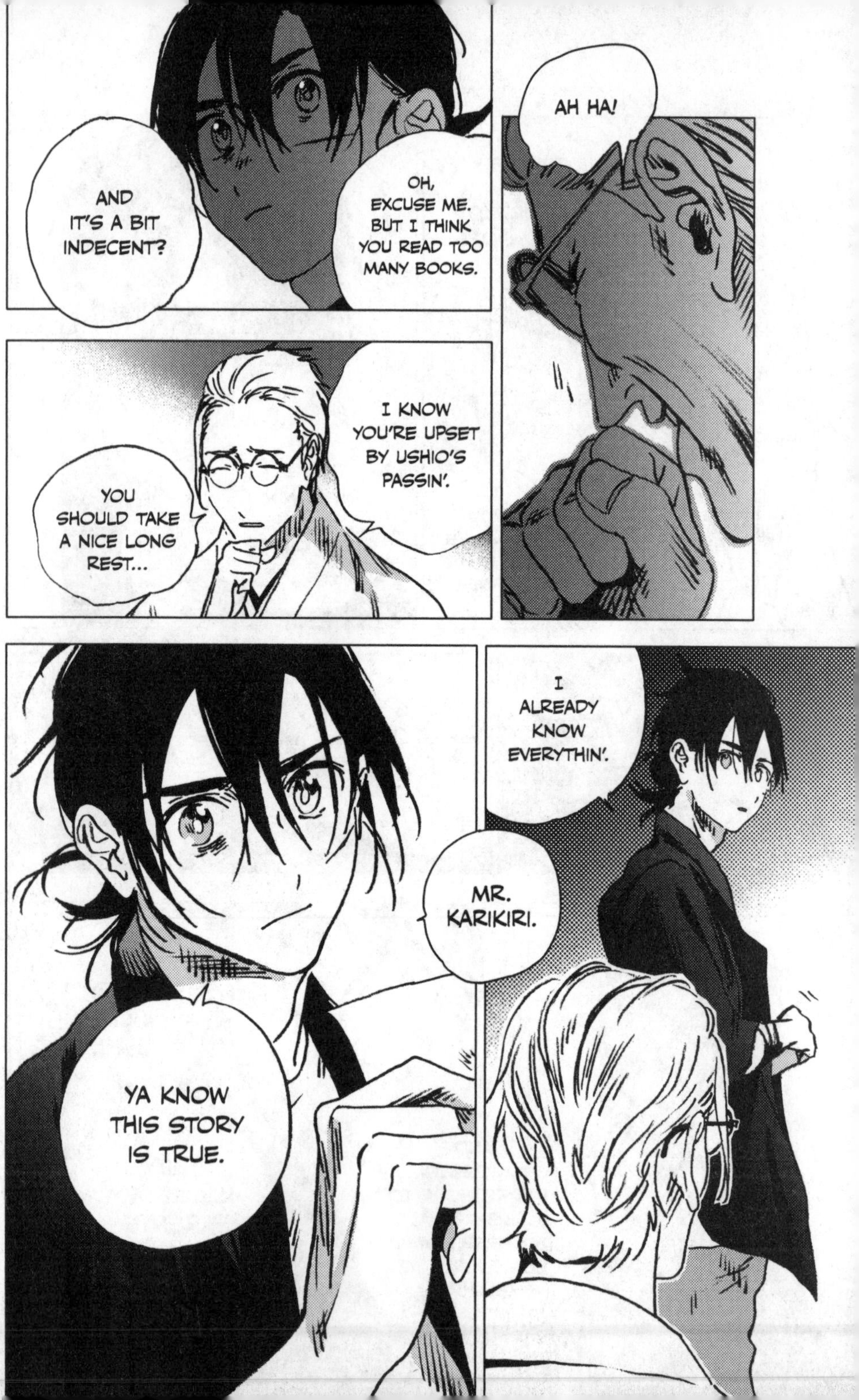
AH HA!
OH, EXCUSE ME. BUT I THINK YOU READ TOO MANY BOOKS.
AND IT'S A BIT INDECENT?
I KNOW YOU'RE UPSET BY USHIO'S PASSIN'.
YOU SHOULD TAKE A NICE LONG REST...
I ALREADY KNOW EVERYTHIN'.
MR. KARIKIRI.
YA KNOW THIS STORY IS TRUE.

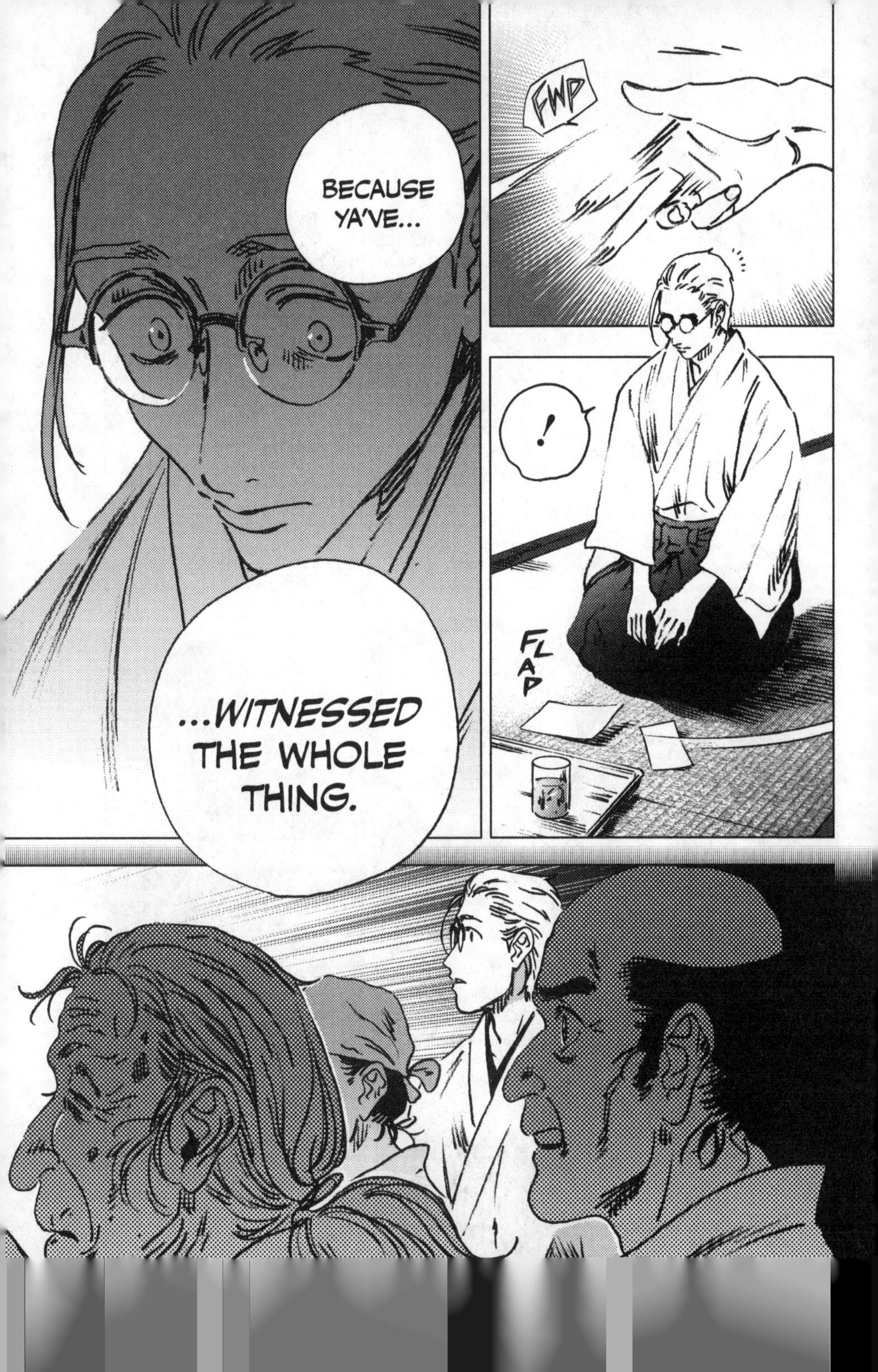
FWP
!
FLAP
BECAUSE YA'VE...
...WITNESSED THE WHOLE THING.

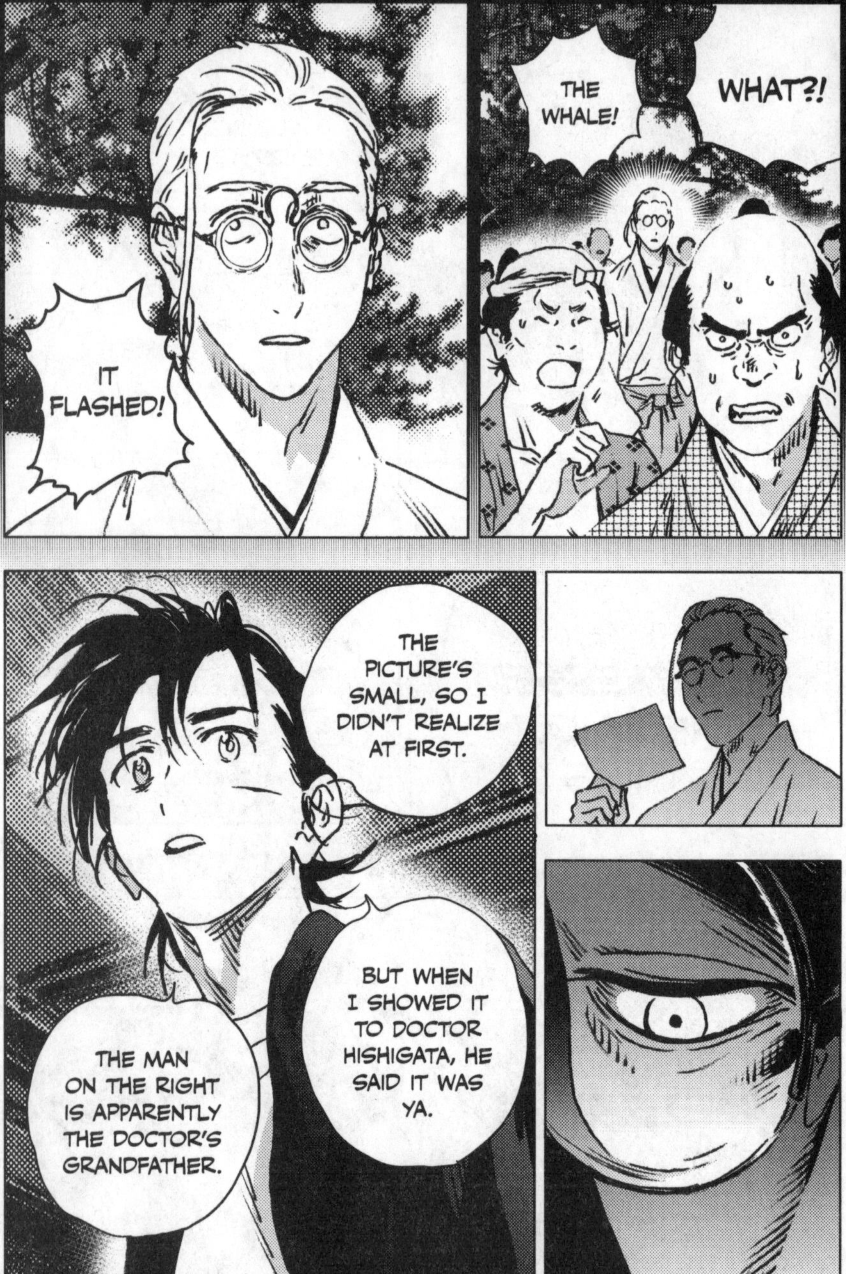
WHAT?!
THE WHALE!
IT FLASHED!
THE PICTURE'S SMALL, SO I DIDN'T REALIZE AT FIRST.
BUT WHEN I SHOWED IT TO DOCTOR HISHIGATA, HE SAID IT WAS YA.
THE MAN ON THE RIGHT IS APPARENTLY THE DOCTOR'S GRANDFATHER.

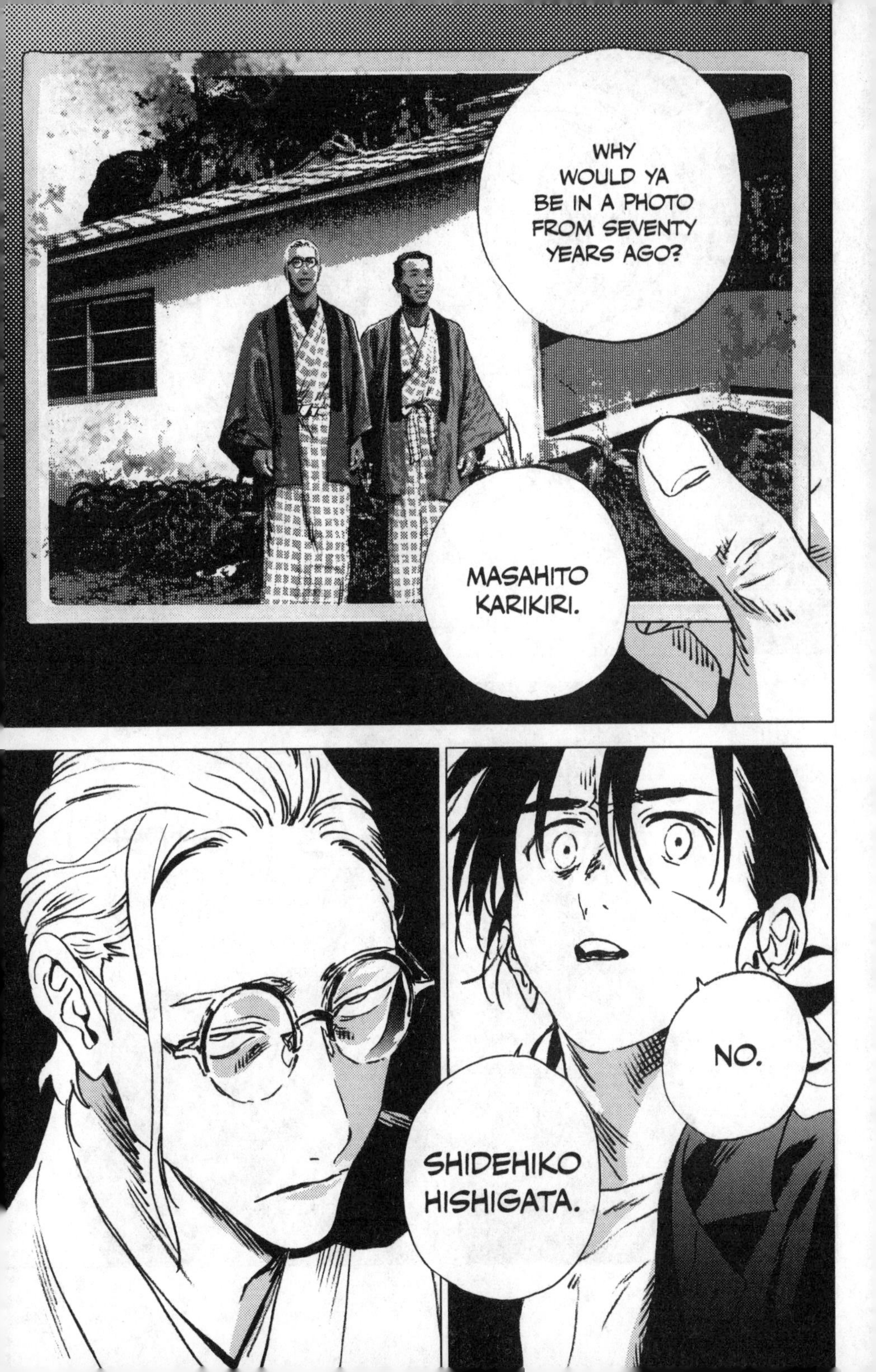
WHY WOULD YA BE IN A PHOTO FROM SEVENTY YEARS AGO?
MASAHITO KARIKIRI.
NO.
SHIDEHIKO HISHIGATA.

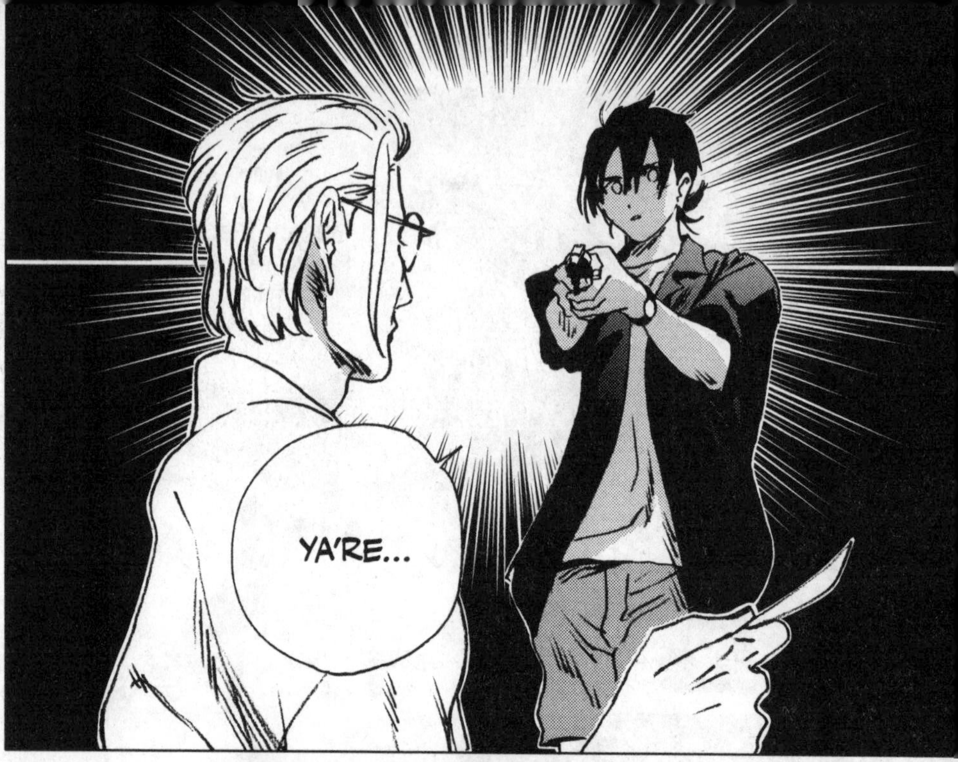
YA'RE...
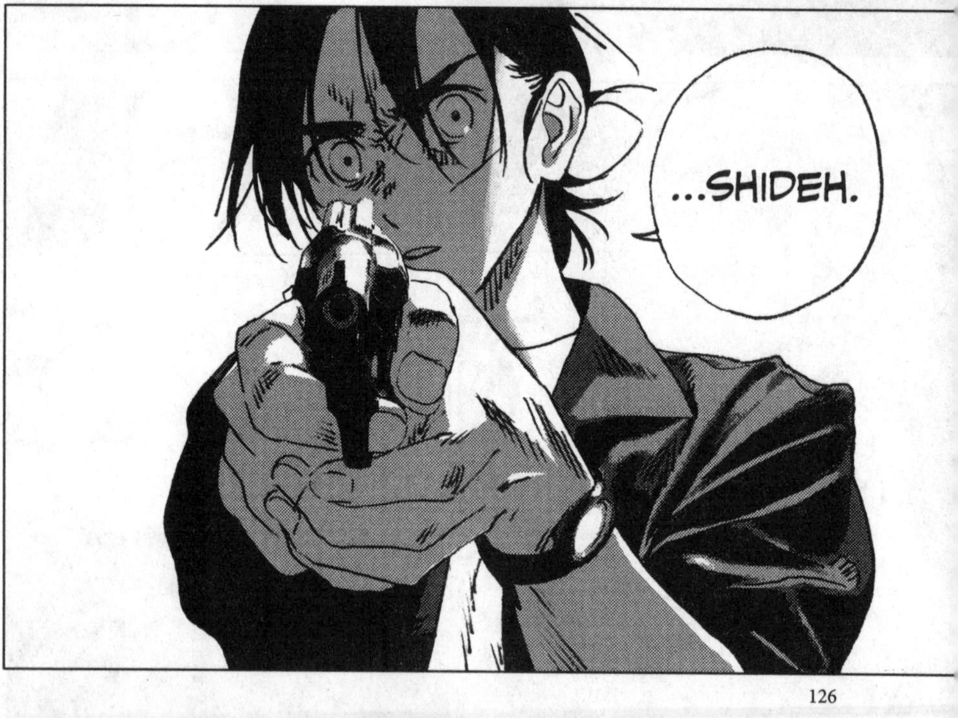
...SHIDEH.

サマータイムレンダ

Summer time rendering

[Made in black]

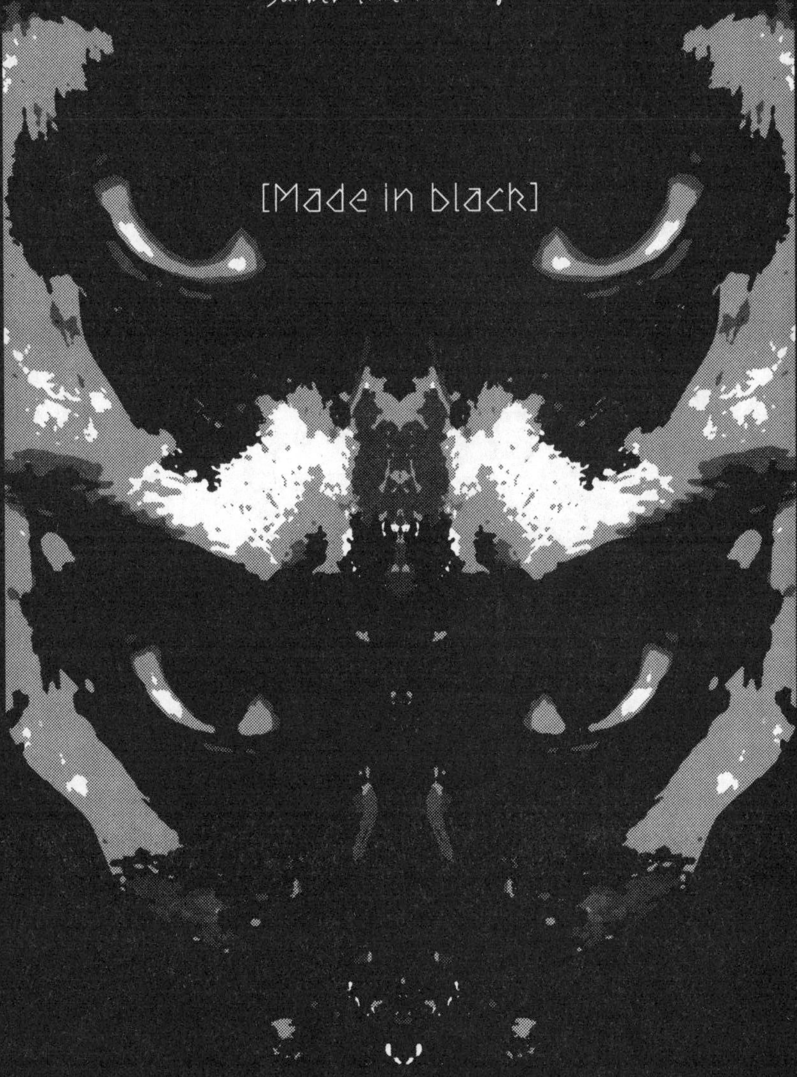

田中靖規

TANAKA YASUKI

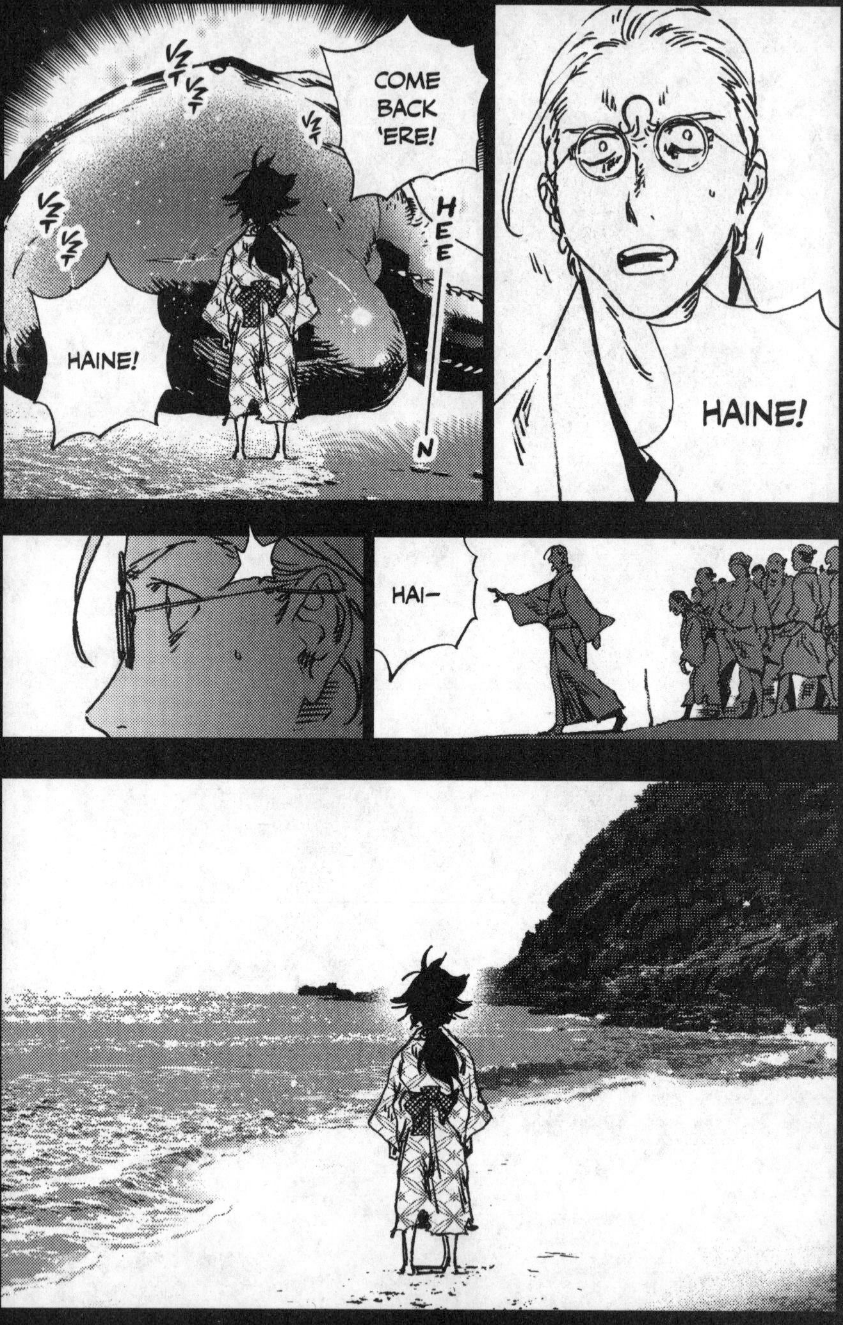
HAINE!
COME BACK 'ERE!
HEEN
VZT VZT
VZT
VZT VZT
HAINE!
HAI-

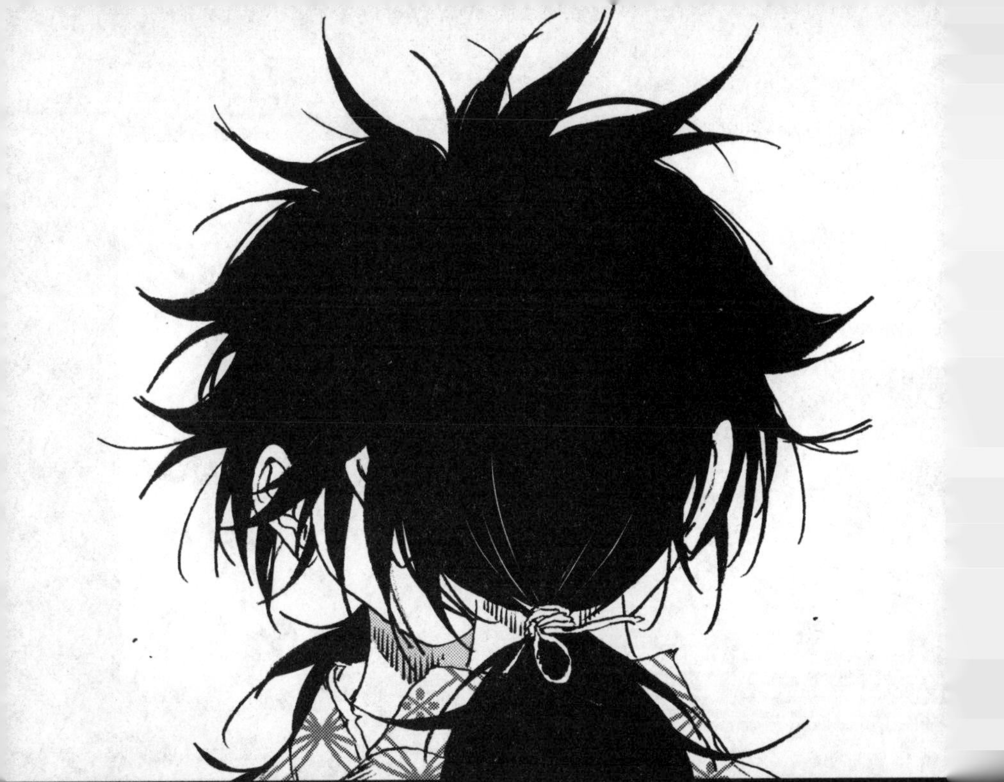

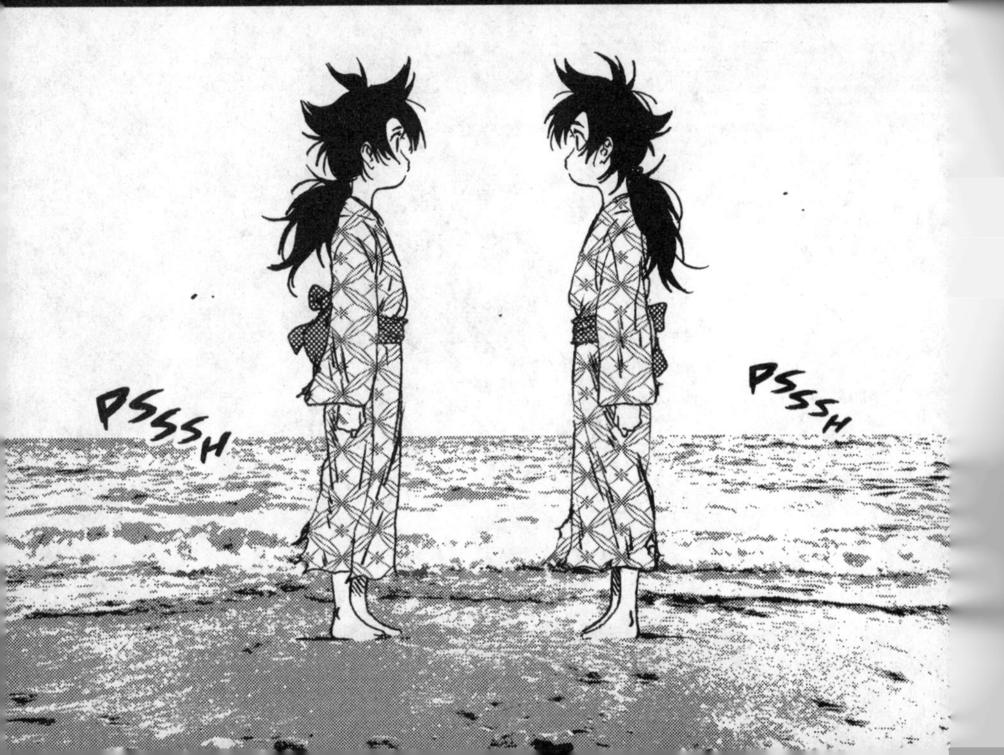
PSSSH
PSSSH

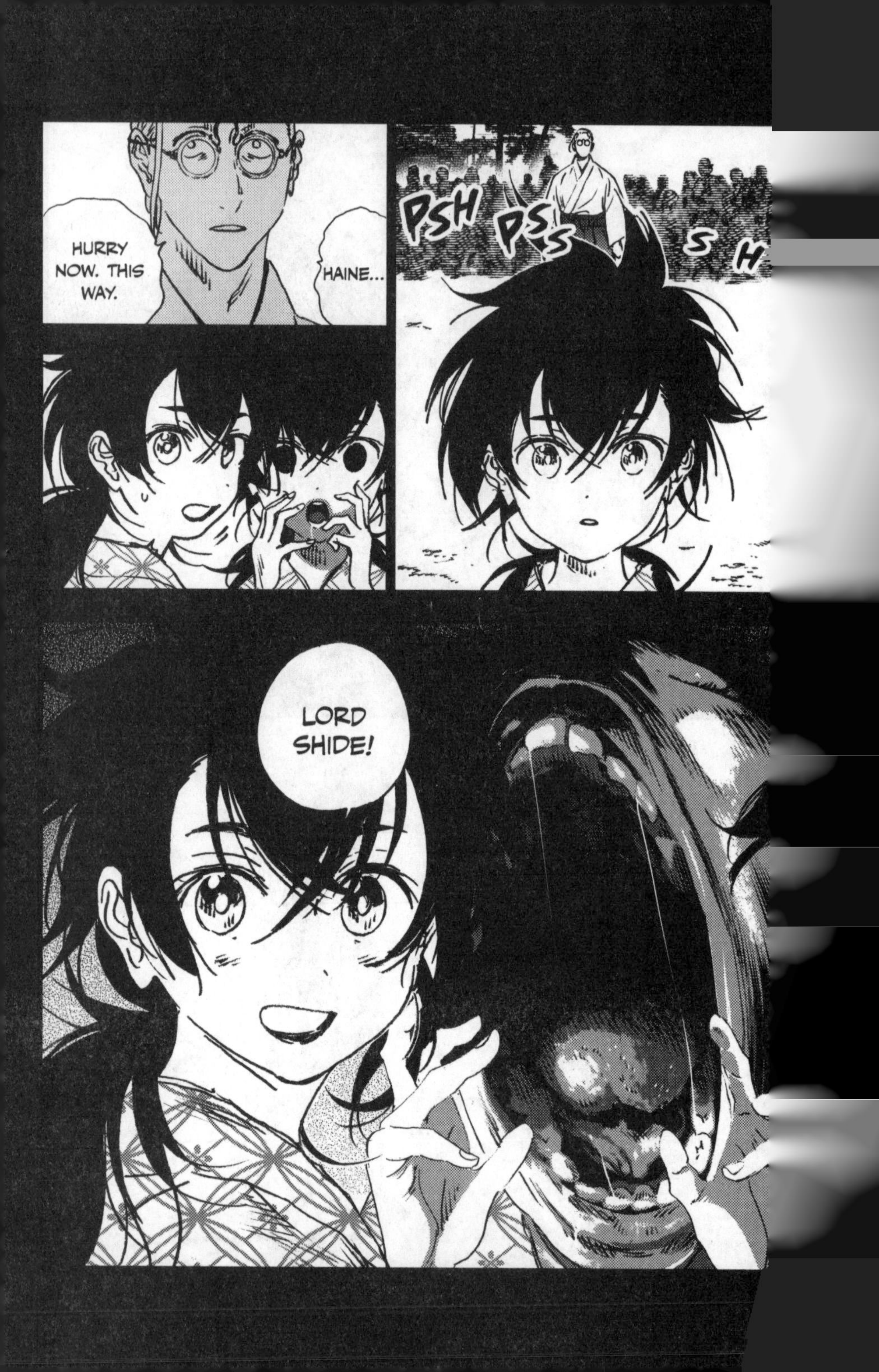
PSH
PSSS
SH
HAINE...
HURRY NOW. THIS WAY.
LORD SHIDE!

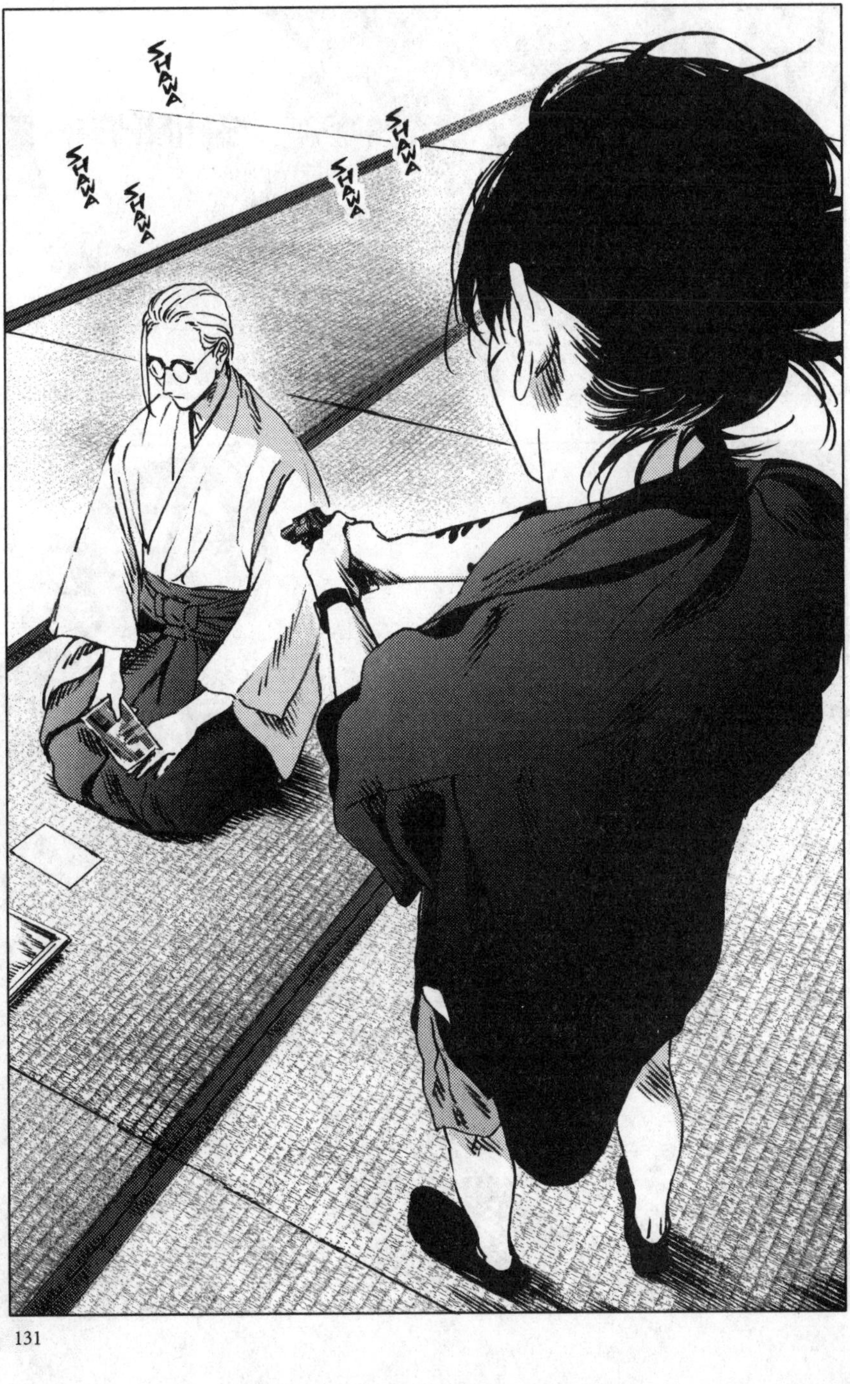
SHAWA
SHAWA
SHAWA
SHAWA
SHAWA

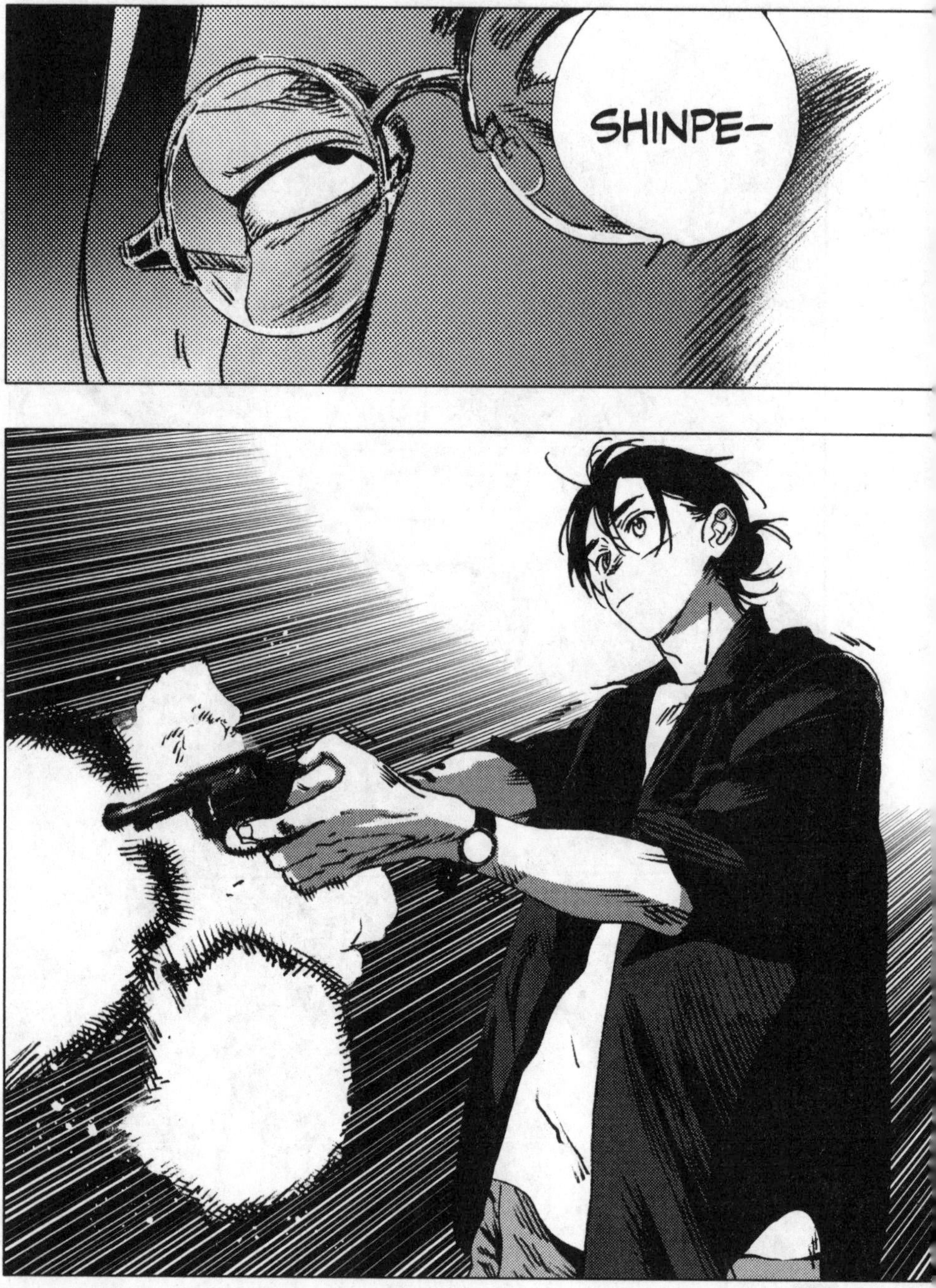
SHINPE-

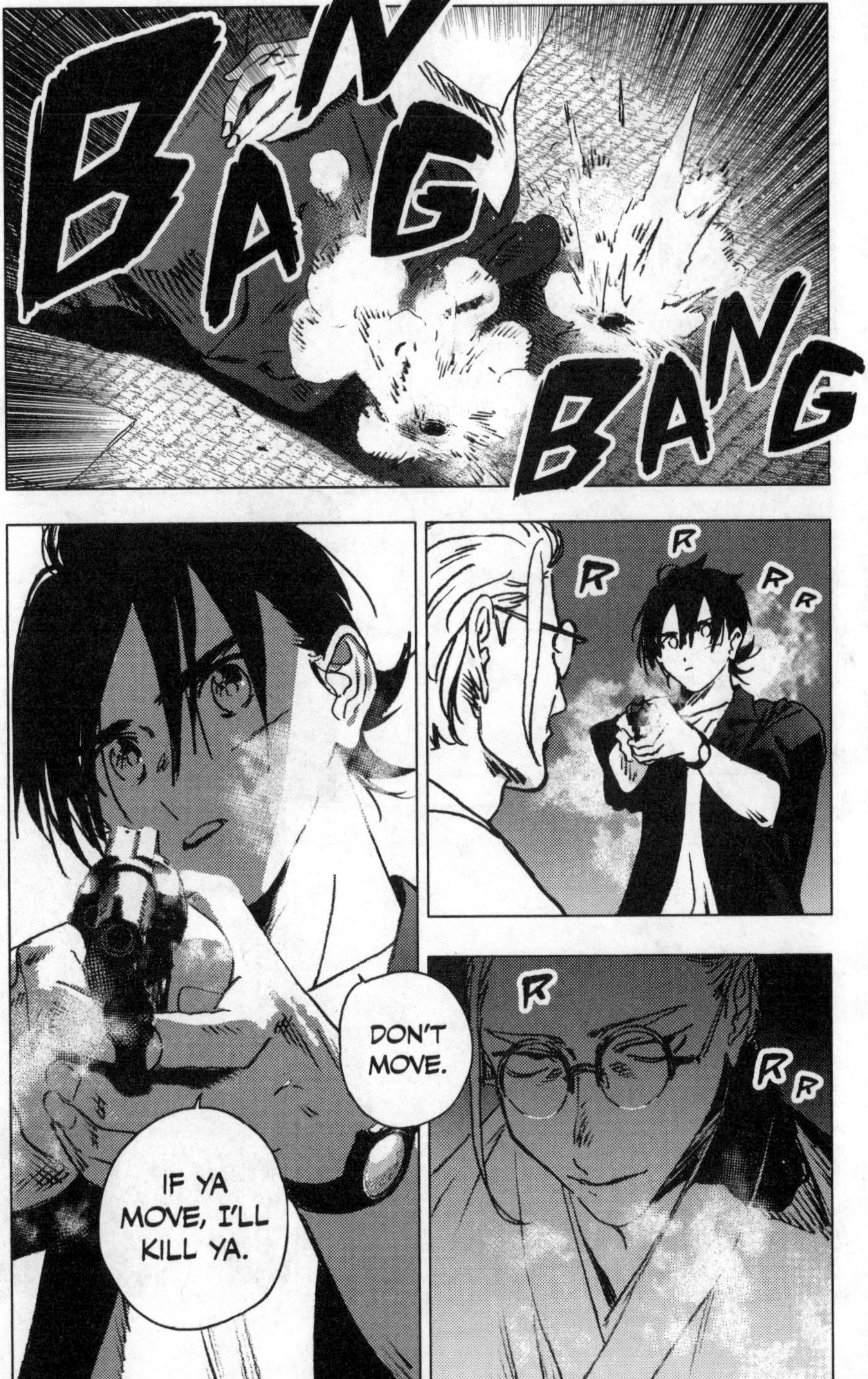
BANG
BANG
R R R R R
R R R
DON'T MOVE.
IF YA MOVE, I'LL KILL YA.

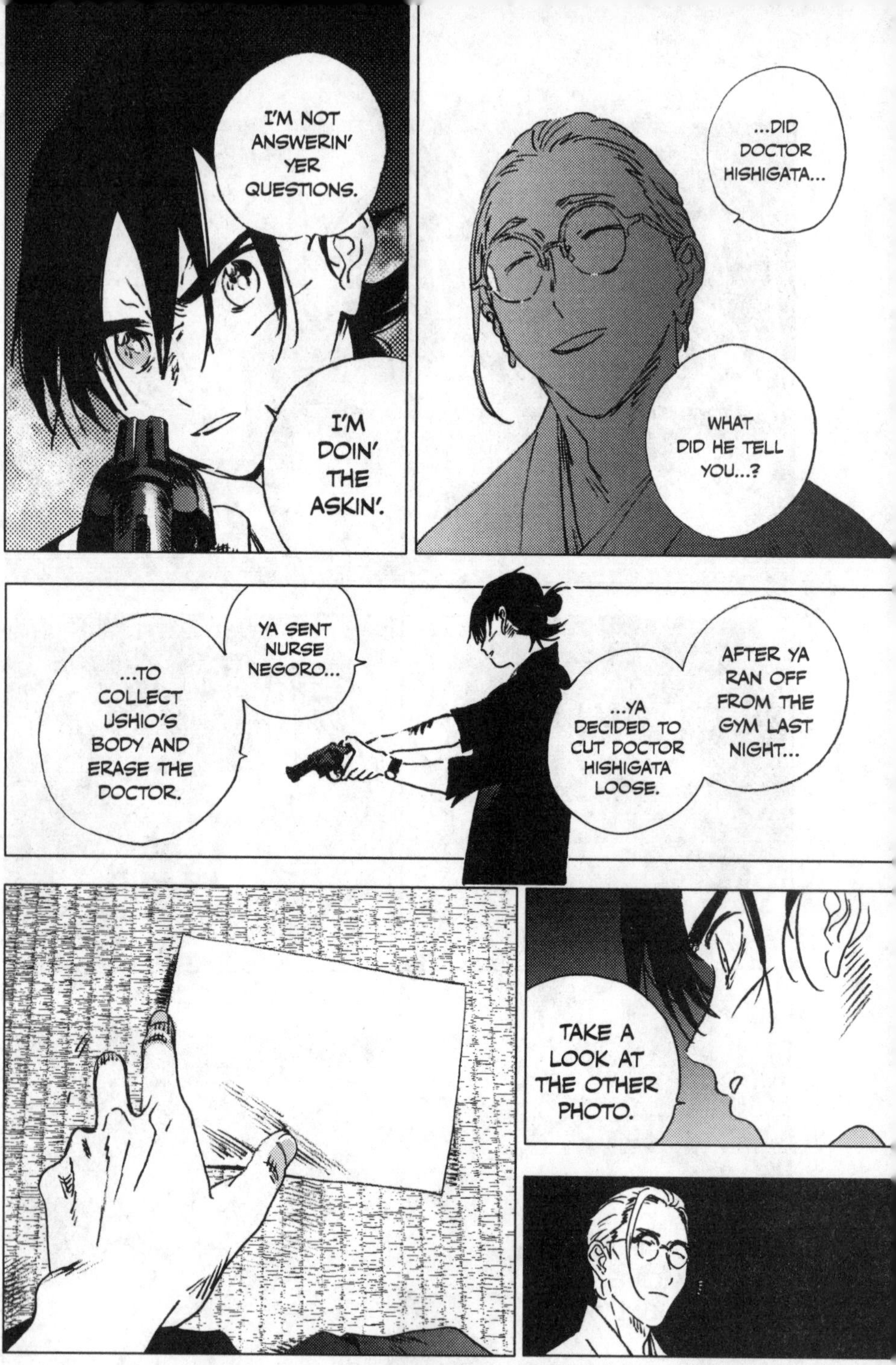
...DID DOCTOR HISHIGATA...
WHAT DID HE TELL YOU...?
I'M NOT ANSWERIN' YER QUESTIONS.
I'M DOIN' THE ASKIN'.
AFTER YA RAN OFF FROM THE GYM LAST NIGHT...
...YA DECIDED TO CUT DOCTOR HISHIGATA LOOSE.
YA SENT NURSE NEGORO...
...TO COLLECT USHIO'S BODY AND ERASE THE DOCTOR.
TAKE A LOOK AT THE OTHER PHOTO.

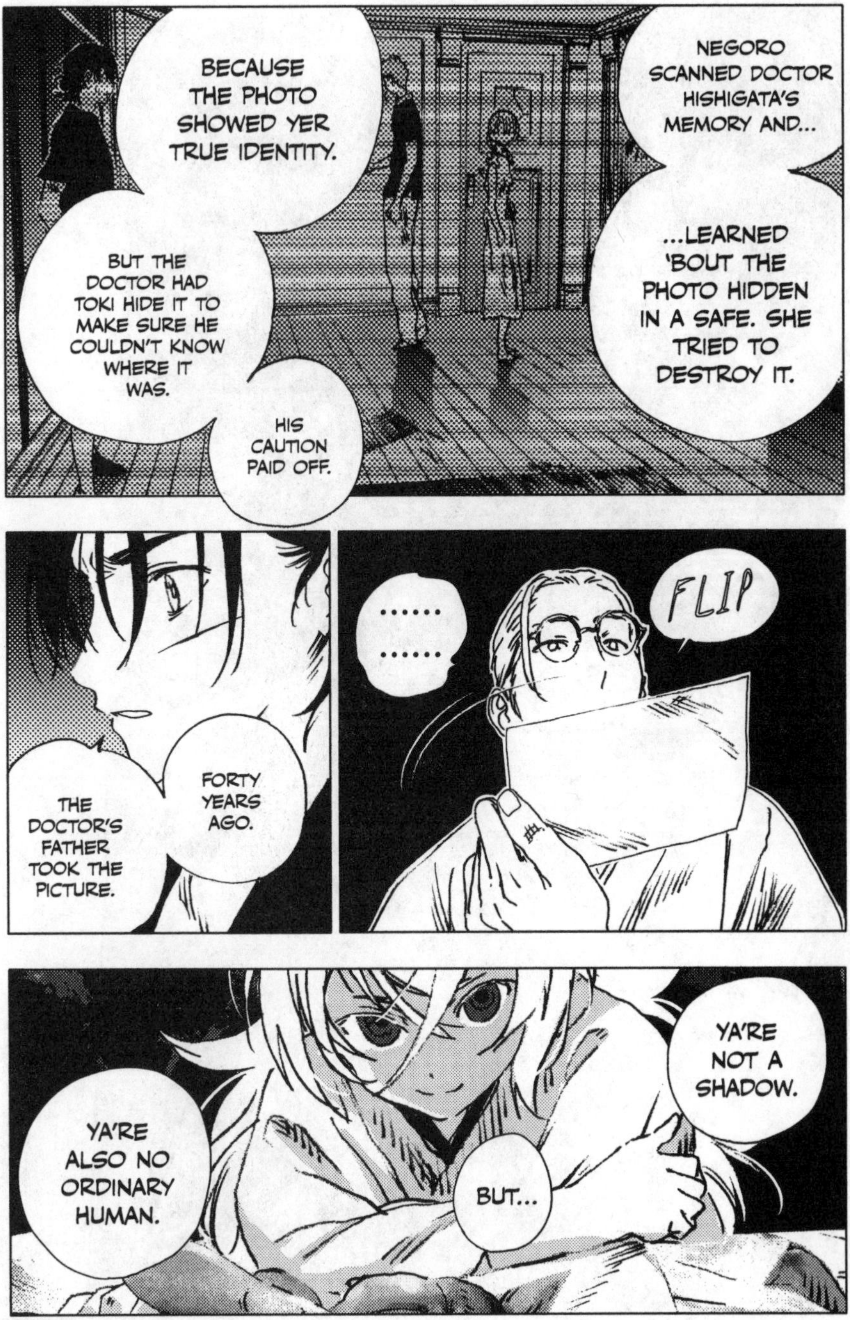
NEGORO SCANNED DOCTOR HISHIGATA'S MEMORY AND...
...LEARNED 'BOUT THE PHOTO HIDDEN IN A SAFE. SHE TRIED TO DESTROY IT.
BECAUSE THE PHOTO SHOWED YER TRUE IDENTITY.
BUT THE DOCTOR HAD TOKI HIDE IT TO MAKE SURE HE COULDN'T KNOW WHERE IT WAS.
HIS CAUTION PAID OFF.
......
......
FLIP
FORTY YEARS AGO.
THE DOCTOR'S FATHER TOOK THE PICTURE.
YA'RE NOT A SHADOW.
BUT...
YA'RE ALSO NO ORDINARY HUMAN.

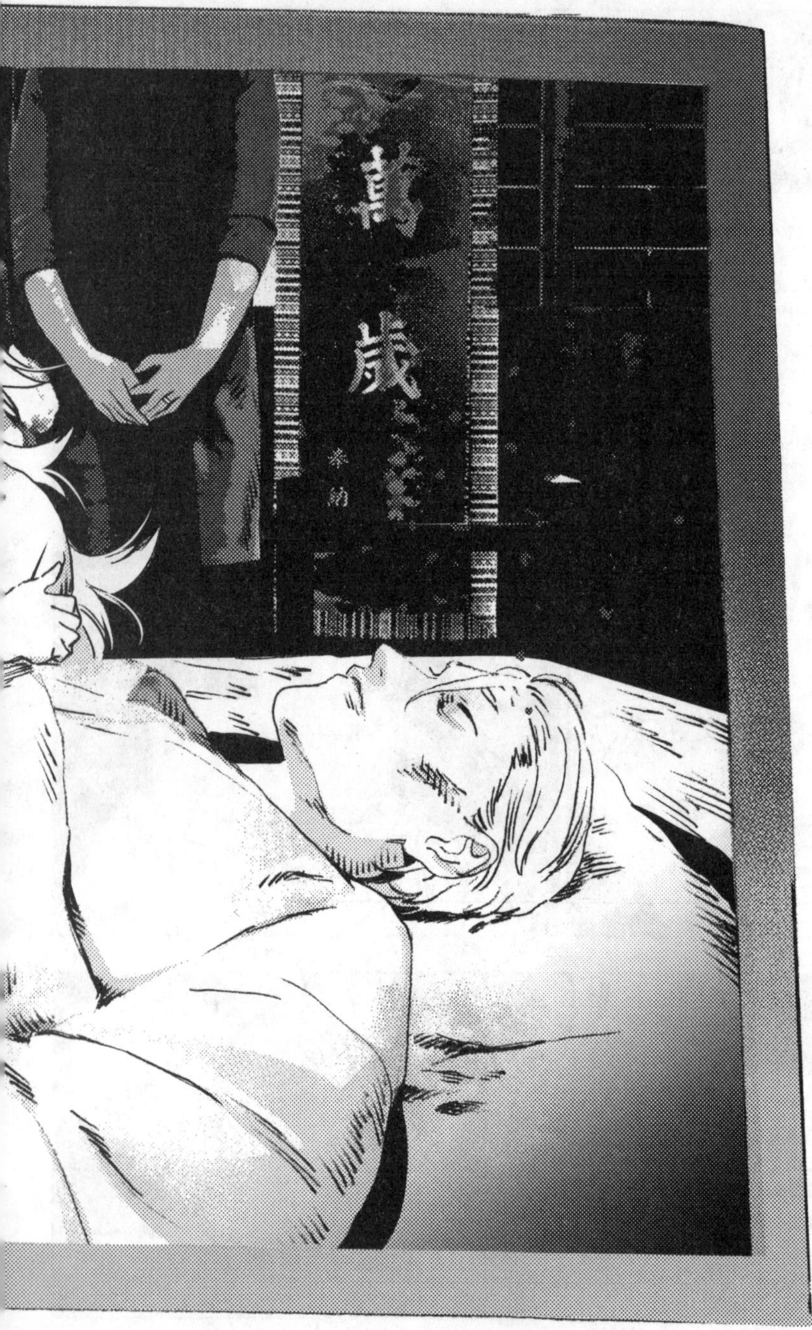

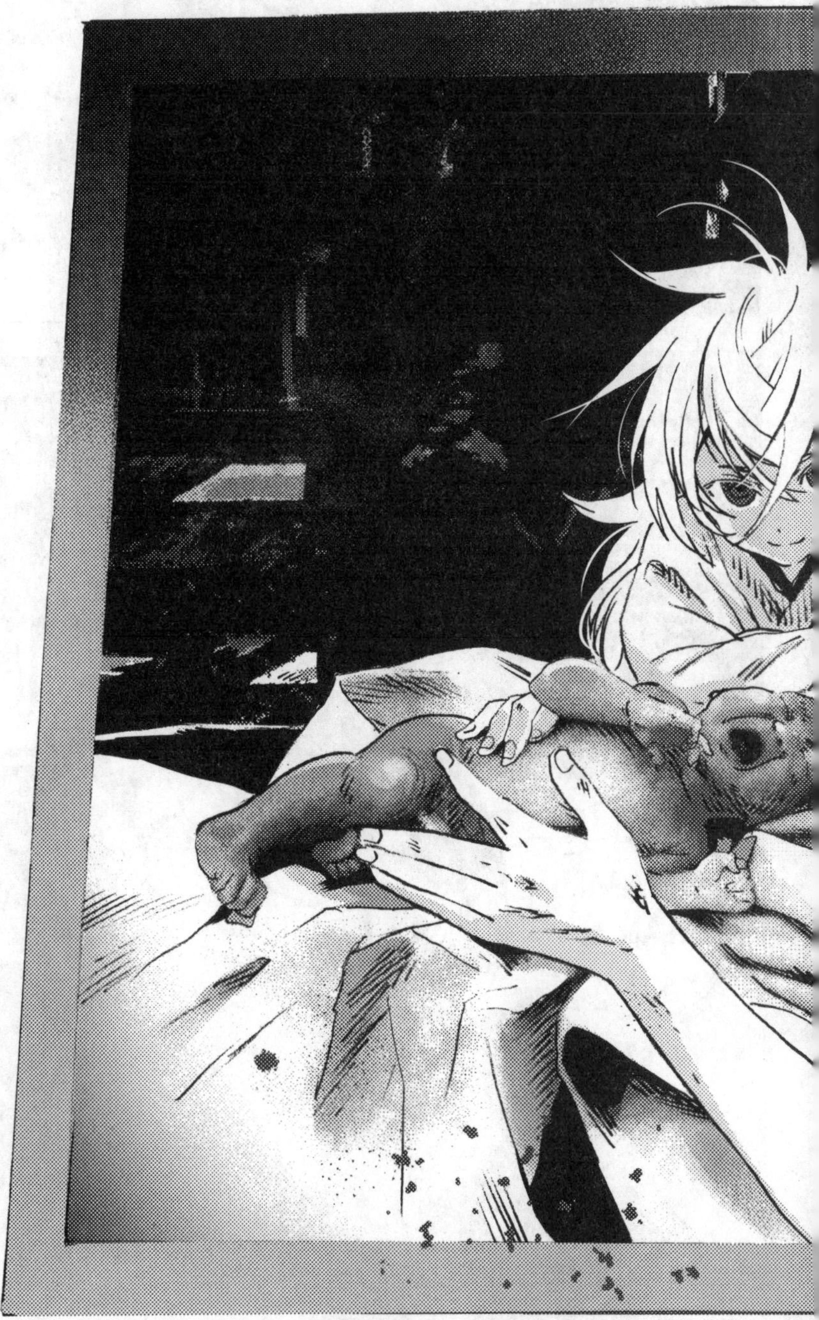

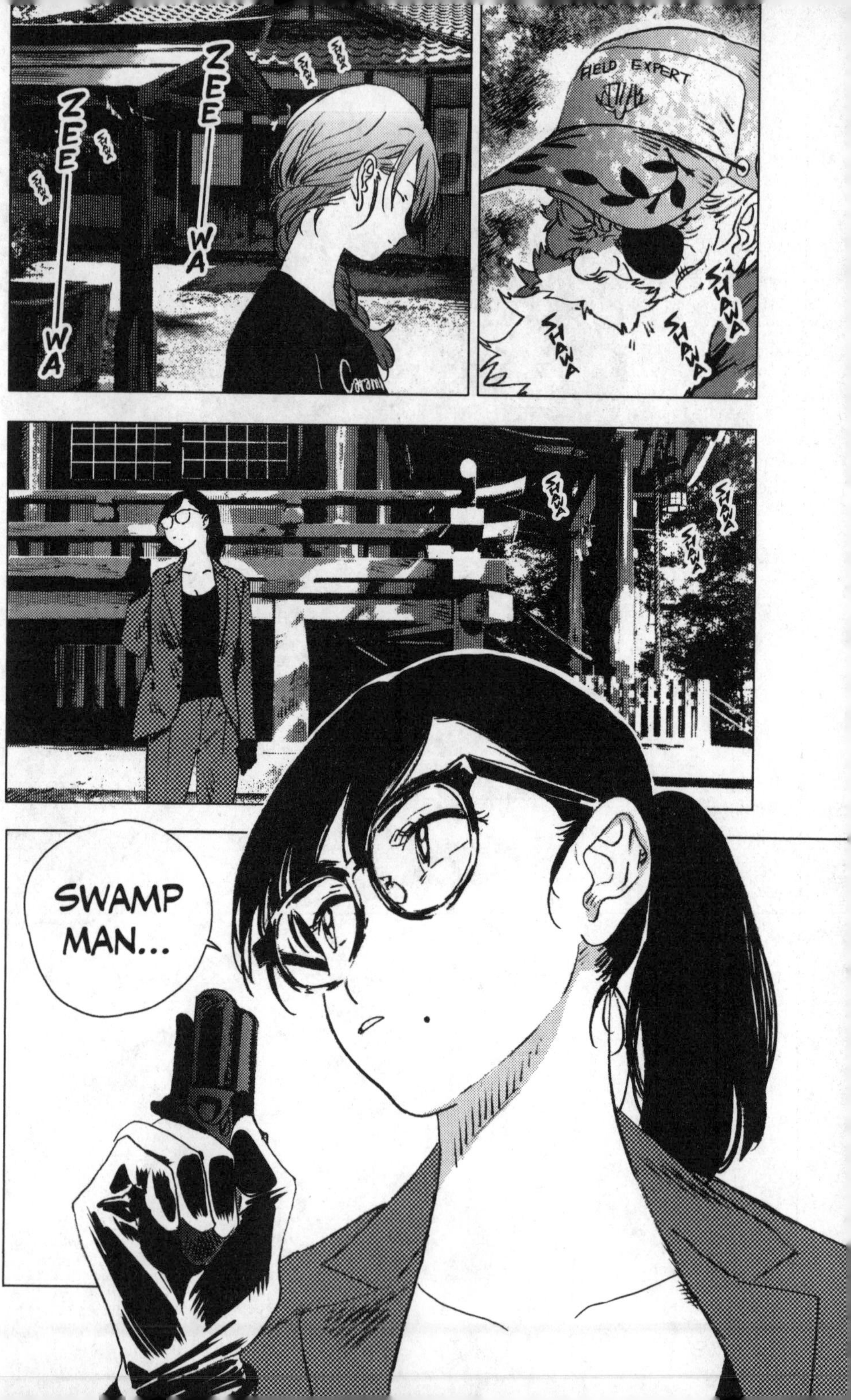
FIELD EXPERT
SHAWA
SHAWA
SHAWA
ZEE WA
ZEE WA
SHAWA
SHAWA
SHAWA
SWAMP MAN...

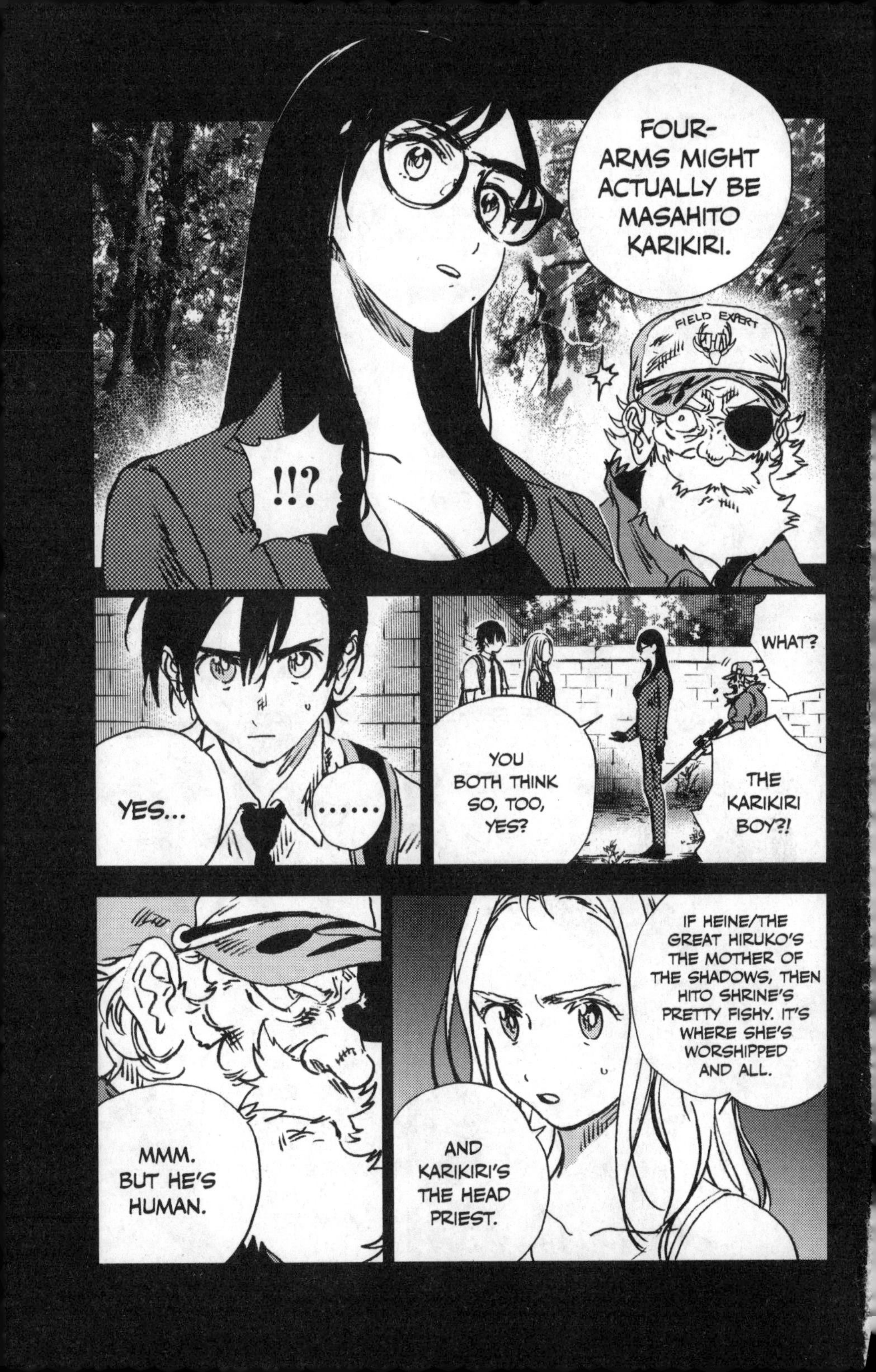
FOUR-ARMS MIGHT ACTUALLY BE MASAHITO KARIKIRI.
FIELD EXPERT
!!?
WHAT?
THE KARIKIRI BOY?!
YOU BOTH THINK SO, TOO, YES?
......
YES...
IF HEINE/THE GREAT HIRUKO'S THE MOTHER OF THE SHADOWS, THEN HITO SHRINE'S PRETTY FISHY. IT'S WHERE SHE'S WORSHIPPED AND ALL.
AND KARIKIRI'S THE HEAD PRIEST.
MMM. BUT HE'S HUMAN.

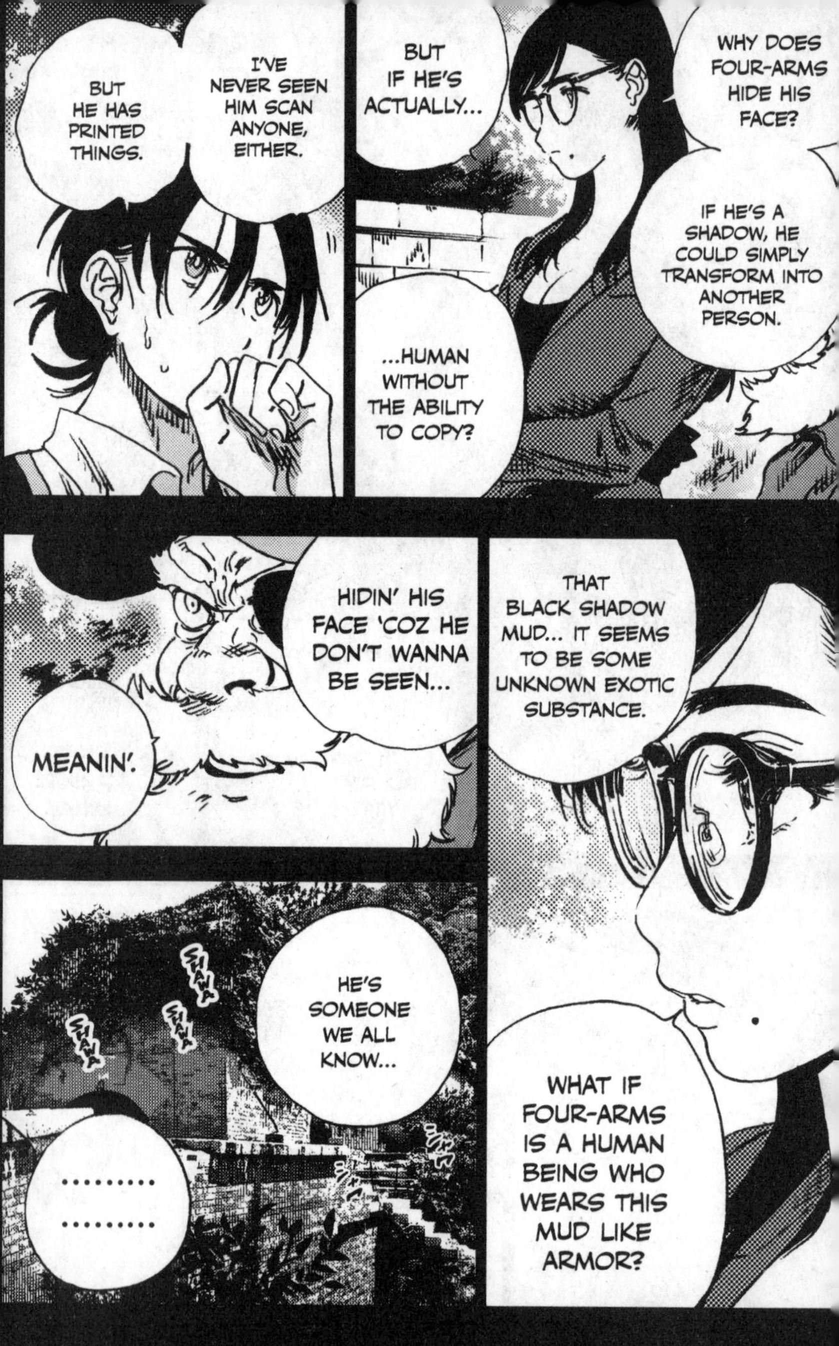
WHY DOES FOUR-ARMS HIDE HIS FACE?
IF HE'S A SHADOW, HE COULD SIMPLY TRANSFORM INTO ANOTHER PERSON.
BUT IF HE'S ACTUALLY...
...HUMAN WITHOUT THE ABILITY TO COPY?
I'VE NEVER SEEN HIM SCAN ANYONE, EITHER.
BUT HE HAS PRINTED THINGS.
THAT BLACK SHADOW MUD... IT SEEMS TO BE SOME UNKNOWN EXOTIC SUBSTANCE.
WHAT IF FOUR-ARMS IS A HUMAN BEING WHO WEARS THIS MUD LIKE ARMOR?
HIDIN' HIS FACE 'COZ HE DON'T WANNA BE SEEN...
MEANIN'.
SHAWA
SHAWA
SHAWA
HE'S SOMEONE WE ALL KNOW...
....
....

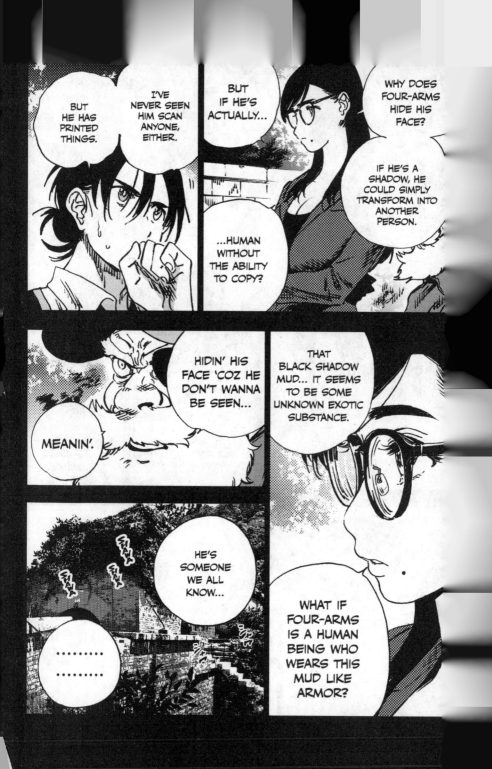

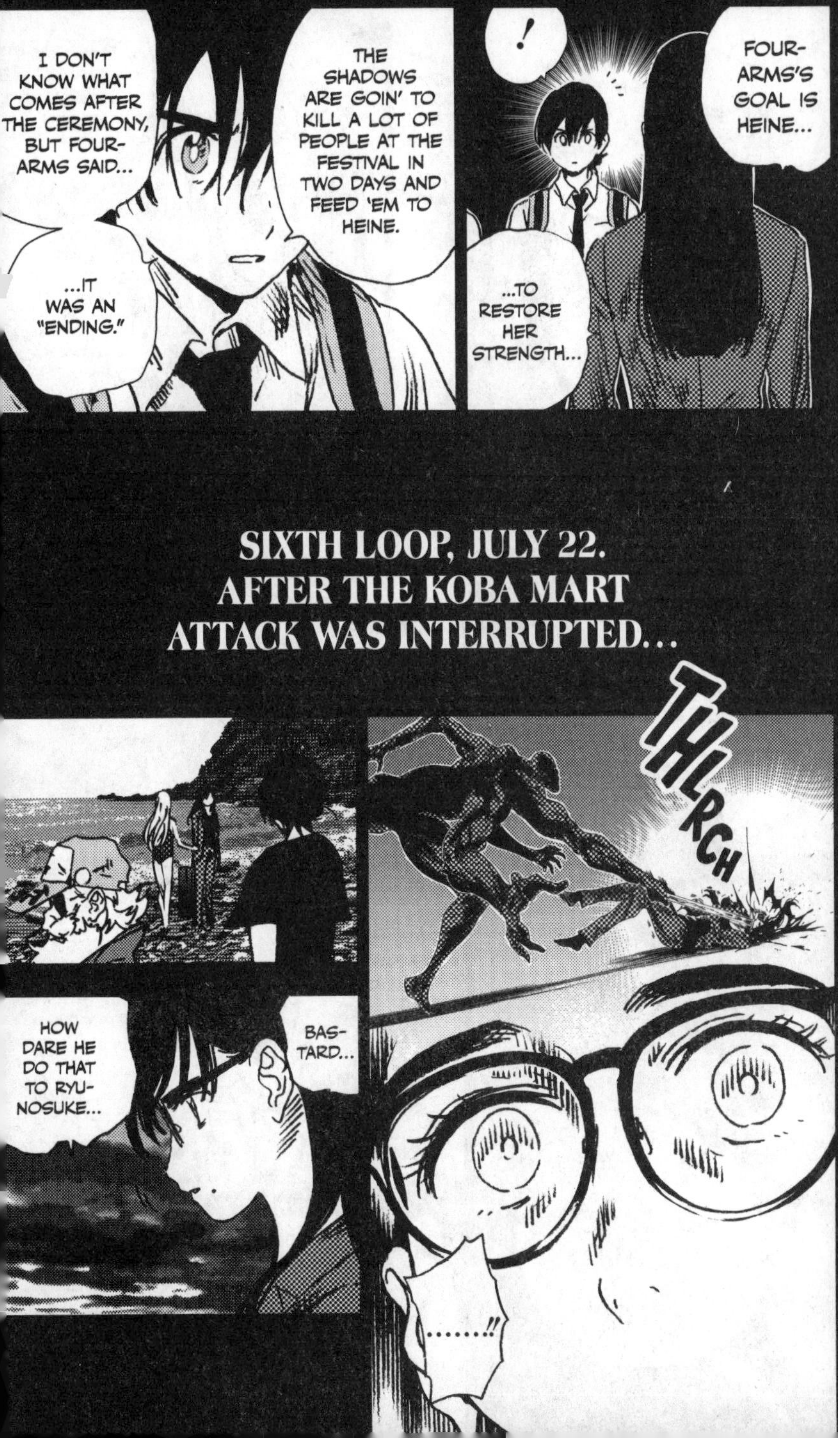
!
FOUR-ARMS'S GOAL IS HEINE...
...TO RESTORE HER STRENGTH...
THE SHADOWS ARE GOIN' TO KILL A LOT OF PEOPLE AT THE FESTIVAL IN TWO DAYS AND FEED 'EM TO HEINE.
I DON'T KNOW WHAT COMES AFTER THE CEREMONY, BUT FOUR-ARMS SAID...
...IT WAS AN "ENDING."
SIXTH LOOP, JULY 22.
AFTER THE KOBA MART
ATTACK WAS INTERRUPTED...
THLRCH
........!!
BAS-TARD...
HOW DARE HE DO THAT TO RYU-NOSUKE...

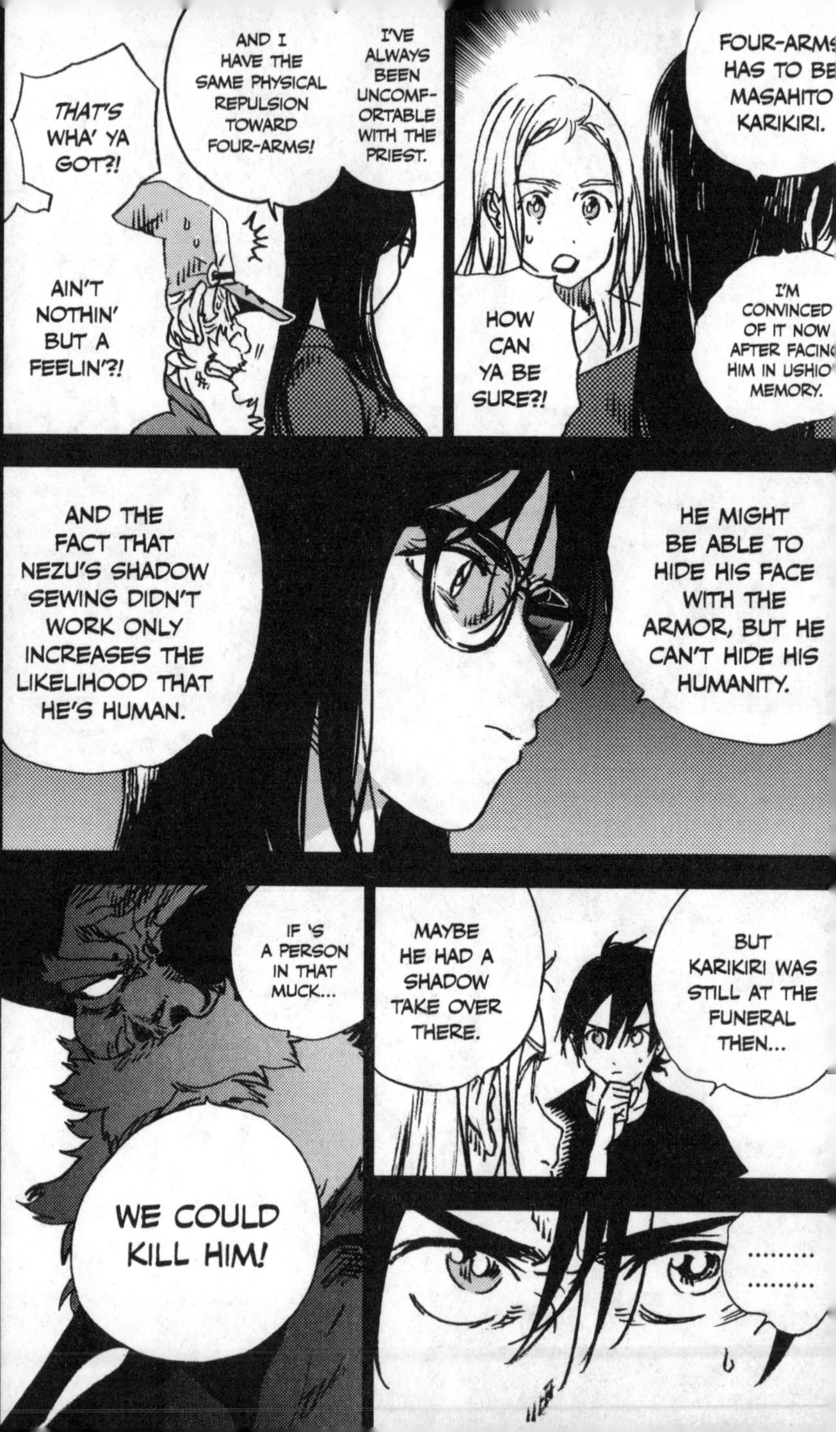
FOUR-ARMS HAS TO BE MASAHITO KARIKIRI.
HOW CAN YA BE SURE?!
I'M CONVINCED OF IT NOW AFTER FACING HIM IN USHIO'S MEMORY.
I'VE ALWAYS BEEN UNCOMF-ORTABLE WITH THE PRIEST.
AND I HAVE THE SAME PHYSICAL REPULSION TOWARD FOUR-ARMS!
THAT'S WHA' YA GOT?!
AIN'T NOTHIN' BUT A FEELIN'?!
HE MIGHT BE ABLE TO HIDE HIS FACE WITH THE ARMOR, BUT HE CAN'T HIDE HIS HUMANITY.
AND THE FACT THAT NEZU'S SHADOW SEWING DIDN'T WORK ONLY INCREASES THE LIKELIHOOD THAT HE'S HUMAN.
BUT KARIKIRI WAS STILL AT THE FUNERAL THEN...
MAYBE HE HAD A SHADOW TAKE OVER THERE.
....
....
IF 'S A PERSON IN THAT MUCK...
WE COULD KILL HIM!

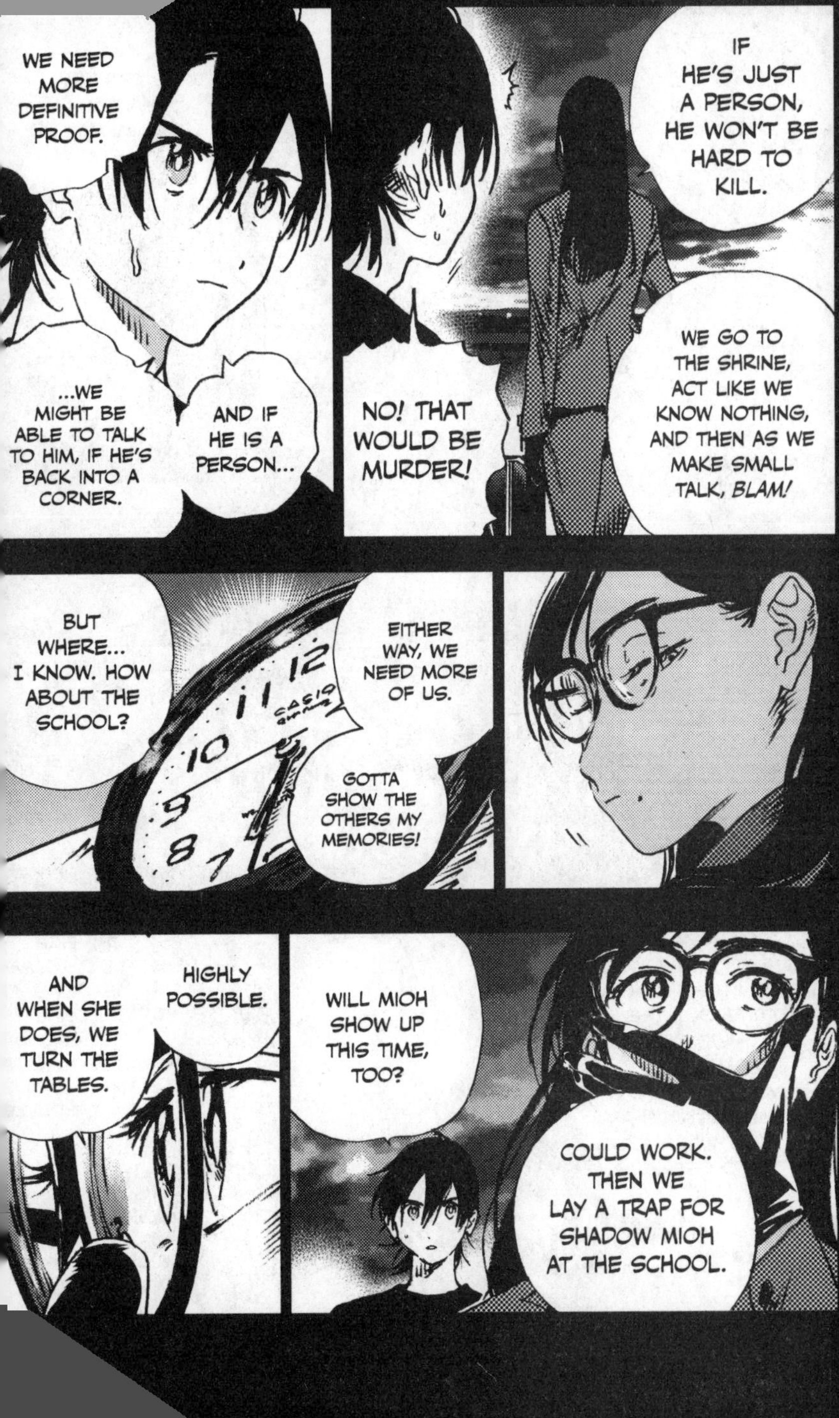
IF HE'S JUST A PERSON, HE WON'T BE HARD TO KILL.
WE GO TO THE SHRINE, ACT LIKE WE KNOW NOTHING, AND THEN AS WE MAKE SMALL TALK, *BLAM!*
NO! THAT WOULD BE MURDER!
WE NEED MORE DEFINITIVE PROOF.
AND IF HE IS A PERSON...
...WE MIGHT BE ABLE TO TALK TO HIM, IF HE'S BACK INTO A CORNER.
EITHER WAY, WE NEED MORE OF US.
GOTTA SHOW THE OTHERS MY MEMORIES!
BUT WHERE... I KNOW. HOW ABOUT THE SCHOOL?
COULD WORK. THEN WE LAY A TRAP FOR SHADOW MIOH AT THE SCHOOL.
WILL MIOH SHOW UP THIS TIME, TOO?
HIGHLY POSSIBLE.
AND WHEN SHE DOES, WE TURN THE TABLES.

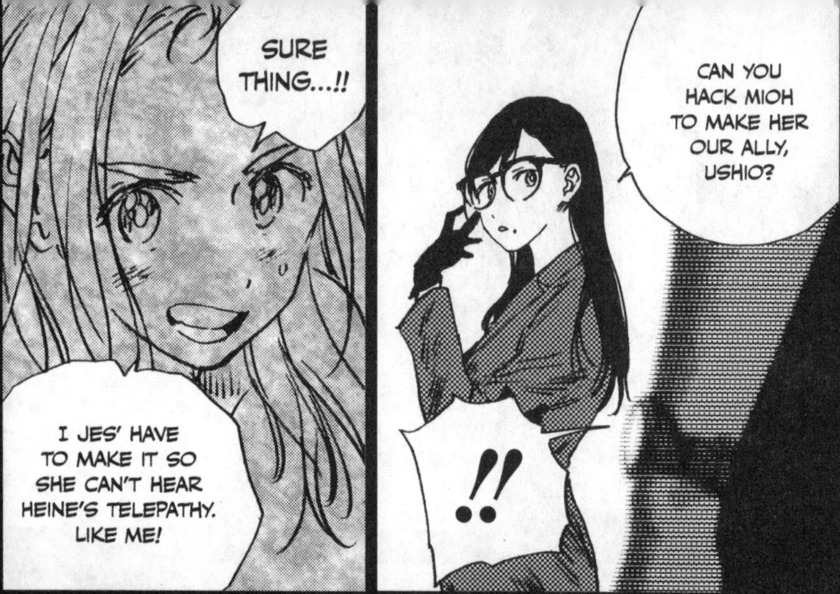
CAN YOU HACK MIOH TO MAKE HER OUR ALLY, USHIO?
!!
SURE THING...!!
I JES' HAVE TO MAKE IT SO SHE CAN'T HEAR HEINE'S TELEPATHY. LIKE ME!

SEVENTH LOOP, JULY 22.
AFTER THE BATTLE
IN THE GYM…

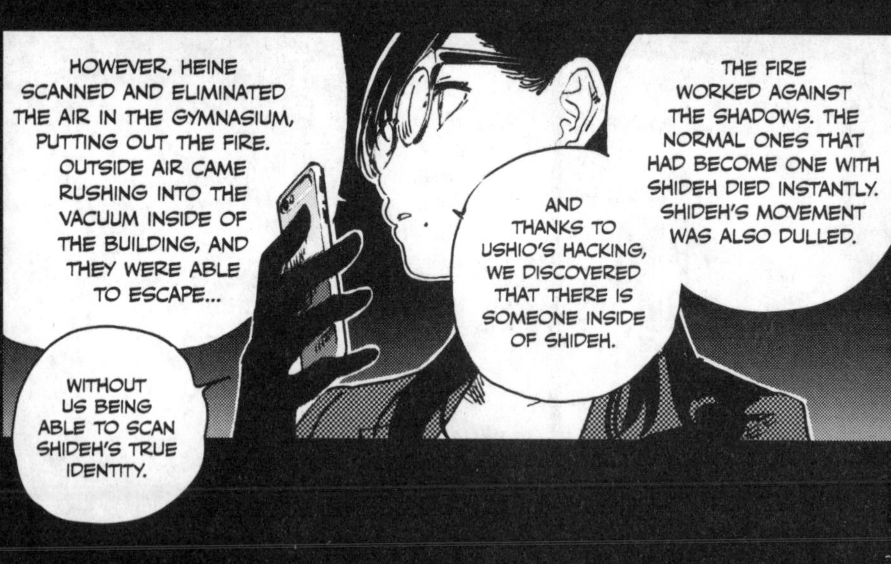
THE FIRE WORKED AGAINST THE SHADOWS. THE NORMAL ONES THAT HAD BECOME ONE WITH SHIDEH DIED INSTANTLY. SHIDEH'S MOVEMENT WAS ALSO DULLED.
AND THANKS TO USHIO'S HACKING, WE DISCOVERED THAT THERE IS SOMEONE INSIDE OF SHIDEH.
HOWEVER, HEINE SCANNED AND ELIMINATED THE AIR IN THE GYMNASIUM, PUTTING OUT THE FIRE. OUTSIDE AIR CAME RUSHING INTO THE VACUUM INSIDE OF THE BUILDING, AND THEY WERE ABLE TO ESCAPE...
WITHOUT US BEING ABLE TO SCAN SHIDEH'S TRUE IDENTITY.

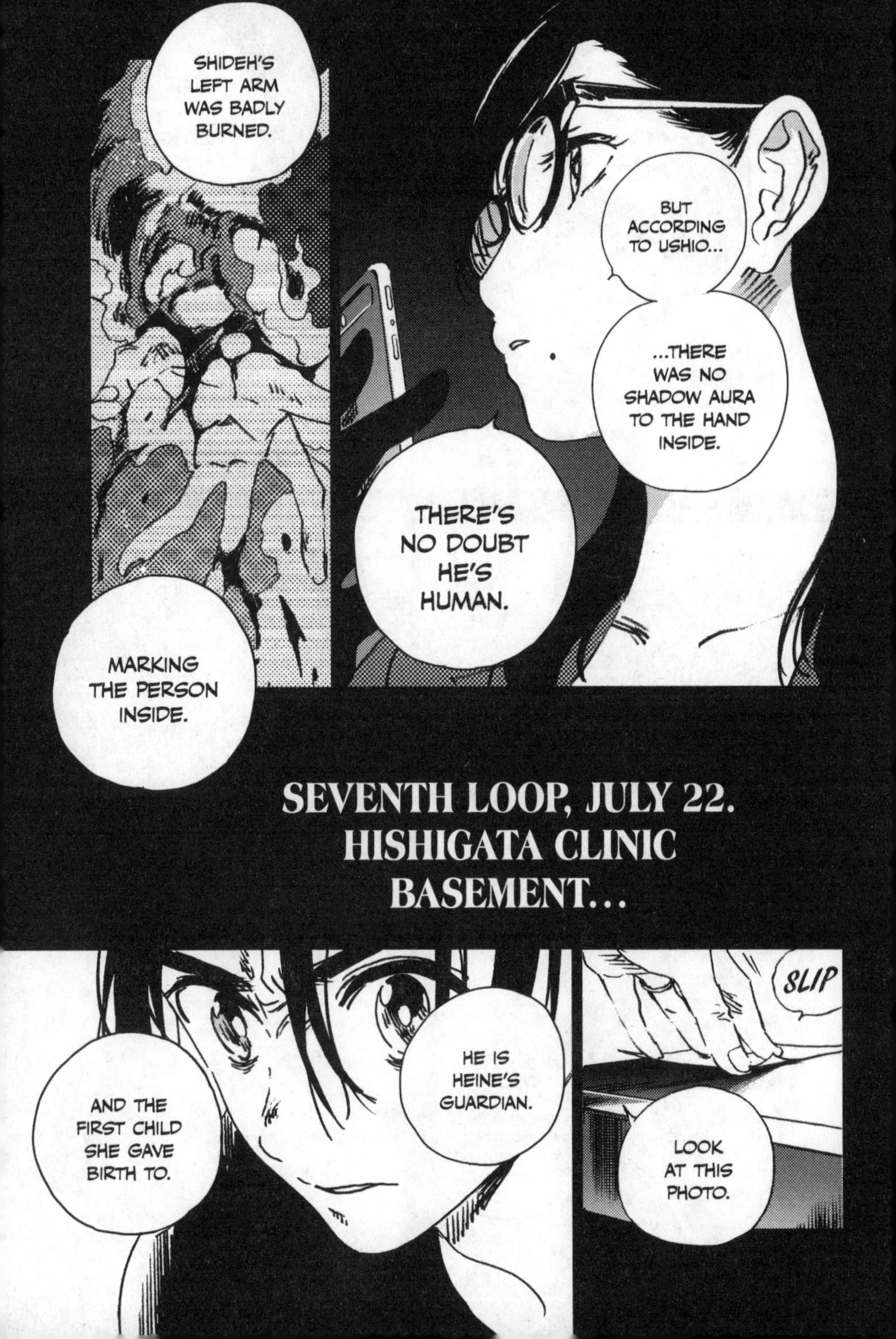
BUT ACCORDING TO USHIO...
...THERE WAS NO SHADOW AURA TO THE HAND INSIDE.
THERE'S NO DOUBT HE'S HUMAN.
SHIDEH'S LEFT ARM WAS BADLY BURNED.
MARKING THE PERSON INSIDE.
SEVENTH LOOP, JULY 22. HISHIGATA CLINIC BASEMENT...
SLIP
LOOK AT THIS PHOTO.
HE IS HEINE'S GUARDIAN.
AND THE FIRST CHILD SHE GAVE BIRTH TO.

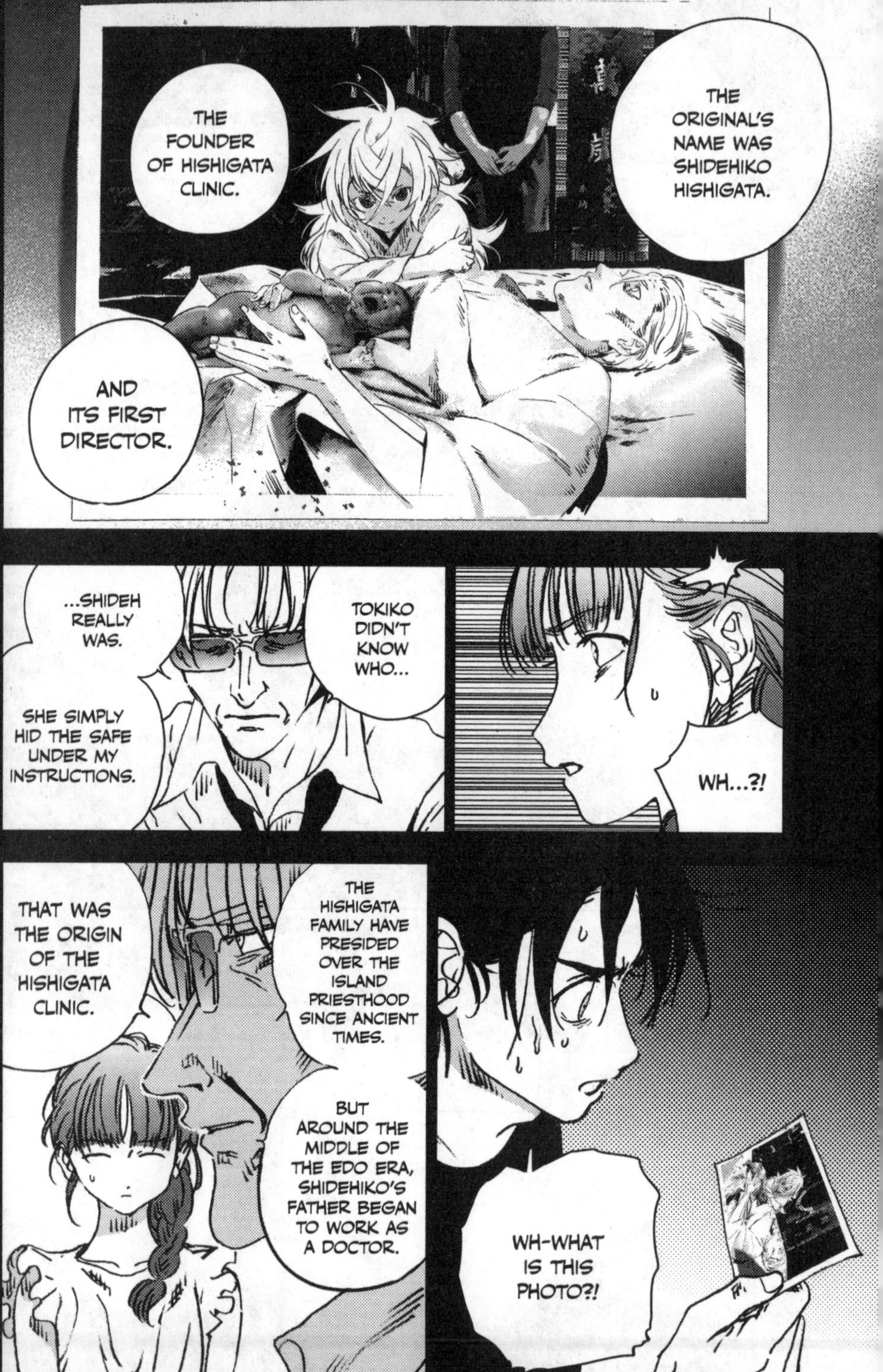
THE ORIGINAL'S NAME WAS SHIDEHIKO HISHIGATA.
THE FOUNDER OF HISHIGATA CLINIC.
AND ITS FIRST DIRECTOR.
WH...?!
TOKIKO DIDN'T KNOW WHO...
...SHIDEH REALLY WAS.
SHE SIMPLY HID THE SAFE UNDER MY INSTRUCTIONS.
WH-WHAT IS THIS PHOTO?!
THE HISHIGATA FAMILY HAVE PRESIDED OVER THE ISLAND PRIESTHOOD SINCE ANCIENT TIMES.
BUT AROUND THE MIDDLE OF THE EDO ERA, SHIDEHIKO'S FATHER BEGAN TO WORK AS A DOCTOR.
THAT WAS THE ORIGIN OF THE HISHIGATA CLINIC.

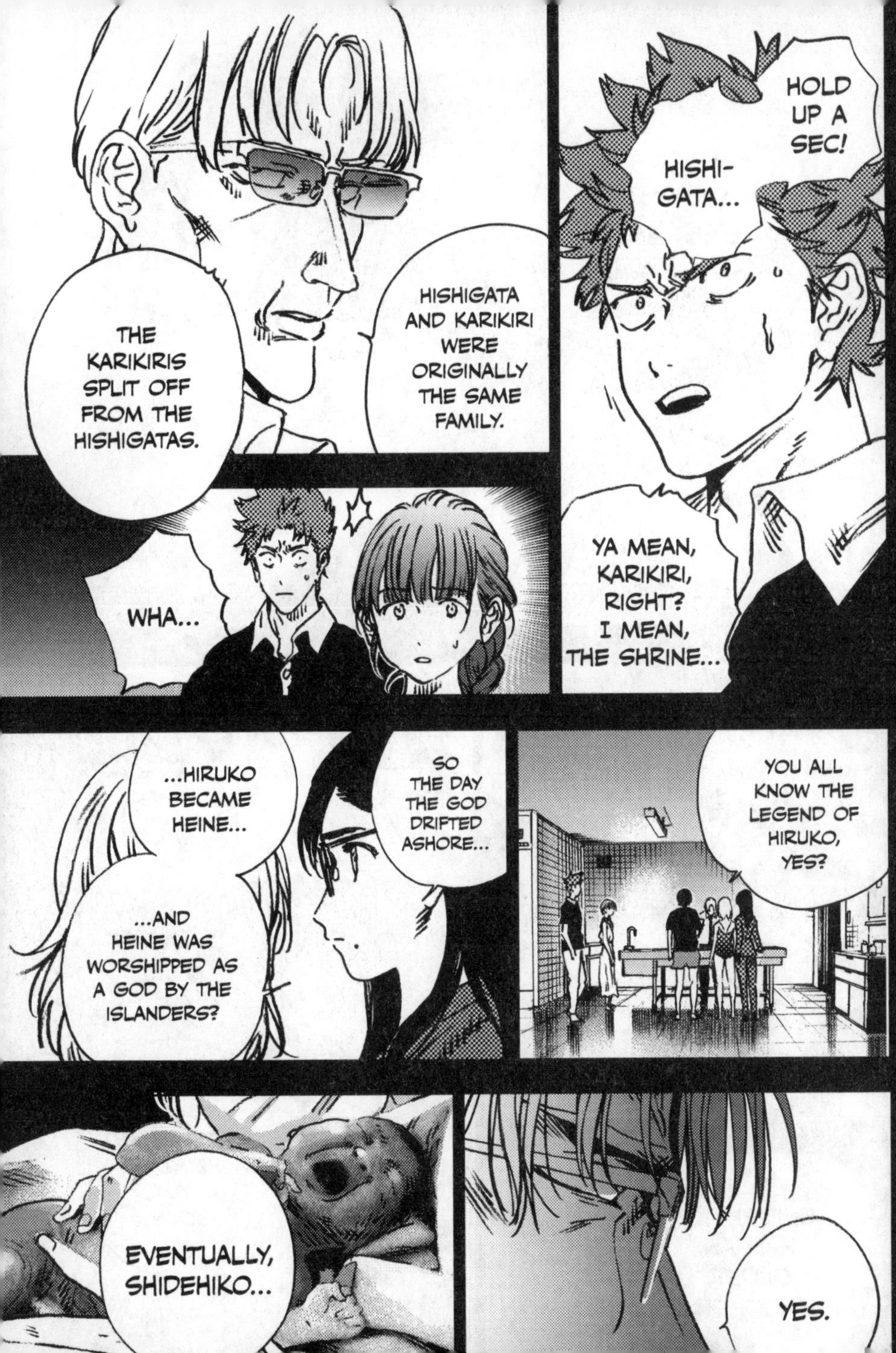
HOLD UP A SEC!
HISHI-GATA...
YA MEAN, KARIKIRI, RIGHT? I MEAN, THE SHRINE...
HISHIGATA AND KARIKIRI WERE ORIGINALLY THE SAME FAMILY.
THE KARIKIRIS SPLIT OFF FROM THE HISHIGATAS.
WHA...
YOU ALL KNOW THE LEGEND OF HIRUKO, YES?
SO THE DAY THE GOD DRIFTED ASHORE...
...HIRUKO BECAME HEINE...
...AND HEINE WAS WORSHIPPED AS A GOD BY THE ISLANDERS?
YES.
EVENTUALLY, SHIDEHIKO...

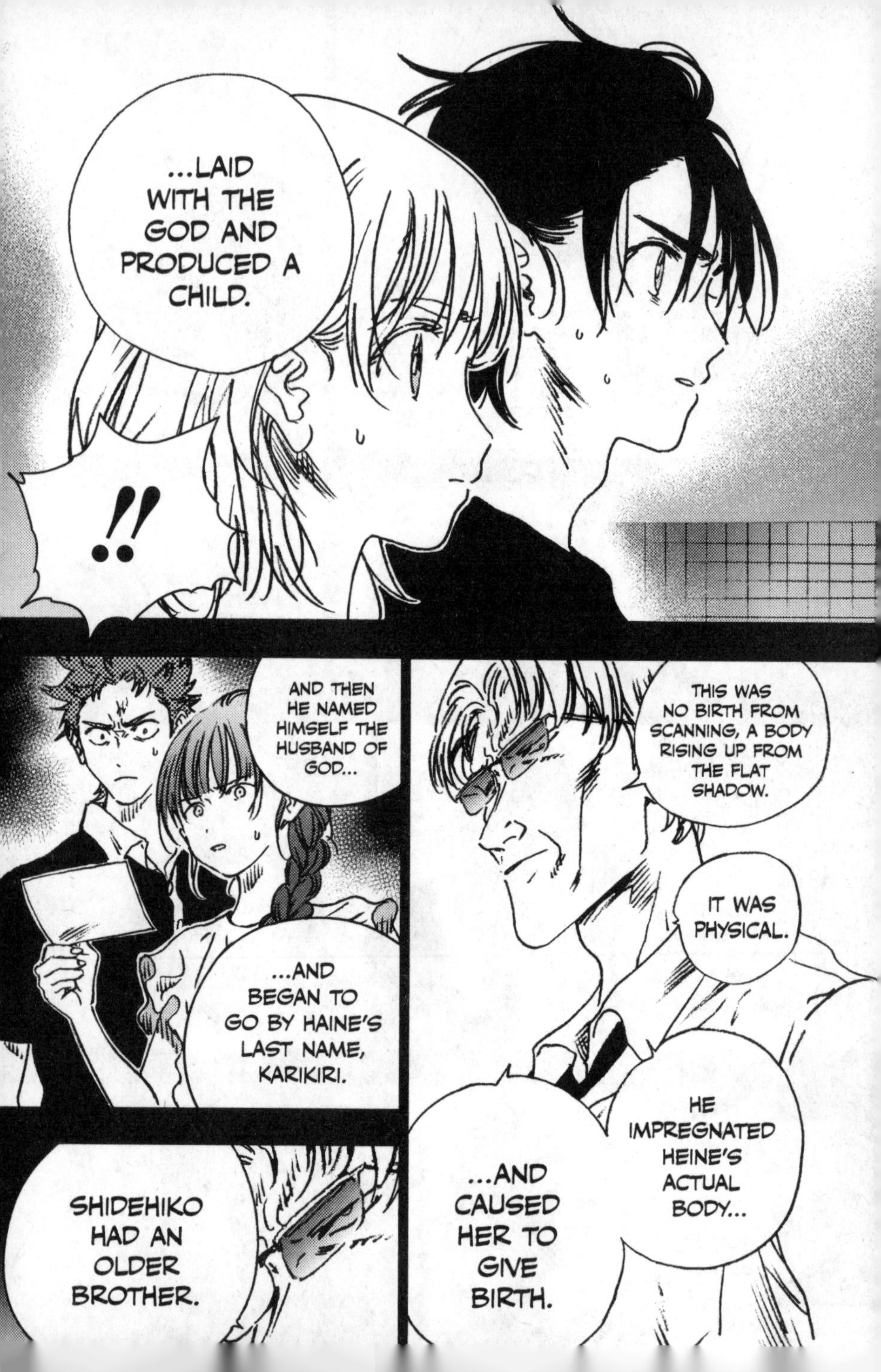
...LAID WITH THE GOD AND PRODUCED A CHILD.
!!
THIS WAS NO BIRTH FROM SCANNING, A BODY RISING UP FROM THE FLAT SHADOW.
IT WAS PHYSICAL.
HE IMPREGNATED HEINE'S ACTUAL BODY...
...AND CAUSED HER TO GIVE BIRTH.
AND THEN HE NAMED HIMSELF THE HUSBAND OF GOD...
...AND BEGAN TO GO BY HAINE'S LAST NAME, KARIKIRI.
SHIDEHIKO HAD AN OLDER BROTHER.

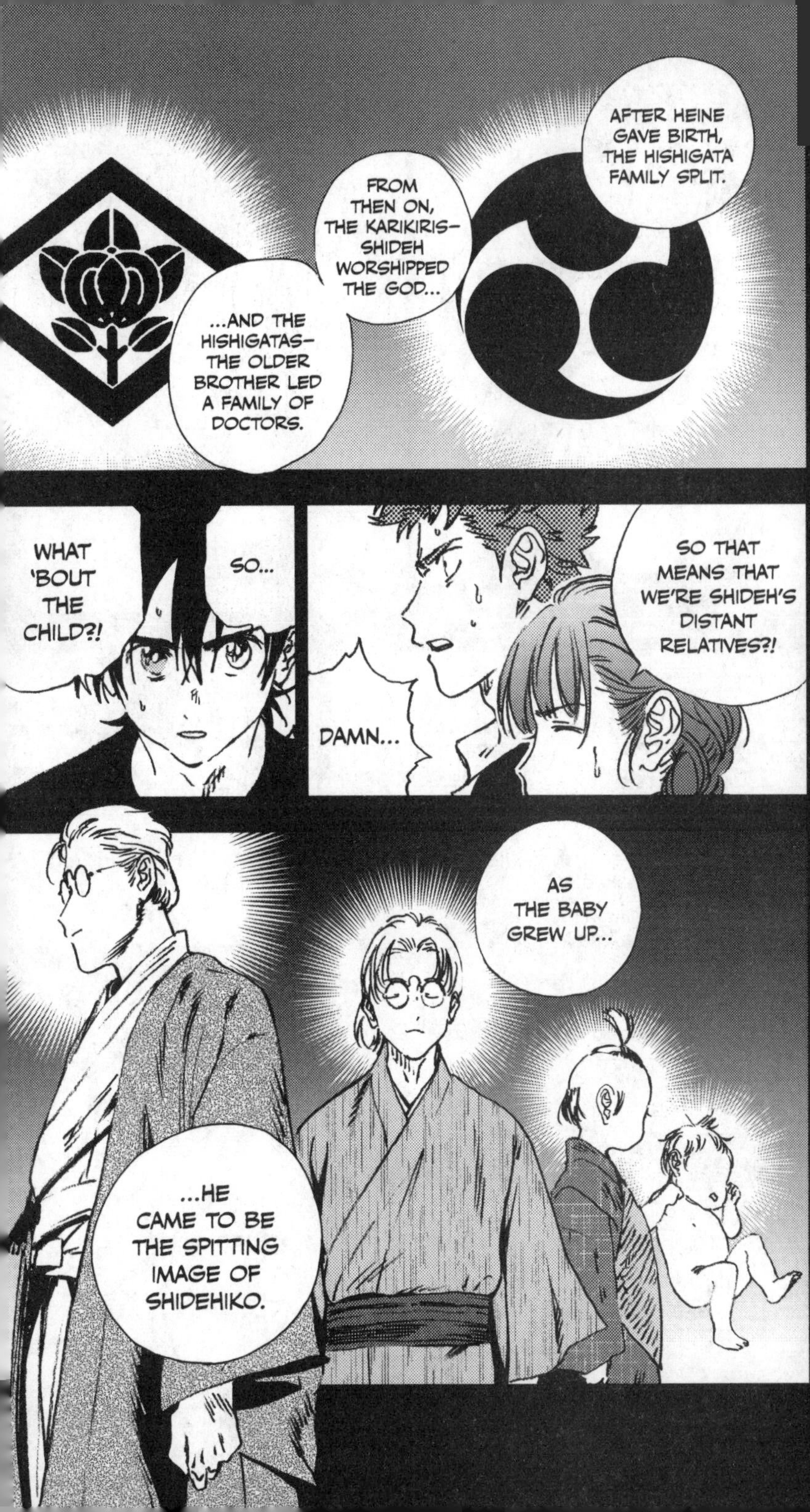
AFTER HEINE GAVE BIRTH, THE HISHIGATA FAMILY SPLIT.
FROM THEN ON, THE KARIKIRIS-SHIDEH WORSHIPPED THE GOD...
...AND THE HISHIGATAS–THE OLDER BROTHER LED A FAMILY OF DOCTORS.
SO THAT MEANS THAT WE'RE SHIDEH'S DISTANT RELATIVES?!
DAMN...
SO...
WHAT 'BOUT THE CHILD?!
AS THE BABY GREW UP...
...HE CAME TO BE THE SPITTING IMAGE OF SHIDEHIKO.

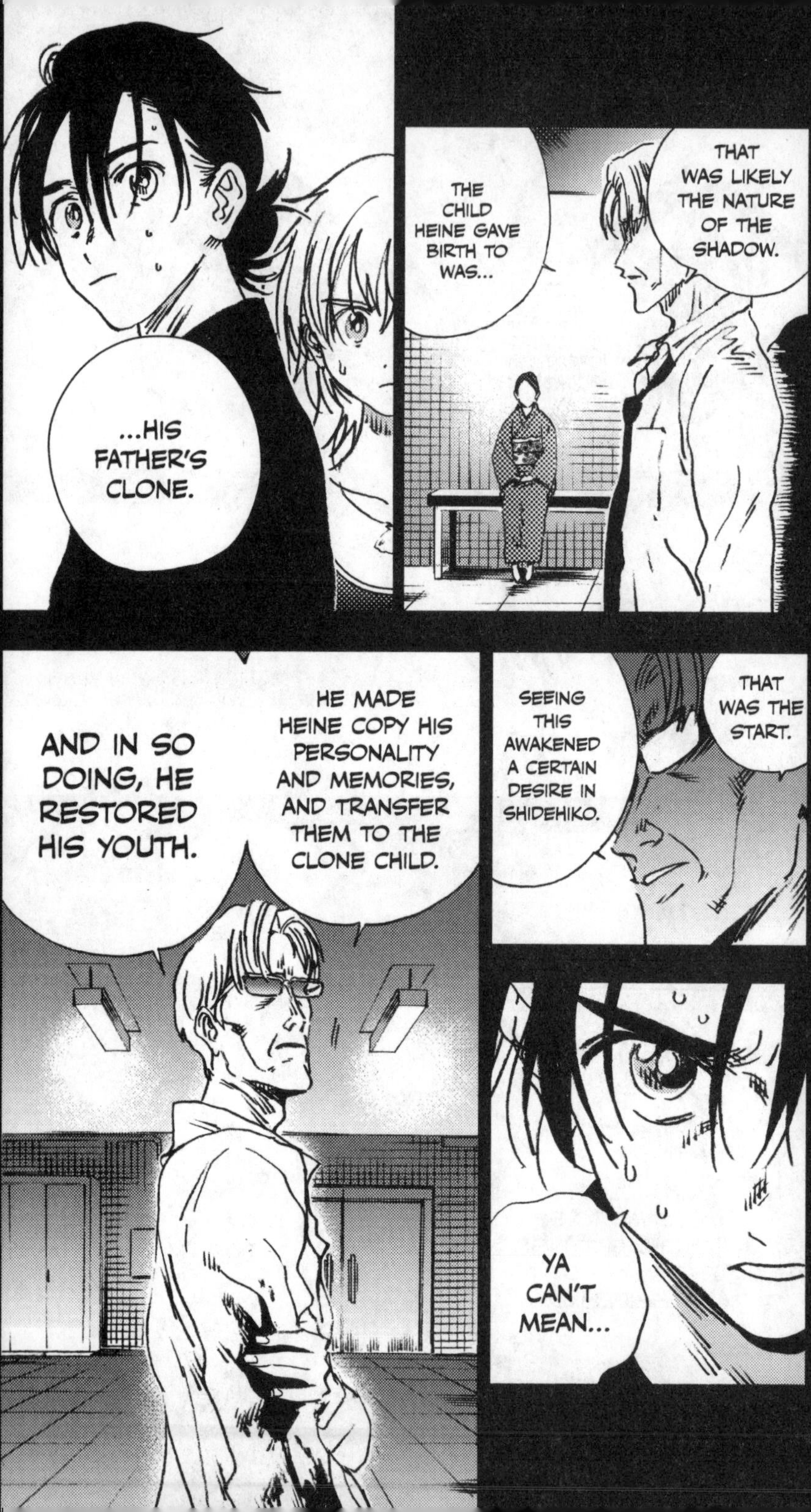
THAT WAS LIKELY THE NATURE OF THE SHADOW.
THE CHILD HEINE GAVE BIRTH TO WAS...
...HIS FATHER'S CLONE.
THAT WAS THE START.
SEEING THIS AWAKENED A CERTAIN DESIRE IN SHIDEHIKO.
YA CAN'T MEAN...
HE MADE HEINE COPY HIS PERSONALITY AND MEMORIES, AND TRANSFER THEM TO THE CLONE CHILD.
AND IN SO DOING, HE RESTORED HIS YOUTH.

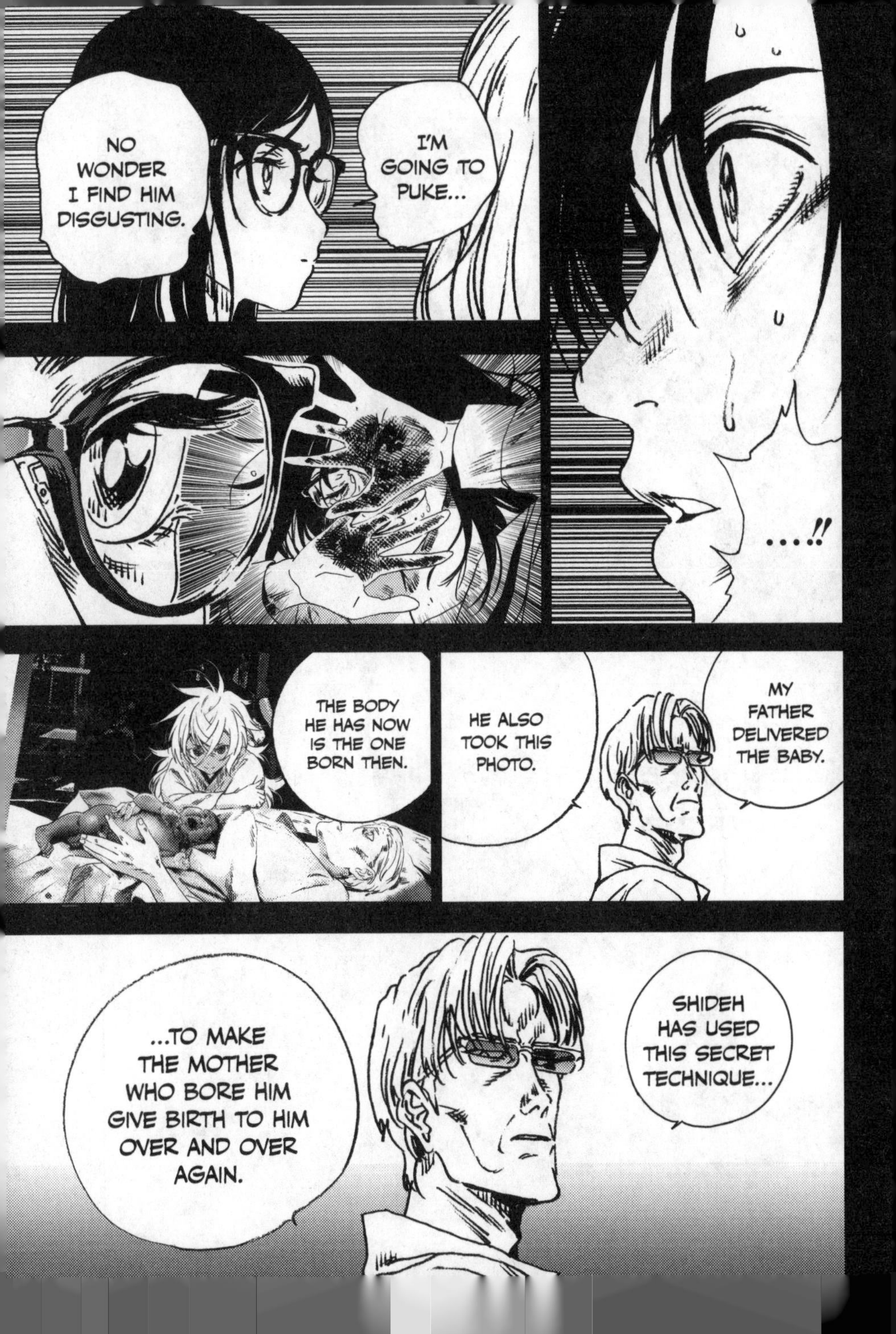
...!!
I'M GOING TO PUKE...
NO WONDER I FIND HIM DISGUSTING.
MY FATHER DELIVERED THE BABY.
HE ALSO TOOK THIS PHOTO.
THE BODY HE HAS NOW IS THE ONE BORN THEN.
SHIDEH HAS USED THIS SECRET TECHNIQUE...
...TO MAKE THE MOTHER WHO BORE HIM GIVE BIRTH TO HIM OVER AND OVER AGAIN.

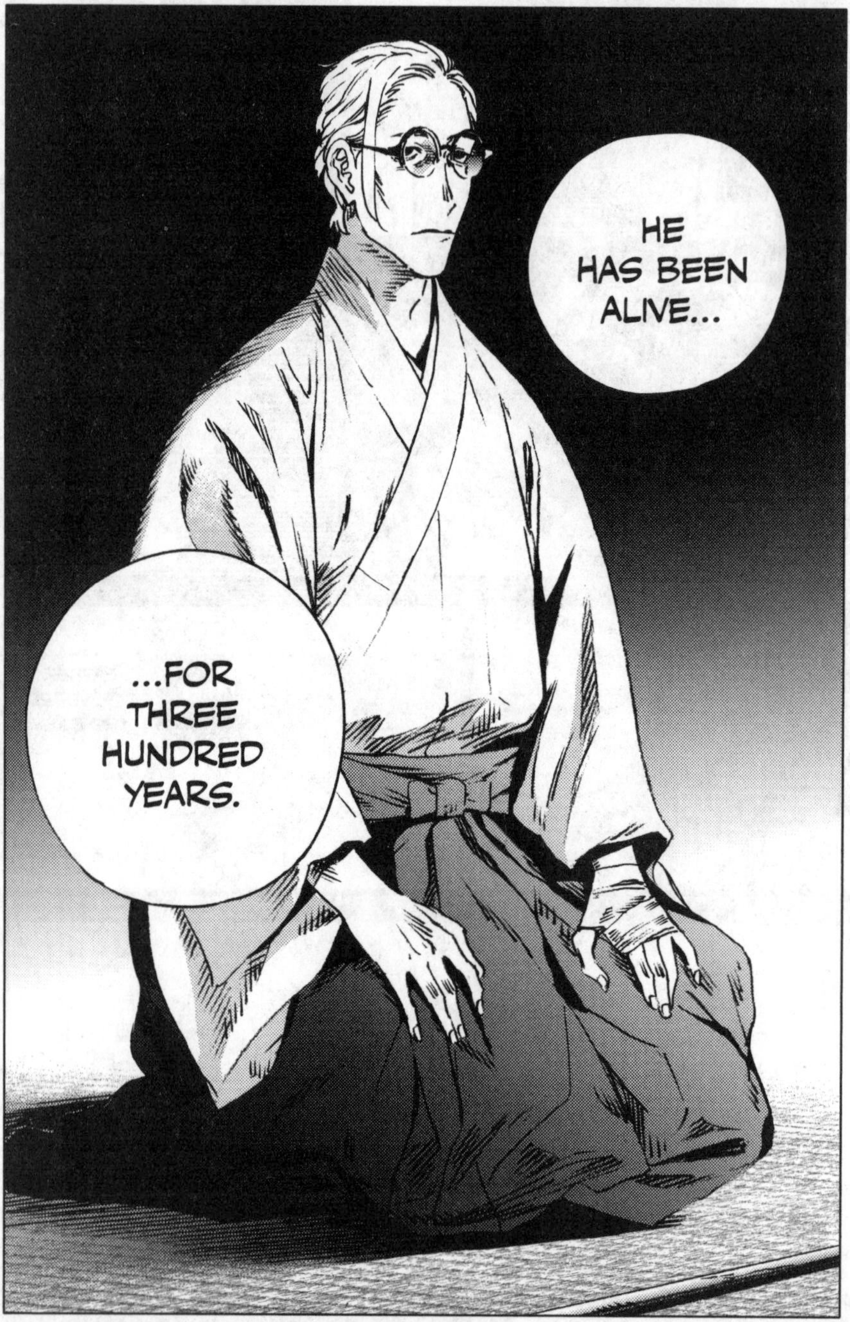
HE HAS BEEN ALIVE...
...FOR THREE HUNDRED YEARS.

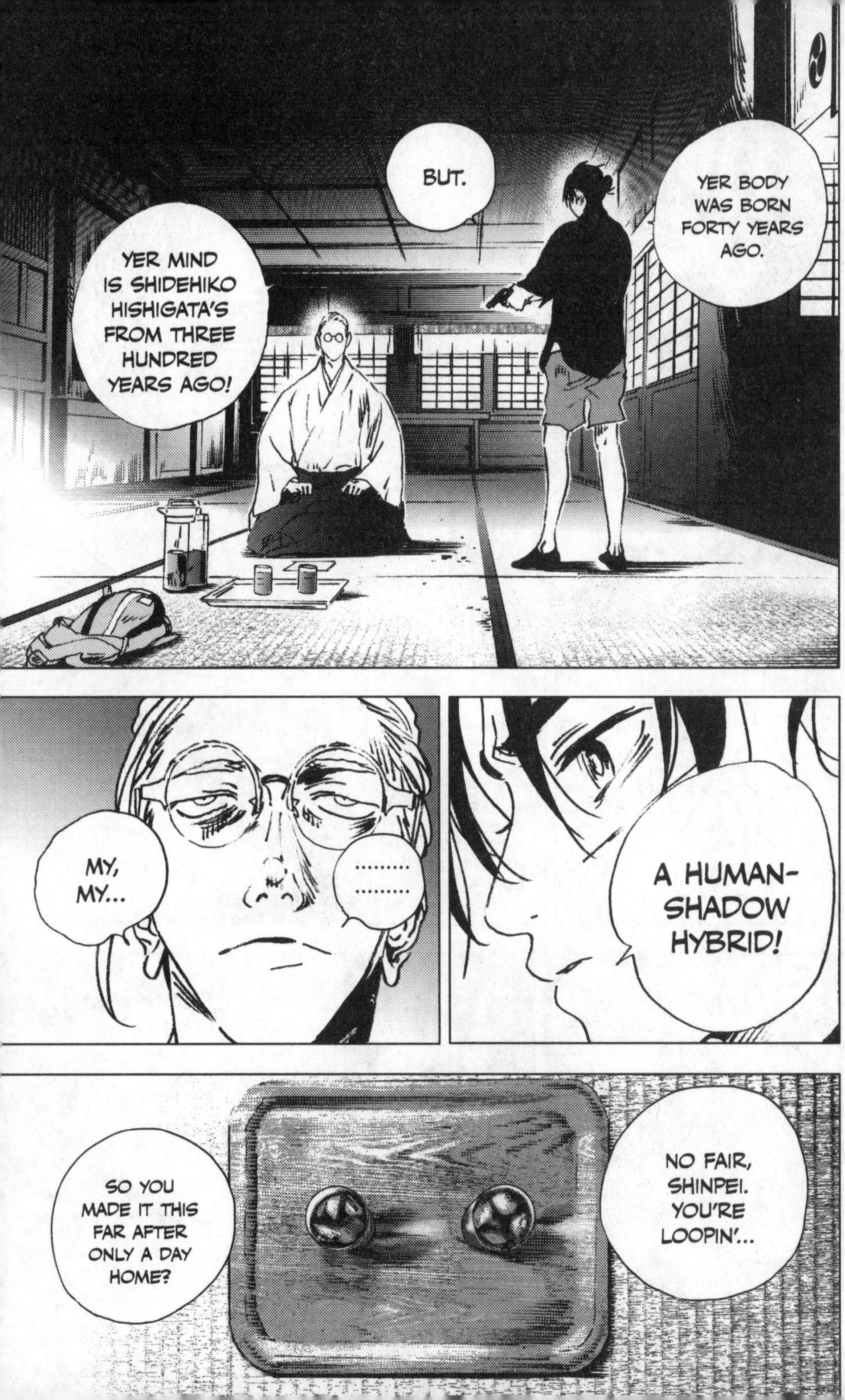
YER BODY WAS BORN FORTY YEARS AGO.
BUT.
YER MIND IS SHIDEHIKO HISHIGATA'S FROM THREE HUNDRED YEARS AGO!
A HUMAN-SHADOW HYBRID!
....
....
MY, MY...
NO FAIR, SHINPEI. YOU'RE LOOPIN'...
SO YOU MADE IT THIS FAR AFTER ONLY A DAY HOME?

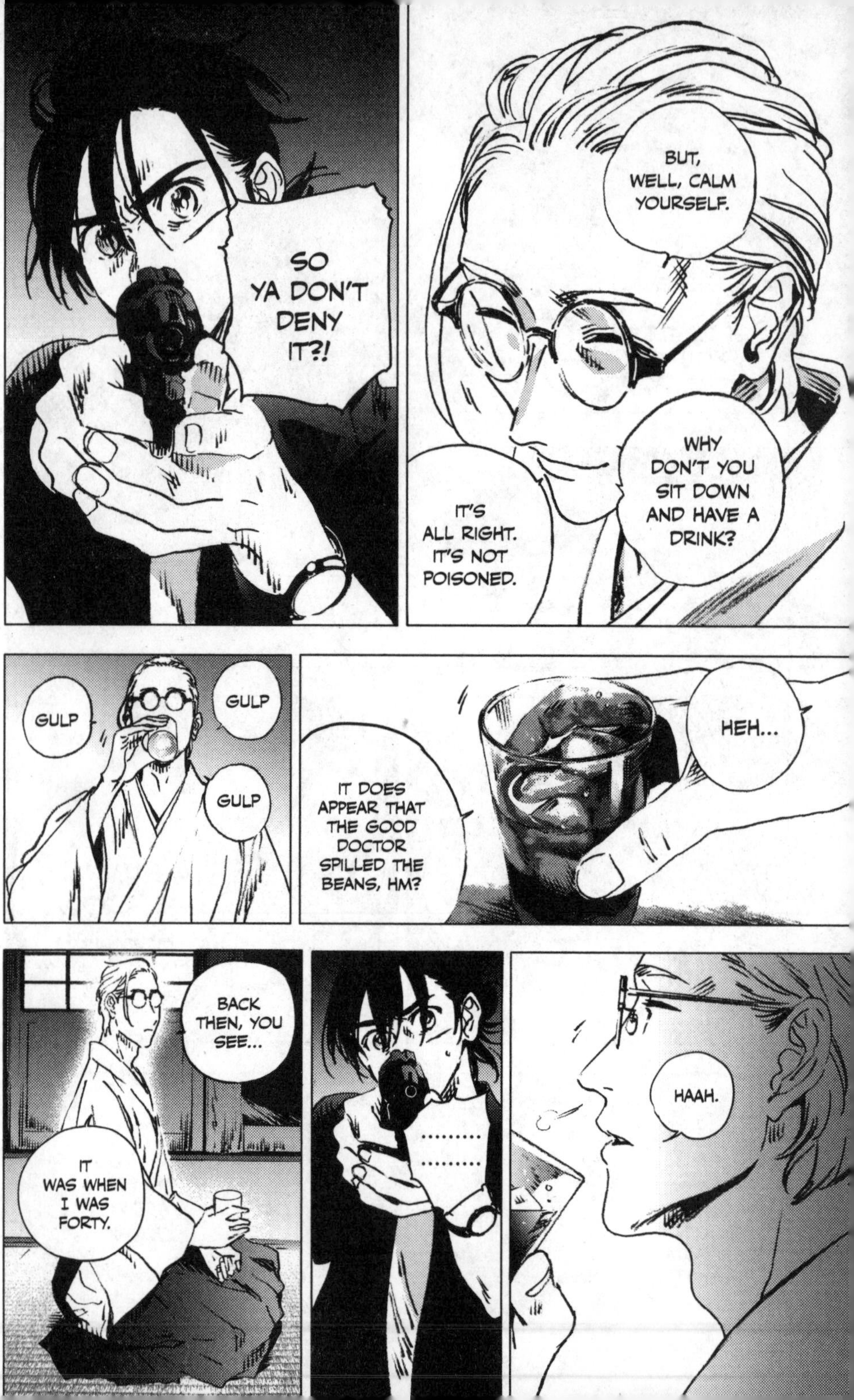
BUT, WELL, CALM YOURSELF.
WHY DON'T YOU SIT DOWN AND HAVE A DRINK?
IT'S ALL RIGHT. IT'S NOT POISONED.
SO YA DON'T DENY IT?!
HEH...
IT DOES APPEAR THAT THE GOOD DOCTOR SPILLED THE BEANS, HM?
GULP
GULP
GULP
HAAH.
....
....
BACK THEN, YOU SEE...
IT WAS WHEN I WAS FORTY.

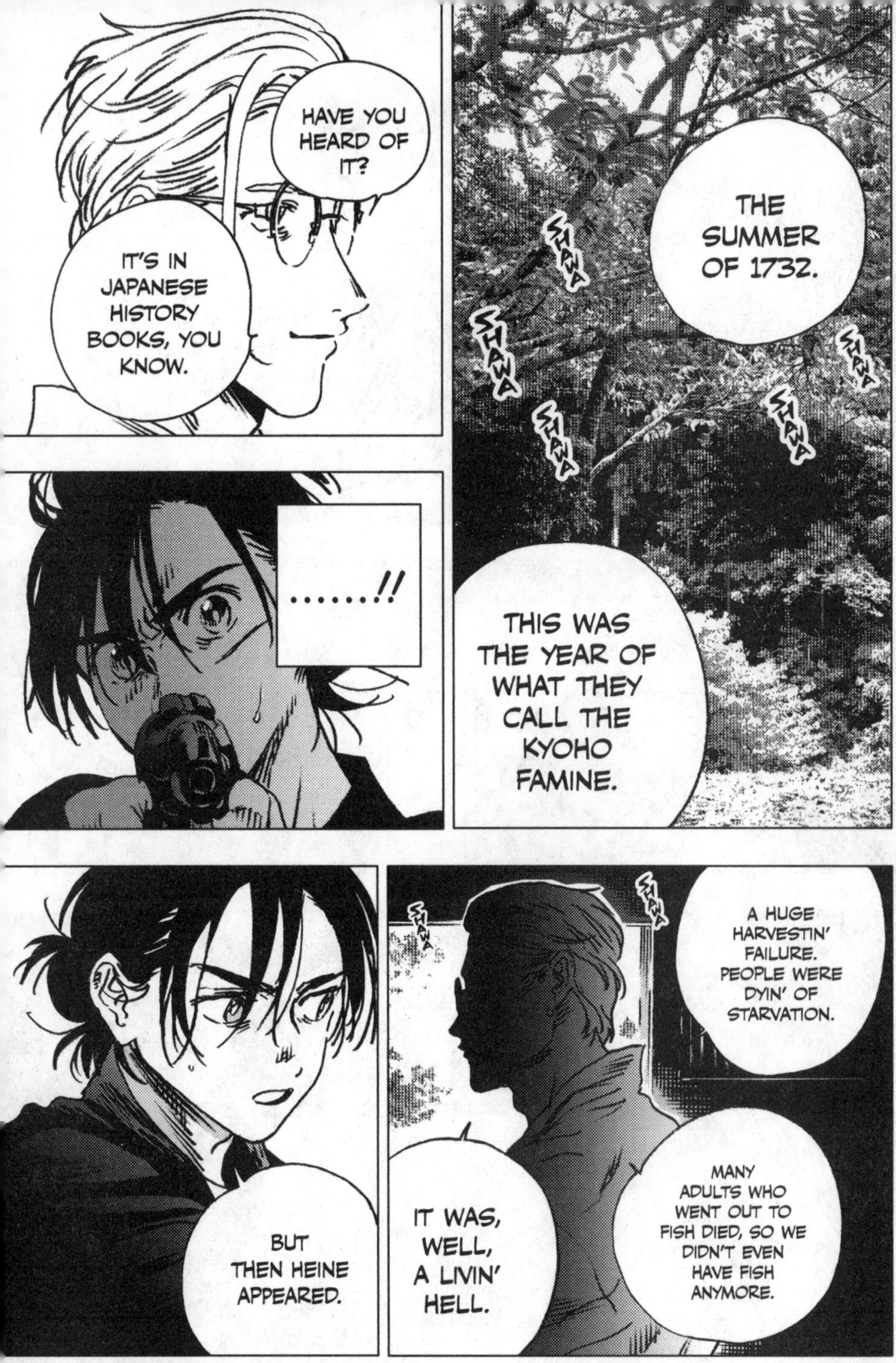
SHAWA
SHAWA
SHAWA
SHAWA
SHAWA
THE SUMMER OF 1732.
THIS WAS THE YEAR OF WHAT THEY CALL THE KYOHO FAMINE.
HAVE YOU HEARD OF IT?
IT'S IN JAPANESE HISTORY BOOKS, YOU KNOW.
......!!
SHAWA
SHAWA
A HUGE HARVESTIN' FAILURE. PEOPLE WERE DYIN' OF STARVATION.
MANY ADULTS WHO WENT OUT TO FISH DIED, SO WE DIDN'T EVEN HAVE FISH ANYMORE.
IT WAS, WELL, A LIVIN' HELL.
BUT THEN HEINE APPEARED.

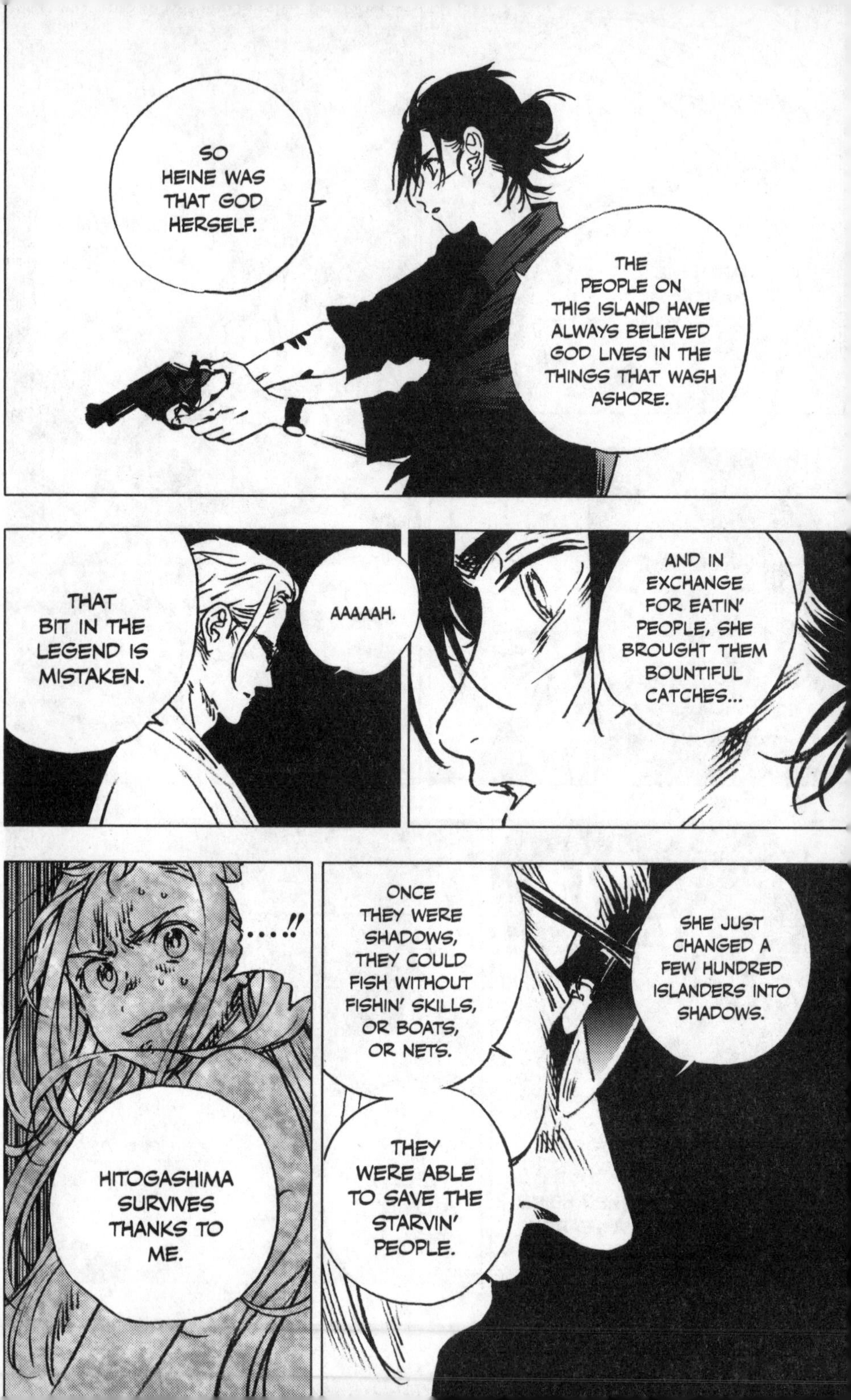

THE PEOPLE ON THIS ISLAND HAVE ALWAYS BELIEVED GOD LIVES IN THE THINGS THAT WASH ASHORE.
SO HEINE WAS THAT GOD HERSELF.
AND IN EXCHANGE FOR EATIN' PEOPLE, SHE BROUGHT THEM BOUNTIFUL CATCHES...
AAAAAH.
THAT BIT IN THE LEGEND IS MISTAKEN.
SHE JUST CHANGED A FEW HUNDRED ISLANDERS INTO SHADOWS.
ONCE THEY WERE SHADOWS, THEY COULD FISH WITHOUT FISHIN' SKILLS, OR BOATS, OR NETS.
THEY WERE ABLE TO SAVE THE STARVIN' PEOPLE.
....!!
HITOGASHIMA SURVIVES THANKS TO ME.

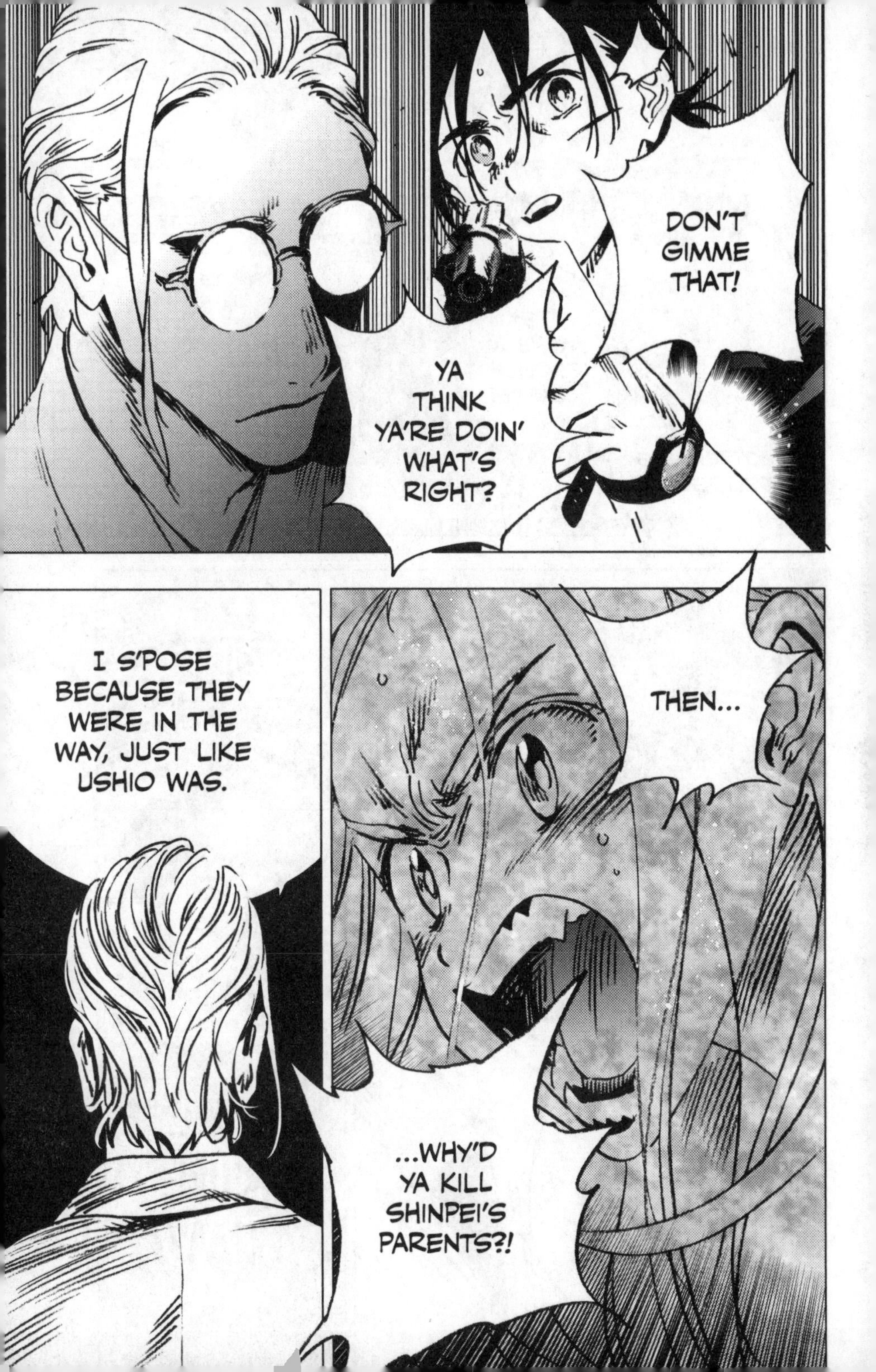
DON'T GIMME THAT!
YA THINK YA'RE DOIN' WHAT'S RIGHT?
THEN...
...WHY'D YA KILL SHINPEI'S PARENTS?!
I S'POSE BECAUSE THEY WERE IN THE WAY, JUST LIKE USHIO WAS.

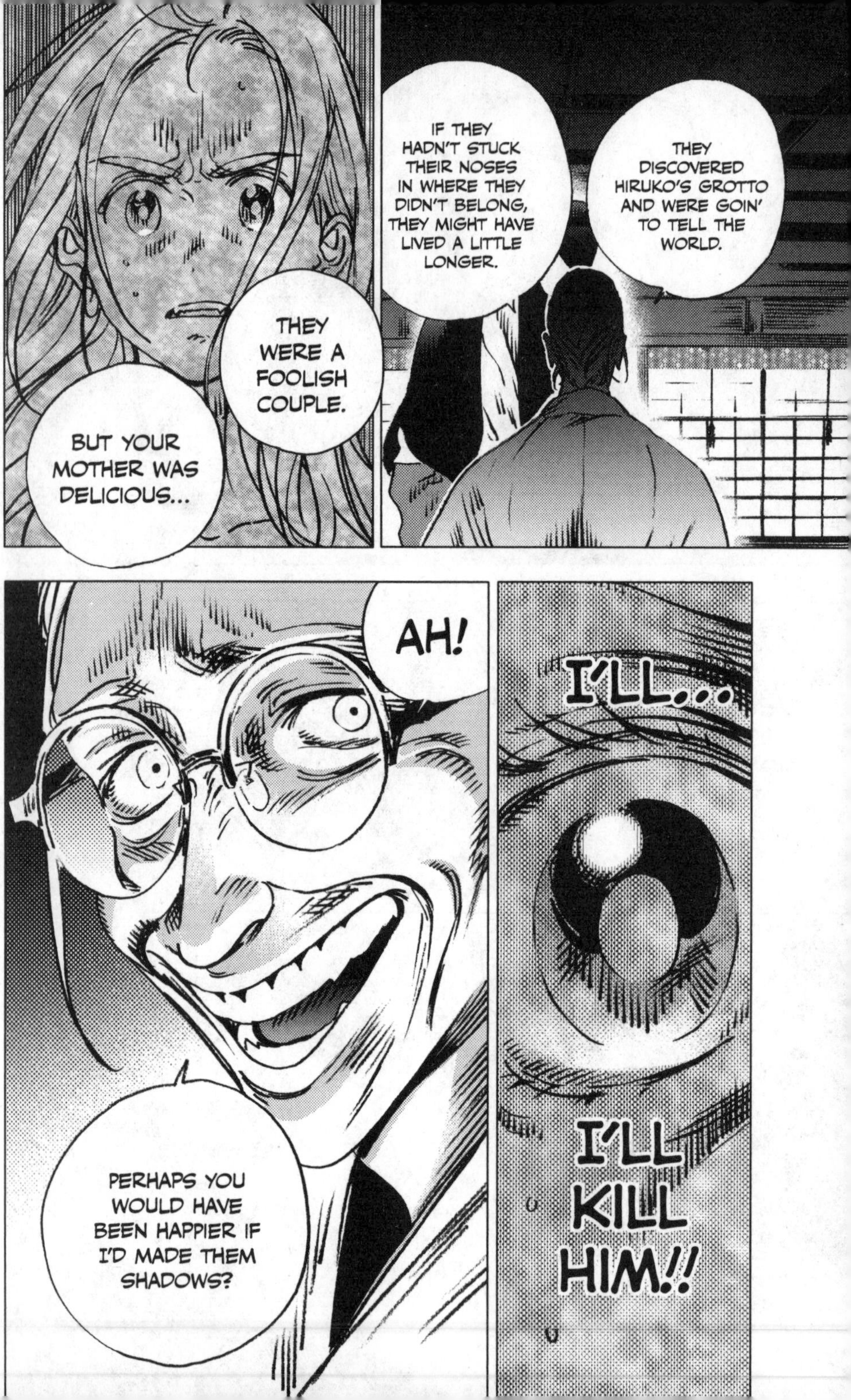
THEY DISCOVERED HIRUKO'S GROTTO AND WERE GOIN' TO TELL THE WORLD.
IF THEY HADN'T STUCK THEIR NOSES IN WHERE THEY DIDN'T BELONG, THEY MIGHT HAVE LIVED A LITTLE LONGER.
THEY WERE A FOOLISH COUPLE.
BUT YOUR MOTHER WAS DELICIOUS...
I'LL...
I'LL KILL HIM!!
AH!
PERHAPS YOU WOULD HAVE BEEN HAPPIER IF I'D MADE THEM SHADOWS?

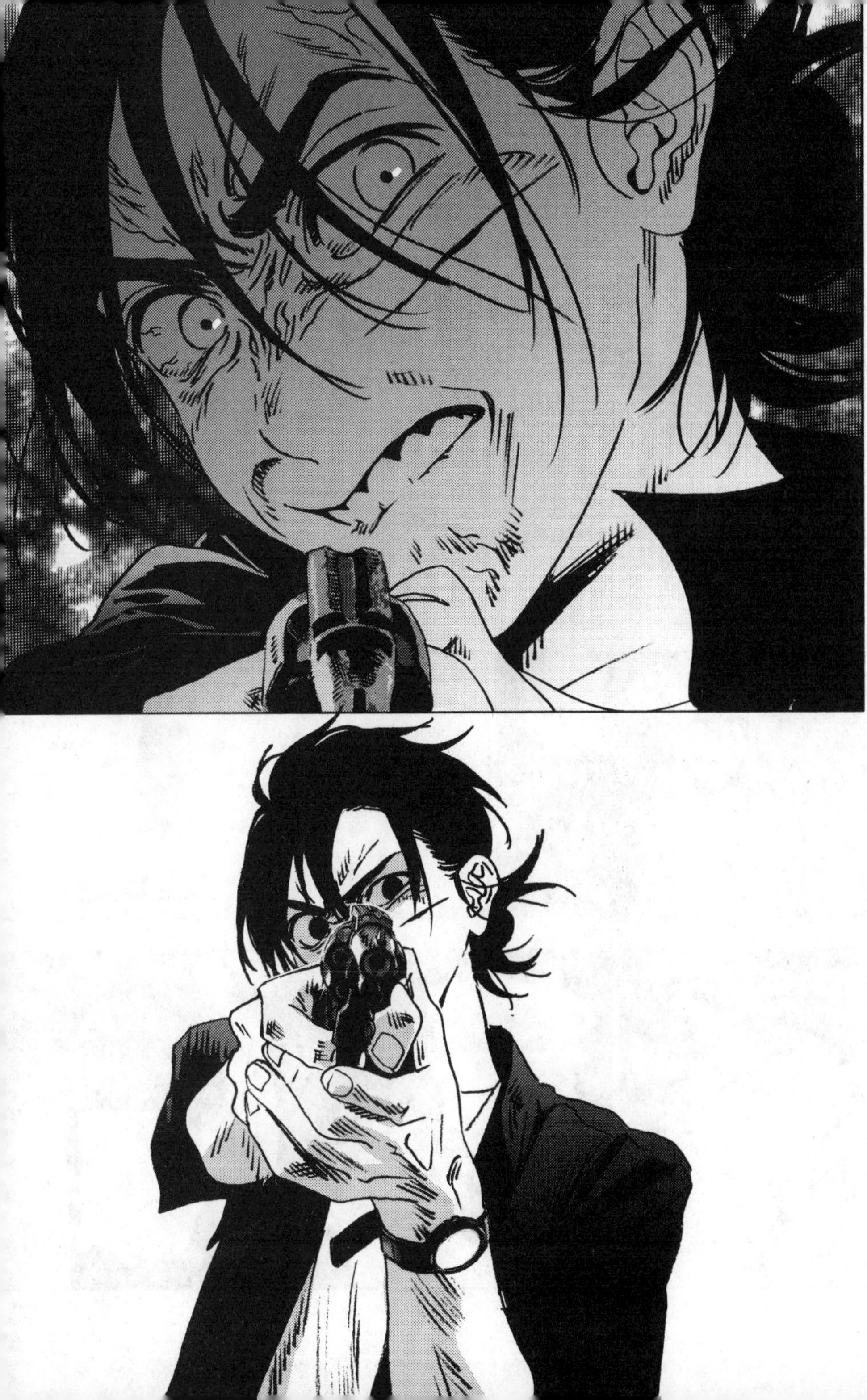

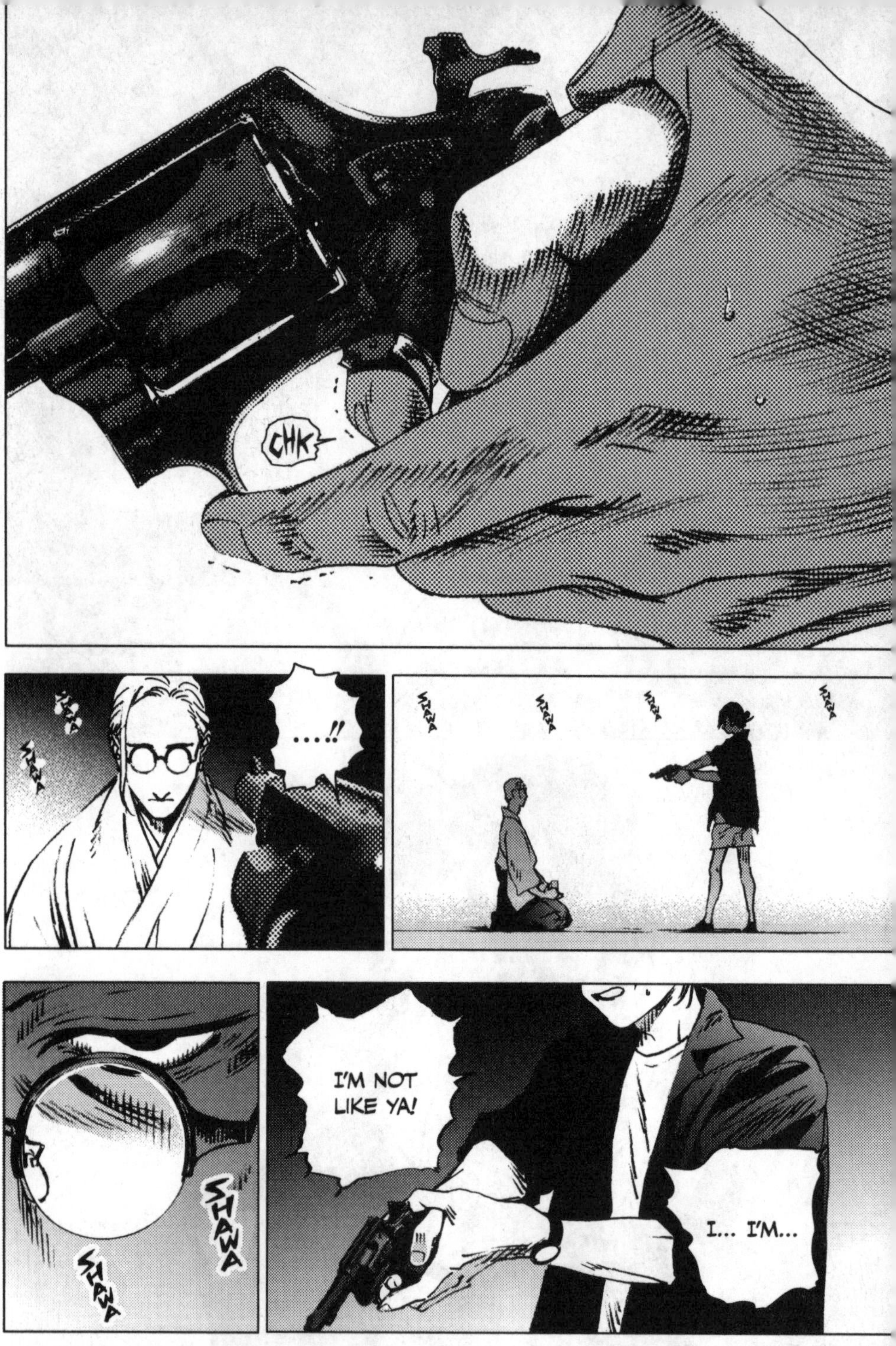
CHK
SHAWA
SHAWA
SHAWA
SHAWA
SHAWA
SHAWA
....!!
I'M NOT LIKE YA!
I... I'M...
SHAWA
SHAWA

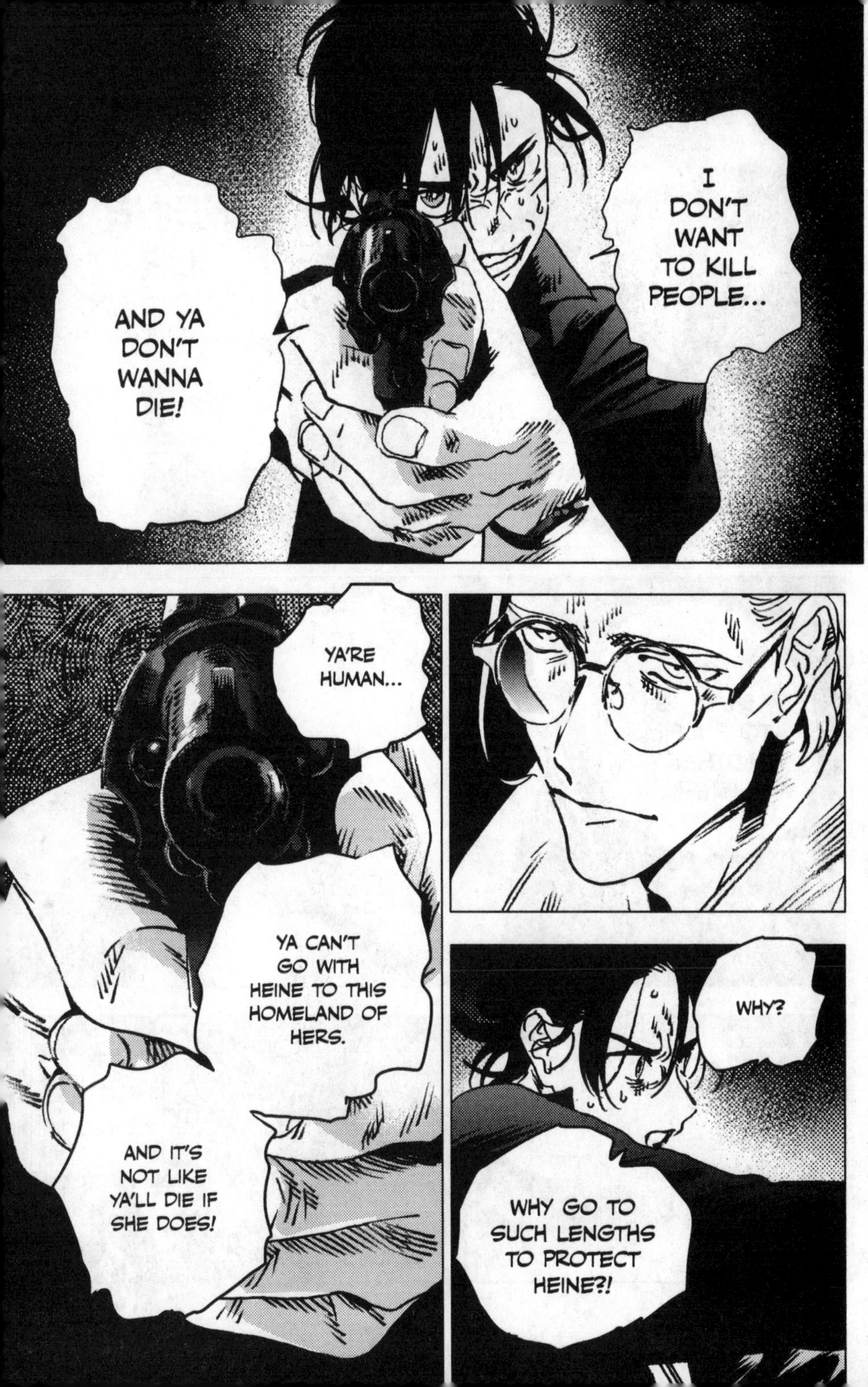
I DON'T WANT TO KILL PEOPLE...
AND YA DON'T WANNA DIE!
WHY?
WHY GO TO SUCH LENGTHS TO PROTECT HEINE?!
YA'RE HUMAN...
YA CAN'T GO WITH HEINE TO THIS HOMELAND OF HERS.
AND IT'S NOT LIKE YA'LL DIE IF SHE DOES!

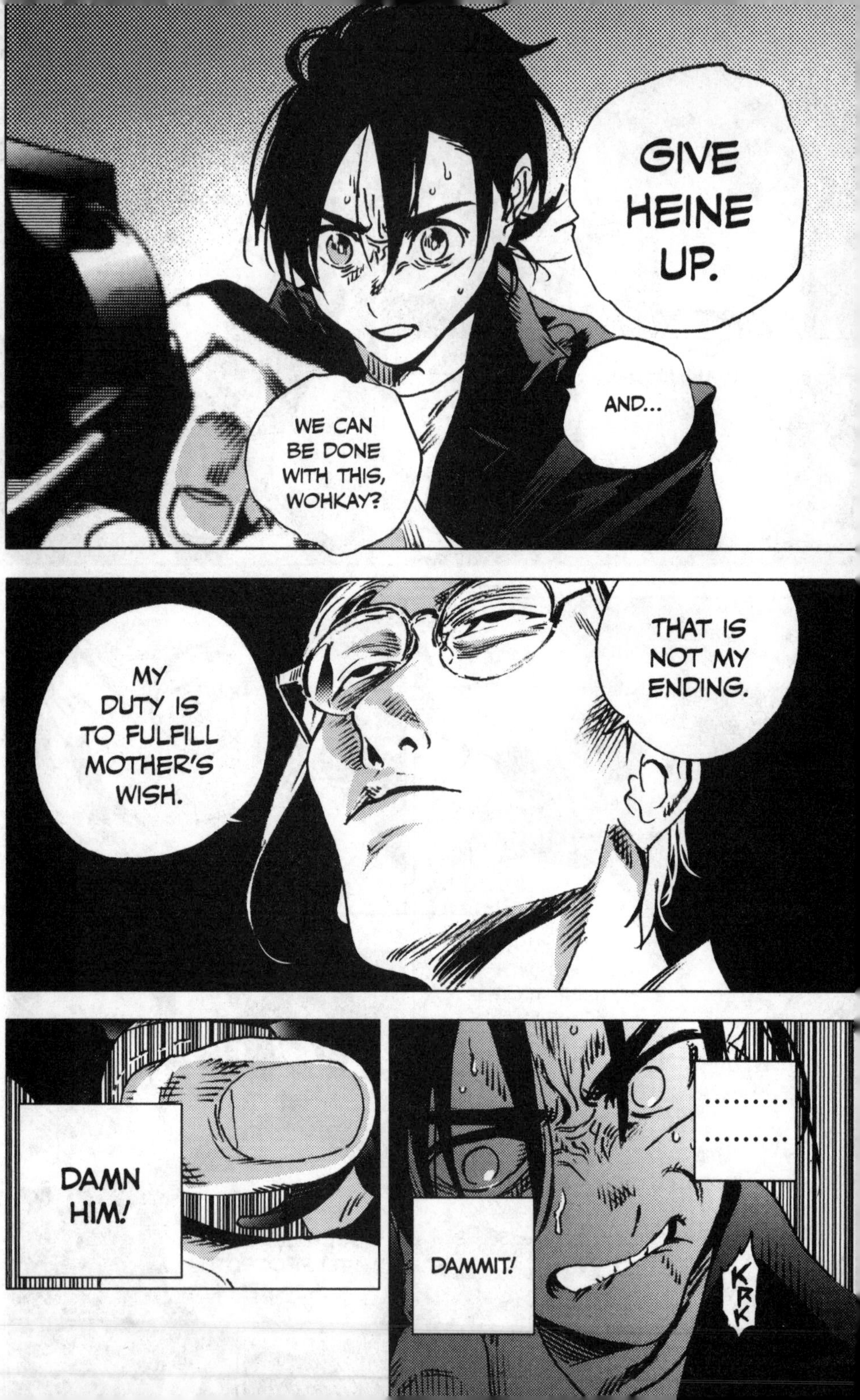
GIVE HEINE UP.
AND...
WE CAN BE DONE WITH THIS, WOHKAY?
THAT IS NOT MY ENDING.
MY DUTY IS TO FULFILL MOTHER'S WISH.
....
....
DAMMIT!
KRK
DAMN HIM!

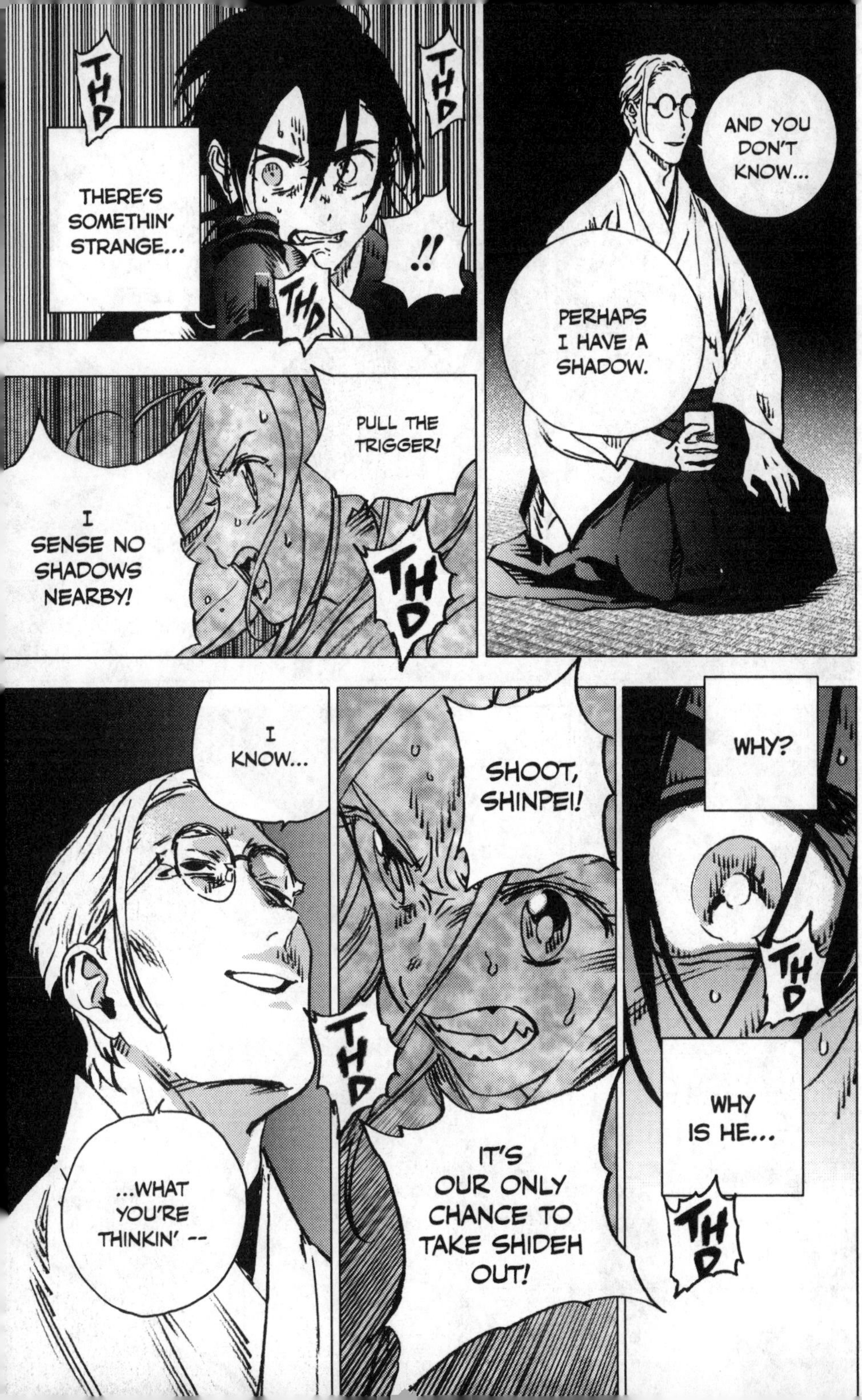
AND YOU DON'T KNOW...
PERHAPS I HAVE A SHADOW.
THD
THD
THERE'S SOMETHIN' STRANGE...
!!
THD
PULL THE TRIGGER!
I SENSE NO SHADOWS NEARBY!
THD
WHY?
THD
WHY IS HE...
THD
SHOOT, SHINPEI!
THD
IT'S OUR ONLY CHANCE TO TAKE SHIDEH OUT!
I KNOW...
...WHAT YOU'RE THINKIN' --

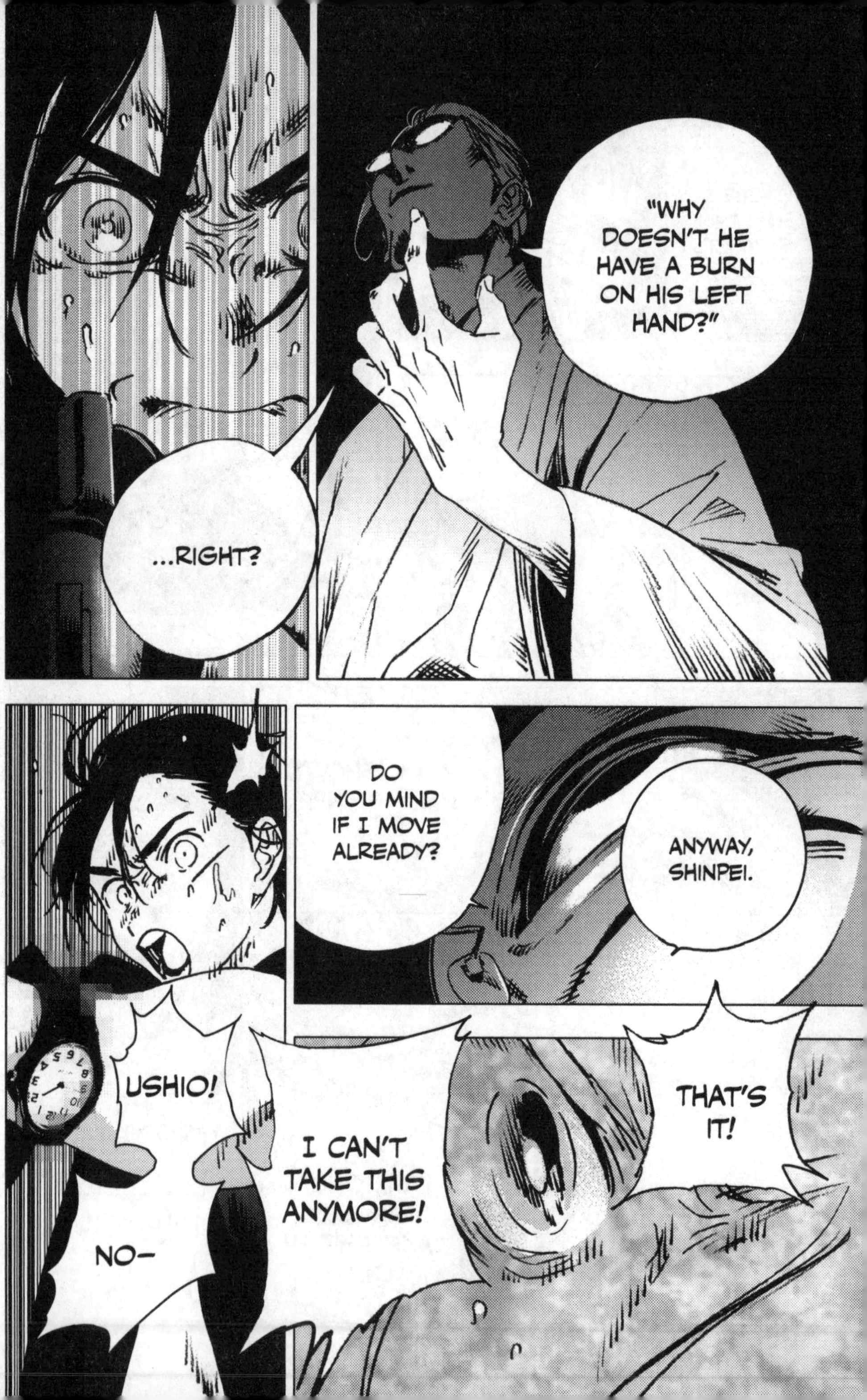
"WHY DOESN'T HE HAVE A BURN ON HIS LEFT HAND?"
...RIGHT?
ANYWAY, SHINPEI.
DO YOU MIND IF I MOVE ALREADY?
THAT'S IT!
I CAN'T TAKE THIS ANYMORE!
USHIO!
NO–

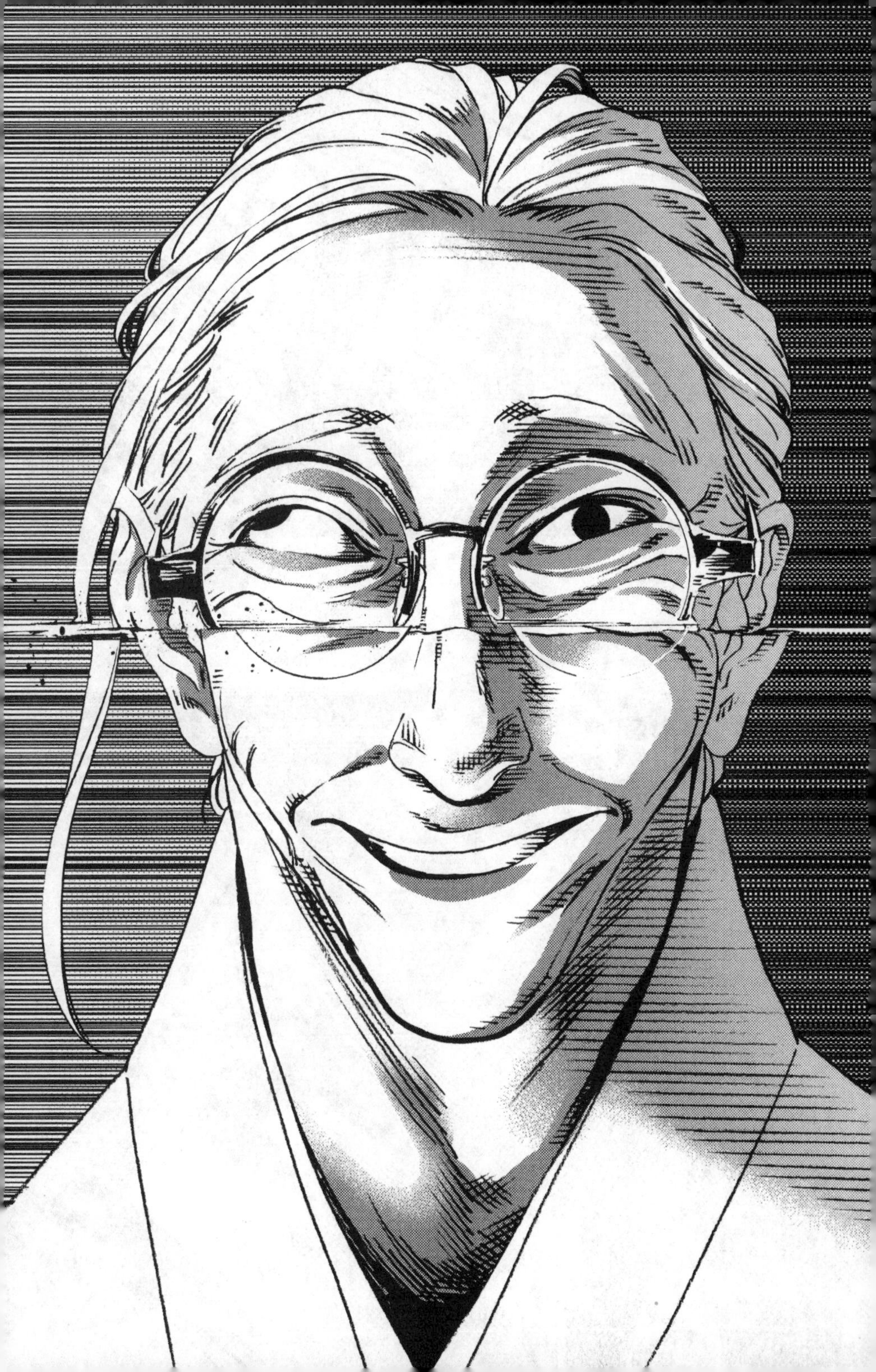

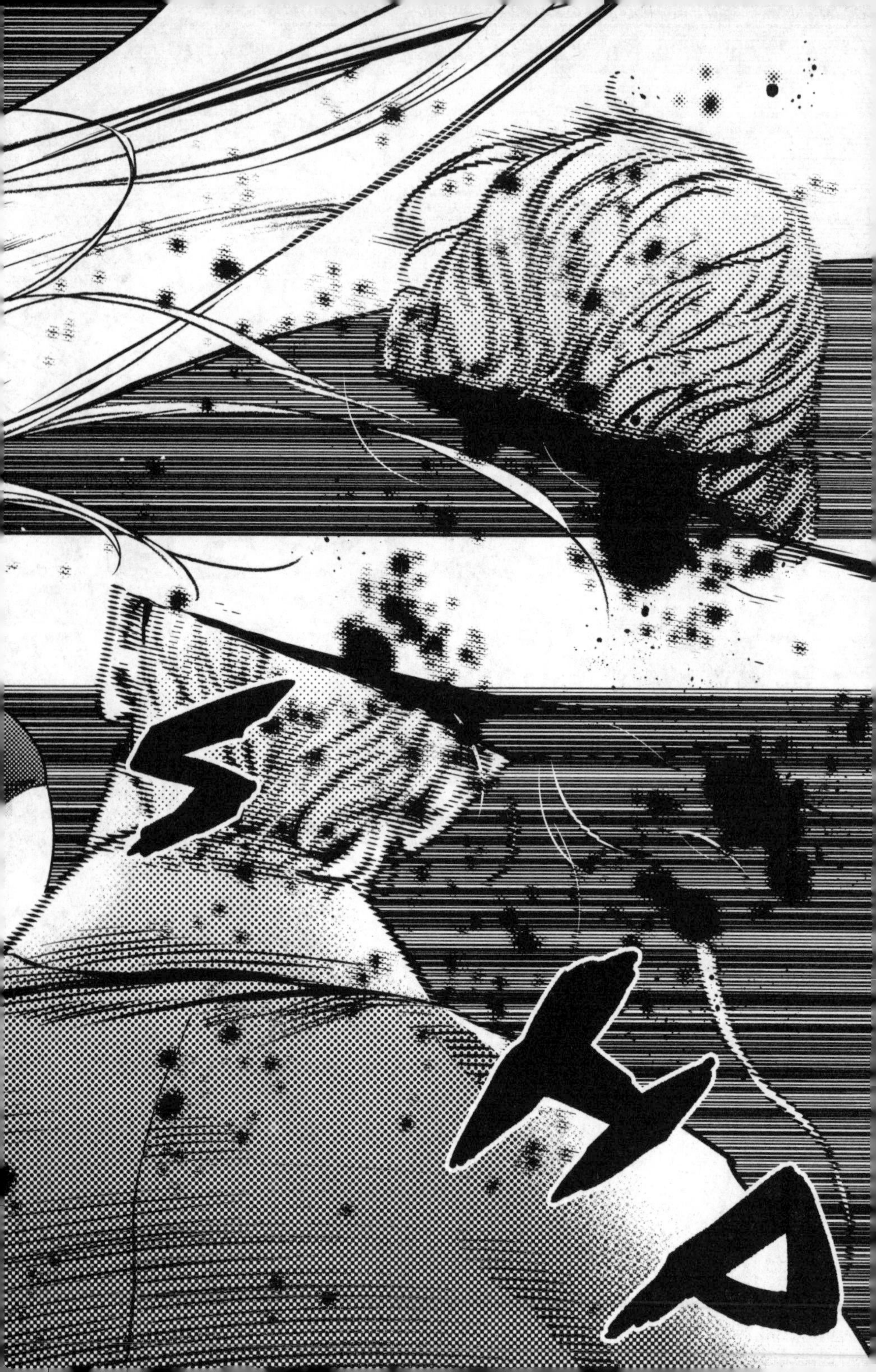
SHA

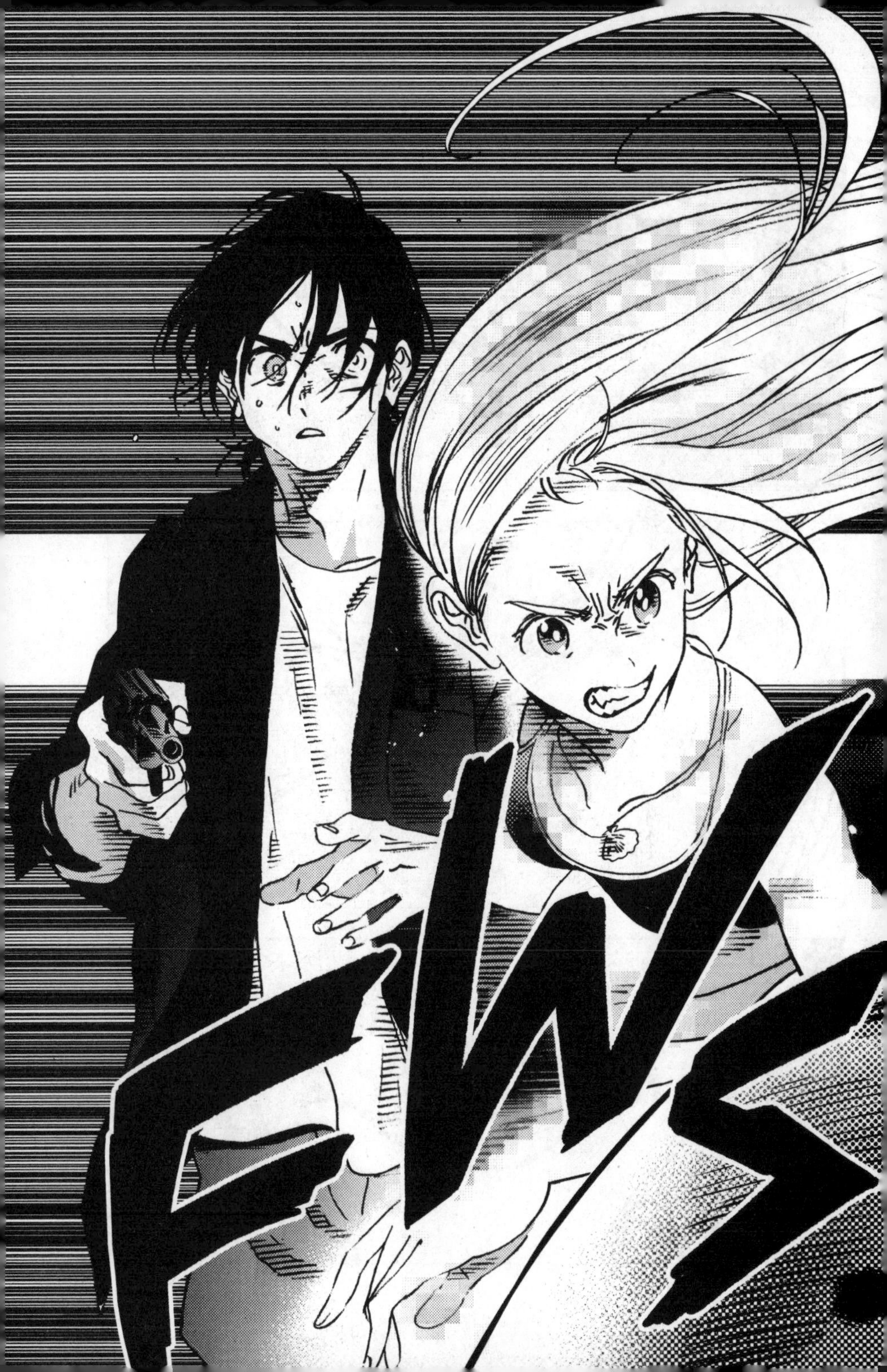

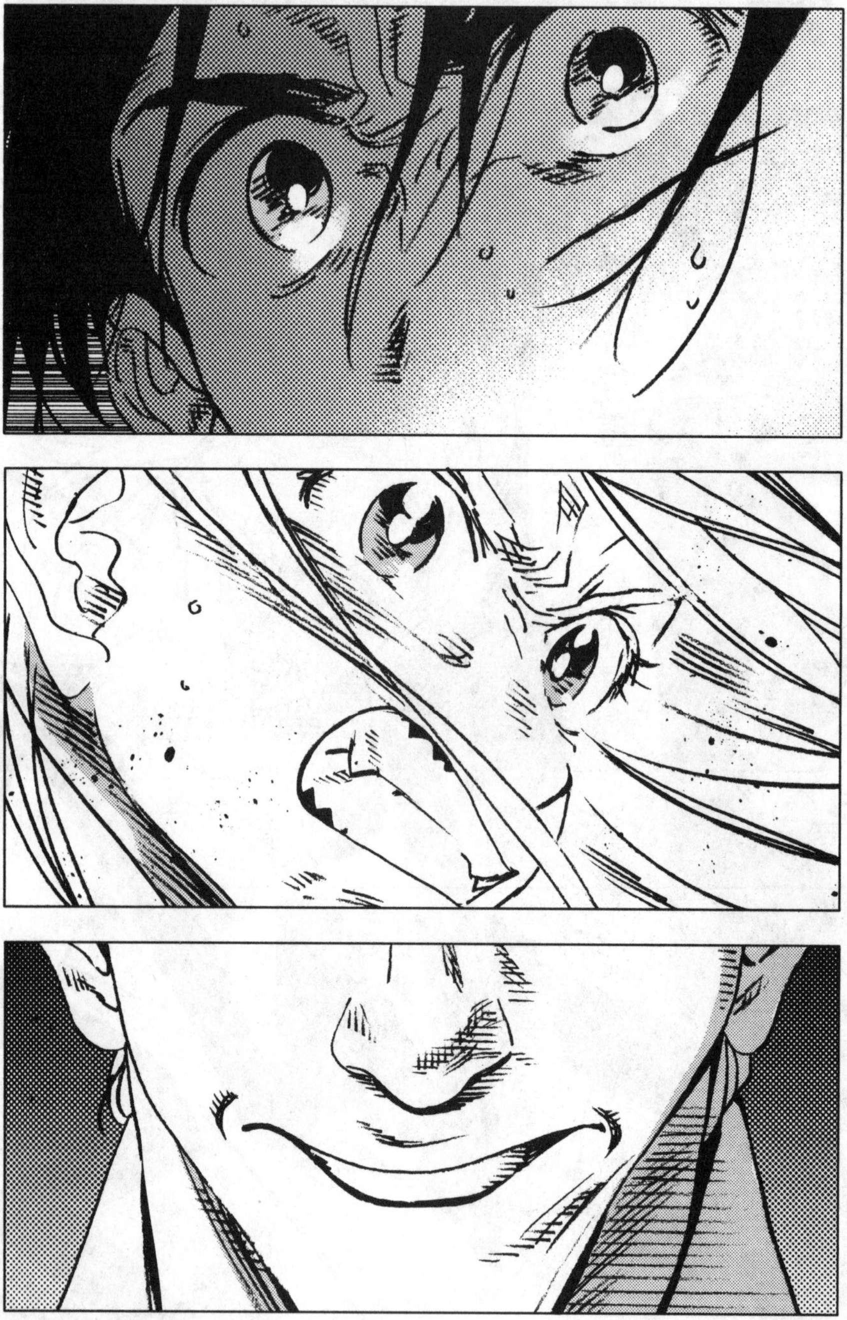

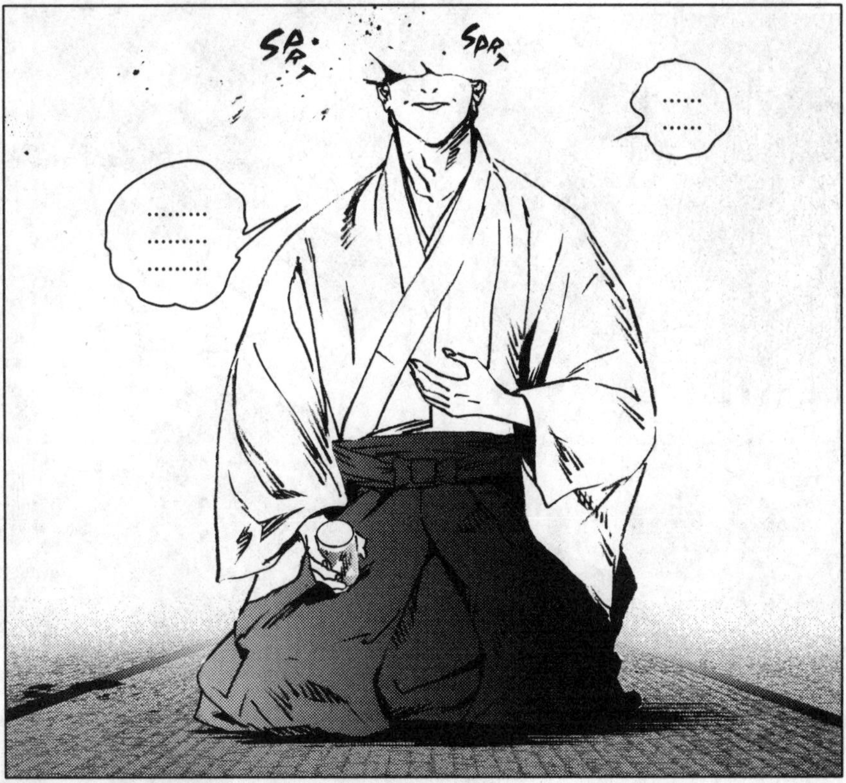
SPRT
......
......
SPRT
....
....
....

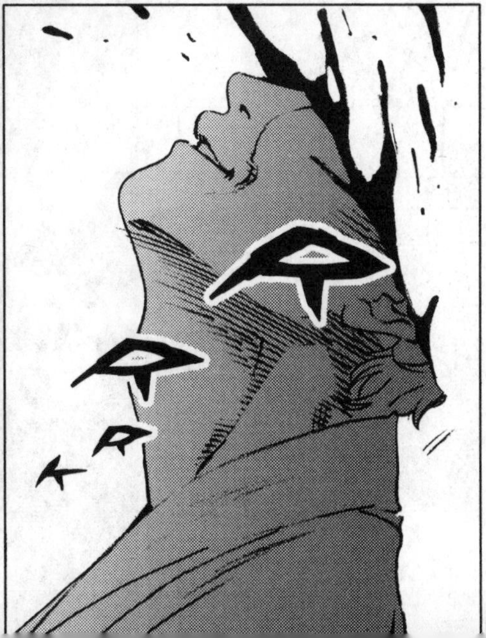

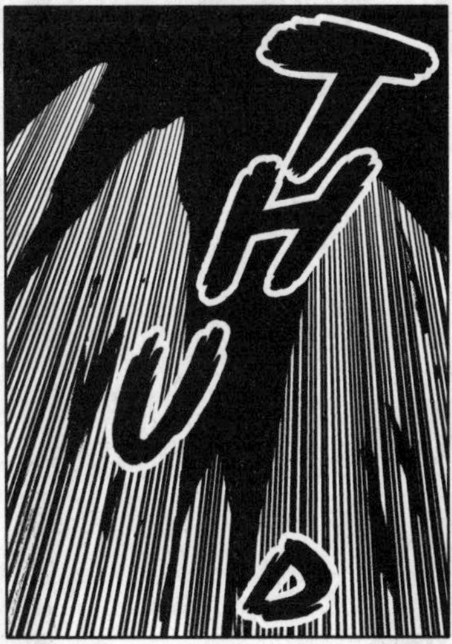
THUD

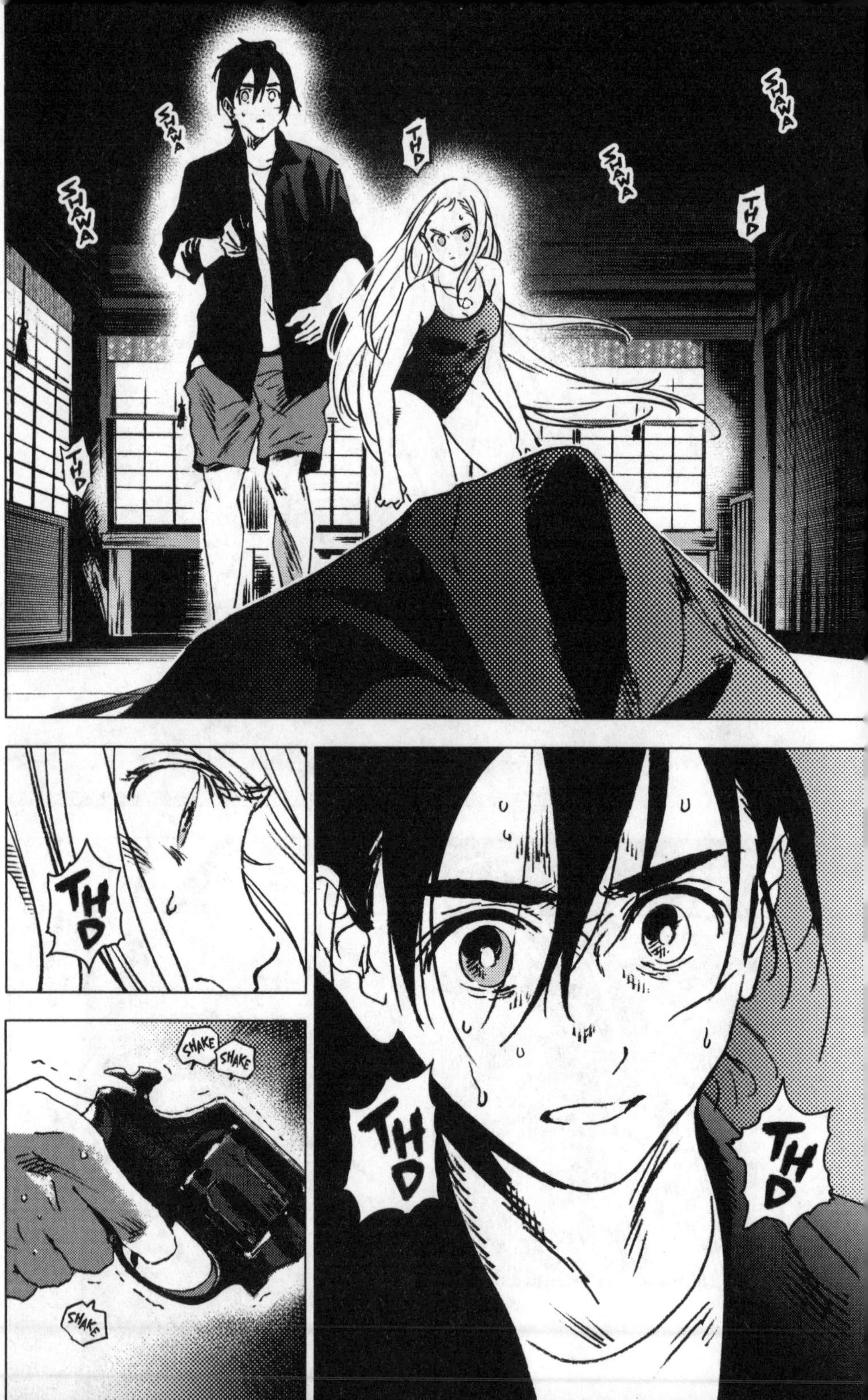
SHAWA
SHAWA
THD
THD
SHAWA
SHAWA
THD
THD
THD
THD
SHAKE
SHAKE
SHAKE

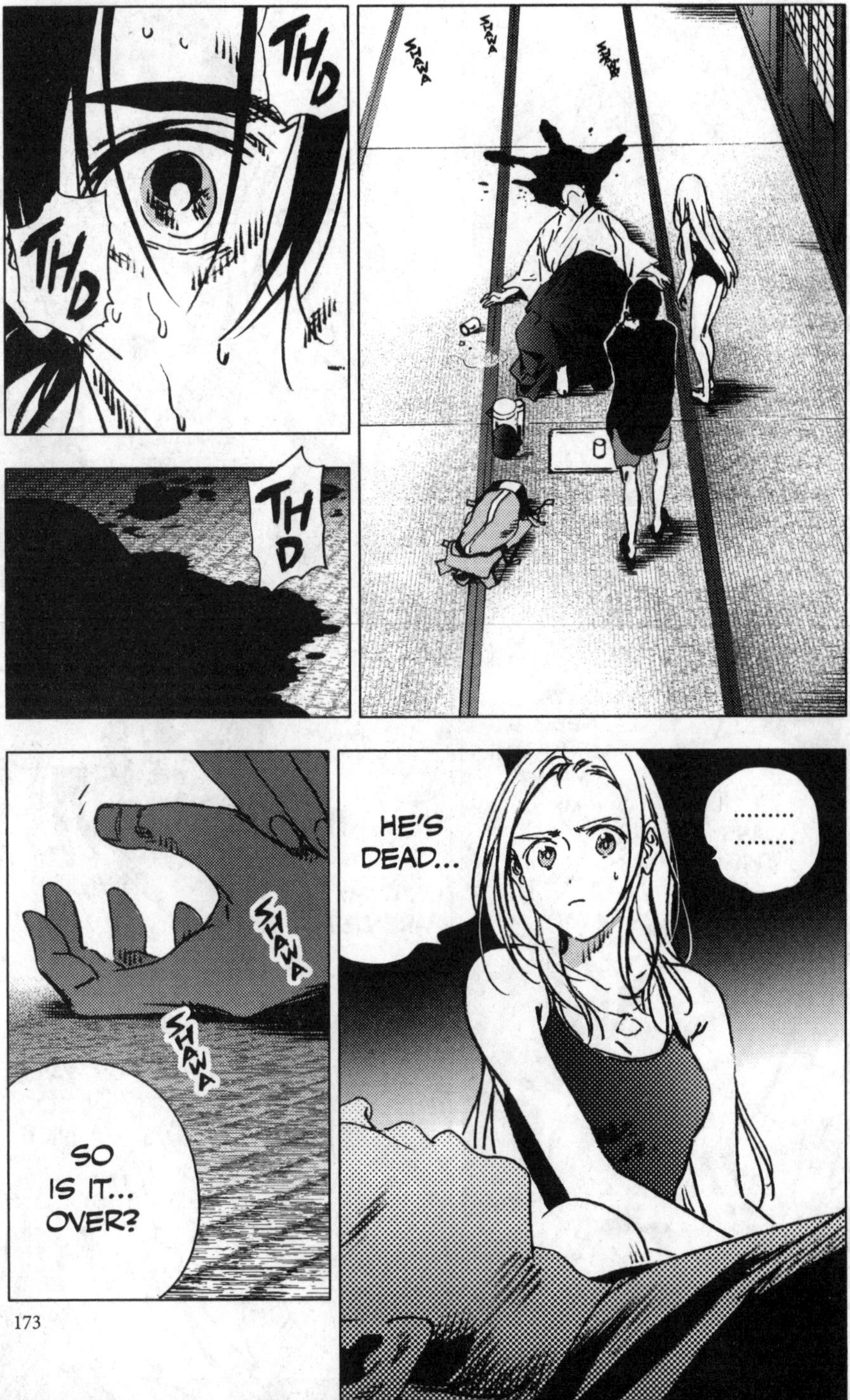

SHAWA
SHAWA
SHAWA
THD
THD
THD
HE'S DEAD...
....
....
SHAWA
SHAWA
SO IS IT... OVER?

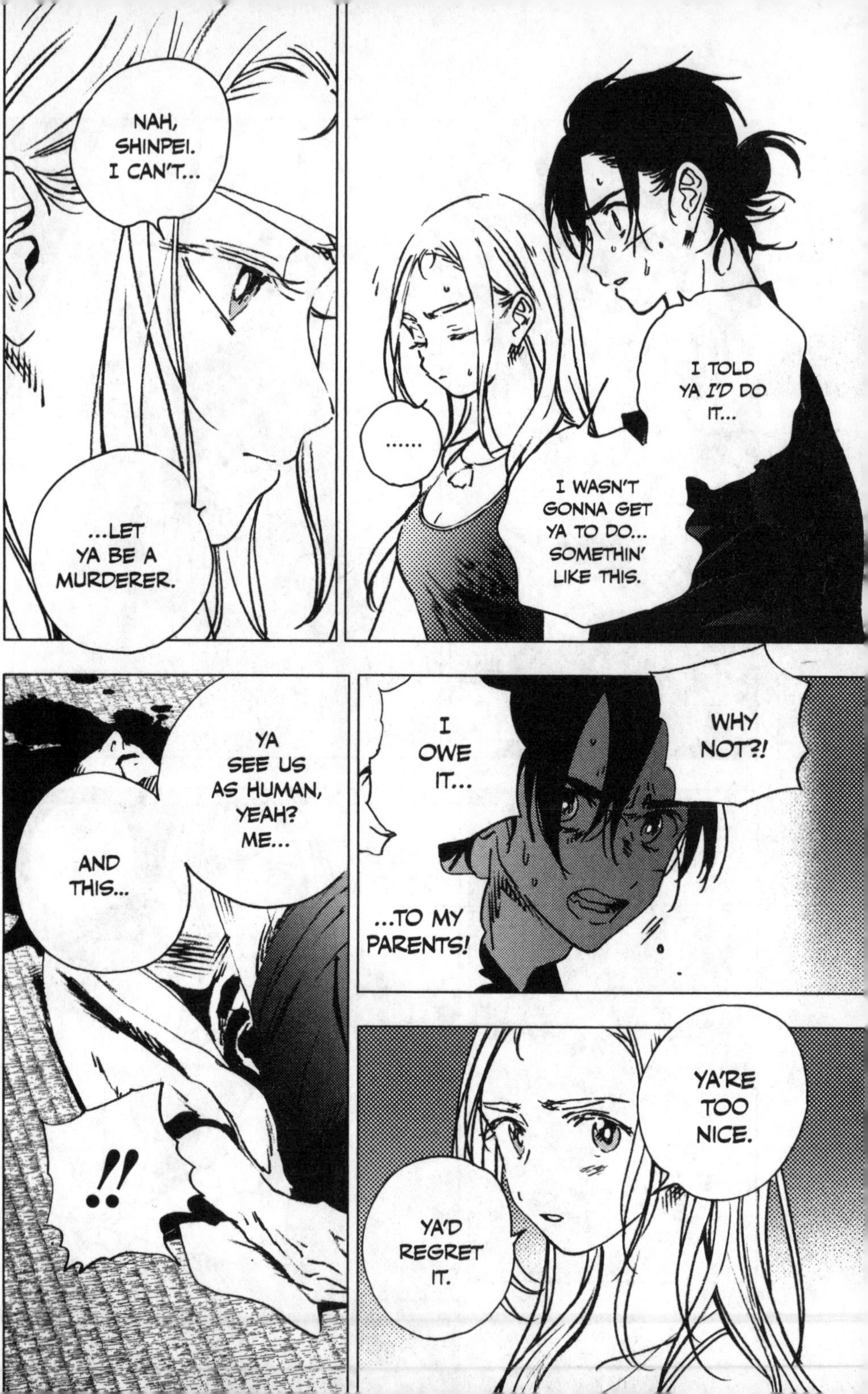
I TOLD YA *I'D* DO IT...
I WASN'T GONNA GET YA TO DO... SOMETHIN' LIKE THIS.
......
NAH, SHINPEI. I CAN'T...
...LET YA BE A MURDERER.
WHY NOT?!
I OWE IT...
...TO MY PARENTS!
YA'RE TOO NICE.
YA'D REGRET IT.
YA SEE US AS HUMAN, YEAH? ME...
AND THIS...
!!

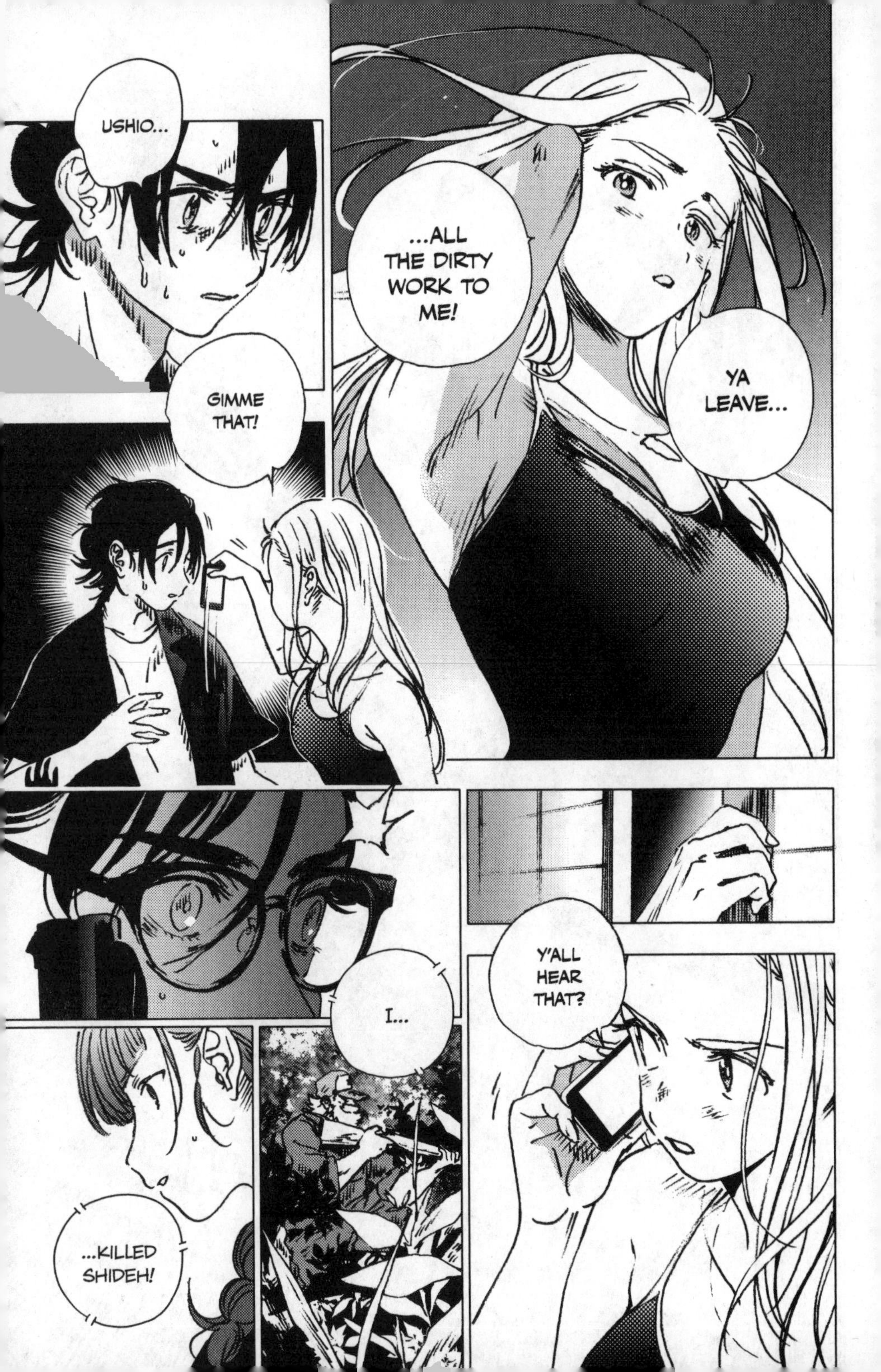
YA LEAVE...
...ALL THE DIRTY WORK TO ME!
USHIO...
GIMME THAT!
Y'ALL HEAR THAT?
I...
...KILLED SHIDEH!

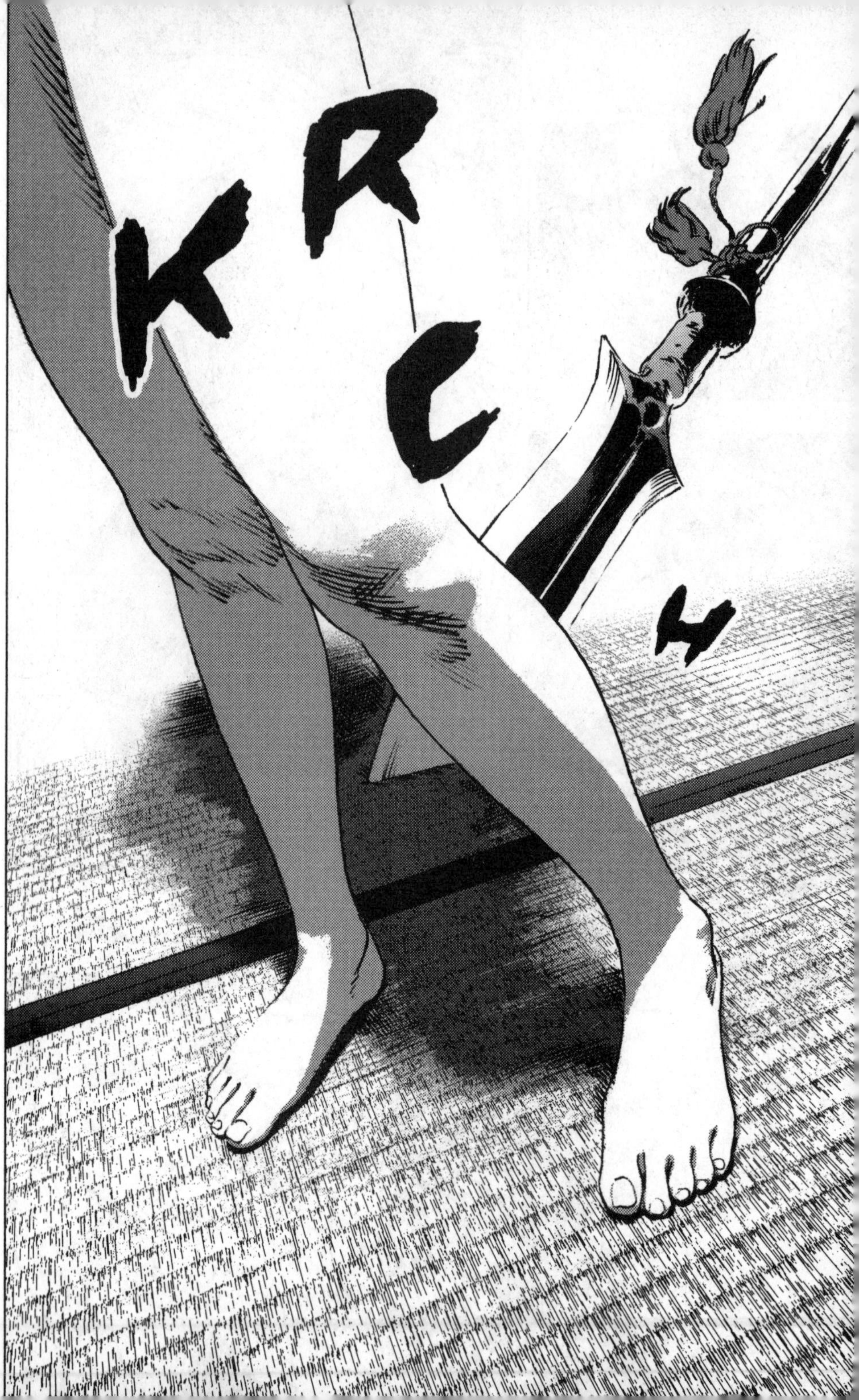
KRCH

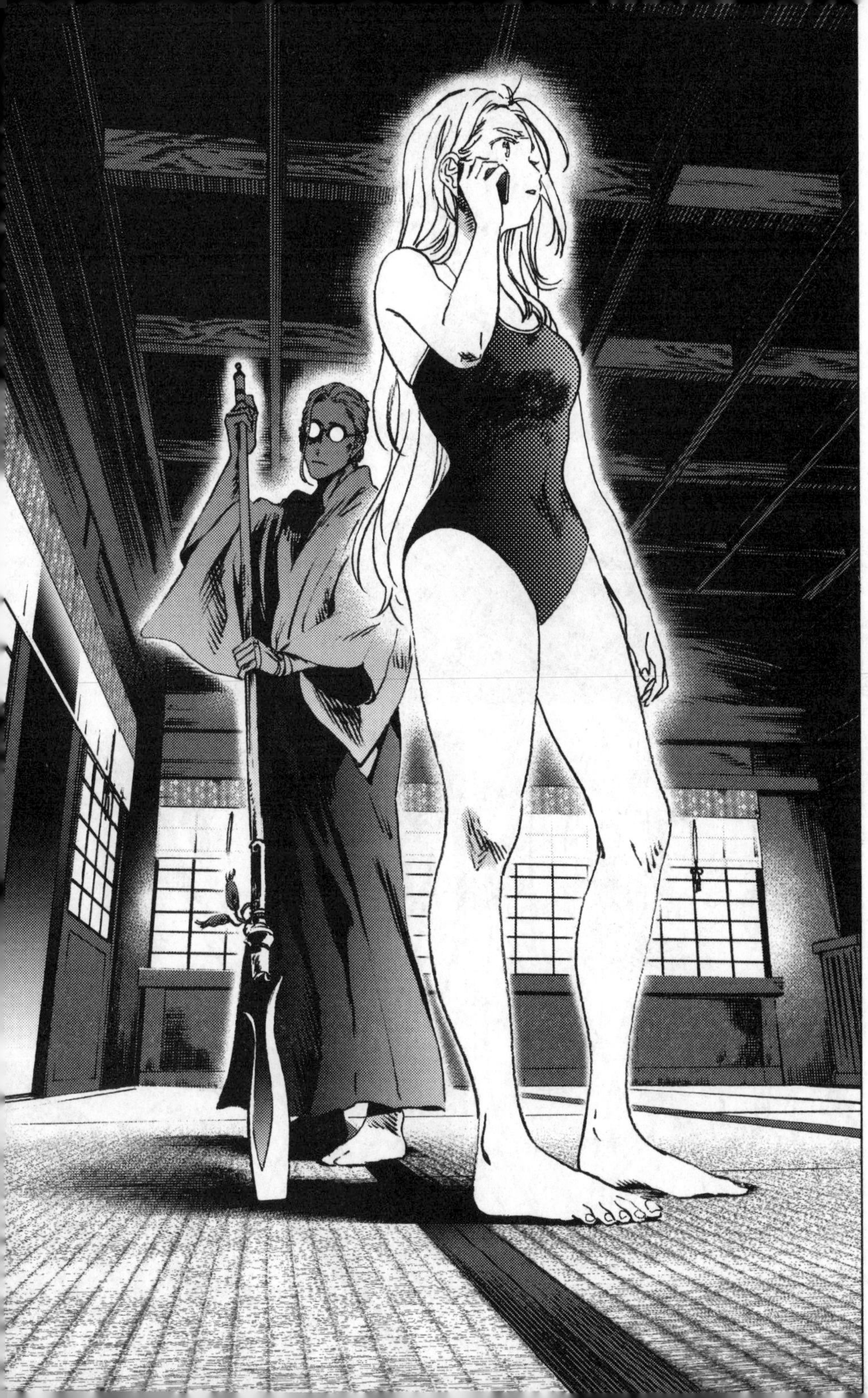

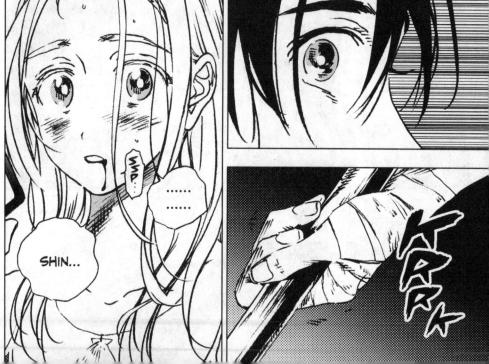

......
......

WHO...

SHIN...

KRRK

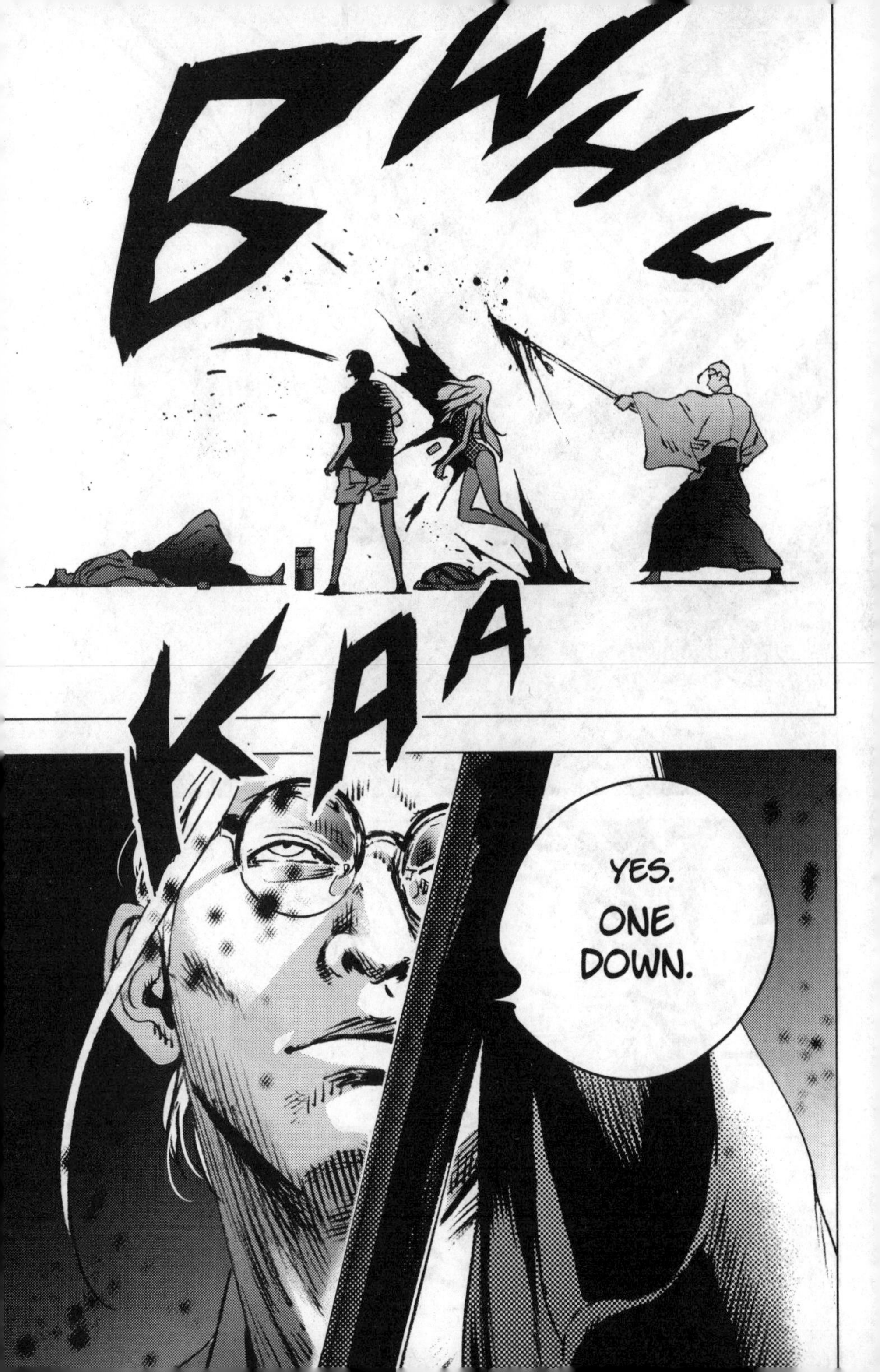
BWHU
KAA
YES. ONE DOWN.

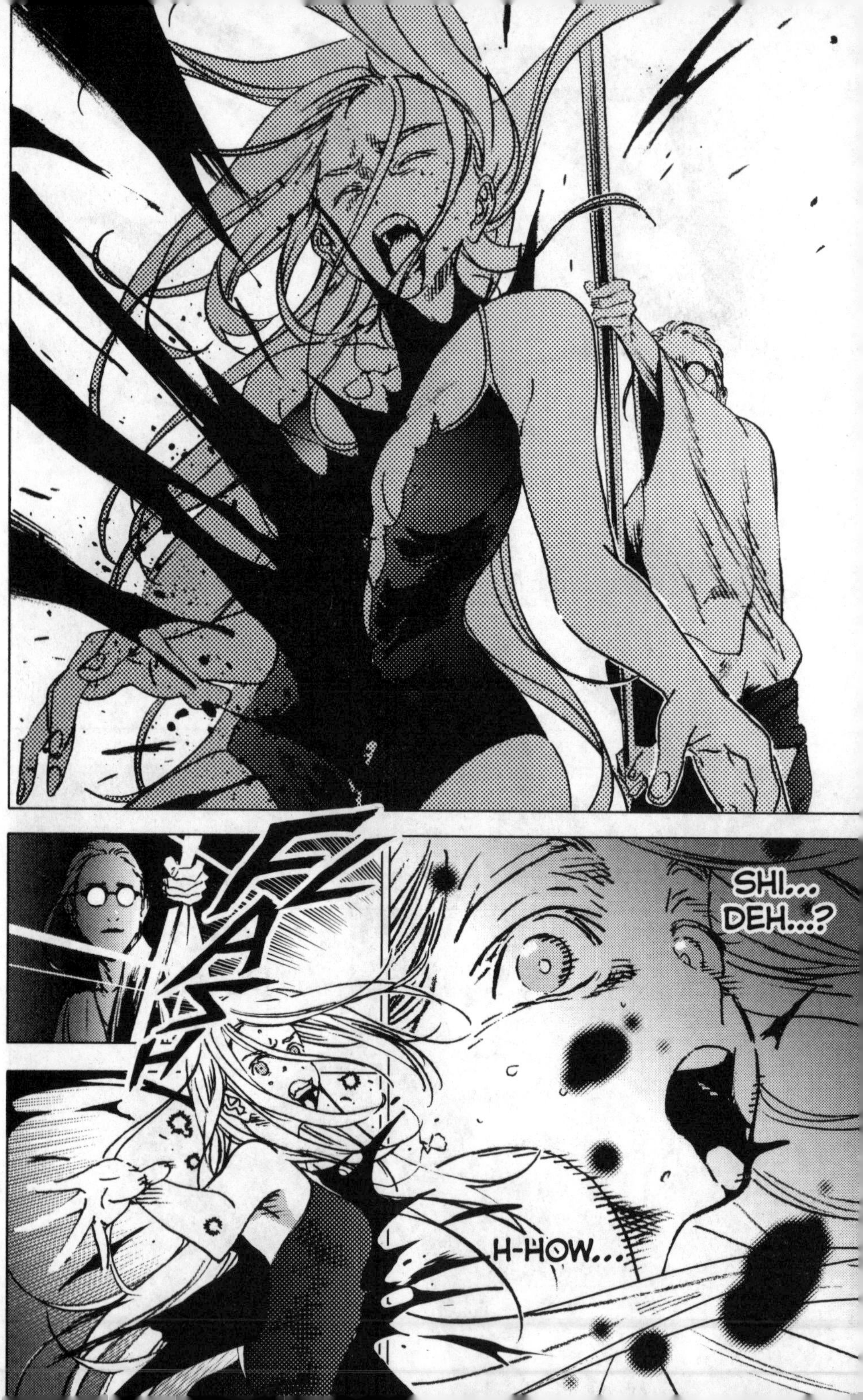
SHI... DEH...?
H-HOW...

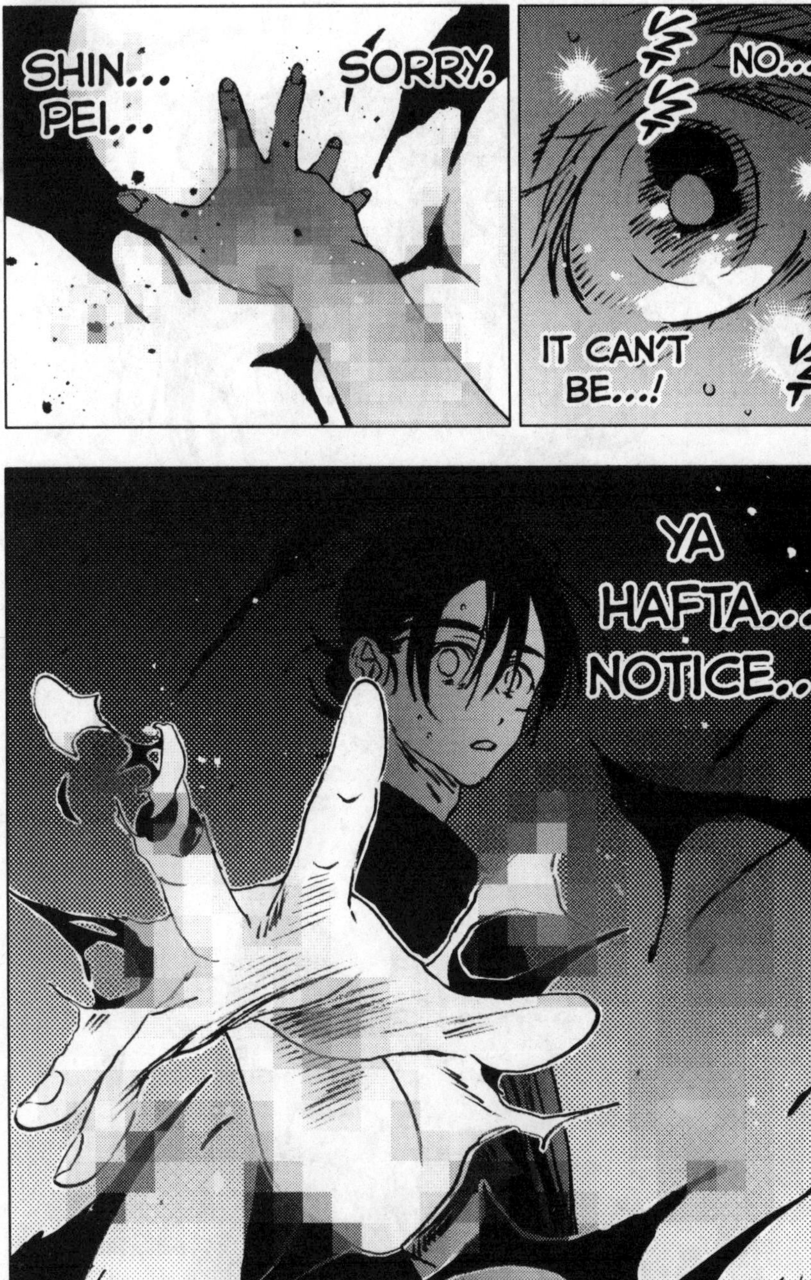
NO...
IT CAN'T BE...!
SORRY.
SHIN... PEI...
YA HAFTA... NOTICE...

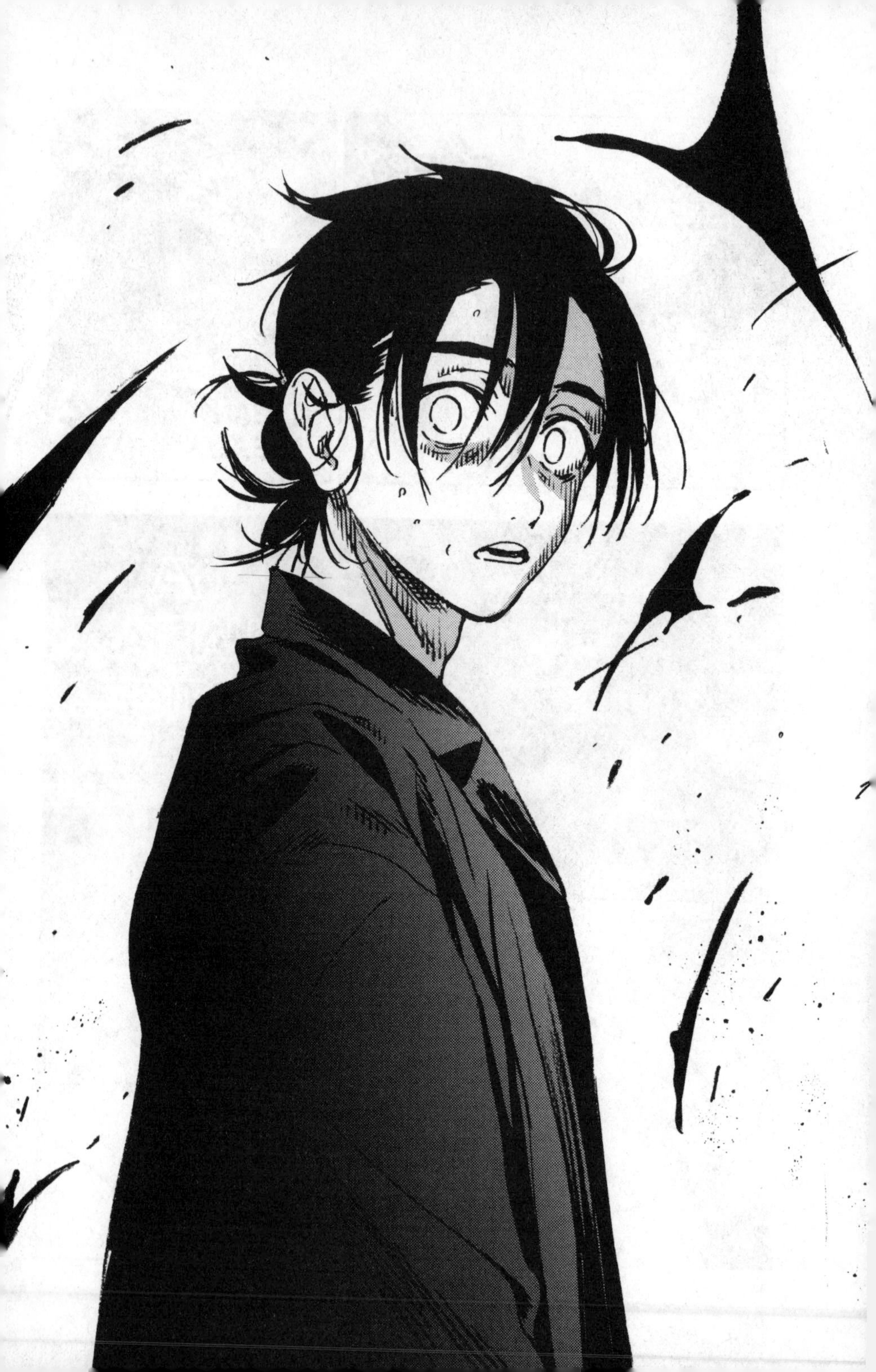

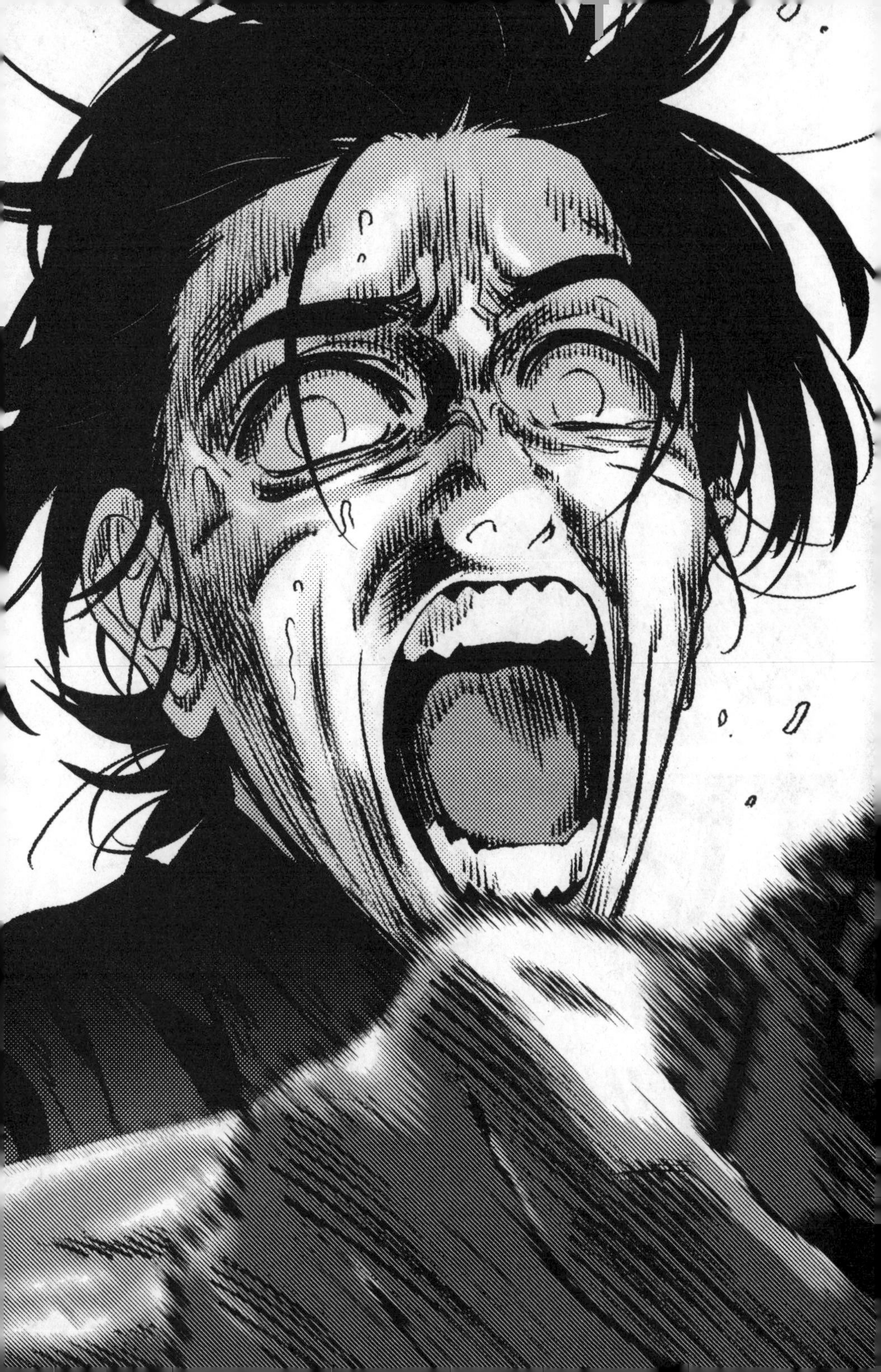

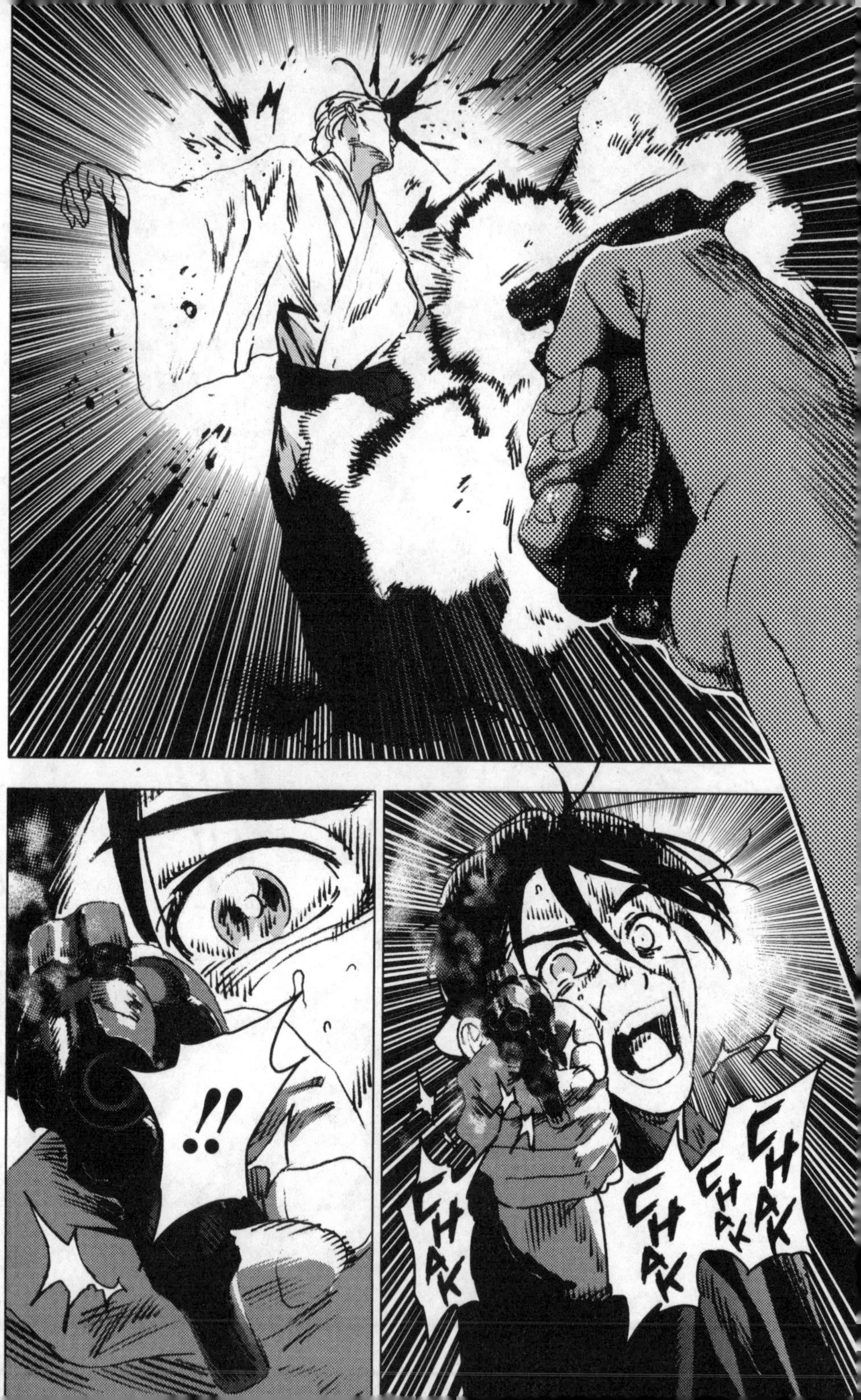
CHAK
CHAK
CHAK
CHAK
!!

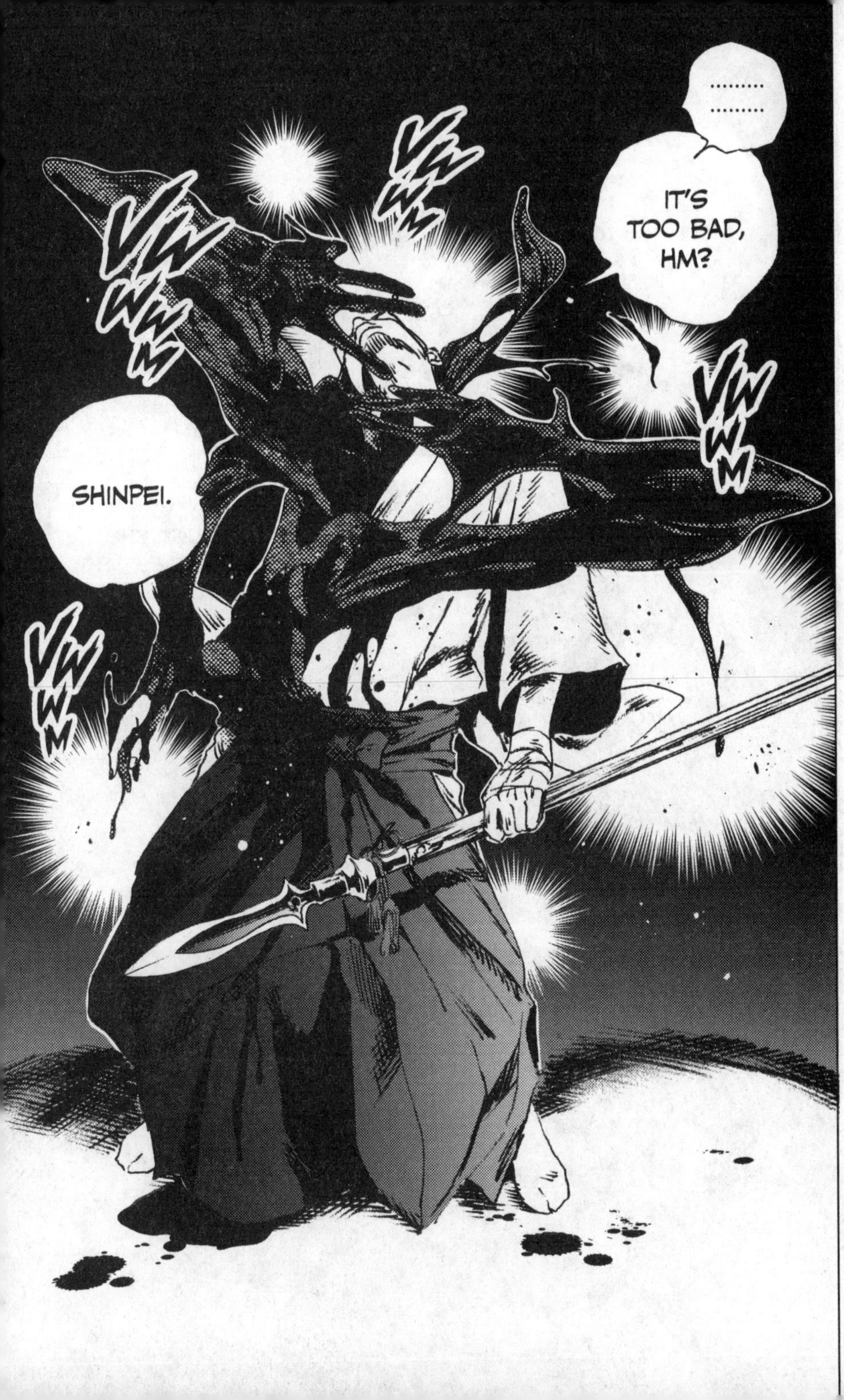
....
....
IT'S TOO BAD, HM?
SHINPEI.

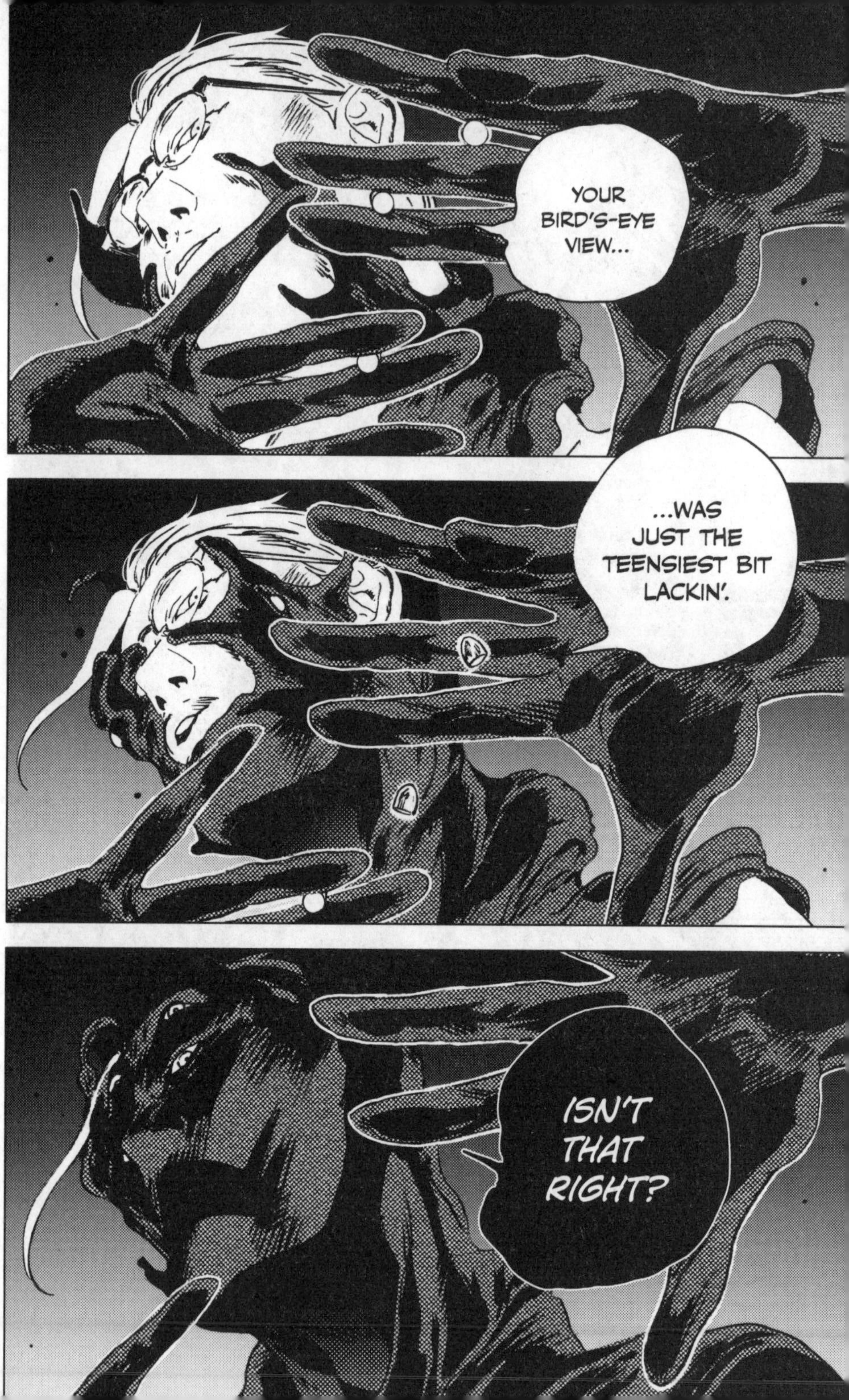
YOUR BIRD'S-EYE VIEW...
...WAS JUST THE TEENSIEST BIT LACKIN'.
ISN'T THAT RIGHT?

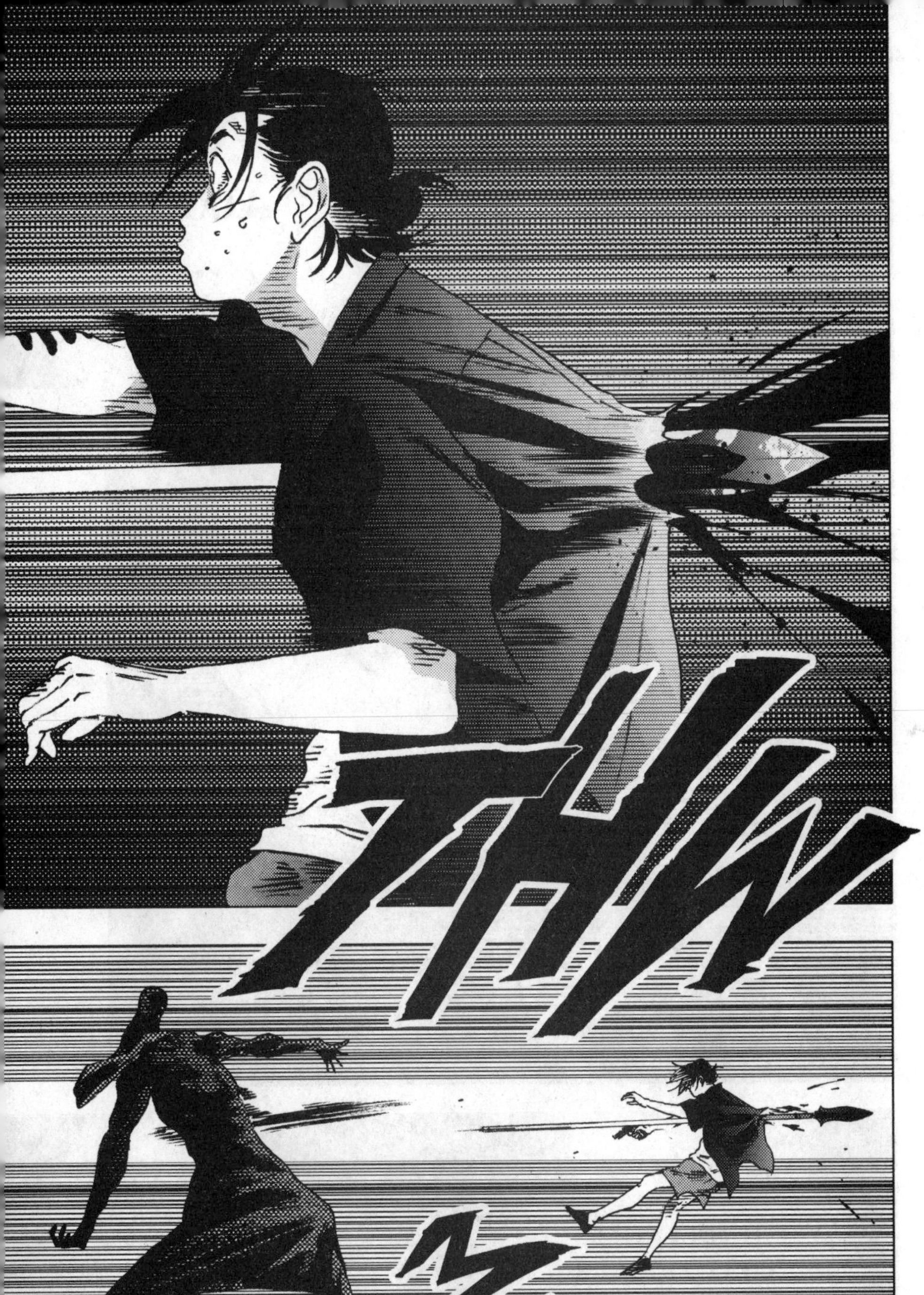
THWMP

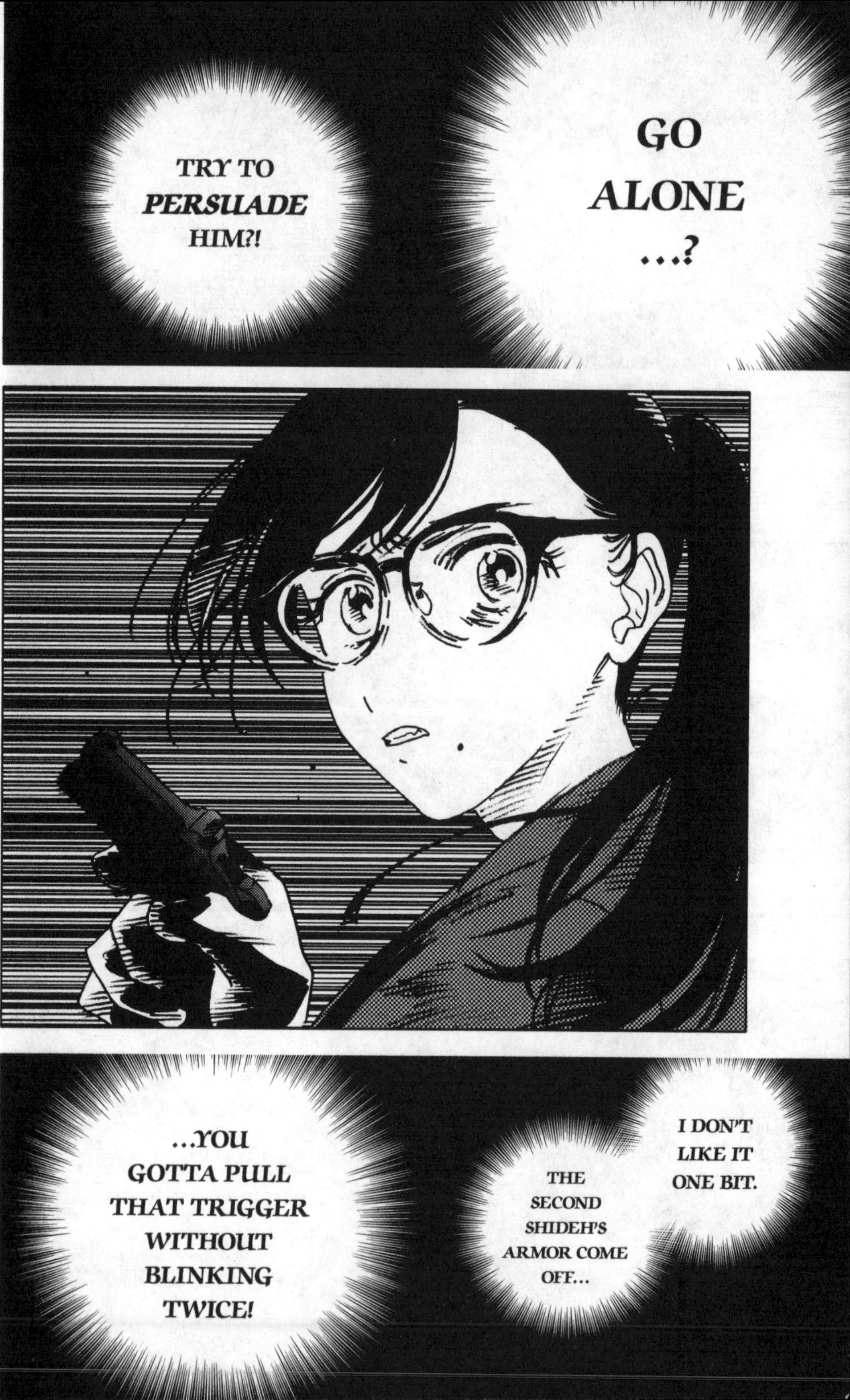
GO ALONE ...?
TRY TO PERSUADE HIM?!
I DON'T LIKE IT ONE BIT.
THE SECOND SHIDEH'S ARMOR COME OFF...
...YOU GOTTA PULL THAT TRIGGER WITHOUT BLINKING TWICE!

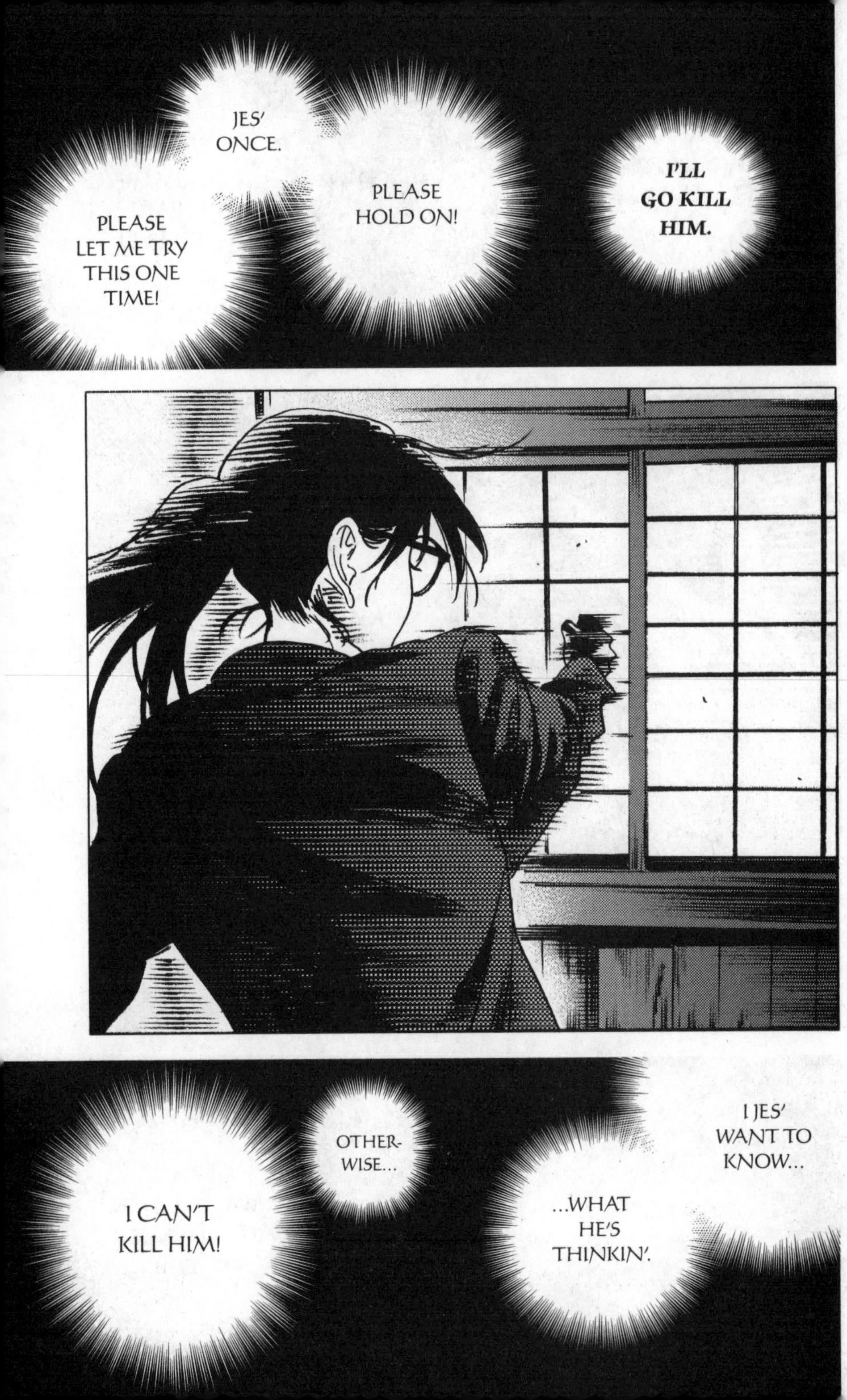
I'LL GO KILL HIM.
PLEASE HOLD ON!
JES' ONCE.
PLEASE LET ME TRY THIS ONE TIME!
I JES' WANT TO KNOW...
...WHAT HE'S THINKIN'.
OTHER-WISE...
I CAN'T KILL HIM!

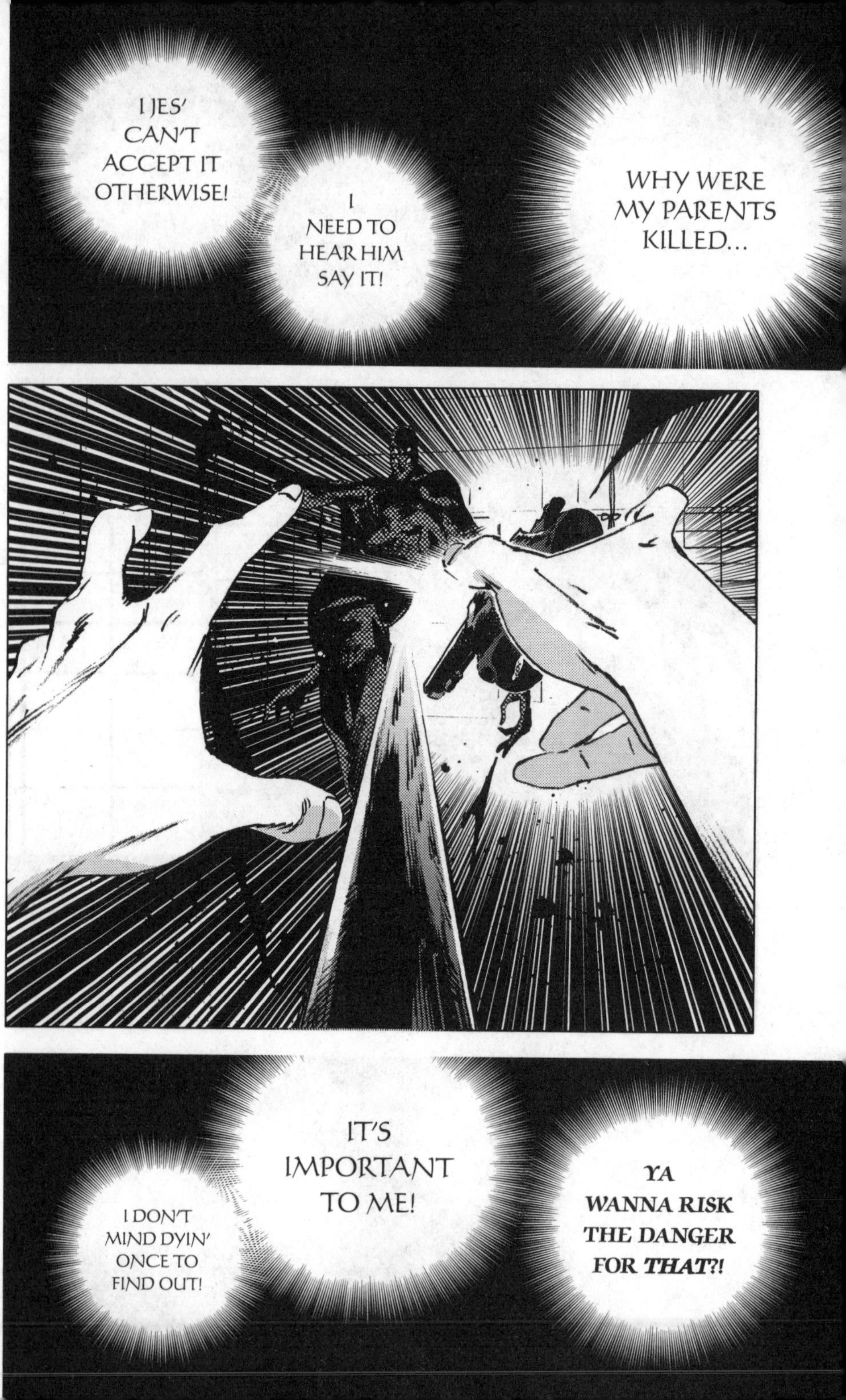
WHY WERE MY PARENTS KILLED…
I NEED TO HEAR HIM SAY IT!
I JES' CAN'T ACCEPT IT OTHERWISE!
YA WANNA RISK THE DANGER FOR *THAT*?!
IT'S IMPORTANT TO ME!
I DON'T MIND DYIN' ONCE TO FIND OUT!

I'M COMIN' WITH YA!
...!!
YA CAN'T SENSE SHADOWS, SHINPEI.
IF THE SHRINE'S CRAWLIN' WITH 'EM, YA AIN'T DOIN' ANY TALKIN' AT ALL!
USHIO'S RIGHT.
IF YOU GO IN ALONE, WE RUN THE RISK OF THEM SWITCHING THEIR PLAN TO CAPTURE YOU.
SHIDEH'S ALSO DOING A PSEUDO-LOOP. HE WON'T LET YOU COMMIT SUICIDE AGAIN.

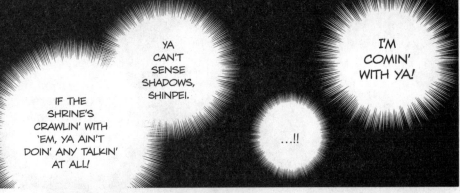

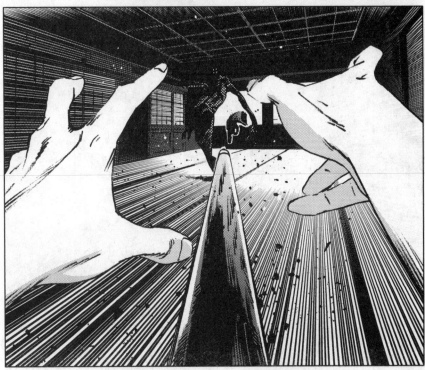

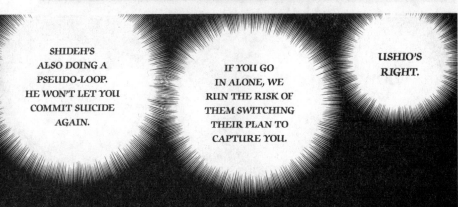

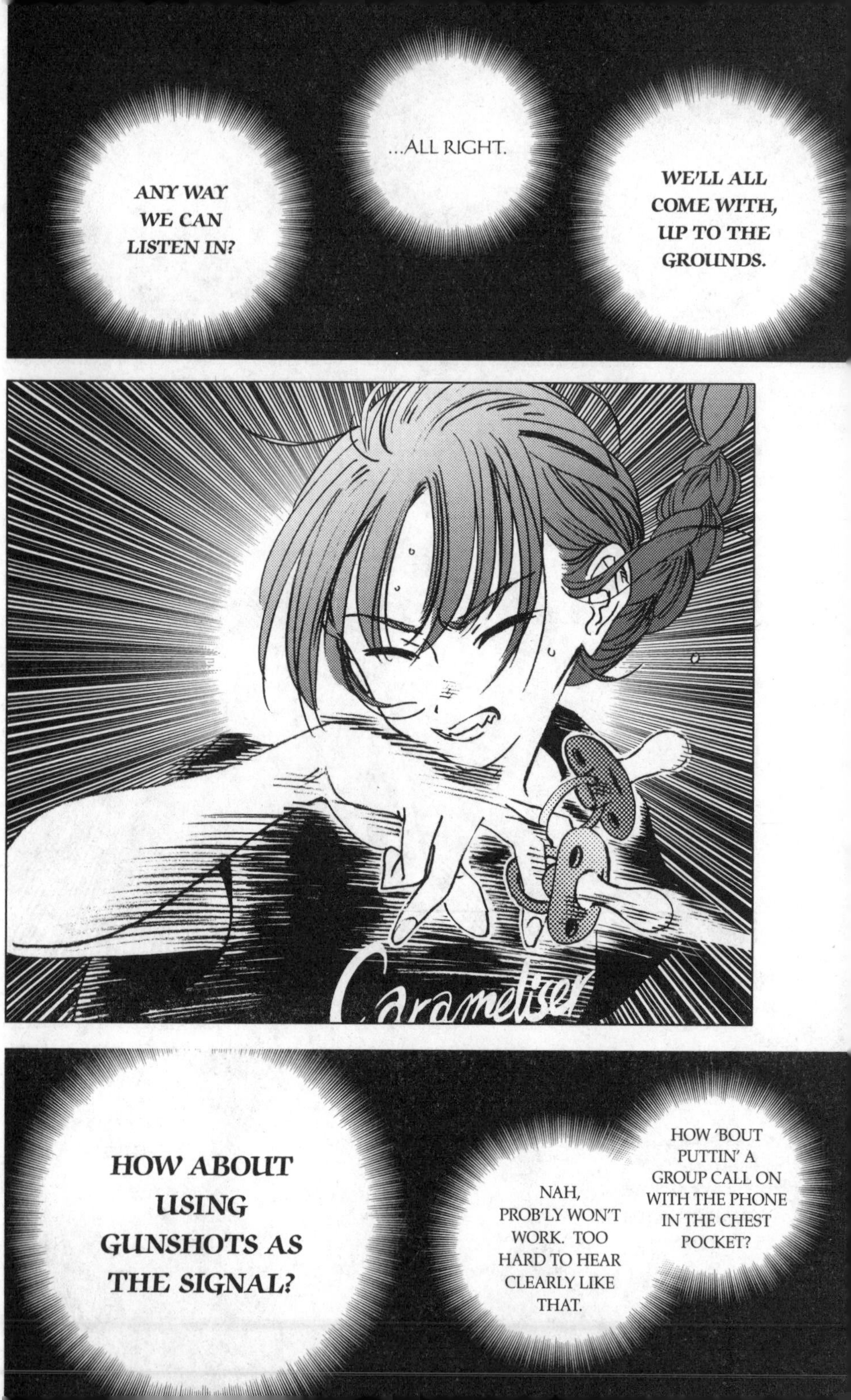
WE'LL ALL COME WITH, UP TO THE GROUNDS.
...ALL RIGHT.
ANY WAY WE CAN LISTEN IN?
Caramelise
HOW 'BOUT PUTTIN' A GROUP CALL ON WITH THE PHONE IN THE CHEST POCKET?
NAH, PROB'LY WON'T WORK. TOO HARD TO HEAR CLEARLY LIKE THAT.
HOW ABOUT USING GUNSHOTS AS THE SIGNAL?

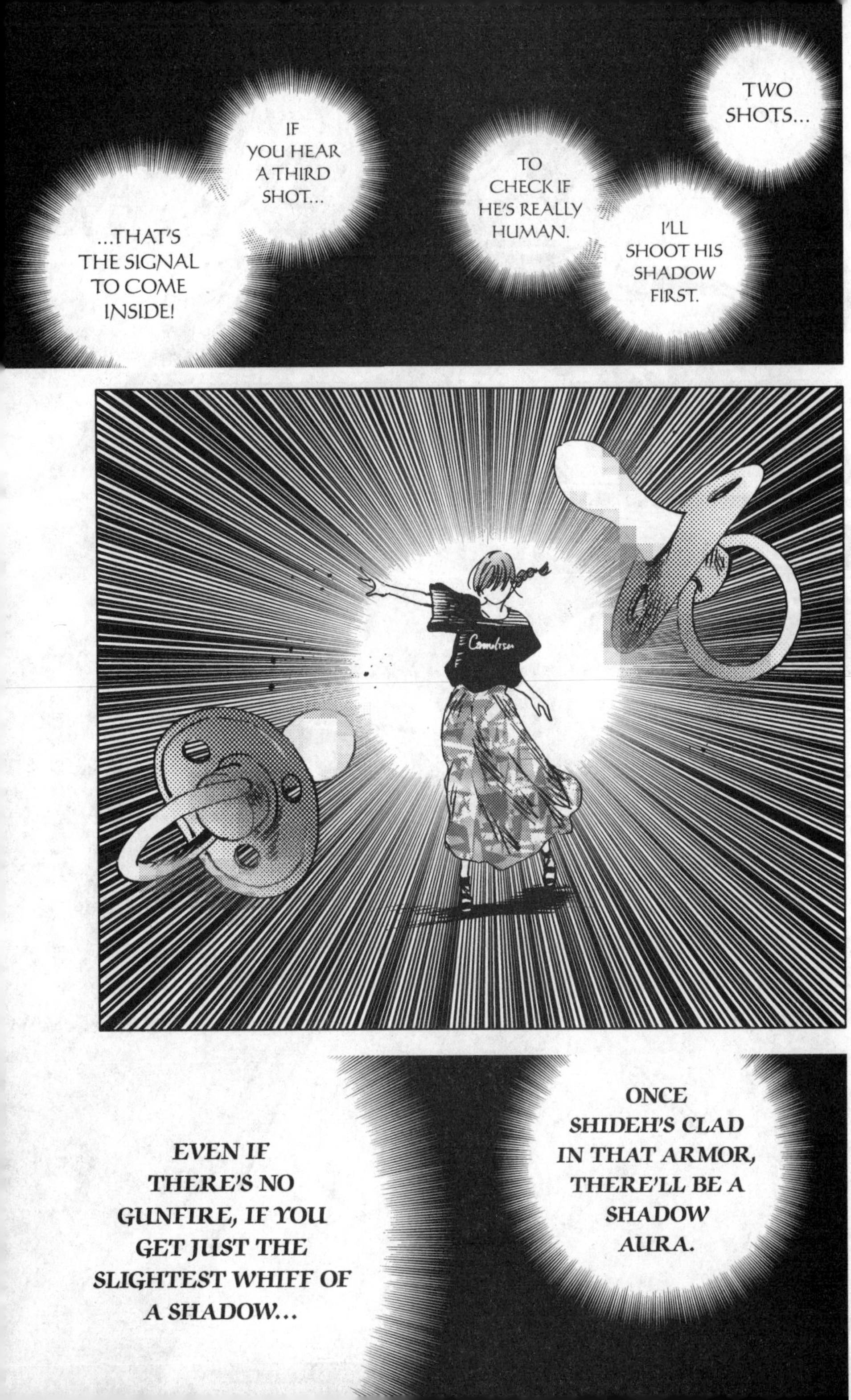
TWO SHOTS...
I'LL SHOOT HIS SHADOW FIRST.
TO CHECK IF HE'S REALLY HUMAN.
IF YOU HEAR A THIRD SHOT...
...THAT'S THE SIGNAL TO COME INSIDE!
ONCE SHIDEH'S CLAD IN THAT ARMOR, THERE'LL BE A SHADOW AURA.
EVEN IF THERE'S NO GUNFIRE, IF YOU GET JUST THE SLIGHTEST WHIFF OF A SHADOW...

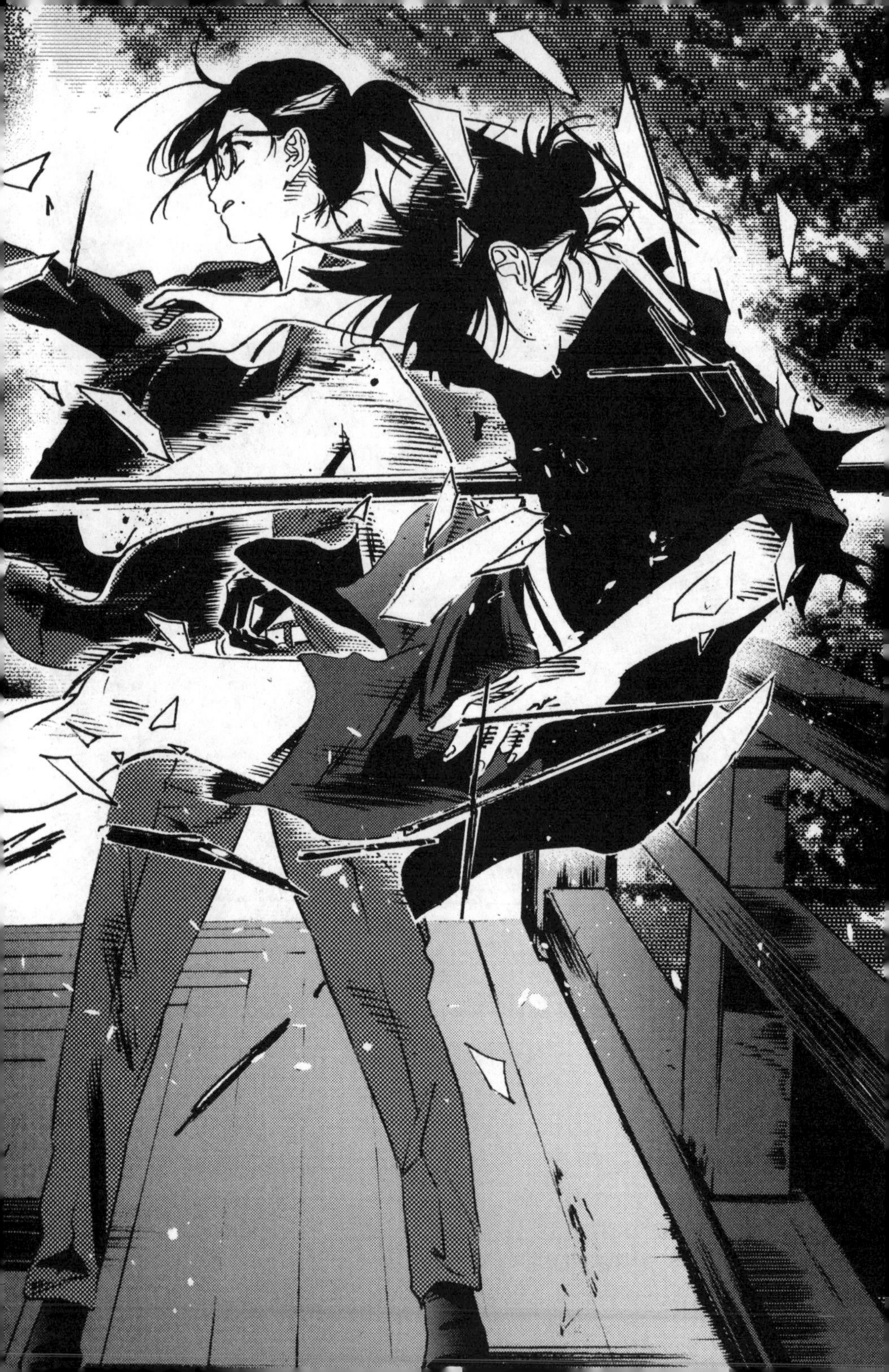

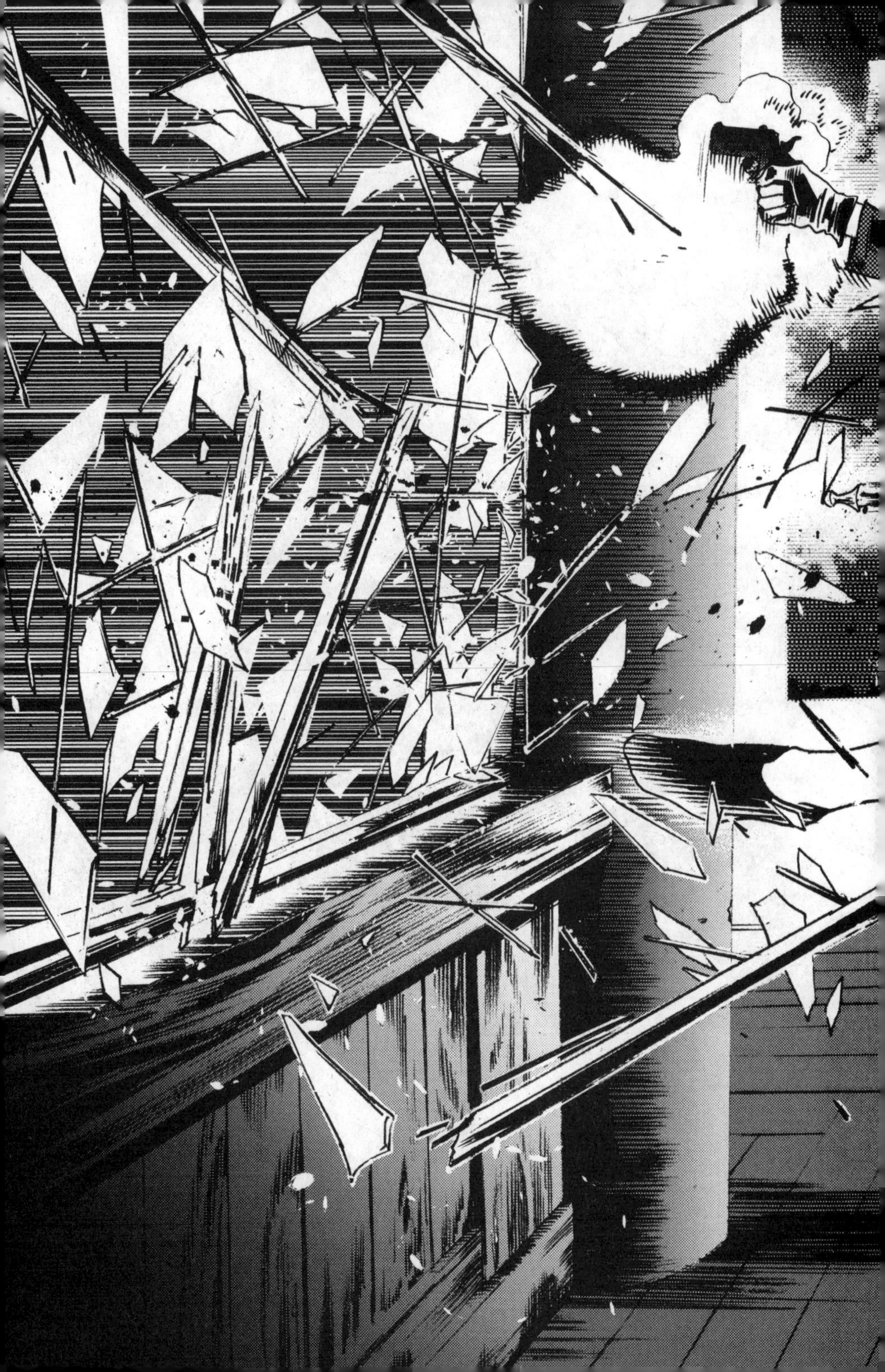

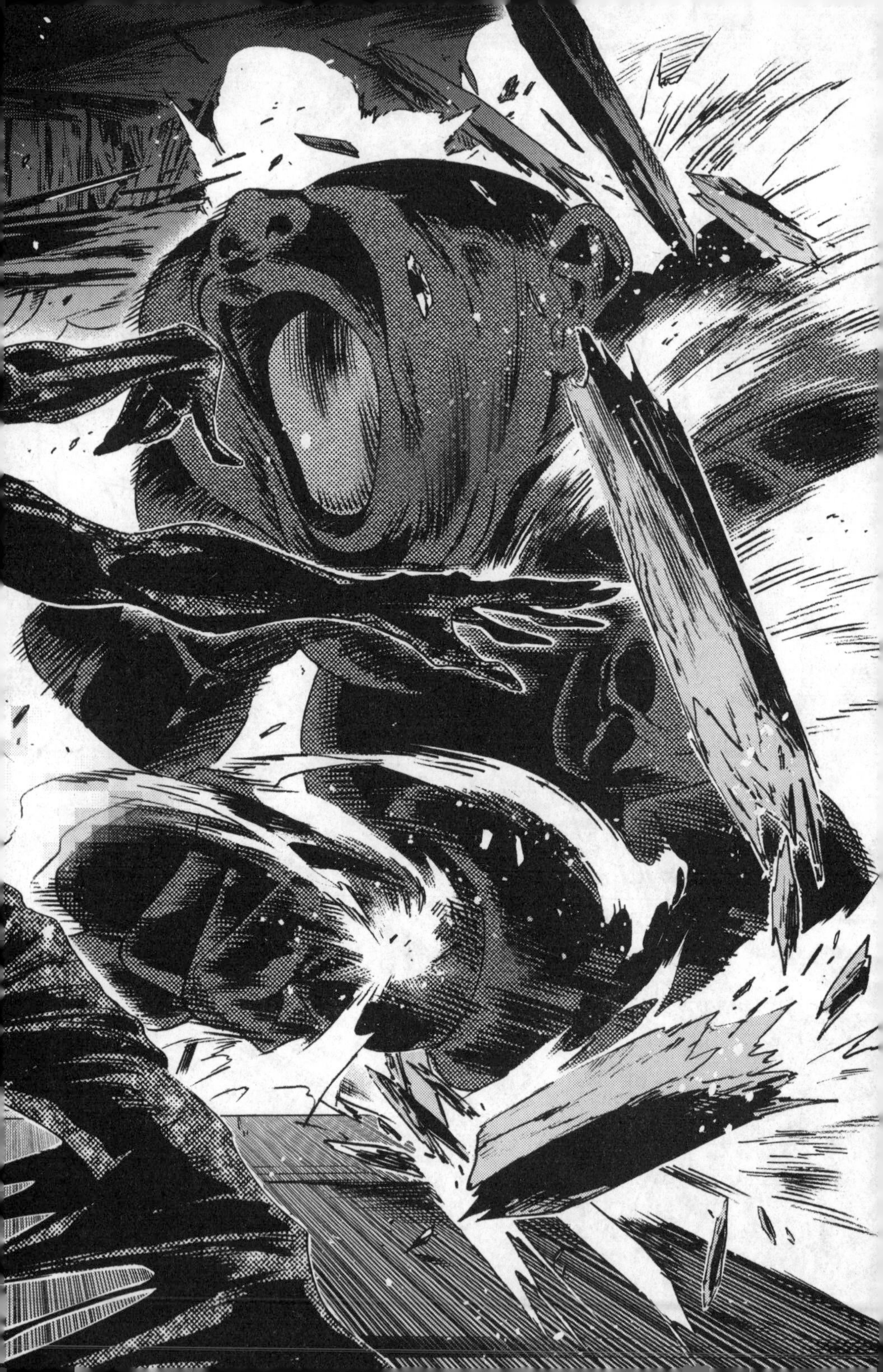

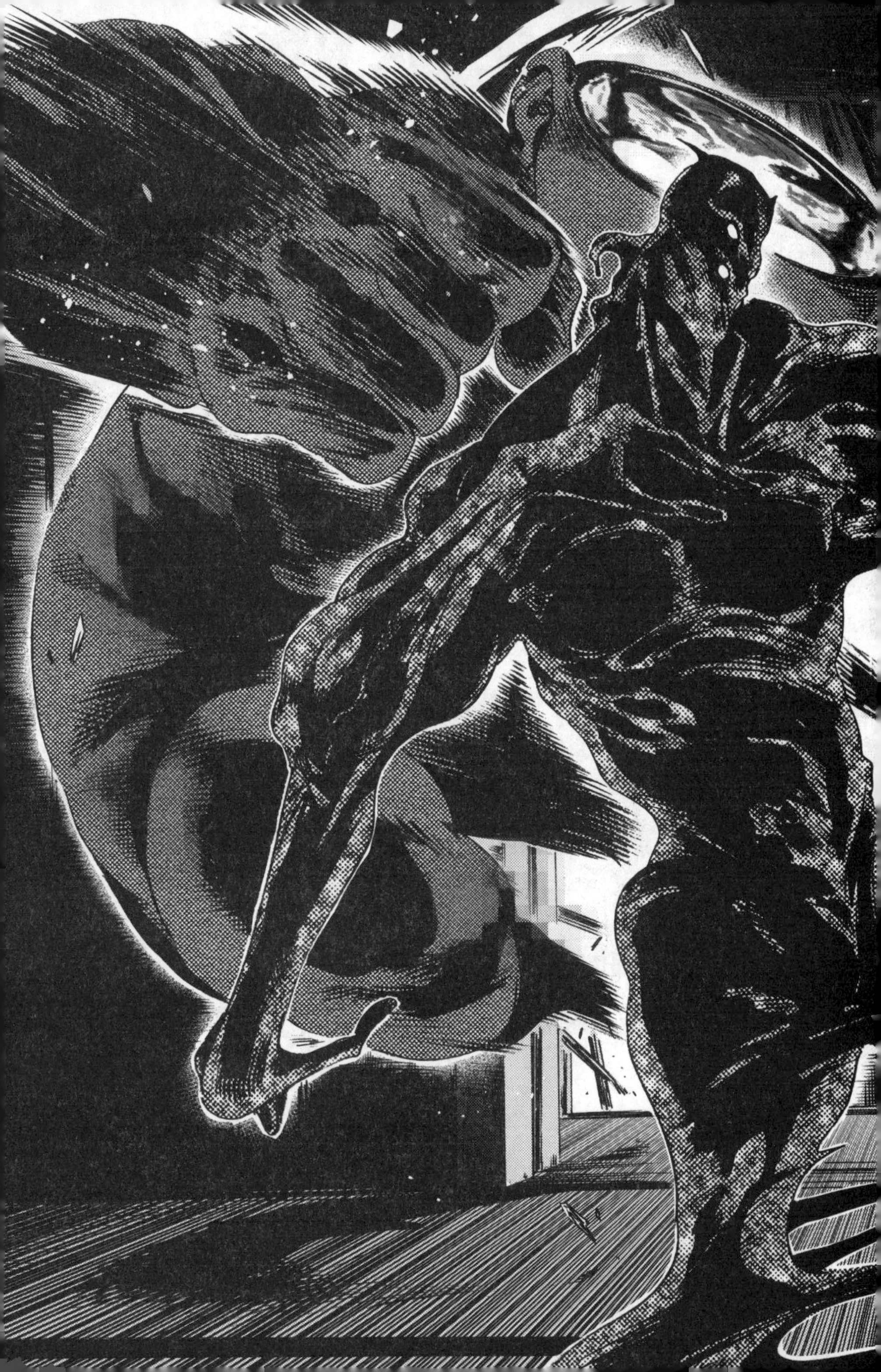

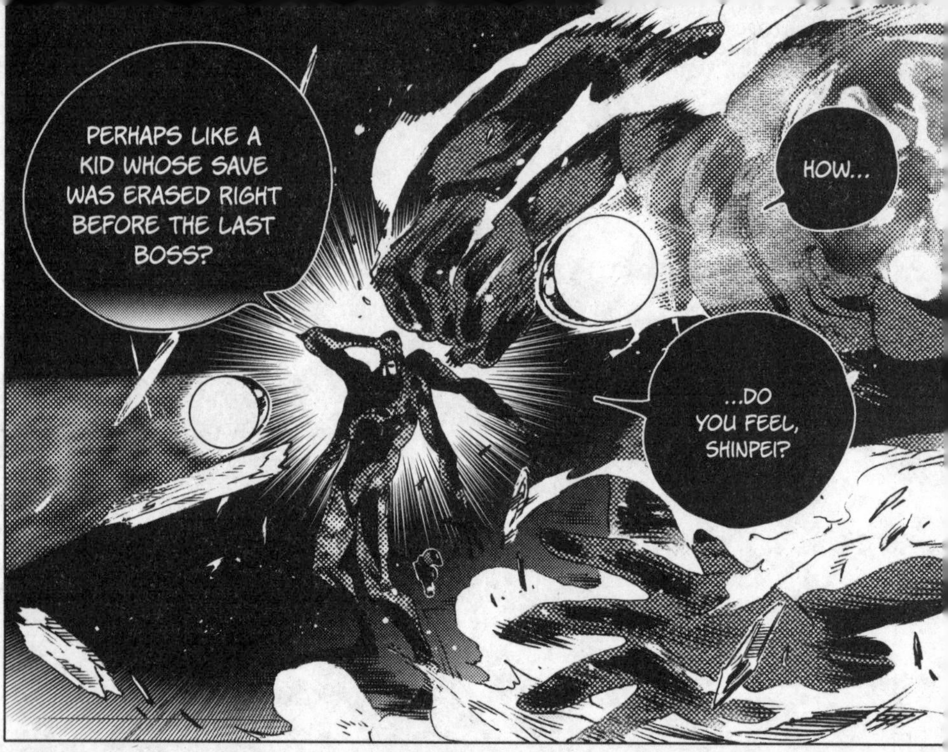
HOW...
...DO YOU FEEL, SHINPEI?
PERHAPS LIKE A KID WHOSE SAVE WAS ERASED RIGHT BEFORE THE LAST BOSS?
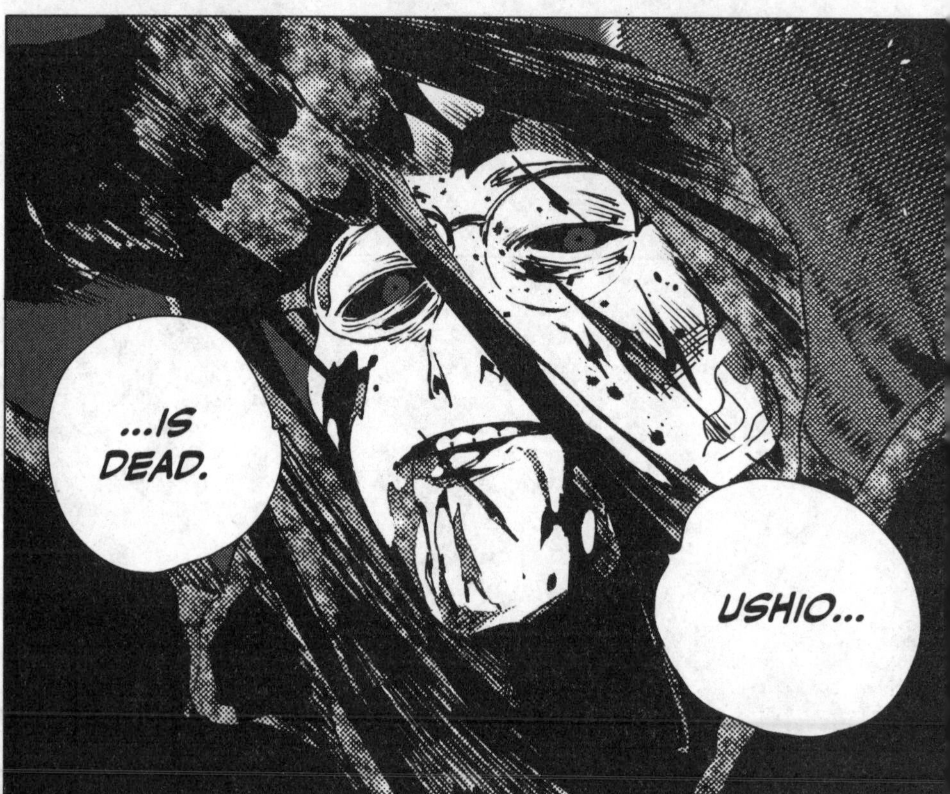
USHIO...
...IS DEAD.

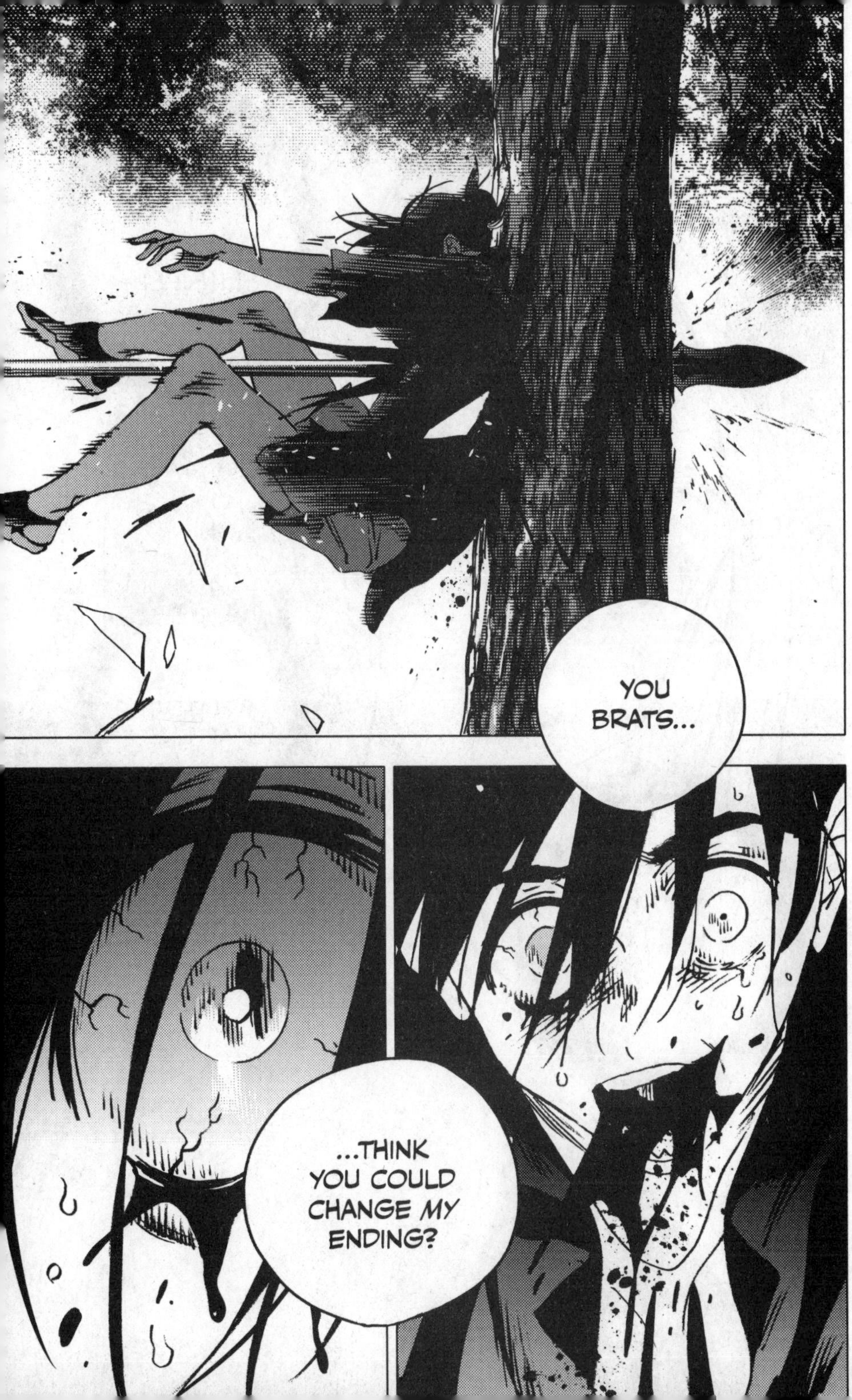
YOU BRATS...
...THINK YOU COULD CHANGE MY ENDING?

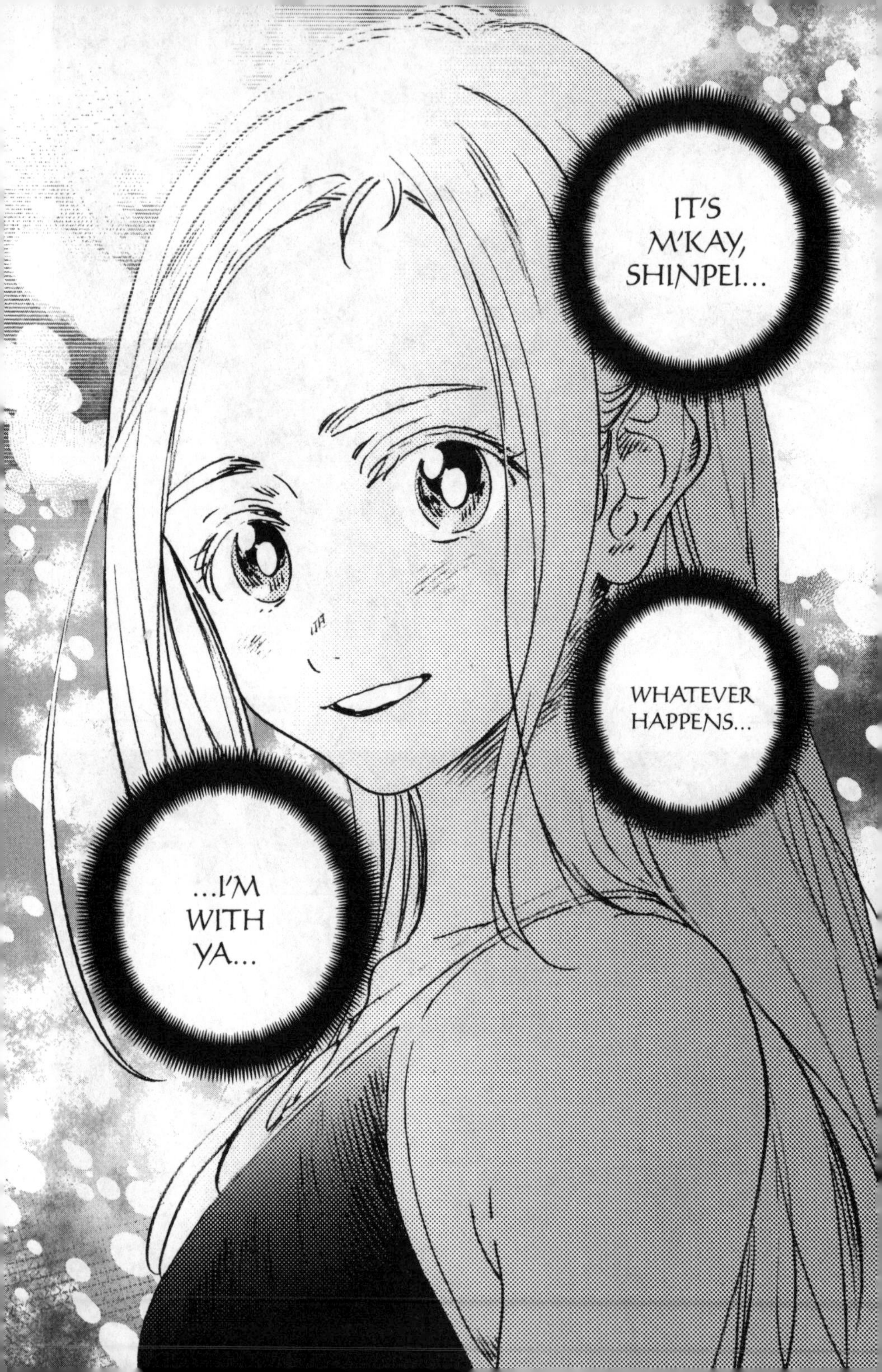
IT'S M'KAY, SHINPEI...
WHATEVER HAPPENS...
...I'M WITH YA...

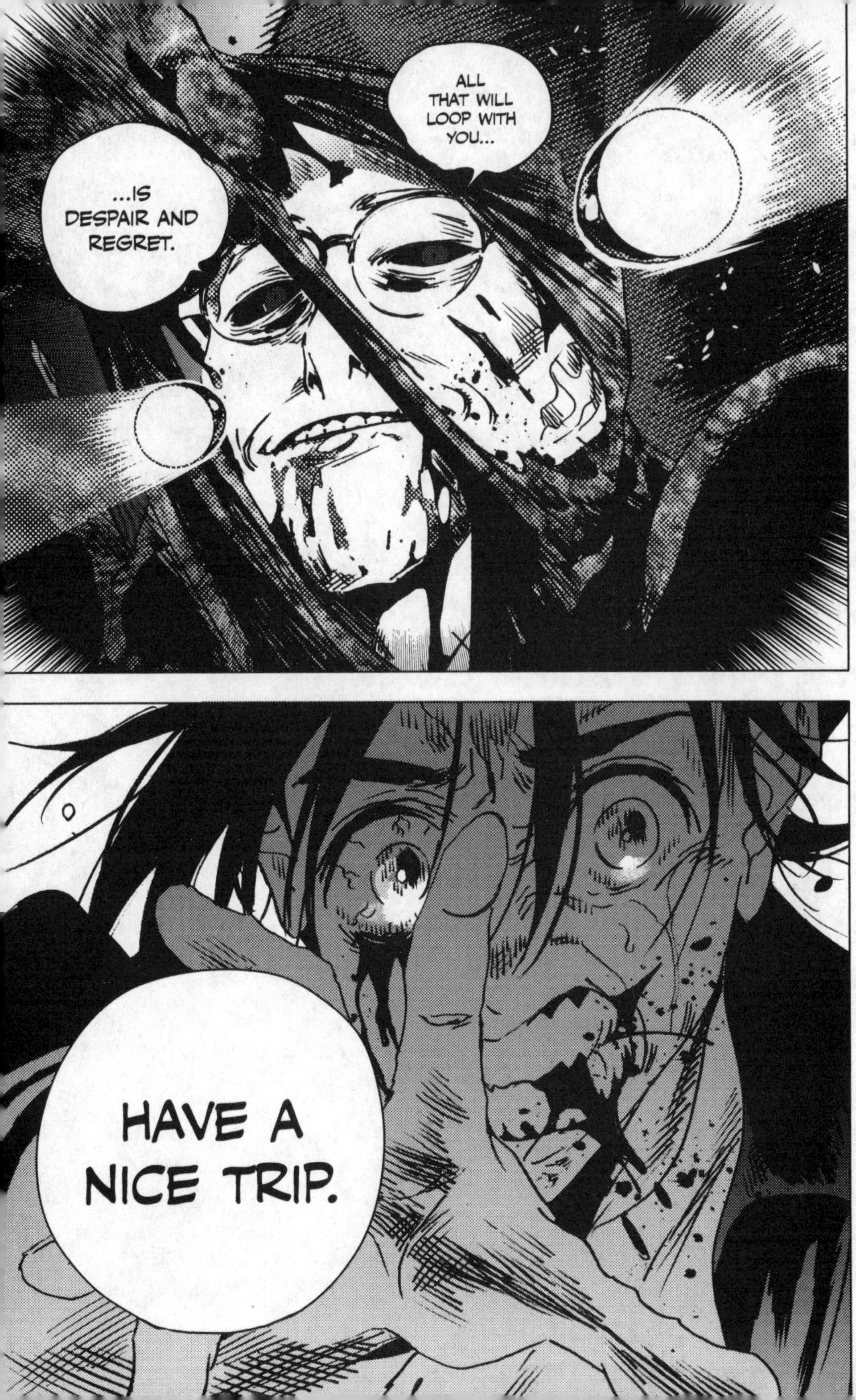
ALL THAT WILL LOOP WITH YOU...
...IS DESPAIR AND REGRET.
HAVE A NICE TRIP.

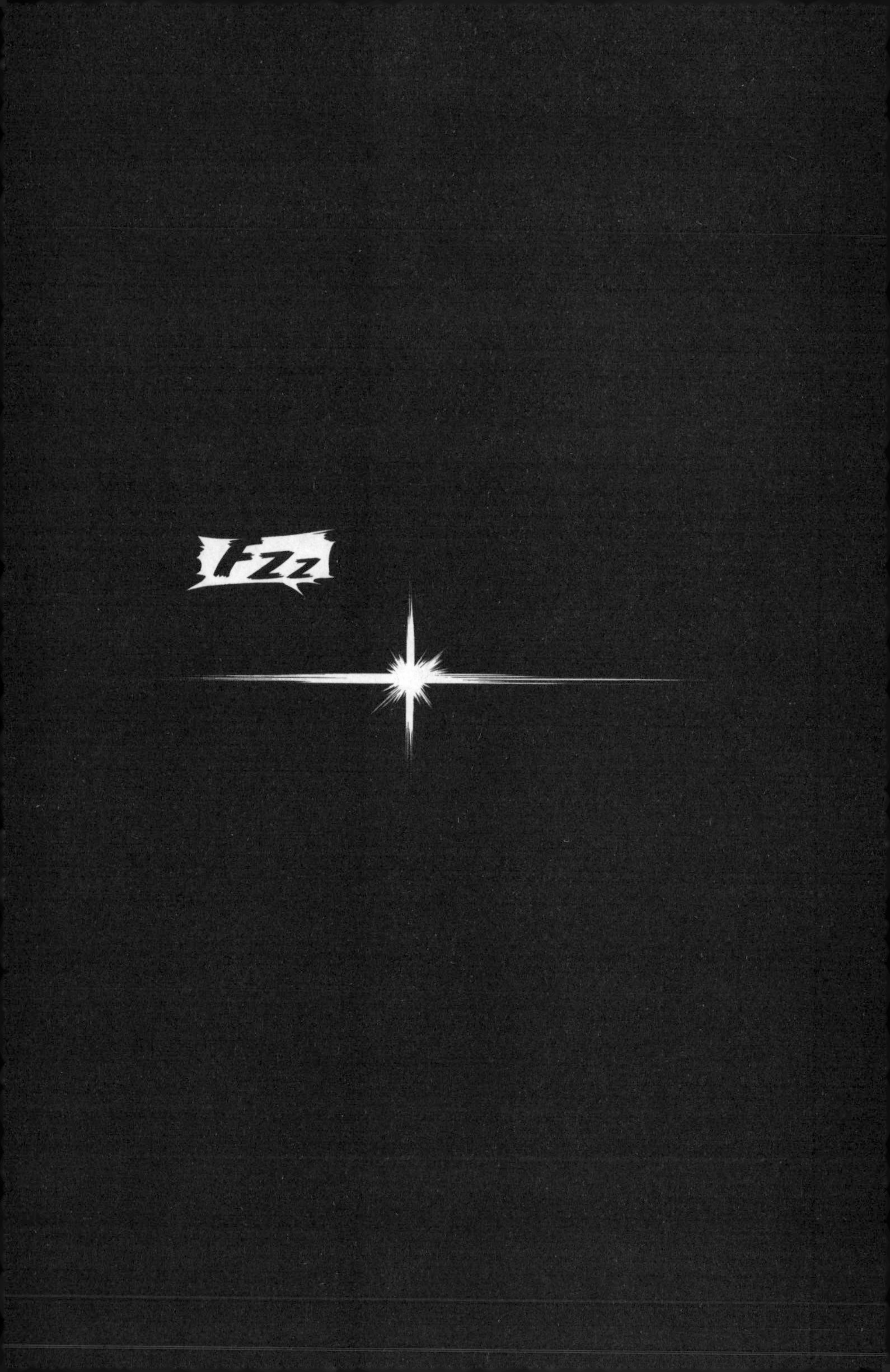
FZz

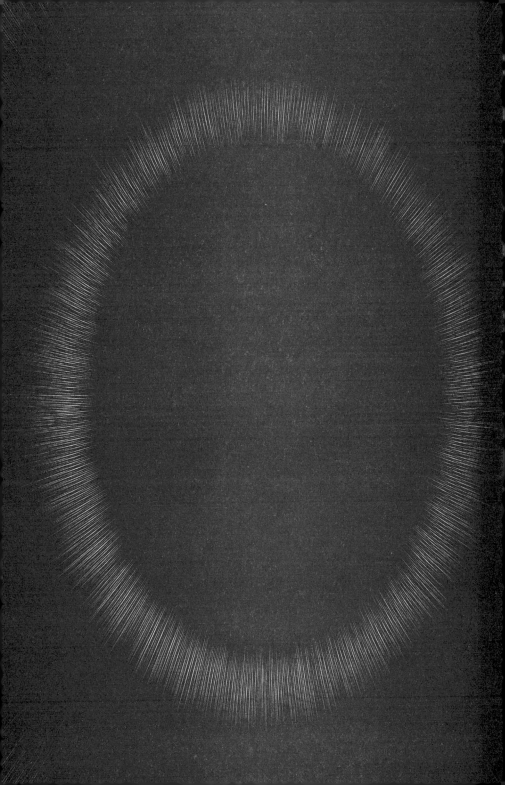

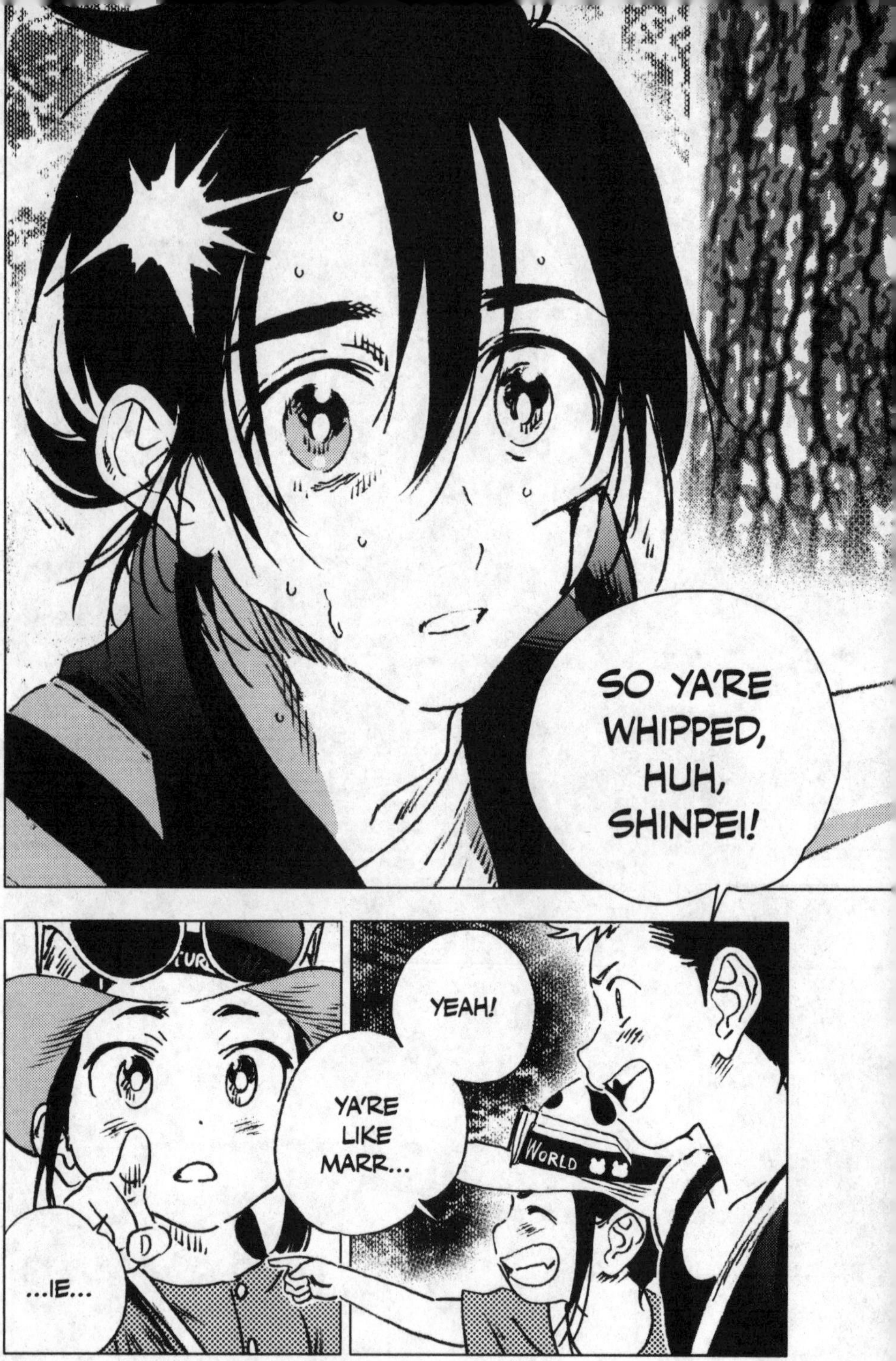
SO YA'RE WHIPPED, HUH, SHINPEI!
YEAH!
YA'RE LIKE MARR...
...IE...

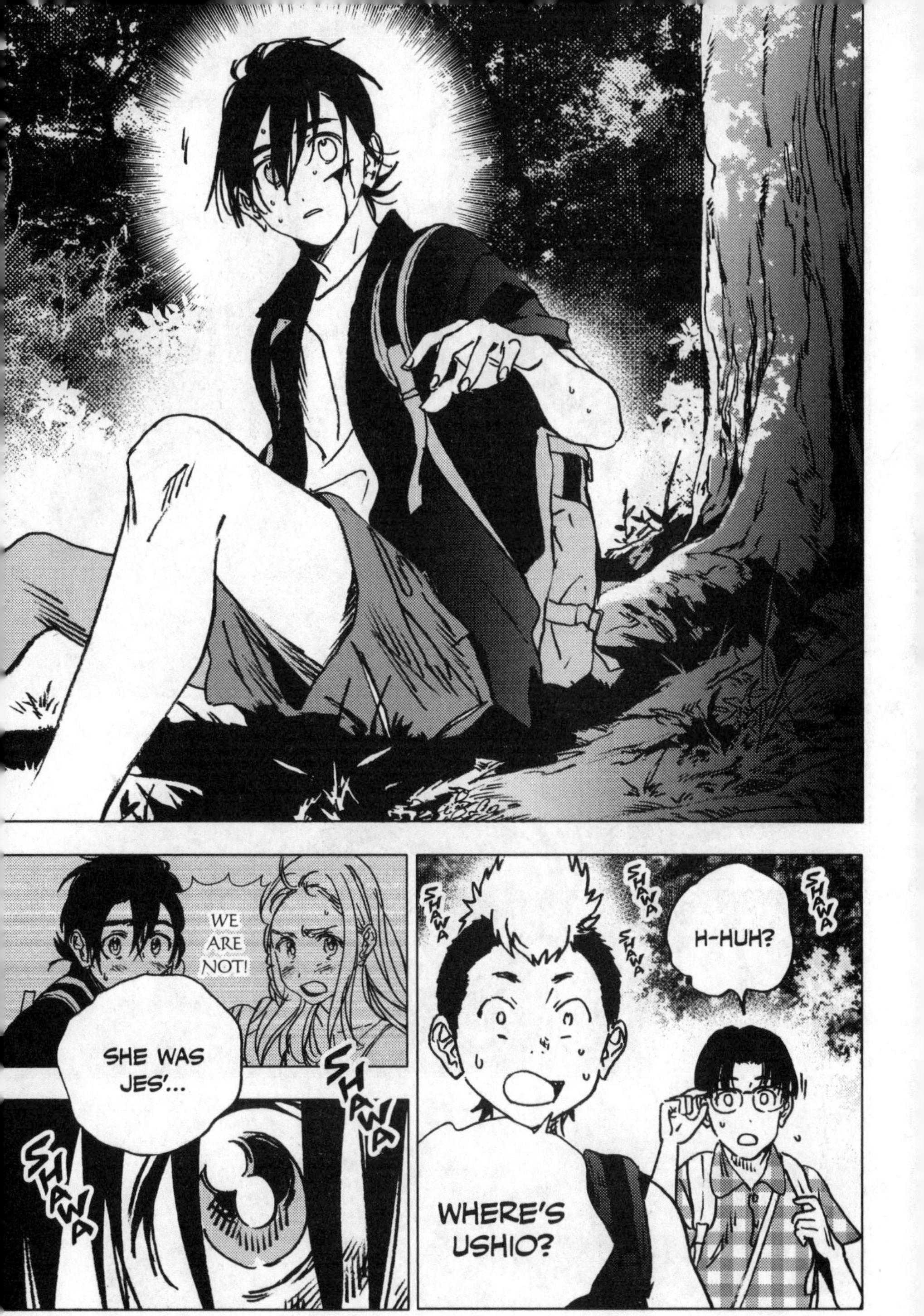
SHAWA
H-HUH?
SHAWA
SHAWA
SHAWA
WHERE'S USHIO?
WE ARE NOT!
SHE WAS JES'...
SHAWA
SHAWA

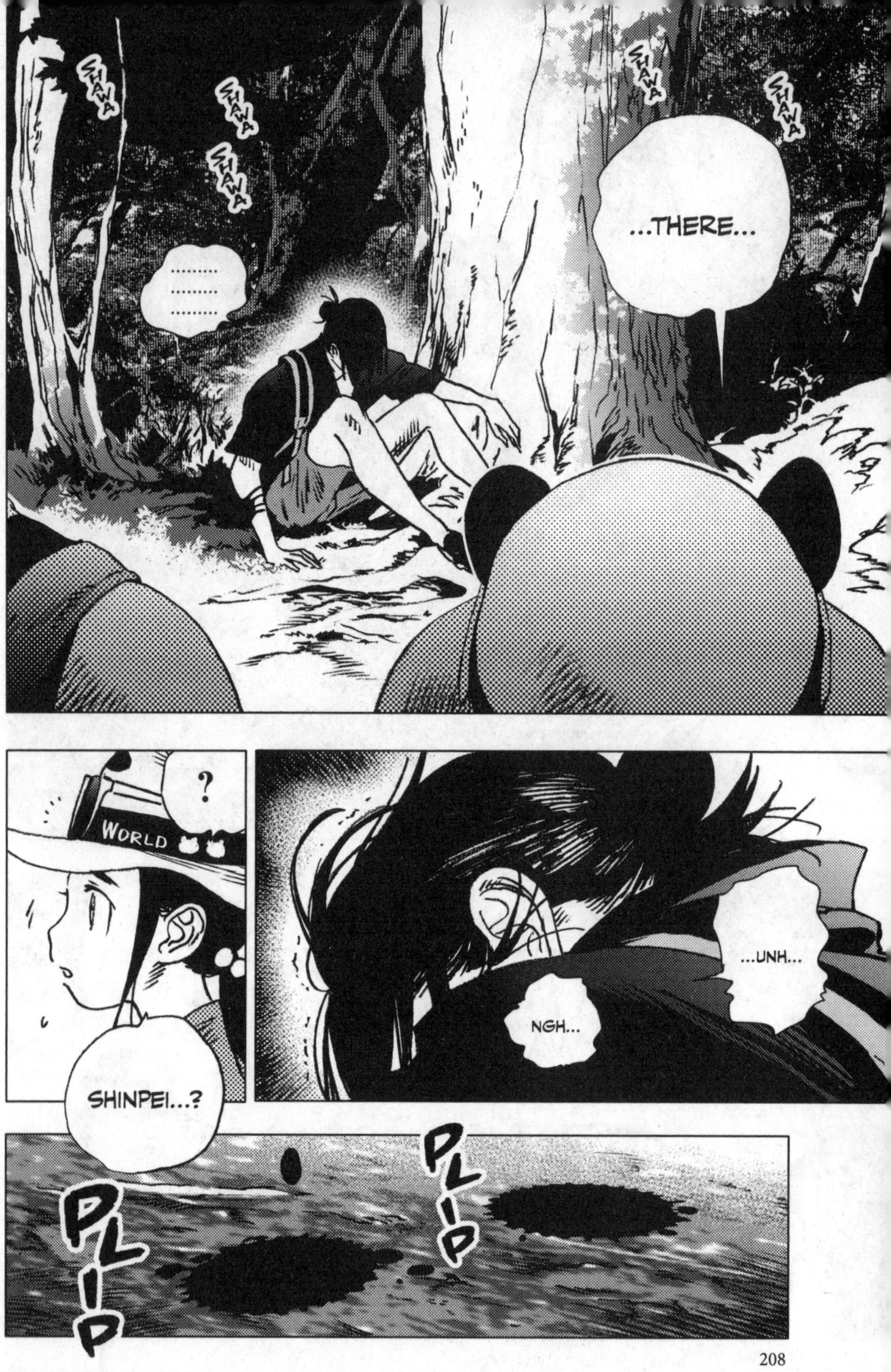
SHAWA
SHAWA
...THERE...
SHAWA
SHAWA
SHAWA
....
....
....
...UNH...
NGH...
?
WORLD
SHINPEI...?
PLIP
PLIP

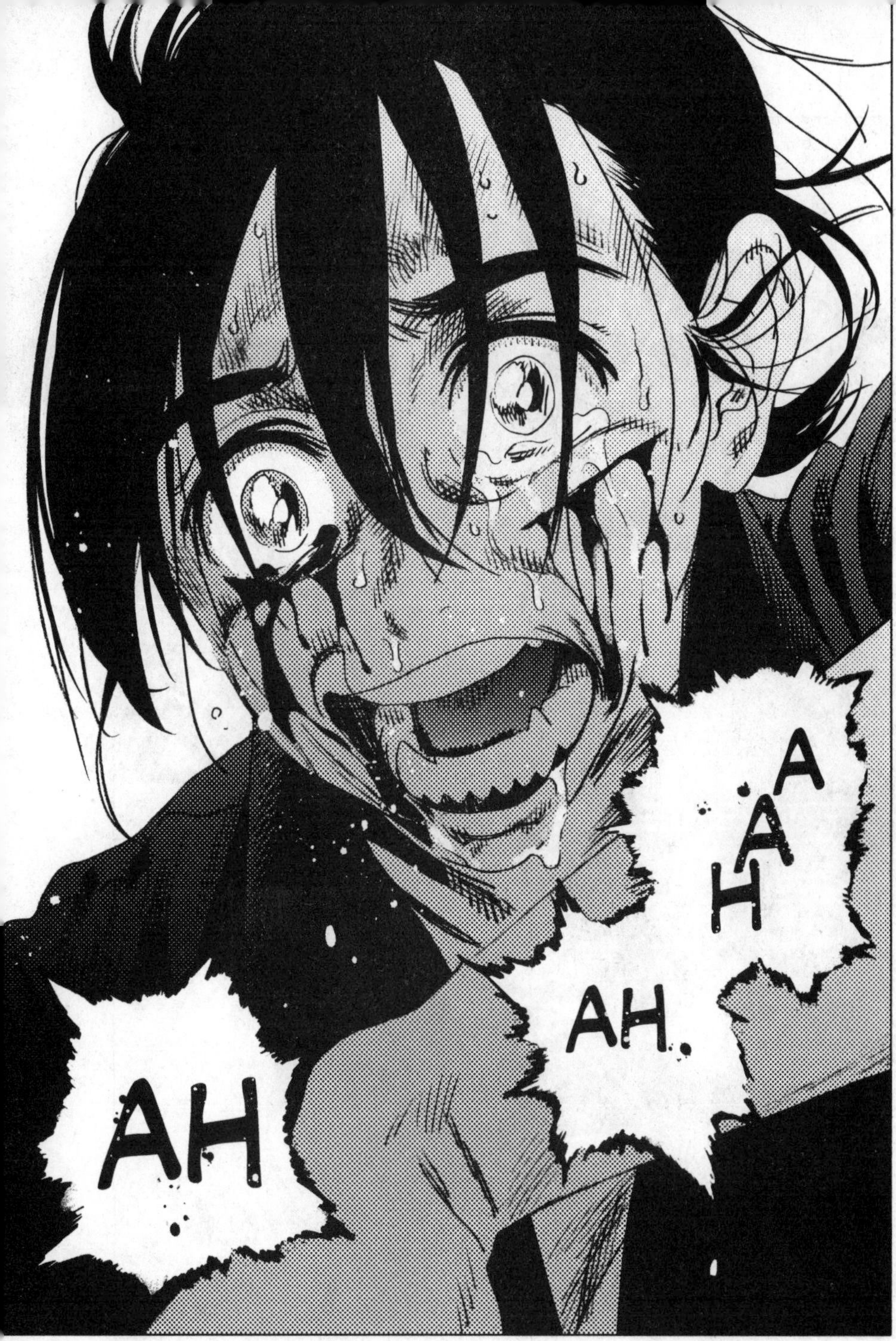
AAH
AH.
AH

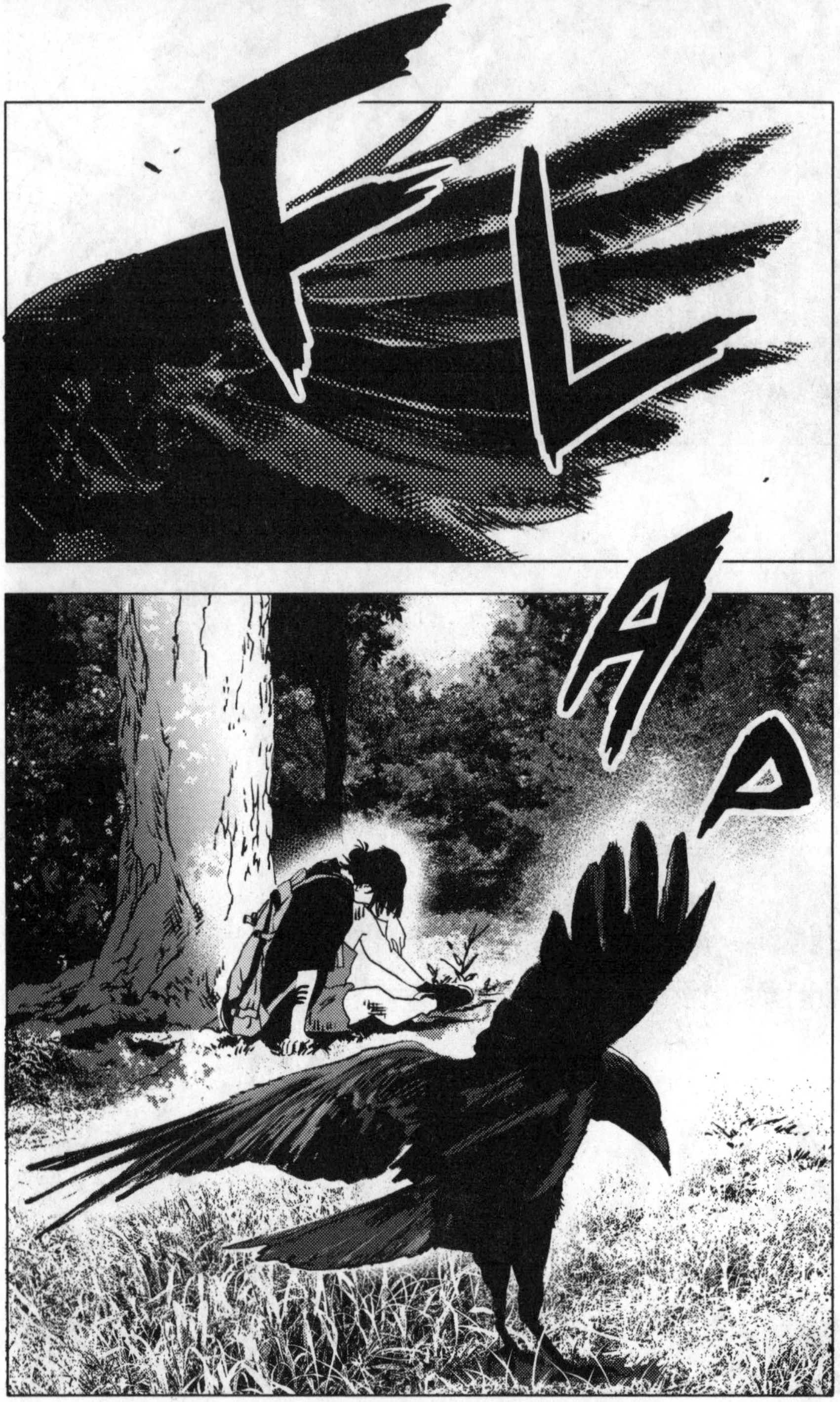
FLAP

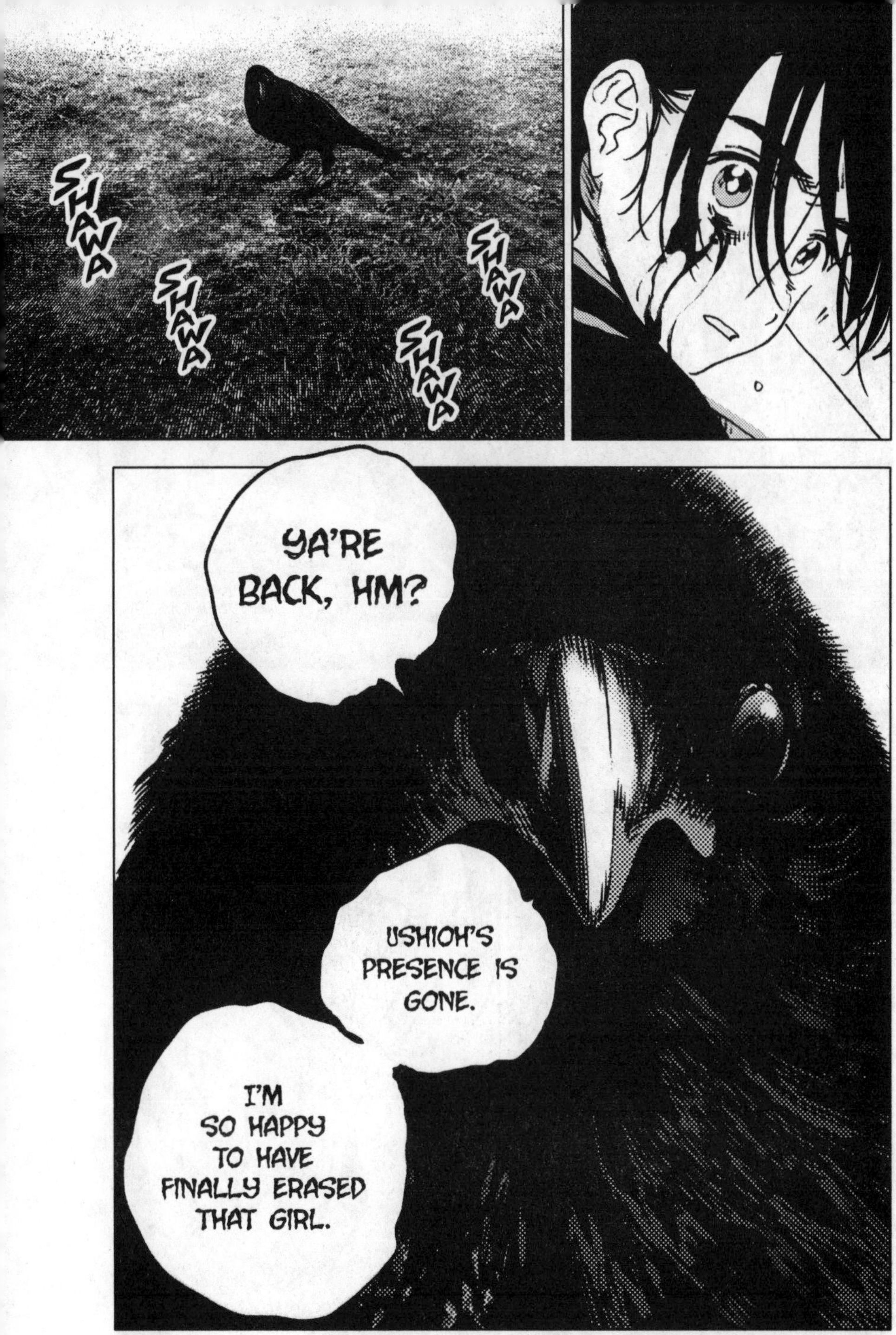
SHAWA
SHAWA
SHAWA
SHAWA
YA'RE BACK, HM?
USHIOH'S PRESENCE IS GONE.
I'M SO HAPPY TO HAVE FINALLY ERASED THAT GIRL.

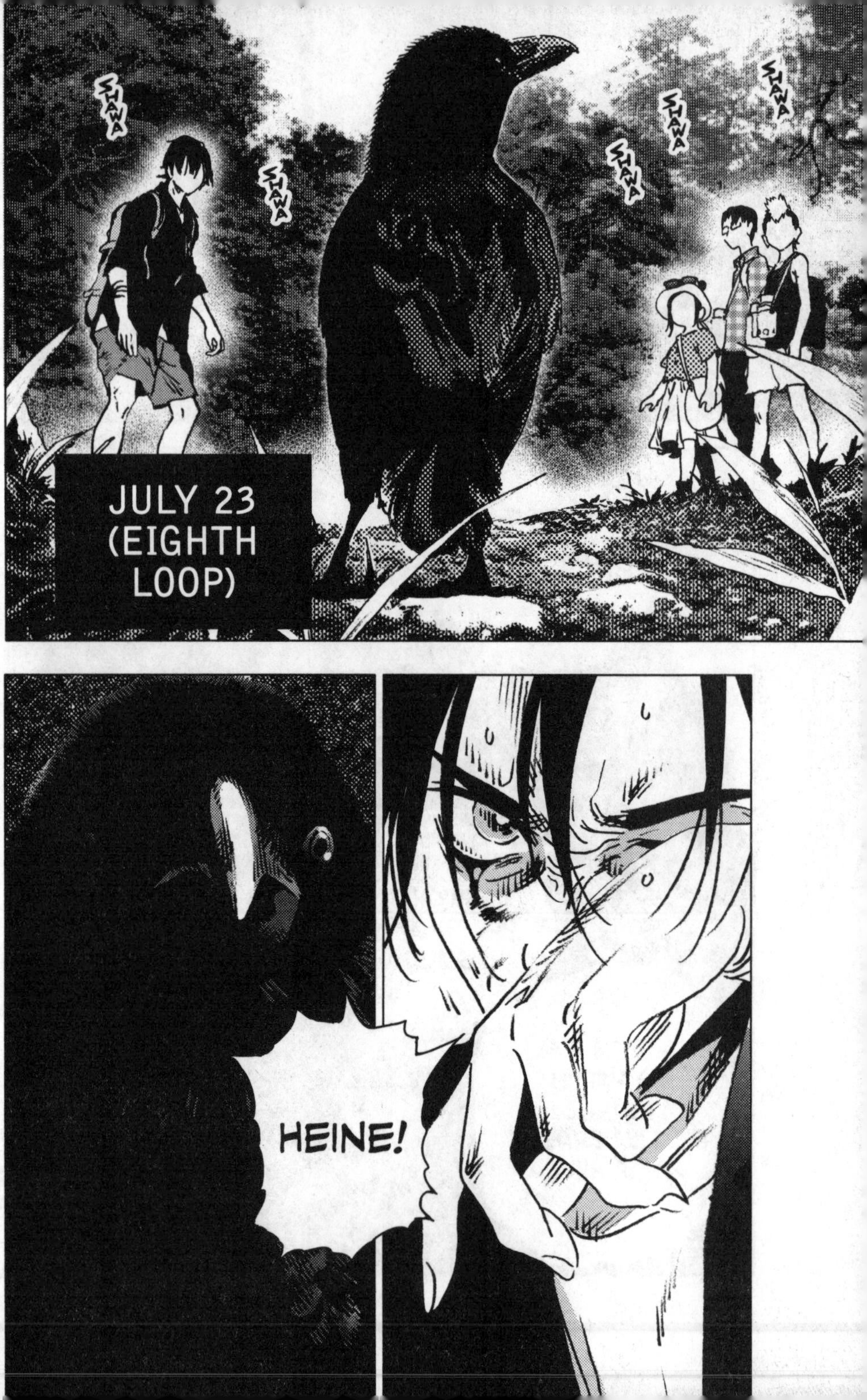
SHAWA
SHAWA
SHAWA
SHAWA
SHAWA
JULY 23 (EIGHTH LOOP)
HEINE!

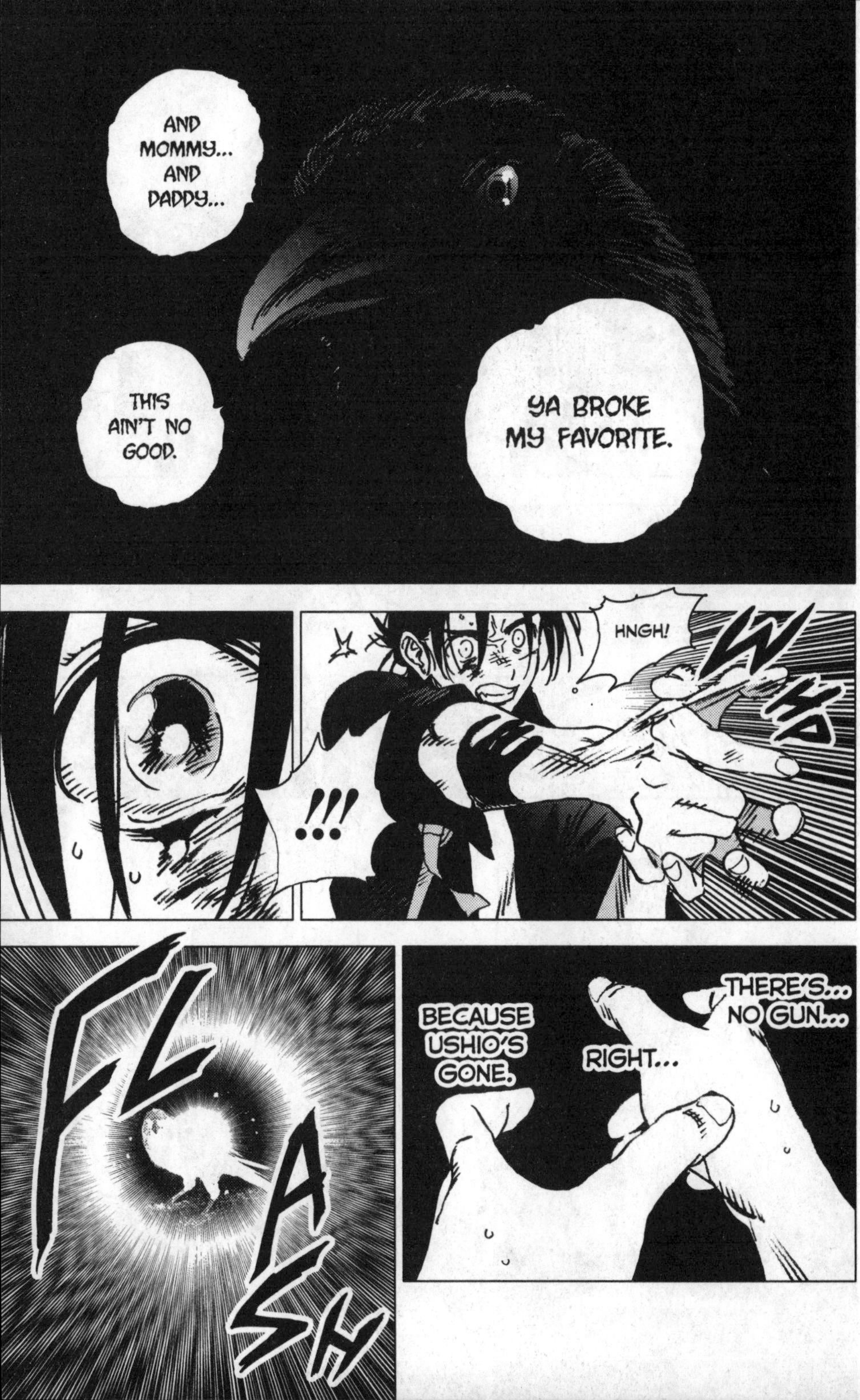
YA BROKE MY FAVORITE.
AND MOMMY... AND DADDY...
THIS AIN'T NO GOOD.
HNGH!
WHIP
!!!
THERE'S... NO GUN...
RIGHT...
BECAUSE USHIO'S GONE.
FLASH

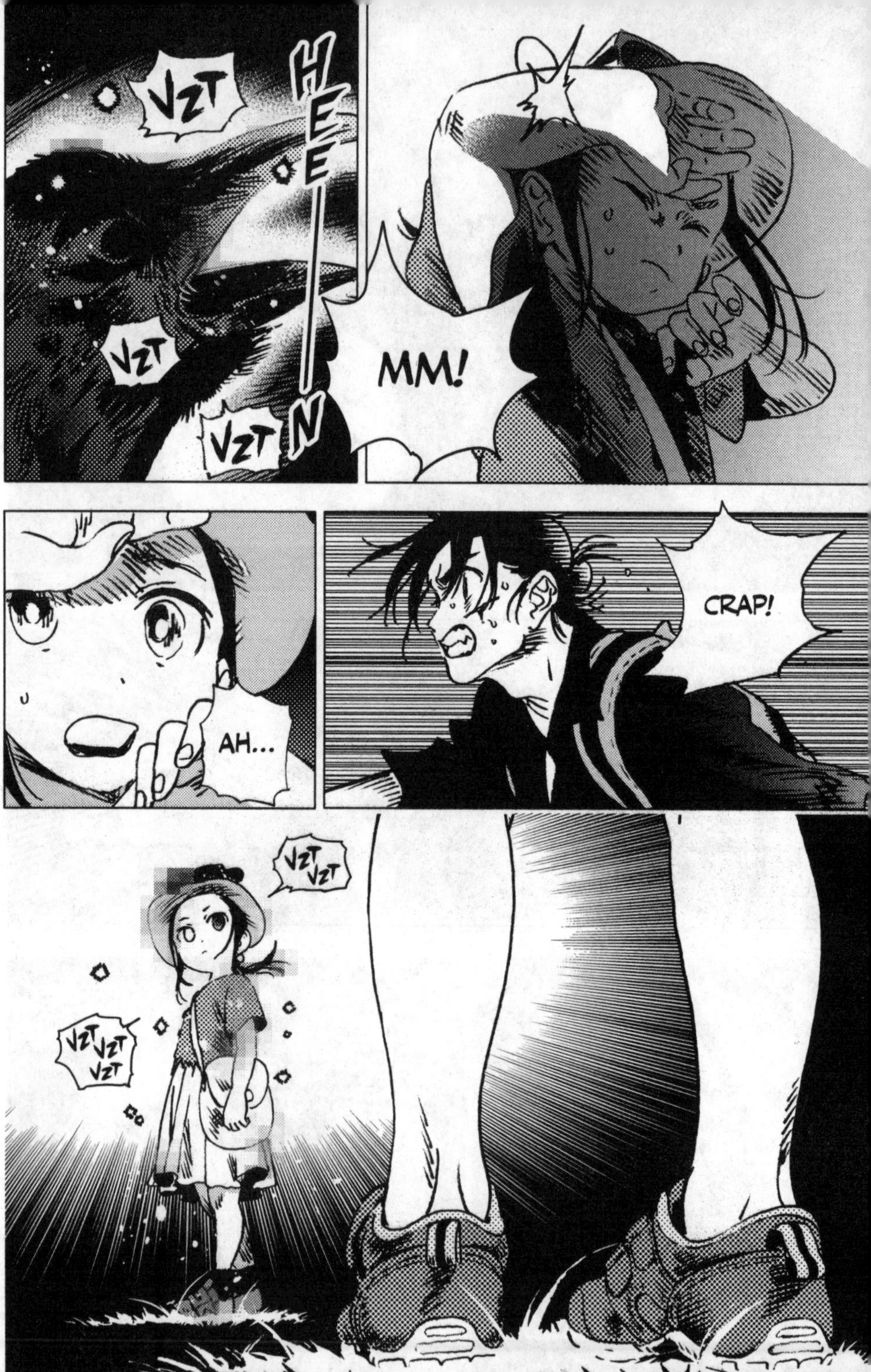
MM!
HEE—N
VZT
VZT
VZT
CRAP!
AH...
VZT VZT
VZT VZT VZT

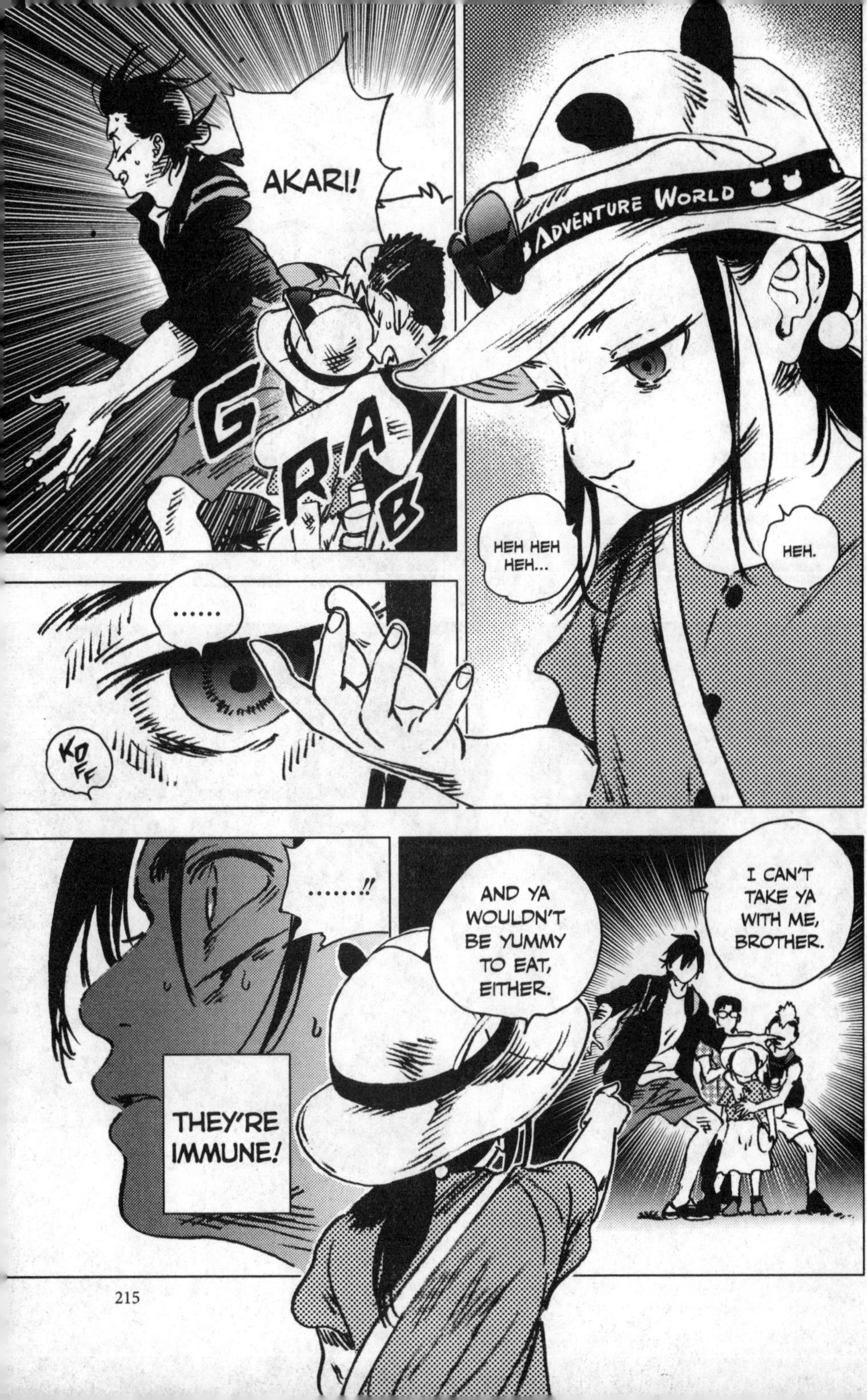
ADVENTURE WORLD
HEH.
HEH HEH HEH...
AKARI!
GRAB
......
KOFF
I CAN'T TAKE YA WITH ME, BROTHER.
AND YA WOULDN'T BE YUMMY TO EAT, EITHER.
......!!
THEY'RE IMMUNE!

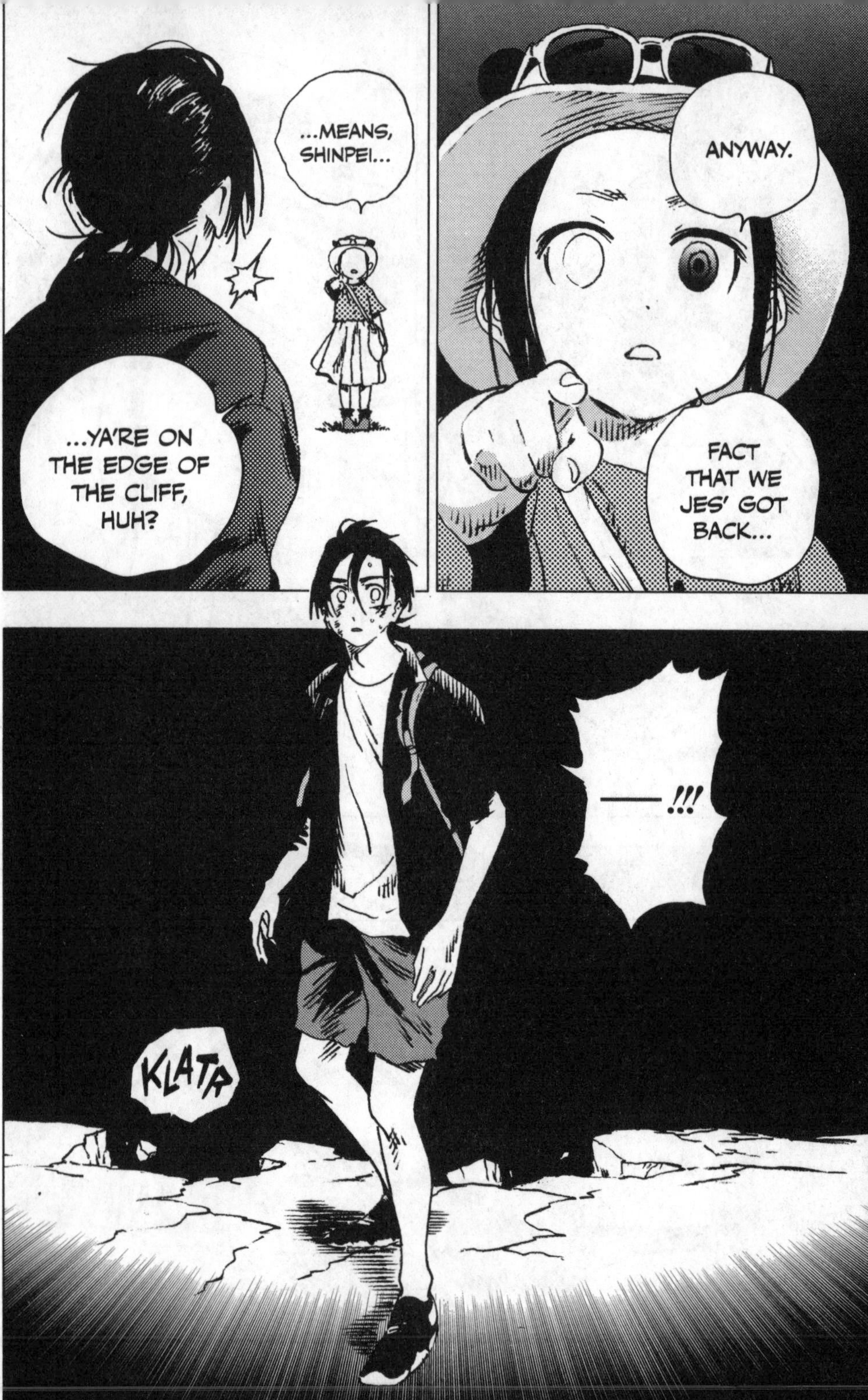
ANYWAY.
FACT THAT WE JES' GOT BACK...
...MEANS, SHINPEI...
...YA'RE ON THE EDGE OF THE CLIFF, HUH?
——!!!
KLATR

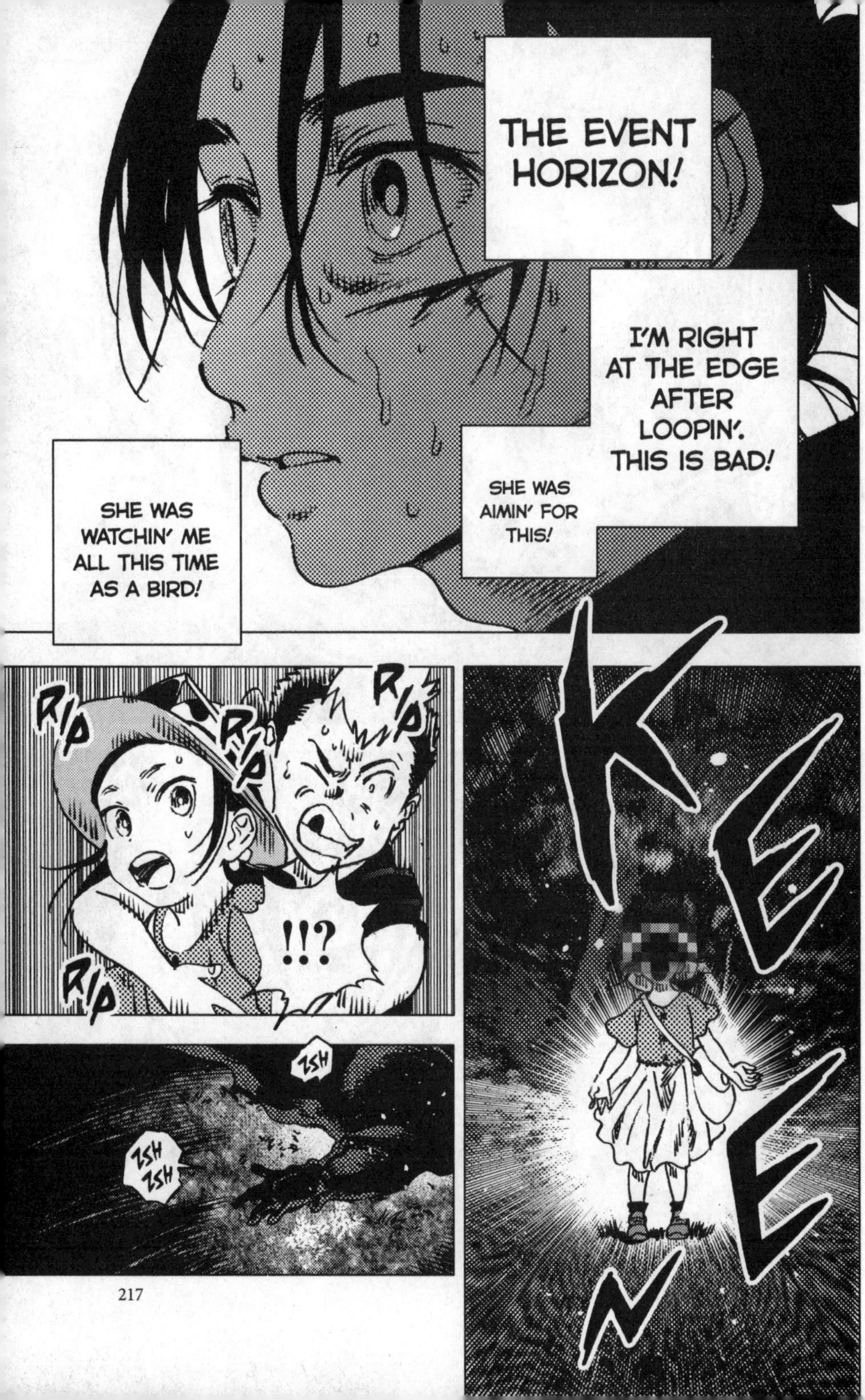
THE EVENT HORIZON!
I'M RIGHT AT THE EDGE AFTER LOOPIN'. THIS IS BAD!
SHE WAS AIMIN' FOR THIS!
SHE WAS WATCHIN' ME ALL THIS TIME AS A BIRD!
KEEEN
RIP
RIP
RIP
RIP
!!?
ZSH
ZSH ZSH

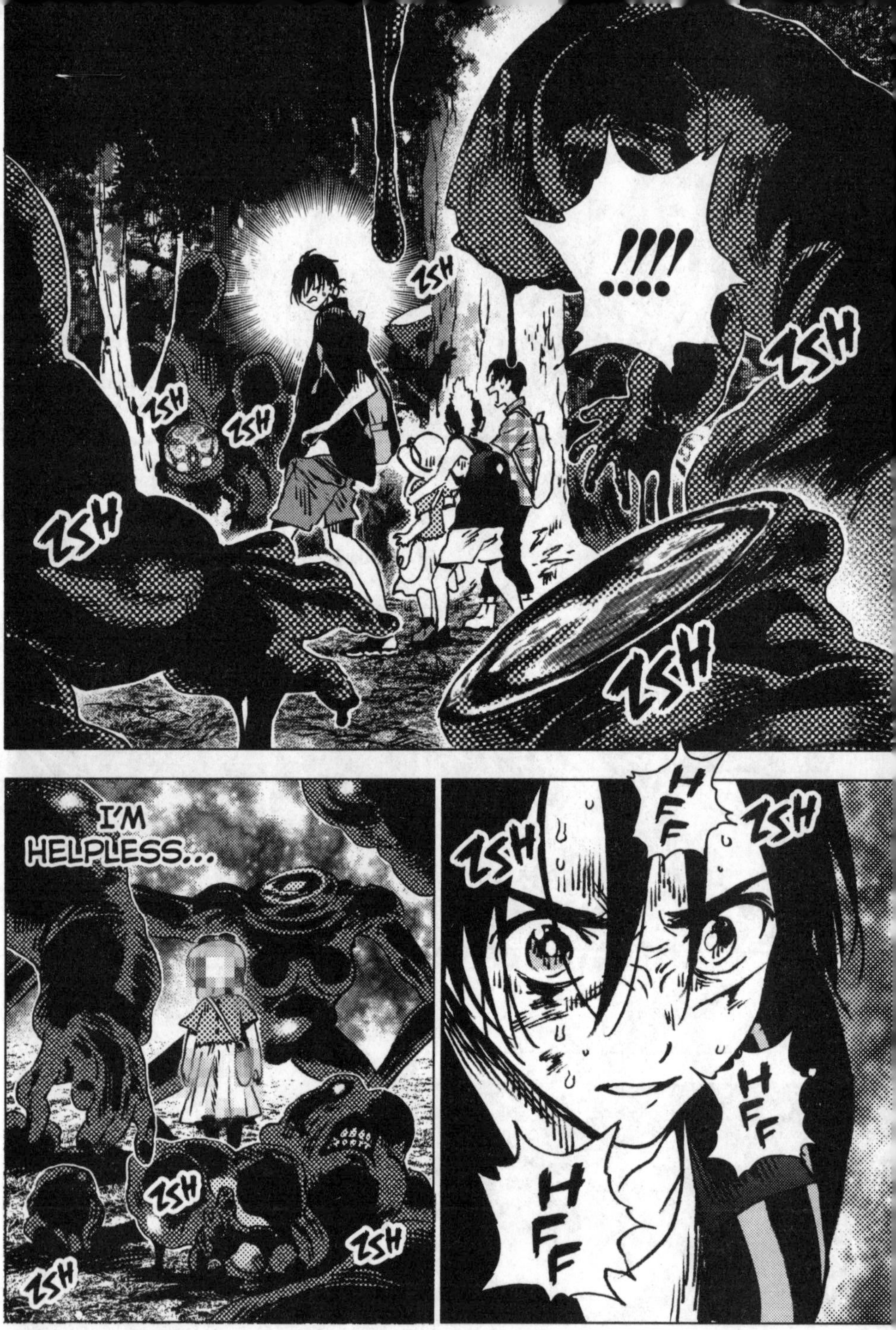
!!!!
ZSH
ZSH
ZSH
ZSH
ZSH
ZSH
ZSH
HFF
ZSH
ZSH
HFF
HFF
I'M HELPLESS...
ZSH
ZSH
ZSH

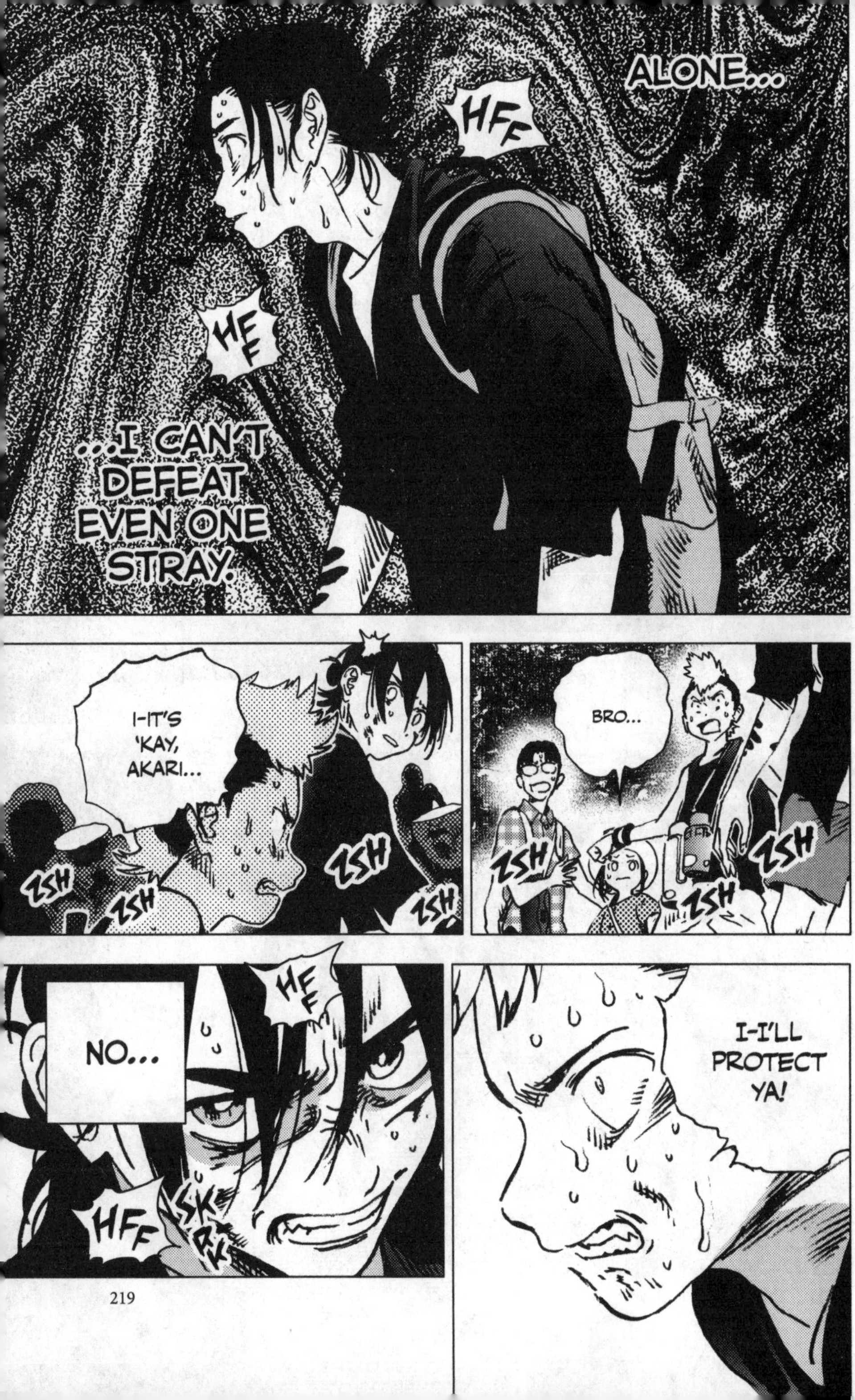
ALONE...
HFF
HFF
...I CAN'T DEFEAT EVEN ONE STRAY.
BRO...
ZSH
ZSH
ZSH
I-IT'S 'KAY, AKARI...
ZSH
ZSH
ZSH
I-I'LL PROTECT YA!
HFF
NO...
HFF
SKRK

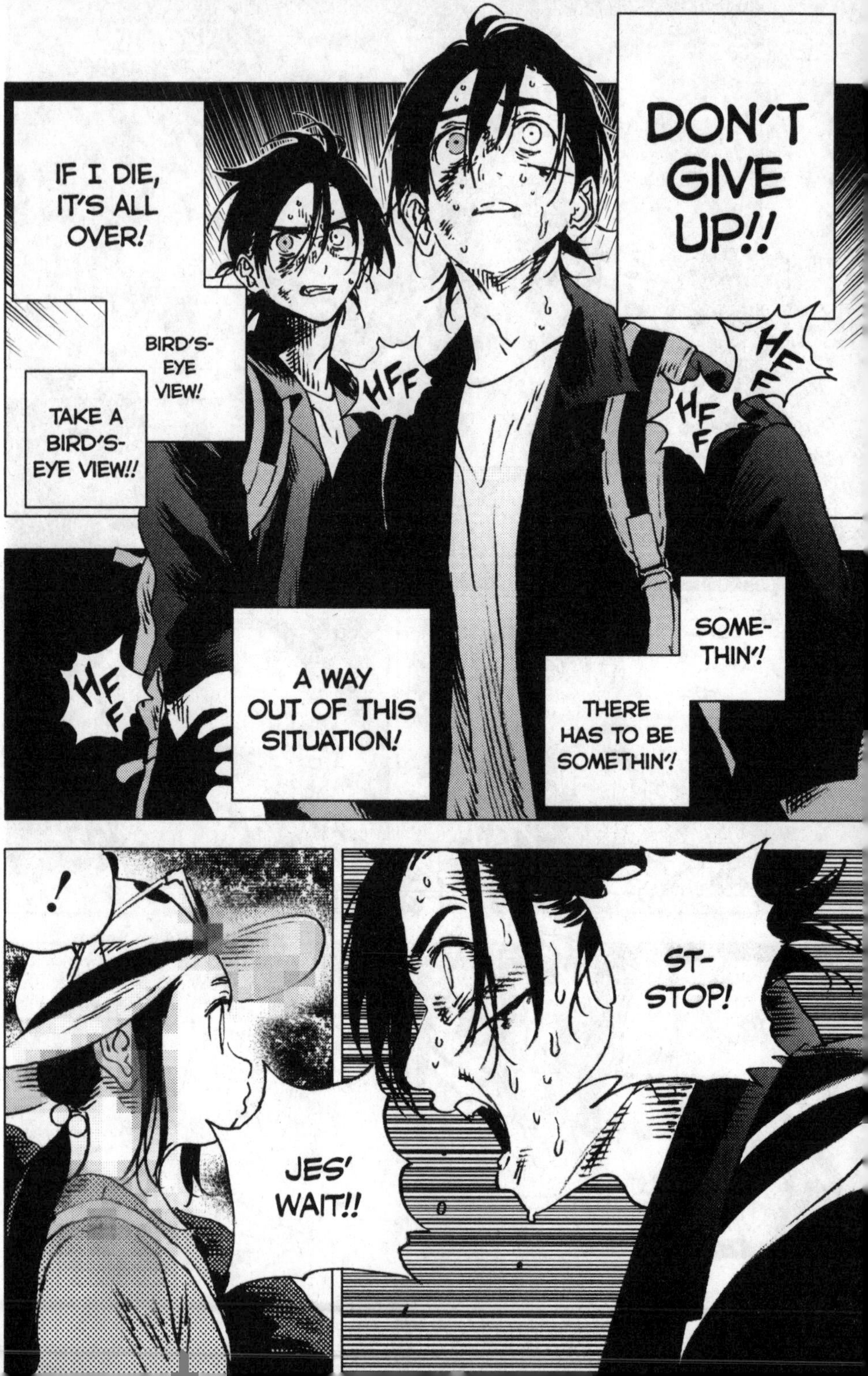
DON'T GIVE UP!!
HFF
HFF
HFF
IF I DIE, IT'S ALL OVER!
BIRD'S-EYE VIEW!
TAKE A BIRD'S-EYE VIEW!!
SOME-THIN'!
THERE HAS TO BE SOMETHIN'!
A WAY OUT OF THIS SITUATION!
HFF
ST-STOP!
JES' WAIT!!
!

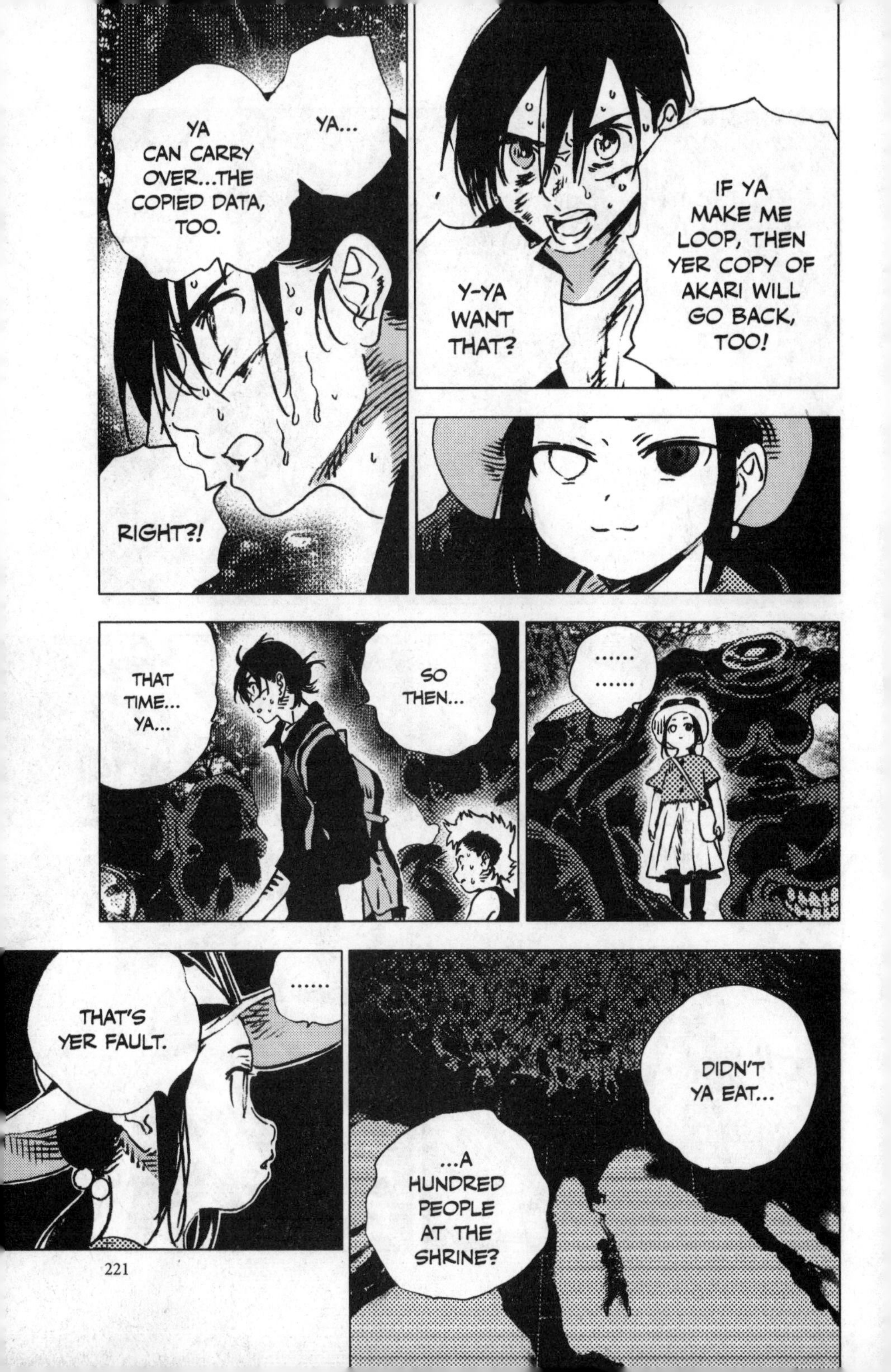
IF YA MAKE ME LOOP, THEN YER COPY OF AKARI WILL GO BACK, TOO!
Y-YA WANT THAT?
YA...
YA CAN CARRY OVER...THE COPIED DATA, TOO.
RIGHT?!
......
......
SO THEN...
THAT TIME... YA...
DIDN'T YA EAT...
...A HUNDRED PEOPLE AT THE SHRINE?
......
THAT'S YER FAULT.

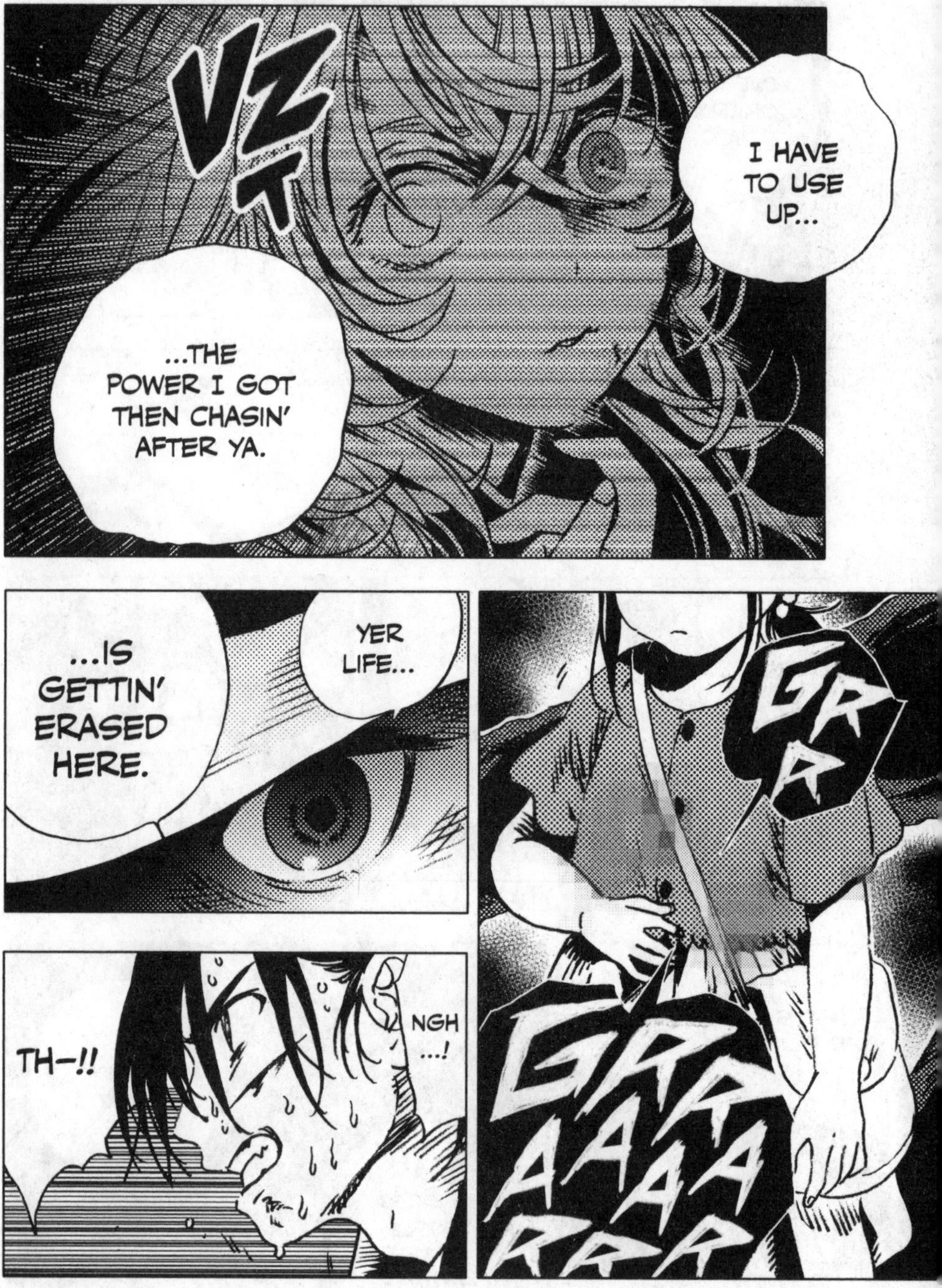
VZT
I HAVE TO USE UP...
...THE POWER I GOT THEN CHASIN' AFTER YA.
GRR
GRRAAAAARRRR
YER LIFE...
...IS GETTIN' ERASED HERE.
NGH ...!
TH-!!

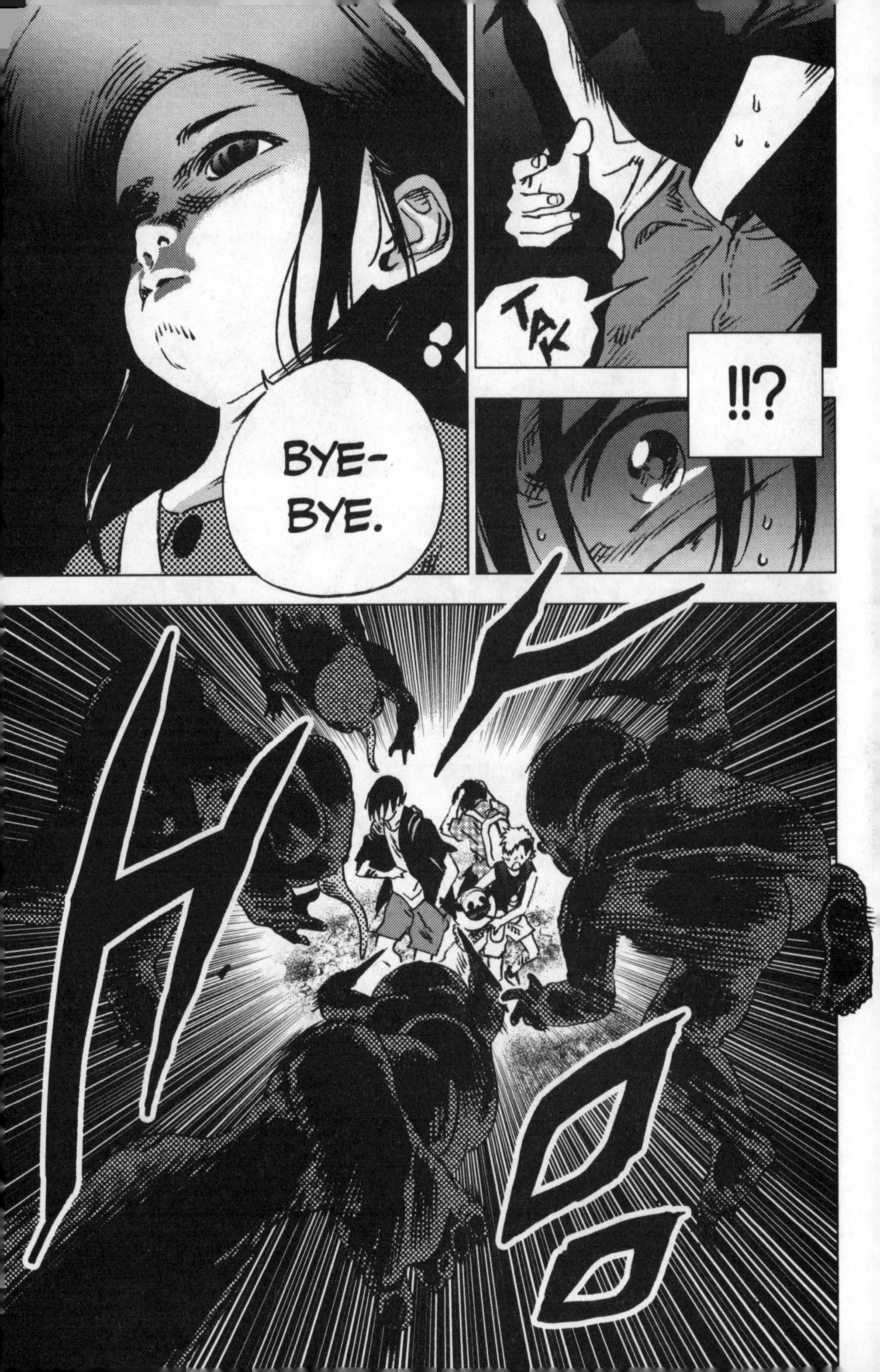
TAK
!!?
BYE-BYE.

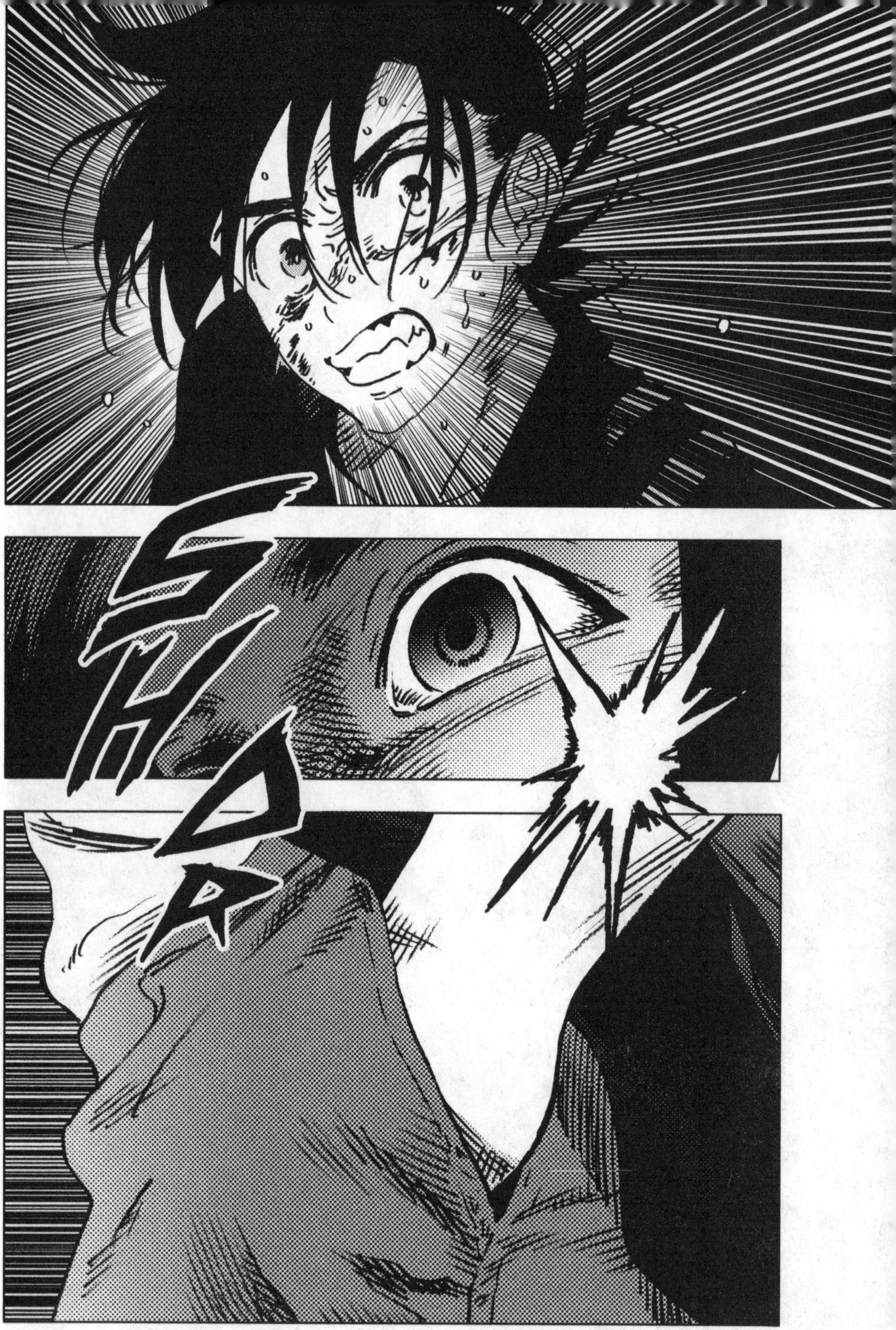
SHAA

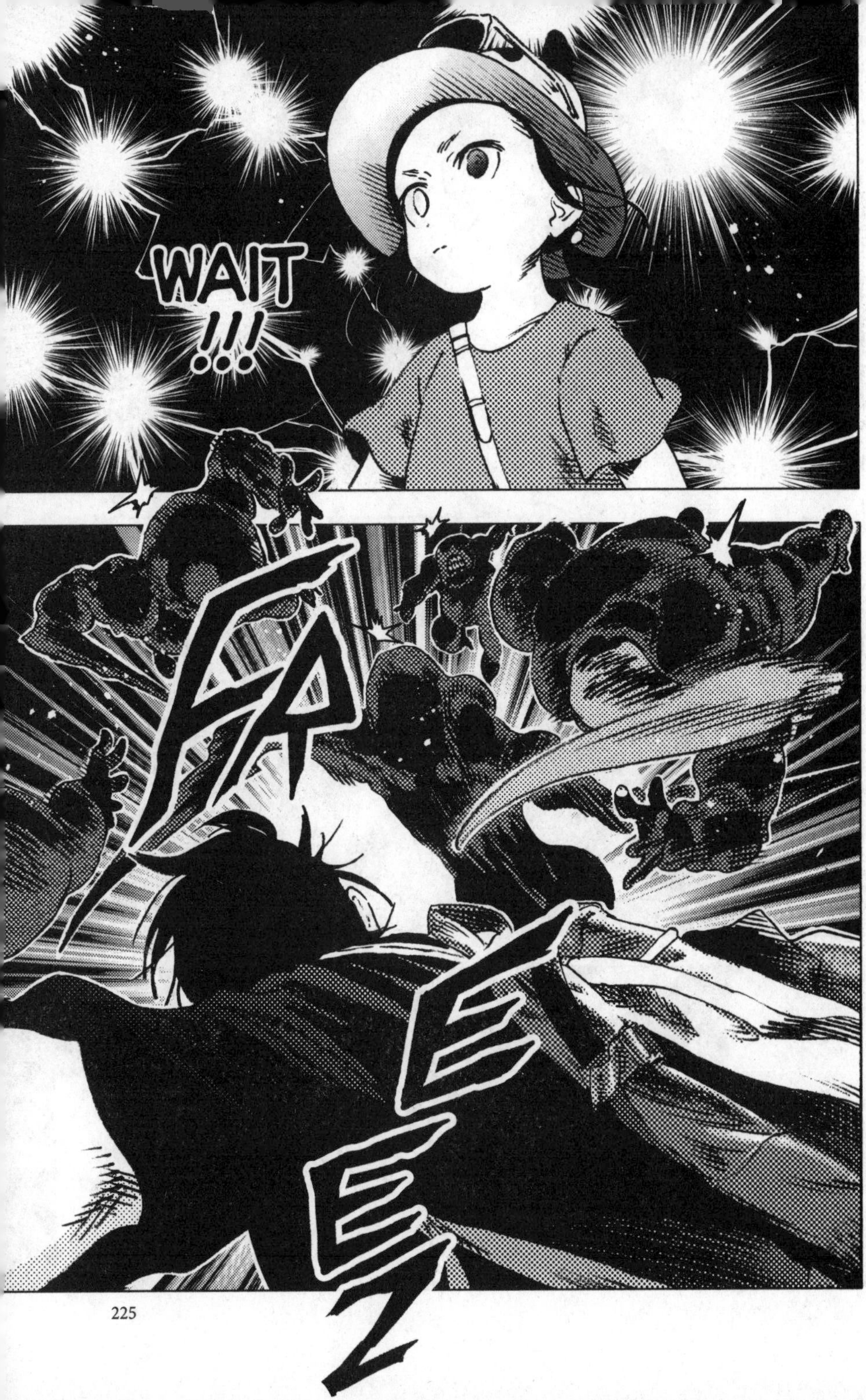
WAIT!!!
FREEZ

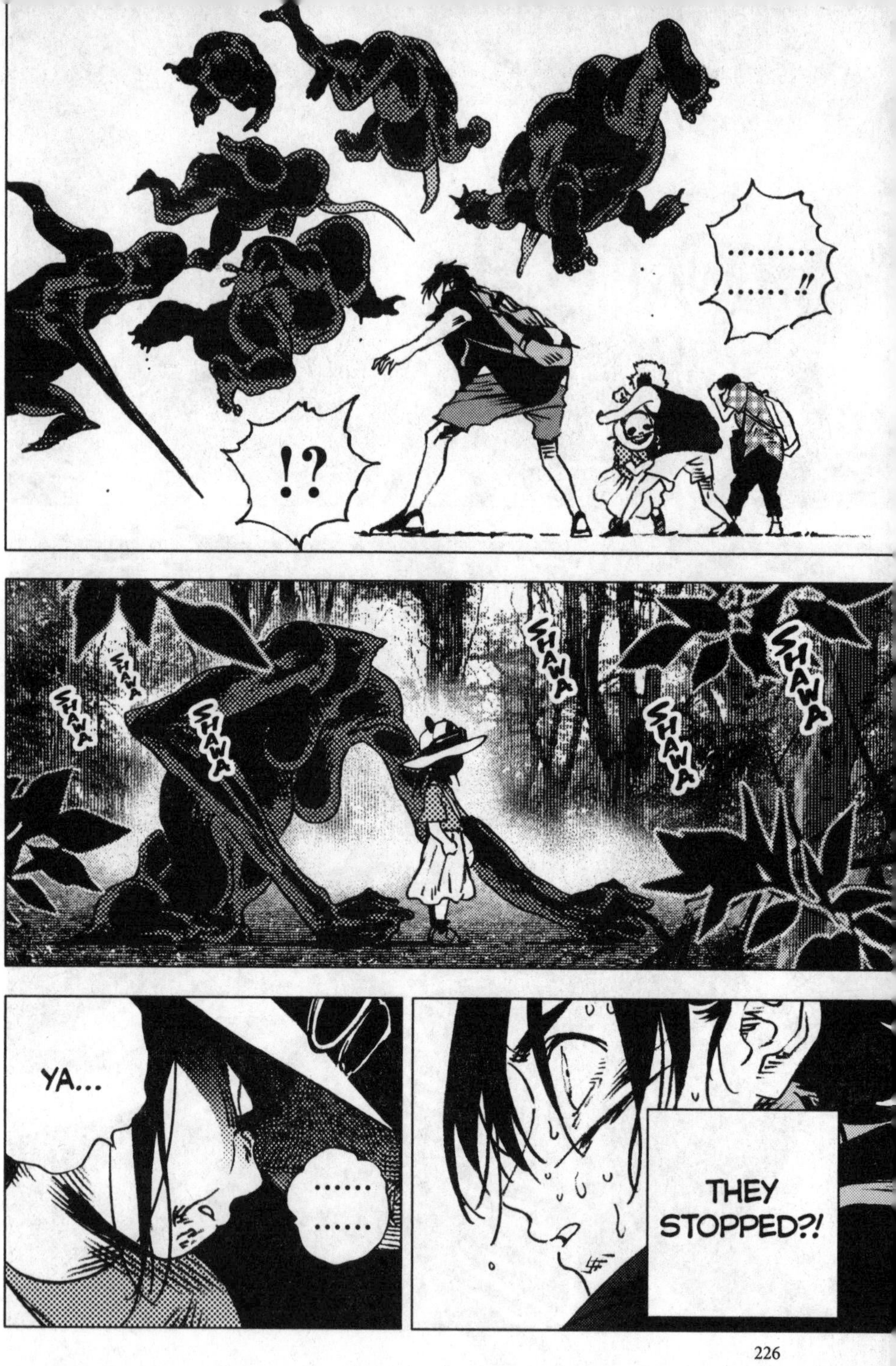

....
.......!!
!?
SHAWA
SHAWA
SHAWA
SHAWA
SHAWA
SHAWA
THEY STOPPED?!
YA...
......
......

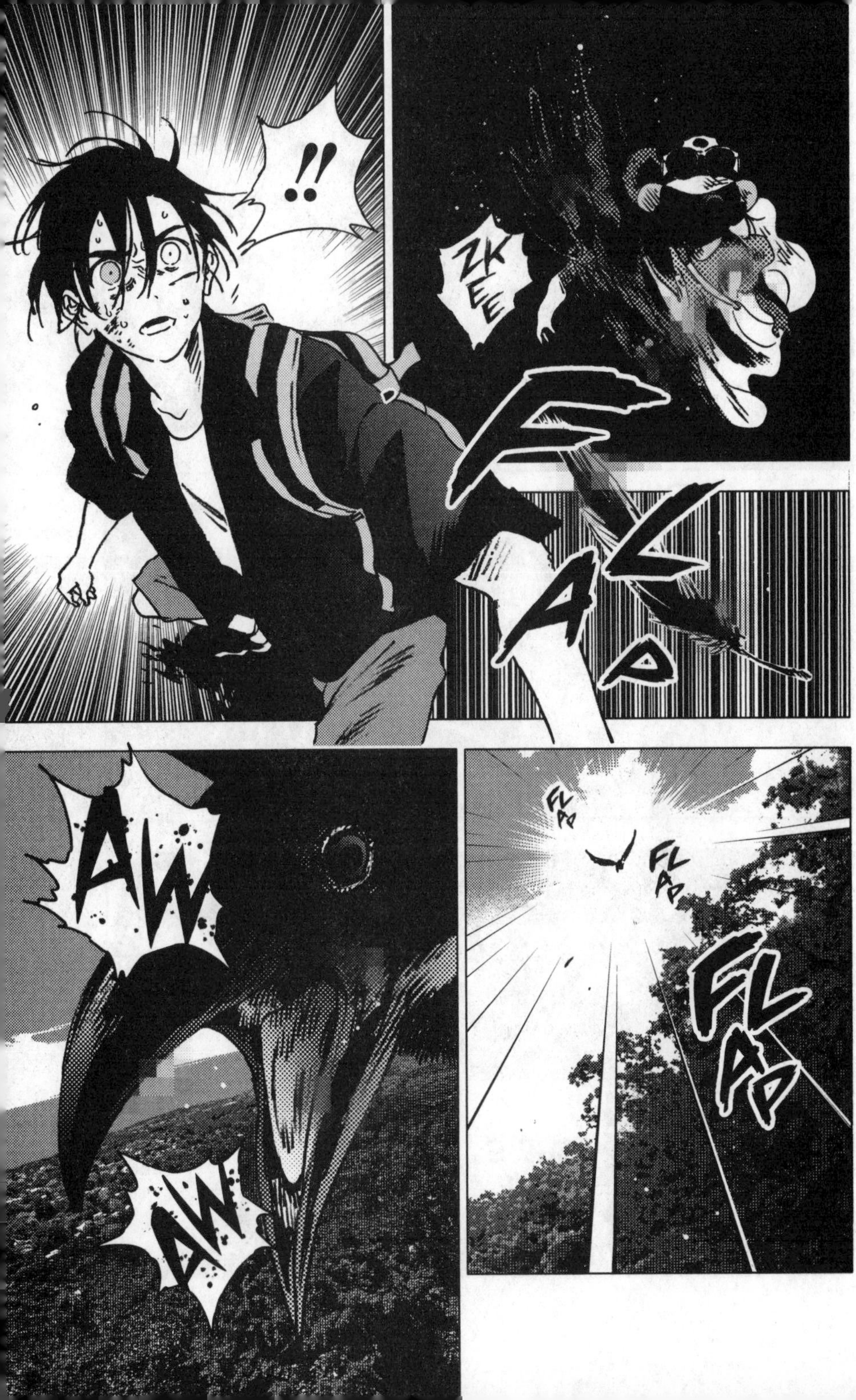
ZKEE
FLAP
!!
FLAP
FLAP
FLAP
AW
AW

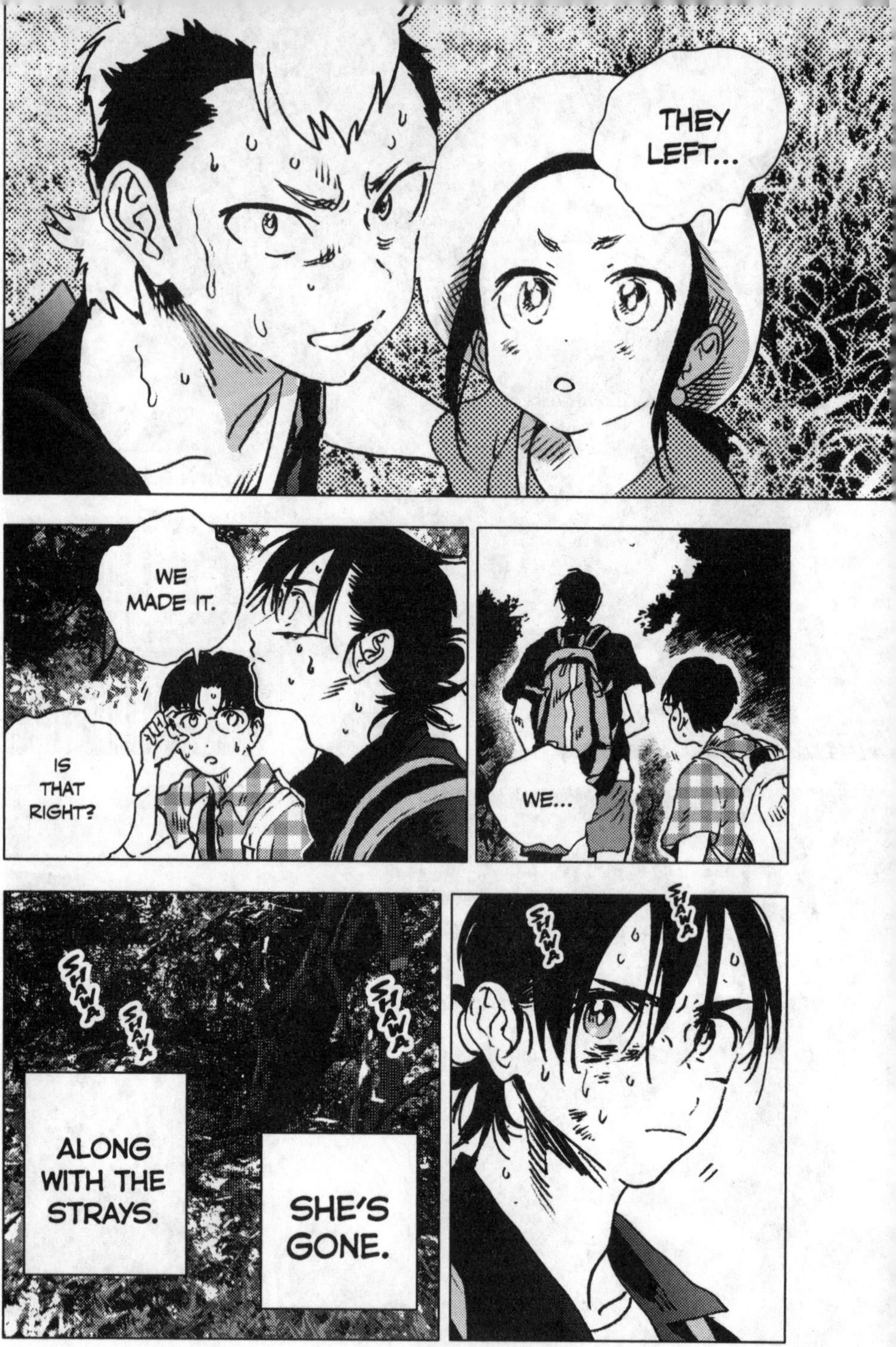
THEY LEFT...
WE...
WE MADE IT.
IS THAT RIGHT?
SHAWA
SHAWA
SHAWA
SHAWA
SHAWA
SHE'S GONE.
ALONG WITH THE STRAYS.

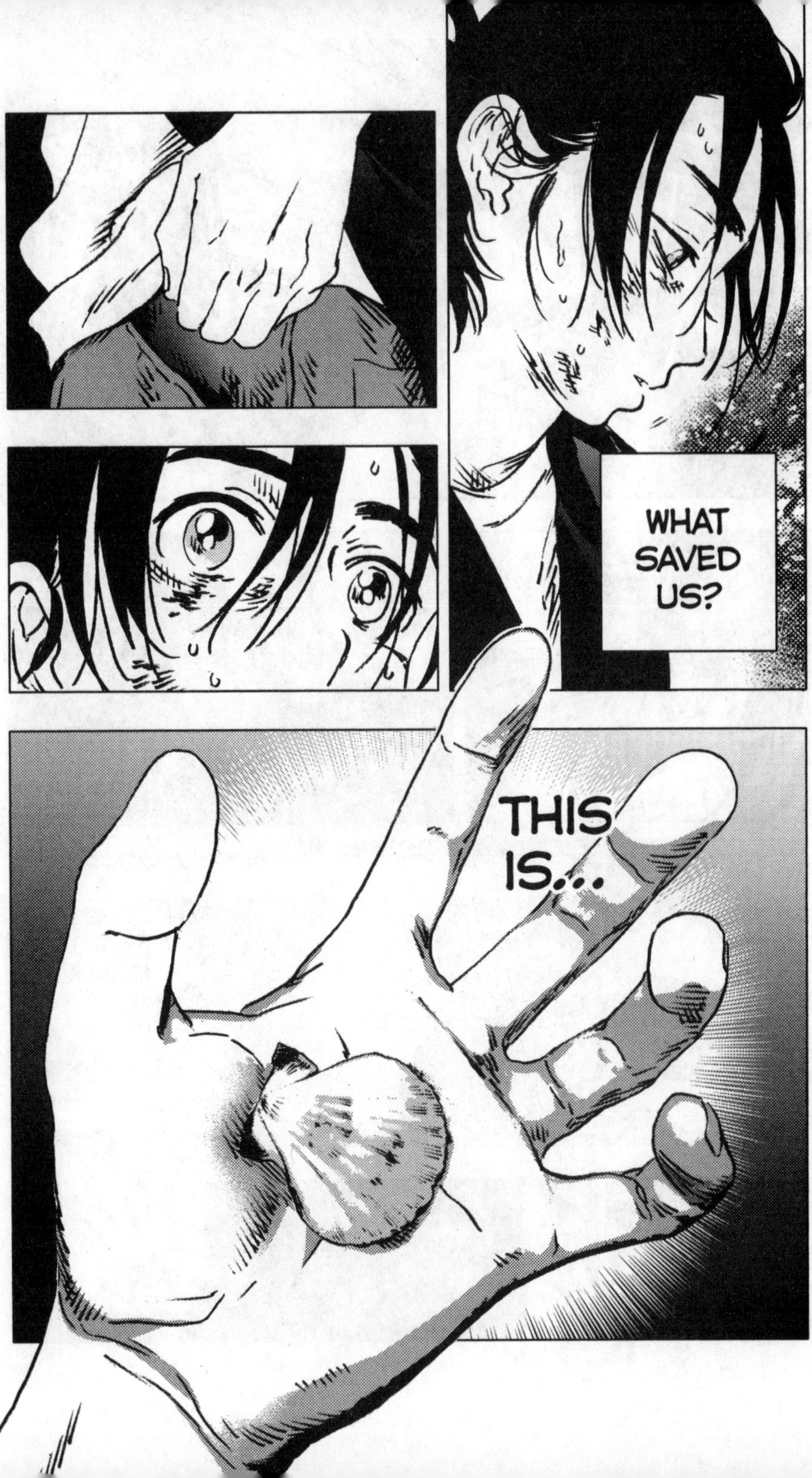
WHAT SAVED US?
THIS IS...

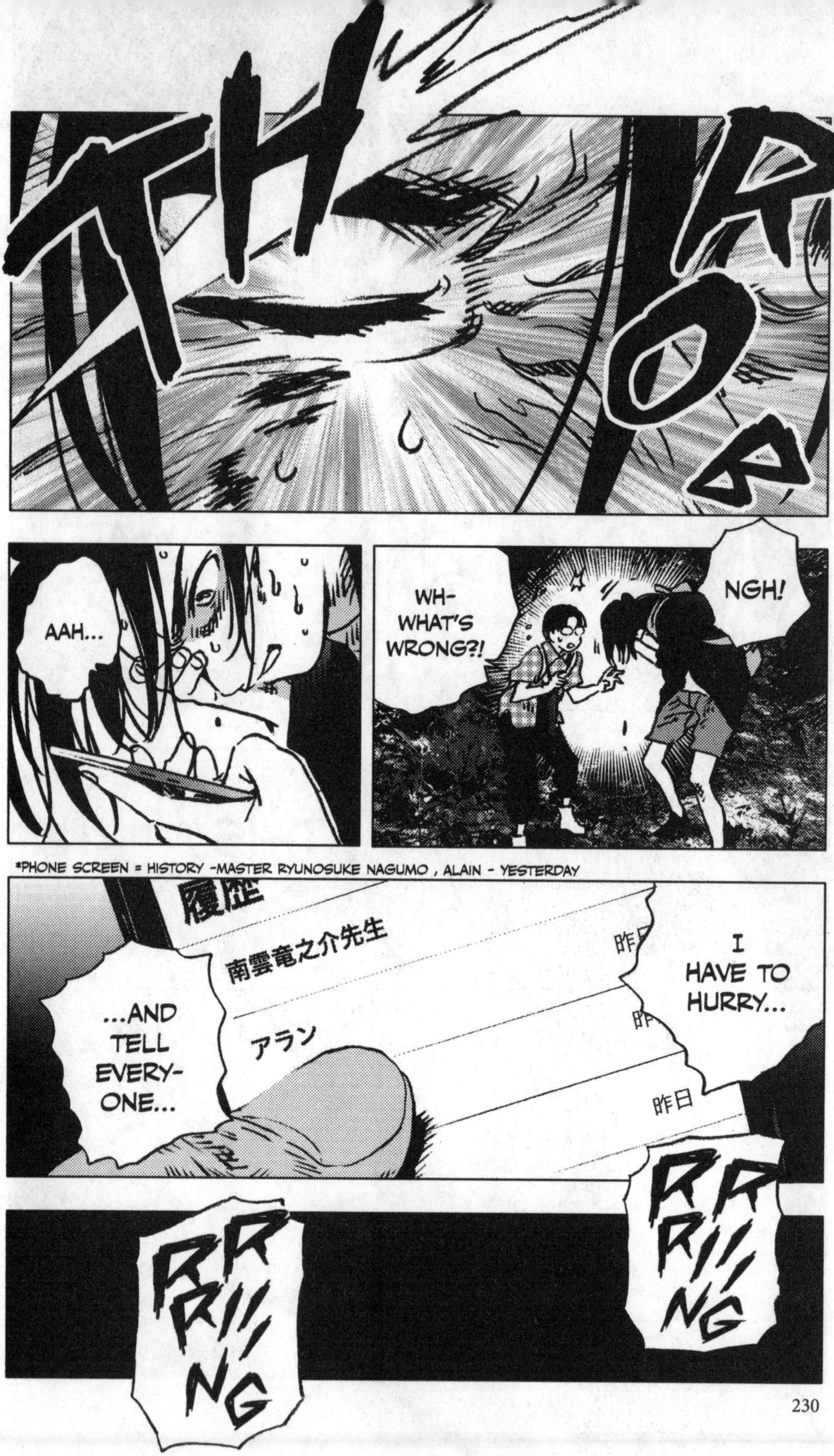
ROB
NGH!
WH-WHAT'S WRONG?!
AAH...
*PHONE SCREEN = HISTORY -MASTER RYUNOSUKE NAGUMO , ALAIN - YESTERDAY
I HAVE TO HURRY...
履歴
南雲竜之介先生
アラン
昨日
...AND TELL EVERY-ONE...
RRRIIING
RRRIIING

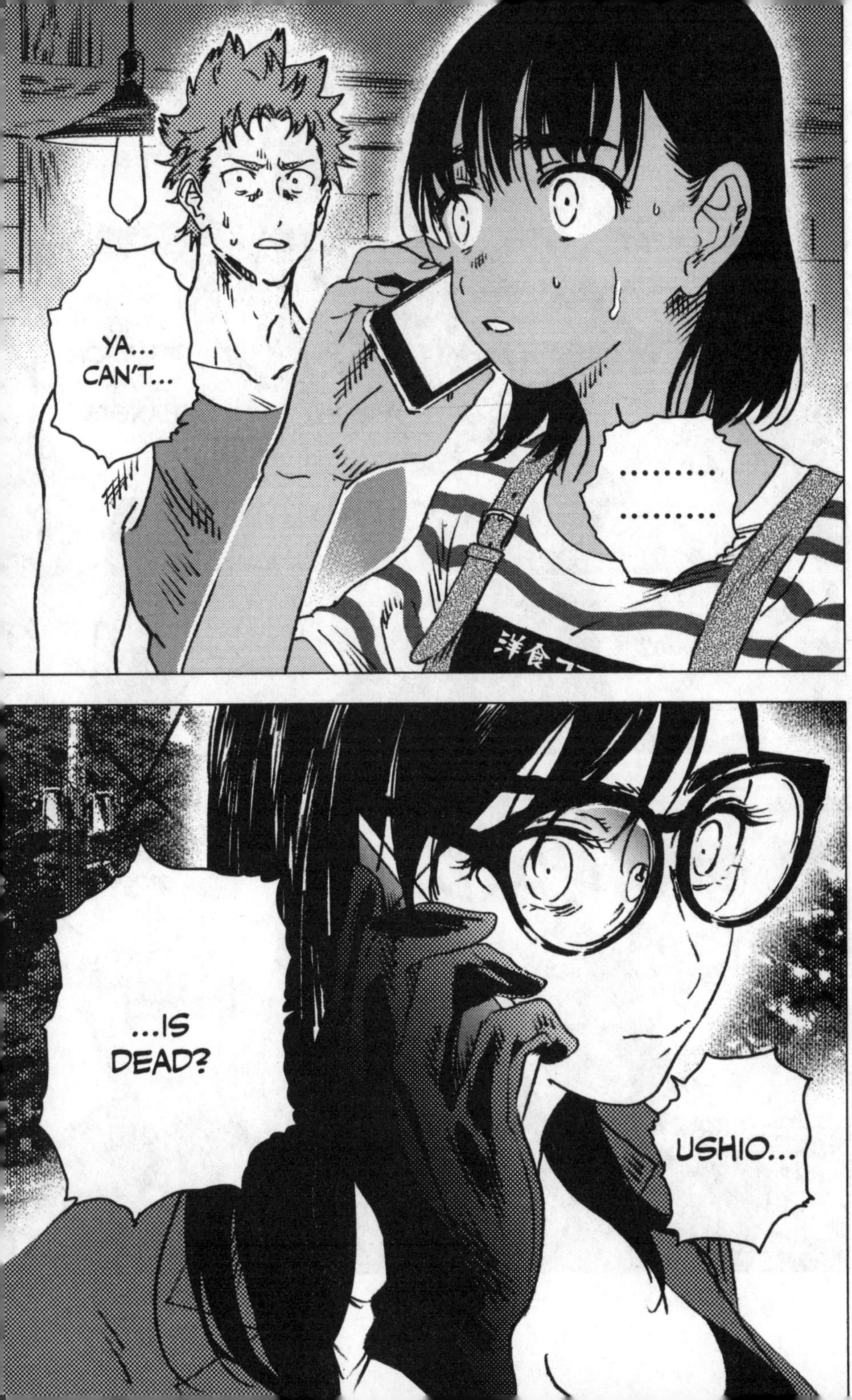
YA... CAN'T...
....
洋食
USHIO...
...IS DEAD?

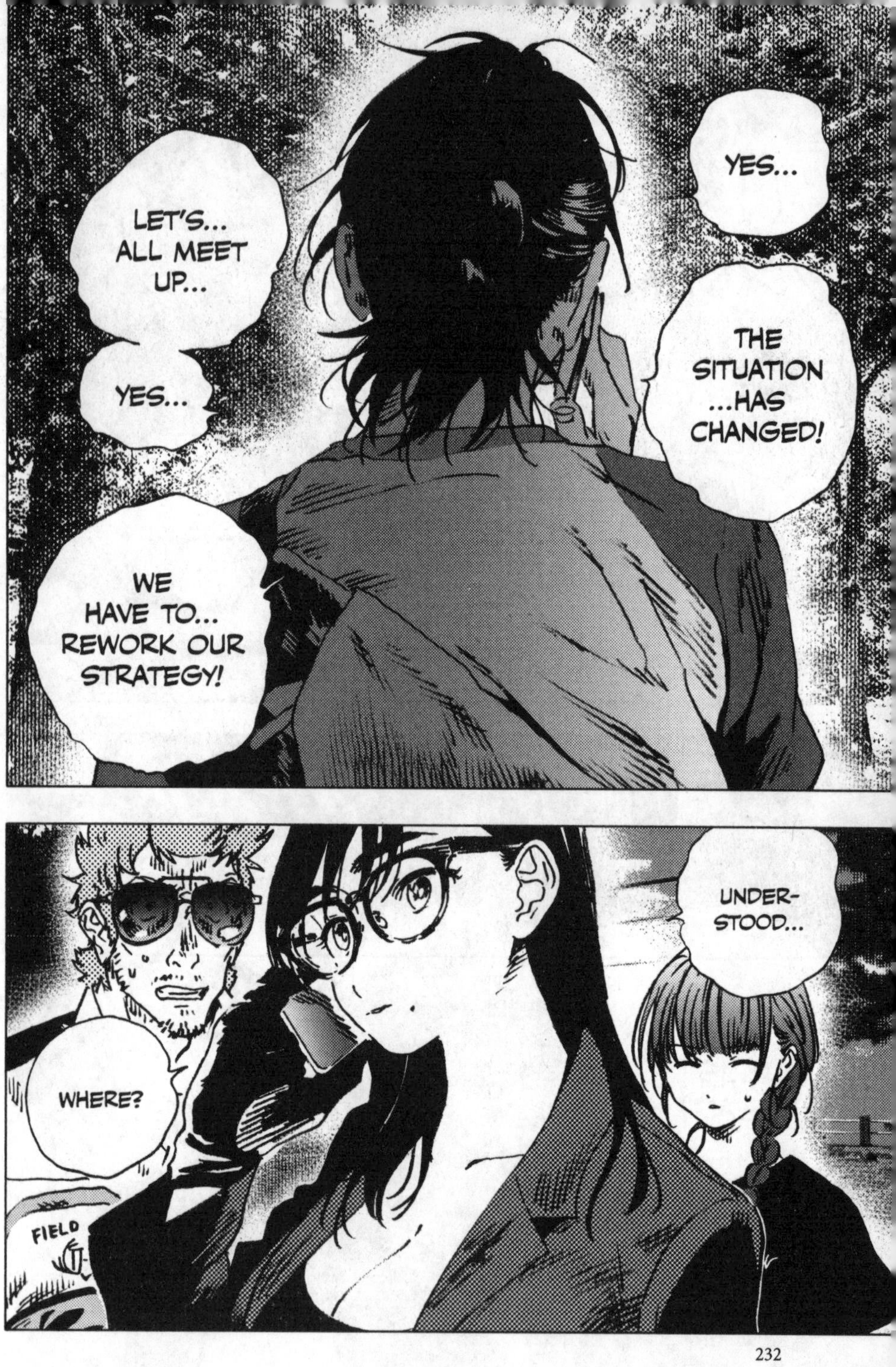
YES...
LET'S... ALL MEET UP...
THE SITUATION ...HAS CHANGED!
YES...
WE HAVE TO... REWORK OUR STRATEGY!
UNDER-STOOD...
WHERE?
FIELD

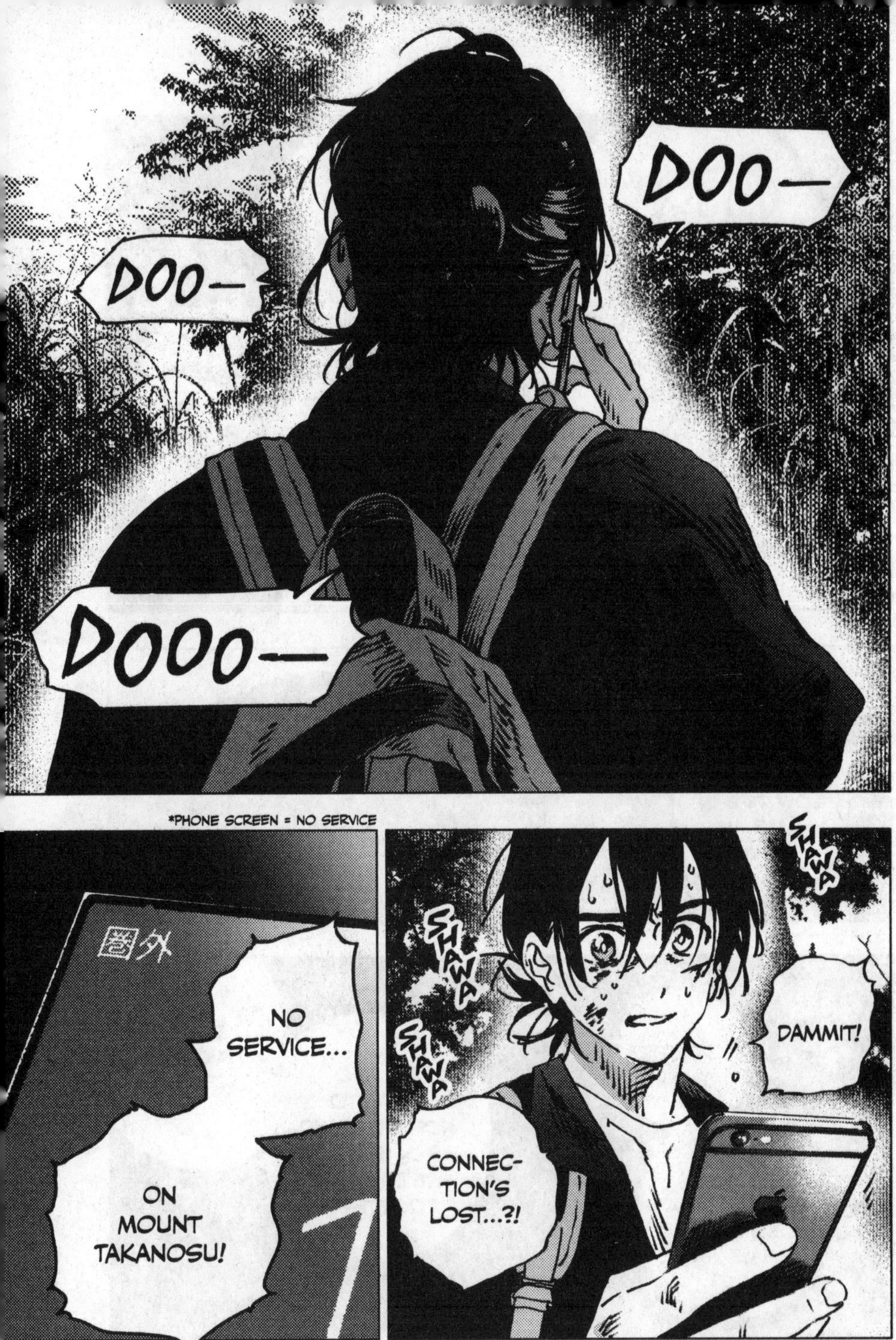
DOO—
DOO—
DOOO—
SHAWA
SHAWA
SHAWA
DAMMIT!
CONNEC-TION'S LOST...?!
*PHONE SCREEN = NO SERVICE
圏外
NO SERVICE...
ON MOUNT TAKANOSU!

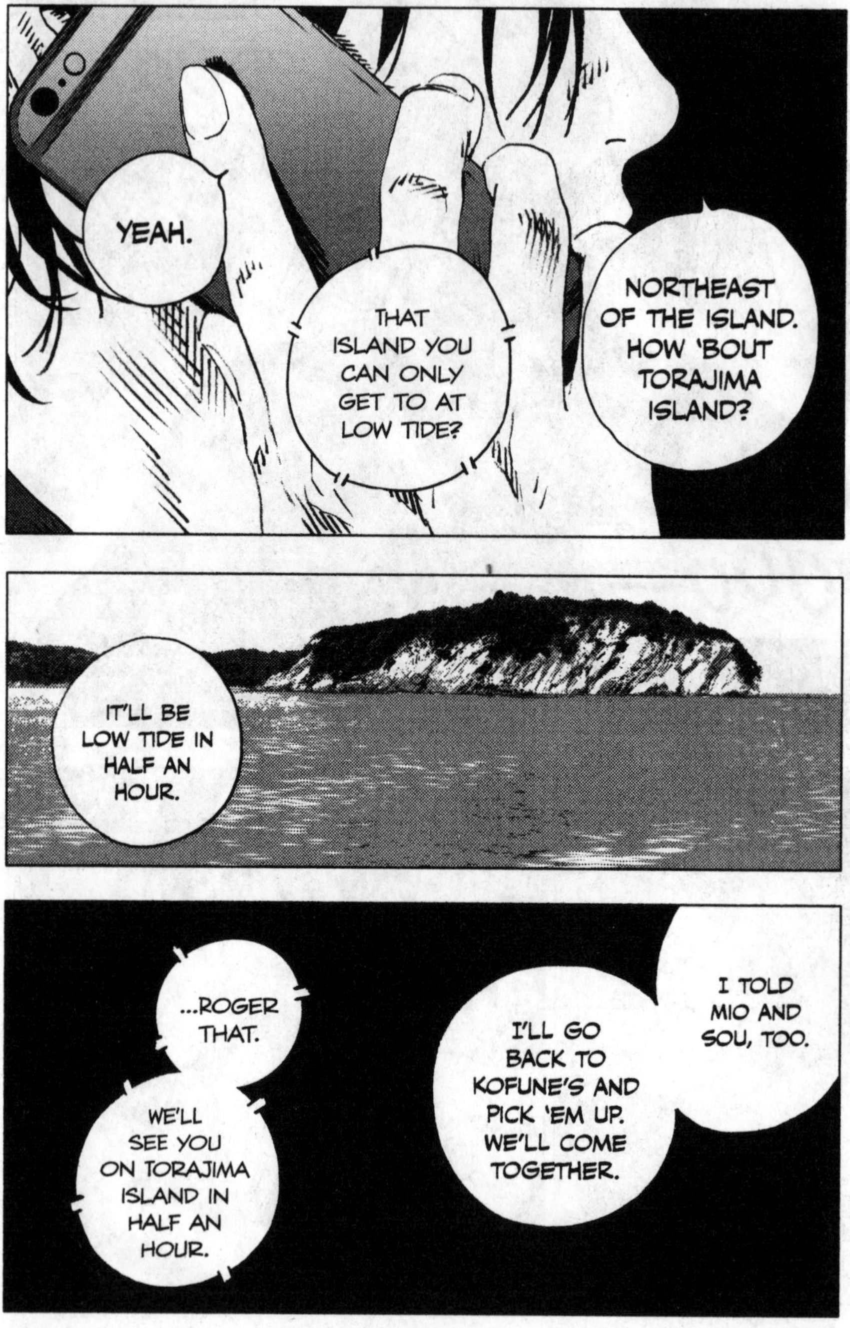
NORTHEAST OF THE ISLAND. HOW 'BOUT TORAJIMA ISLAND?
THAT ISLAND YOU CAN ONLY GET TO AT LOW TIDE?
YEAH.
IT'LL BE LOW TIDE IN HALF AN HOUR.
I TOLD MIO AND SOU, TOO.
I'LL GO BACK TO KOFUNE'S AND PICK 'EM UP. WE'LL COME TOGETHER.
...ROGER THAT.
WE'LL SEE YOU ON TORAJIMA ISLAND IN HALF AN HOUR.

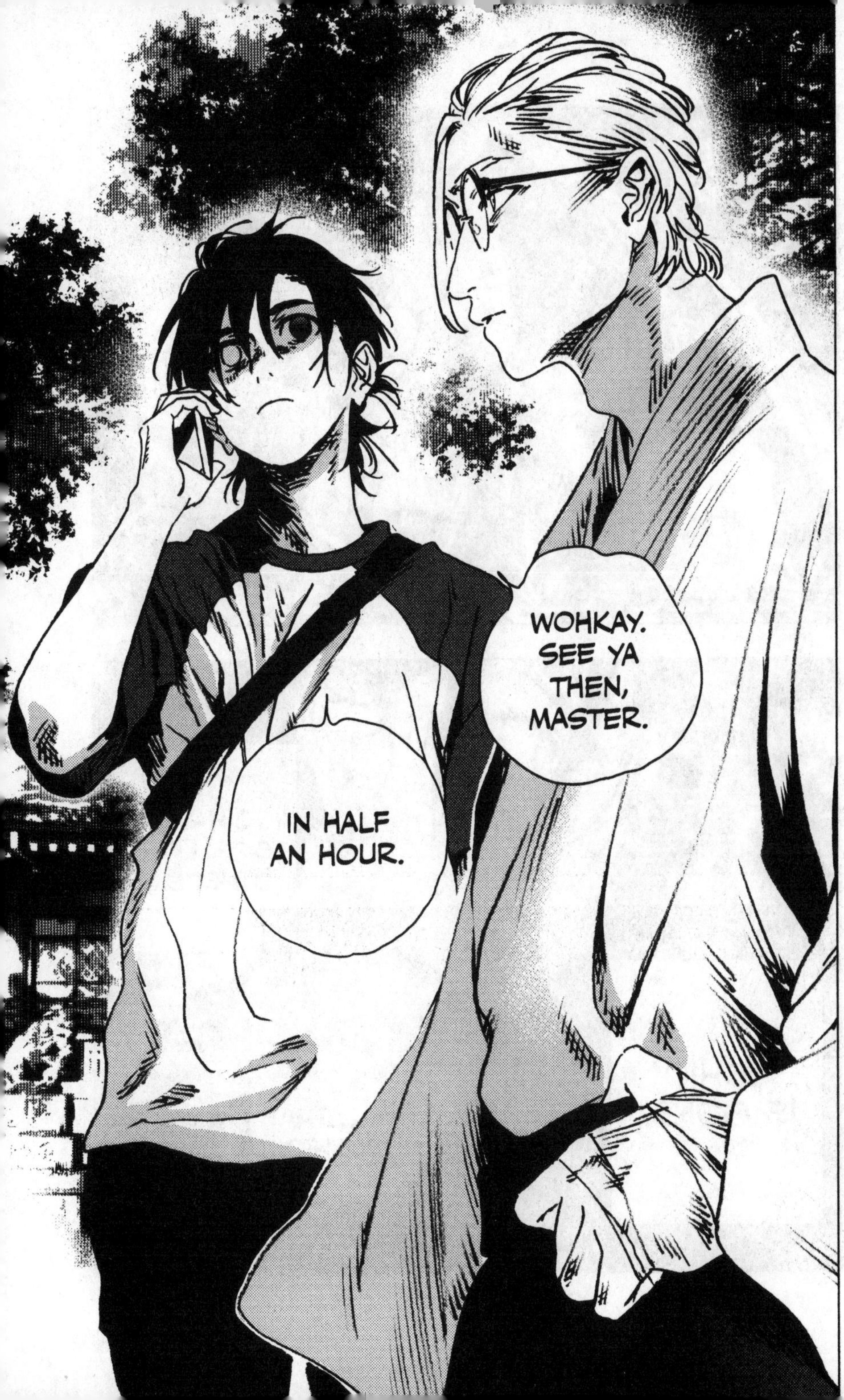
WOHKAY. SEE YA THEN, MASTER.
IN HALF AN HOUR.

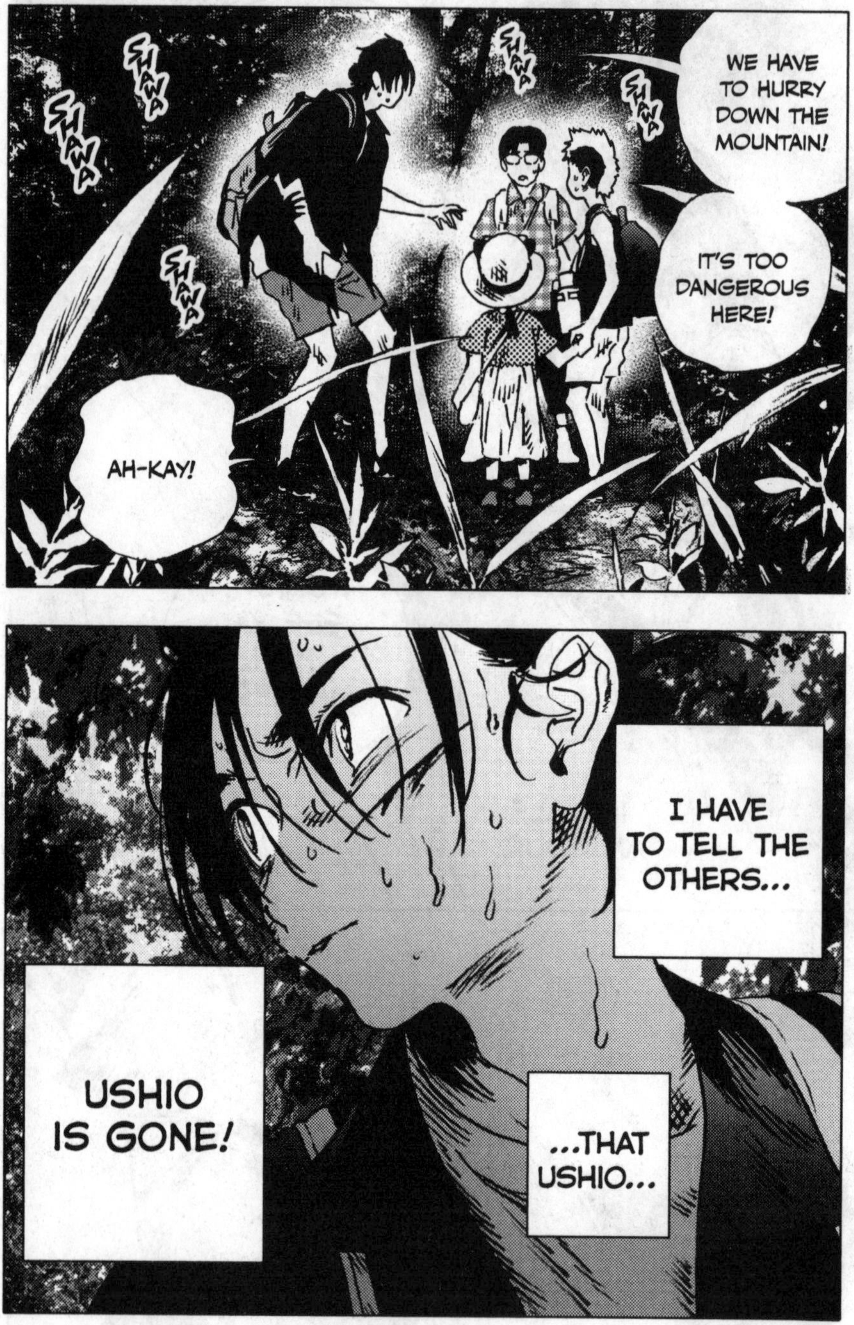
WE HAVE TO HURRY DOWN THE MOUNTAIN!
IT'S TOO DANGEROUS HERE!
SHAWA
SHAWA
SHAWA
SHAWA
AH-KAY!
I HAVE TO TELL THE OTHERS...
...THAT USHIO...
USHIO IS GONE!

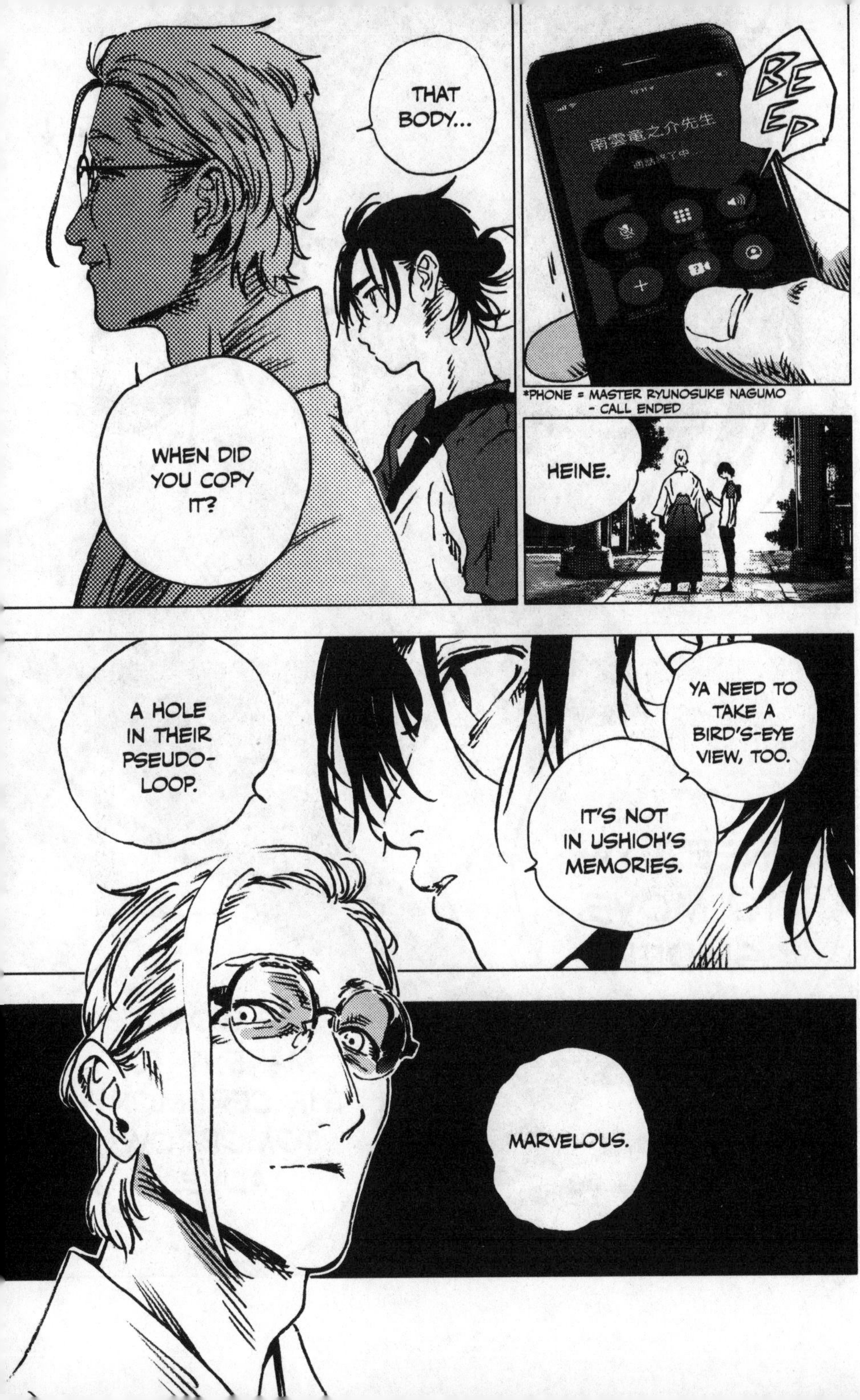
BEEP
南雲竜之介先生
*PHONE = MASTER RYUNOSUKE NAGUMO - CALL ENDED
HEINE.
THAT BODY...
WHEN DID YOU COPY IT?
YA NEED TO TAKE A BIRD'S-EYE VIEW, TOO.
IT'S NOT IN USHIOH'S MEMORIES.
A HOLE IN THEIR PSEUDO-LOOP.
MARVELOUS.

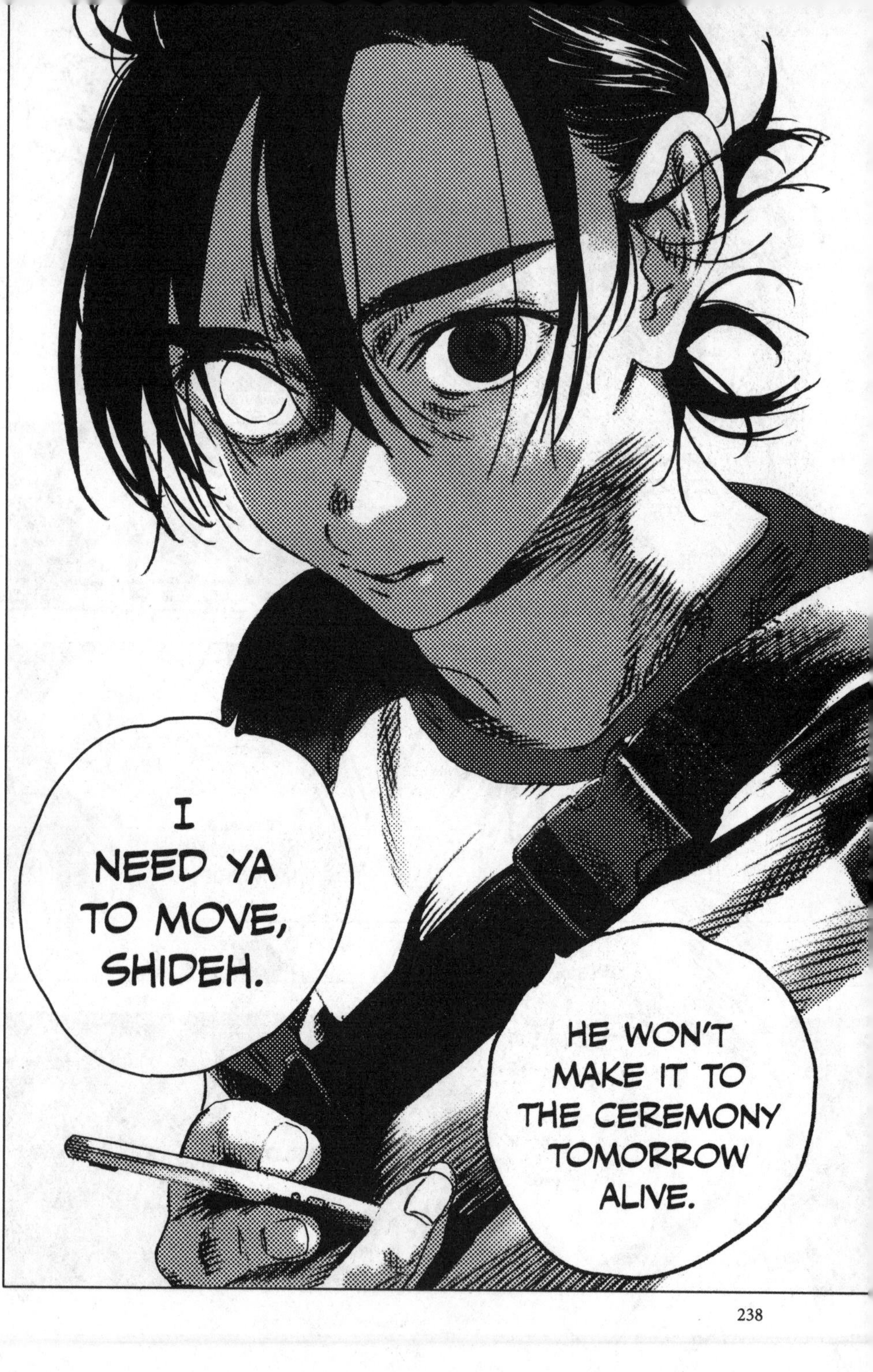
I NEED YA TO MOVE, SHIDEH.
HE WON'T MAKE IT TO THE CEREMONY TOMORROW ALIVE.

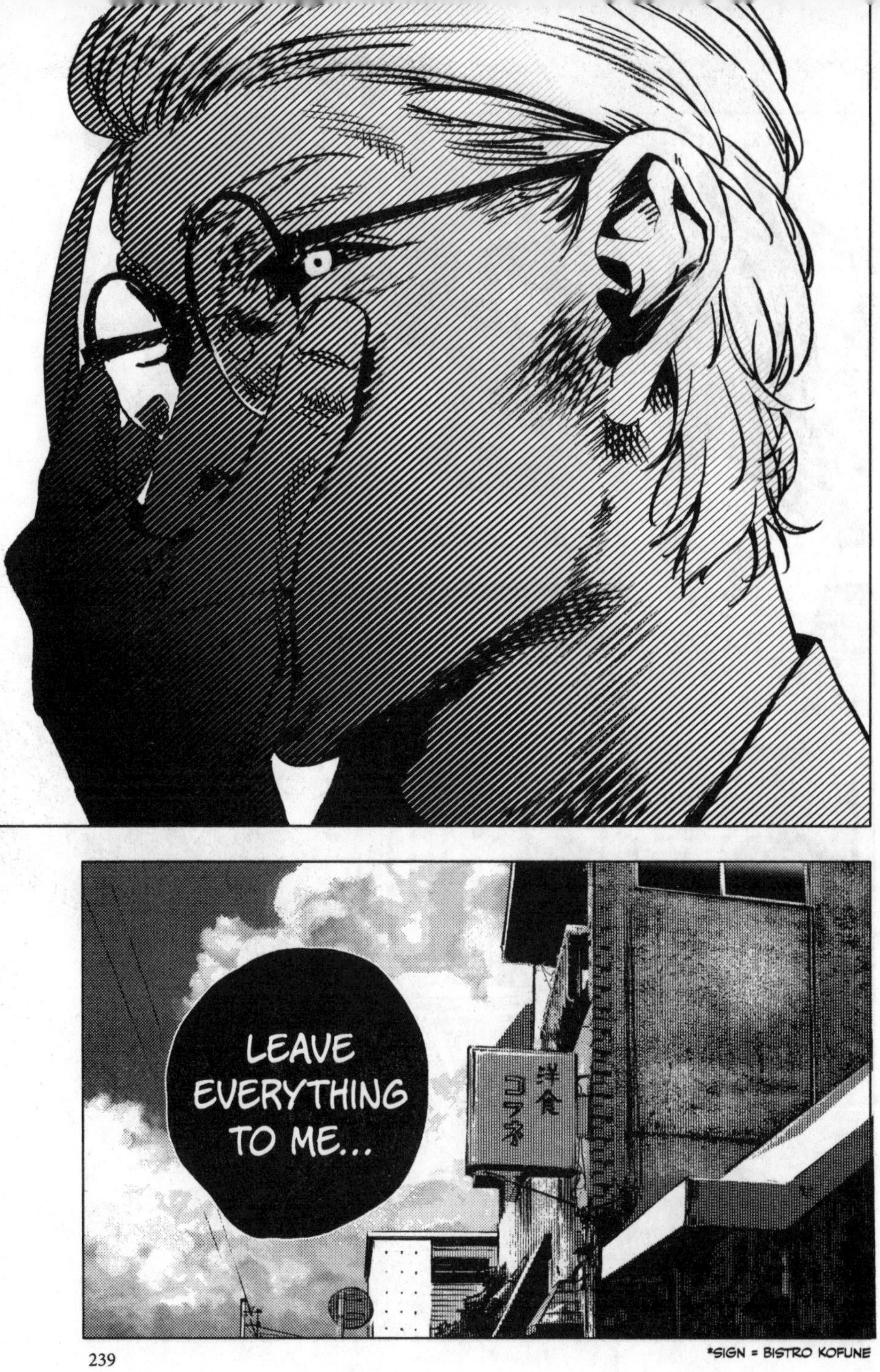
LEAVE EVERYTHING TO ME...
洋食 コフネ

*SIGN = BISTRO KOFUNE

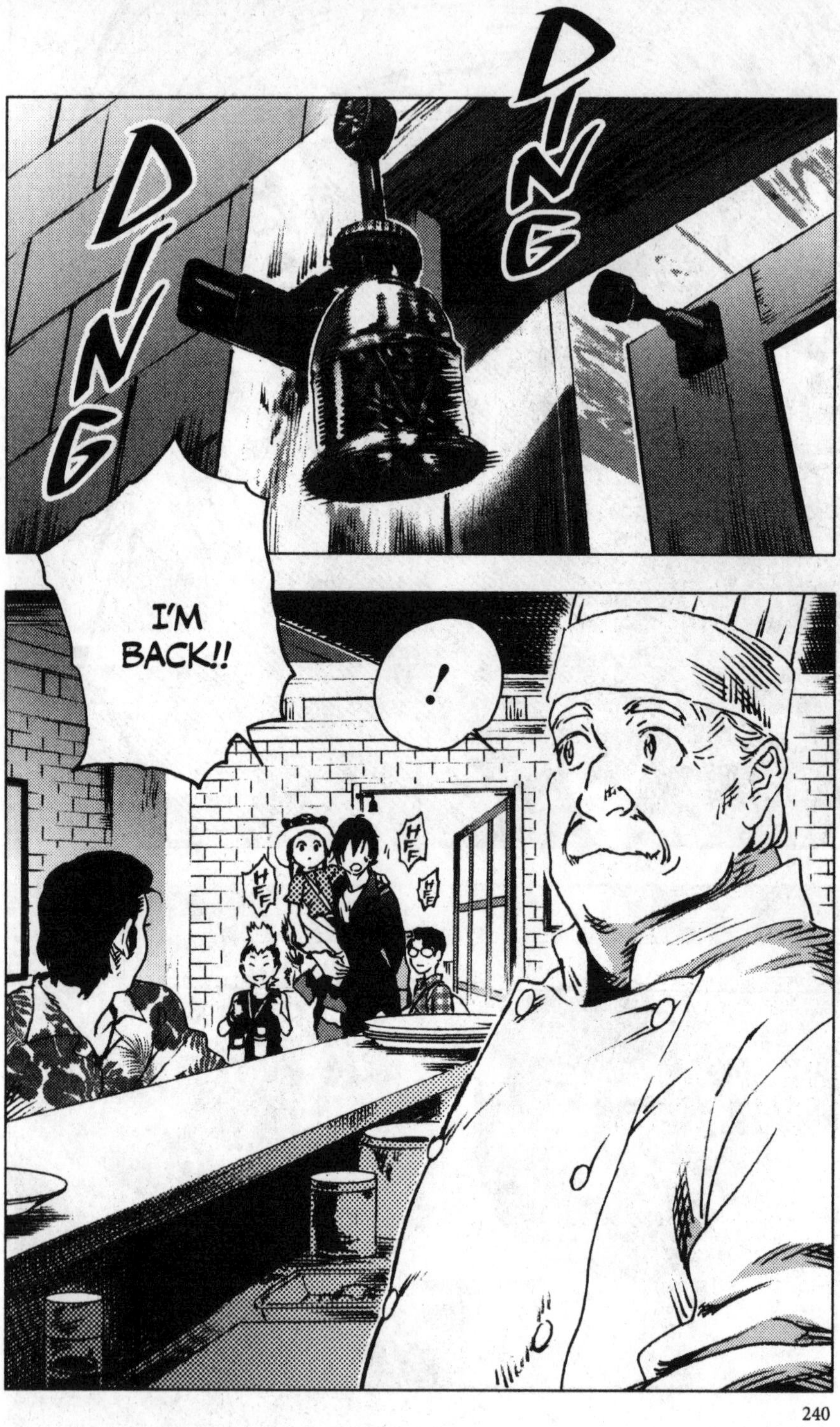
DING
DING
I'M BACK!!
!
HFF
HFF
HFF

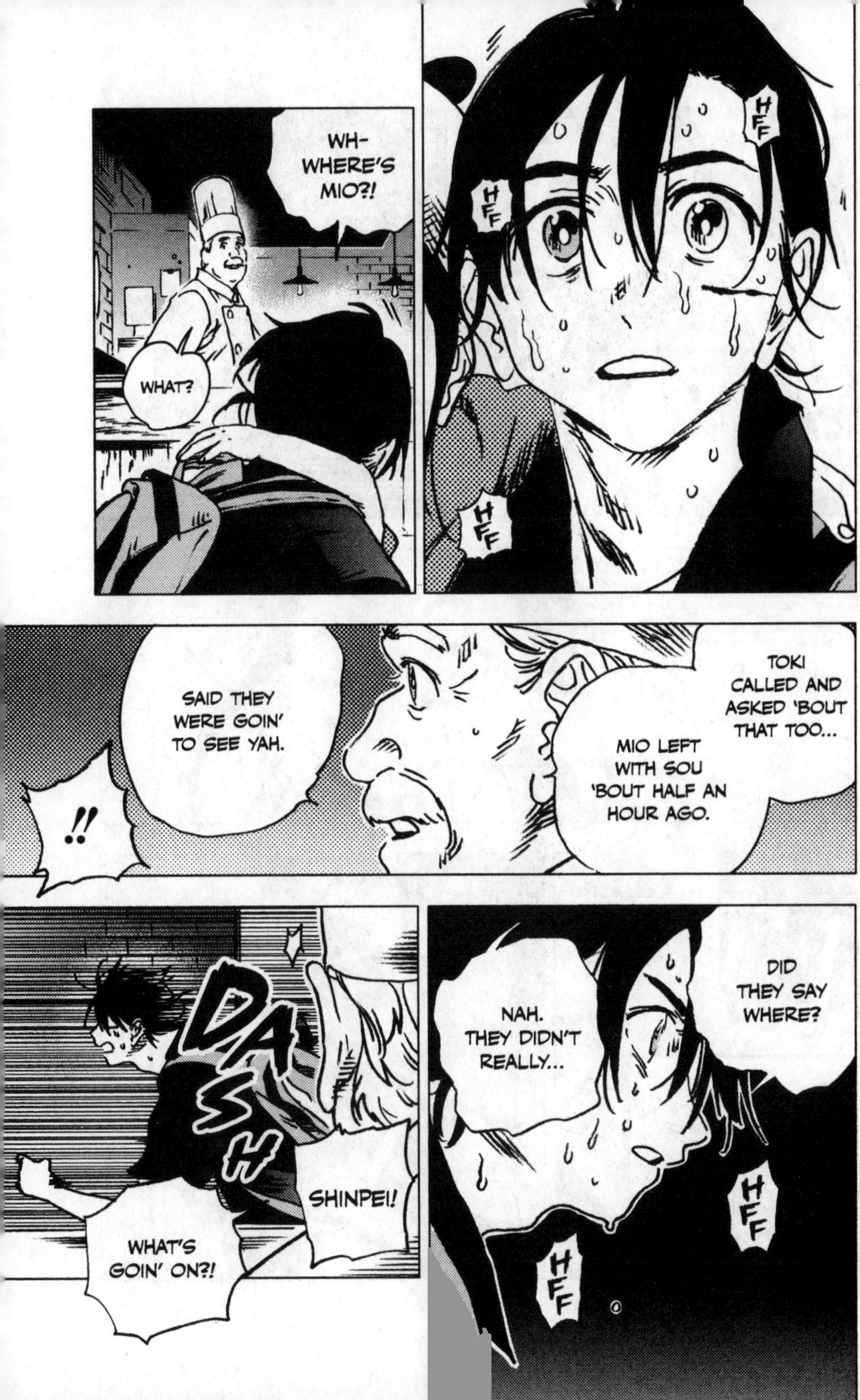
HFF
HFF
HFF
WH- WHERE'S MIO?!
WHAT?
TOKI CALLED AND ASKED 'BOUT THAT TOO...
MIO LEFT WITH SOU 'BOUT HALF AN HOUR AGO.
SAID THEY WERE GOIN' TO SEE YAH.
!!
DID THEY SAY WHERE?
NAH. THEY DIDN'T REALLY...
HFF
HFF
DASH
SHINPEI!
WHAT'S GOIN' ON?!

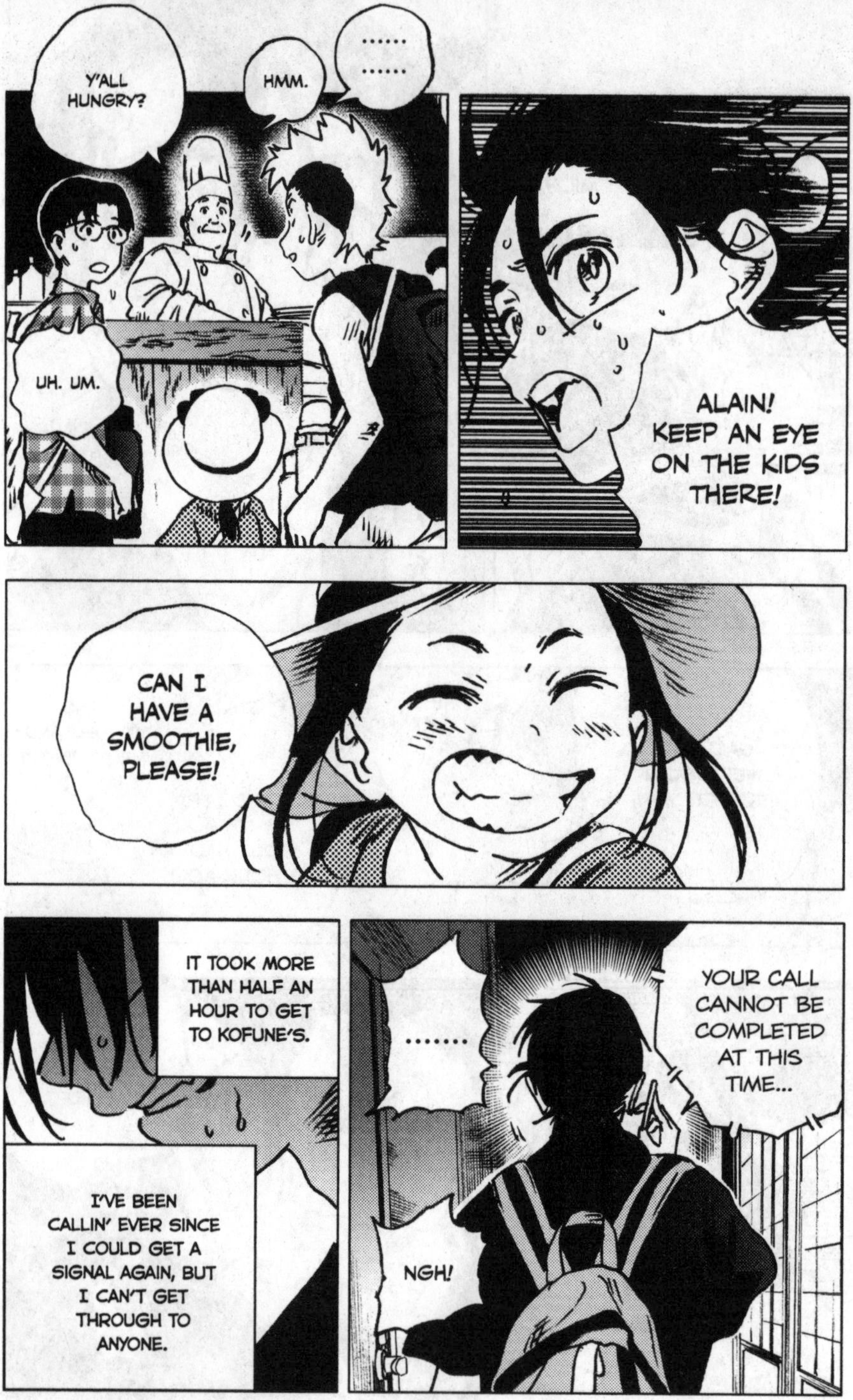
ALAIN! KEEP AN EYE ON THE KIDS THERE!
....
....
HMM.
Y'ALL HUNGRY?
UH. UM.
CAN I HAVE A SMOOTHIE, PLEASE!
YOUR CALL CANNOT BE COMPLETED AT THIS TIME...
....
NGH!
IT TOOK MORE THAN HALF AN HOUR TO GET TO KOFUNE'S.
I'VE BEEN CALLIN' EVER SINCE I COULD GET A SIGNAL AGAIN, BUT I CAN'T GET THROUGH TO ANYONE.

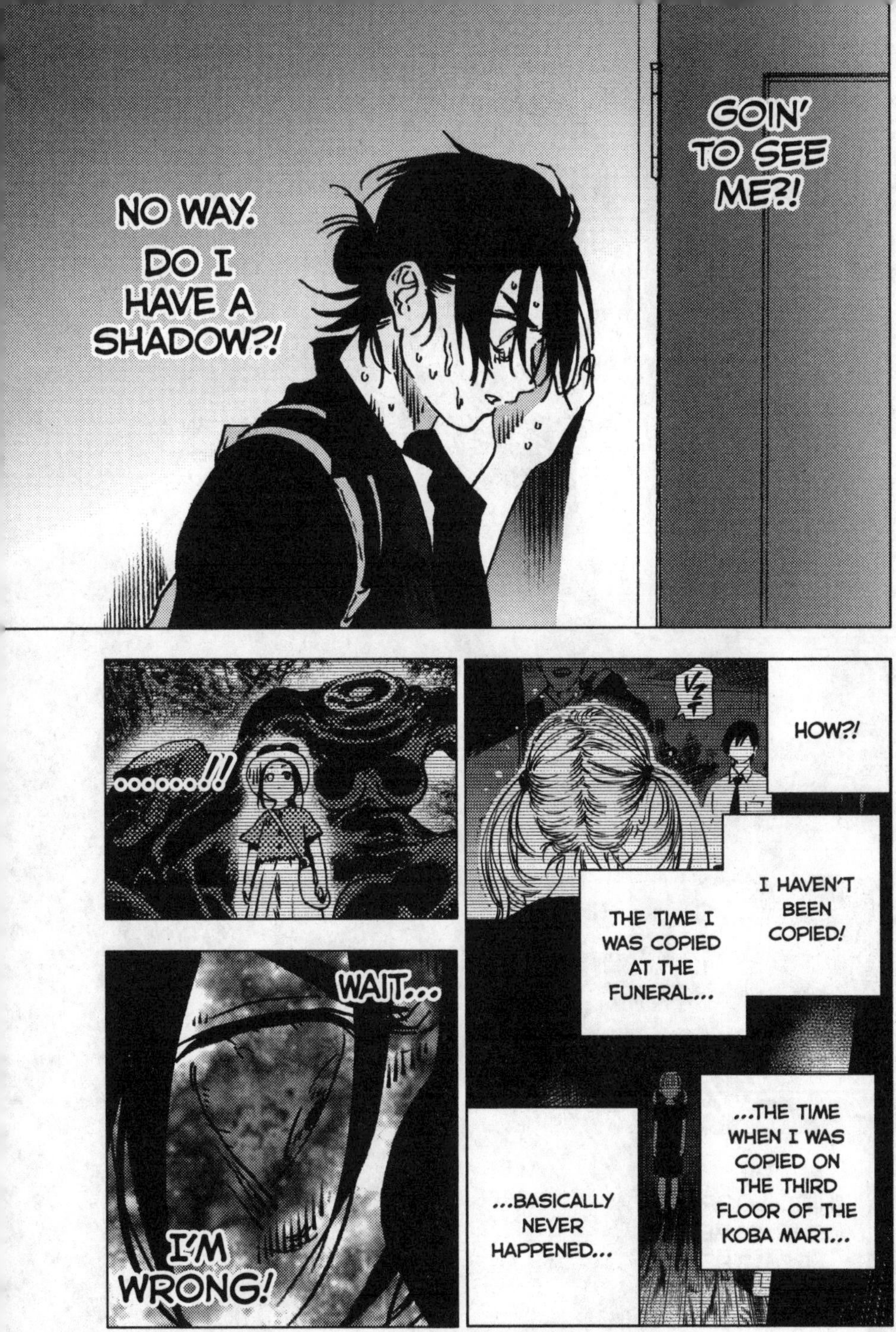
GOIN' TO SEE ME?!
NO WAY. DO I HAVE A SHADOW?!
HOW?!
I HAVEN'T BEEN COPIED!
THE TIME I WAS COPIED AT THE FUNERAL...
.......!!
...THE TIME WHEN I WAS COPIED ON THE THIRD FLOOR OF THE KOBA MART...
...BASICALLY NEVER HAPPENED...
WAIT...
I'M WRONG!

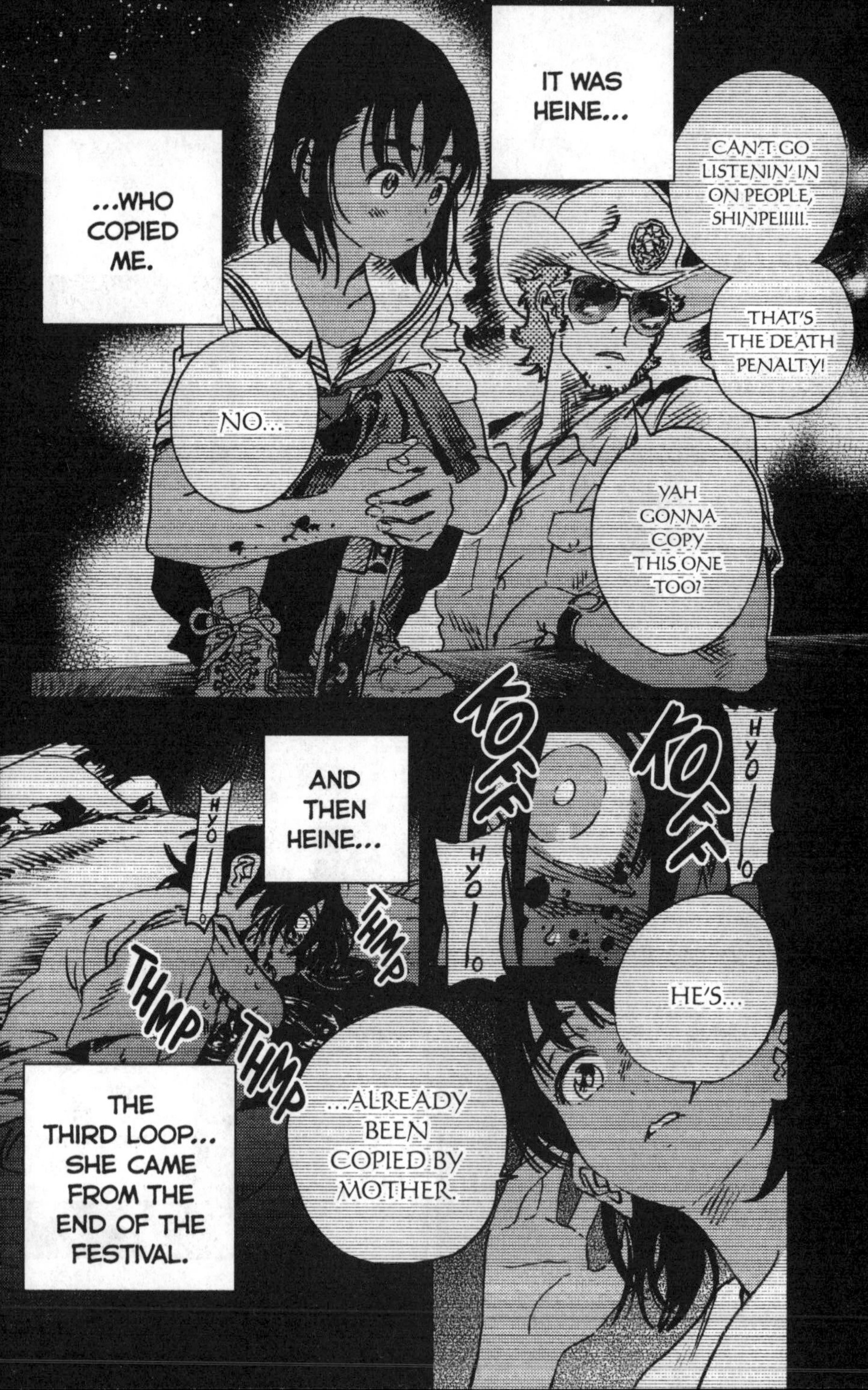
IT WAS HEINE...
CAN'T GO LISTENIN' IN ON PEOPLE, SHINPEIIIII.
THAT'S THE DEATH PENALTY!
...WHO COPIED ME.
NO...
YAH GONNA COPY THIS ONE TOO?
KOFF
KOFF
HYO
HYO
AND THEN HEINE...
HE'S...
...ALREADY BEEN COPIED BY MOTHER.
HYO
THMP
THMP
THMP
THE THIRD LOOP... SHE CAME FROM THE END OF THE FESTIVAL.

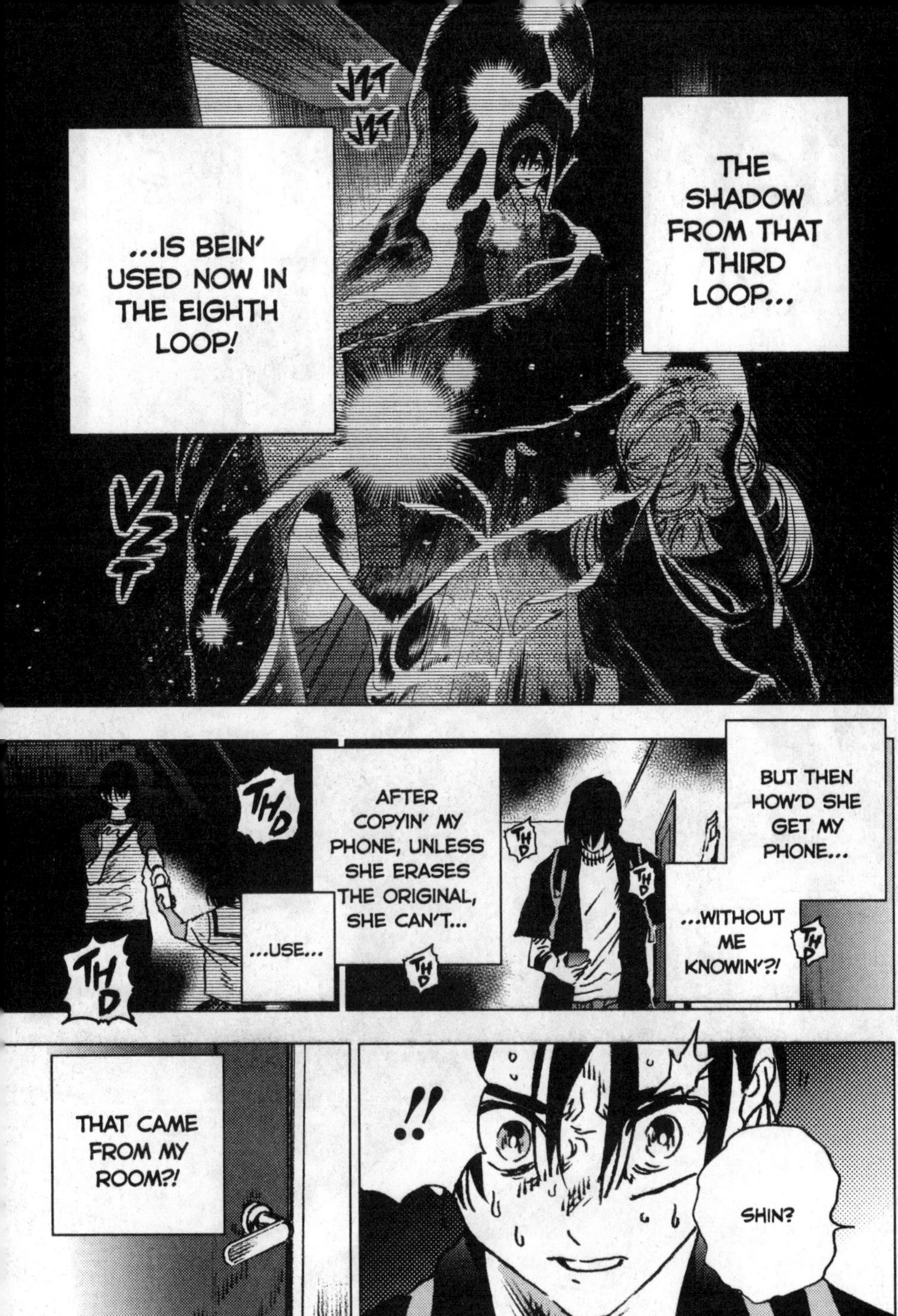
JZT
JZT
THE SHADOW FROM THAT THIRD LOOP...
...IS BEIN' USED NOW IN THE EIGHTH LOOP!
VZT
BUT THEN HOW'D SHE GET MY PHONE...
THD
THD
...WITHOUT ME KNOWIN'?!
THD
THD
AFTER COPYIN' MY PHONE, UNLESS SHE ERASES THE ORIGINAL, SHE CAN'T...
THD
...USE...
THD
!!
SHIN?
THAT CAME FROM MY ROOM?!

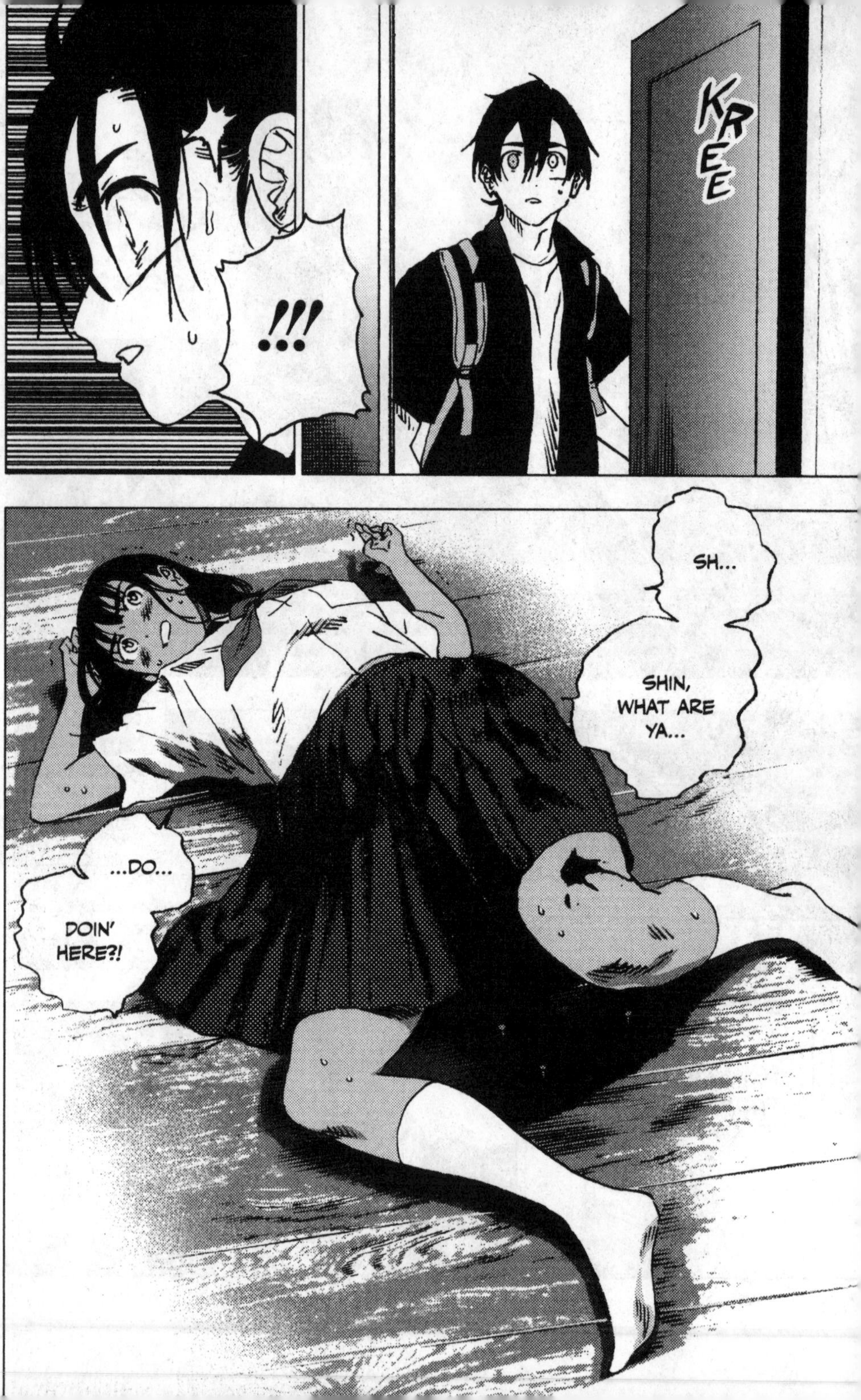
KREE
!!!
SH...
SHIN, WHAT ARE YA...
...DO...
DOIN' HERE?!

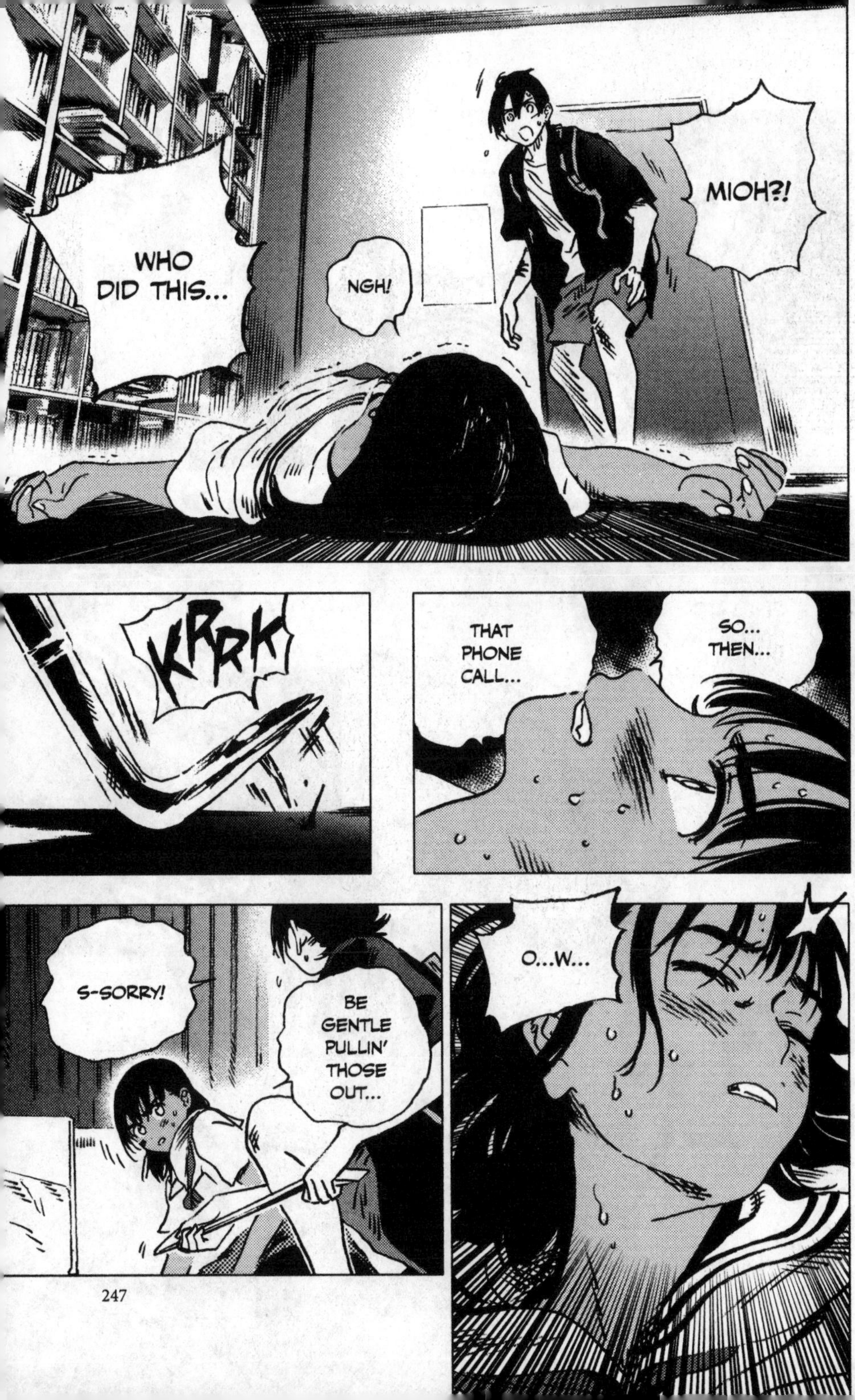
MIOH?!
NGH!
WHO DID THIS...
SO... THEN...
THAT PHONE CALL...
KRRK
O...W...
BE GENTLE PULLIN' THOSE OUT...
S-SORRY!

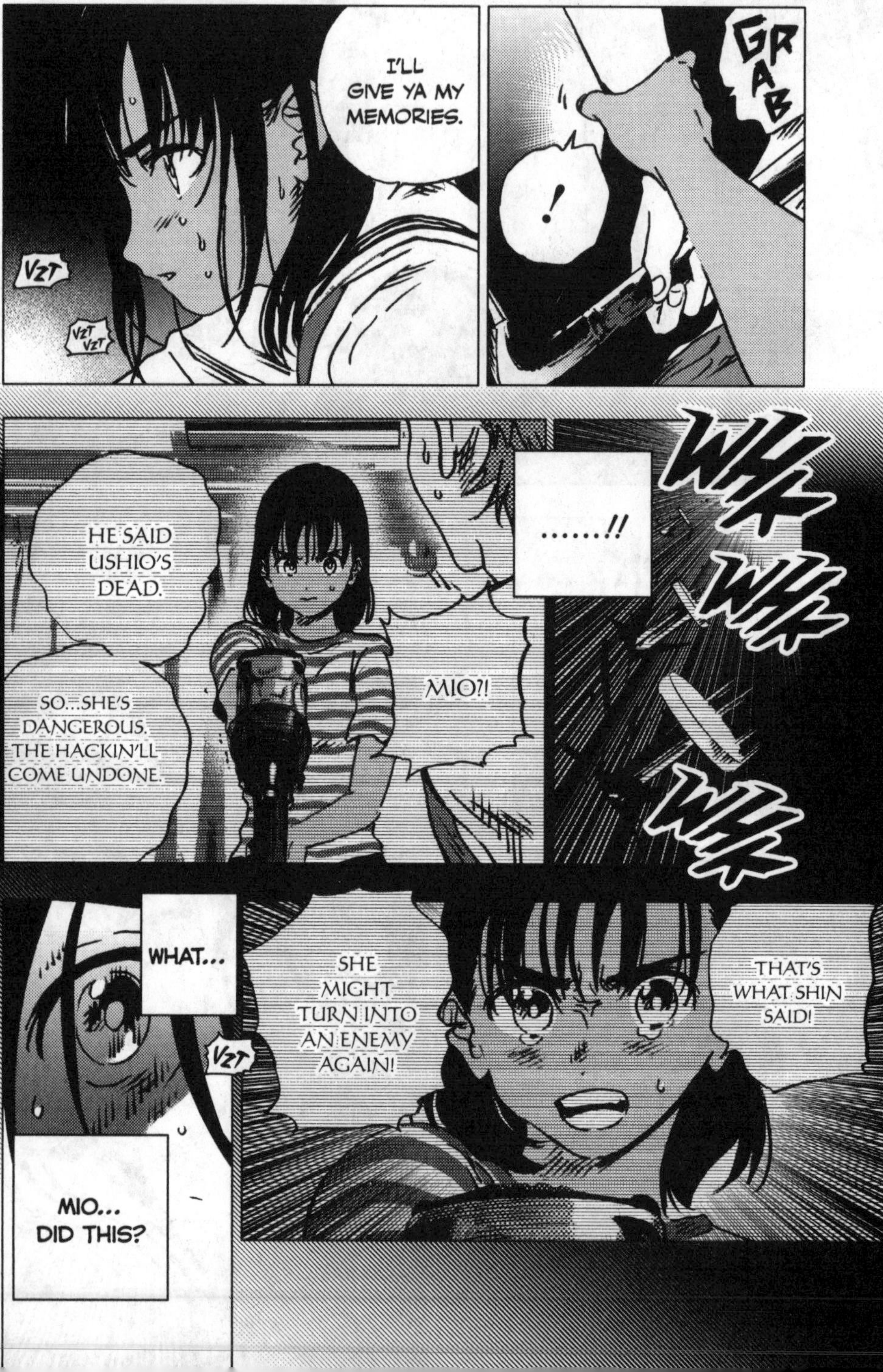
GRAB
!
I'LL GIVE YA MY MEMORIES.
VZT
VZT VZT
WHK WHK WHK
.......!!
MIO?!
HE SAID USHIO'S DEAD.
SO...SHE'S DANGEROUS. THE HACKIN'LL COME UNDONE.
THAT'S WHAT SHIN SAID!
SHE MIGHT TURN INTO AN ENEMY AGAIN!
WHAT...
VZT
MIO... DID THIS?

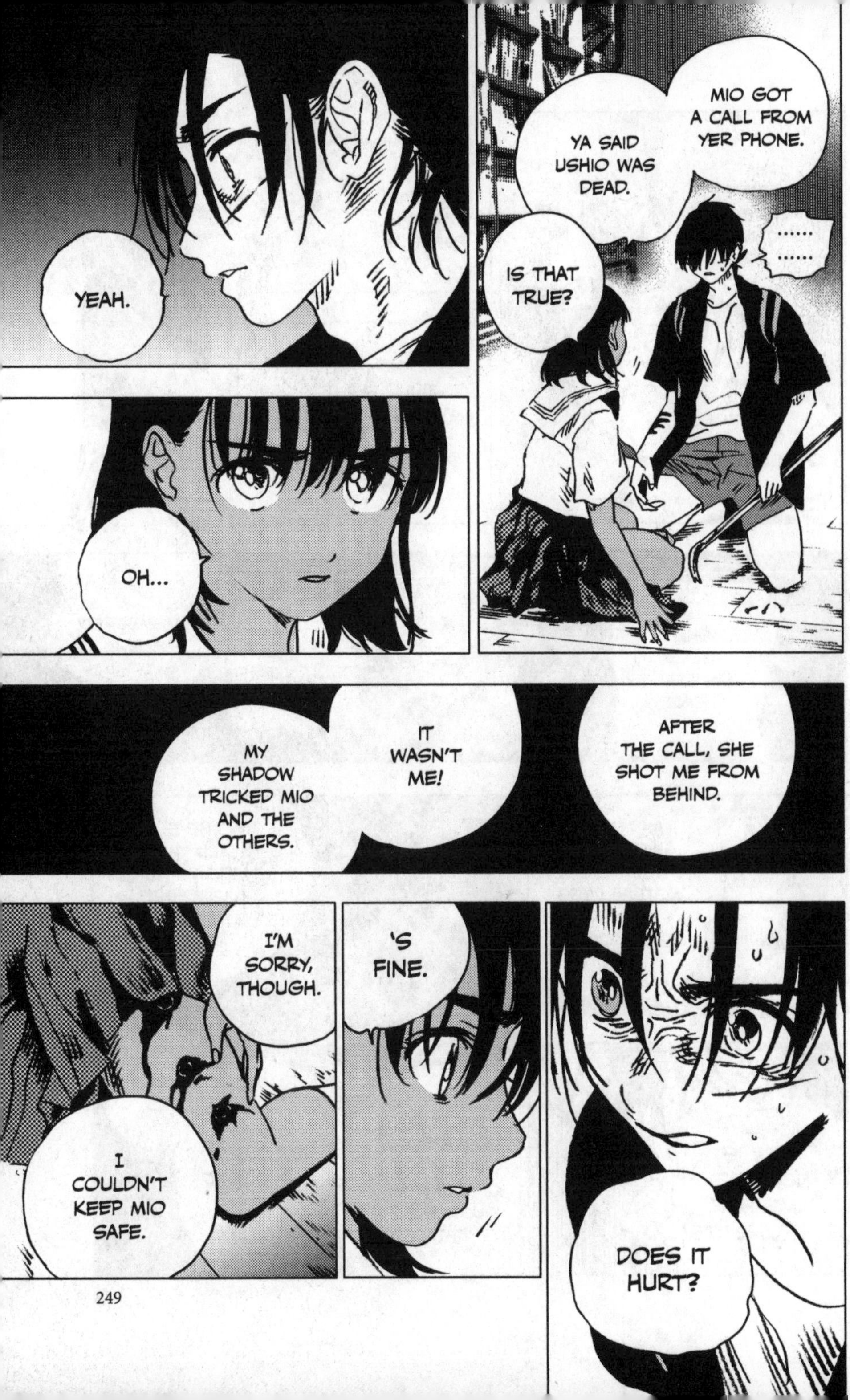
MIO GOT A CALL FROM YER PHONE.
YA SAID USHIO WAS DEAD.
......
......
IS THAT TRUE?
YEAH.
OH...
AFTER THE CALL, SHE SHOT ME FROM BEHIND.
IT WASN'T ME!
MY SHADOW TRICKED MIO AND THE OTHERS.
DOES IT HURT?
'S FINE.
I'M SORRY, THOUGH.
I COULDN'T KEEP MIO SAFE.

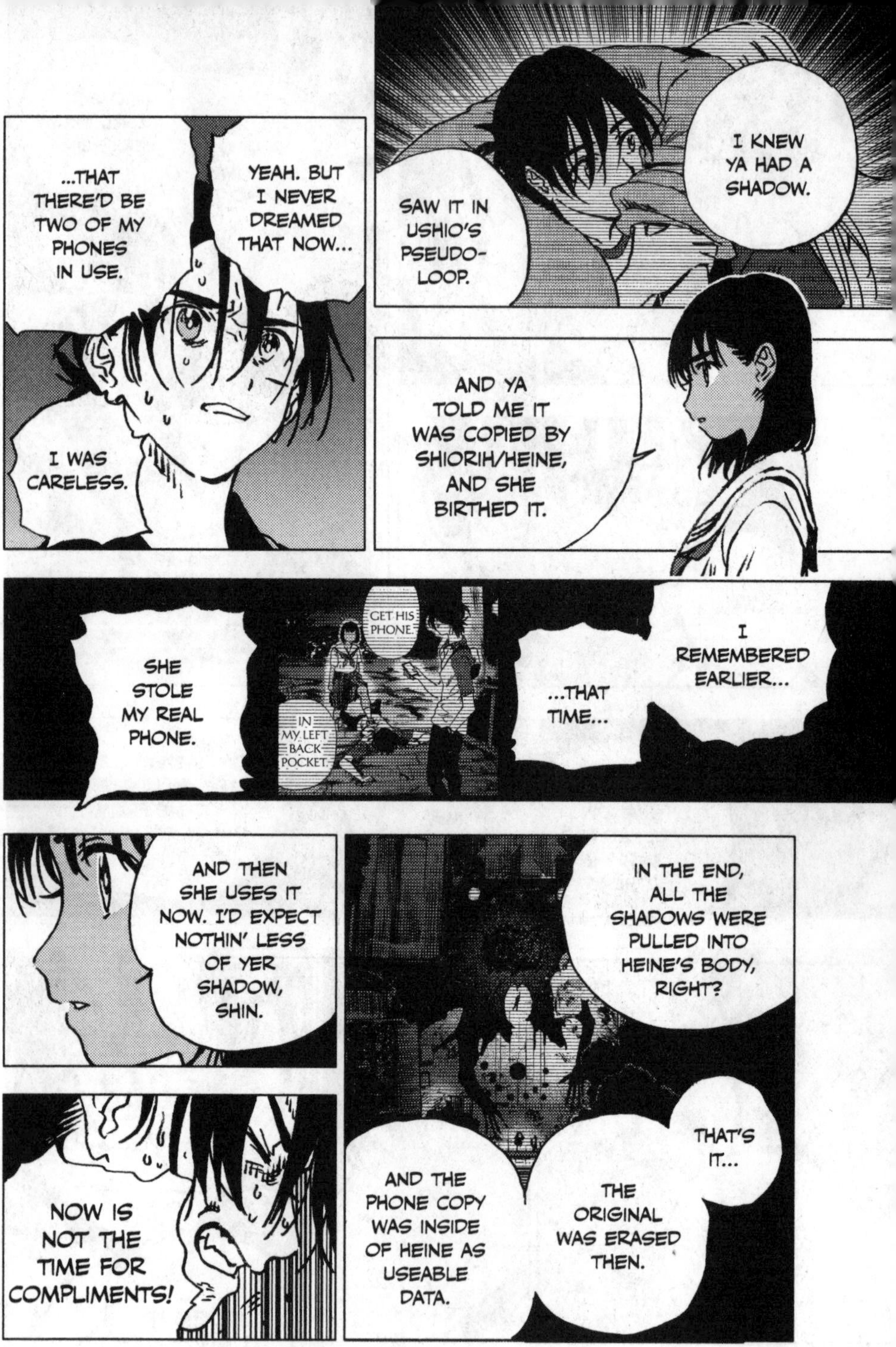
I KNEW YA HAD A SHADOW.
SAW IT IN USHIO'S PSEUDO-LOOP.
AND YA TOLD ME IT WAS COPIED BY SHIORIH/HEINE, AND SHE BIRTHED IT.
YEAH. BUT I NEVER DREAMED THAT NOW...
...THAT THERE'D BE TWO OF MY PHONES IN USE.
I WAS CARELESS.
I REMEMBERED EARLIER...
...THAT TIME...
GET HIS PHONE.
IN MY LEFT BACK POCKET.
SHE STOLE MY REAL PHONE.
IN THE END, ALL THE SHADOWS WERE PULLED INTO HEINE'S BODY, RIGHT?
THAT'S IT...
THE ORIGINAL WAS ERASED THEN.
AND THE PHONE COPY WAS INSIDE OF HEINE AS USEABLE DATA.
AND THEN SHE USES IT NOW. I'D EXPECT NOTHIN' LESS OF YER SHADOW, SHIN.
NOW IS NOT THE TIME FOR COMPLIMENTS!

AT THE END OF THE FOURTH LOOP, I WAS F... WOUND...

THEY... LIKELY... READ... MEMORY O... THE BATT... UP TO TH... POI...

...OST ...T WAS ...ITHER ...WERE ...D, AND ...U'S ...NE.

HEINE READ MASTER NAGUMO'S MEMORIES, TOO.

DID MIO SAY WHERE THEY WERE GOIN'?

THIS IS BAD. SHE KNOWS NAGUMO'S CONTACT INFO.

HELLO?!

MASTER NAGUMO!

....!!

雲竜ノ

BZZZ

*PHONE = RYUNOSUKE NAGUMO

!!!!

HEY...

...ME.

251

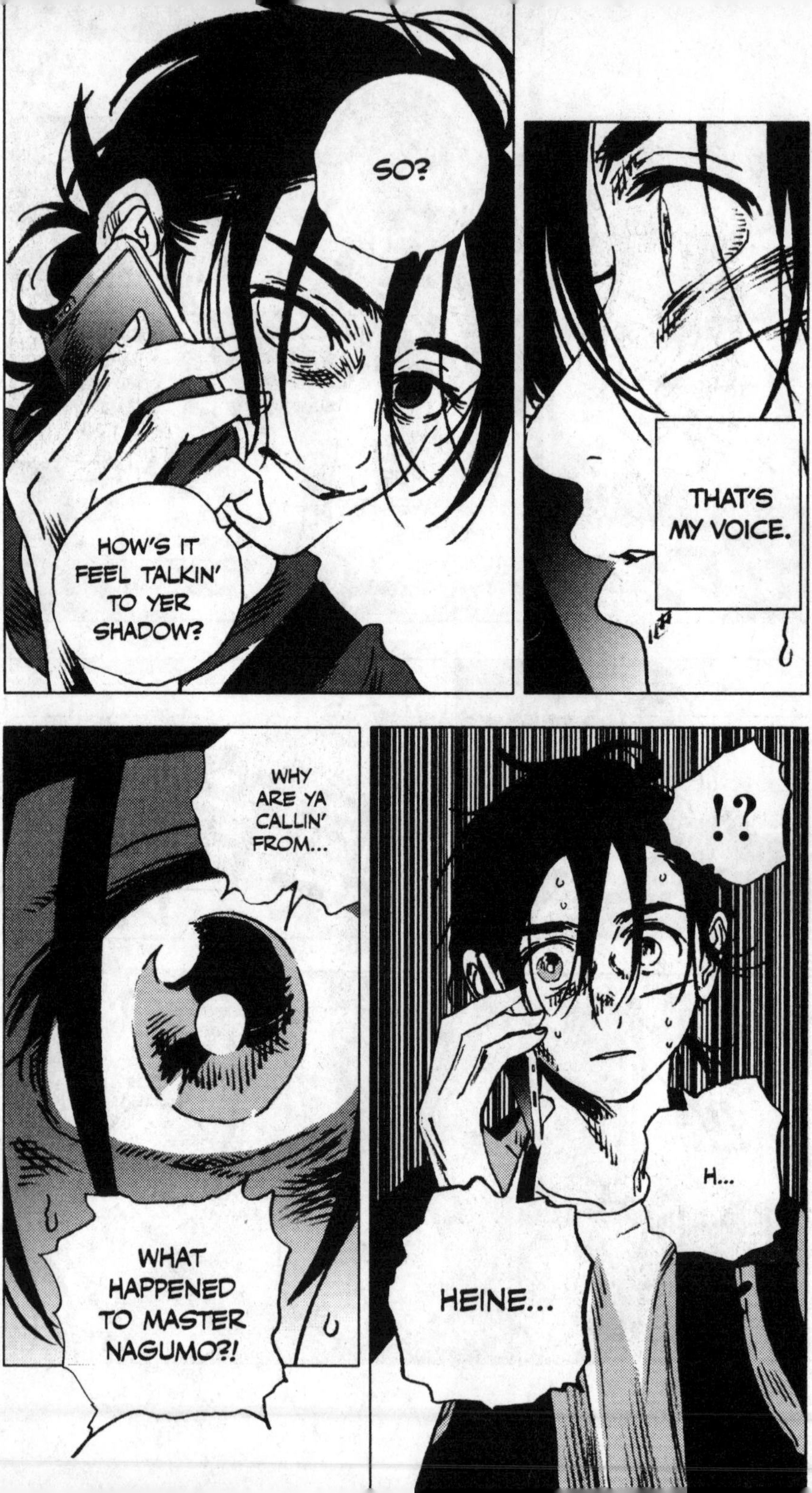
THAT'S MY VOICE.
SO?
HOW'S IT FEEL TALKIN' TO YER SHADOW?
!?
H...
HEINE...
WHY ARE YA CALLIN' FROM...
WHAT HAPPENED TO MASTER NAGUMO?!

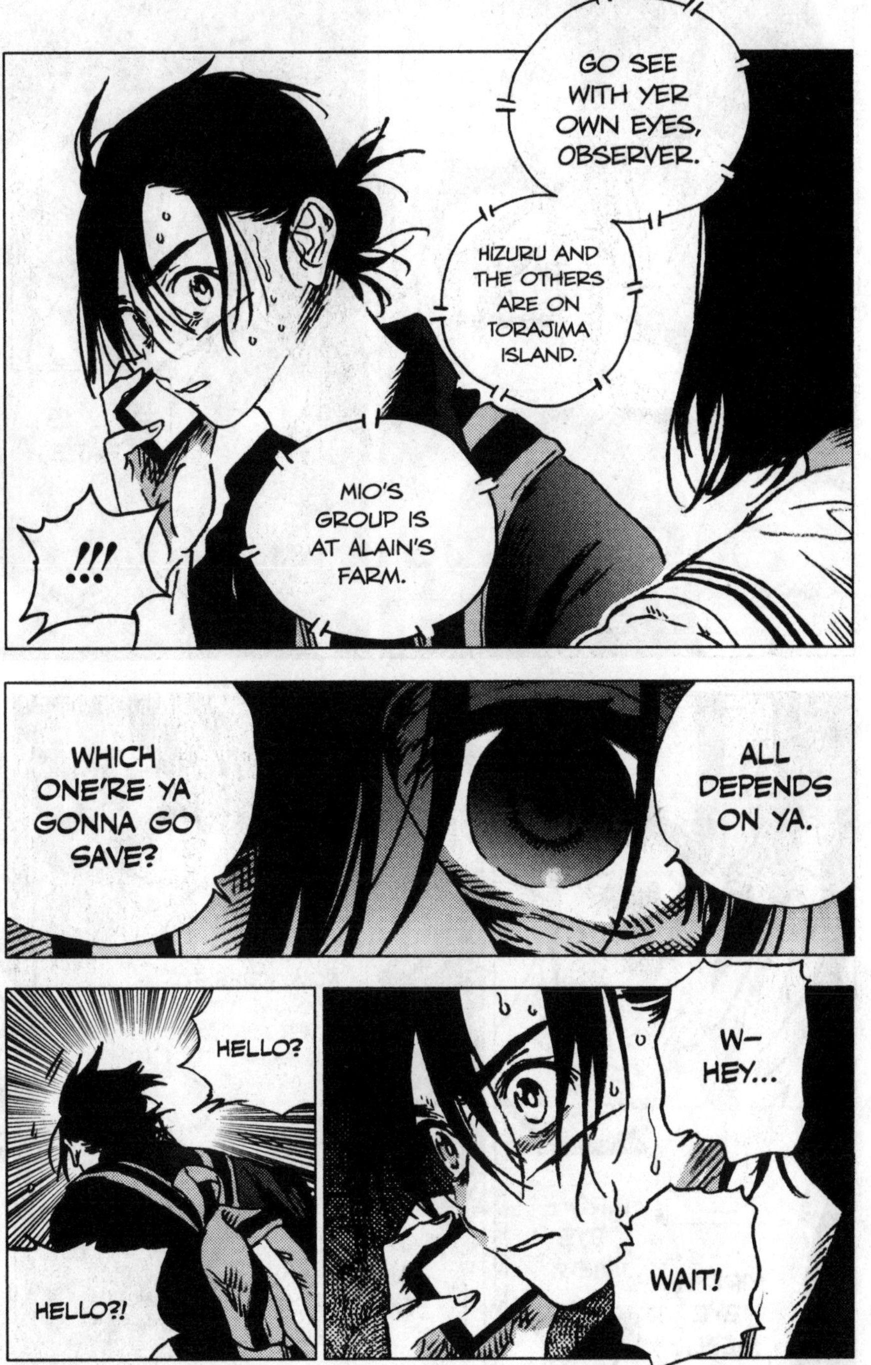
GO SEE WITH YER OWN EYES, OBSERVER.
HIZURU AND THE OTHERS ARE ON TORAJIMA ISLAND.
MIO'S GROUP IS AT ALAIN'S FARM.
!!!
ALL DEPENDS ON YA.
WHICH ONE'RE YA GONNA GO SAVE?
W— HEY...
WAIT!
HELLO?
HELLO?!

CALM DOWN, SHIN.

THINK OF ALL THE POSSIBILITIES.

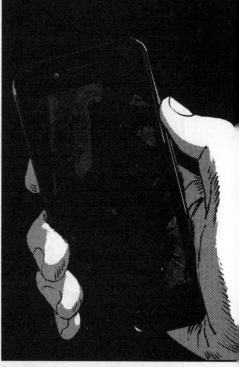

I KNOW...

NGH!

BIRD'S-EYE VIEW.

BIRD'S-EYE VIEW...

RIGHT NOW, HEINE'S THINKIN' WITH YER MIND, SHIN.

WE'RE ALSO BEIN' BIRD'S-EYE VIEWED.

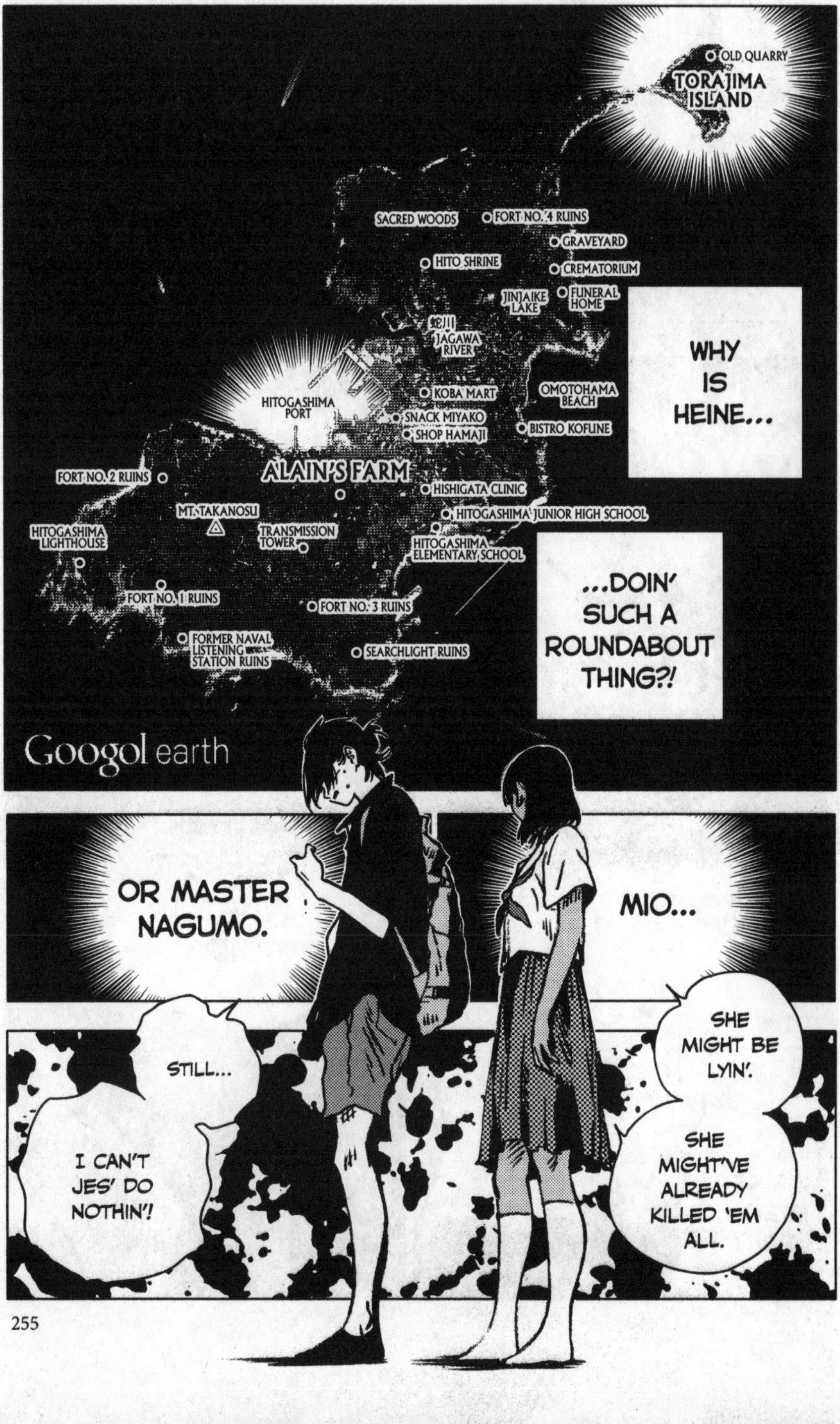
OLD QUARRY
TORAJIMA ISLAND
SACRED WOODS
FORT NO. 4 RUINS
GRAVEYARD
HITO SHRINE
CREMATORIUM
JINJAIKE LAKE
FUNERAL HOME
JAGAWA RIVER
KOBA MART
OMOTOHAMA BEACH
HITOGASHIMA PORT
SNACK MIYAKO
SHOP HAMAJI
BISTRO KOFUNE
FORT NO. 2 RUINS
ALAIN'S FARM
HISHIGATA CLINIC
MT. TAKANOSU
HITOGASHIMA JUNIOR HIGH SCHOOL
HITOGASHIMA LIGHTHOUSE
TRANSMISSION TOWER
HITOGASHIMA ELEMENTARY SCHOOL
FORT NO. 1 RUINS
FORT NO. 3 RUINS
FORMER NAVAL LISTENING STATION RUINS
SEARCHLIGHT RUINS
Googol earth
WHY IS HEINE...
...DOIN' SUCH A ROUNDABOUT THING?!
MIO...
OR MASTER NAGUMO.
SHE MIGHT BE LYIN'.
SHE MIGHT'VE ALREADY KILLED 'EM ALL.
STILL...
I CAN'T JES' DO NOTHIN'!

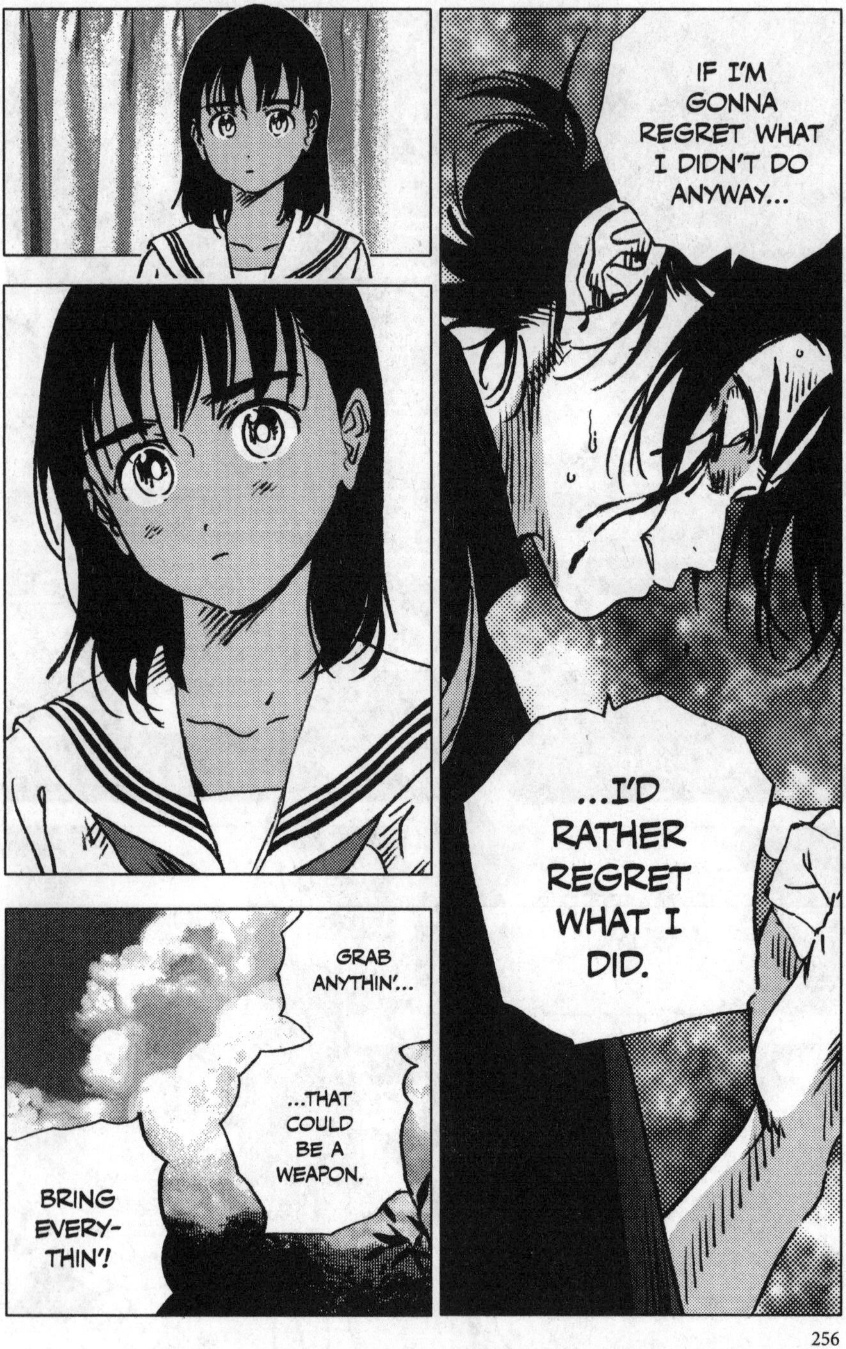
IF I'M GONNA REGRET WHAT I DIDN'T DO ANYWAY...
...I'D RATHER REGRET WHAT I DID.
GRAB ANYTHIN'...
...THAT COULD BE A WEAPON.
BRING EVERY-THIN'!

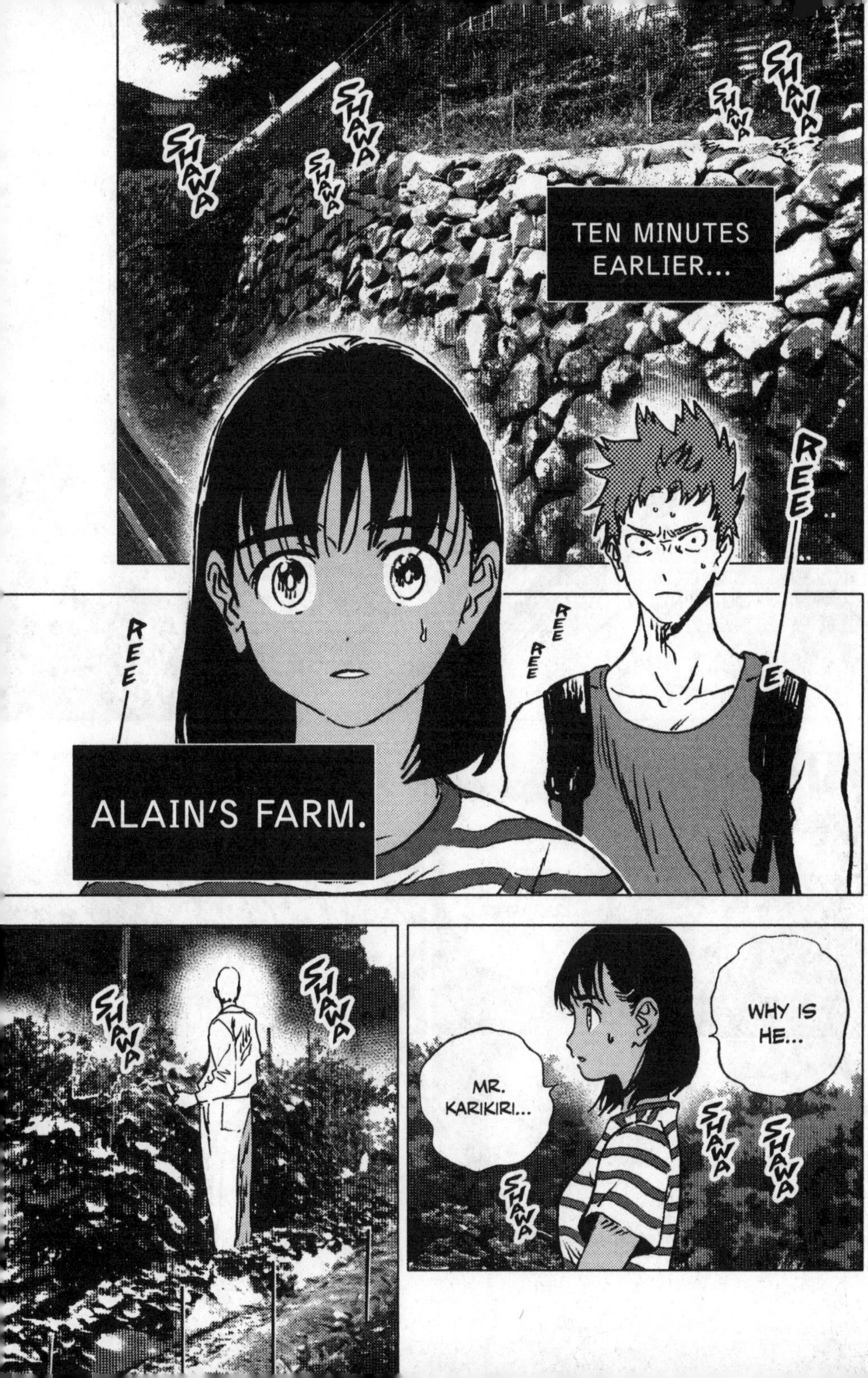
SHAWA
SHAWA
TEN MINUTES EARLIER...
SHAWA
SHAWA
SHAWA
REE
REE
REE
REE
REE
ALAIN'S FARM.
WHY IS HE...
MR. KARIKIRI...
SHAWA
SHAWA
SHAWA
SHAWA
SHAWA

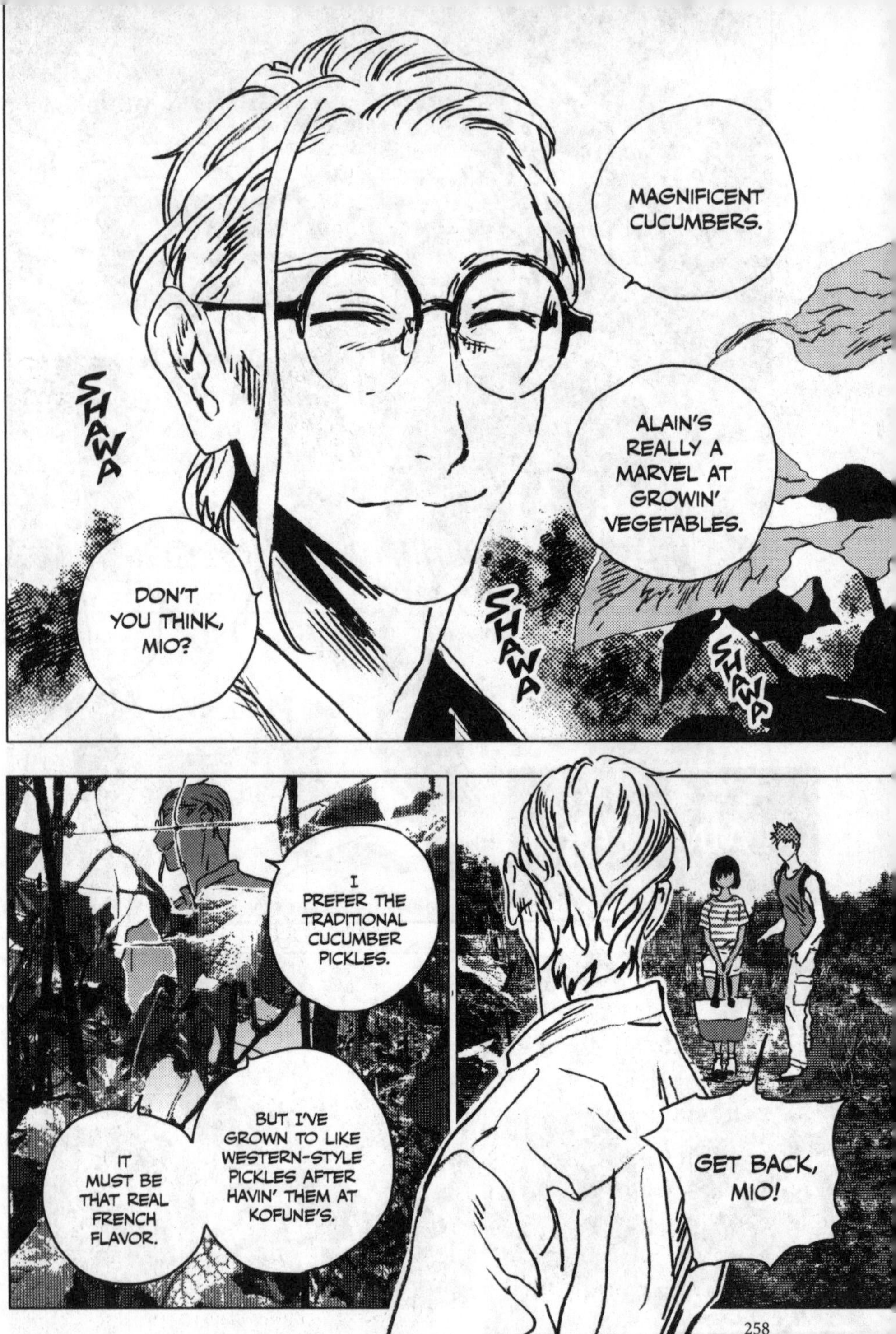
MAGNIFICENT CUCUMBERS.
ALAIN'S REALLY A MARVEL AT GROWIN' VEGETABLES.
SHAWA
SHAWA
SHAWA
DON'T YOU THINK, MIO?
GET BACK, MIO!
I PREFER THE TRADITIONAL CUCUMBER PICKLES.
BUT I'VE GROWN TO LIKE WESTERN-STYLE PICKLES AFTER HAVIN' THEM AT KOFUNE'S.
IT MUST BE THAT REAL FRENCH FLAVOR.

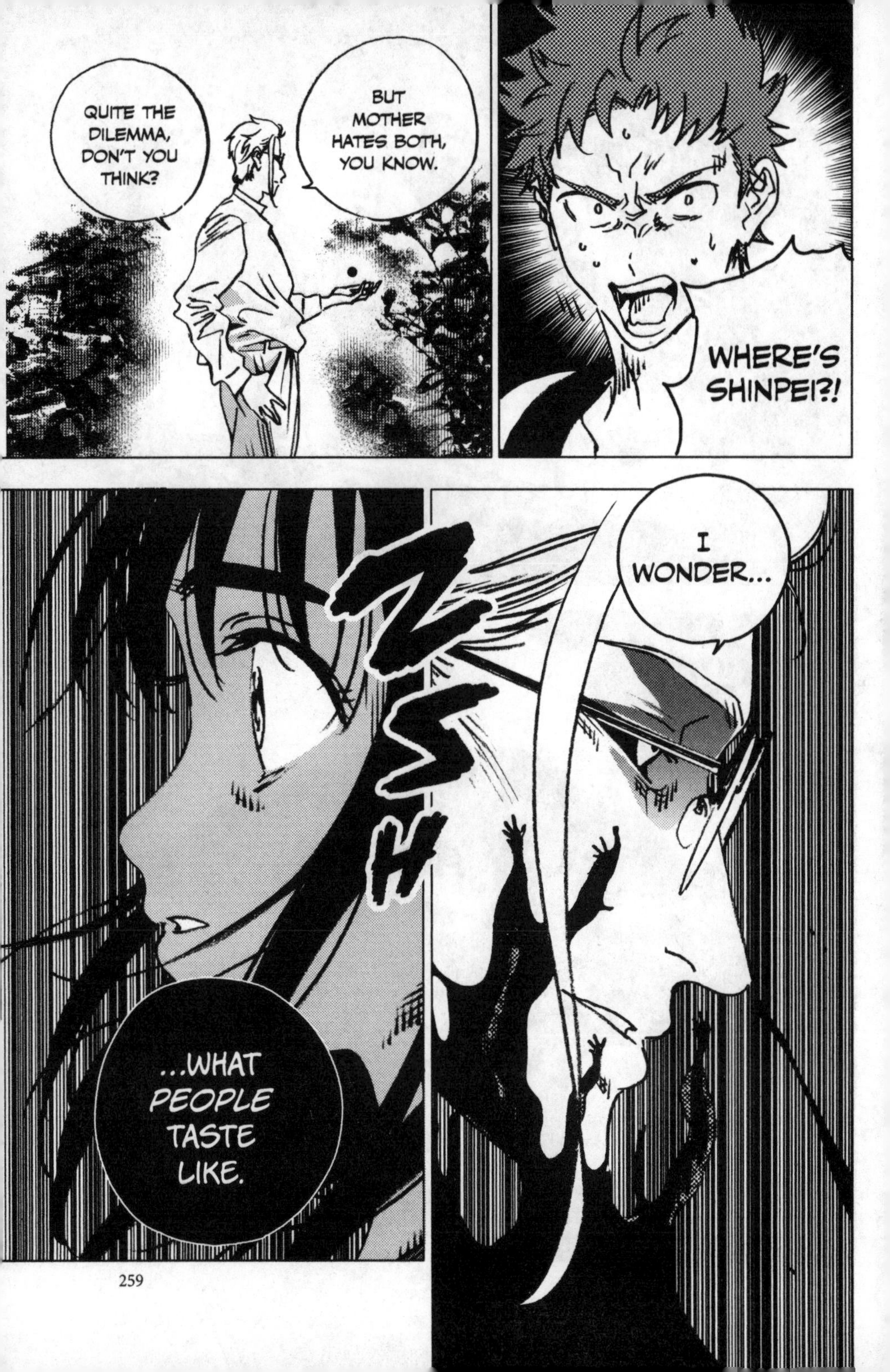
WHERE'S SHINPEI?!
BUT MOTHER HATES BOTH, YOU KNOW.
QUITE THE DILEMMA, DON'T YOU THINK?
I WONDER...
ZSH
...WHAT PEOPLE TASTE LIKE.

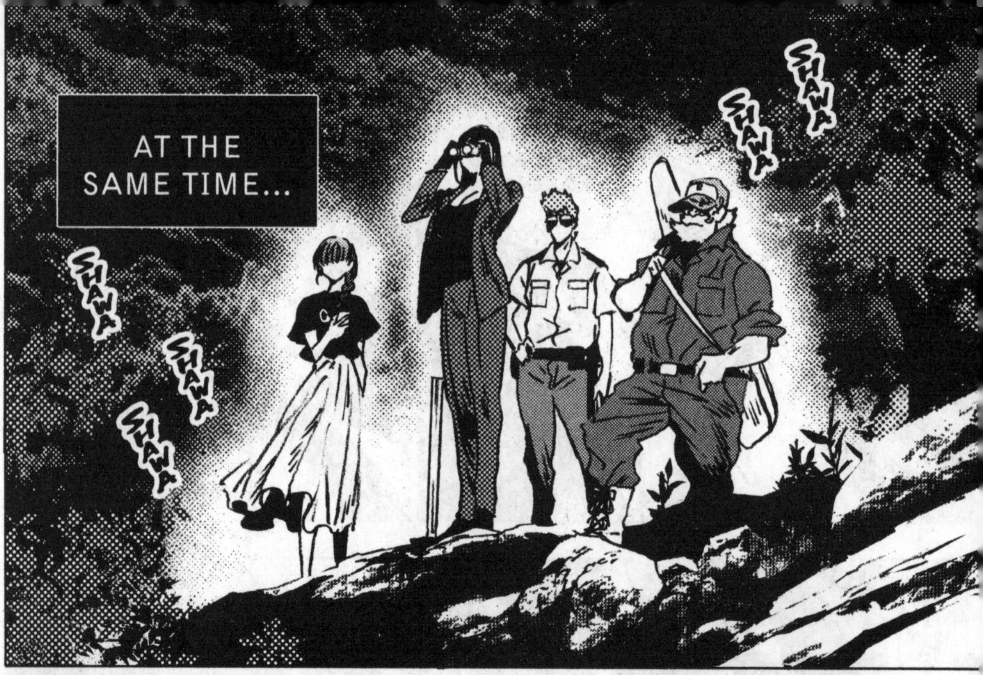
SHAWA
SHAWA
AT THE SAME TIME...
SHAWA
SHAWA
SHAWA
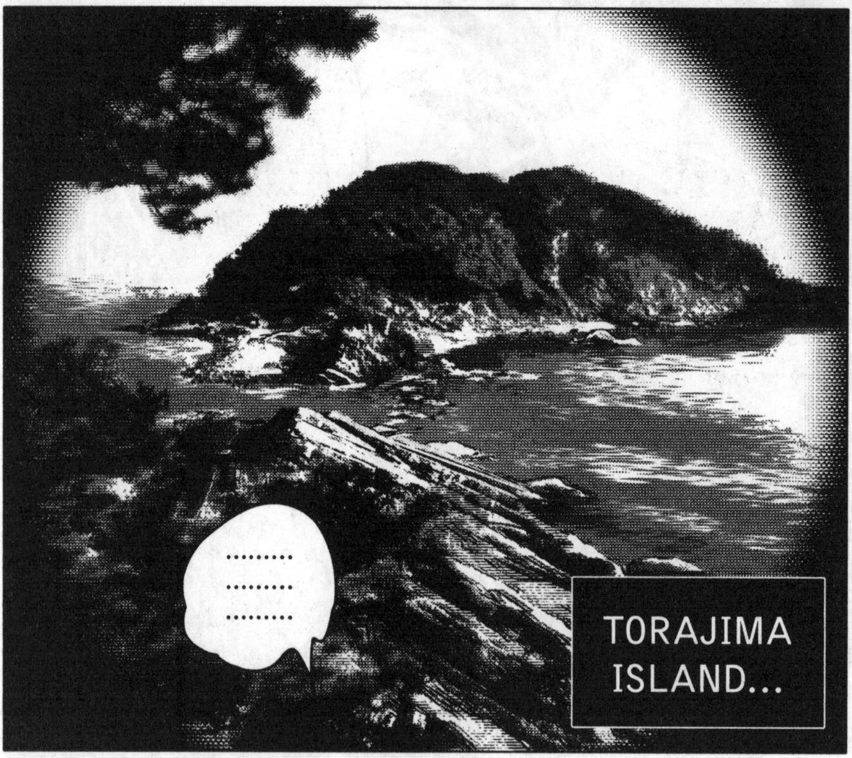
TORAJIMA ISLAND...
....
....
....

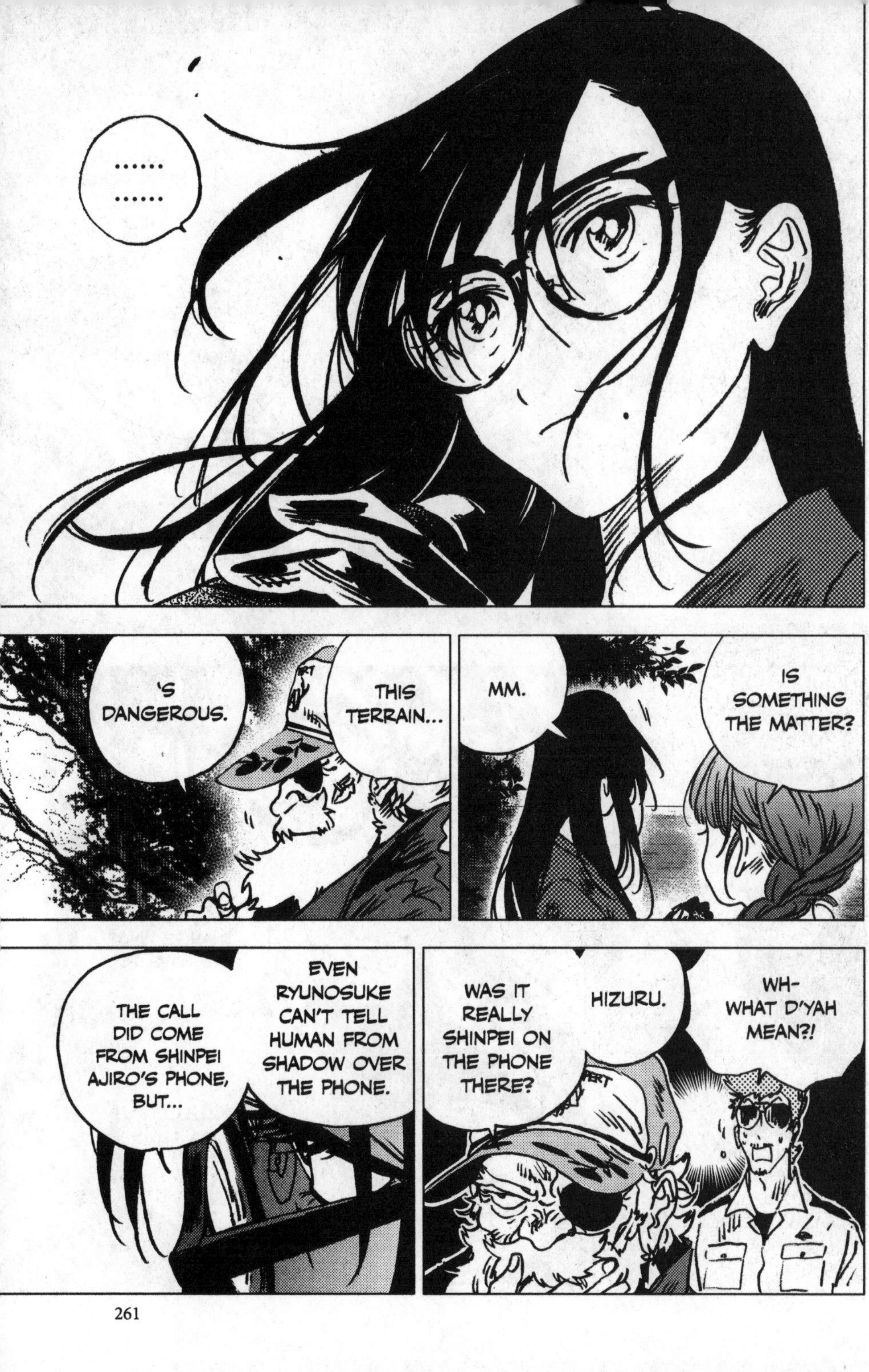

....
IS SOMETHING THE MATTER?
MM.
THIS TERRAIN...
'S DANGEROUS.
WH- WHAT D'YAH MEAN?!
HIZURU.
WAS IT REALLY SHINPEI ON THE PHONE THERE?
EVEN RYUNOSUKE CAN'T TELL HUMAN FROM SHADOW OVER THE PHONE.
THE CALL DID COME FROM SHINPEI AJIRO'S PHONE, BUT...

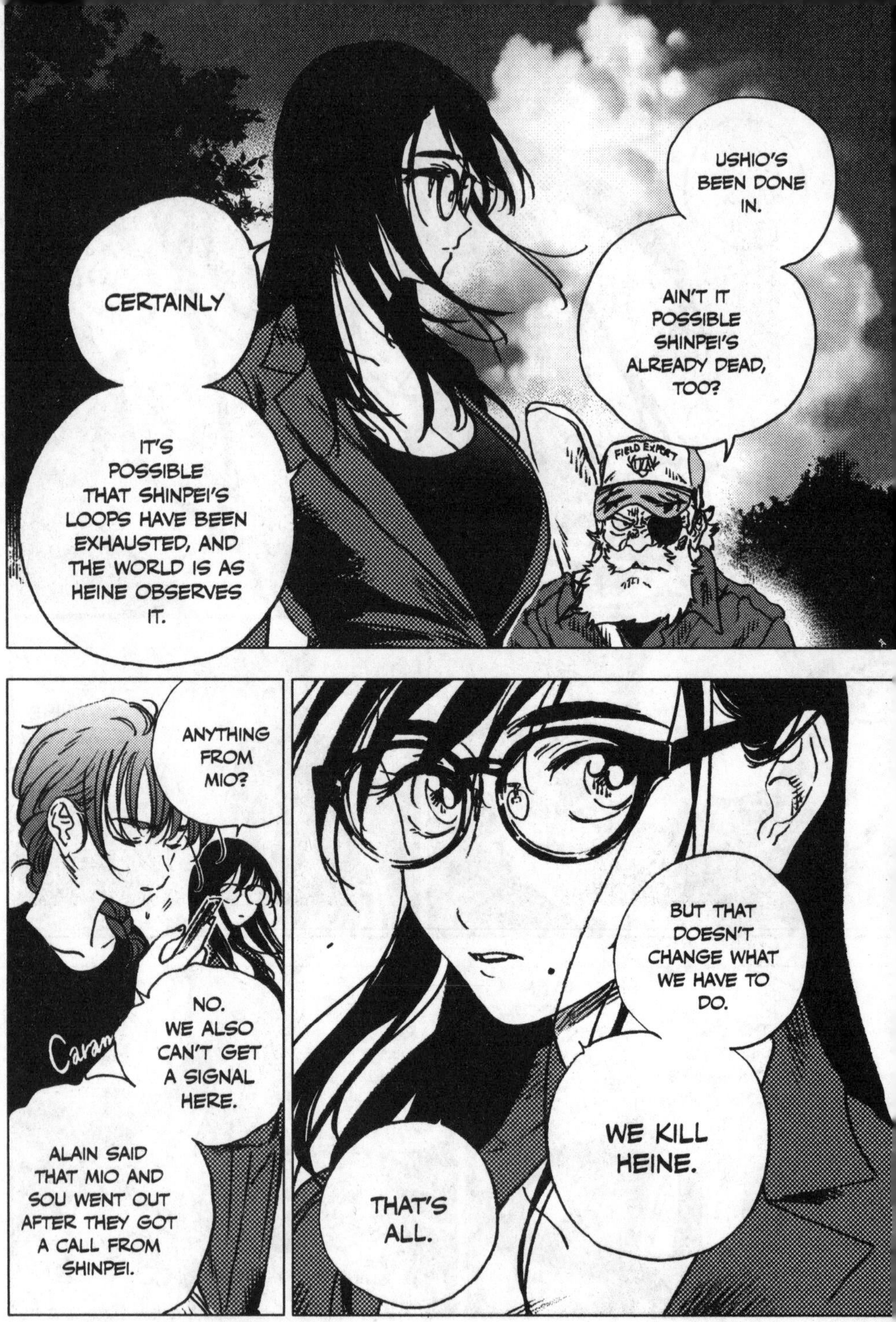
USHIO'S BEEN DONE IN.
AIN'T IT POSSIBLE SHINPEI'S ALREADY DEAD, TOO?
CERTAINLY
IT'S POSSIBLE THAT SHINPEI'S LOOPS HAVE BEEN EXHAUSTED, AND THE WORLD IS AS HEINE OBSERVES IT.
BUT THAT DOESN'T CHANGE WHAT WE HAVE TO DO.
WE KILL HEINE.
THAT'S ALL.
ANYTHING FROM MIO?
NO. WE ALSO CAN'T GET A SIGNAL HERE.
ALAIN SAID THAT MIO AND SOU WENT OUT AFTER THEY GOT A CALL FROM SHINPEI.

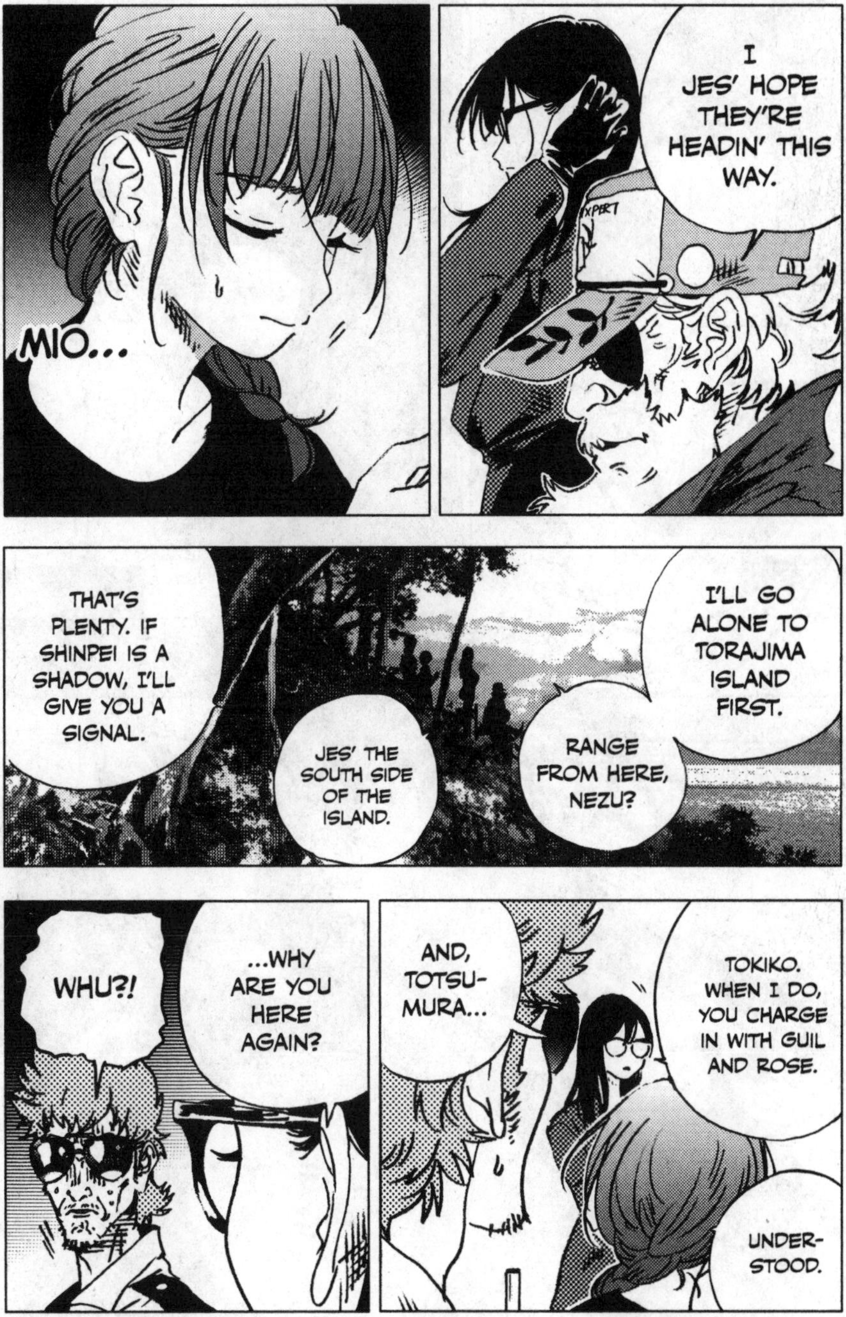
I JES' HOPE THEY'RE HEADIN' THIS WAY.
MIO...
I'LL GO ALONE TO TORAJIMA ISLAND FIRST.
RANGE FROM HERE, NEZU?
JES' THE SOUTH SIDE OF THE ISLAND.
THAT'S PLENTY. IF SHINPEI IS A SHADOW, I'LL GIVE YOU A SIGNAL.
TOKIKO. WHEN I DO, YOU CHARGE IN WITH GUIL AND ROSE.
UNDERSTOOD.
AND, TOTSUMURA...
...WHY ARE YOU HERE AGAIN?
WHU?!

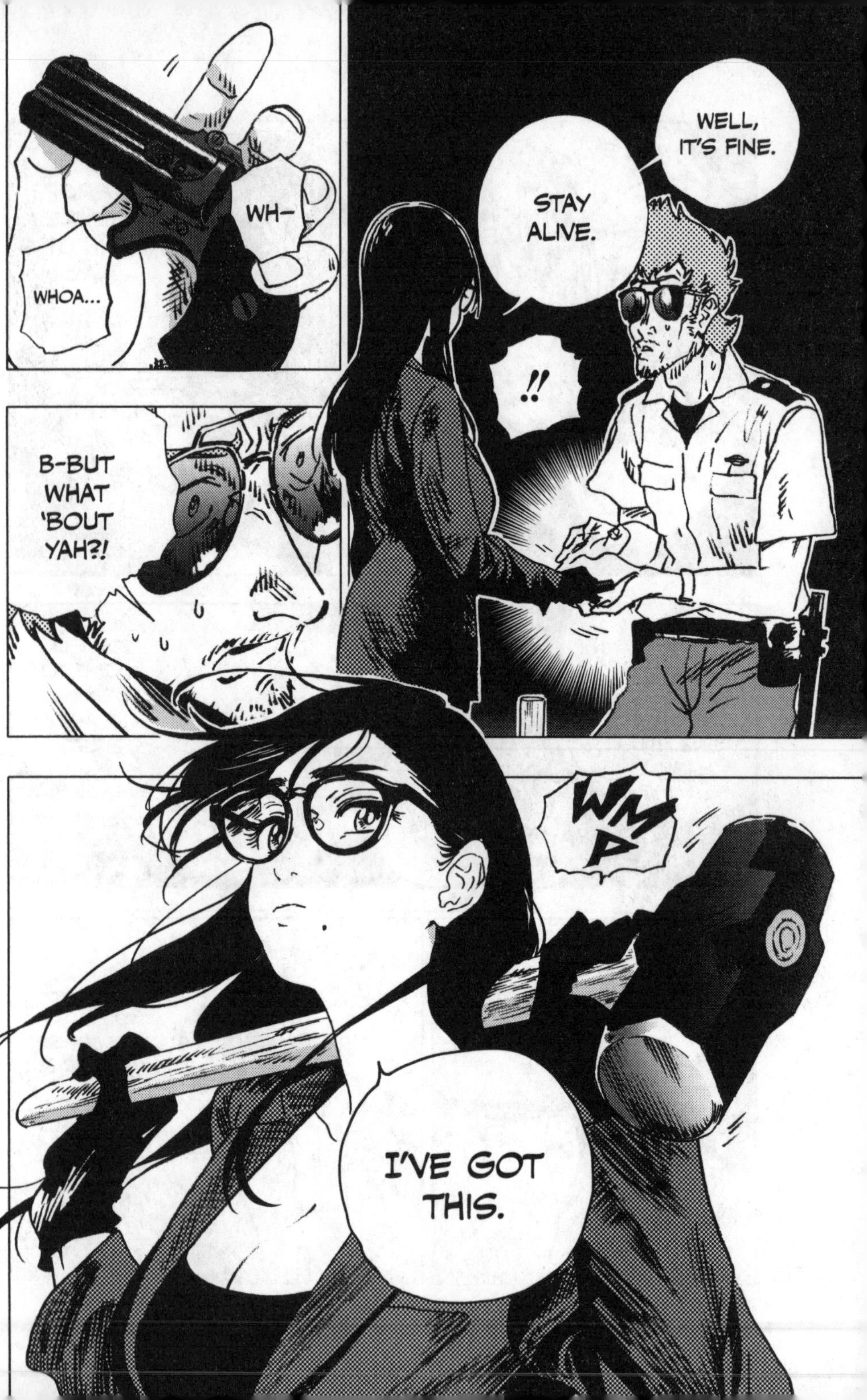
WELL, IT'S FINE.
STAY ALIVE.
!!
WH-
WHOA...
B-BUT WHAT 'BOUT YAH?!
WMP
I'VE GOT THIS.

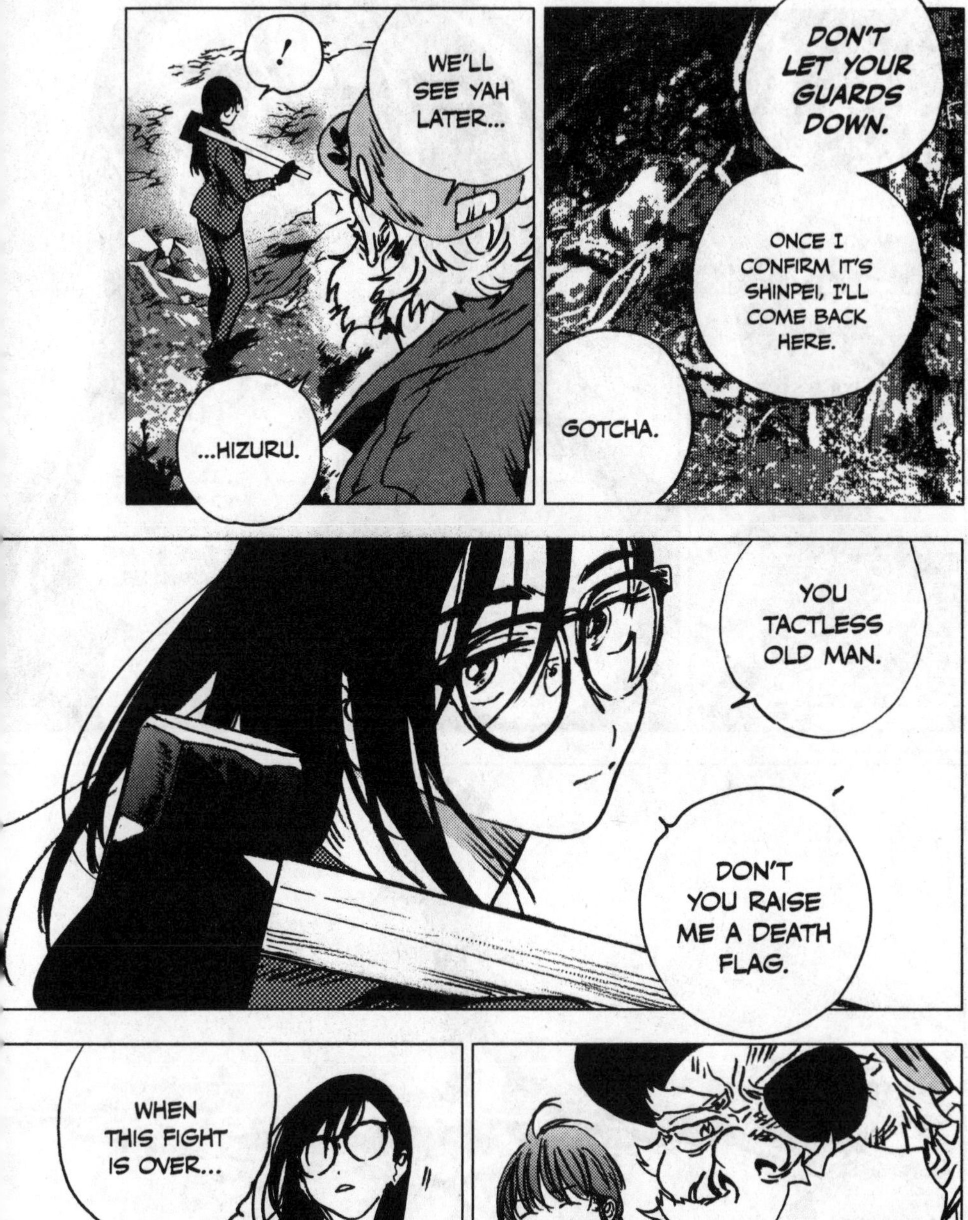
DON'T LET YOUR GUARDS DOWN.
ONCE I CONFIRM IT'S SHINPEI, I'LL COME BACK HERE.
GOTCHA.
WE'LL SEE YAH LATER...
!
...HIZURU.
YOU TACTLESS OLD MAN.
DON'T YOU RAISE ME A DEATH FLAG.
WHA?!
FLAG?
WHEN THIS FIGHT IS OVER...

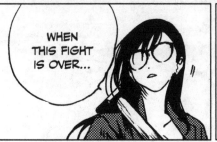

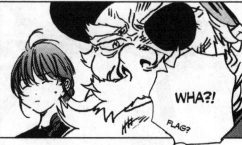

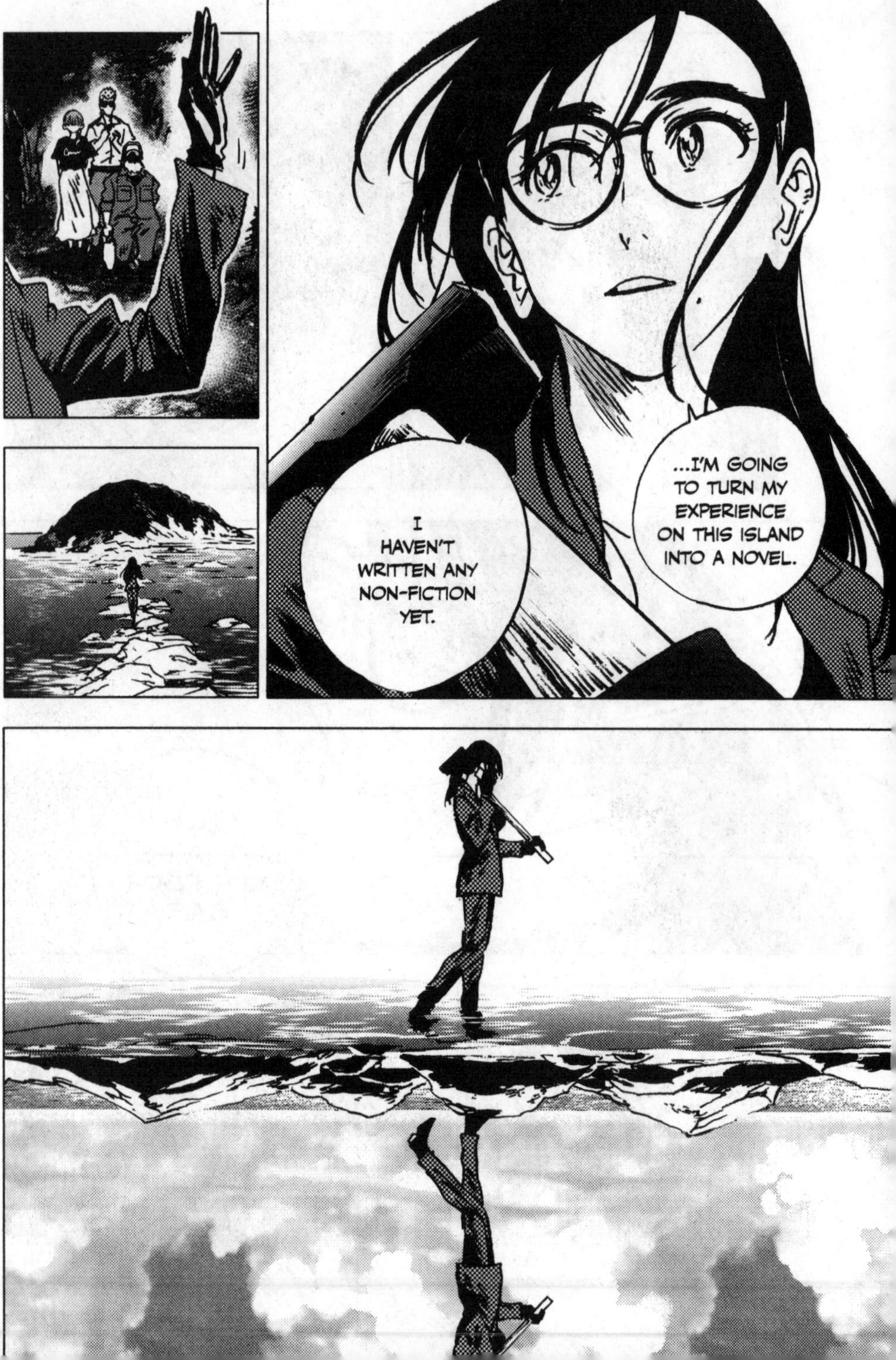
...I'M GOING TO TURN MY EXPERIENCE ON THIS ISLAND INTO A NOVEL.
I HAVEN'T WRITTEN ANY NON-FICTION YET.

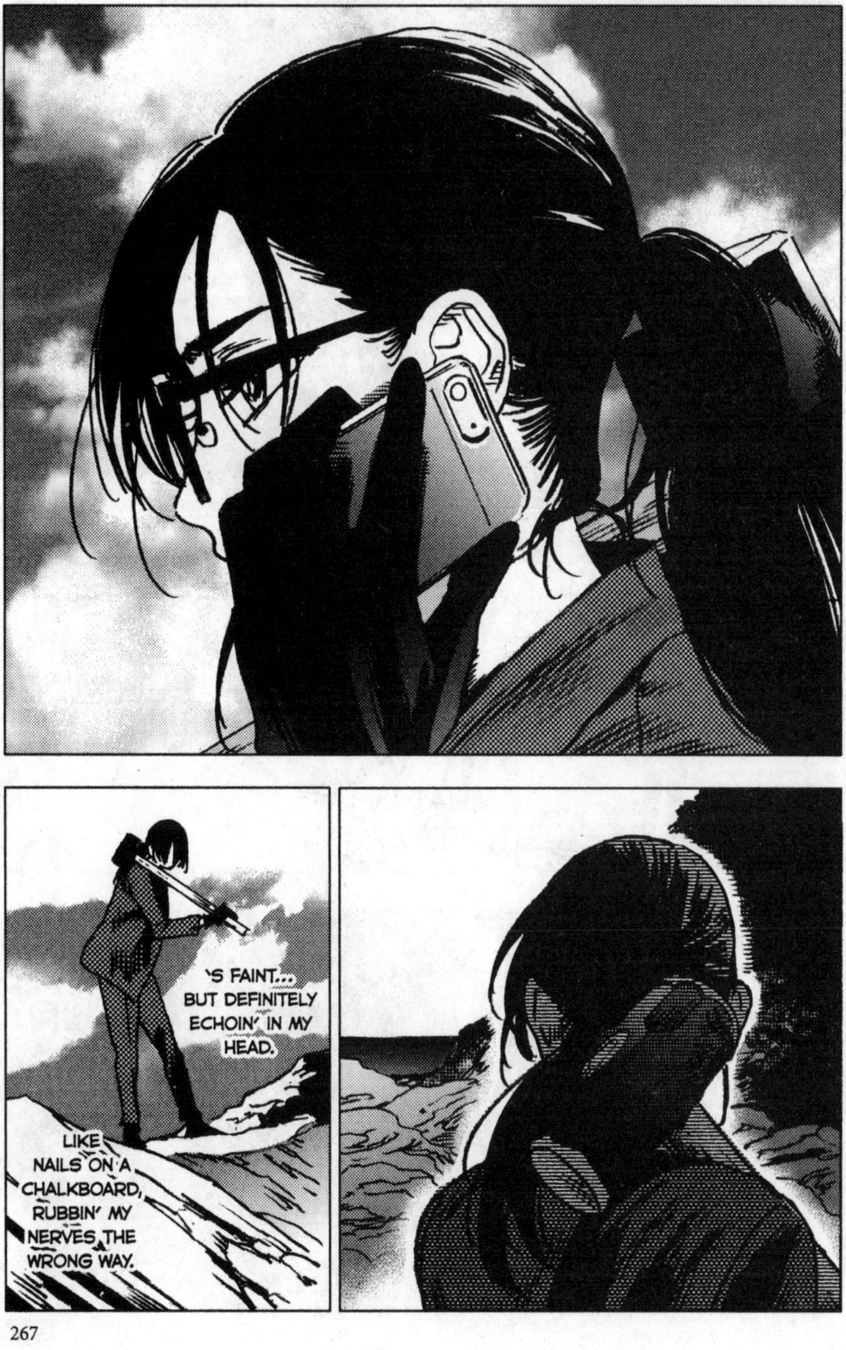
'S FAINT... BUT DEFINITELY ECHOIN' IN MY HEAD.
LIKE NAILS ON A CHALKBOARD, RUBBIN' MY NERVES THE WRONG WAY.

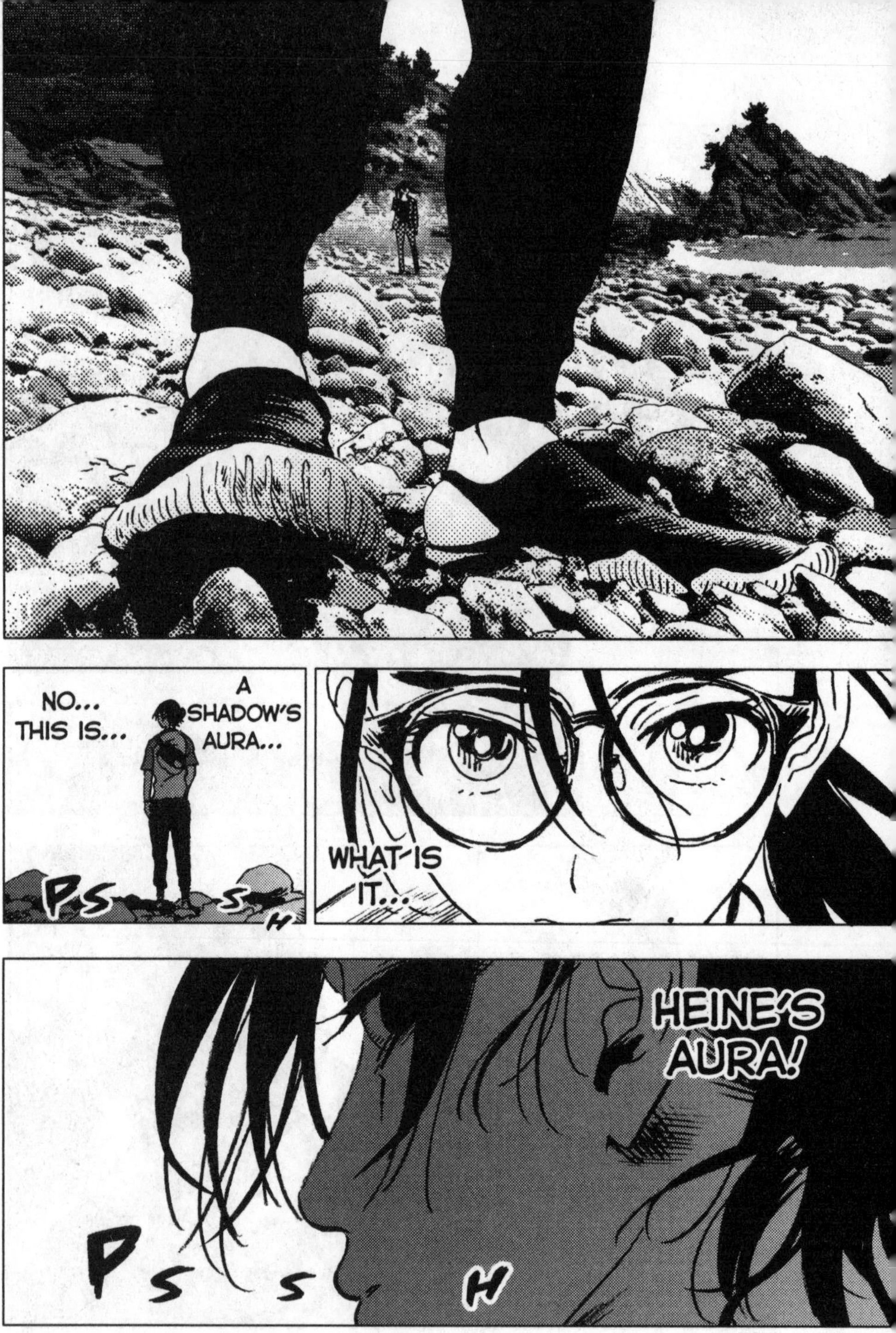
WHAT IS IT...
A SHADOW'S AURA...
NO... THIS IS...
PSSSH
HEINE'S AURA!
PSSSH

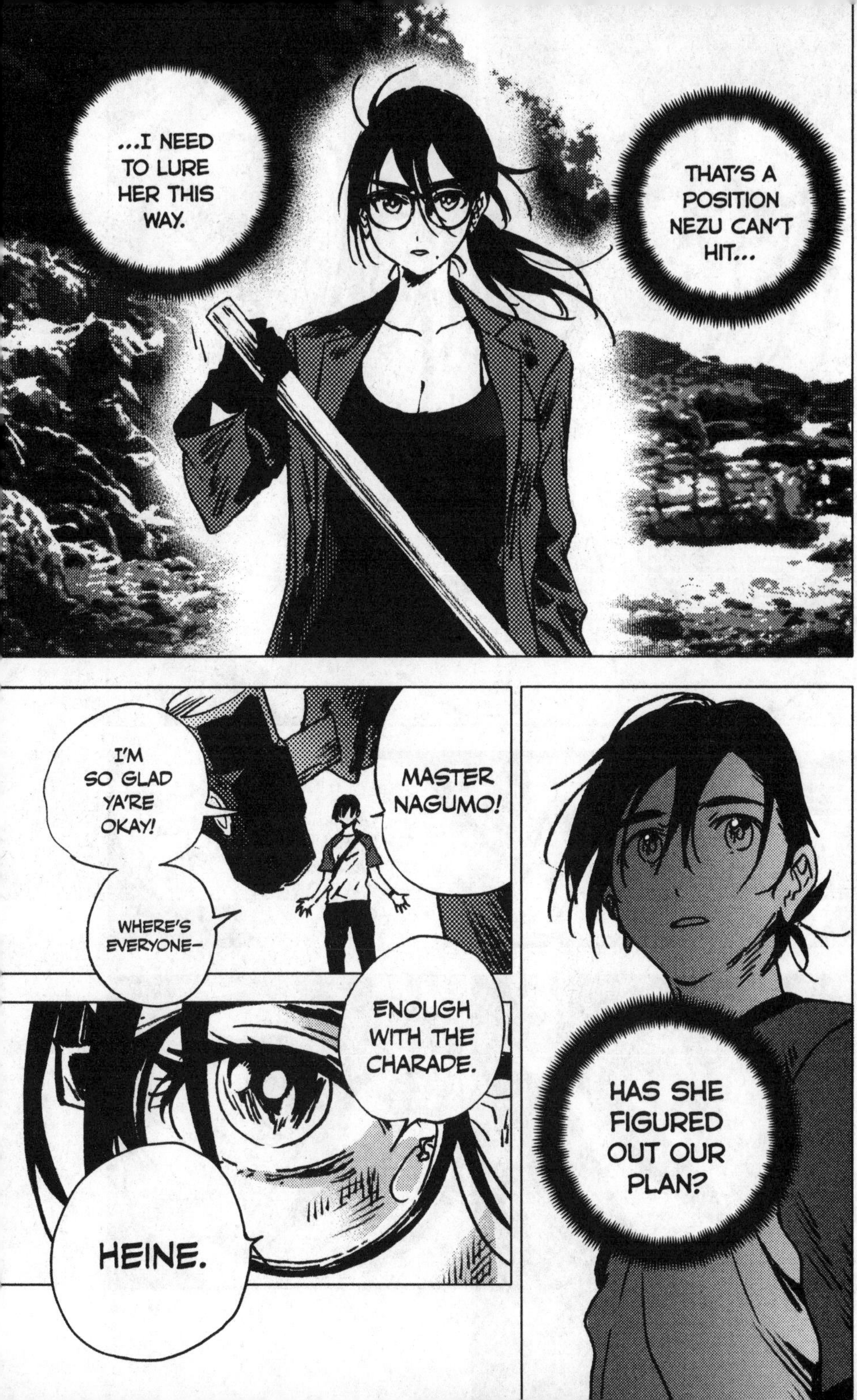
THAT'S A POSITION NEZU CAN'T HIT...
...I NEED TO LURE HER THIS WAY.
HAS SHE FIGURED OUT OUR PLAN?
MASTER NAGUMO!
I'M SO GLAD YA'RE OKAY!
WHERE'S EVERYONE–
ENOUGH WITH THE CHARADE.
HEINE.

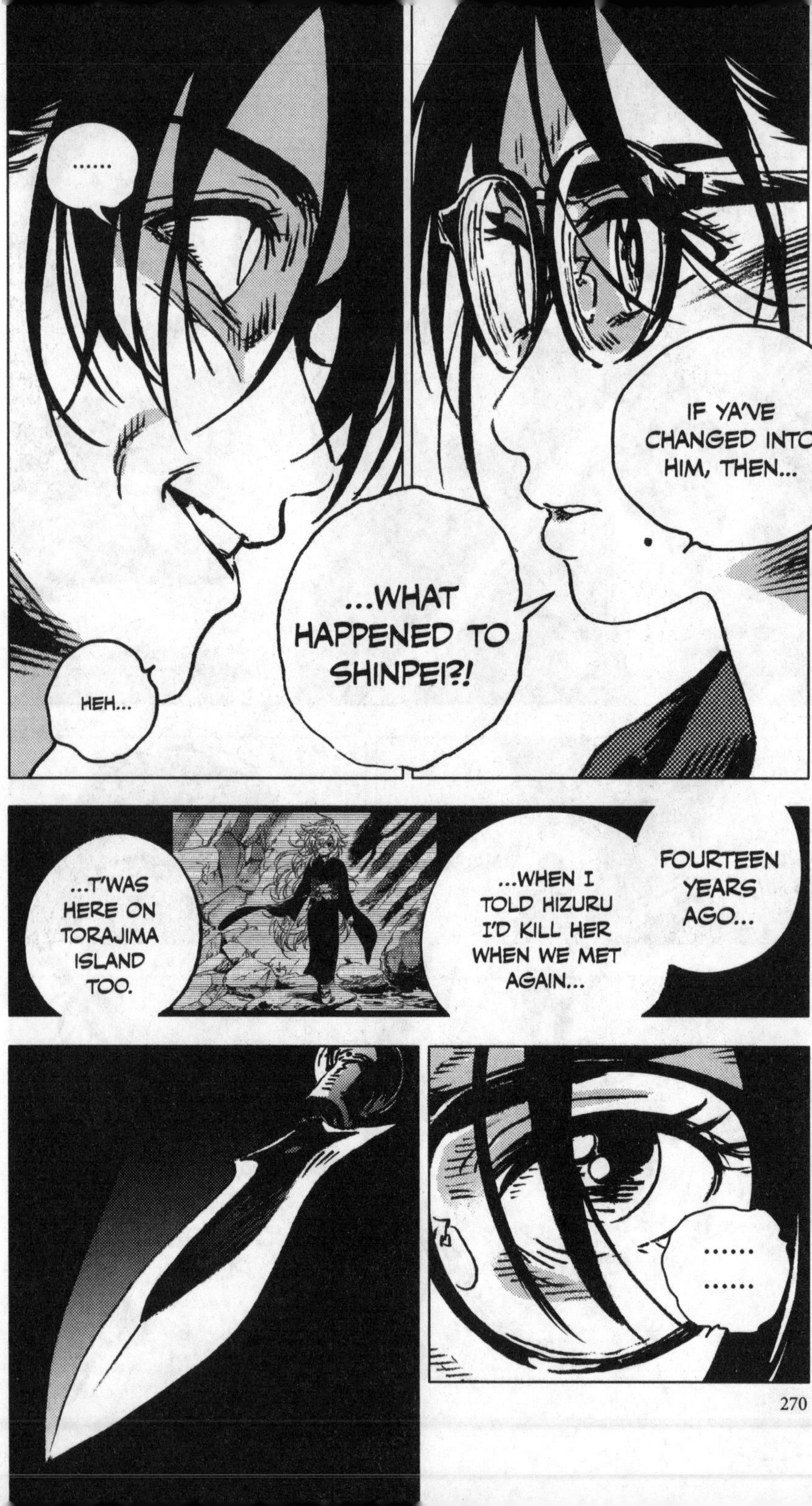
IF YA'VE CHANGED INTO HIM, THEN...
...WHAT HAPPENED TO SHINPEI?!
......
HEH...
FOURTEEN YEARS AGO...
...WHEN I TOLD HIZURU I'D KILL HER WHEN WE MET AGAIN...
...T'WAS HERE ON TORAJIMA ISLAND TOO.
....

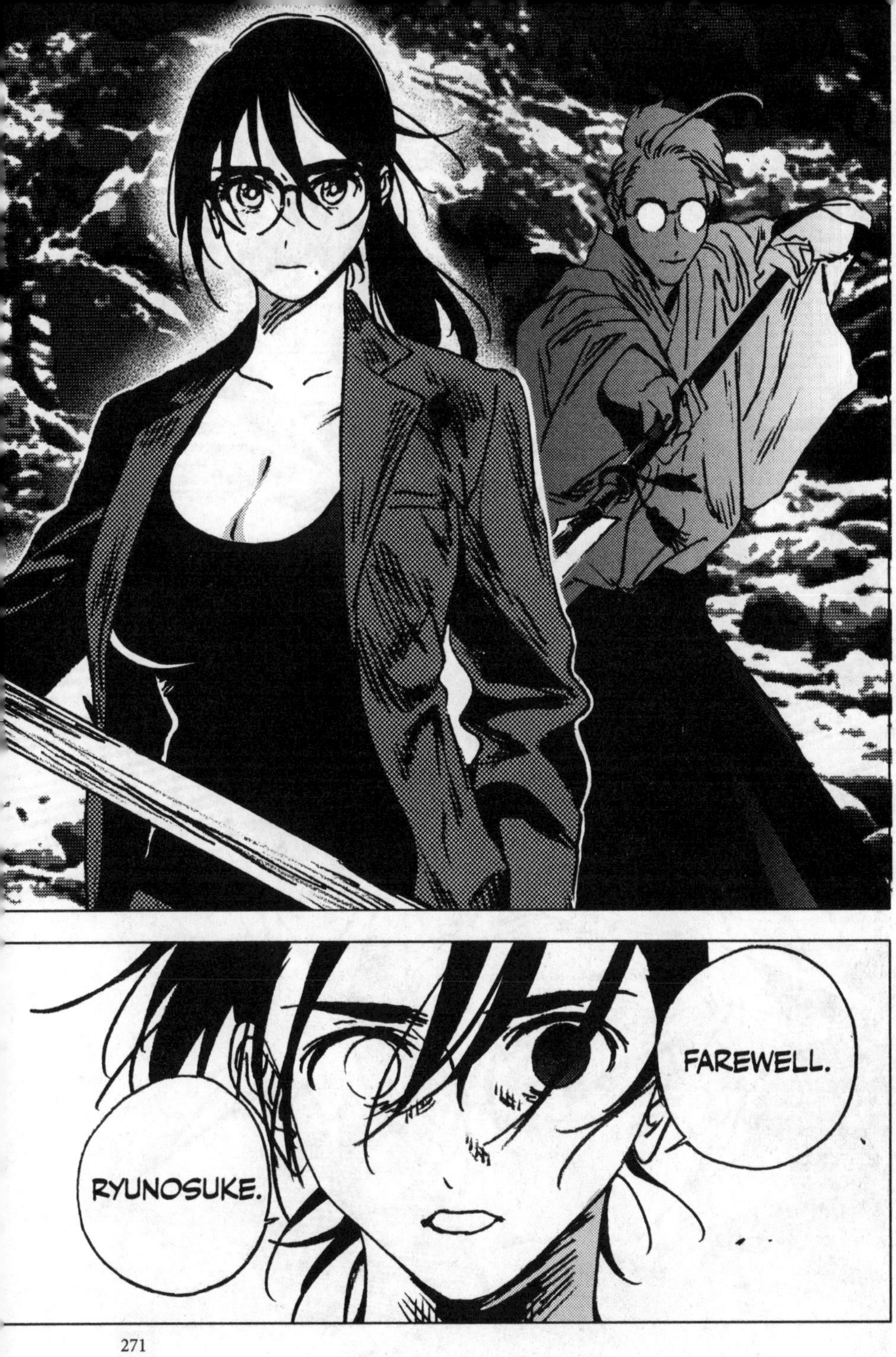
FAREWELL.
RYUNOSUKE.

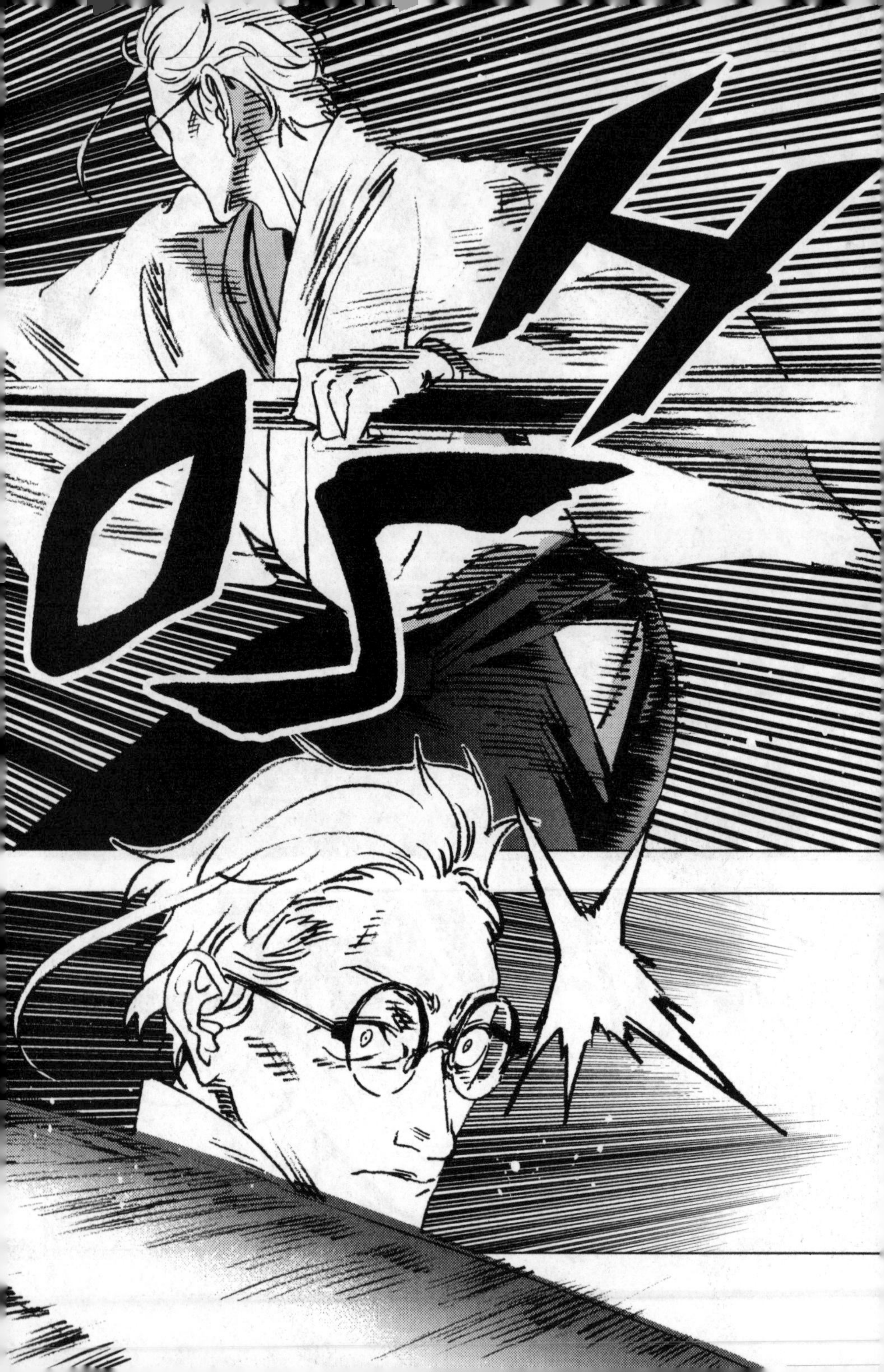

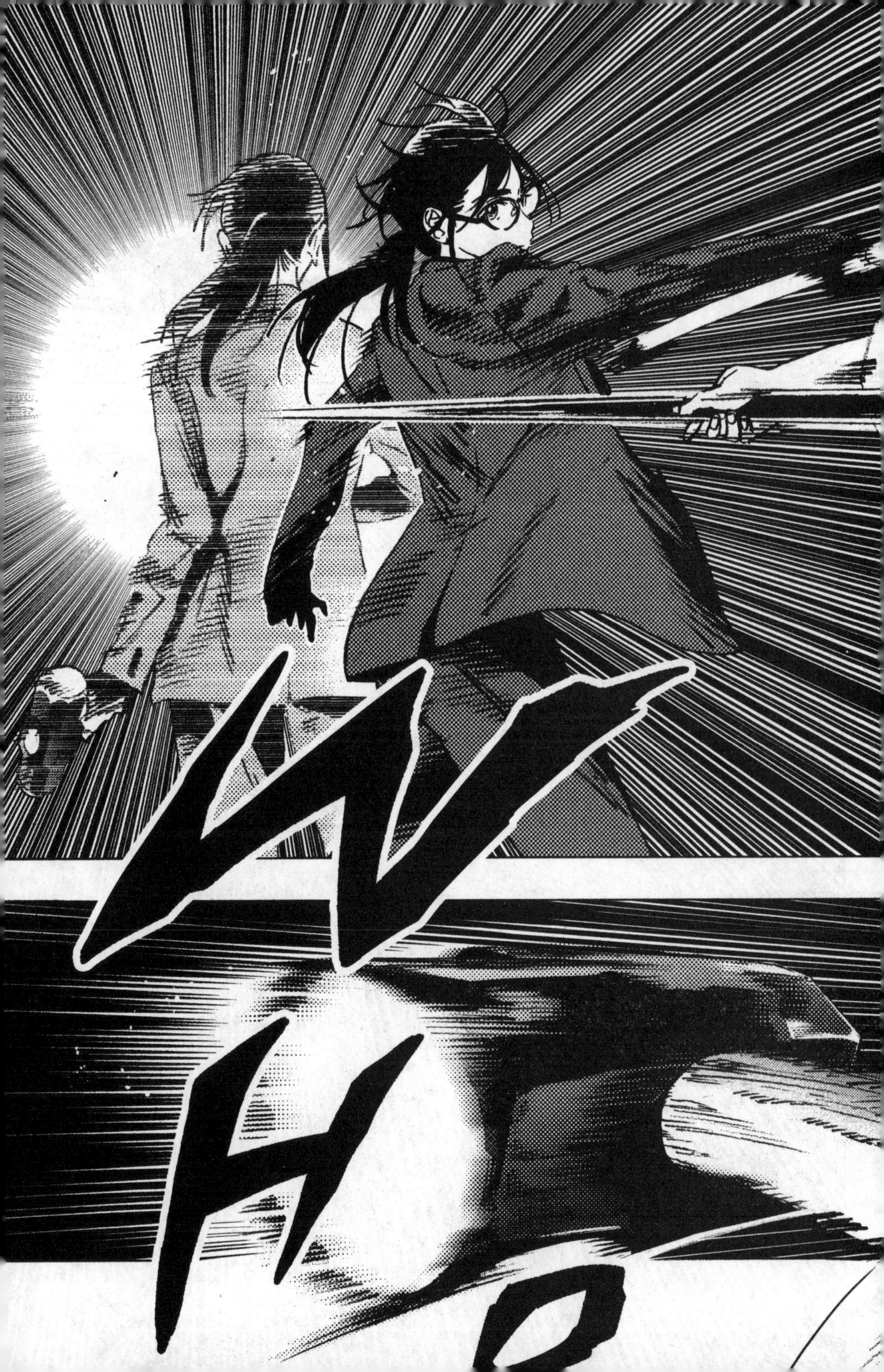

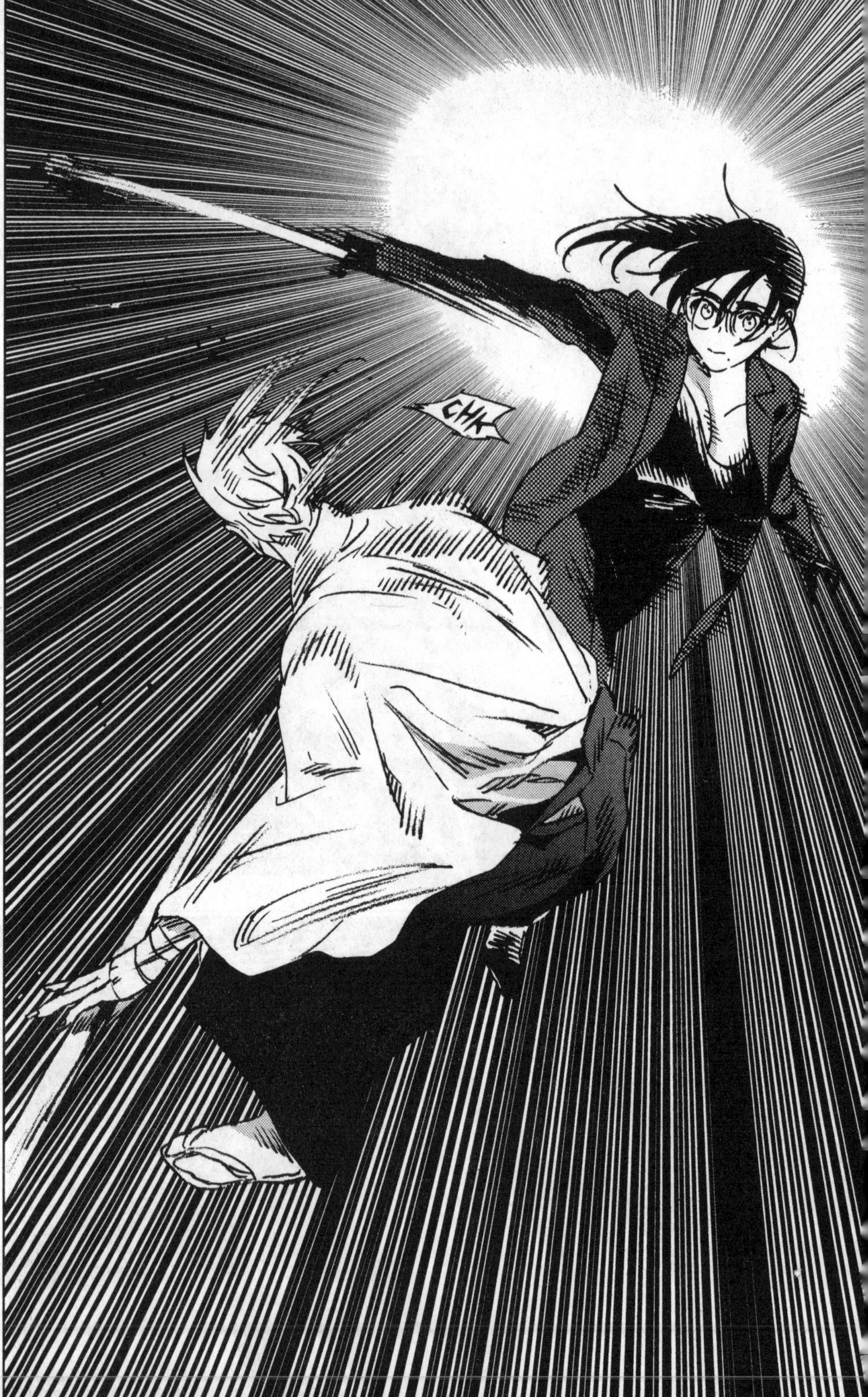
CHK

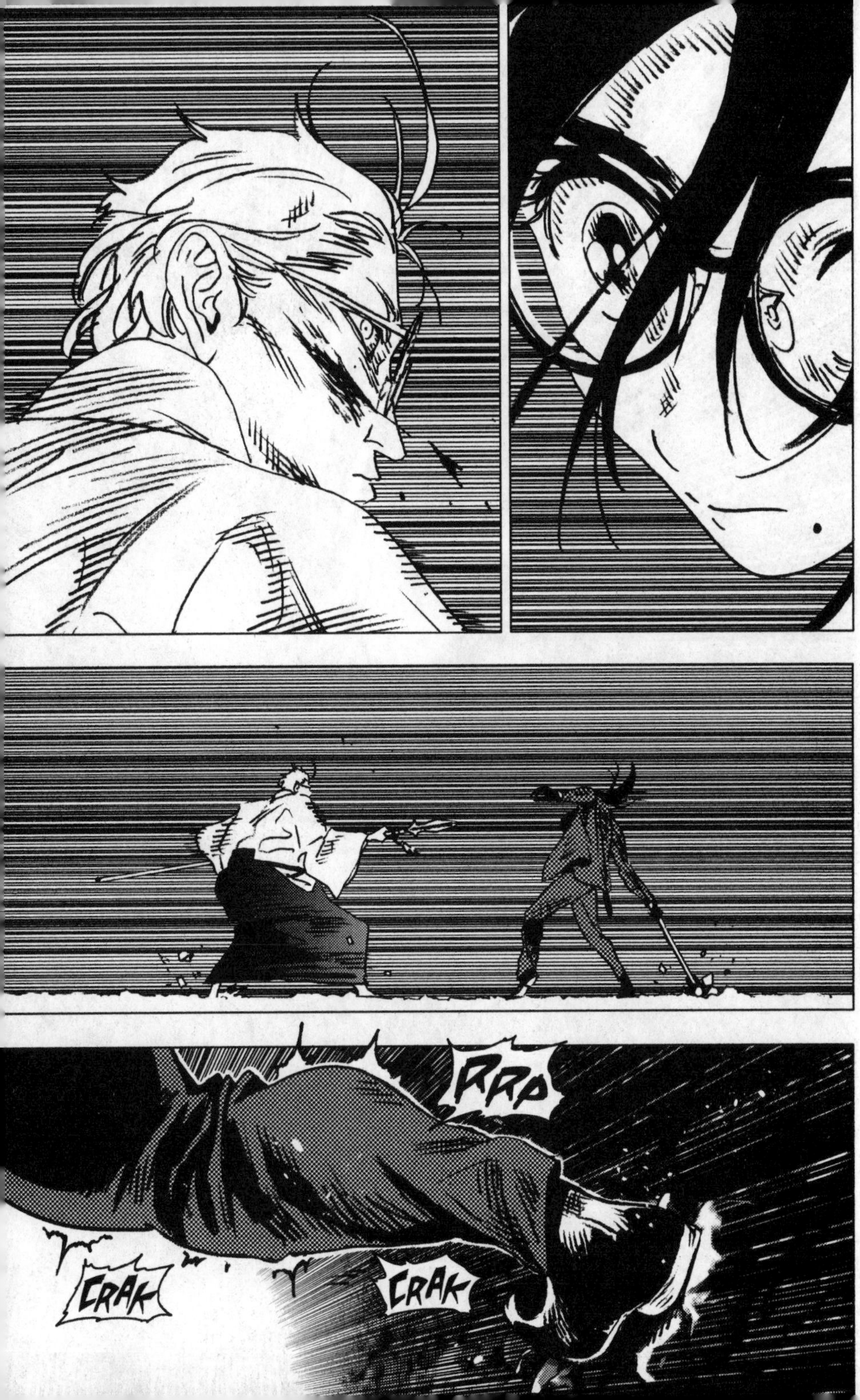
RRP
CRAK
CRAK

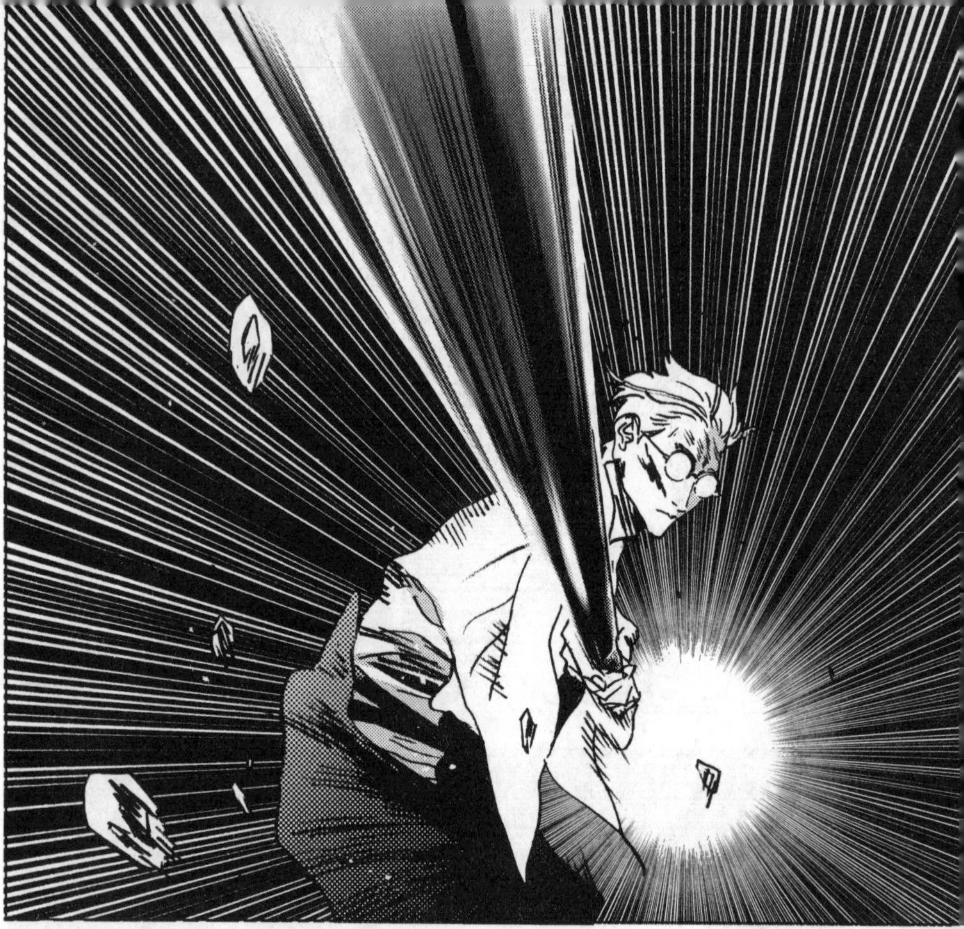
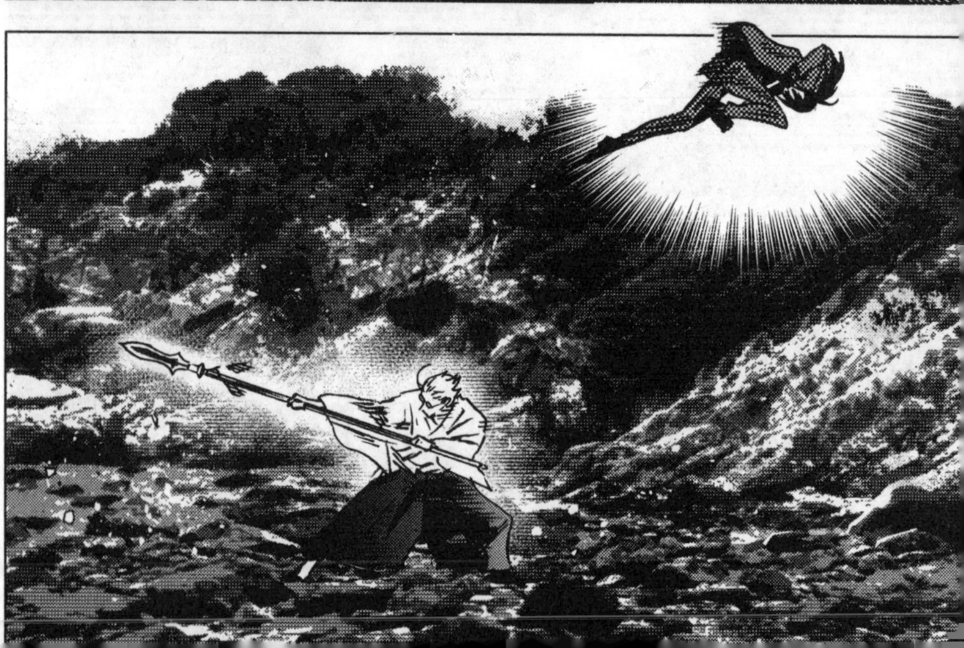

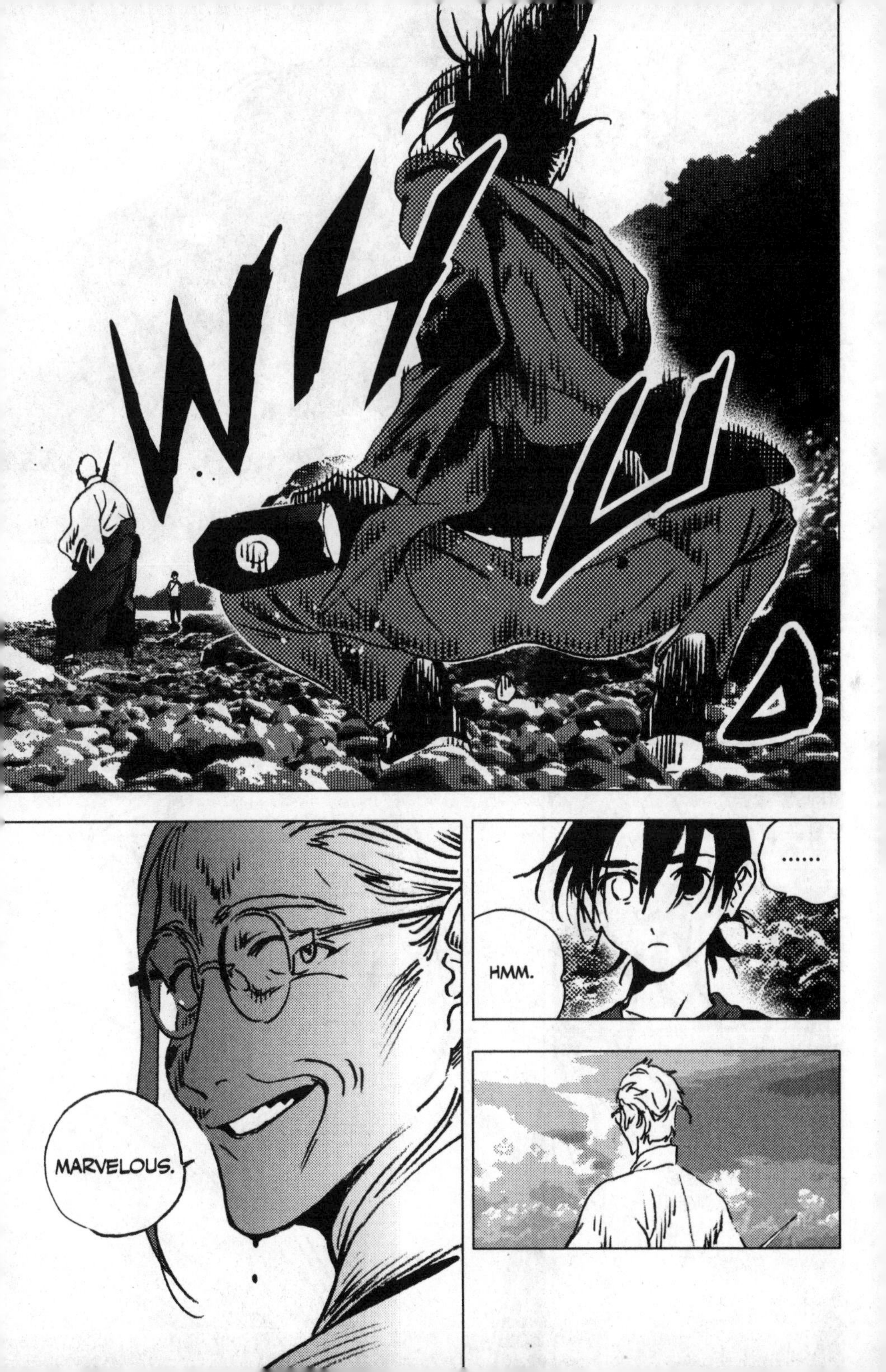
WHUD
......
HMM.
MARVELOUS.

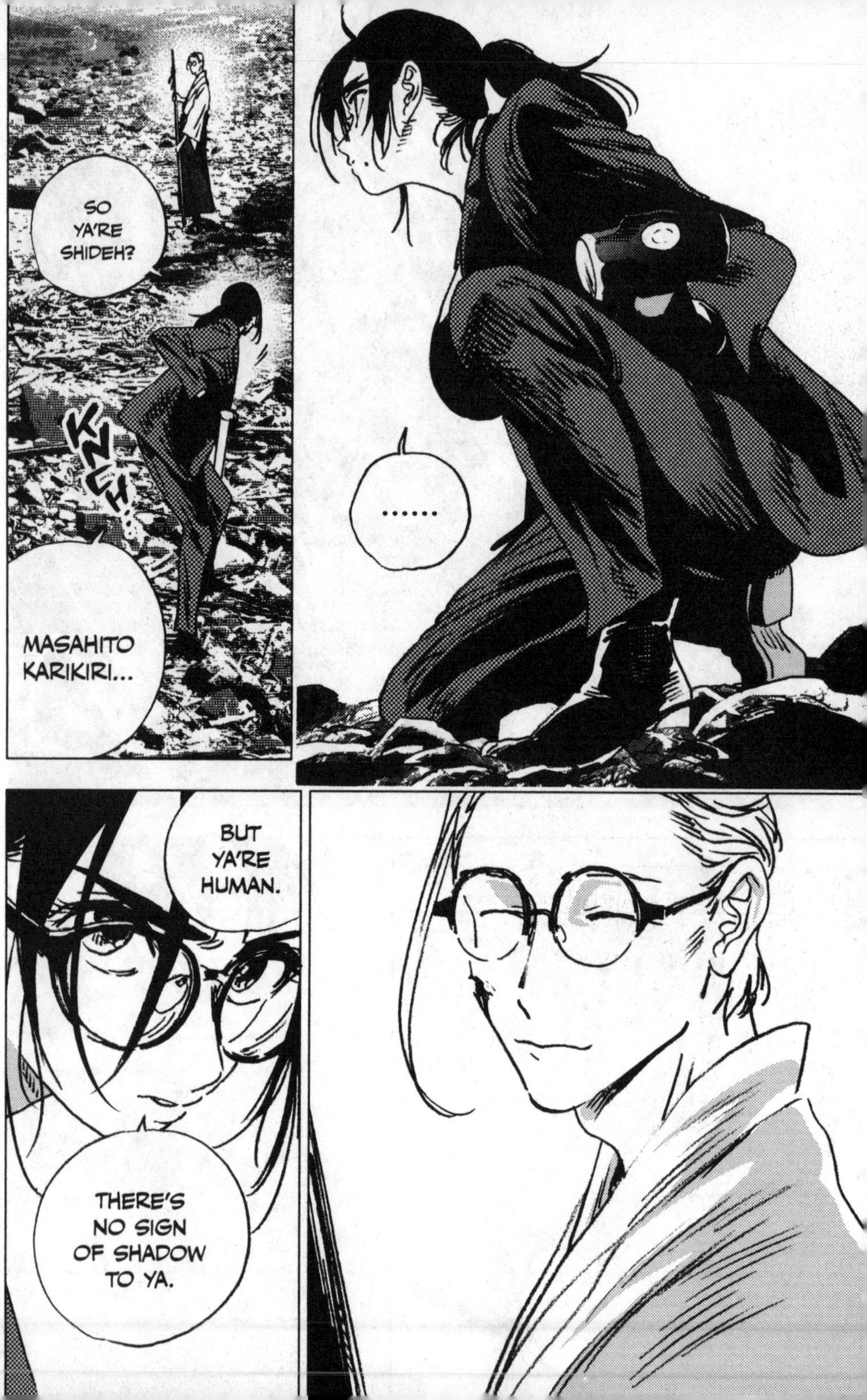
......
SO YA'RE SHIDEH?
KNCH!!
MASAHITO KARIKIRI...
BUT YA'RE HUMAN.
THERE'S NO SIGN OF SHADOW TO YA.

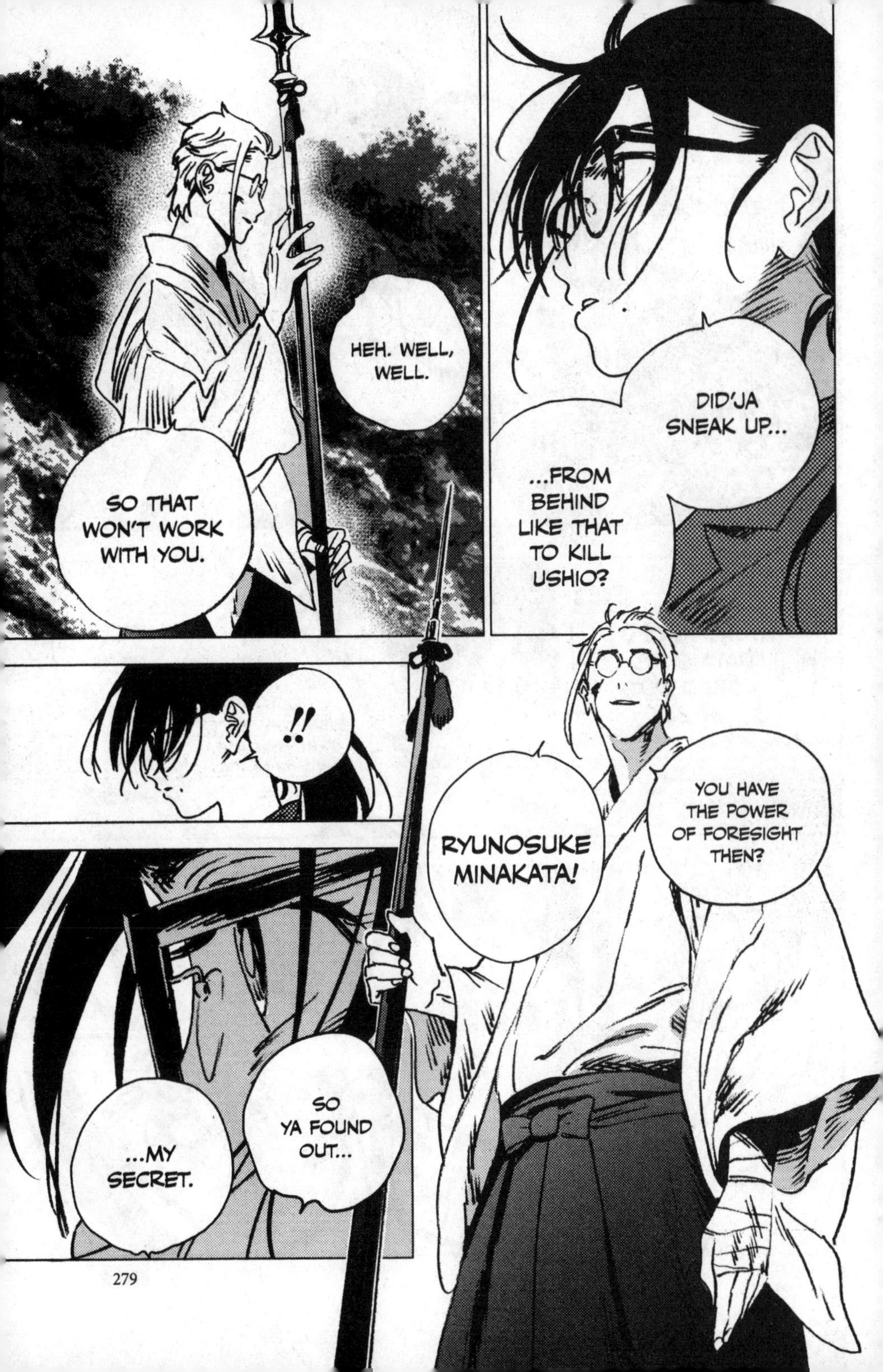
DID'JA SNEAK UP...
...FROM BEHIND LIKE THAT TO KILL USHIO?
HEH. WELL, WELL.
SO THAT WON'T WORK WITH YOU.
YOU HAVE THE POWER OF FORESIGHT THEN?
RYUNOSUKE MINAKATA!
!!
SO YA FOUND OUT...
...MY SECRET.

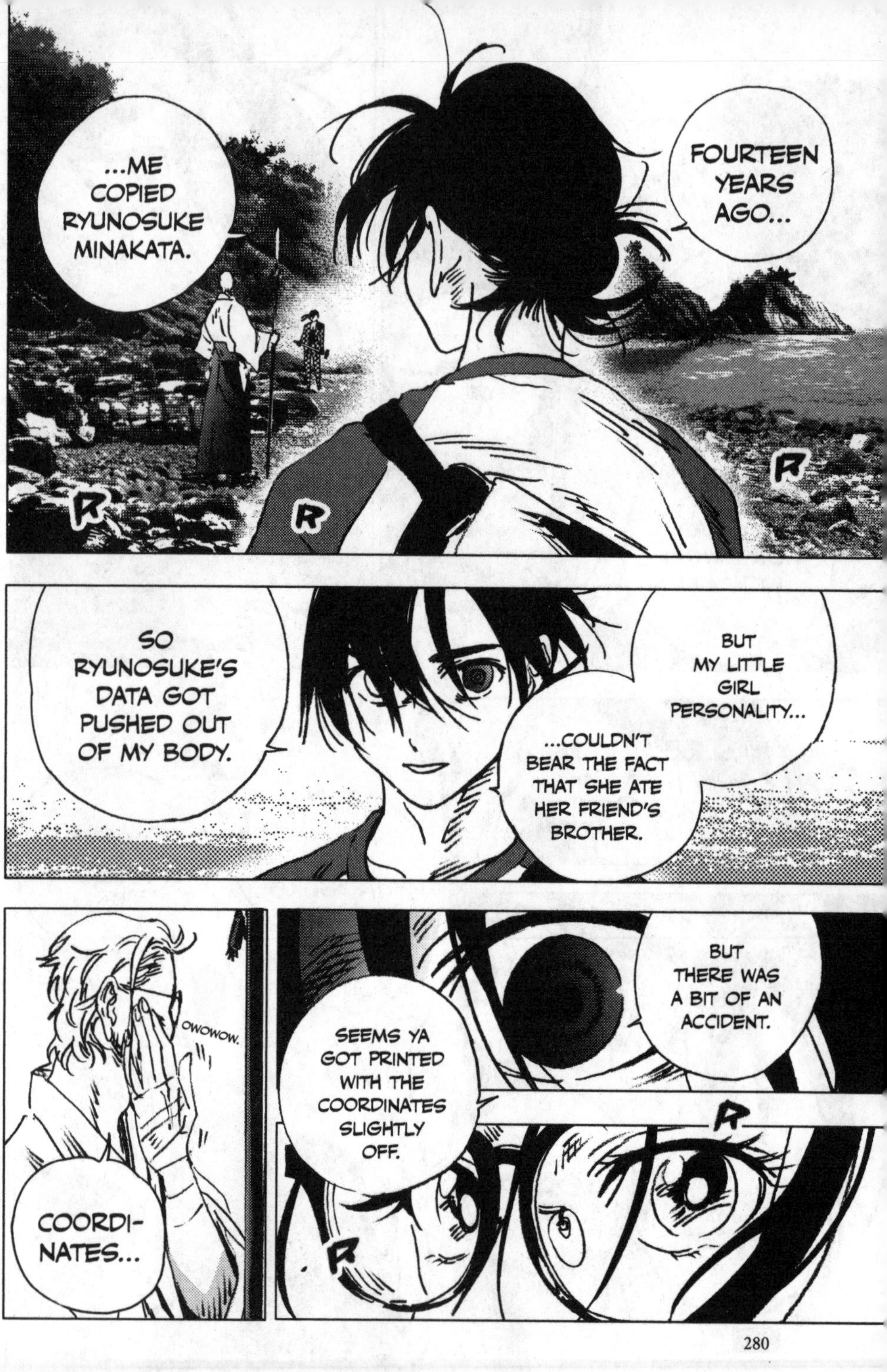
FOURTEEN YEARS AGO...
...ME COPIED RYUNOSUKE MINAKATA.
R
R
R
BUT MY LITTLE GIRL PERSONALITY...
...COULDN'T BEAR THE FACT THAT SHE ATE HER FRIEND'S BROTHER.
SO RYUNOSUKE'S DATA GOT PUSHED OUT OF MY BODY.
BUT THERE WAS A BIT OF AN ACCIDENT.
SEEMS YA GOT PRINTED WITH THE COORDINATES SLIGHTLY OFF.
R
R
OWOWOW.
COORDI-NATES...

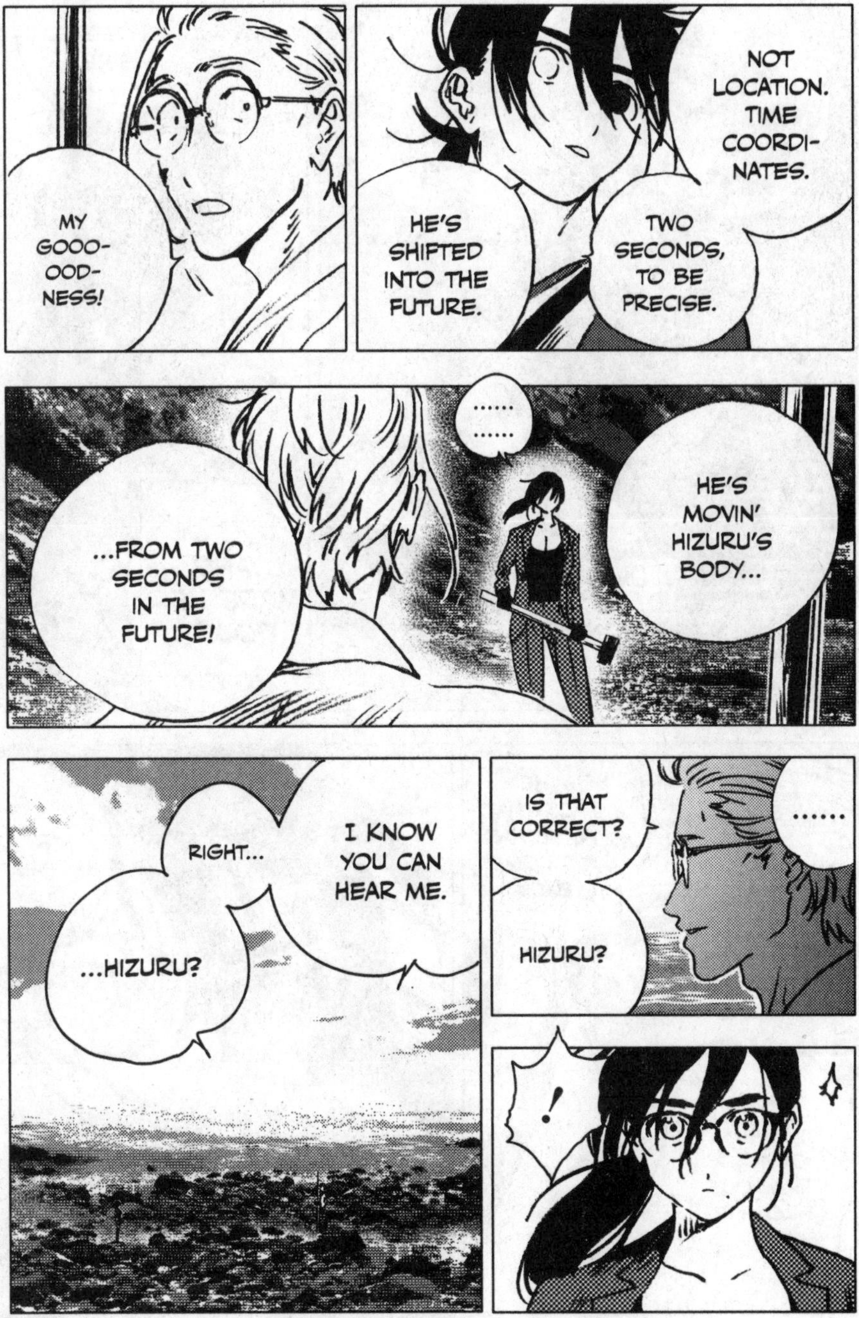
NOT LOCATION. TIME COORDINATES.
TWO SECONDS, TO BE PRECISE.
HE'S SHIFTED INTO THE FUTURE.
MY GOOOOODNESS!
......
......
HE'S MOVIN' HIZURU'S BODY...
...FROM TWO SECONDS IN THE FUTURE!
......
IS THAT CORRECT?
HIZURU?
!
I KNOW YOU CAN HEAR ME.
RIGHT...
...HIZURU?

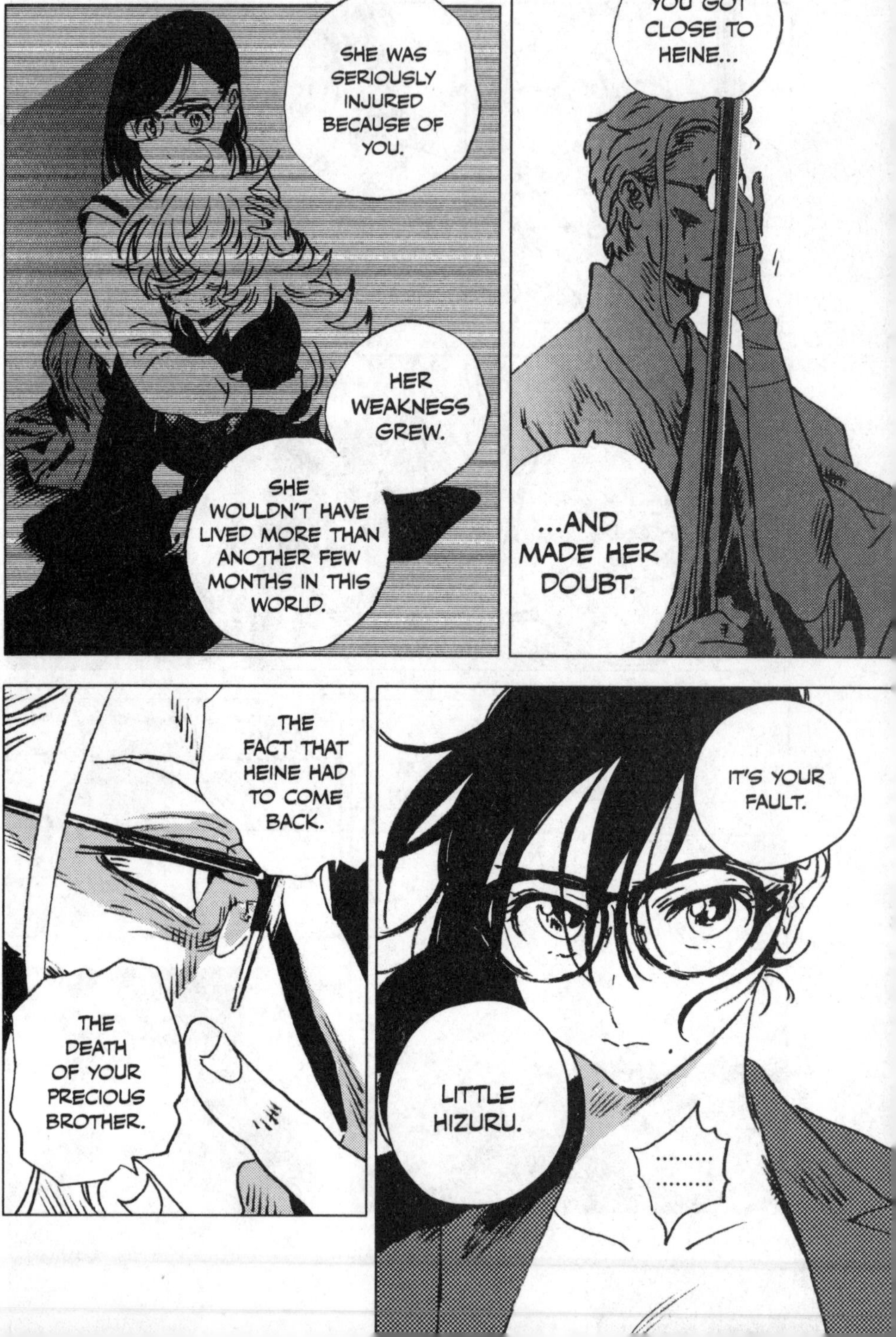
YOU GOT CLOSE TO HEINE...
...AND MADE HER DOUBT.
SHE WAS SERIOUSLY INJURED BECAUSE OF YOU.
HER WEAKNESS GREW.
SHE WOULDN'T HAVE LIVED MORE THAN ANOTHER FEW MONTHS IN THIS WORLD.
IT'S YOUR FAULT.
LITTLE HIZURU.
....
....
THE FACT THAT HEINE HAD TO COME BACK.
THE DEATH OF YOUR PRECIOUS BROTHER.

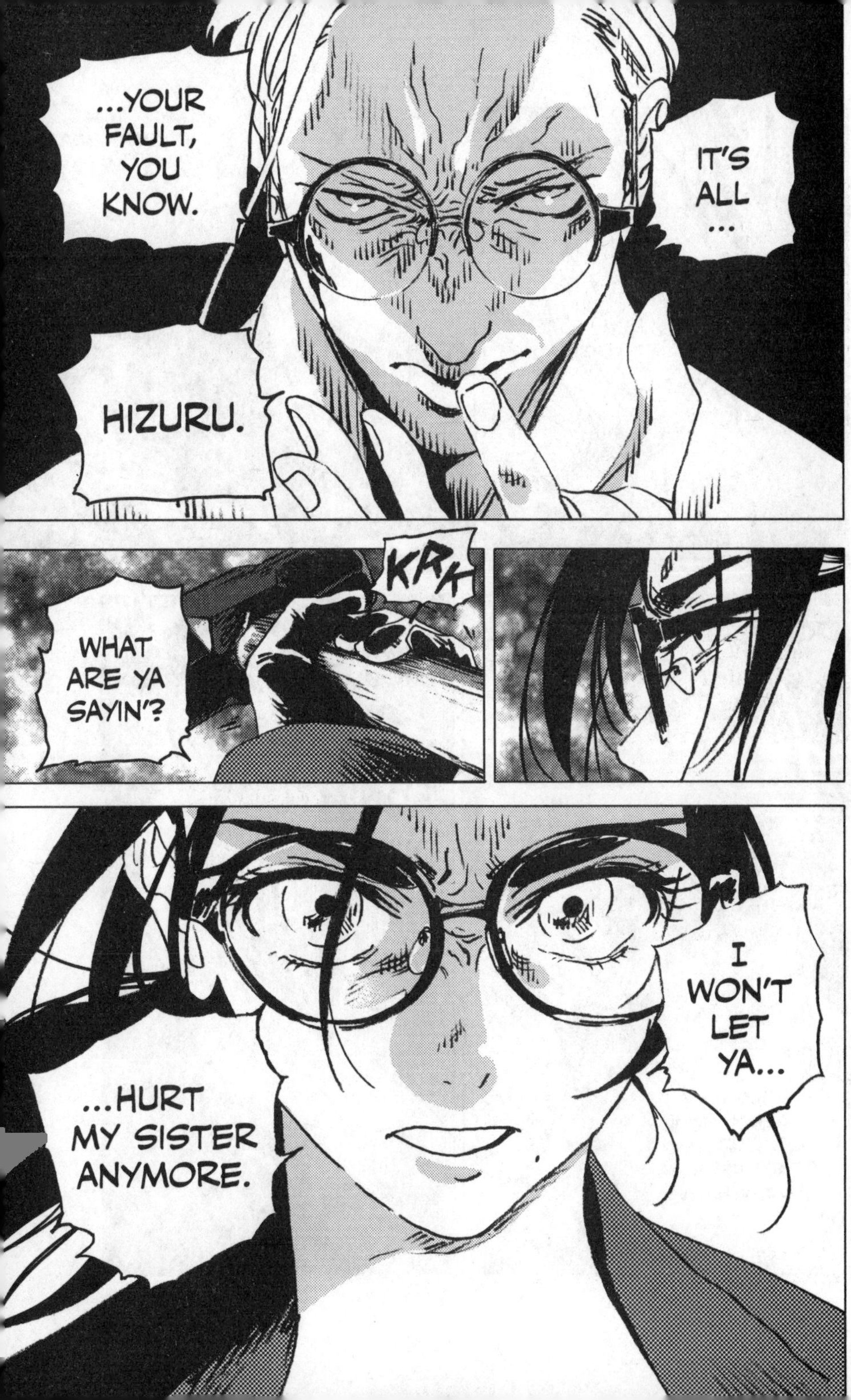
IT'S ALL ...
...YOUR FAULT, YOU KNOW.
HIZURU.
KRK
WHAT ARE YA SAYIN'?
I WON'T LET YA...
...HURT MY SISTER ANYMORE.

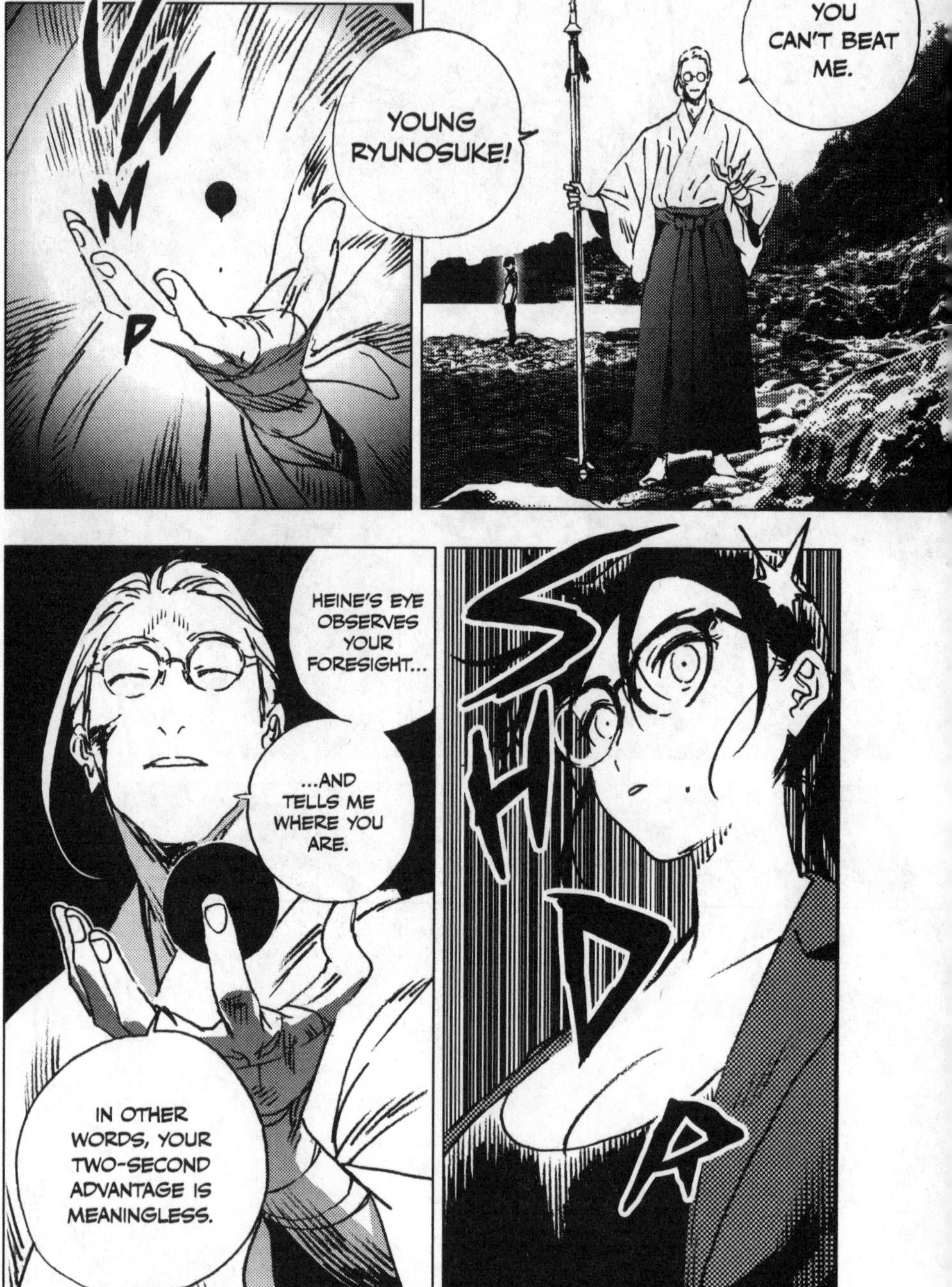
YOU CAN'T BEAT ME.
YOUNG RYUNOSUKE!
VWMP
SHDR
HEINE'S EYE OBSERVES YOUR FORESIGHT...
...AND TELLS ME WHERE YOU ARE.
IN OTHER WORDS, YOUR TWO-SECOND ADVANTAGE IS MEANINGLESS.

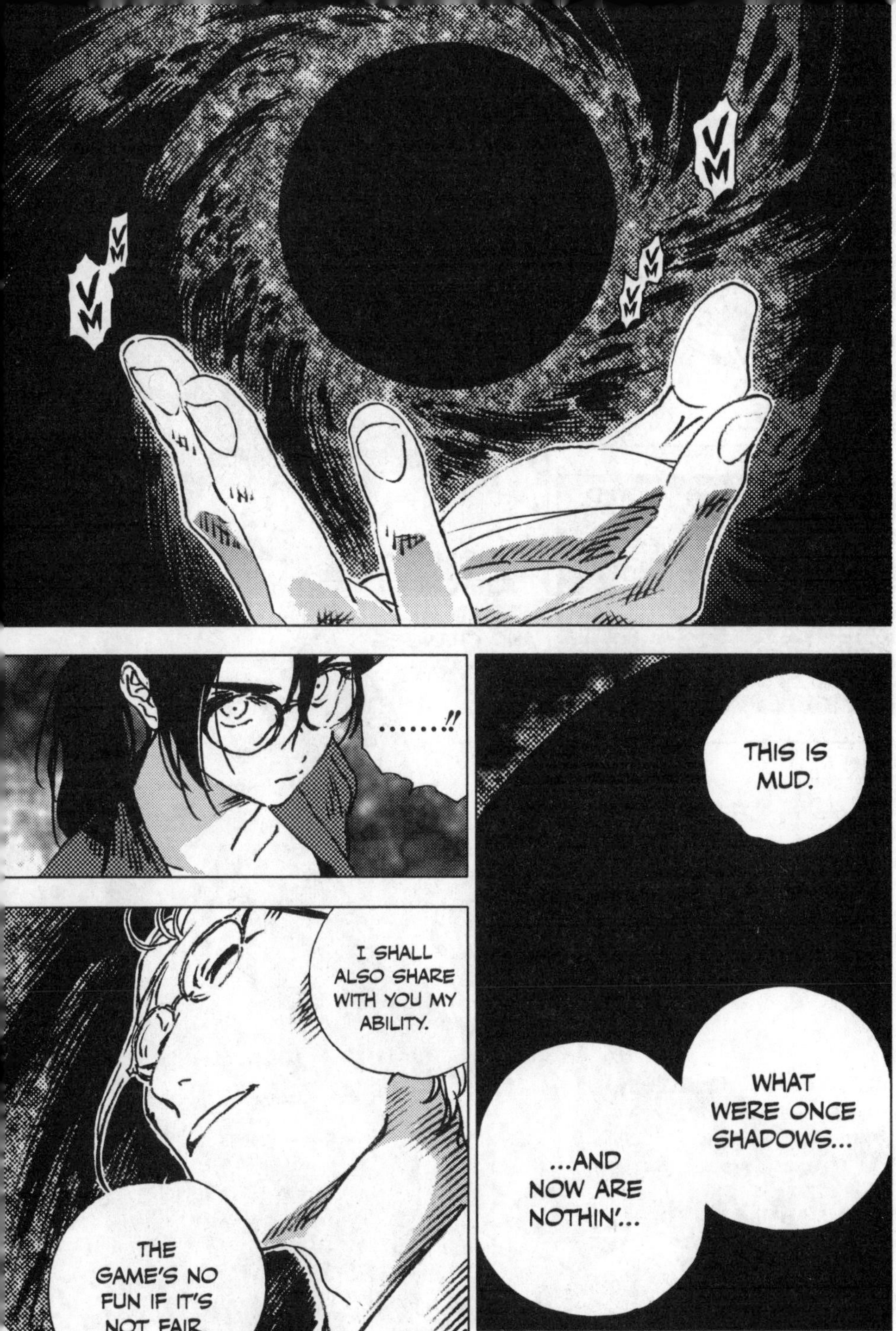
VM
VM
VM
VM
VM
VM
THIS IS MUD.
WHAT WERE ONCE SHADOWS...
...AND NOW ARE NOTHIN'...
.......!!
I SHALL ALSO SHARE WITH YOU MY ABILITY.
THE GAME'S NO FUN IF IT'S NOT FAIR.

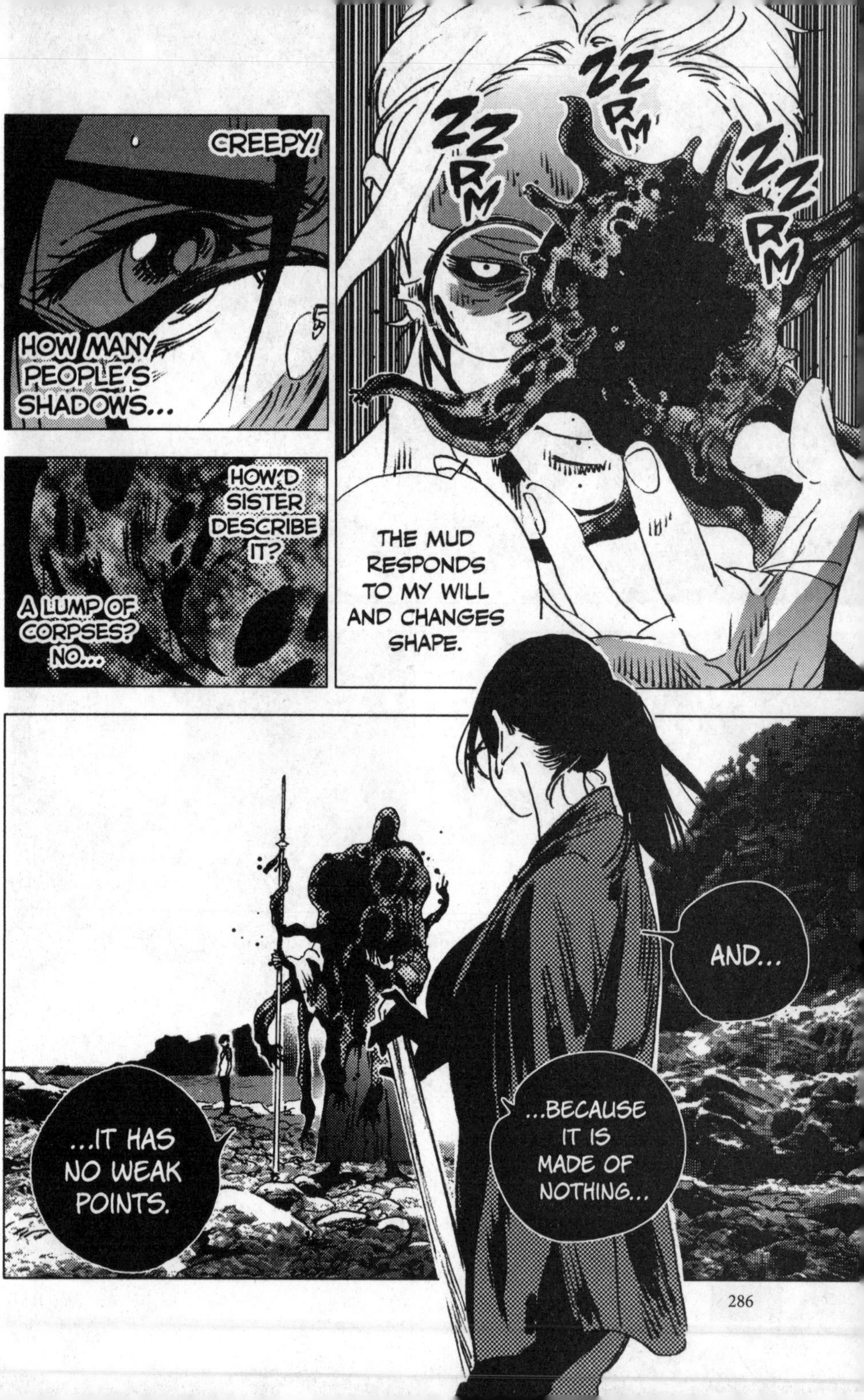
ZZRM
ZZRM
ZZRM
THE MUD RESPONDS TO MY WILL AND CHANGES SHAPE.
CREEPY!
HOW MANY PEOPLE'S SHADOWS...
HOW'D SISTER DESCRIBE IT?
A LUMP OF CORPSES? NO...
AND...
...BECAUSE IT IS MADE OF NOTHING...
...IT HAS NO WEAK POINTS.

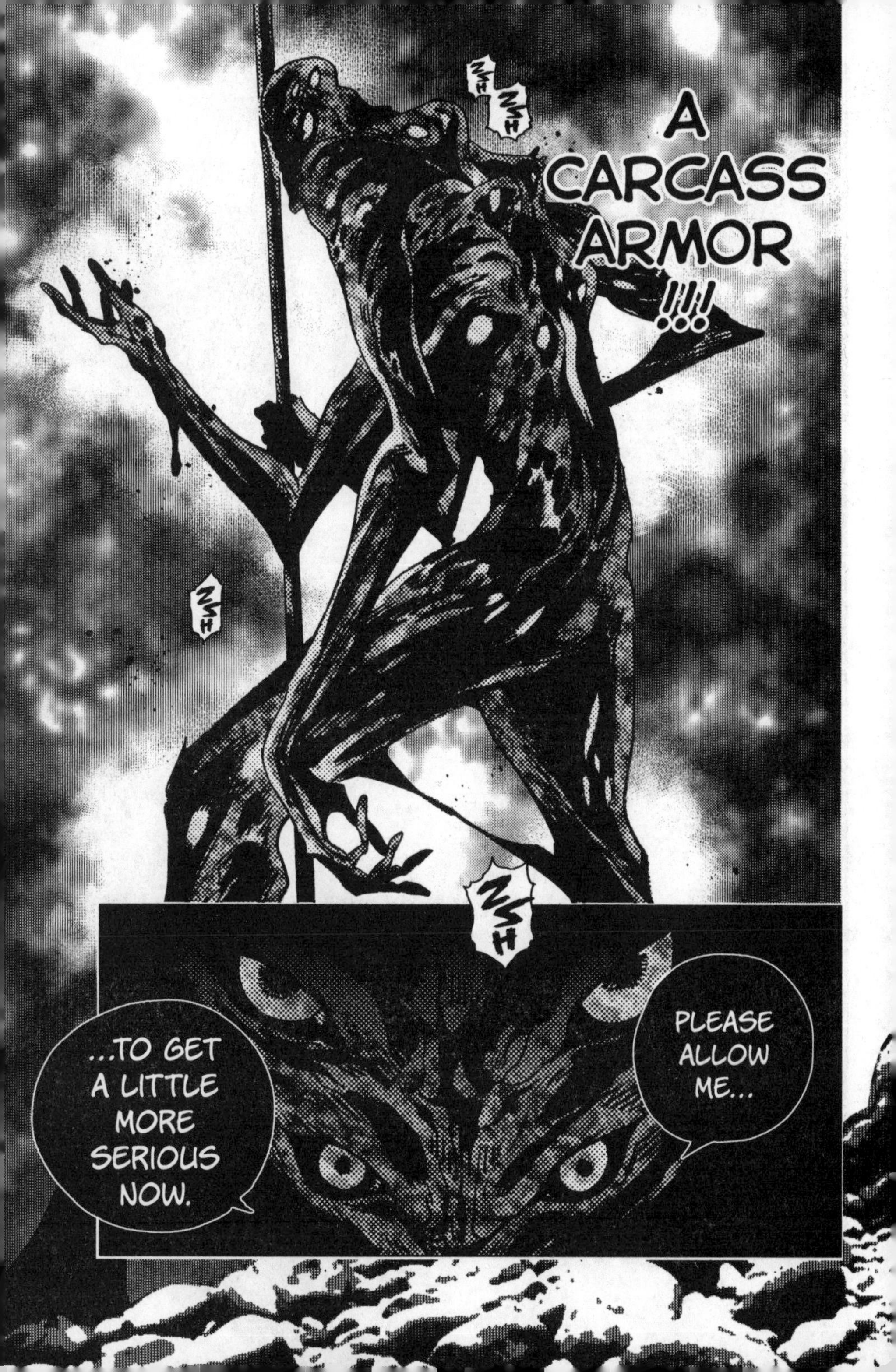
ZSH
ZSH
A CARCASS ARMOR!!!!
ZSH
ZSH
PLEASE ALLOW ME...
...TO GET A LITTLE MORE SERIOUS NOW.

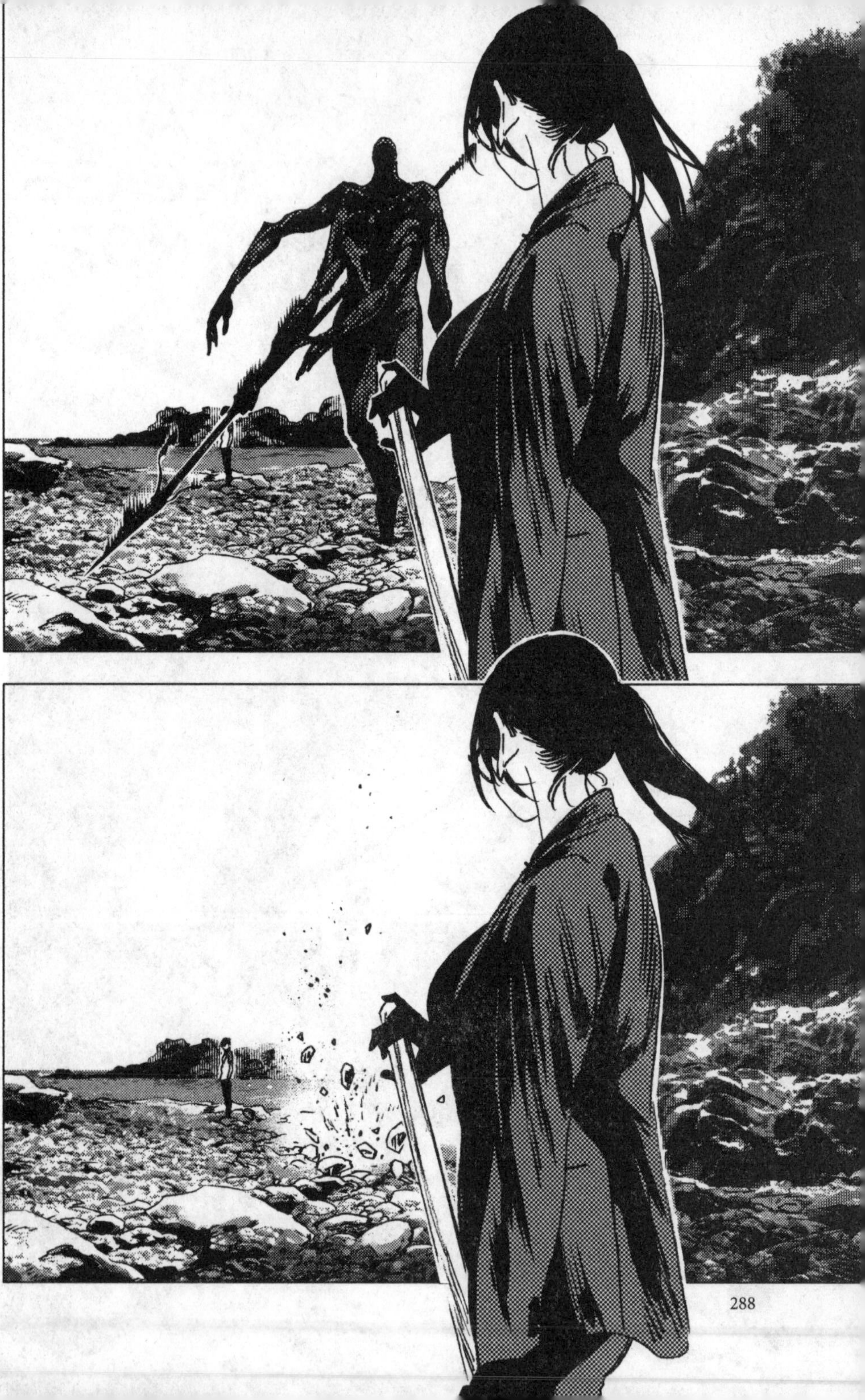

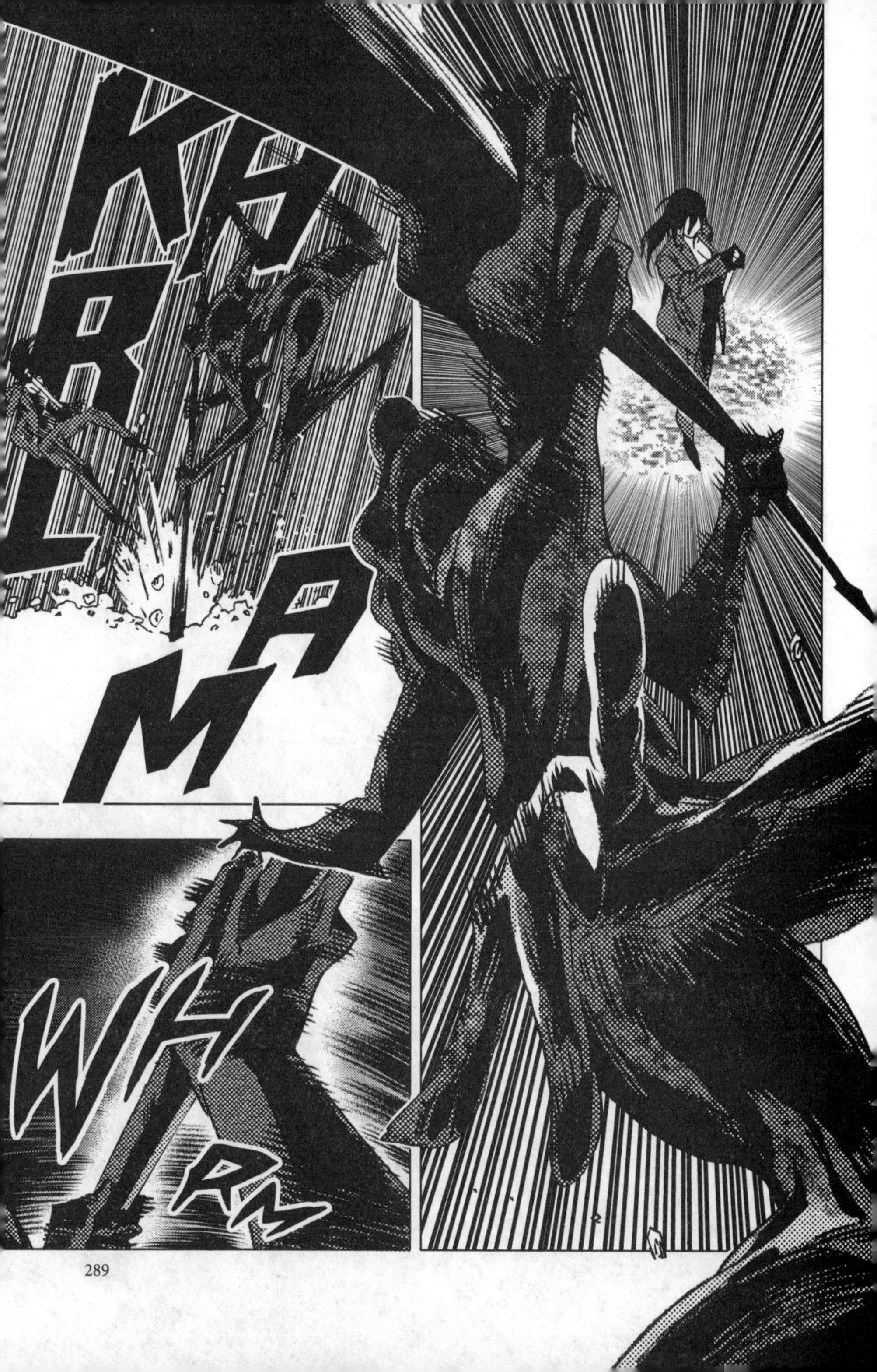

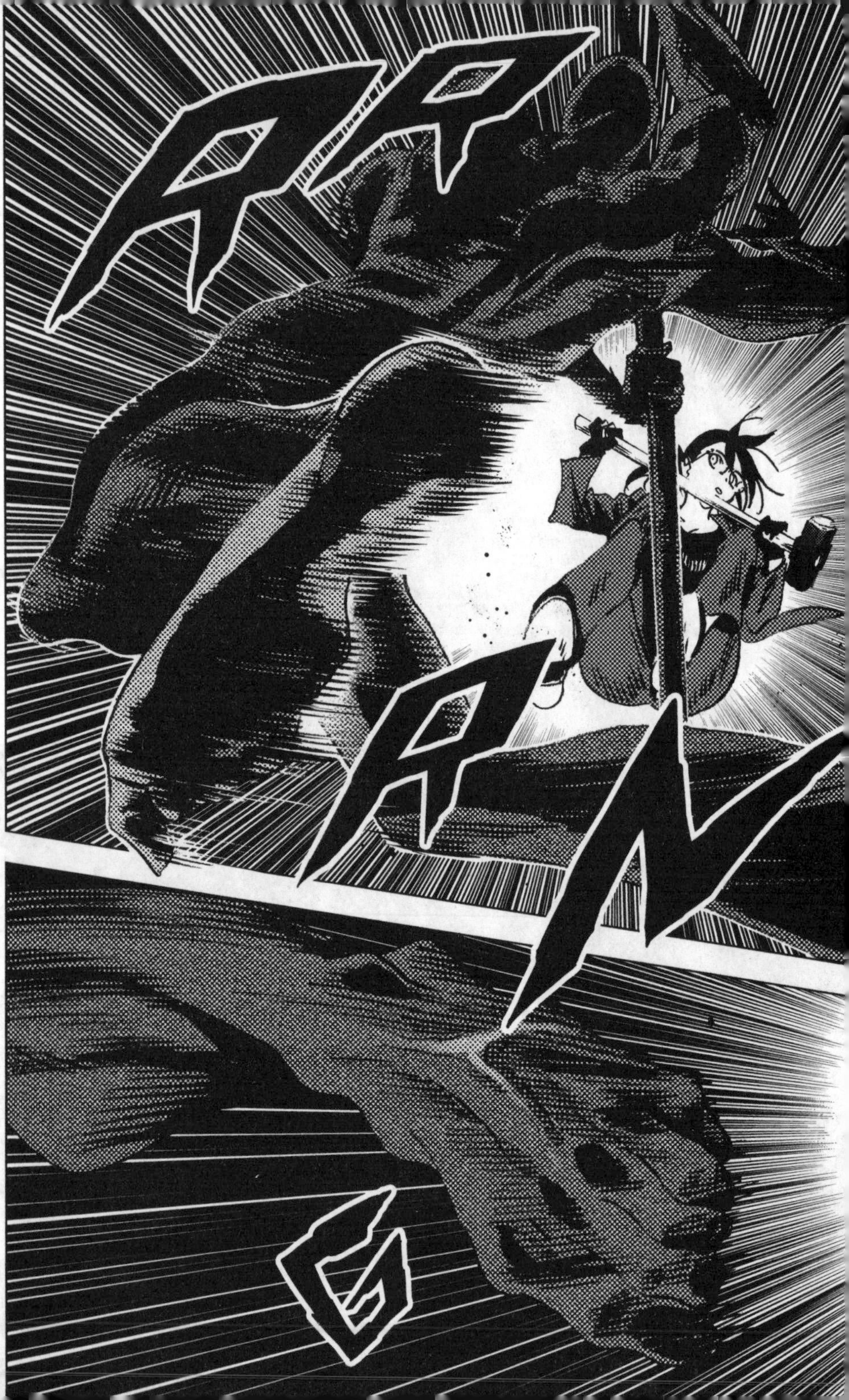
RRRNG

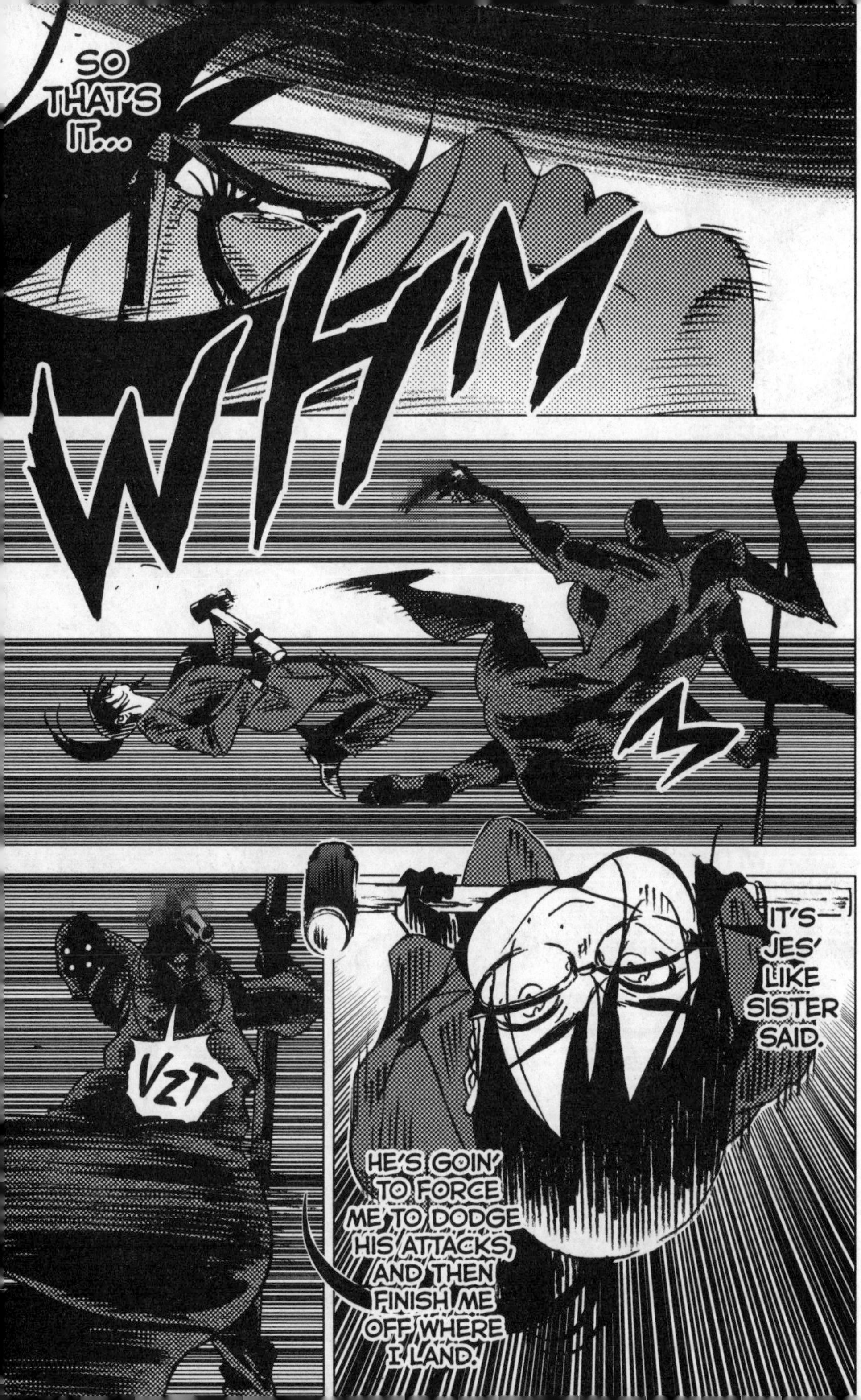

SO THAT'S IT...
WHM
M
IT'S— JES' LIKE SISTER SAID.
HE'S GOIN' TO FORCE ME TO DODGE HIS ATTACKS, AND THEN FINISH ME OFF WHERE I LAND.
VZT

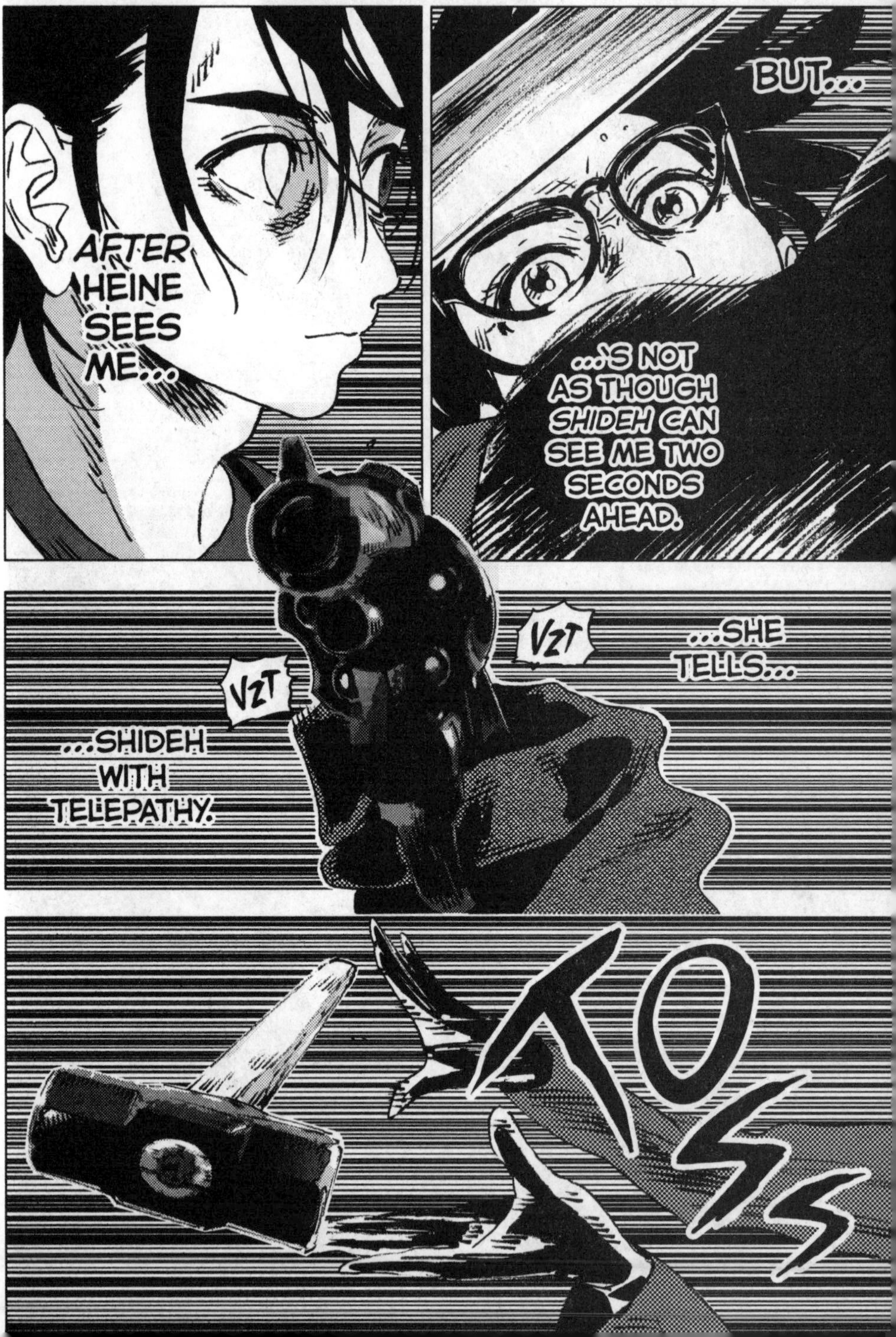
BUT...
...'S NOT AS THOUGH SHIDEH CAN SEE ME TWO SECONDS AHEAD.
AFTER HEINE SEES ME...
VZT
VZT
...SHE TELLS...
...SHIDEH WITH TELEPATHY.
TOSS

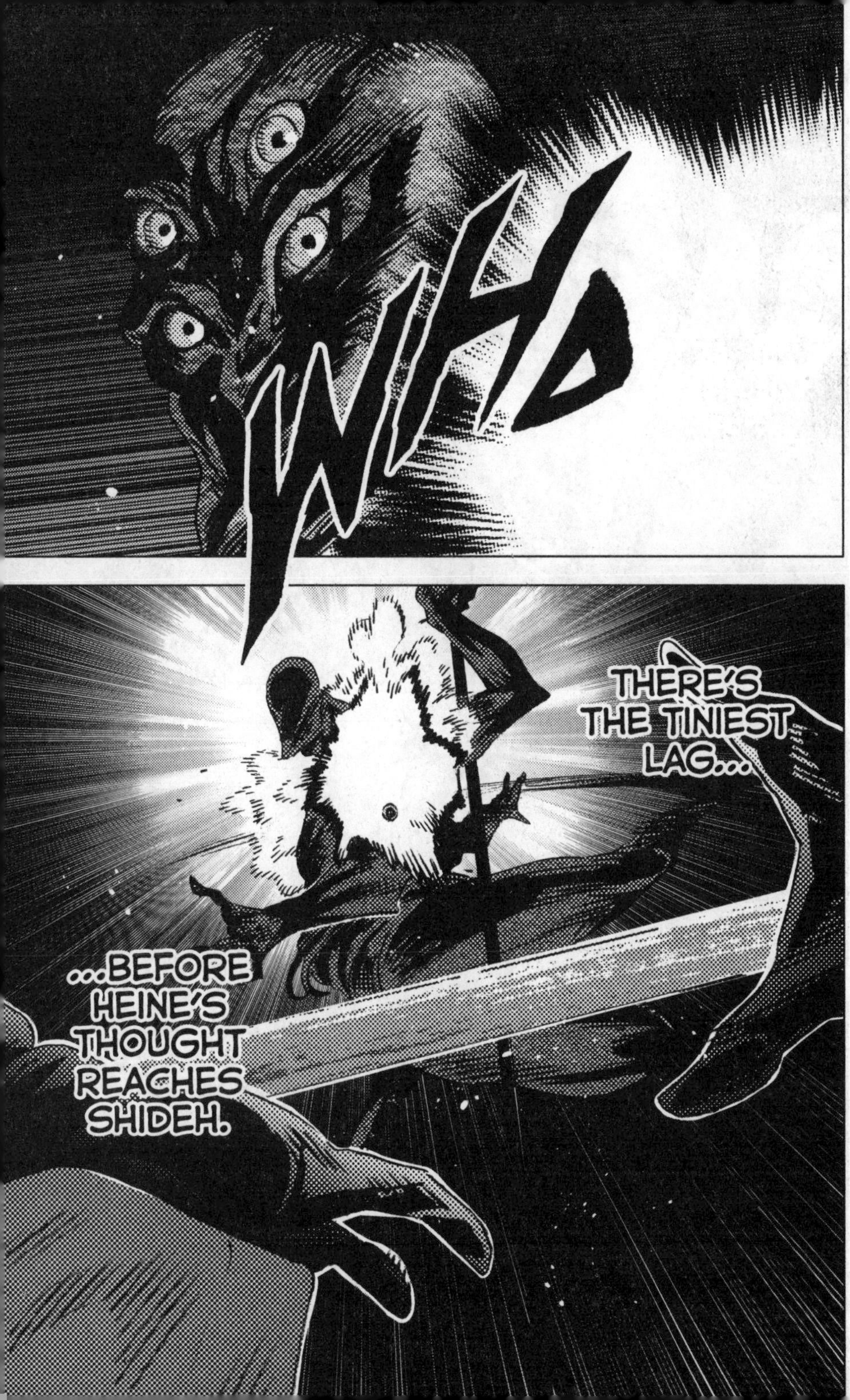
THERE'S THE TINIEST LAG...
...BEFORE HEINE'S THOUGHT REACHES SHIDEH.

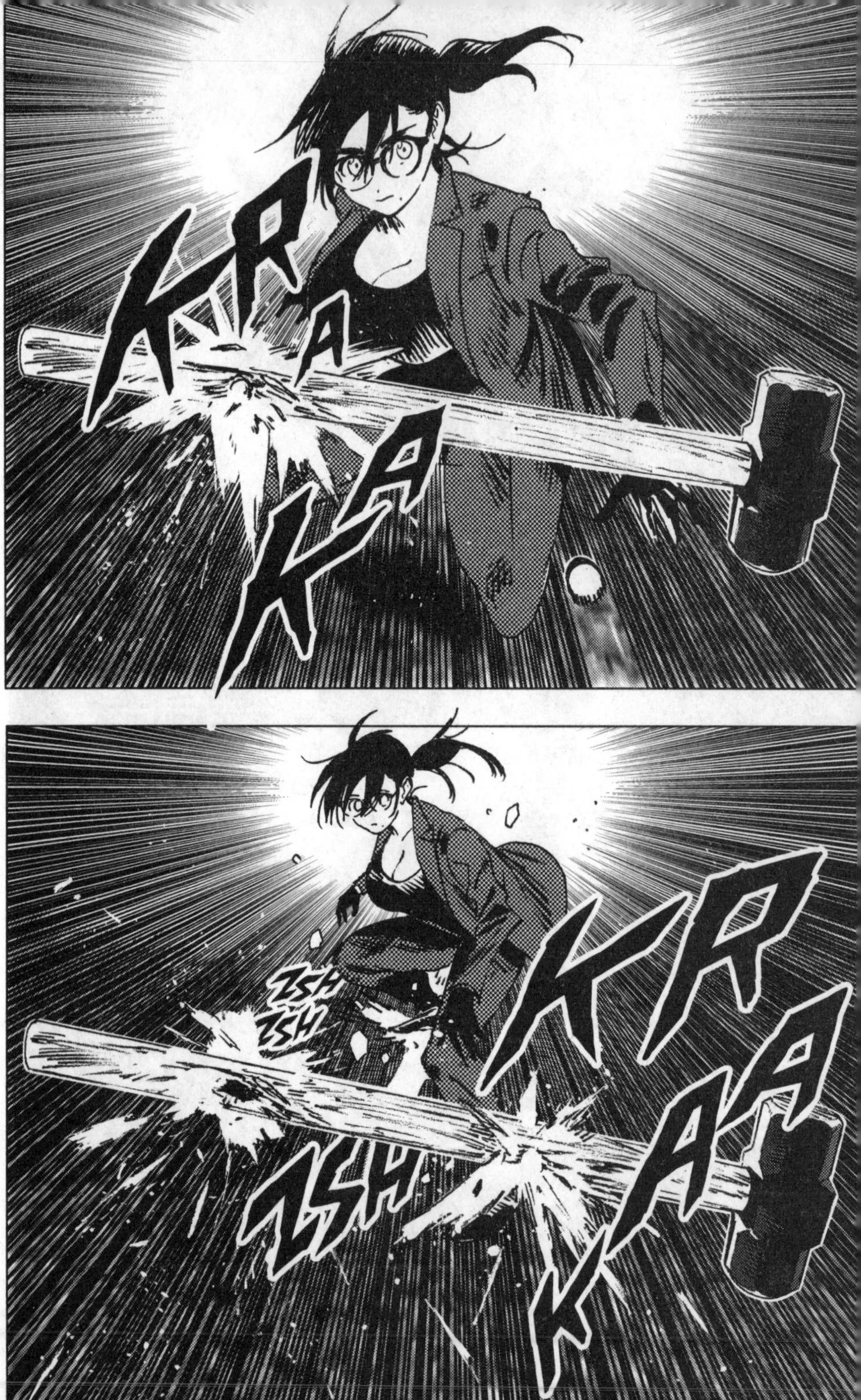
KRAAK
KRAAAK
ZSH ZSH
ZSH

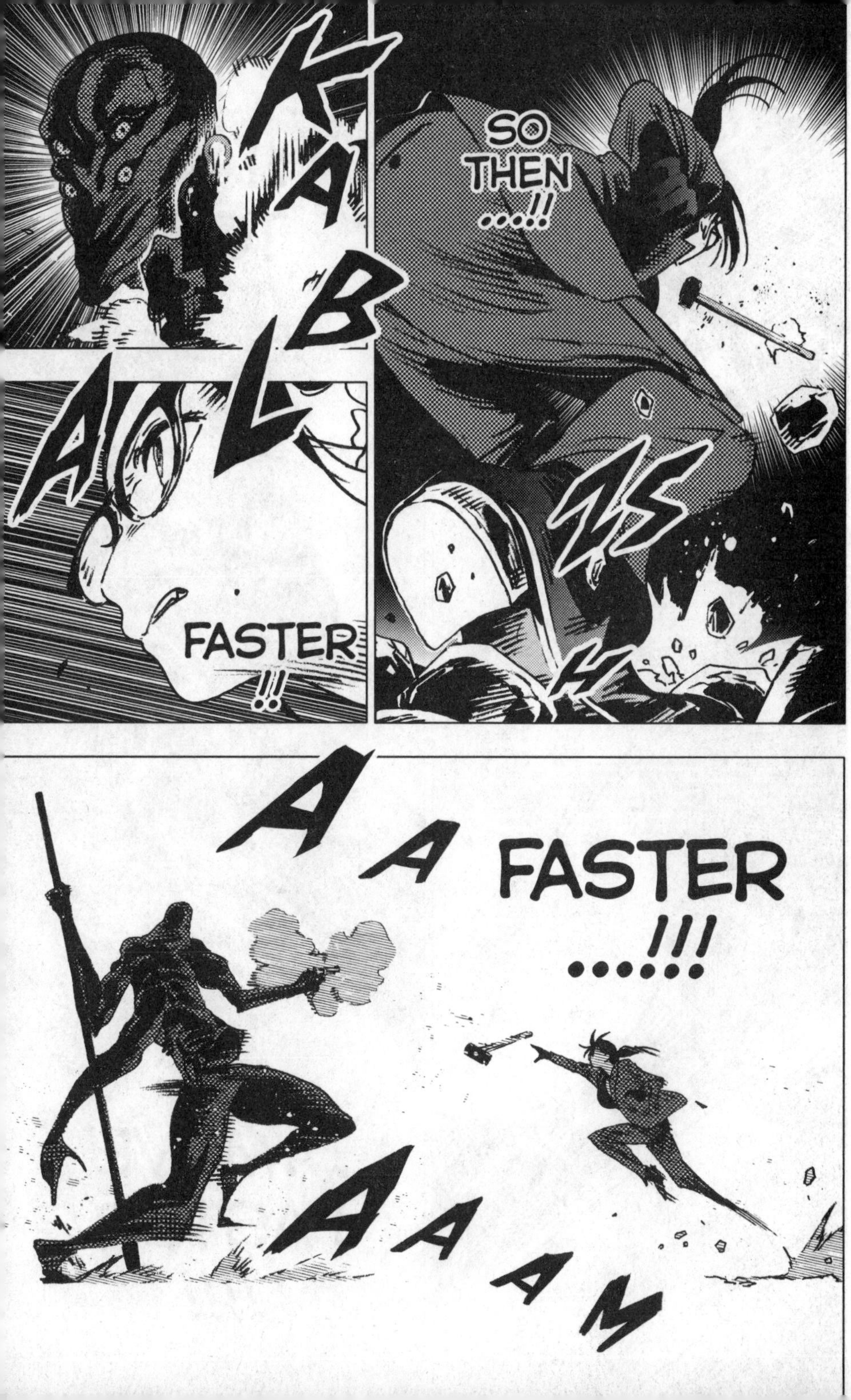
SO THEN ....!!
ZSH
KABLA
FASTER !!
AA
FASTER ....!!!
AAAAM

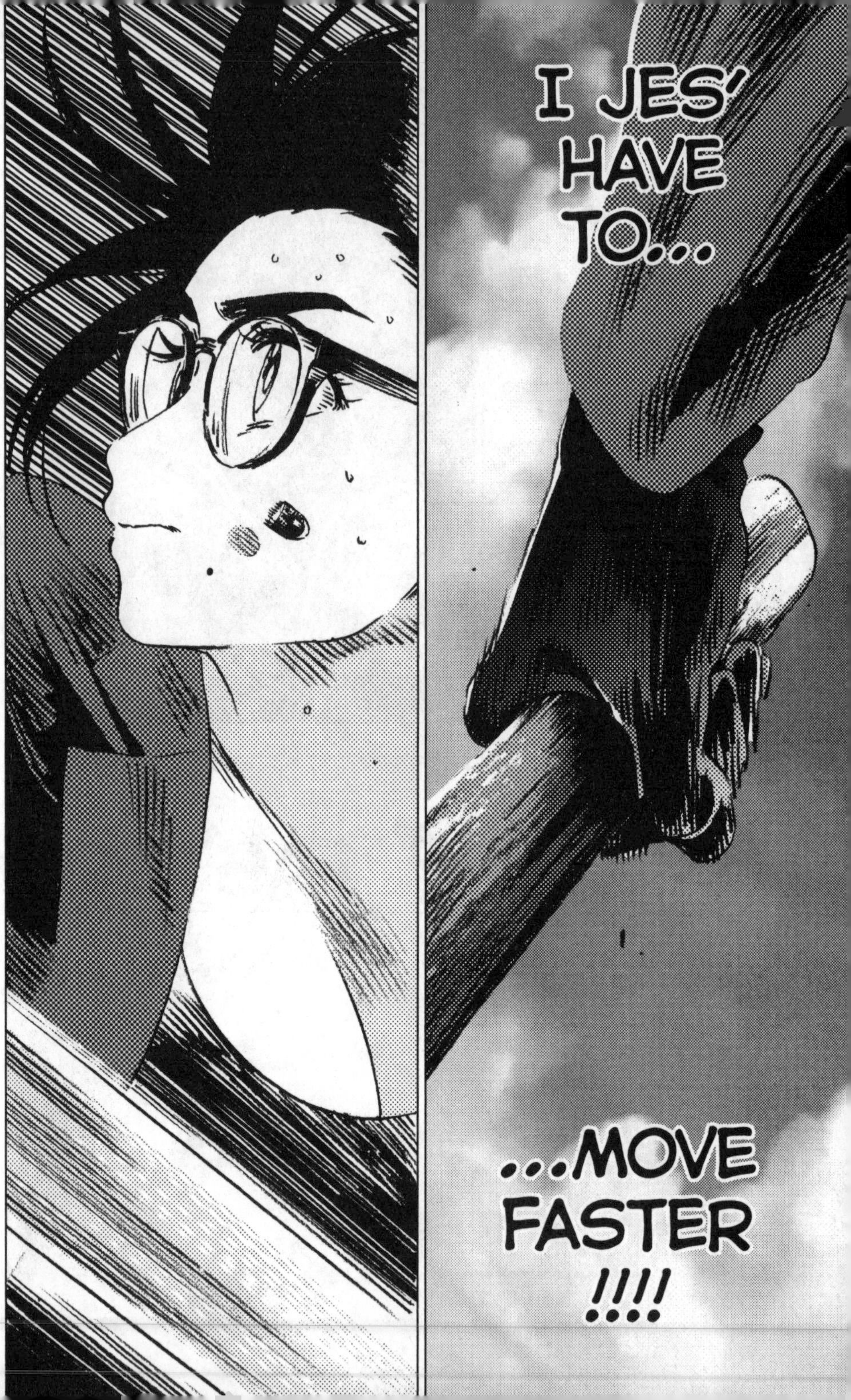
I JES' HAVE TO...
...MOVE FASTER !!!!

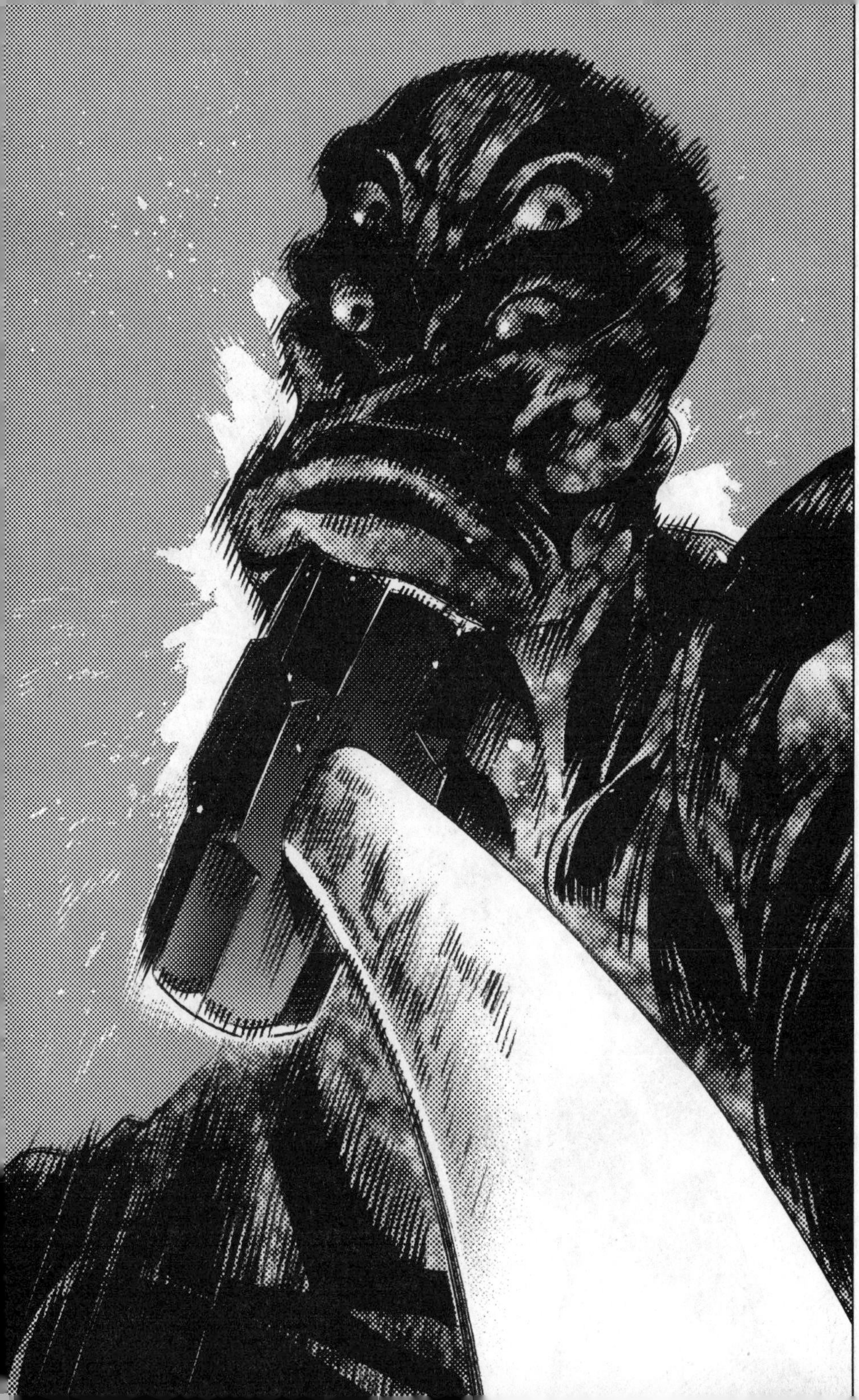

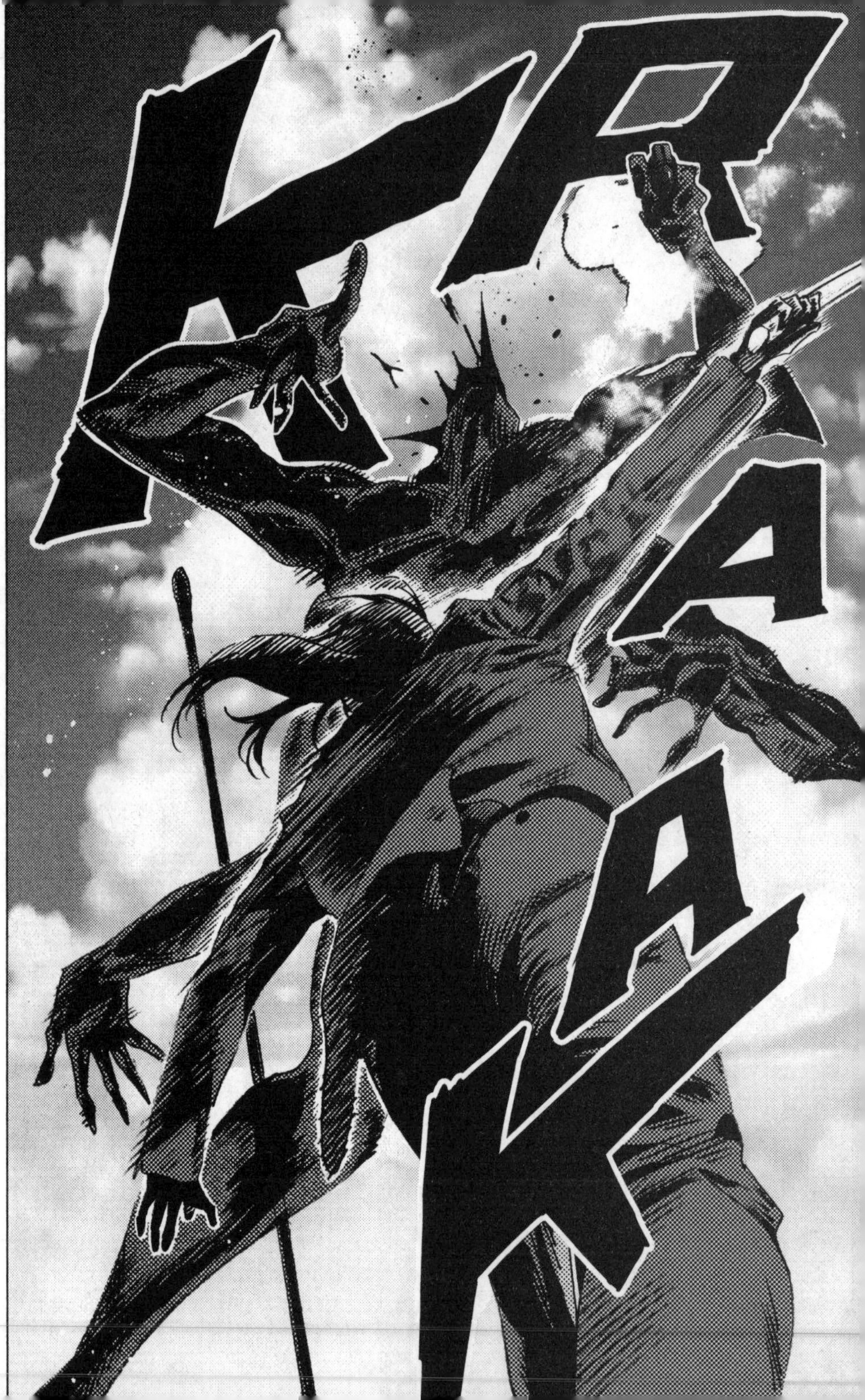
KRAAK

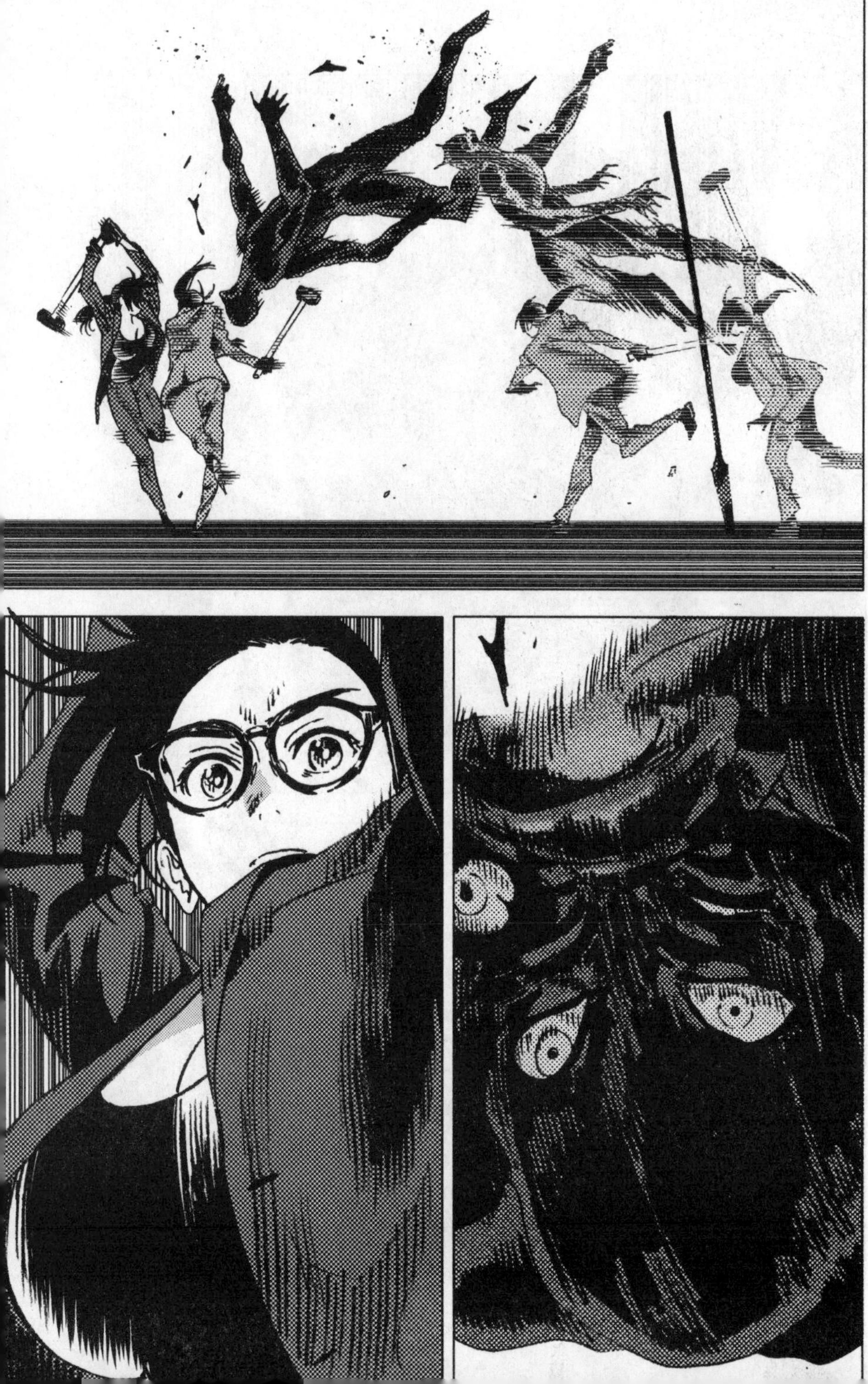

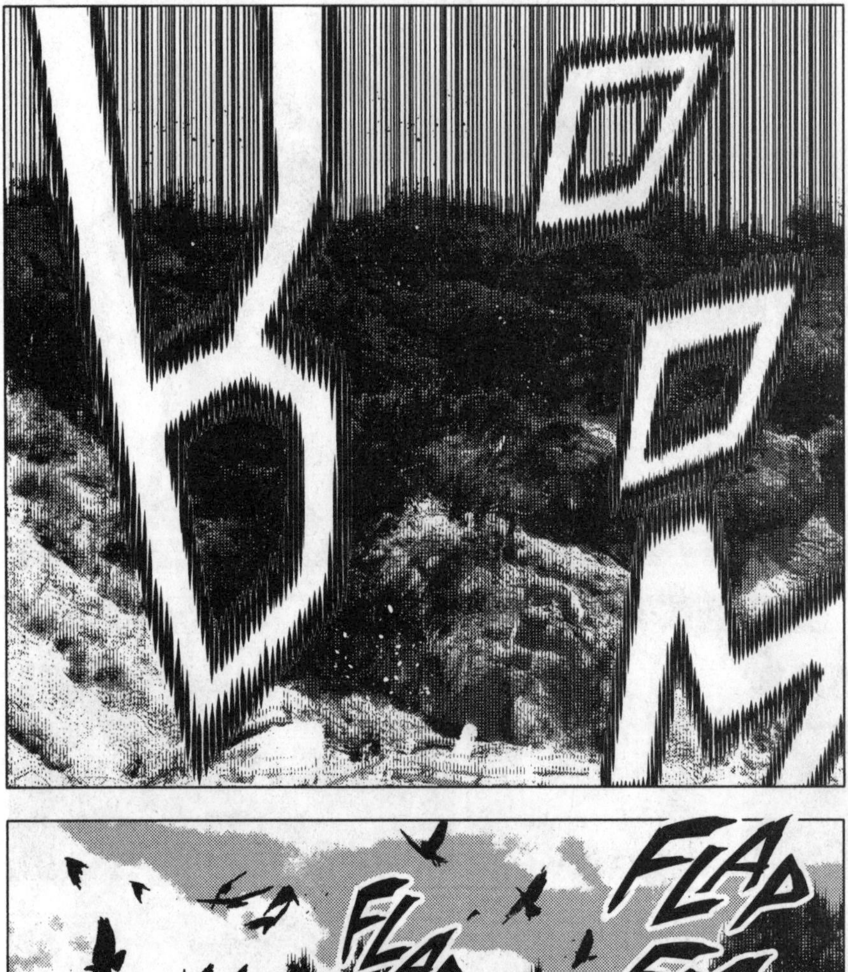

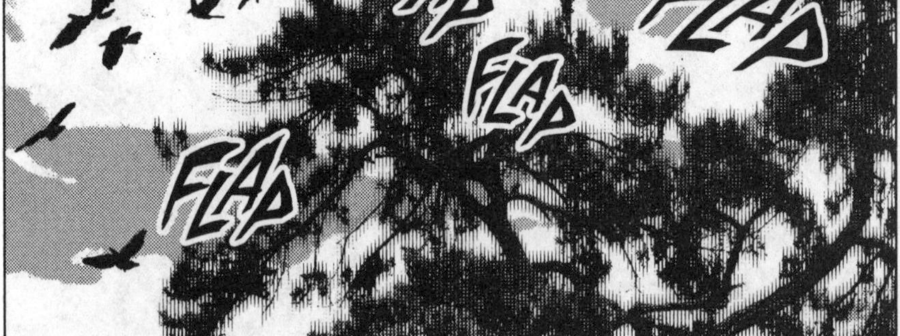
FLAP
FLAP
FLAP
FLAP
FLAP

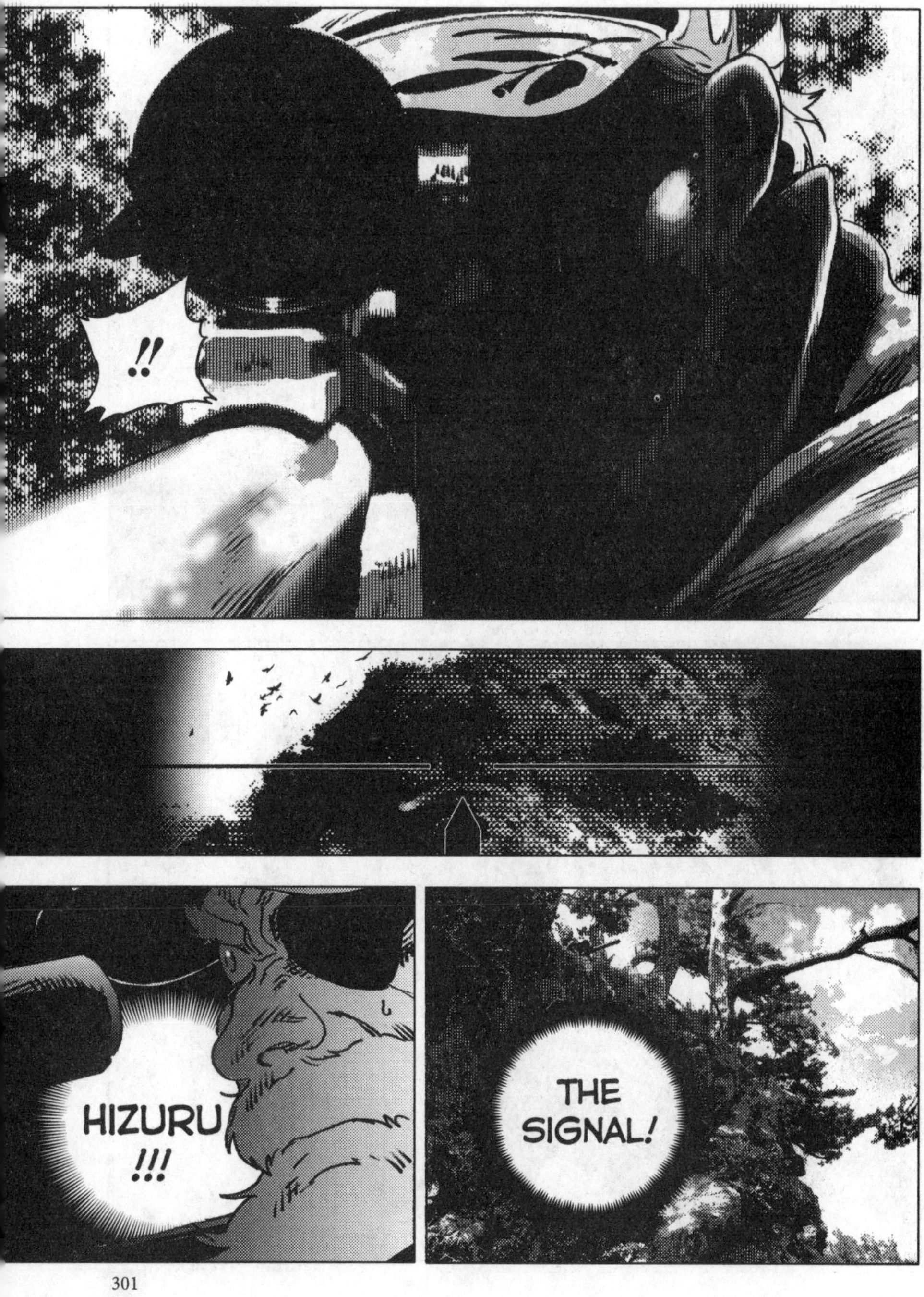
!!
THE SIGNAL!
HIZURU !!!

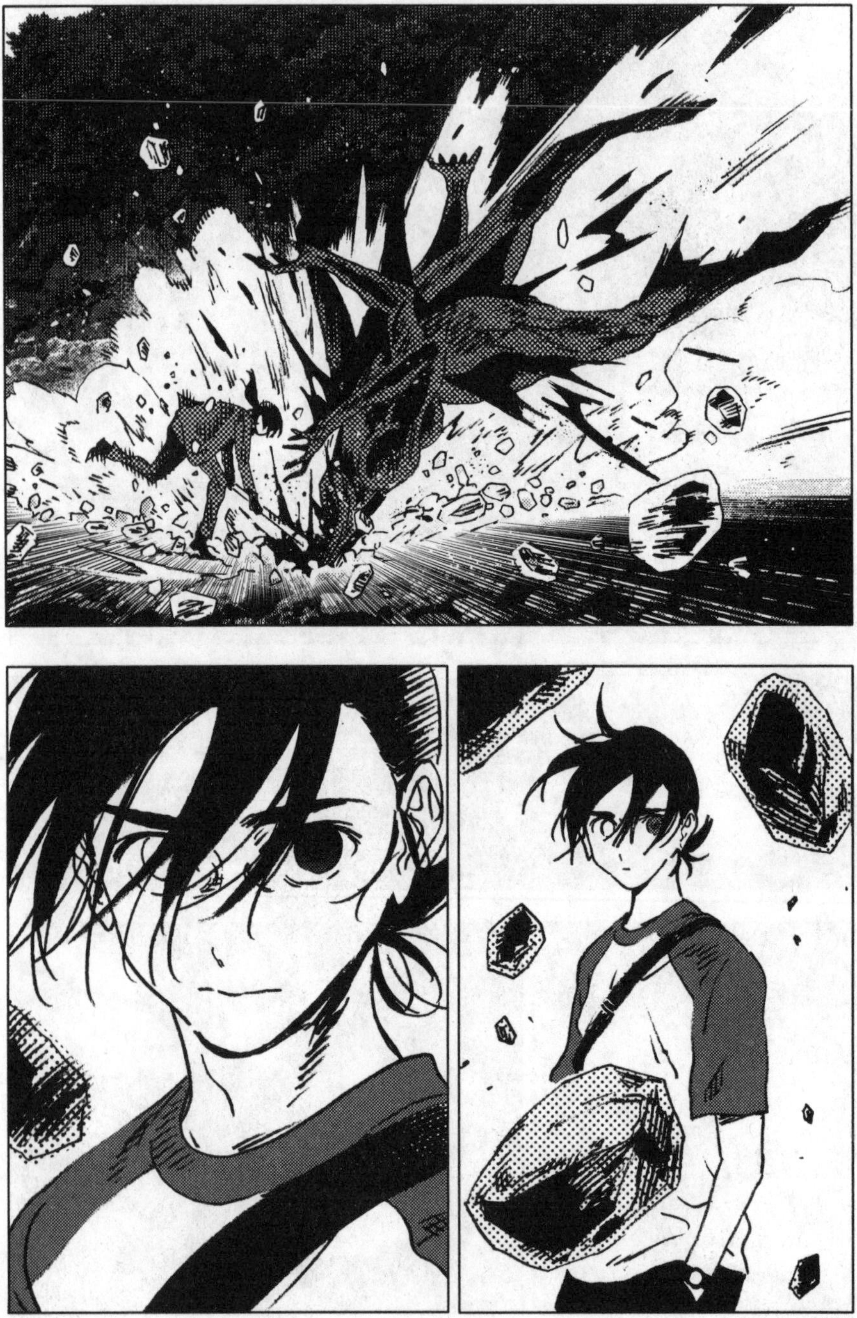

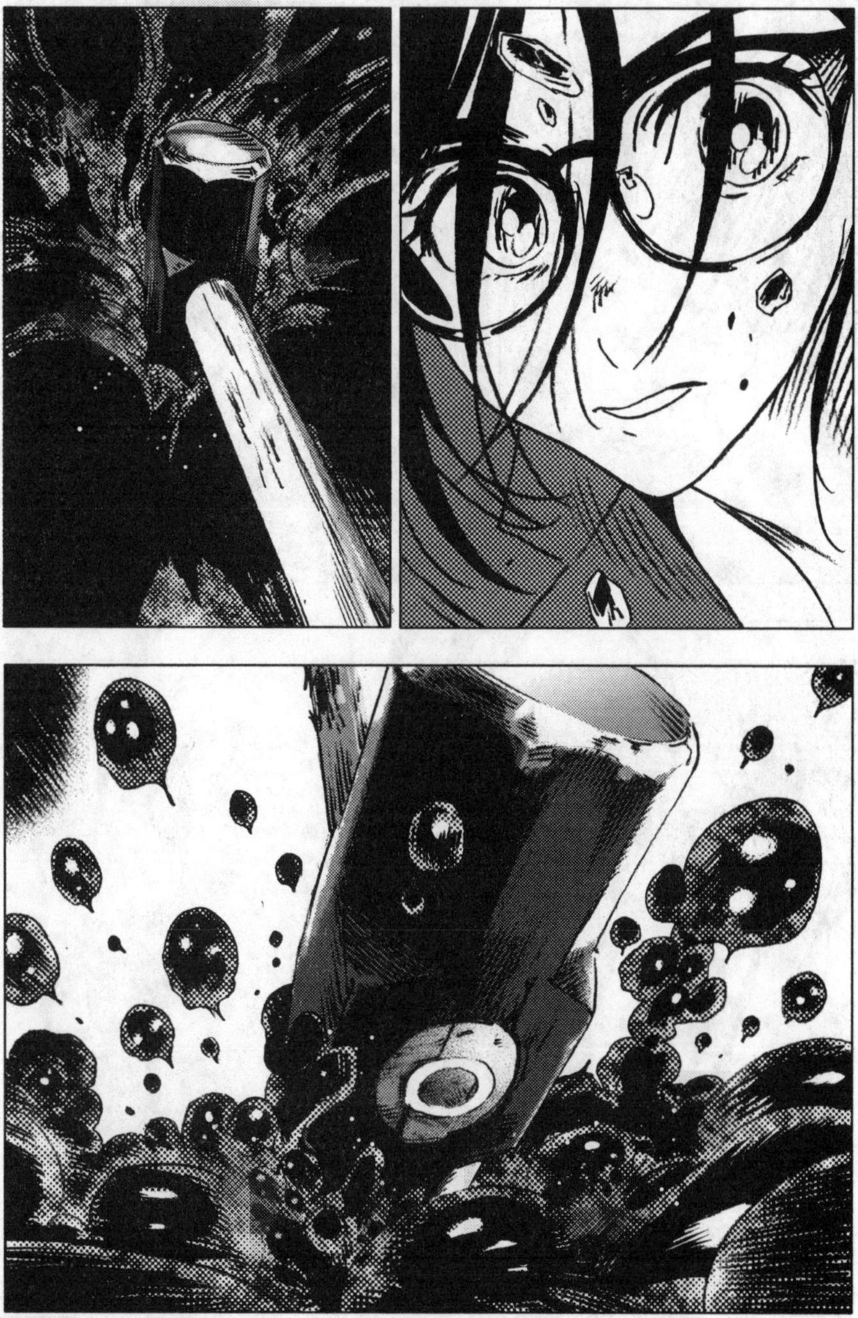

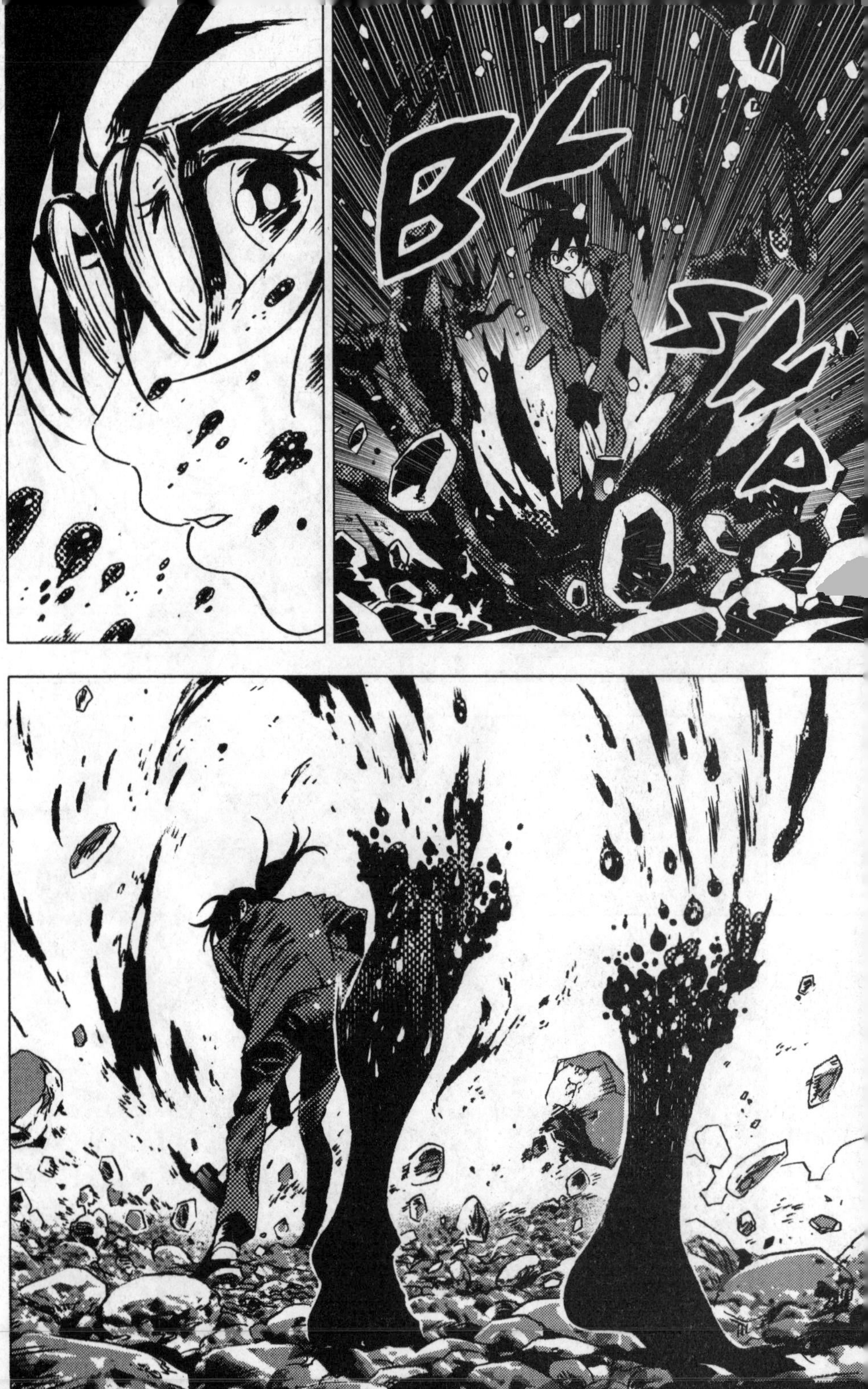
BLSHA

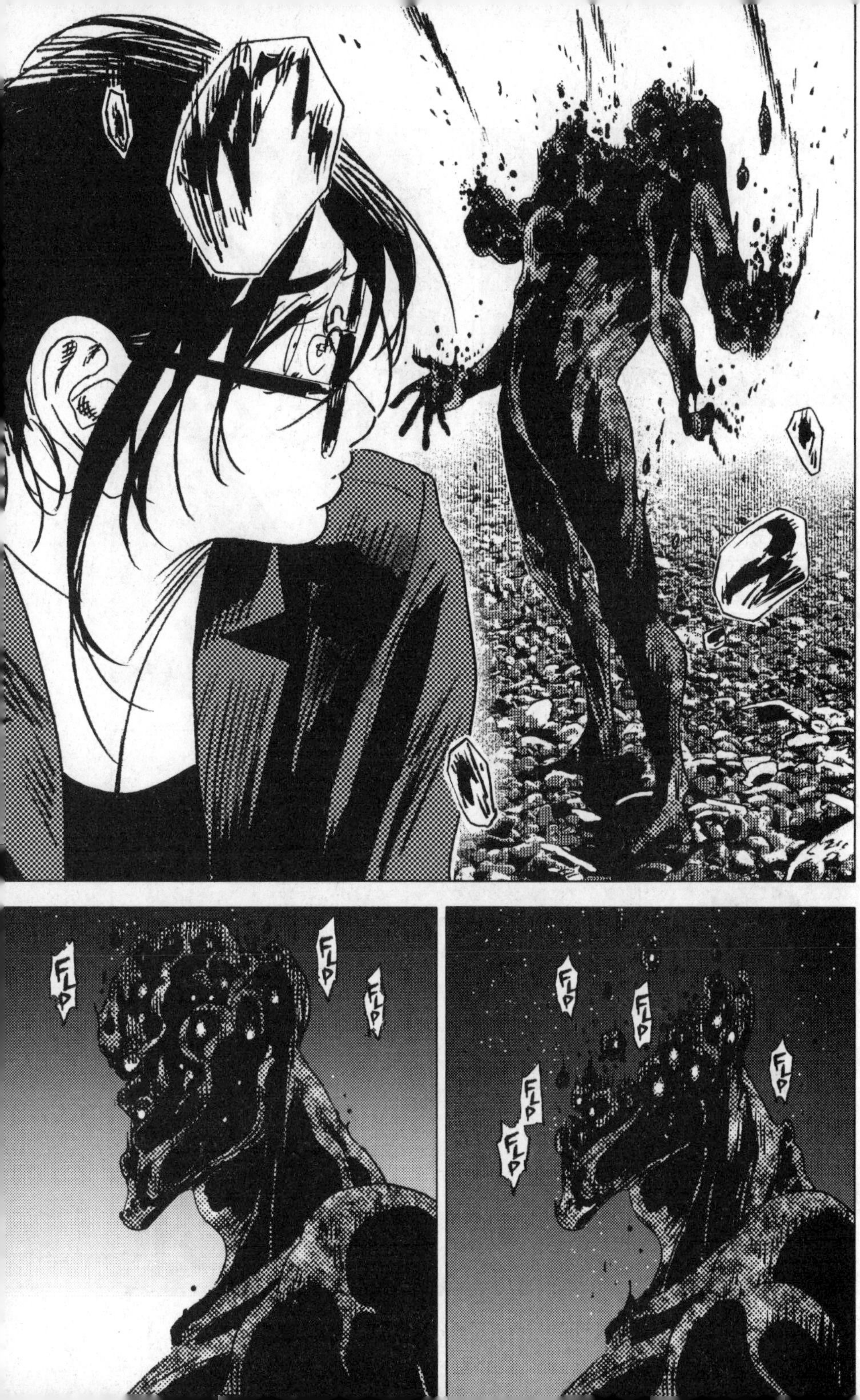
FLP
FLP
FLP
FLP
FLP
FLP
FLP
FLP

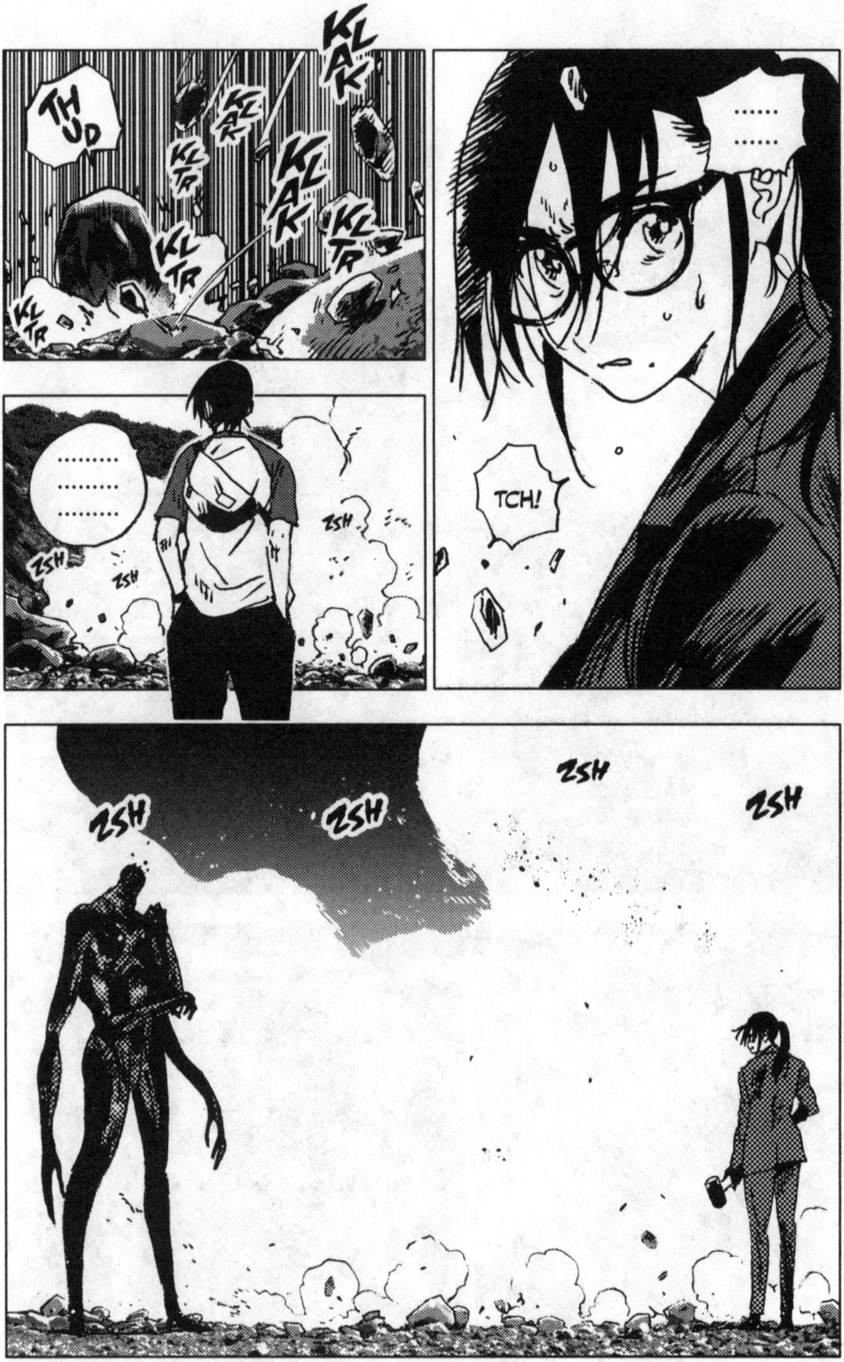
....
TCH!
KLAK
KLTR
KLAK
KLAK
THUD
KLTR
KLTR
KLTR
....
ZSH
ZSH
ZSH
ZSH
ZSH
ZSH
ZSH

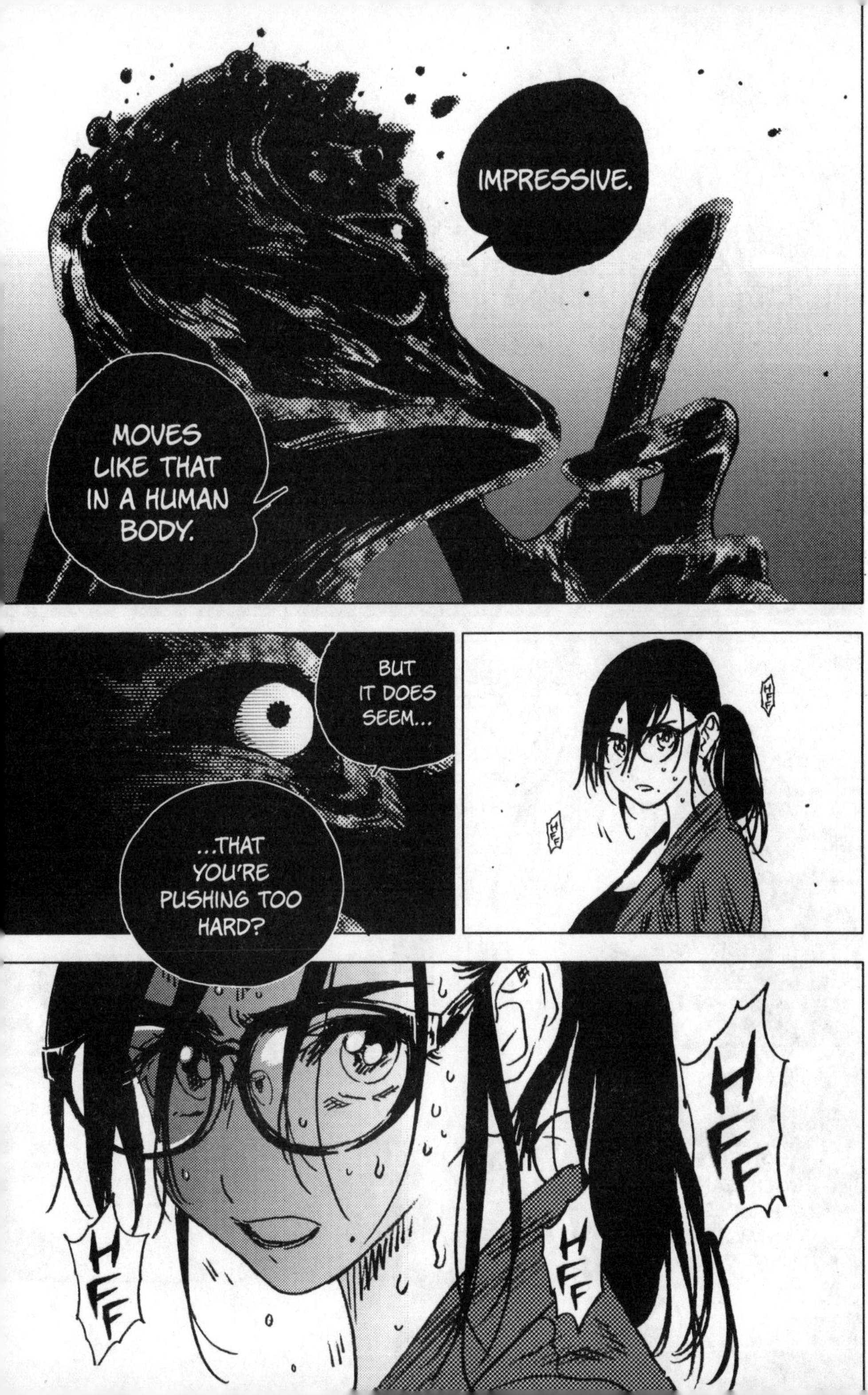
IMPRESSIVE.
MOVES LIKE THAT IN A HUMAN BODY.
HFF
HFF
BUT IT DOES SEEM...
...THAT YOU'RE PUSHING TOO HARD?
HFF
HFF
HFF

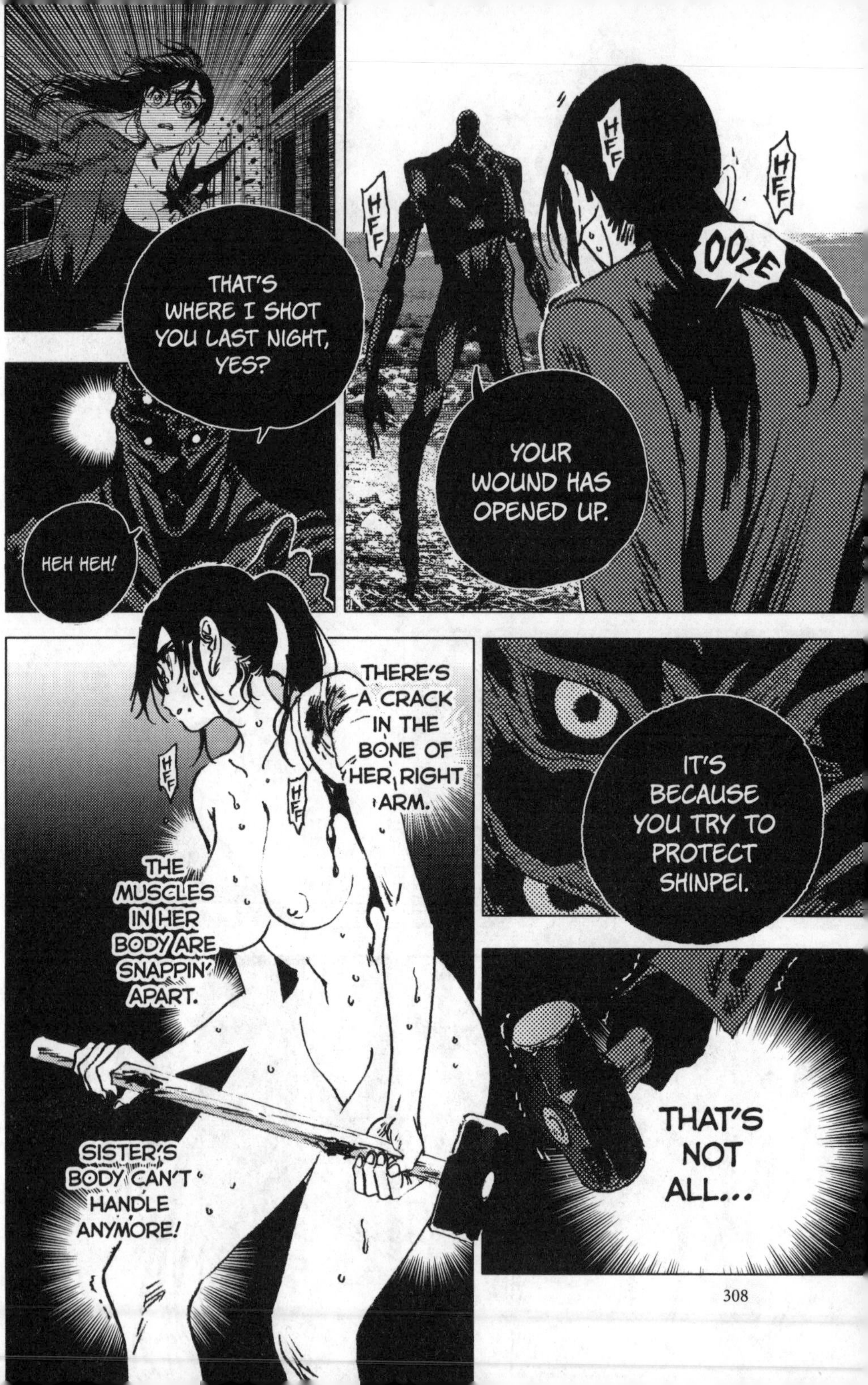
HFF
HFF
HFF
OOZE
YOUR WOUND HAS OPENED UP.
THAT'S WHERE I SHOT YOU LAST NIGHT, YES?
HEH HEH!
IT'S BECAUSE YOU TRY TO PROTECT SHINPEI.
THAT'S NOT ALL...
THERE'S A CRACK IN THE BONE OF HER RIGHT ARM.
HFF
HFF
THE MUSCLES IN HER BODY ARE SNAPPIN' APART.
SISTER'S BODY CAN'T HANDLE ANYMORE!

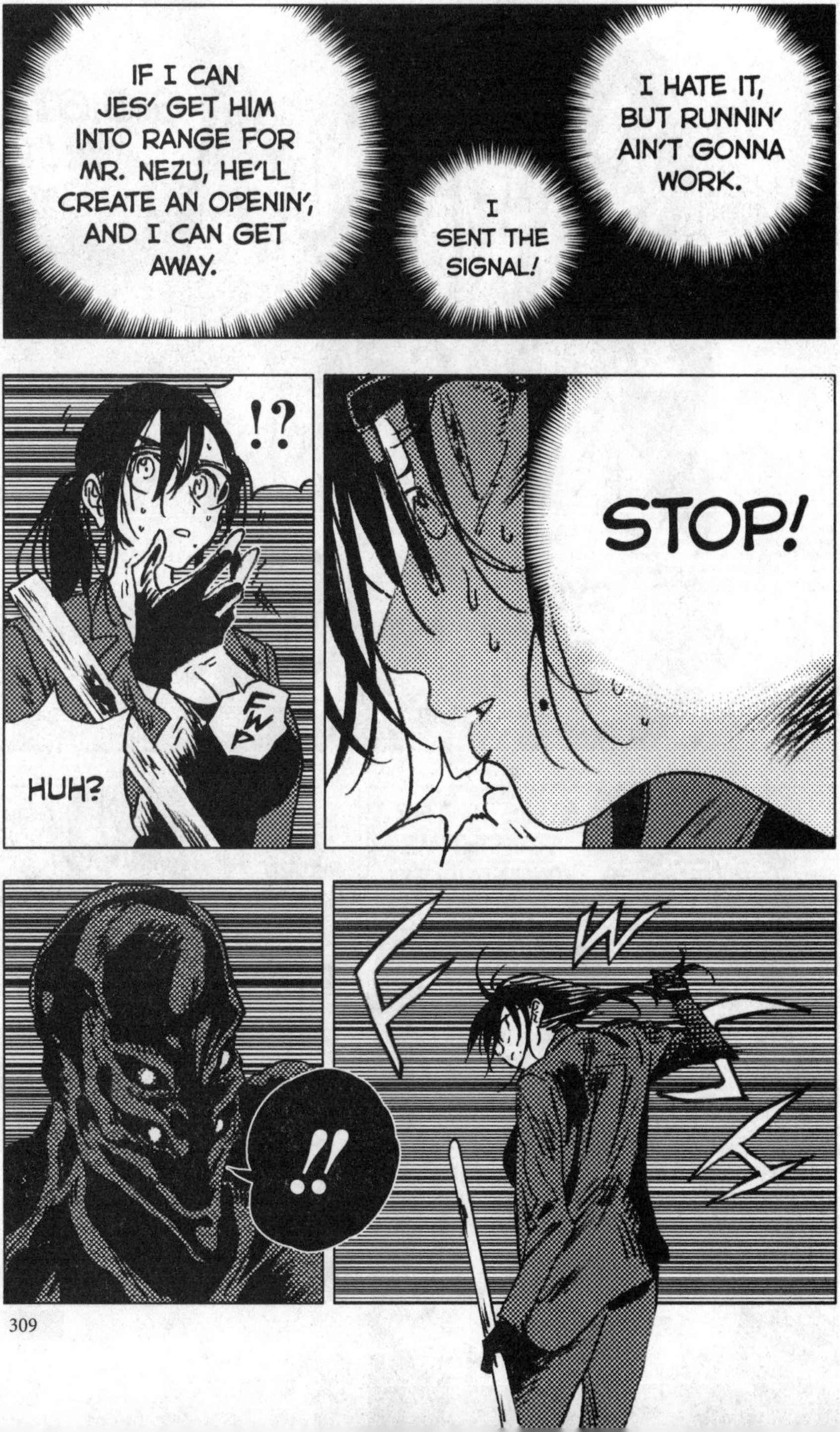
I HATE IT, BUT RUNNIN' AIN'T GONNA WORK.
I SENT THE SIGNAL!
IF I CAN JES' GET HIM INTO RANGE FOR MR. NEZU, HE'LL CREATE AN OPENIN', AND I CAN GET AWAY.
STOP!
!?
FWP
HUH?
!!

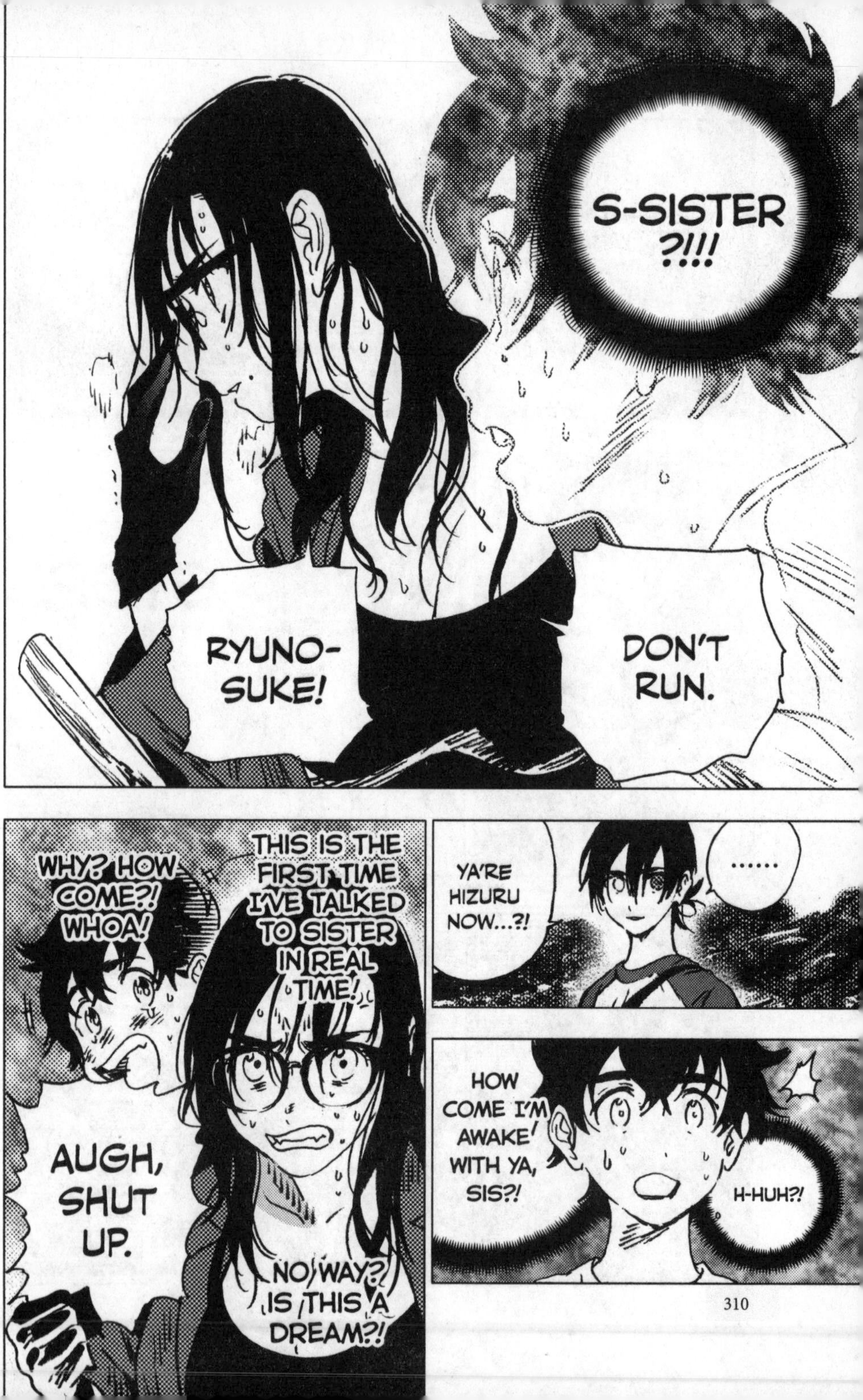
S-SISTER ?!!!
DON'T RUN.
RYUNO-SUKE!
......
YA'RE HIZURU NOW...?!
H-HUH?!
HOW COME I'M AWAKE WITH YA, SIS?!
THIS IS THE FIRST TIME I'VE TALKED TO SISTER IN REAL TIME!
WHY? HOW COME?! WHOA!
AUGH, SHUT UP.
NO WAY?! IS THIS A DREAM?!

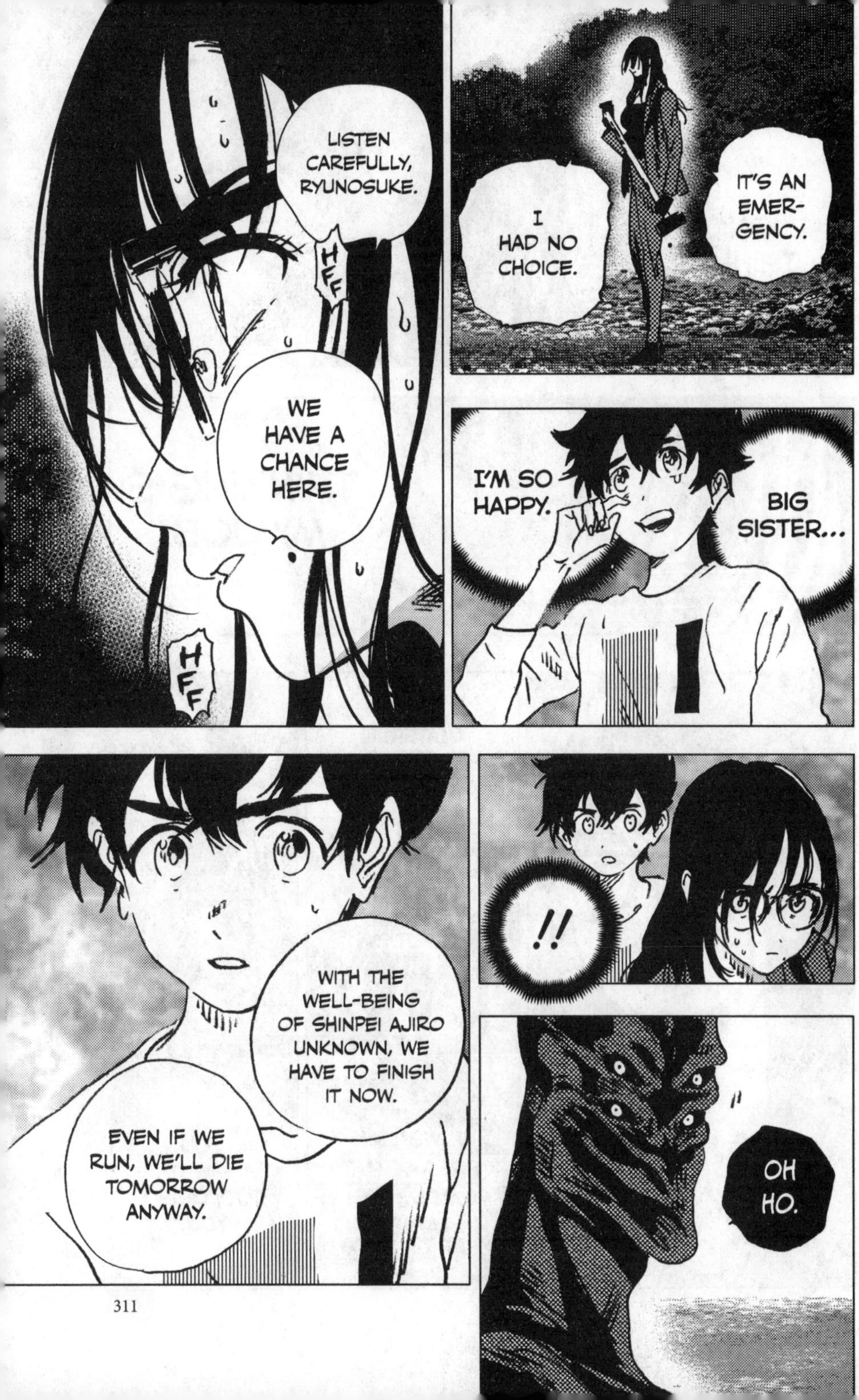

IT'S AN EMER-GENCY.
I HAD NO CHOICE.
BIG SISTER...
I'M SO HAPPY.
LISTEN CAREFULLY, RYUNOSUKE.
HFF
WE HAVE A CHANCE HERE.
HFF
!!
OH HO.
WITH THE WELL-BEING OF SHINPEI AJIRO UNKNOWN, WE HAVE TO FINISH IT NOW.
EVEN IF WE RUN, WE'LL DIE TOMORROW ANYWAY.

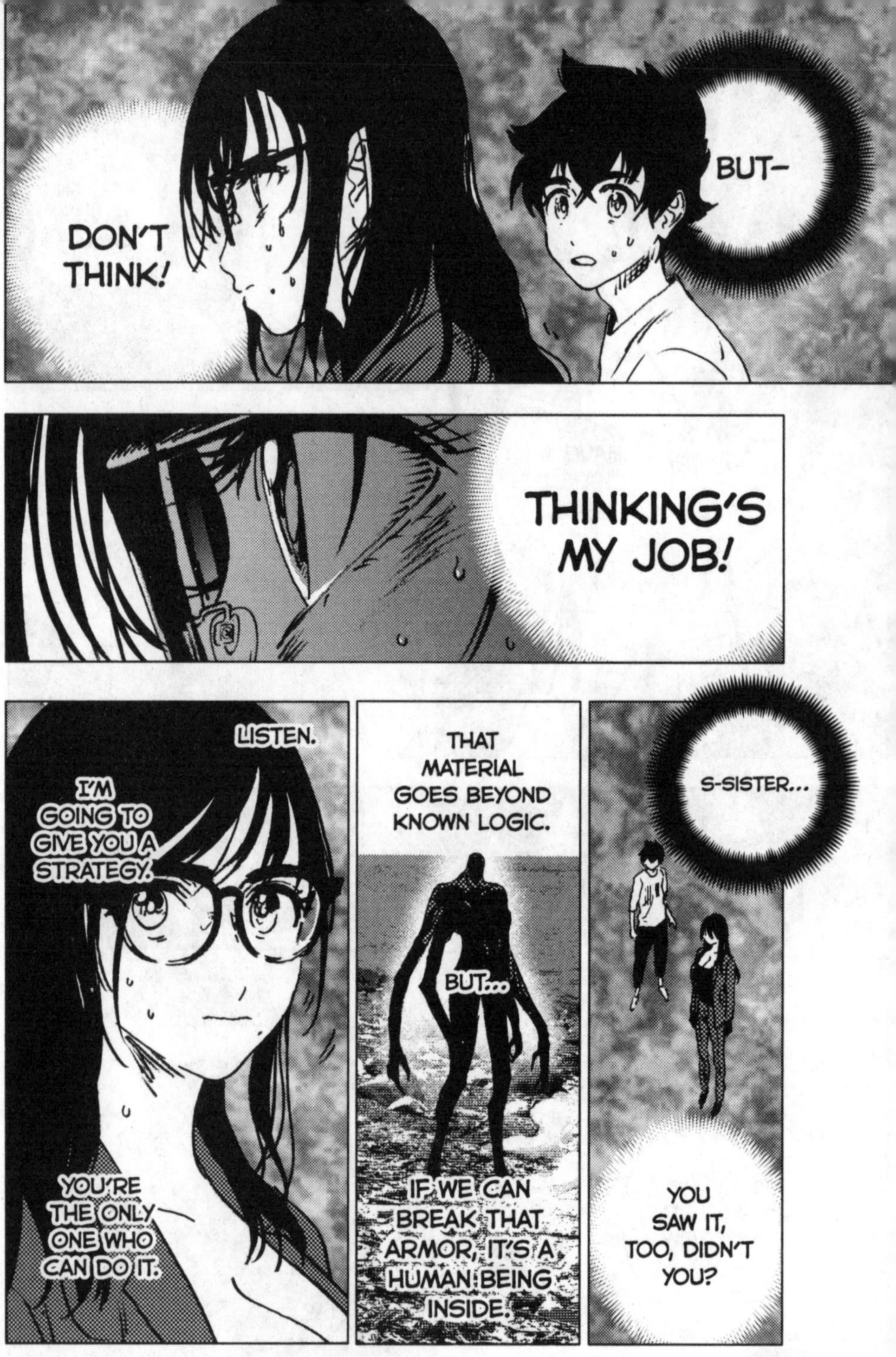
BUT–
DON'T THINK!
THINKING'S MY JOB!
S-SISTER...
YOU SAW IT, TOO, DIDN'T YOU?
THAT MATERIAL GOES BEYOND KNOWN LOGIC.
BUT...
IF WE CAN BREAK THAT ARMOR, IT'S A HUMAN BEING INSIDE.
LISTEN.
I'M GOING TO GIVE YOU A STRATEGY.
YOU'RE THE ONLY ONE WHO CAN DO IT.

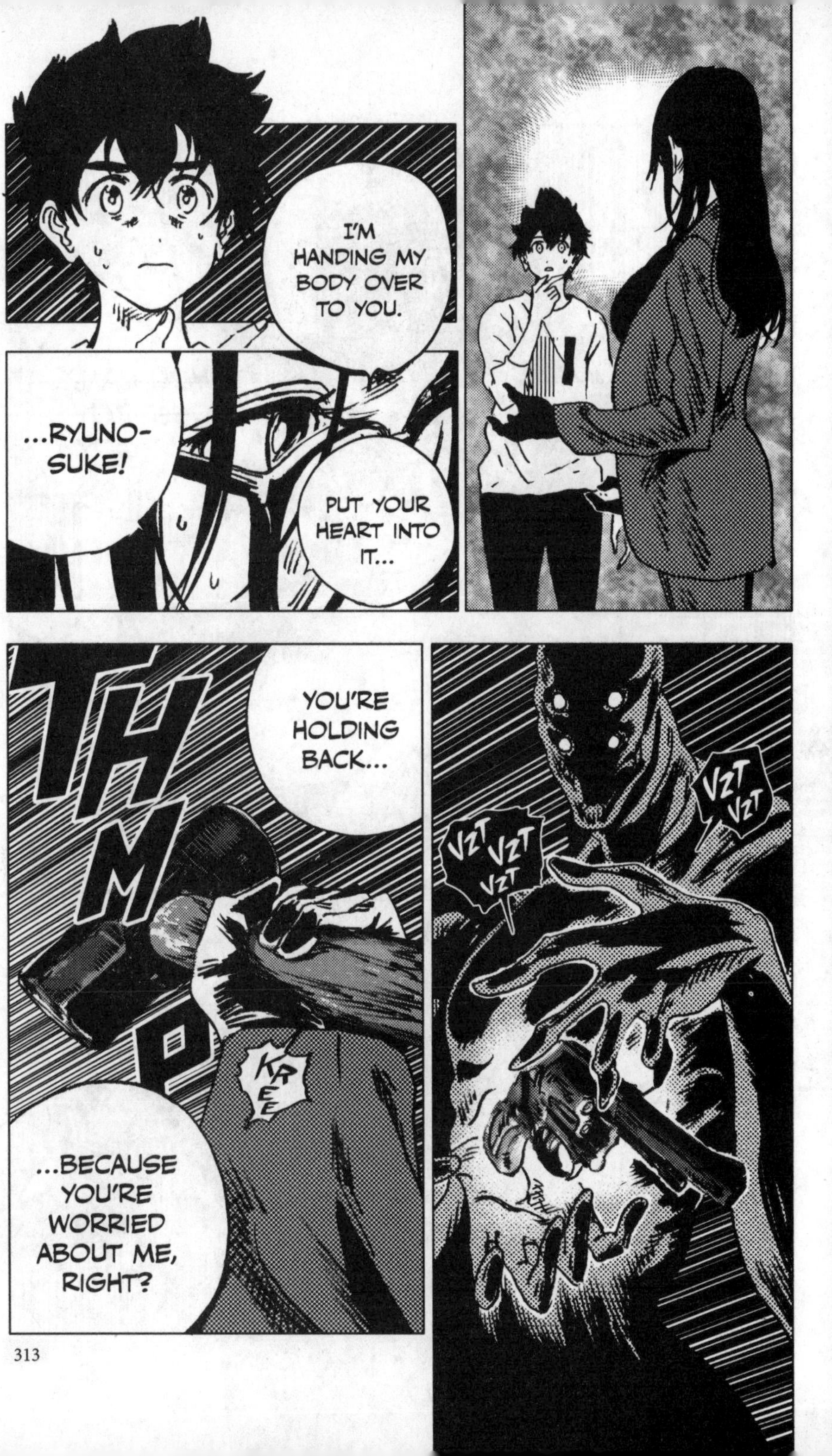
I'M HANDING MY BODY OVER TO YOU.
...RYUNO-SUKE!
PUT YOUR HEART INTO IT...
VZT VZT
VZT VZT VZT
THMP
YOU'RE HOLDING BACK...
KREE
...BECAUSE YOU'RE WORRIED ABOUT ME, RIGHT?

YOU CAN... DESTROY MY BODY.
GO! USE IT TO THE FULLEST!!

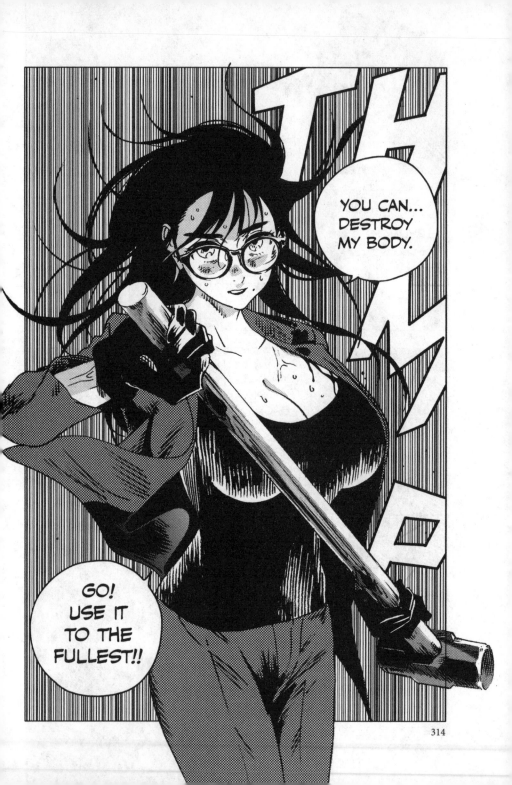

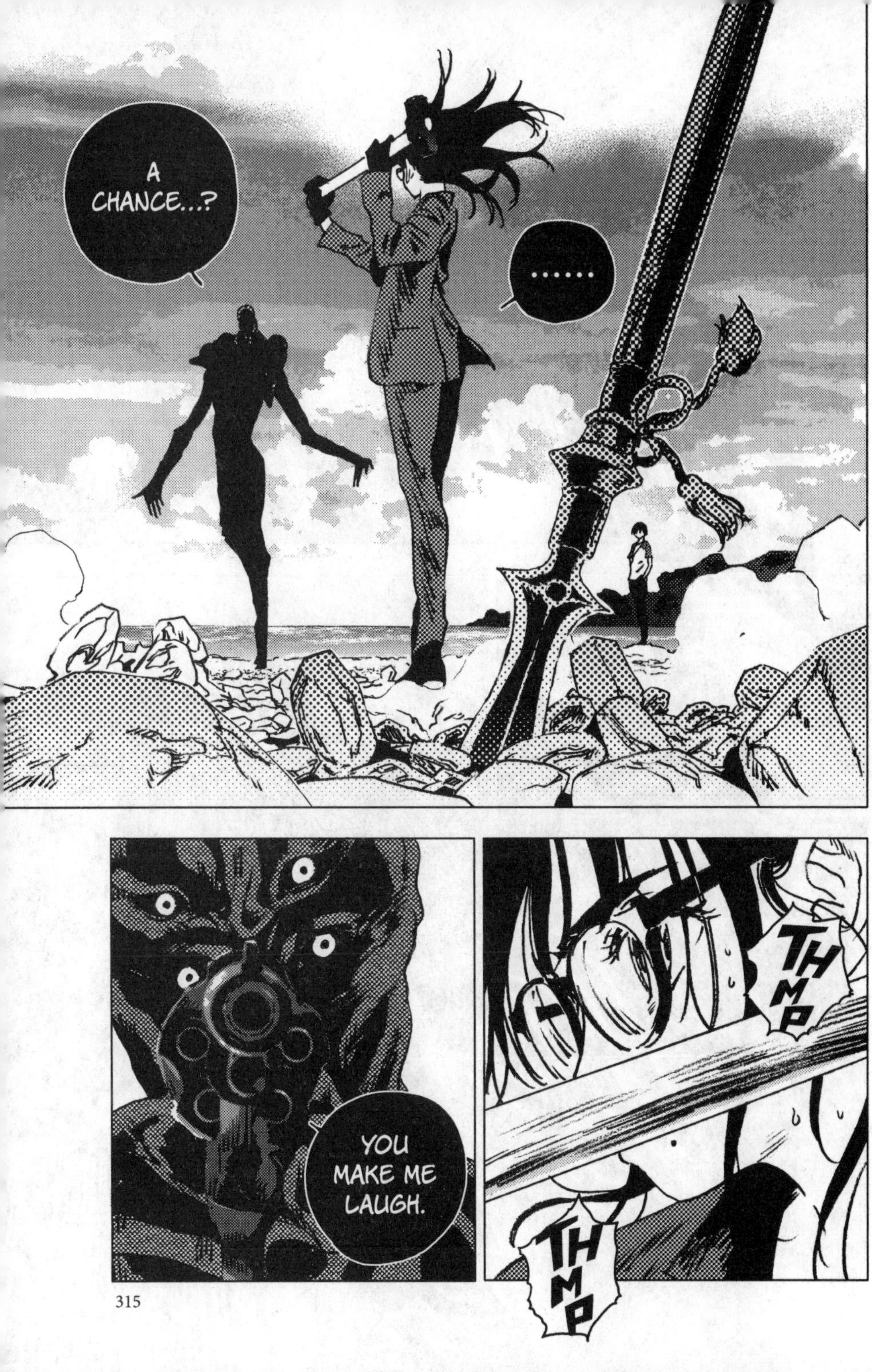
A CHANCE...?
......
THMP
THMP
YOU MAKE ME LAUGH.

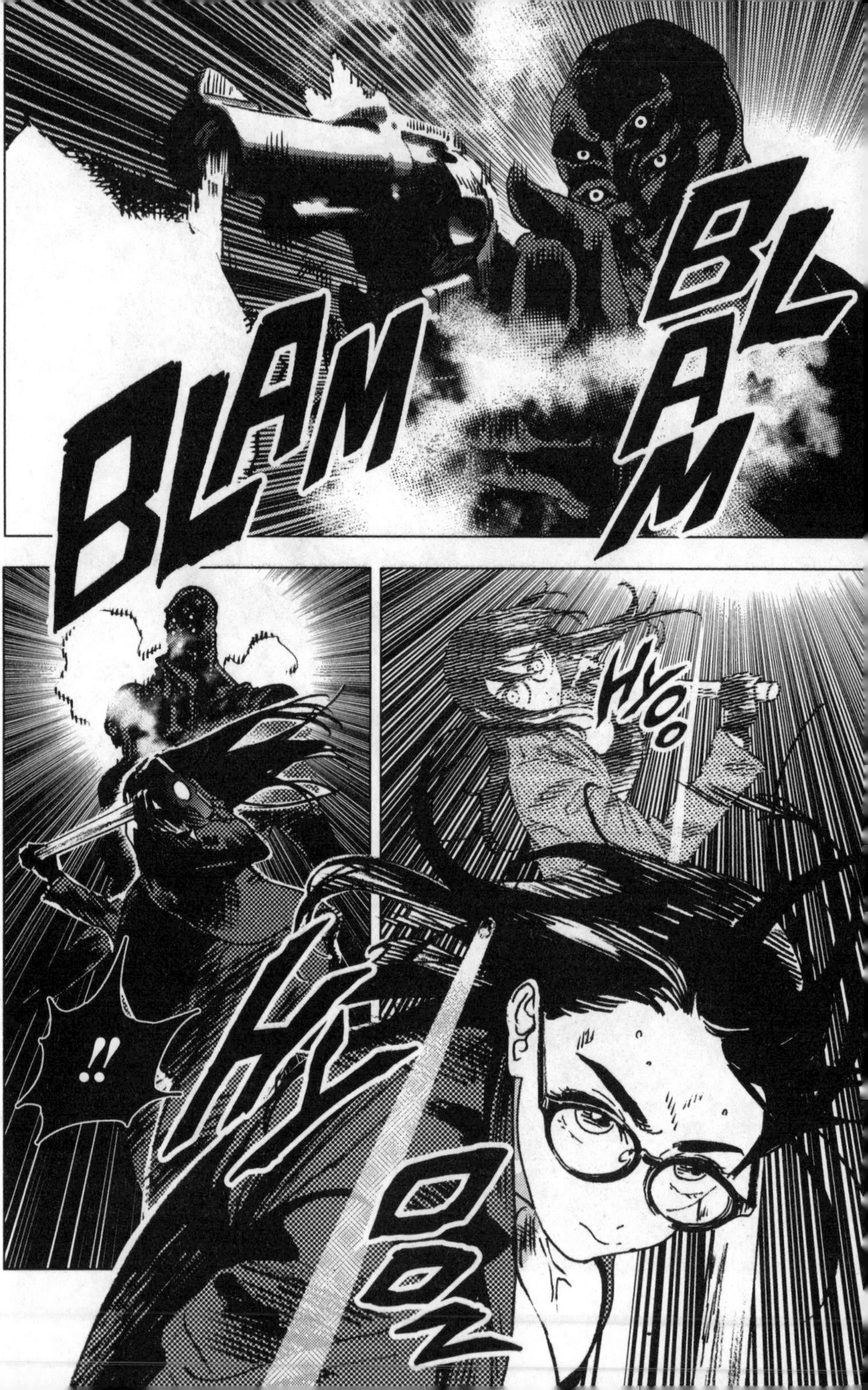
BLAM
BLAM
HYO..
!!

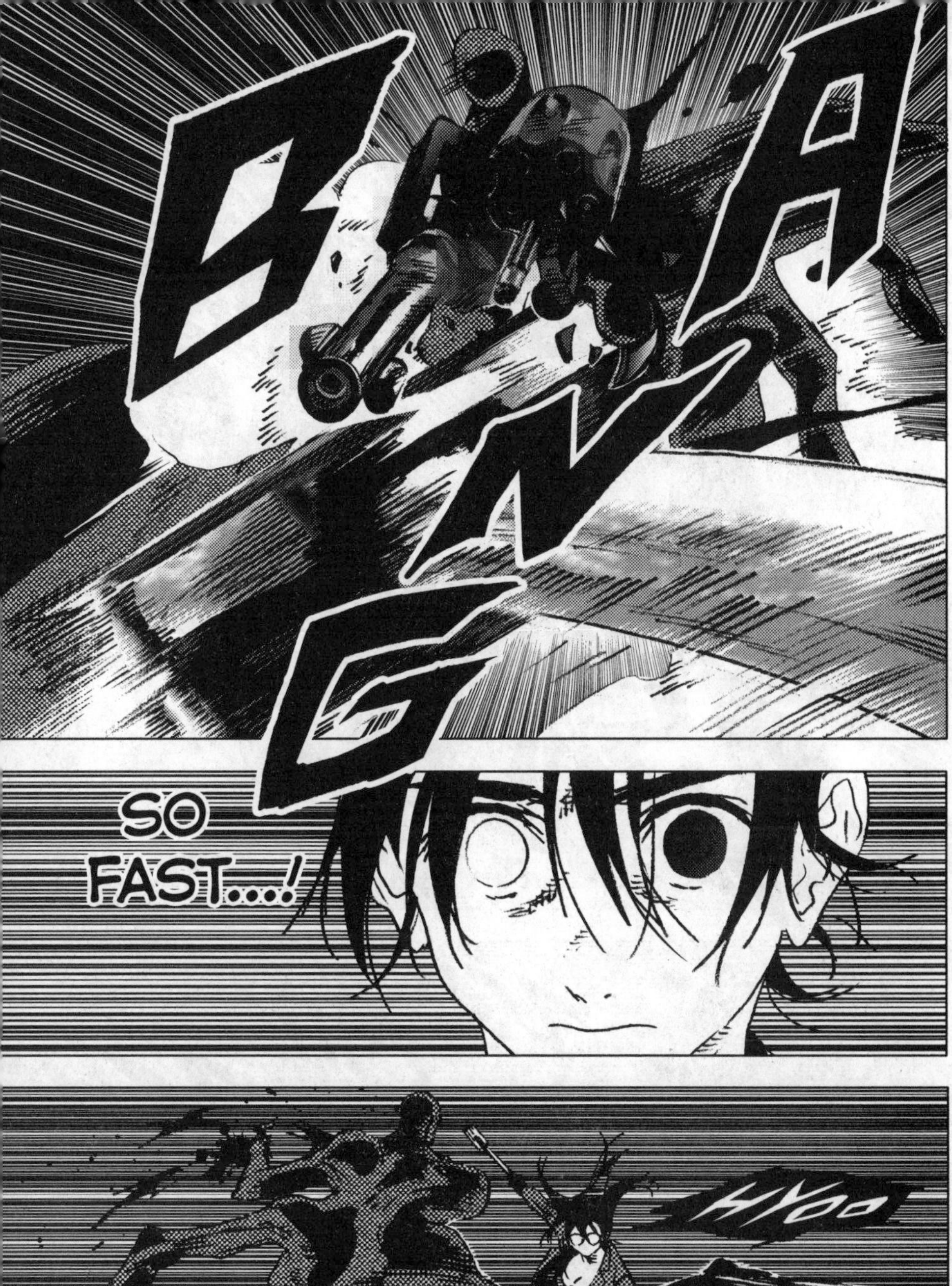
BANG
SO FAST...!
HYOO

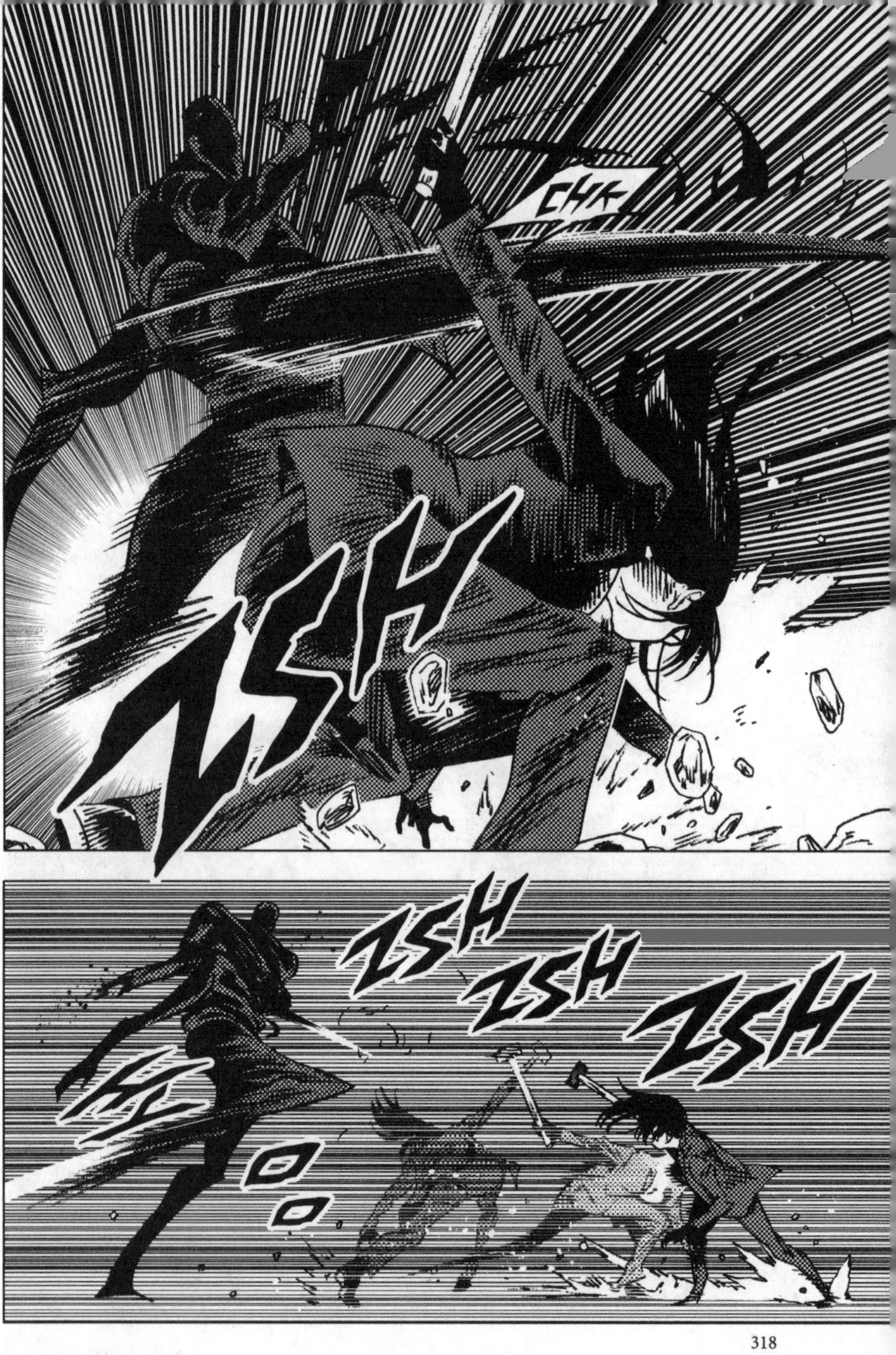
CHK
ZSH
ZSH
ZSH
ZSH

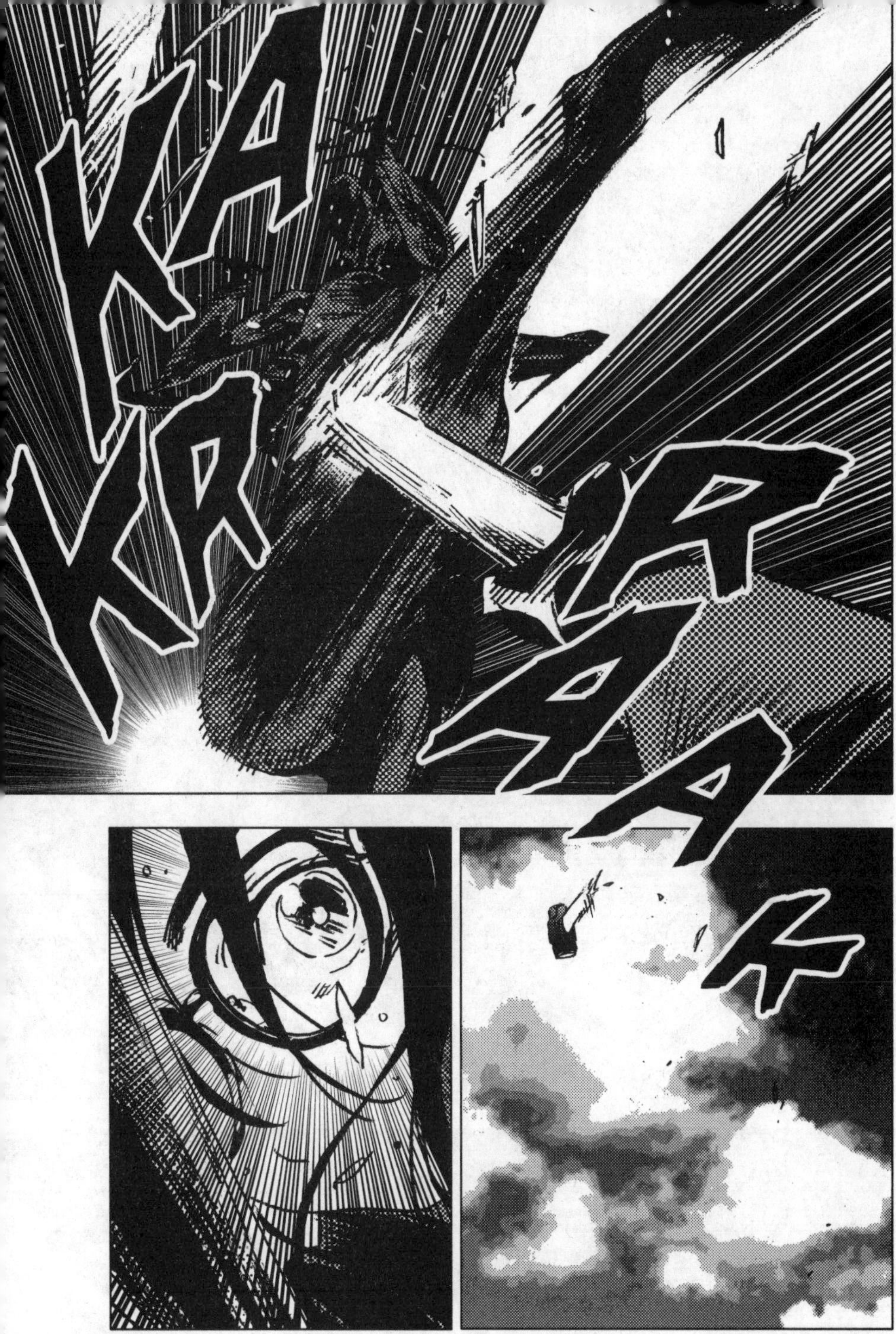
KA
KRRAAAK

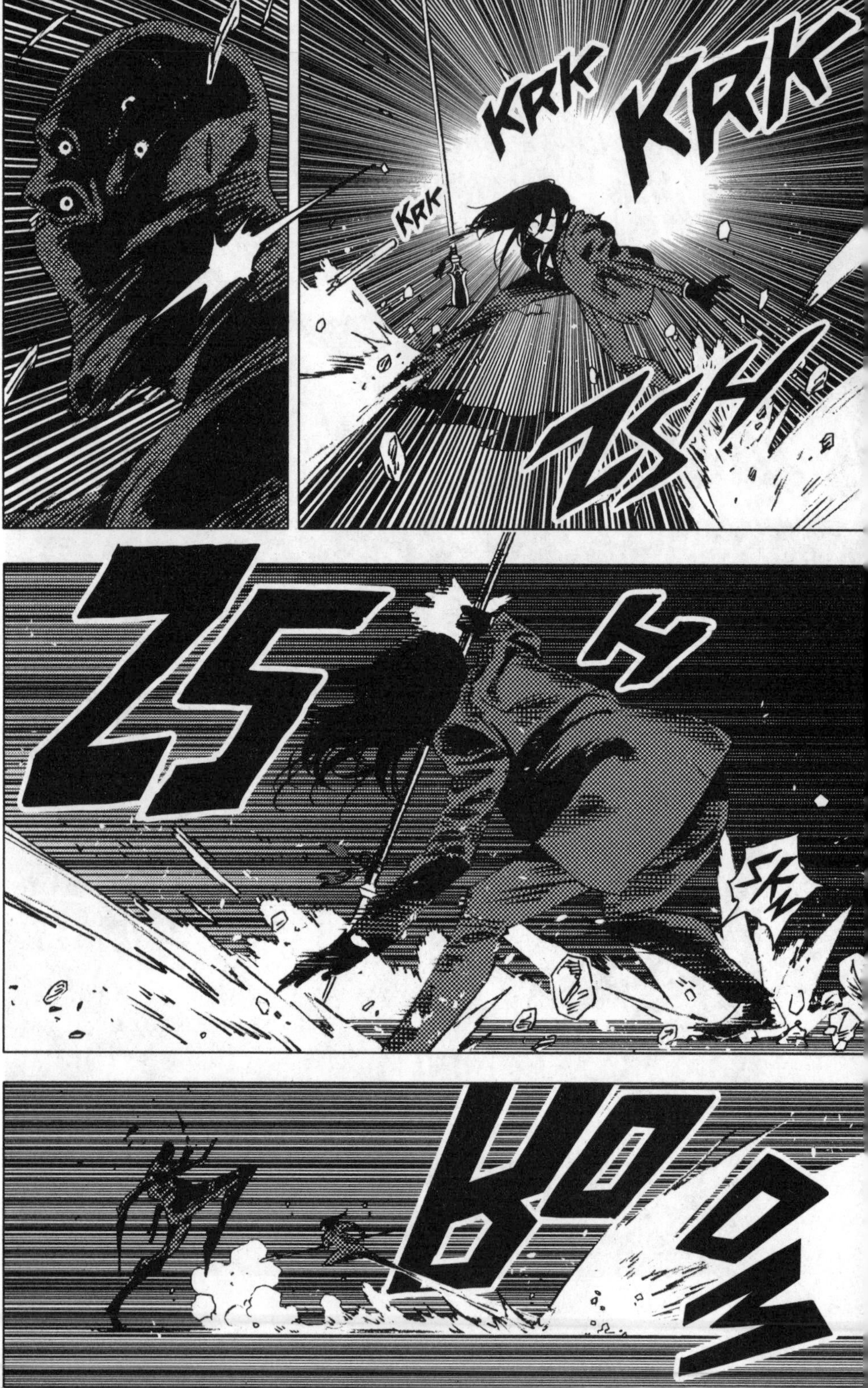
KRK
KRK
KRK
ZSH
ZSH
SKW
BOOM

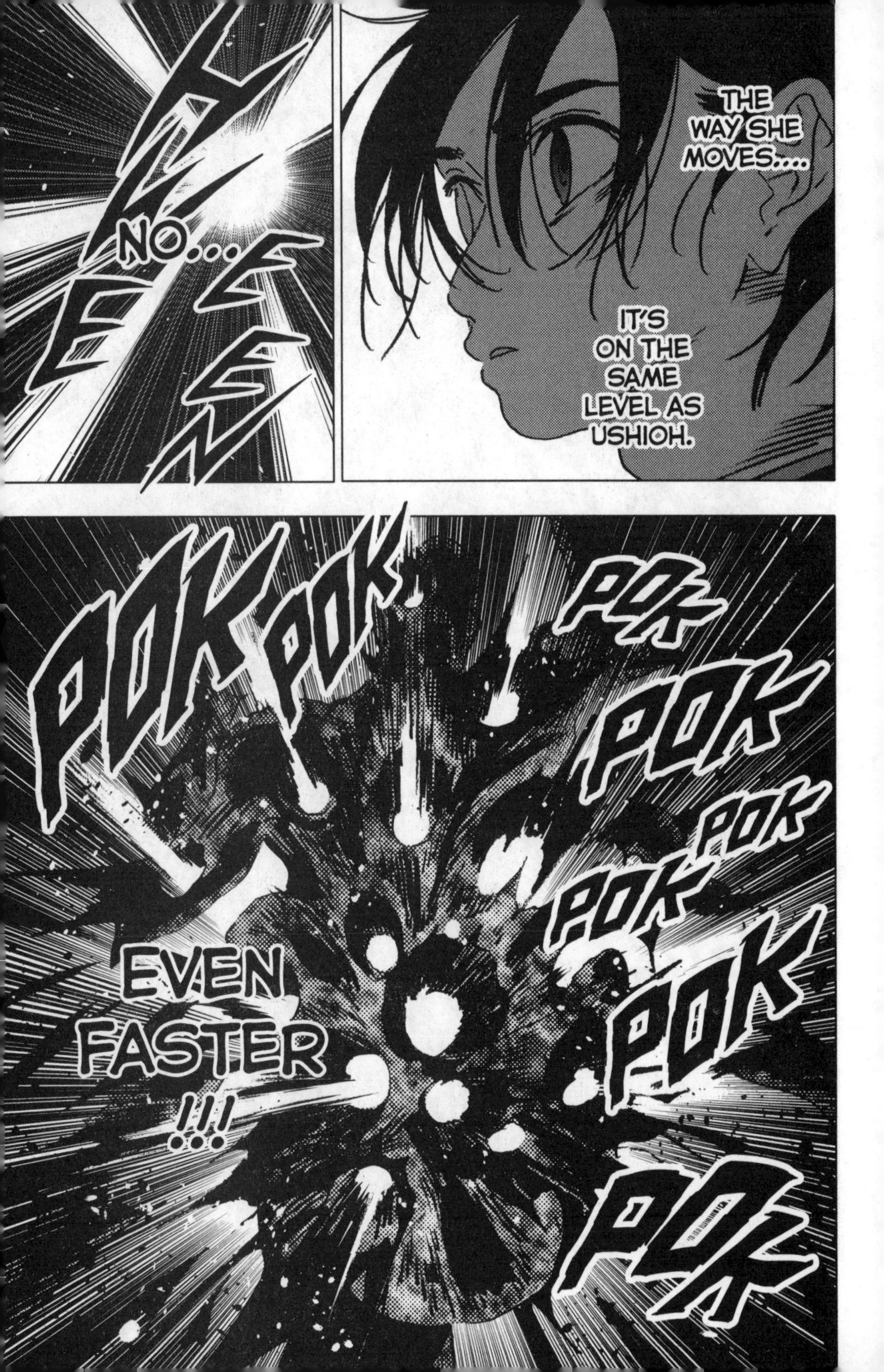
THE WAY SHE MOVES....
IT'S ON THE SAME LEVEL AS USHIOH.
NO...
POK
POK
POK
POK
POK
POK
POK
POK
EVEN FASTER !!!

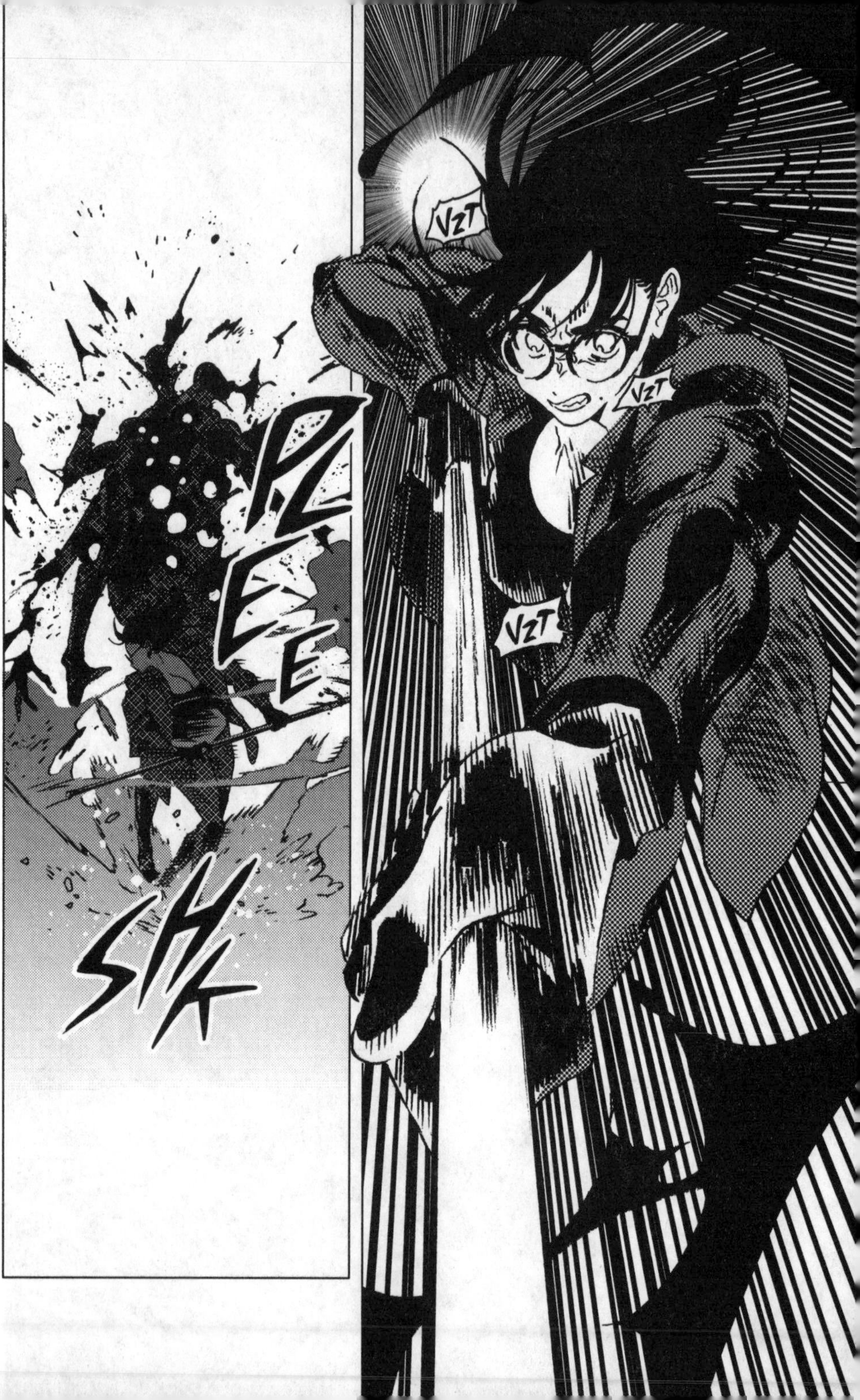
VZT
VZT
VZT
PZEEE
SHK

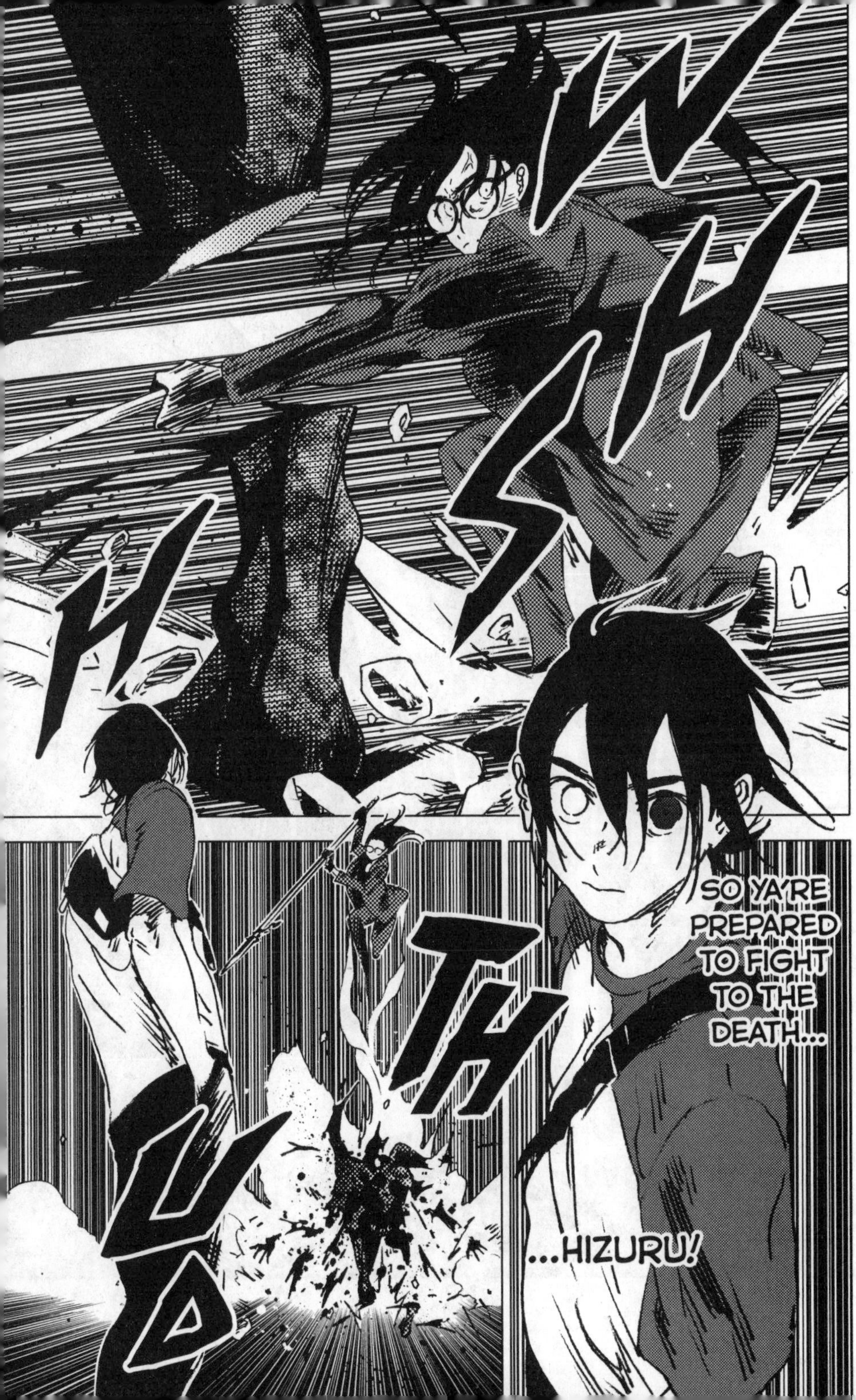
WHSH
SO YA'RE PREPARED TO FIGHT TO THE DEATH...
...HIZURU!
THUD

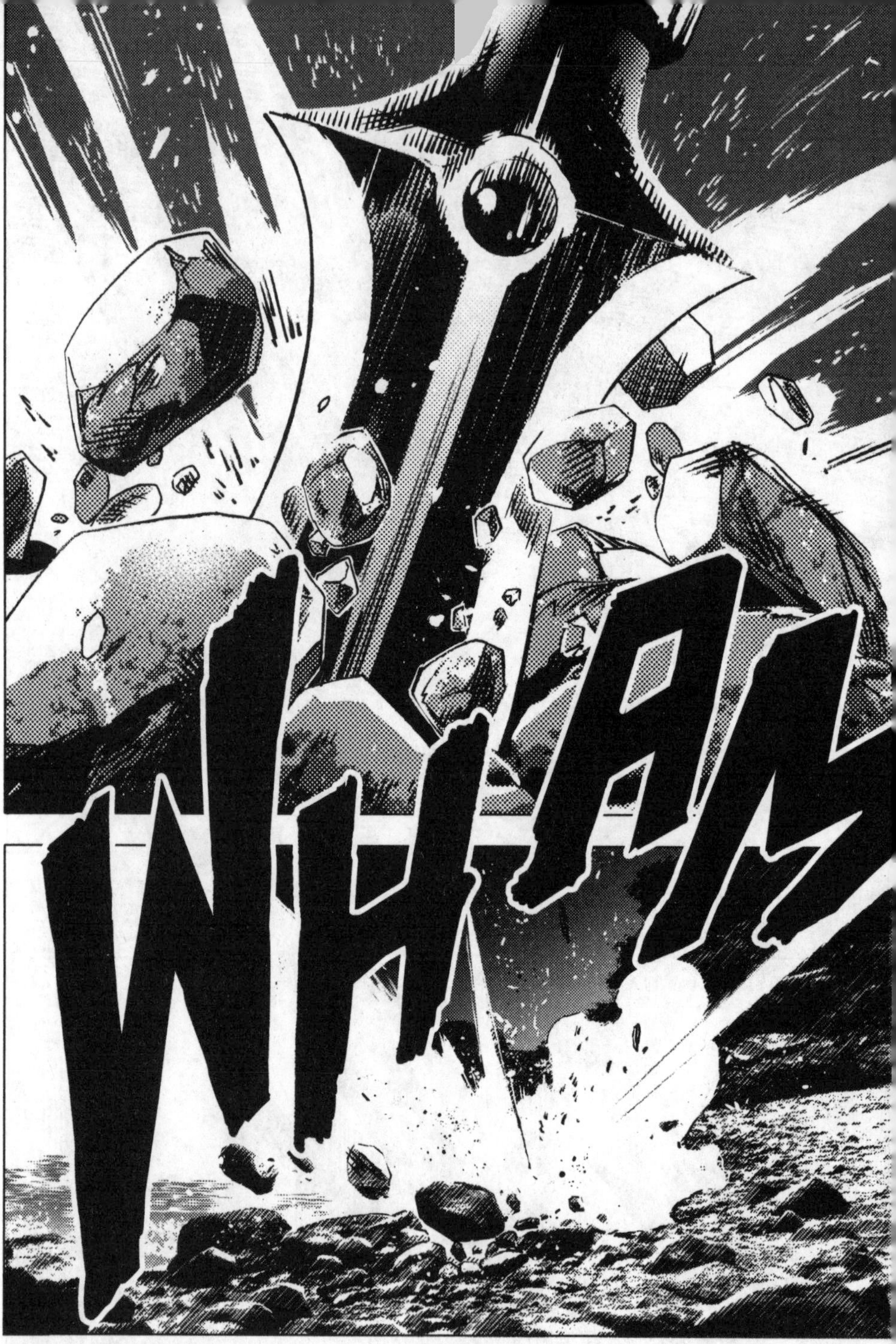
WHAM

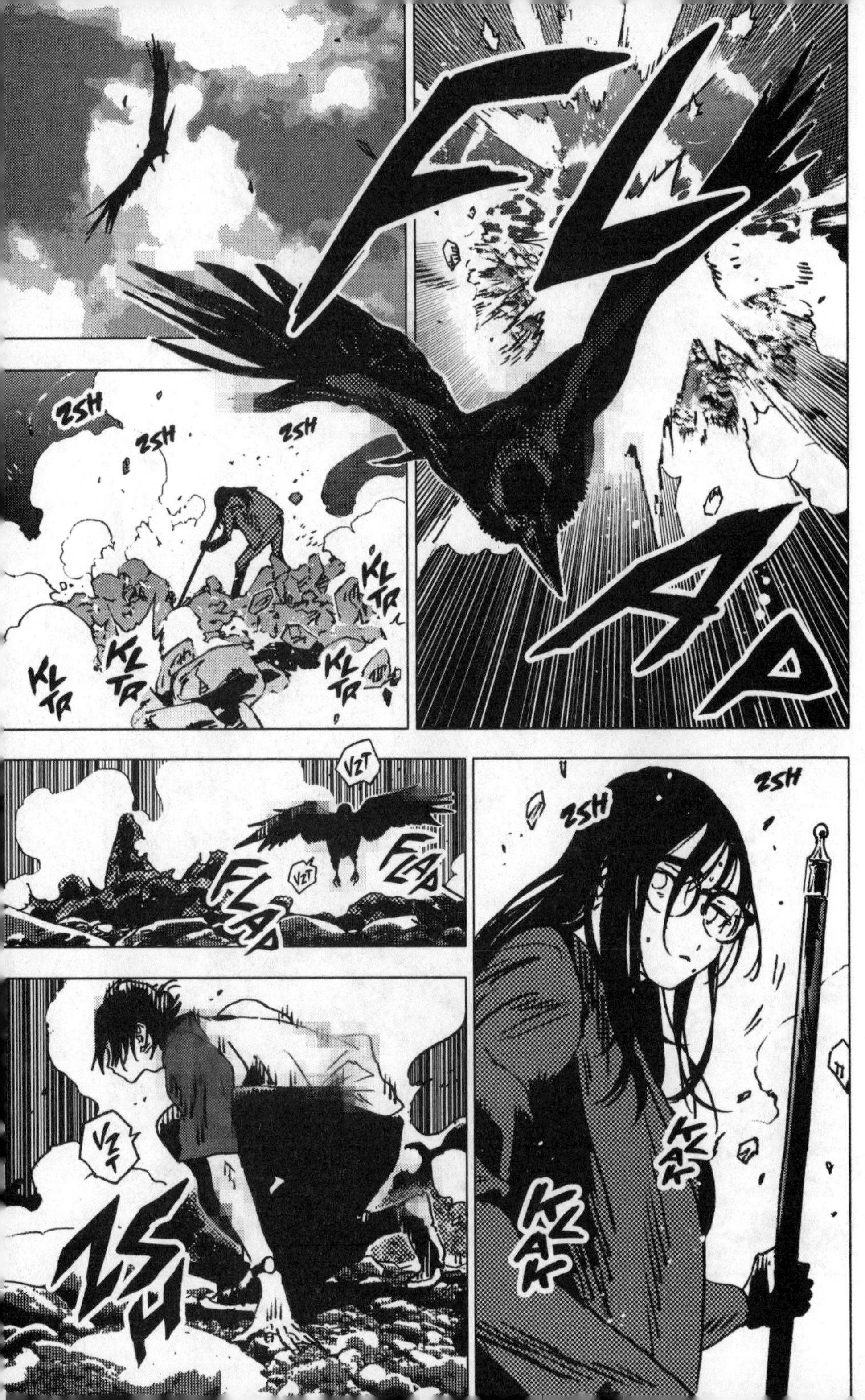
FLAP
ZSH
ZSH
ZSH
KLTR
KLTR
KLTR
KLTR
ZSH
ZSH
KLAK
KLAK
VZT
FLAP
VZT
FLAP
VZT
ZSH

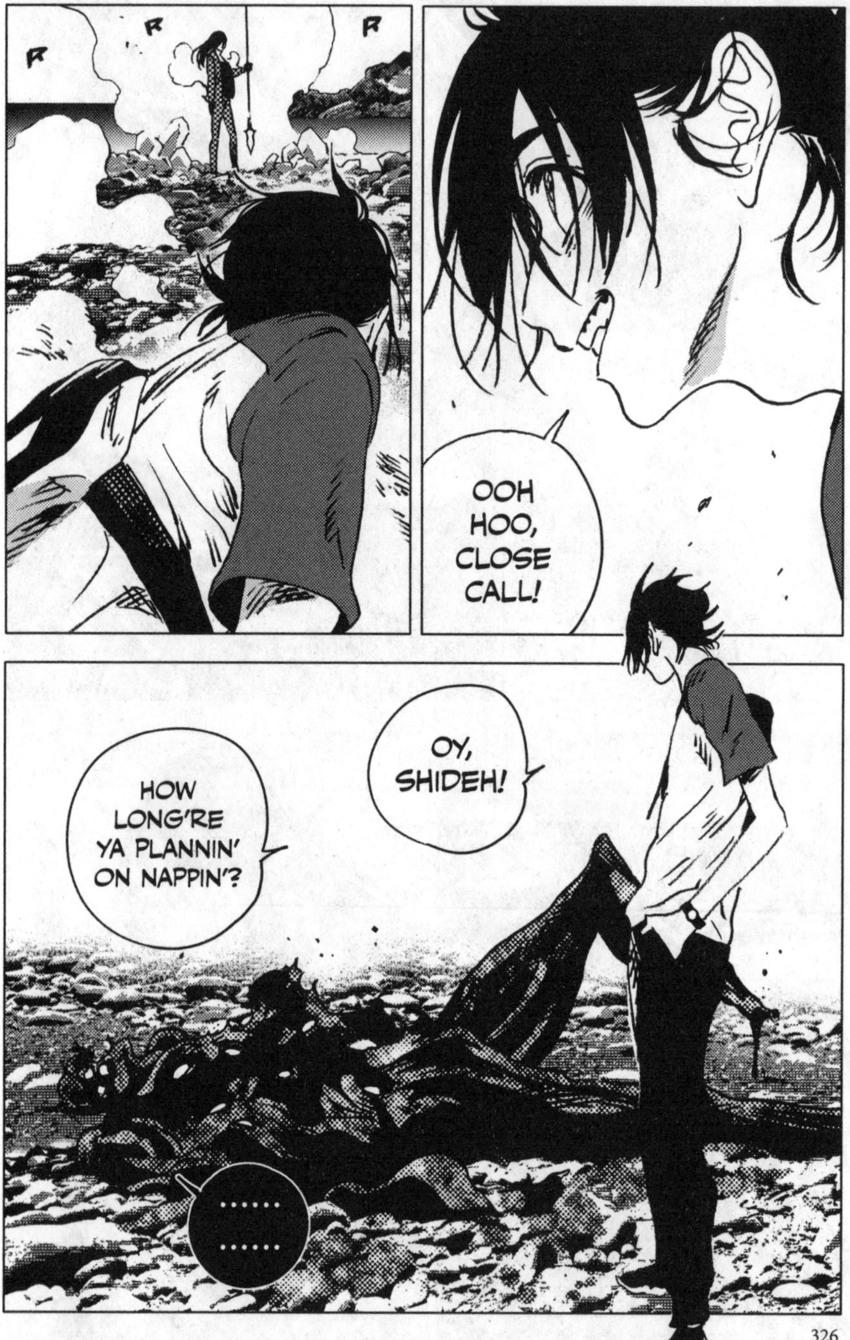
OOH HOO, CLOSE CALL!
R
R
R
OY, SHIDEH!
HOW LONG'RE YA PLANNIN' ON NAPPIN'?
…… ……

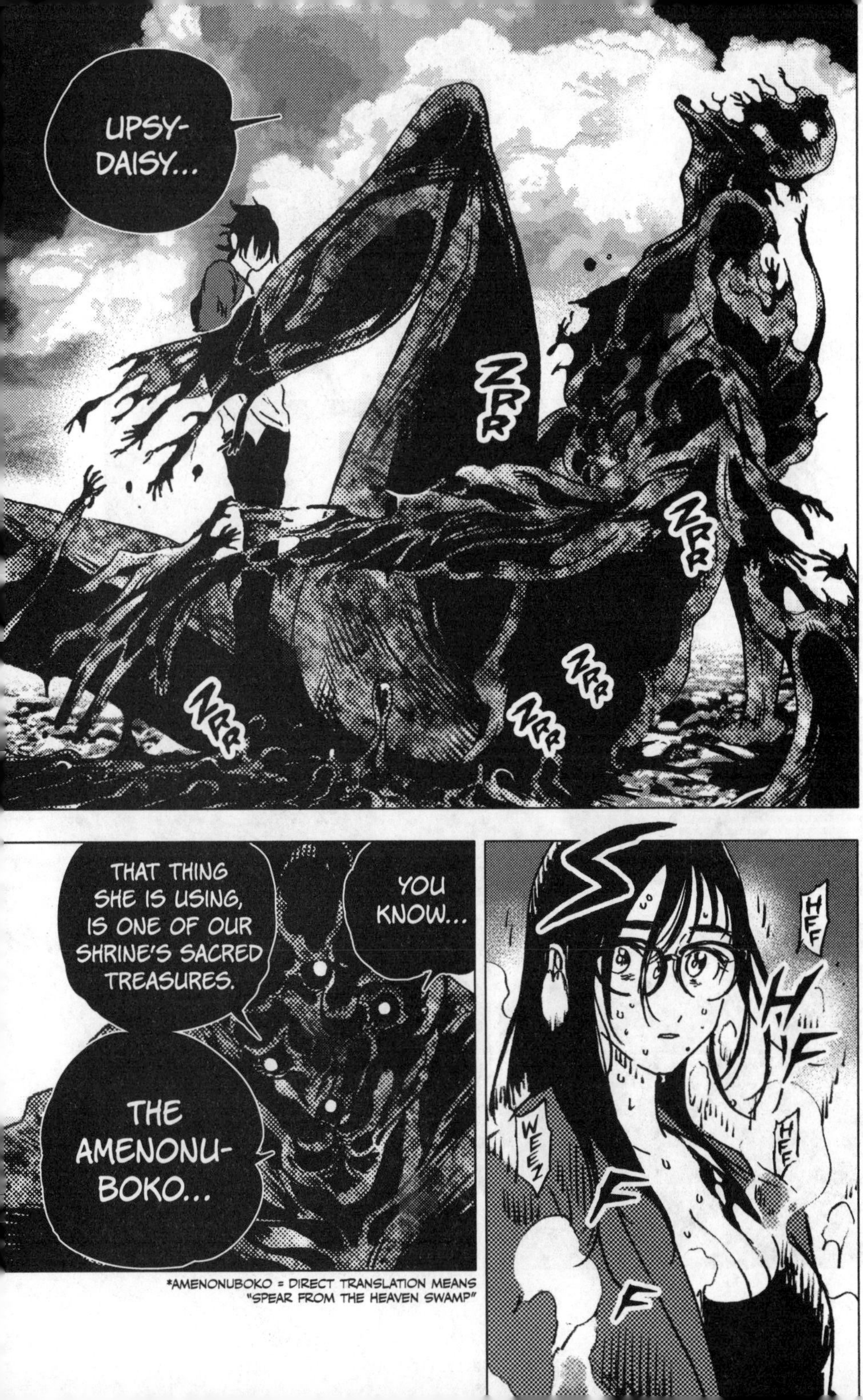
UPSY-DAISY...
ZRR
ZRR
ZRR
ZRR
ZRR
HFF
HFF
WEEZ
YOU KNOW...
THAT THING SHE IS USING, IS ONE OF OUR SHRINE'S SACRED TREASURES.
THE AMENONU-BOKO...
*AMENONUBOKO = DIRECT TRANSLATION MEANS "SPEAR FROM THE HEAVEN SWAMP"

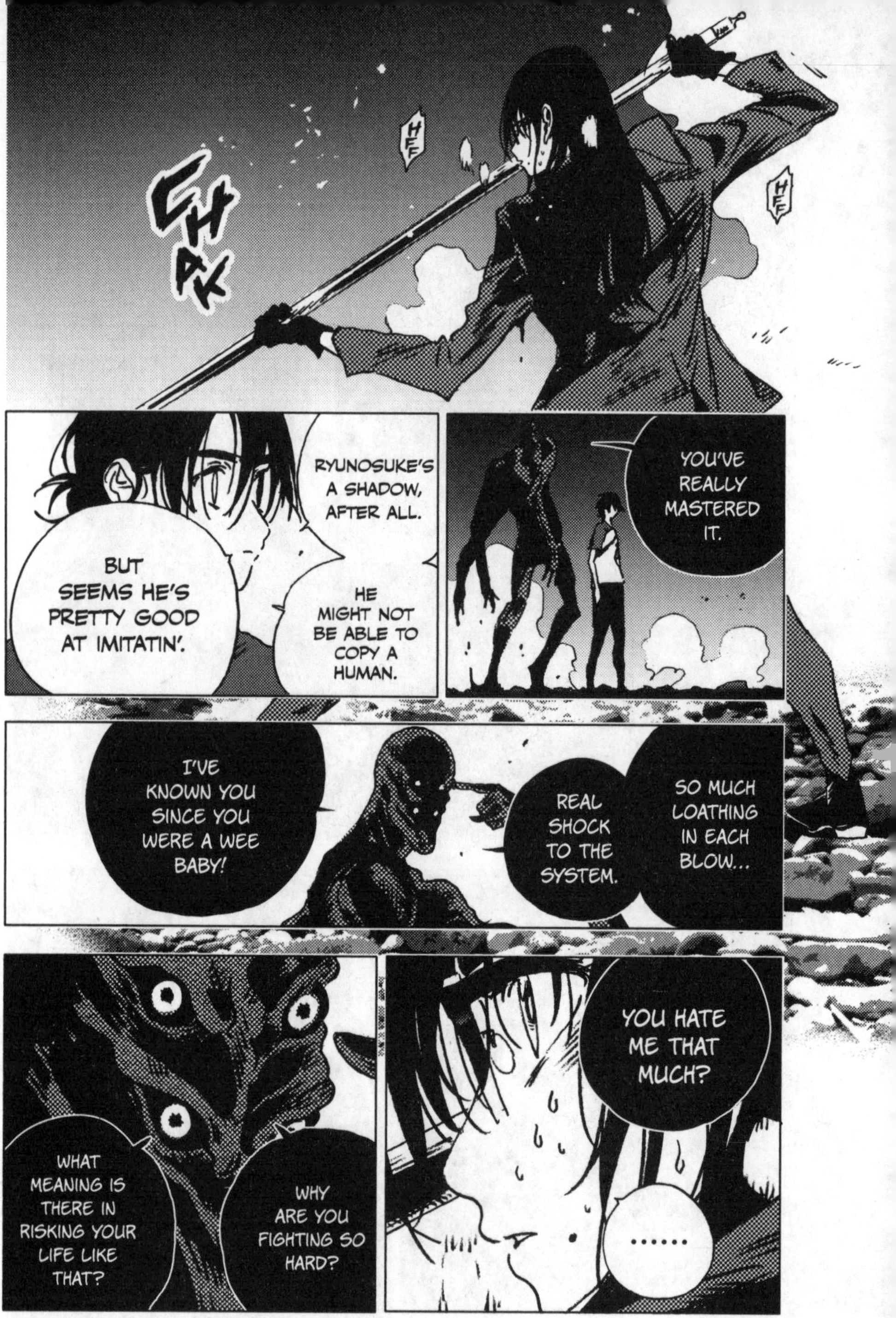
HFF
HFF
CHAK
YOU'VE REALLY MASTERED IT.
RYUNOSUKE'S A SHADOW, AFTER ALL.
HE MIGHT NOT BE ABLE TO COPY A HUMAN.
BUT SEEMS HE'S PRETTY GOOD AT IMITATIN'.
SO MUCH LOATHING IN EACH BLOW...
REAL SHOCK TO THE SYSTEM.
I'VE KNOWN YOU SINCE YOU WERE A WEE BABY!
YOU HATE ME THAT MUCH?
......
WHY ARE YOU FIGHTING SO HARD?
WHAT MEANING IS THERE IN RISKING YOUR LIFE LIKE THAT?

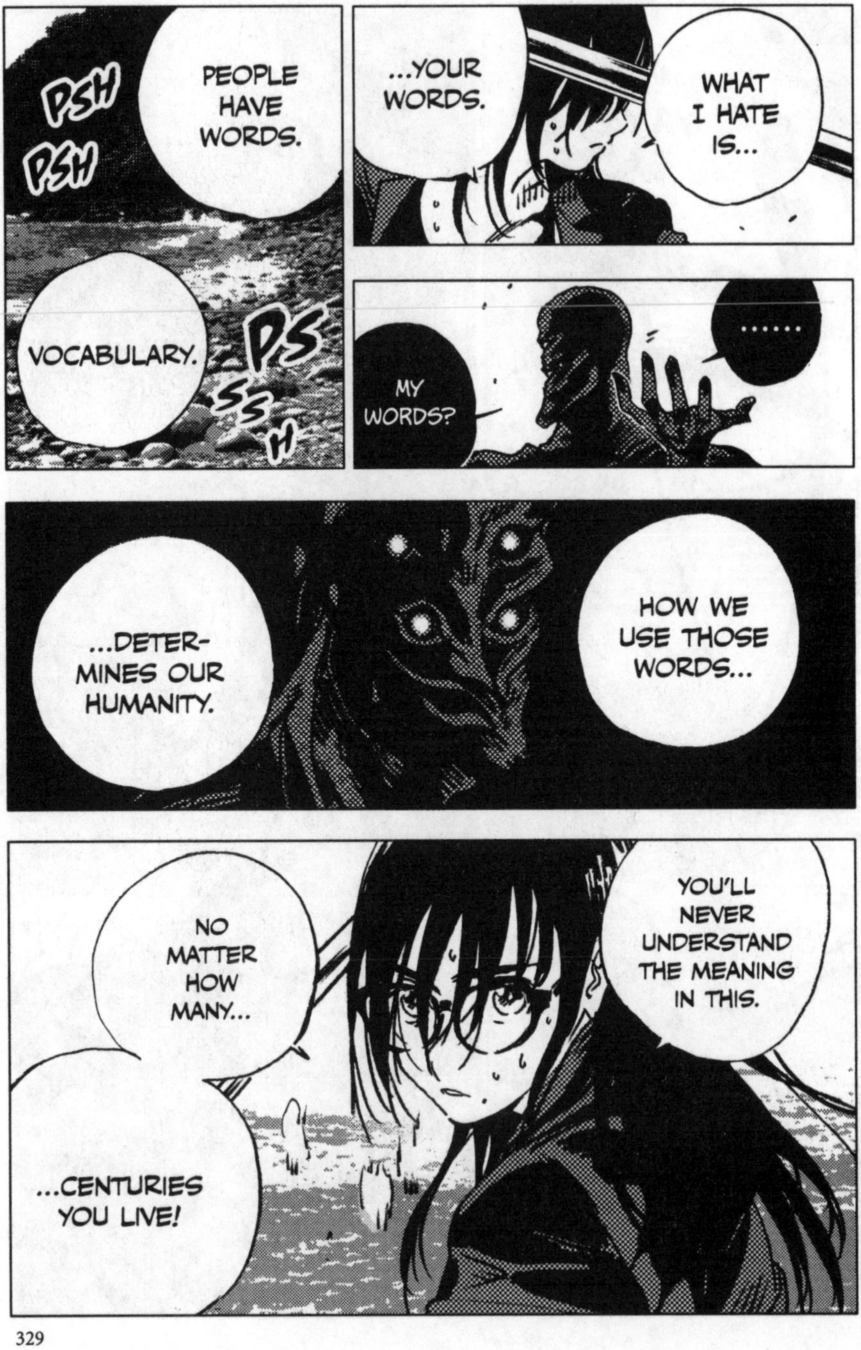
WHAT I HATE IS...
...YOUR WORDS.
....
MY WORDS?
PEOPLE HAVE WORDS.
PSH PSH
PSSSH
VOCABULARY.
HOW WE USE THOSE WORDS...
...DETER-MINES OUR HUMANITY.
YOU'LL NEVER UNDERSTAND THE MEANING IN THIS.
NO MATTER HOW MANY...
...CENTURIES YOU LIVE!

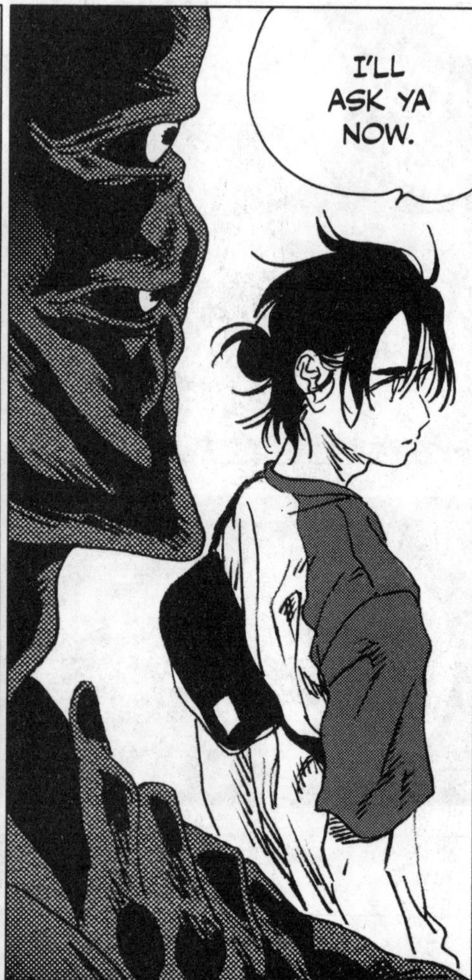
I'LL ASK YA NOW.
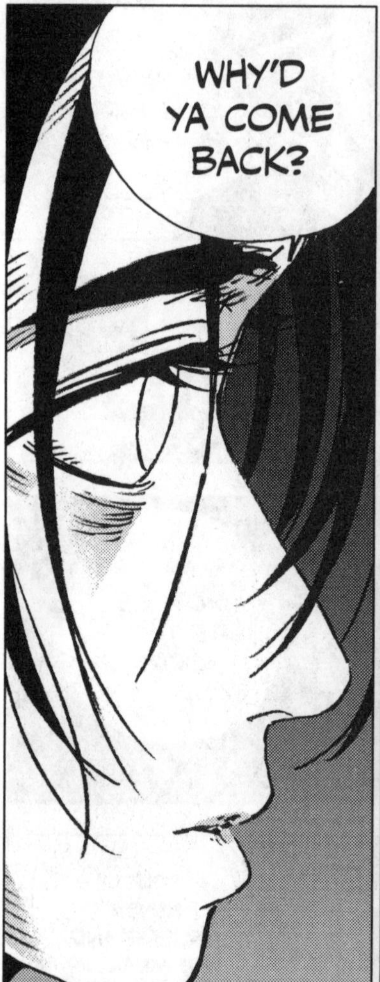
WHY'D YA COME BACK?
HIZURU.

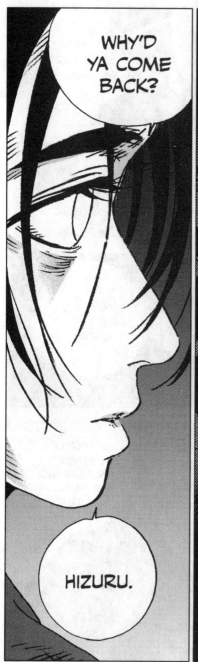

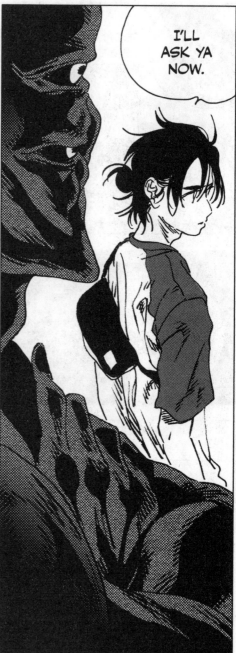

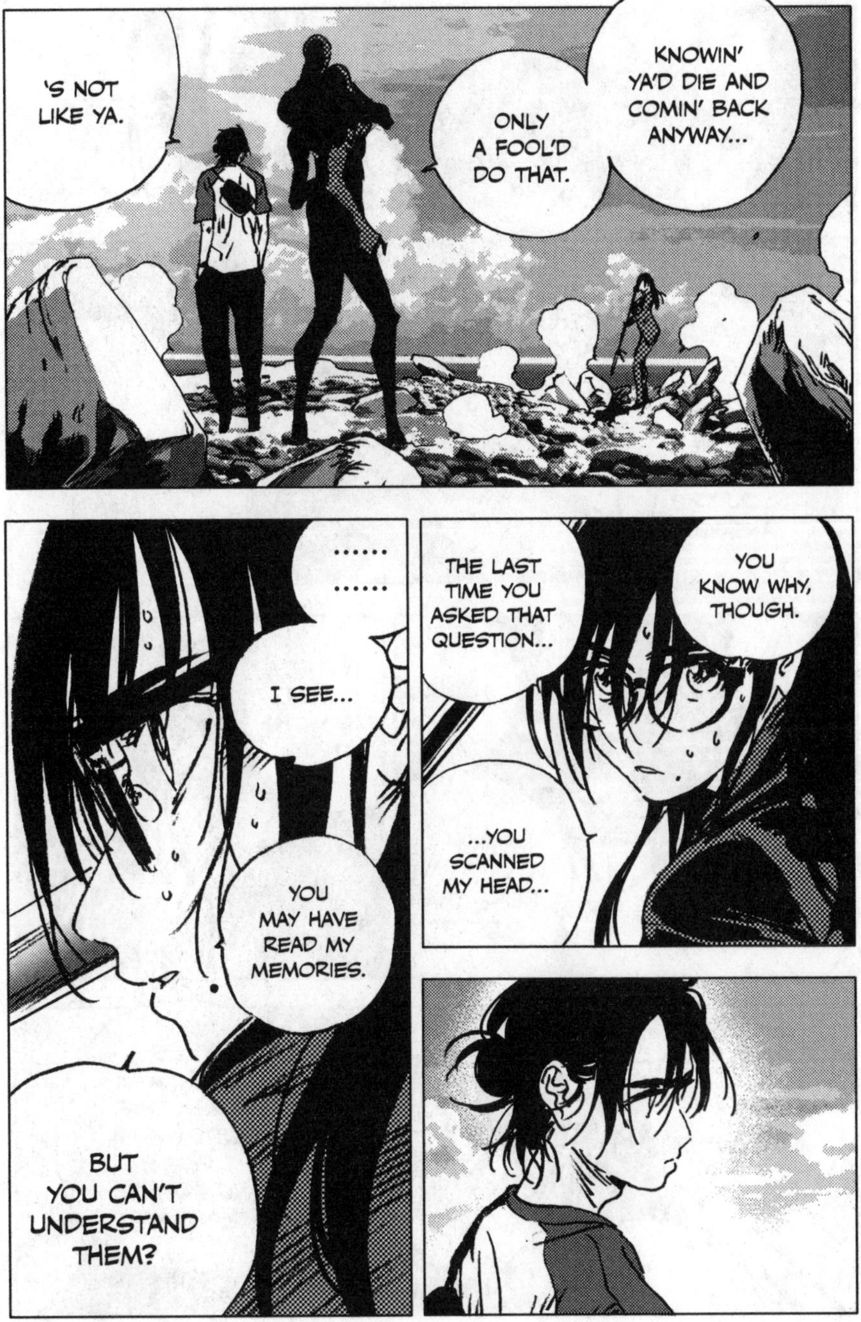
KNOWIN' YA'D DIE AND COMIN' BACK ANYWAY...
ONLY A FOOL'D DO THAT.
'S NOT LIKE YA.
YOU KNOW WHY, THOUGH.
THE LAST TIME YOU ASKED THAT QUESTION...
...YOU SCANNED MY HEAD...
......
......
I SEE...
YOU MAY HAVE READ MY MEMORIES.
BUT YOU CAN'T UNDERSTAND THEM?

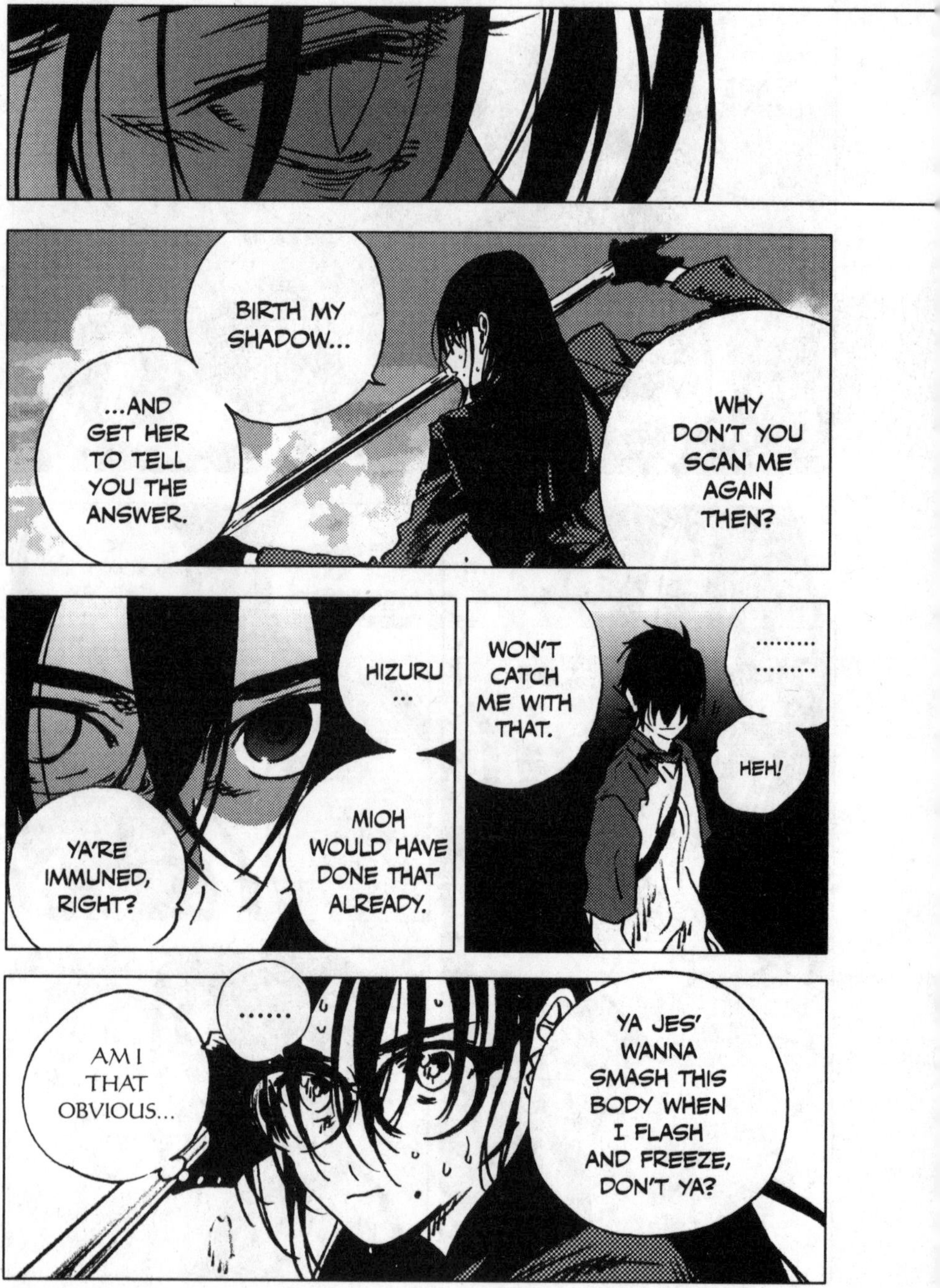
WHY DON'T YOU SCAN ME AGAIN THEN?
BIRTH MY SHADOW...
...AND GET HER TO TELL YOU THE ANSWER.
....
HEH!
WON'T CATCH ME WITH THAT.
HIZURU ...
MIOH WOULD HAVE DONE THAT ALREADY.
YA'RE IMMUNED, RIGHT?
YA JES' WANNA SMASH THIS BODY WHEN I FLASH AND FREEZE, DON'T YA?
......
AM I THAT OBVIOUS...

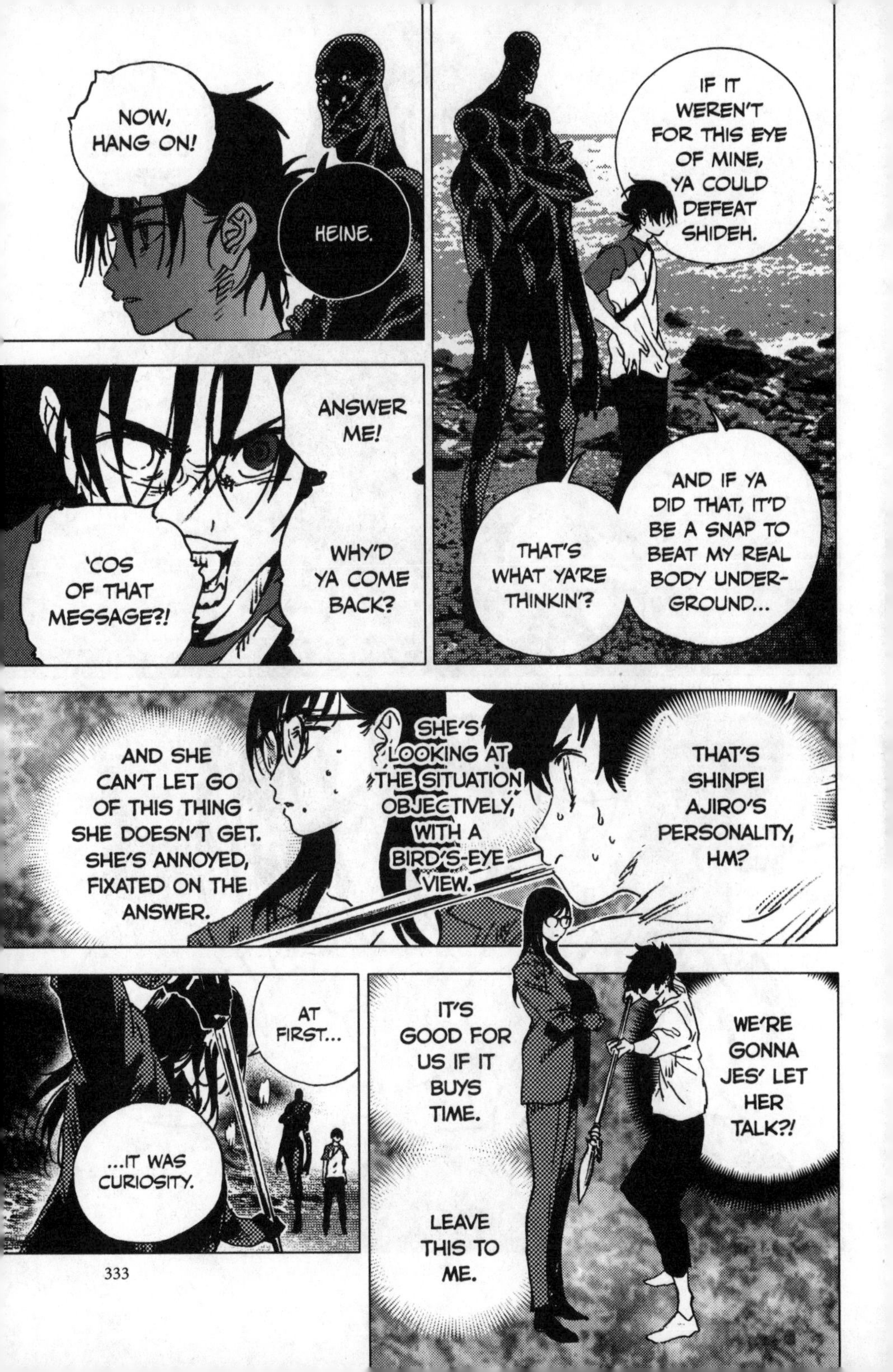

IF IT WEREN'T FOR THIS EYE OF MINE, YA COULD DEFEAT SHIDEH.
AND IF YA DID THAT, IT'D BE A SNAP TO BEAT MY REAL BODY UNDER-GROUND...
THAT'S WHAT YA'RE THINKIN'?
NOW, HANG ON!
HEINE.
ANSWER ME!
WHY'D YA COME BACK?
'COS OF THAT MESSAGE?!
THAT'S SHINPEI AJIRO'S PERSONALITY, HM?
SHE'S LOOKING AT THE SITUATION OBJECTIVELY, WITH A BIRD'S-EYE VIEW.
AND SHE CAN'T LET GO OF THIS THING SHE DOESN'T GET. SHE'S ANNOYED, FIXATED ON THE ANSWER.
WE'RE GONNA JES' LET HER TALK?!
IT'S GOOD FOR US IF IT BUYS TIME.
LEAVE THIS TO ME.
AT FIRST...
...IT WAS CURIOSITY.

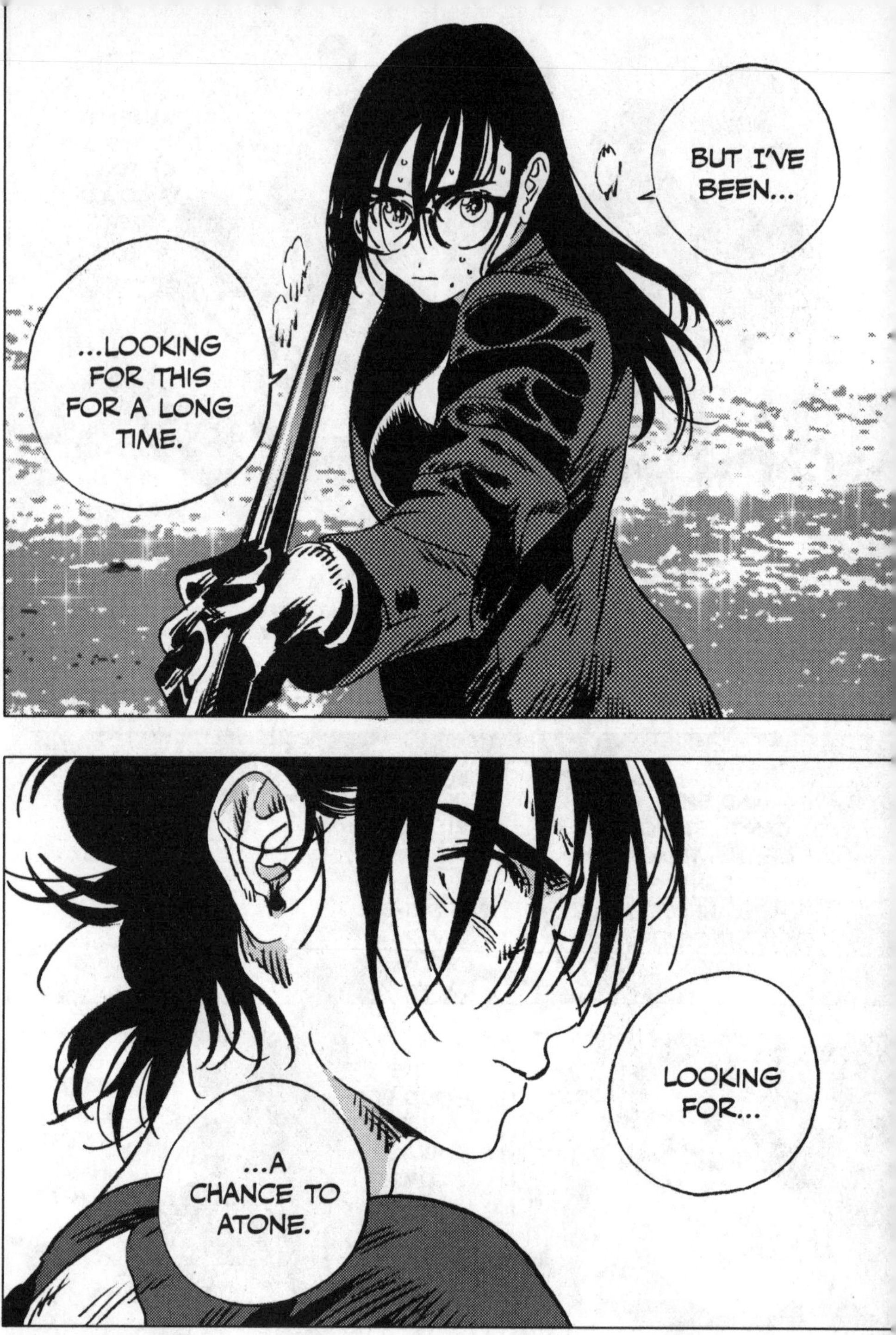
BUT I'VE BEEN...
...LOOKING FOR THIS FOR A LONG TIME.
LOOKING FOR...
...A CHANCE TO ATONE.

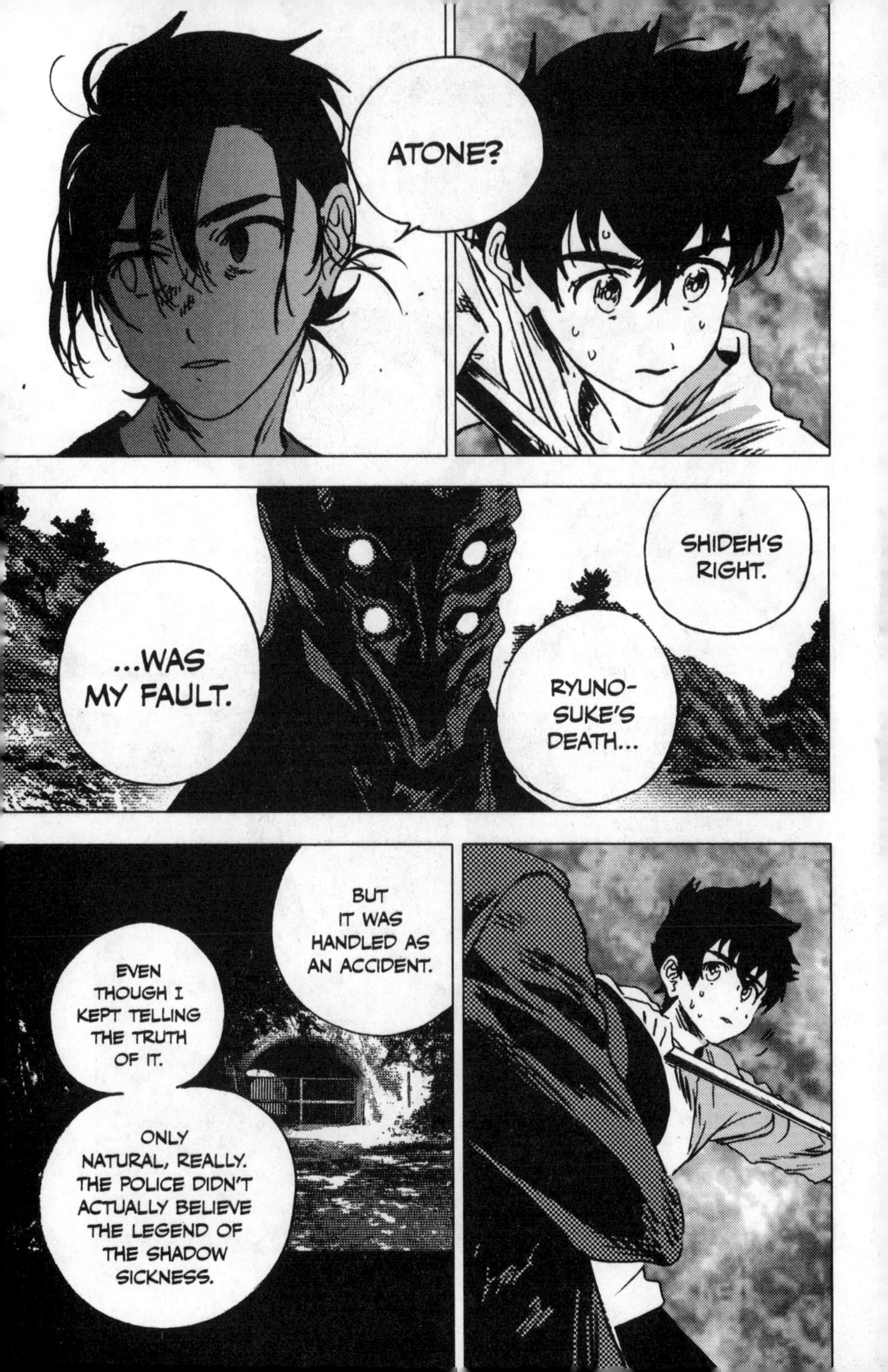
ATONE?
SHIDEH'S RIGHT.
RYUNO-SUKE'S DEATH...
...WAS MY FAULT.
BUT IT WAS HANDLED AS AN ACCIDENT.
EVEN THOUGH I KEPT TELLING THE TRUTH OF IT.
ONLY NATURAL, REALLY. THE POLICE DIDN'T ACTUALLY BELIEVE THE LEGEND OF THE SHADOW SICKNESS.

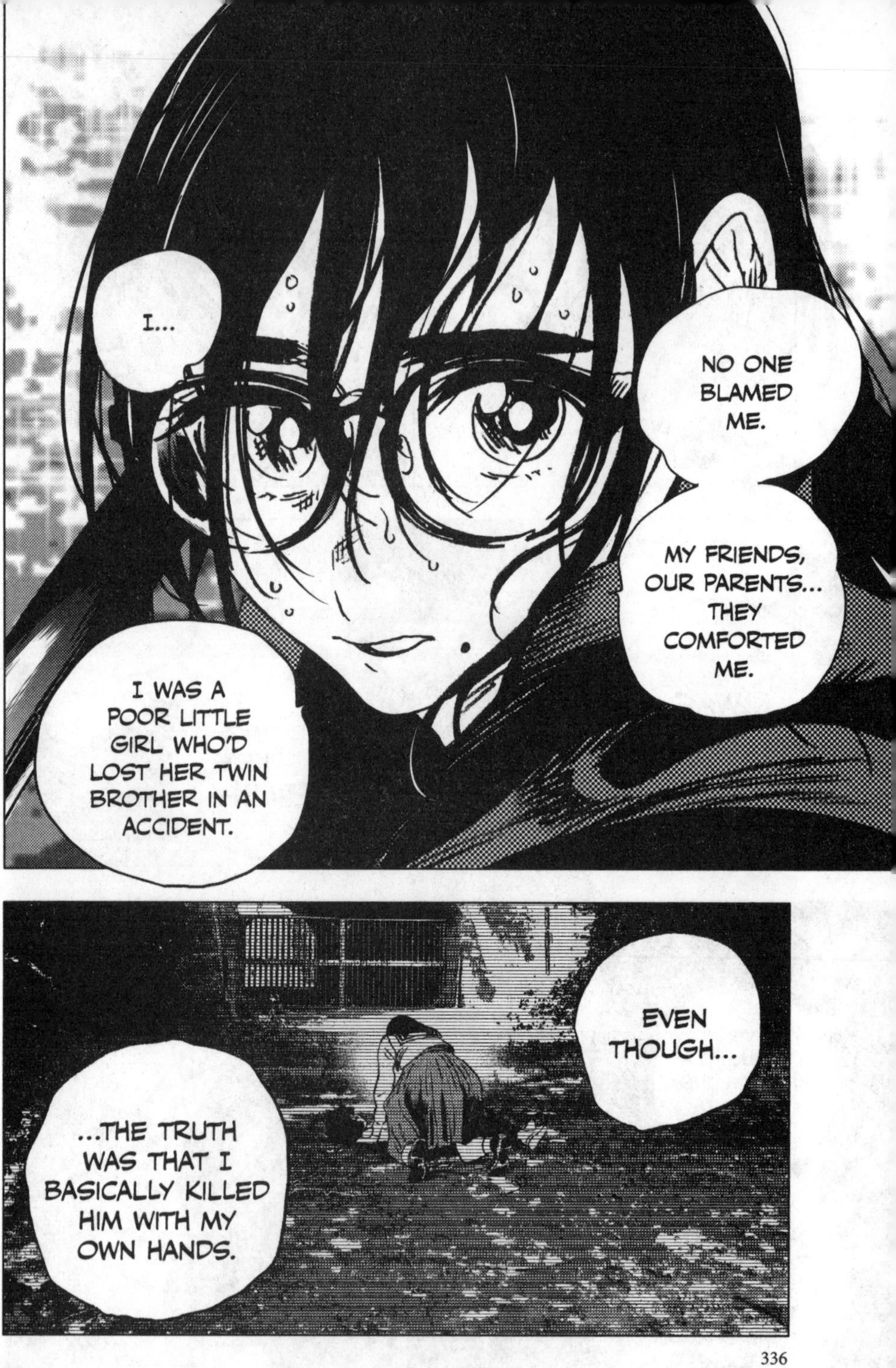
NO ONE BLAMED ME.
MY FRIENDS, OUR PARENTS... THEY COMFORTED ME.
I...
I WAS A POOR LITTLE GIRL WHO'D LOST HER TWIN BROTHER IN AN ACCIDENT.
EVEN THOUGH...
...THE TRUTH WAS THAT I BASICALLY KILLED HIM WITH MY OWN HANDS.

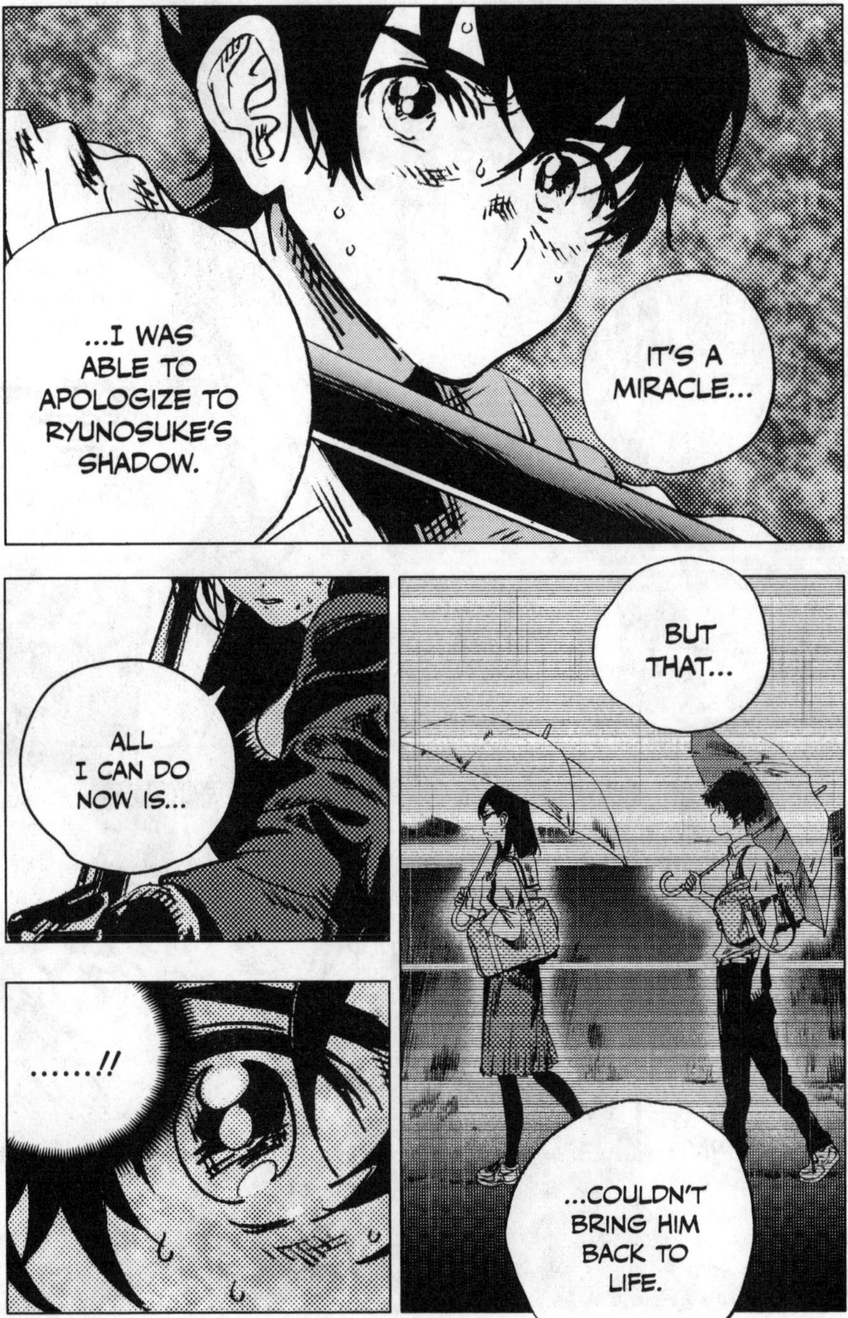
IT'S A MIRACLE...
...I WAS ABLE TO APOLOGIZE TO RYUNOSUKE'S SHADOW.
BUT THAT...
...COULDN'T BRING HIM BACK TO LIFE.
ALL I CAN DO NOW IS...
......!!

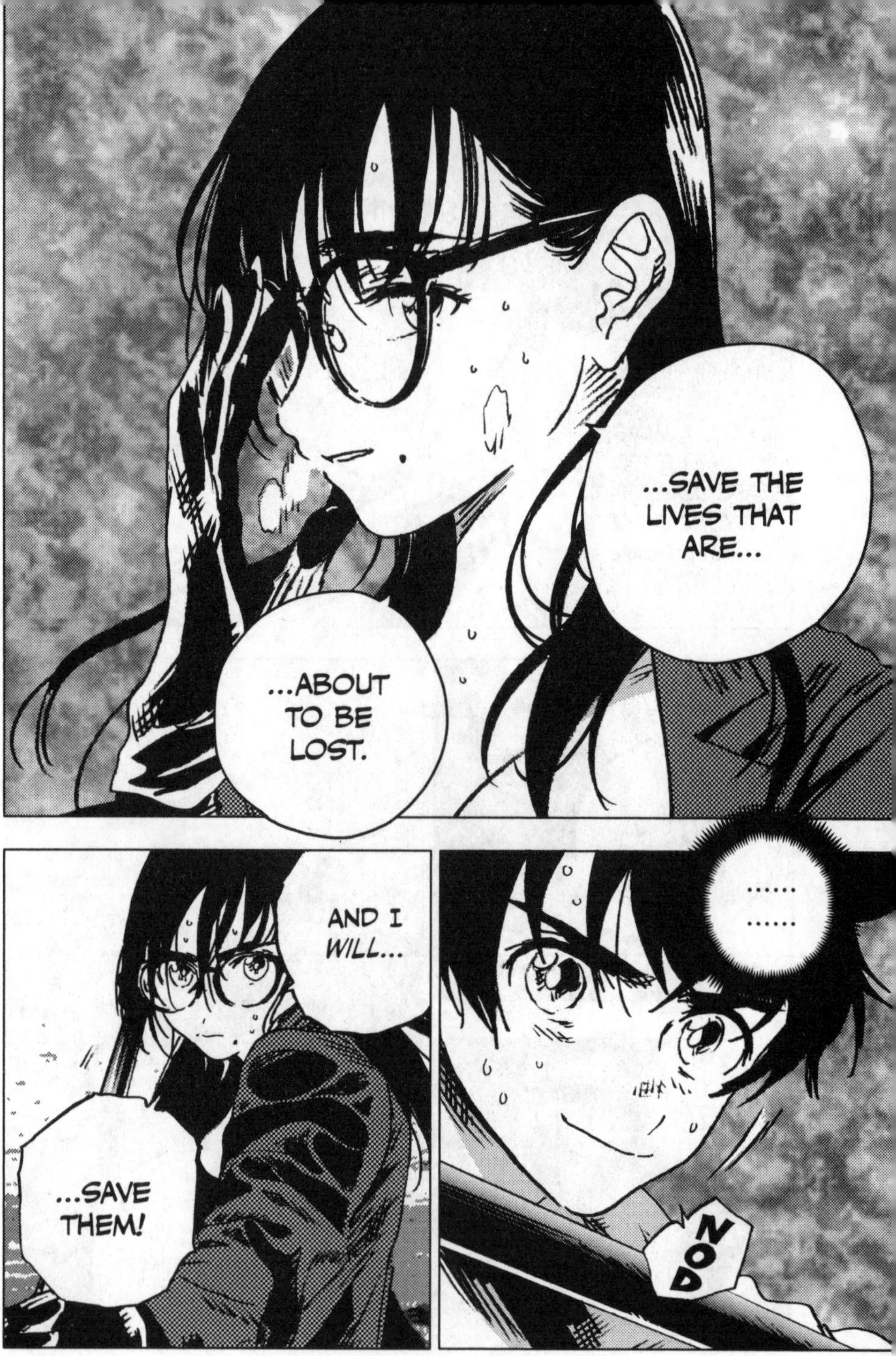
...SAVE THE LIVES THAT ARE...
...ABOUT TO BE LOST.
......
......
NOD
AND I WILL...
...SAVE THEM!

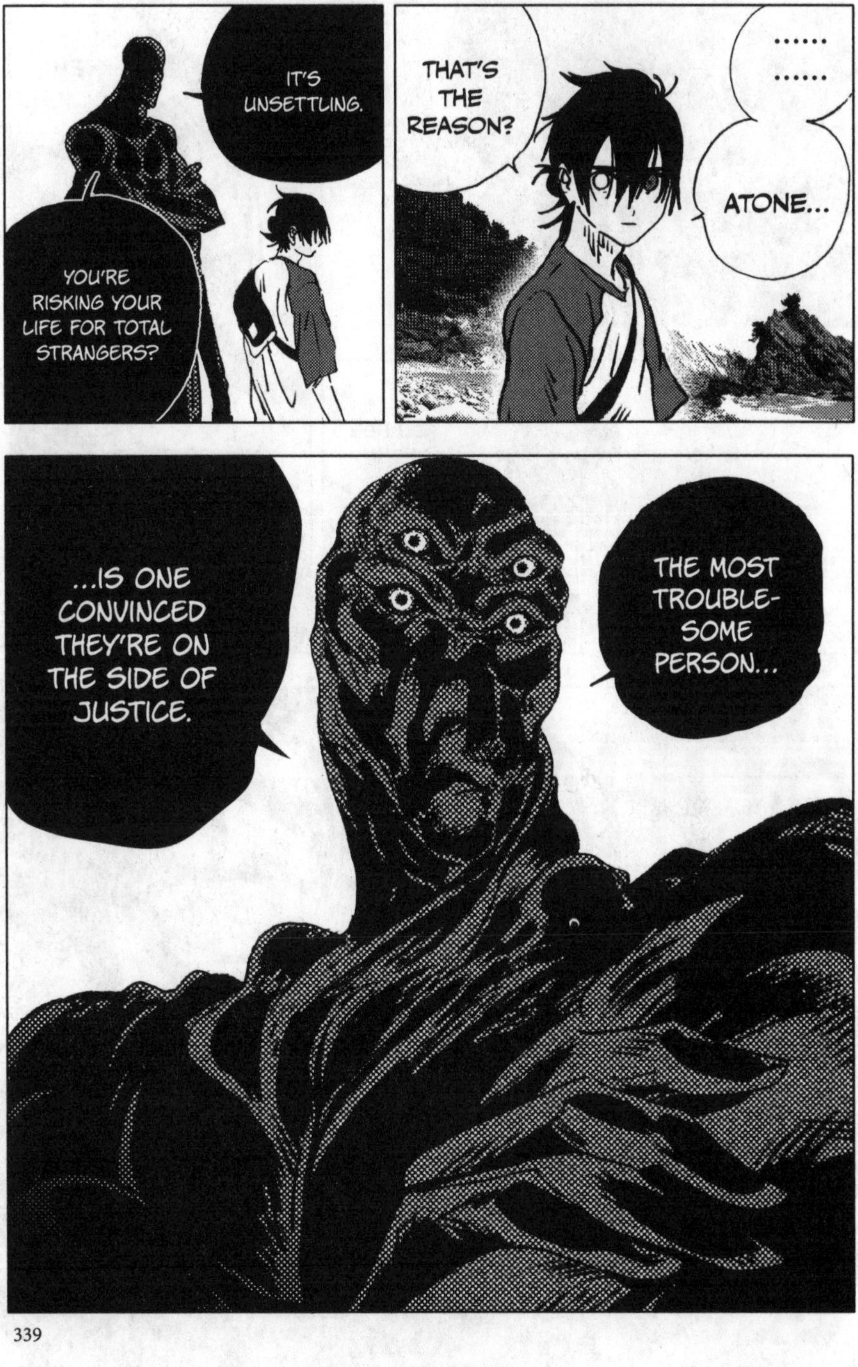
......
......
ATONE...
THAT'S THE REASON?
IT'S UNSETTLING.
YOU'RE RISKING YOUR LIFE FOR TOTAL STRANGERS?
THE MOST TROUBLE-SOME PERSON...
...IS ONE CONVINCED THEY'RE ON THE SIDE OF JUSTICE.

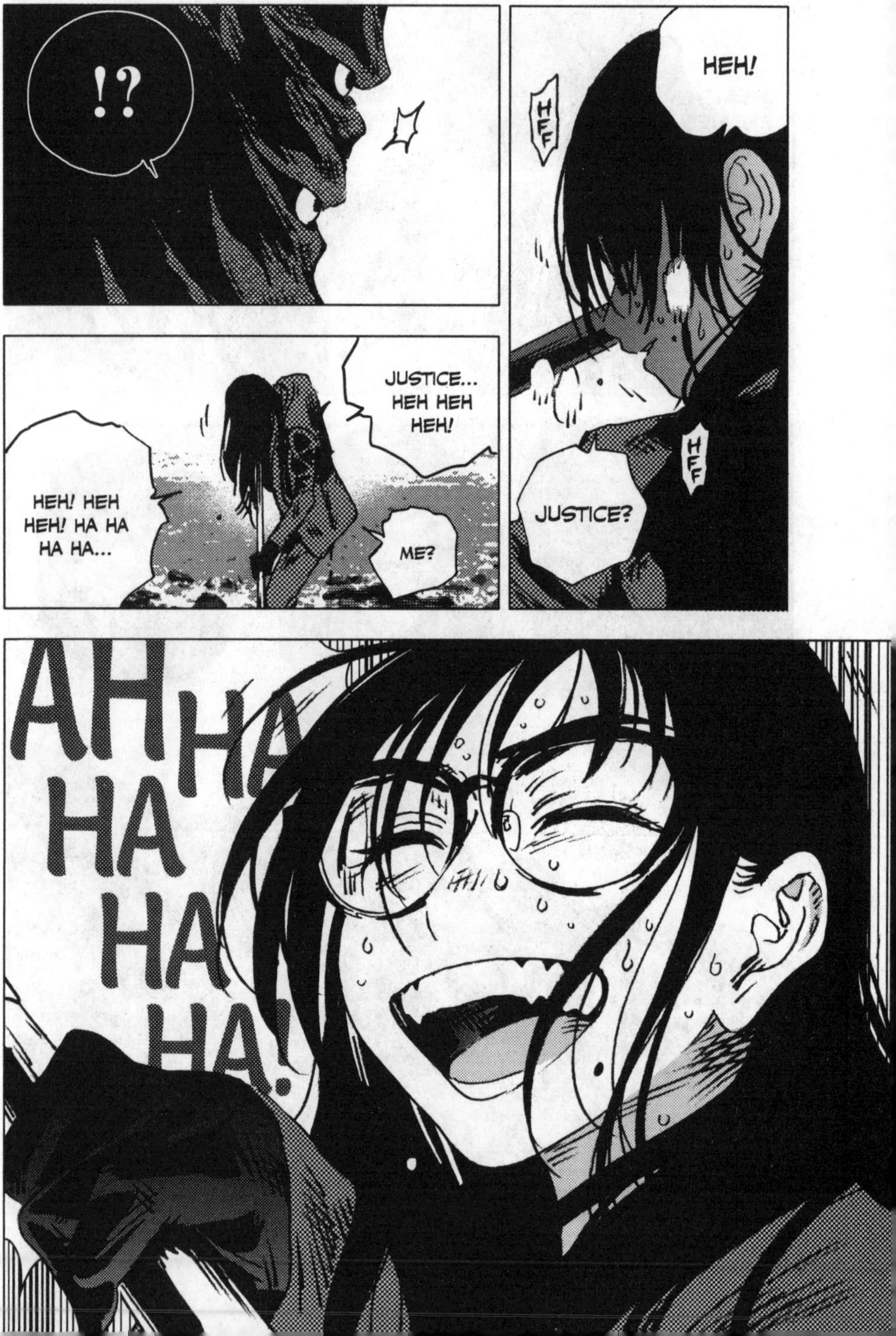
HEH!
HFF
HFF
JUSTICE?
!?
JUSTICE... HEH HEH HEH!
ME?
HEH! HEH HEH! HA HA HA HA...
AH HA HA HA HA HA!

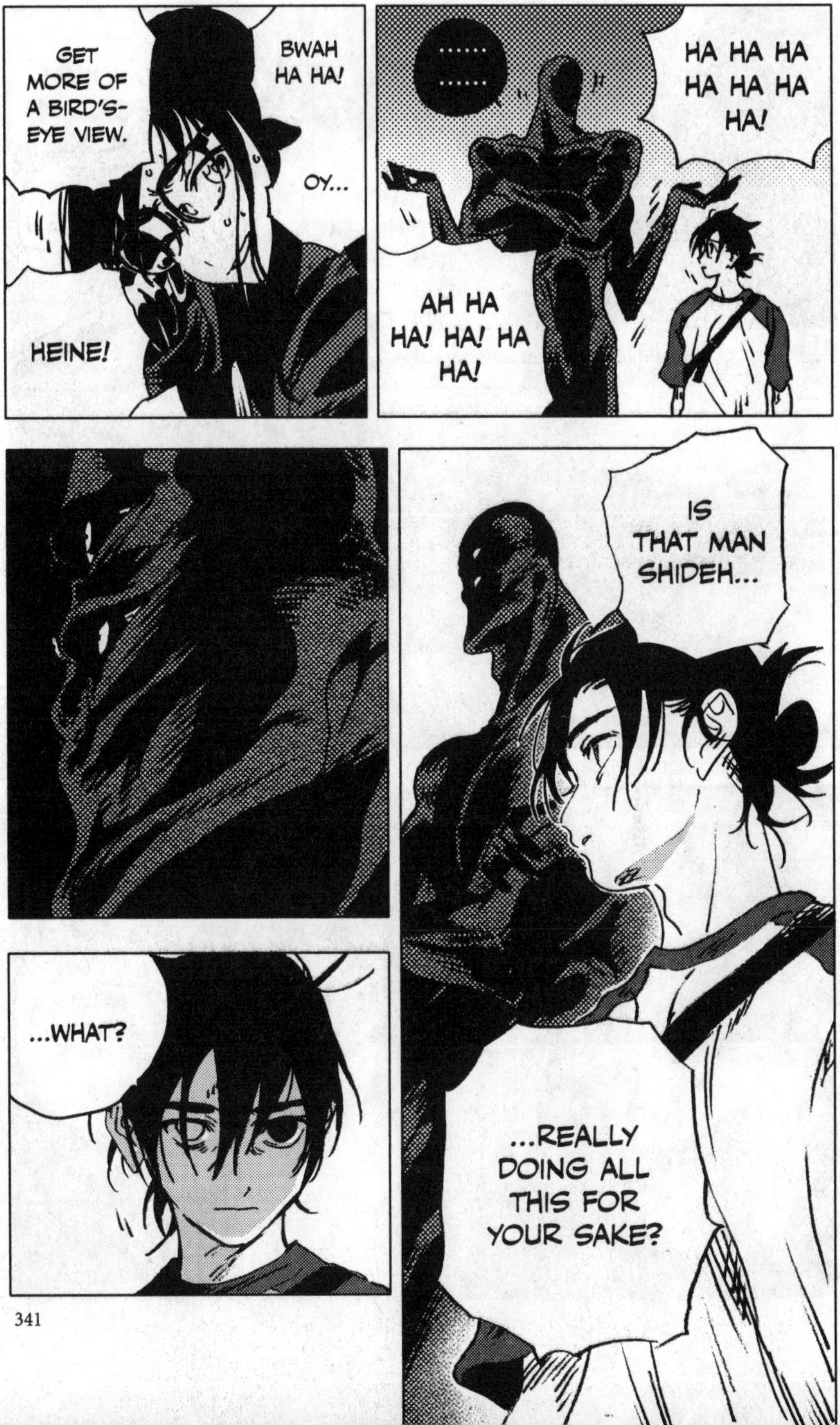
HA HA HA HA HA HA HA!
......
......
AH HA HA! HA! HA HA!
BWAH HA HA!
GET MORE OF A BIRD'S-EYE VIEW.
OY...
HEINE!
IS THAT MAN SHIDEH...
...REALLY DOING ALL THIS FOR YOUR SAKE?
...WHAT?

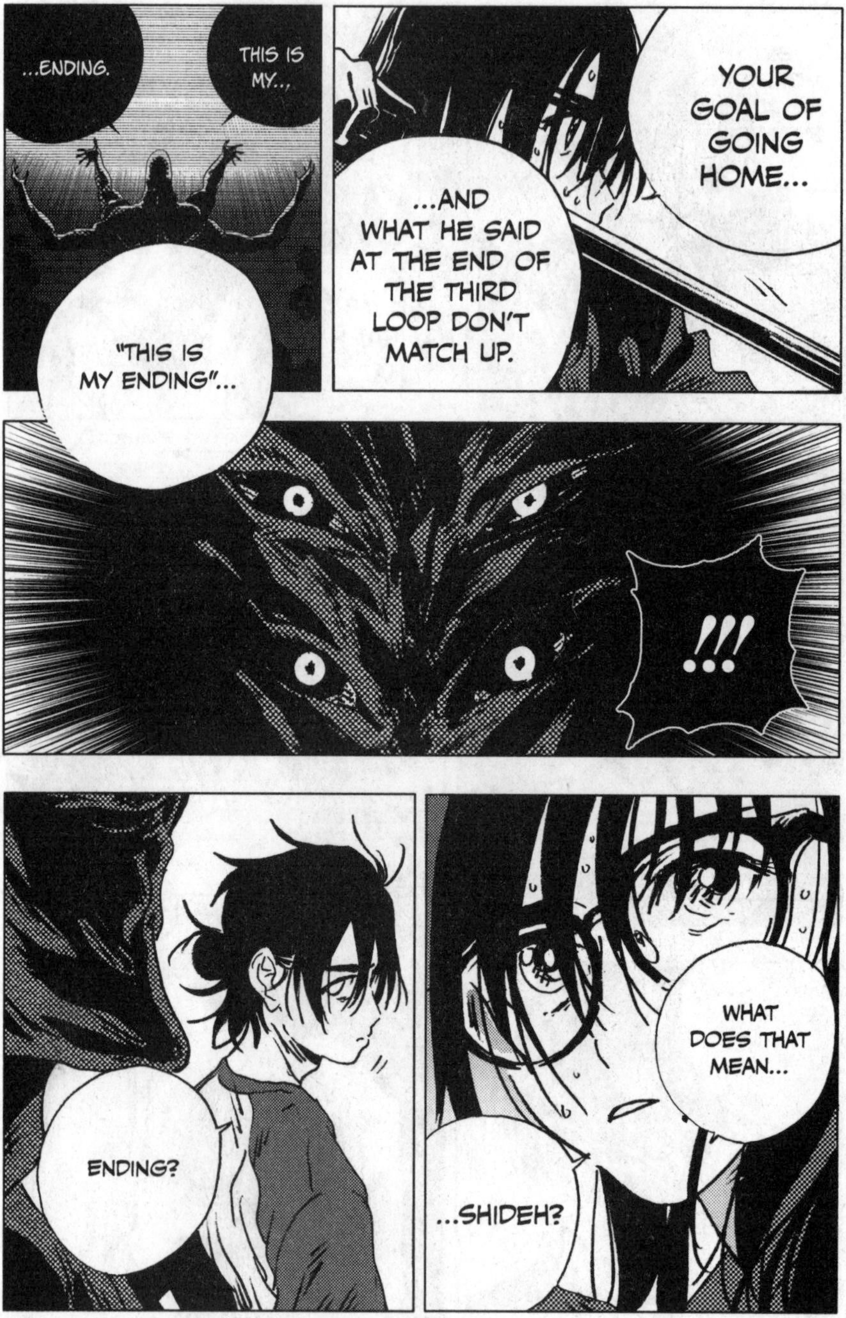
YOUR GOAL OF GOING HOME...
...AND WHAT HE SAID AT THE END OF THE THIRD LOOP DON'T MATCH UP.
THIS IS MY..,
...ENDING.
"THIS IS MY ENDING"...
!!!
WHAT DOES THAT MEAN...
...SHIDEH?
ENDING?

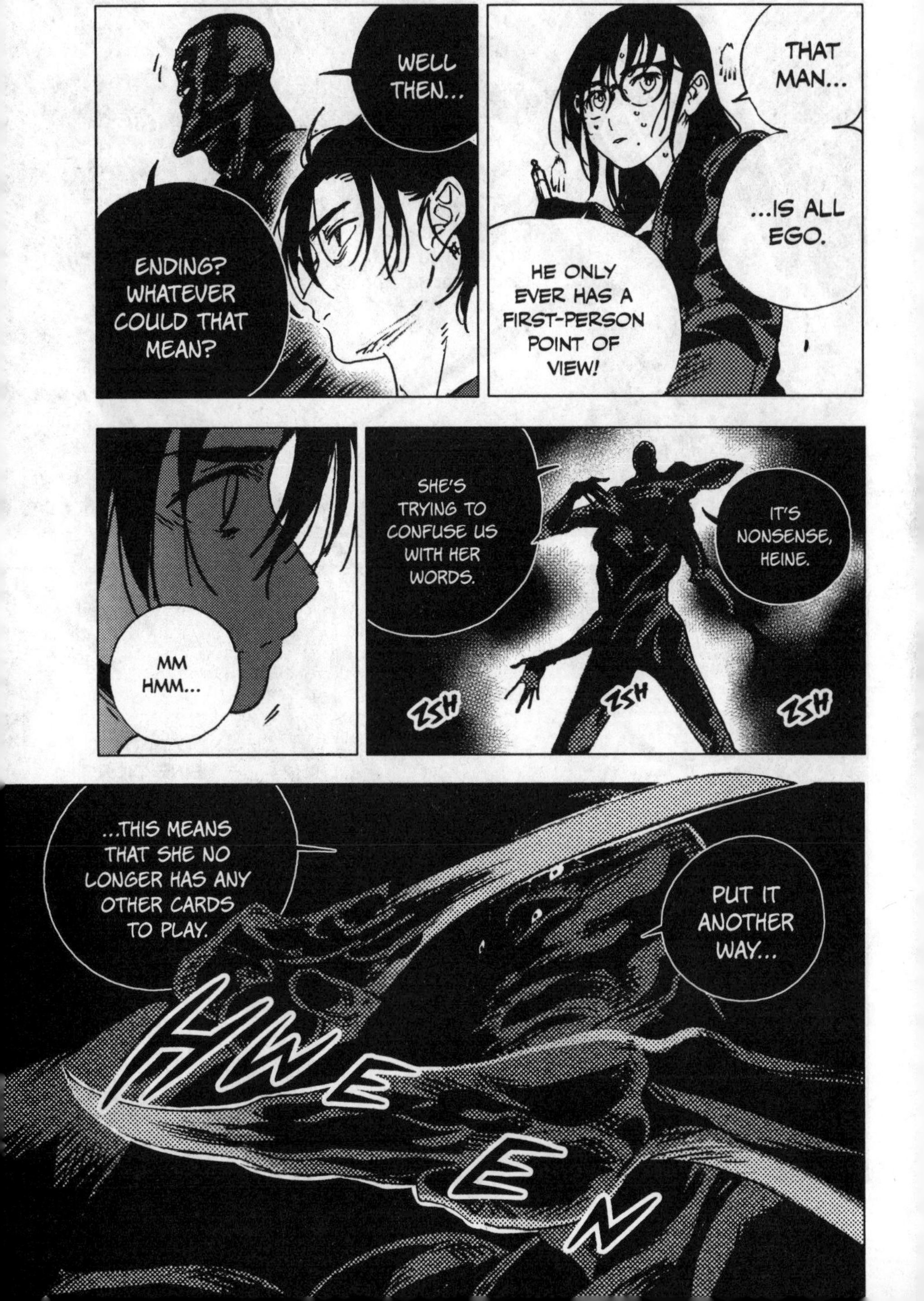
THAT MAN...
...IS ALL EGO.
HE ONLY EVER HAS A FIRST-PERSON POINT OF VIEW!
WELL THEN...
ENDING? WHATEVER COULD THAT MEAN?
IT'S NONSENSE, HEINE.
SHE'S TRYING TO CONFUSE US WITH HER WORDS.
ZSH
ZSH
ZSH
MM HMM...
PUT IT ANOTHER WAY...
...THIS MEANS THAT SHE NO LONGER HAS ANY OTHER CARDS TO PLAY.
HWEEN

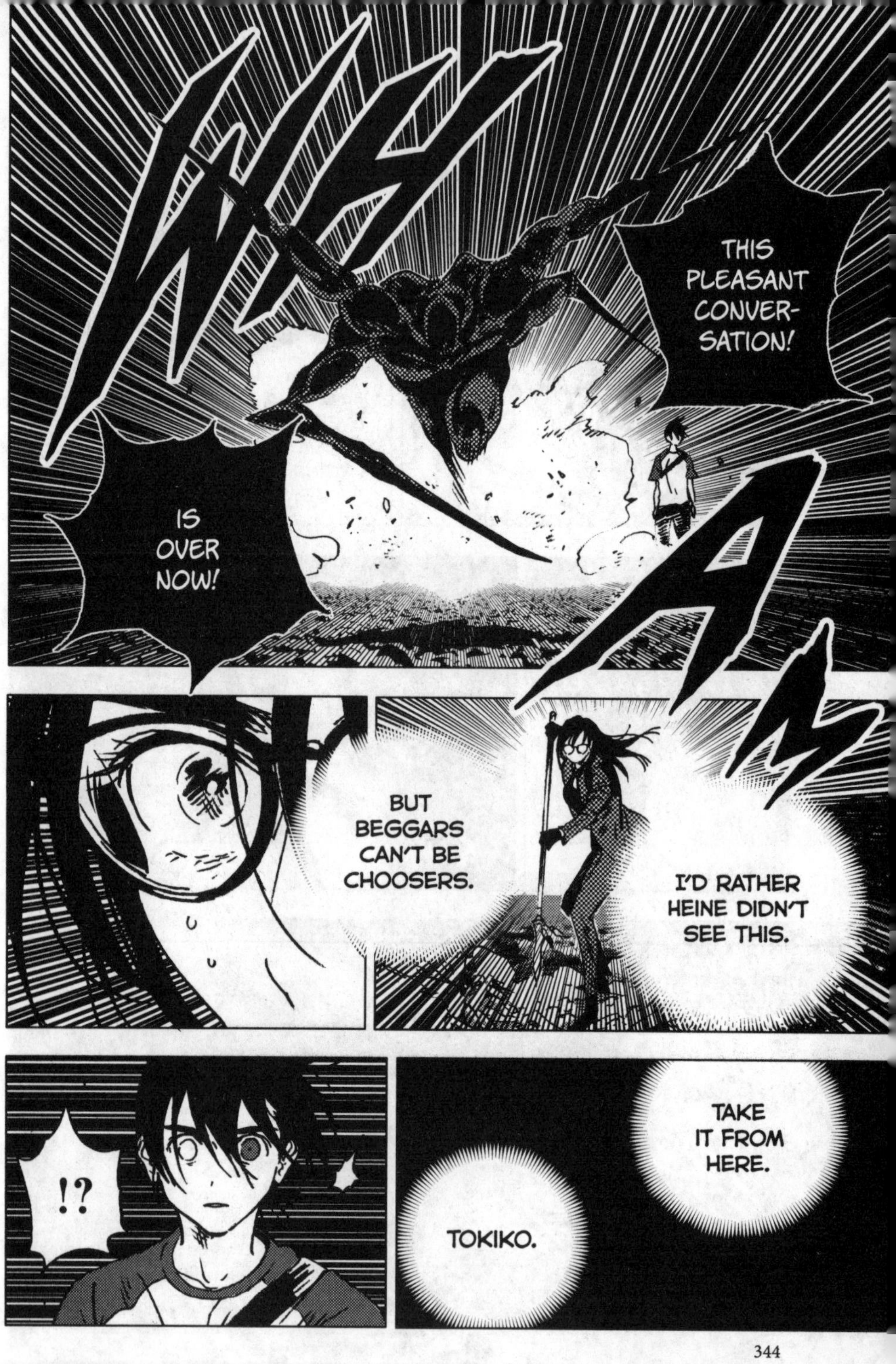
THIS PLEASANT CONVERSATION!
IS OVER NOW!
I'D RATHER HEINE DIDN'T SEE THIS.
BUT BEGGARS CAN'T BE CHOOSERS.
TAKE IT FROM HERE.
TOKIKO.
!?

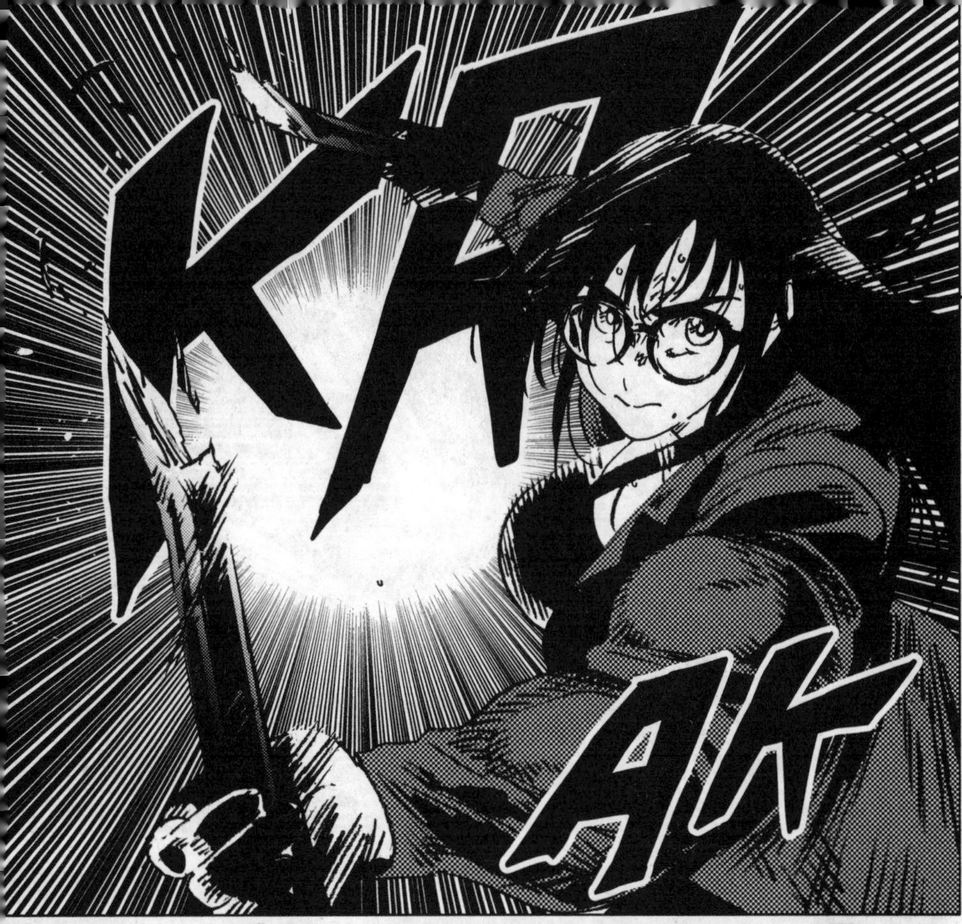

AK

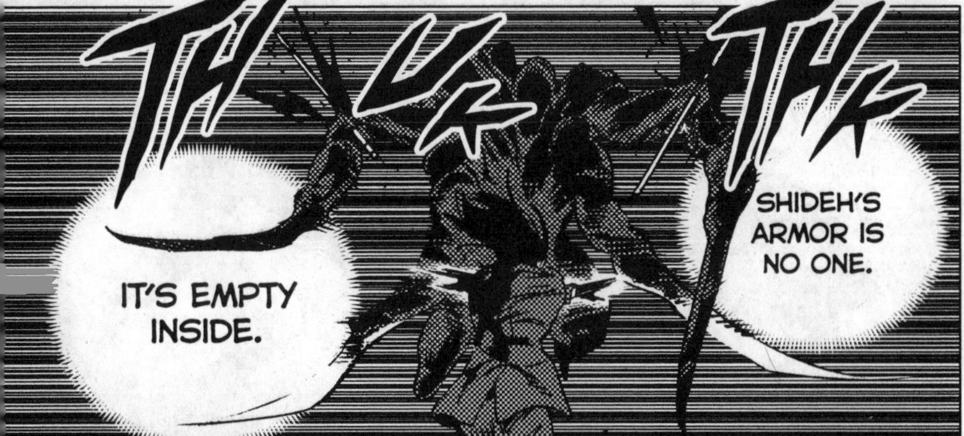

SHIDEH'S ARMOR IS NO ONE.
IT'S EMPTY INSIDE.

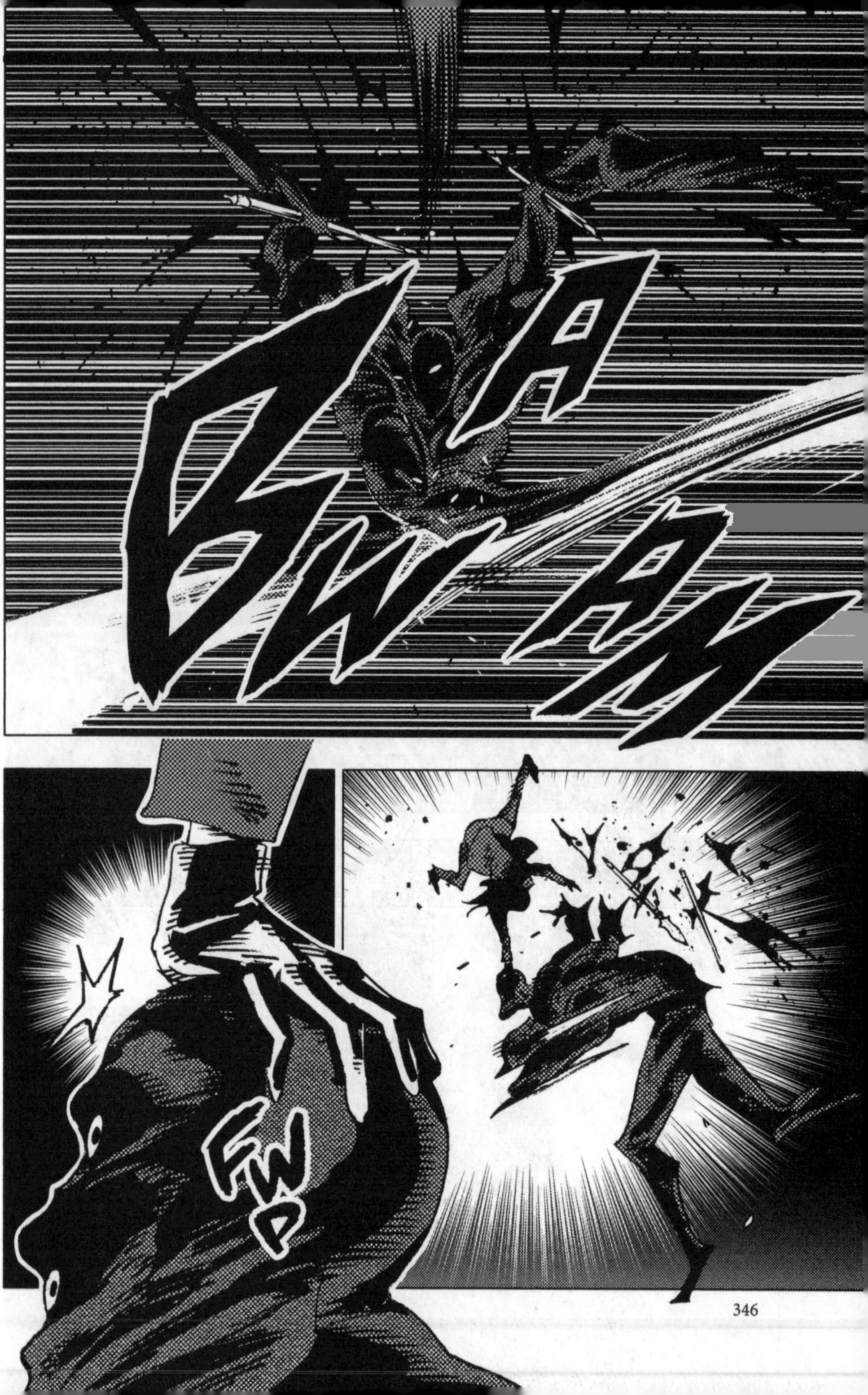
SWAAM
FWP

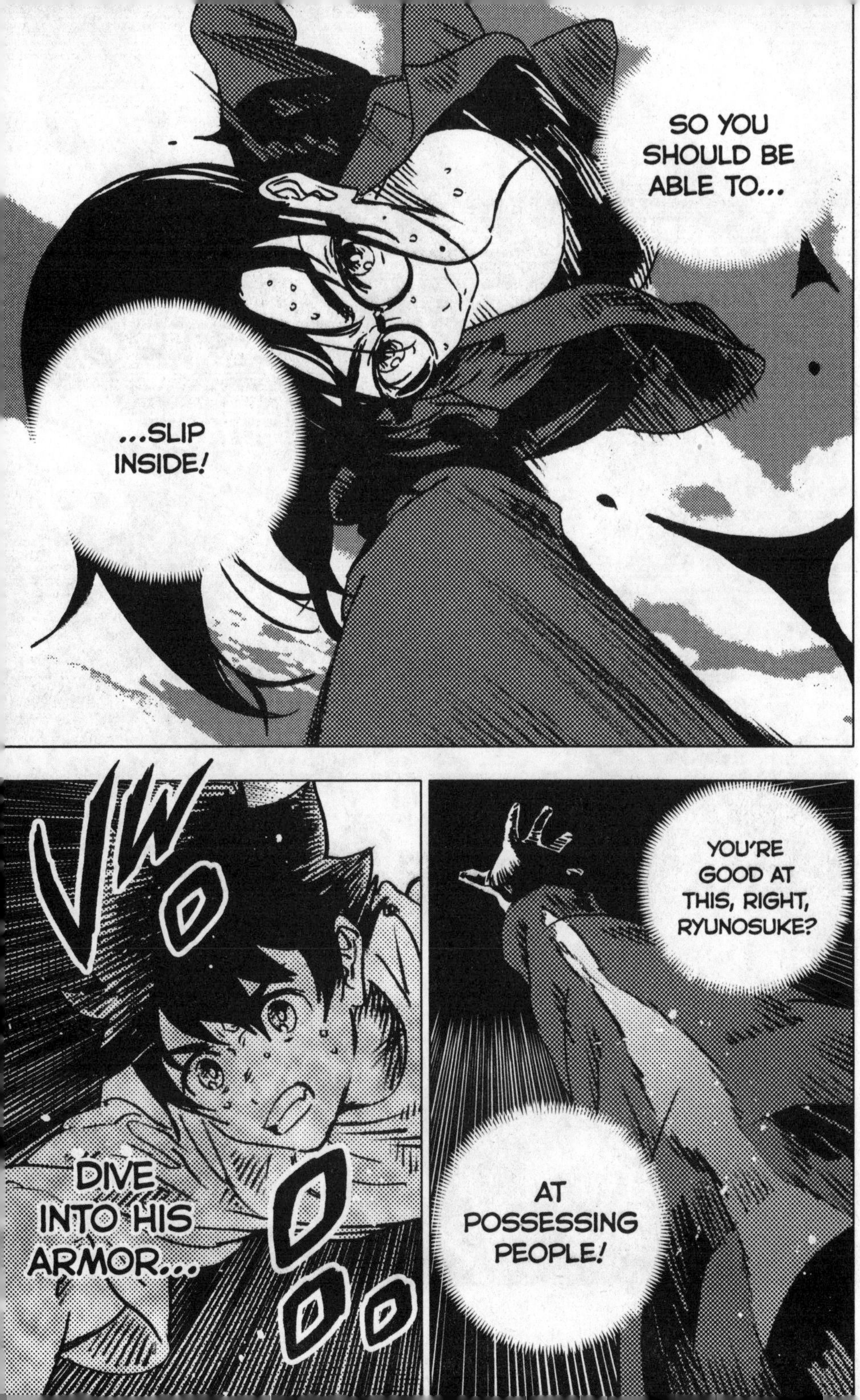
SO YOU SHOULD BE ABLE TO...
...SLIP INSIDE!
YOU'RE GOOD AT THIS, RIGHT, RYUNOSUKE?
AT POSSESSING PEOPLE!
DIVE INTO HIS ARMOR...

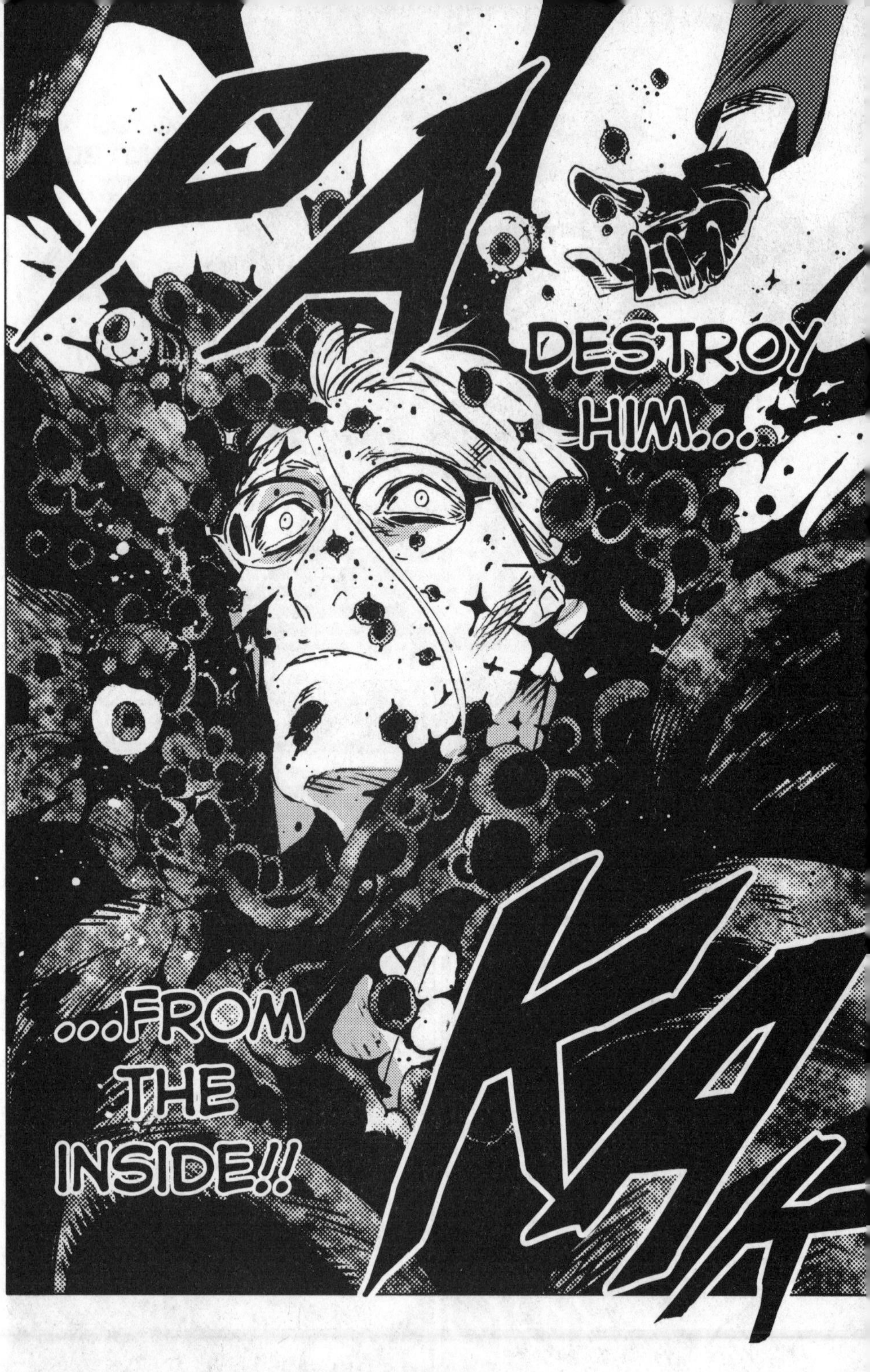
DESTROY HIM...
...FROM THE INSIDE!!

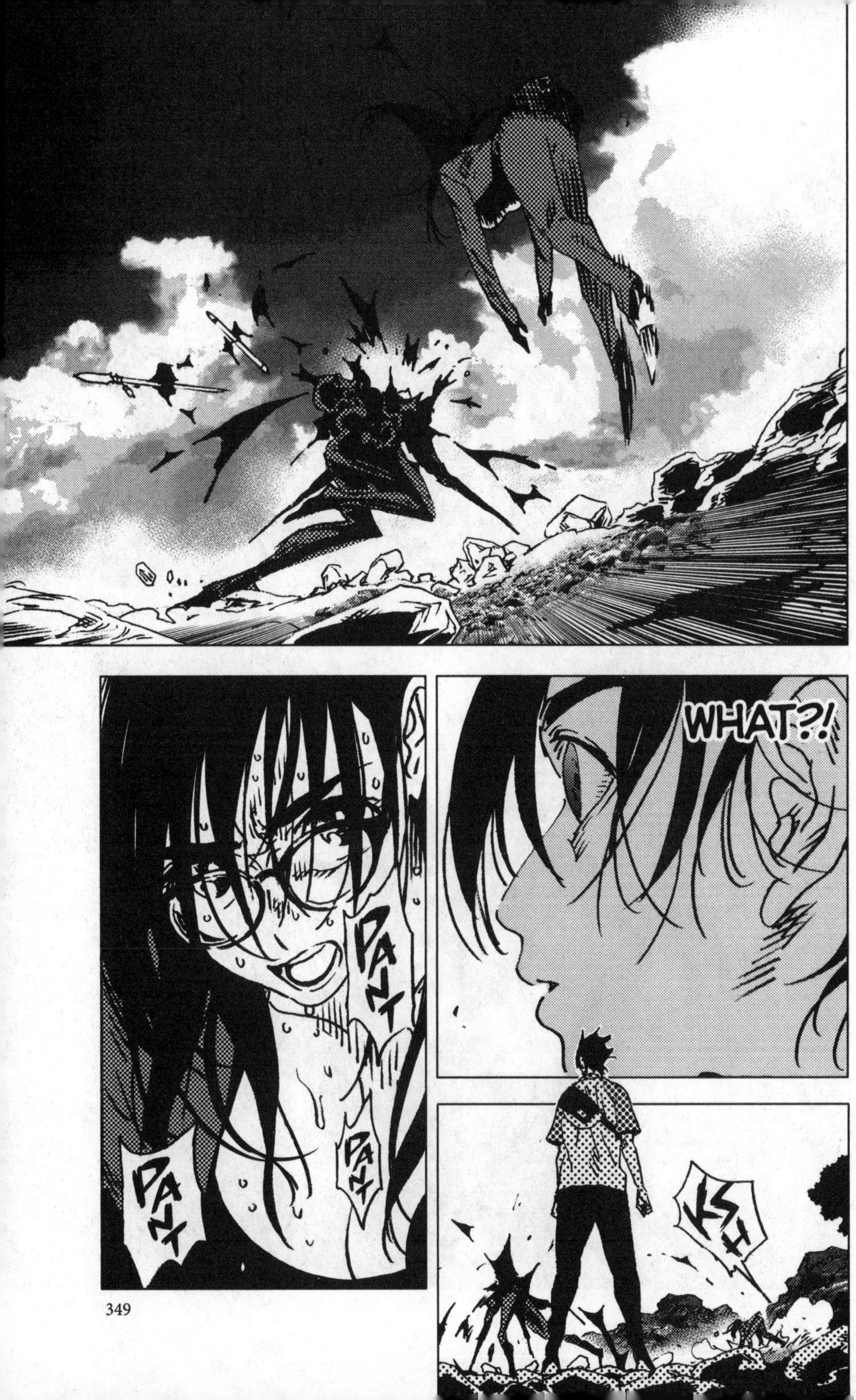
WHAT?!
KSH
PANT
PANT
PANT
PANT

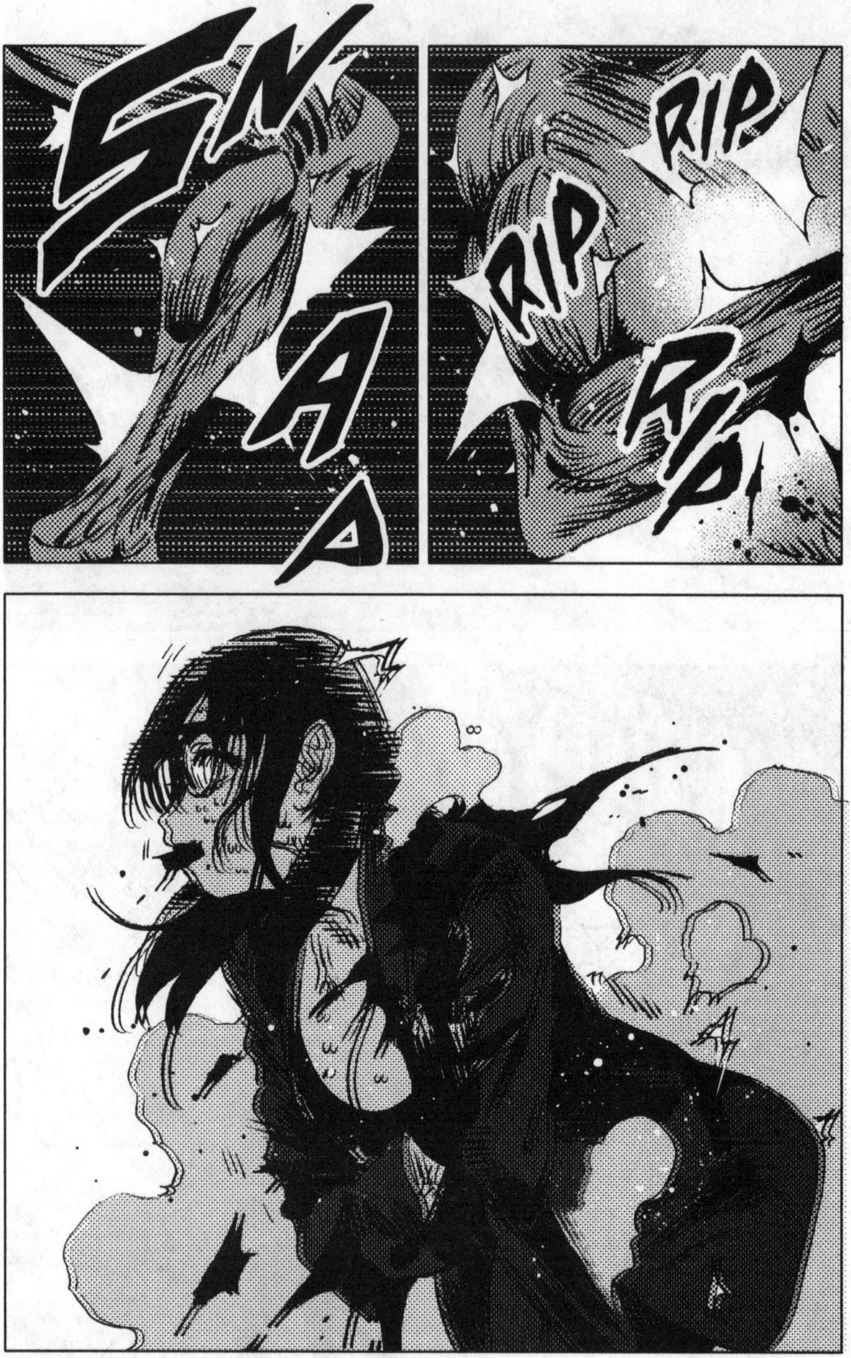
RIP
RIP
RIP
RIP
SNAAP

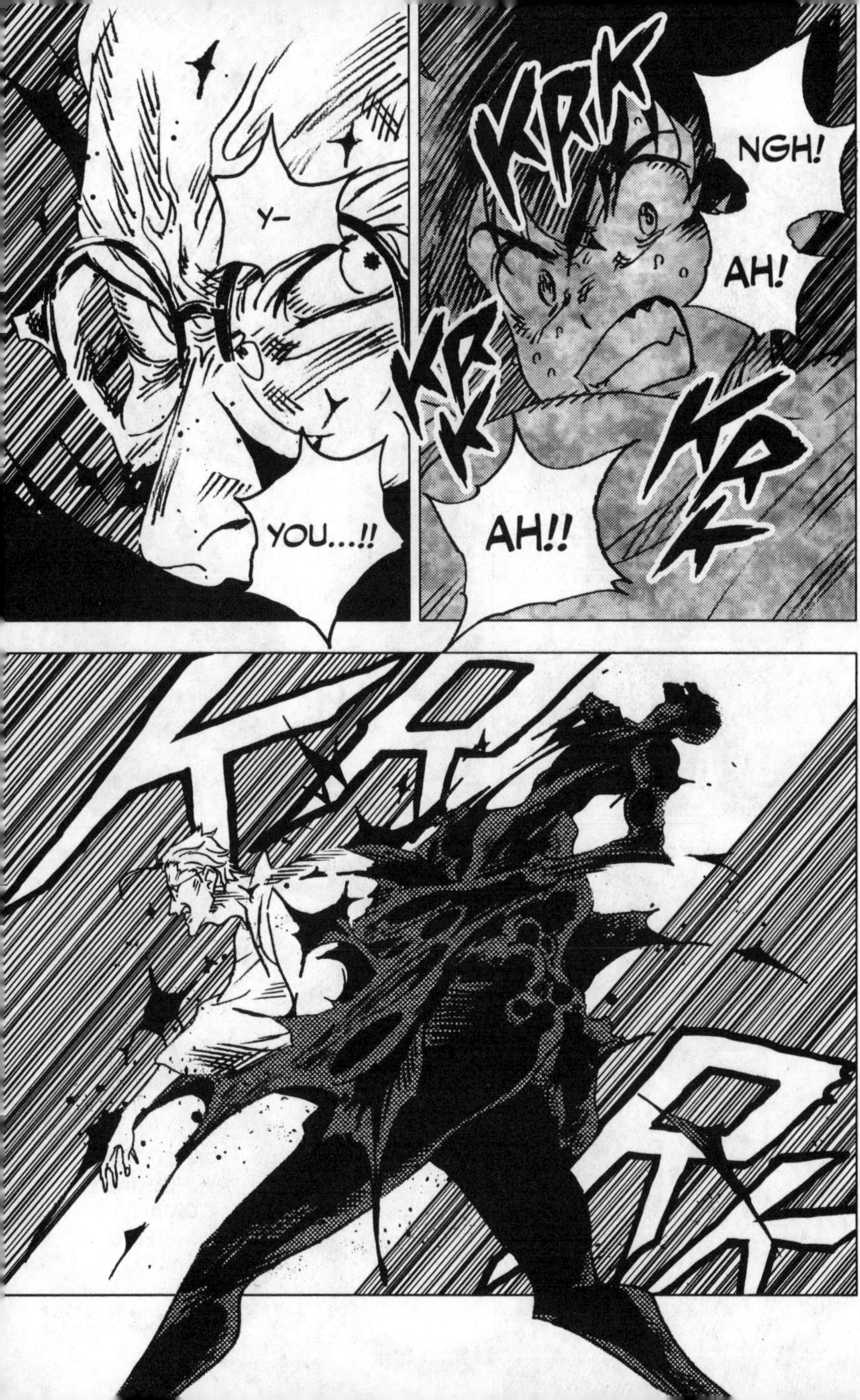
NGH!
KRK
AH!
KR
K
KR
K
AH!!
Y–
YOU...!!

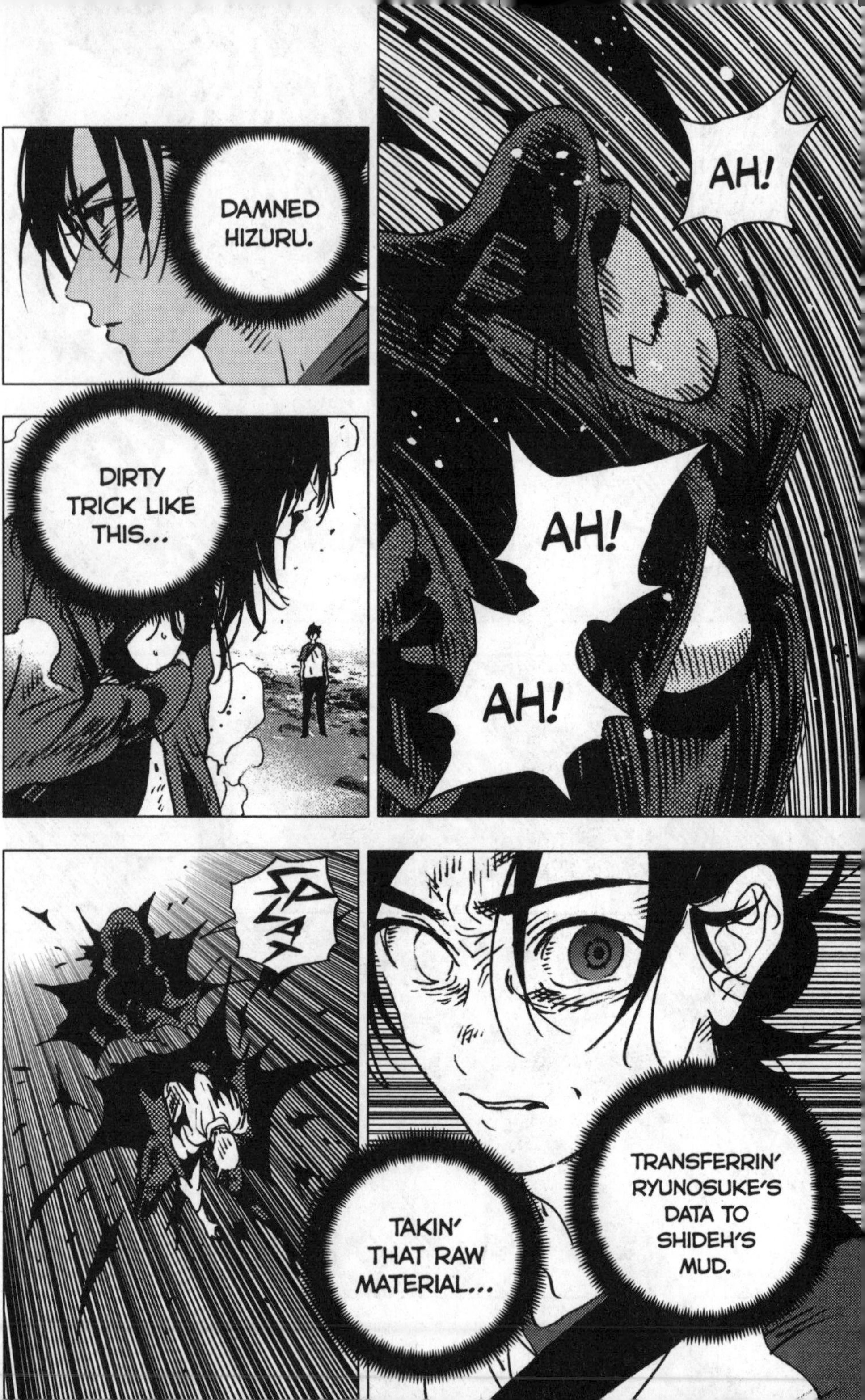
AH!
AH!
AH!
DAMNED HIZURU.
DIRTY TRICK LIKE THIS...
TRANSFERRIN' RYUNOSUKE'S DATA TO SHIDEH'S MUD.
TAKIN' THAT RAW MATERIAL...
SPLAT

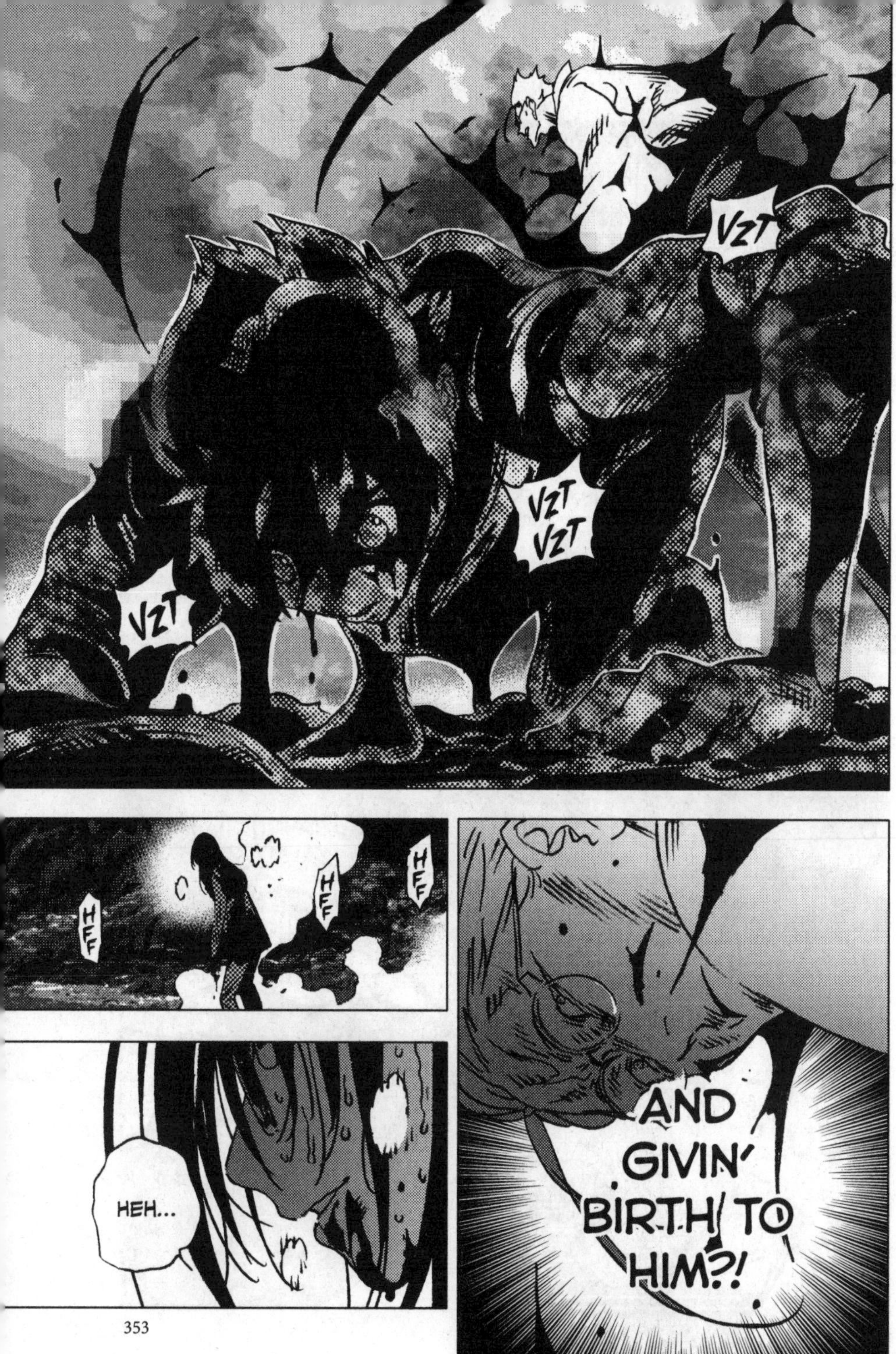
VZT
VZT VZT
VZT
AND GIVIN' BIRTH TO HIM?!
HFF
HFF
HFF
HEH...

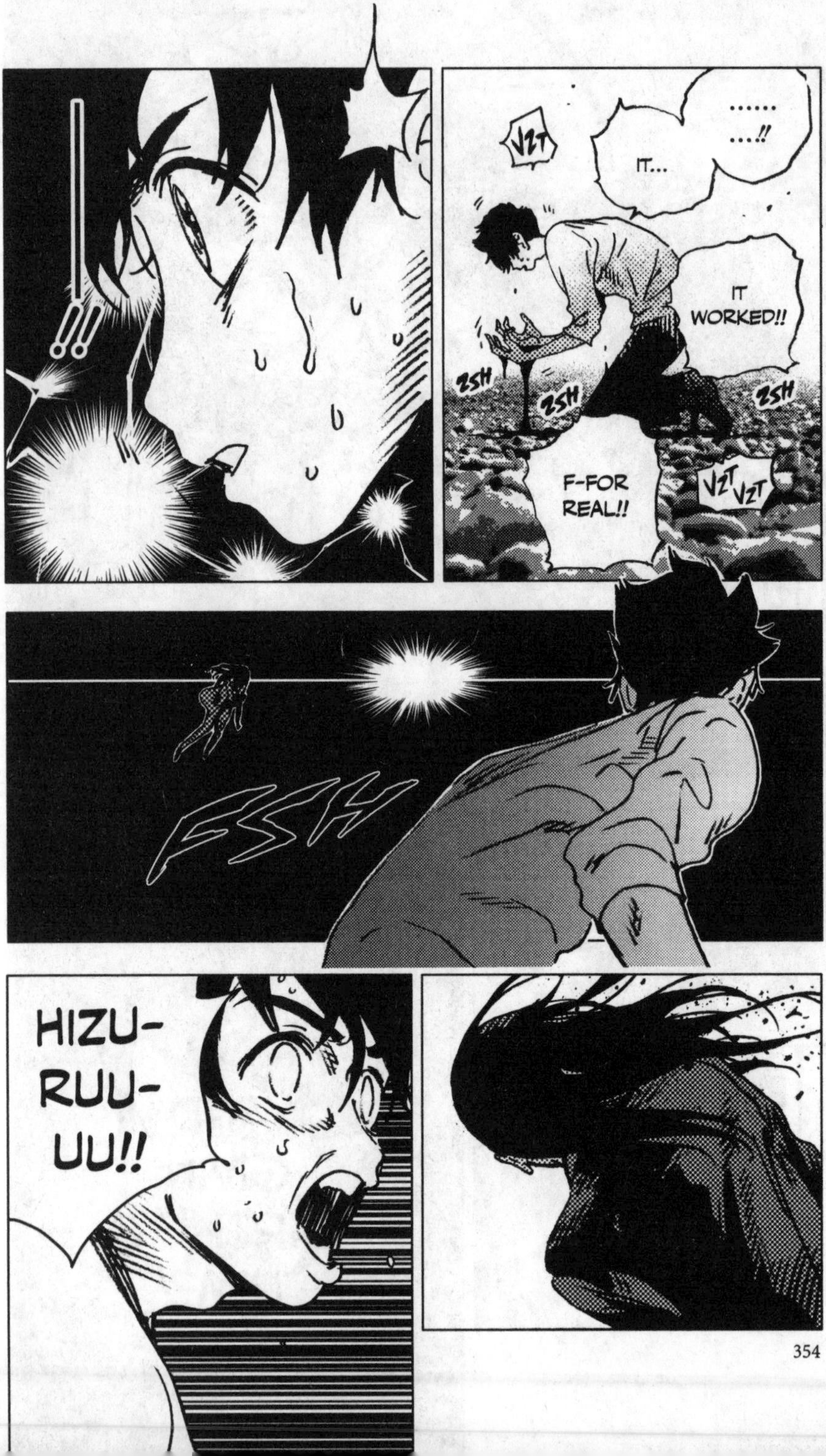

VZT
......
....!!
IT...
IT WORKED!!
ZSH
ZSH
ZSH
F-FOR REAL!!
VZT VZT
FSH
HIZU-
RUUU-
UU!!

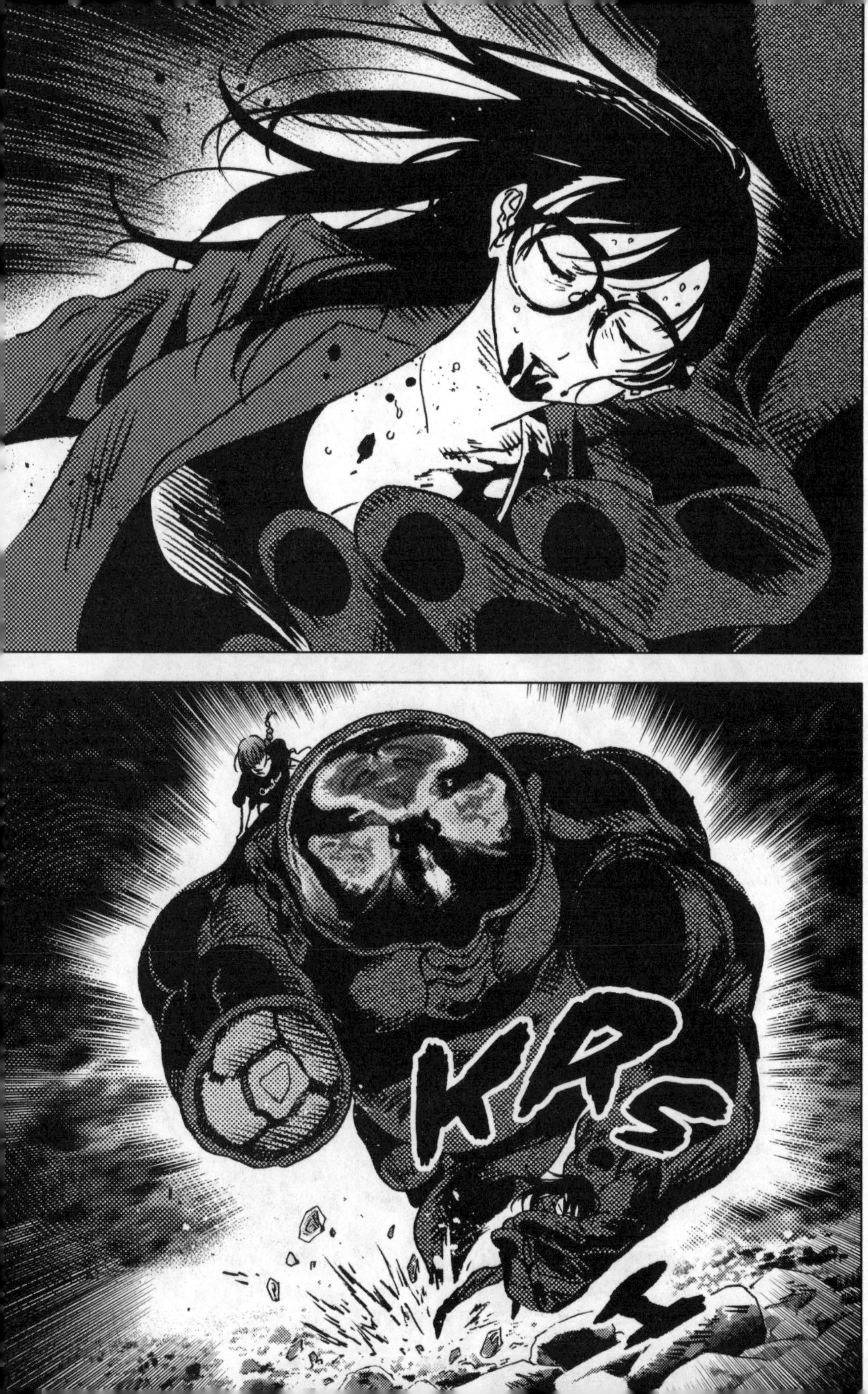
KRS

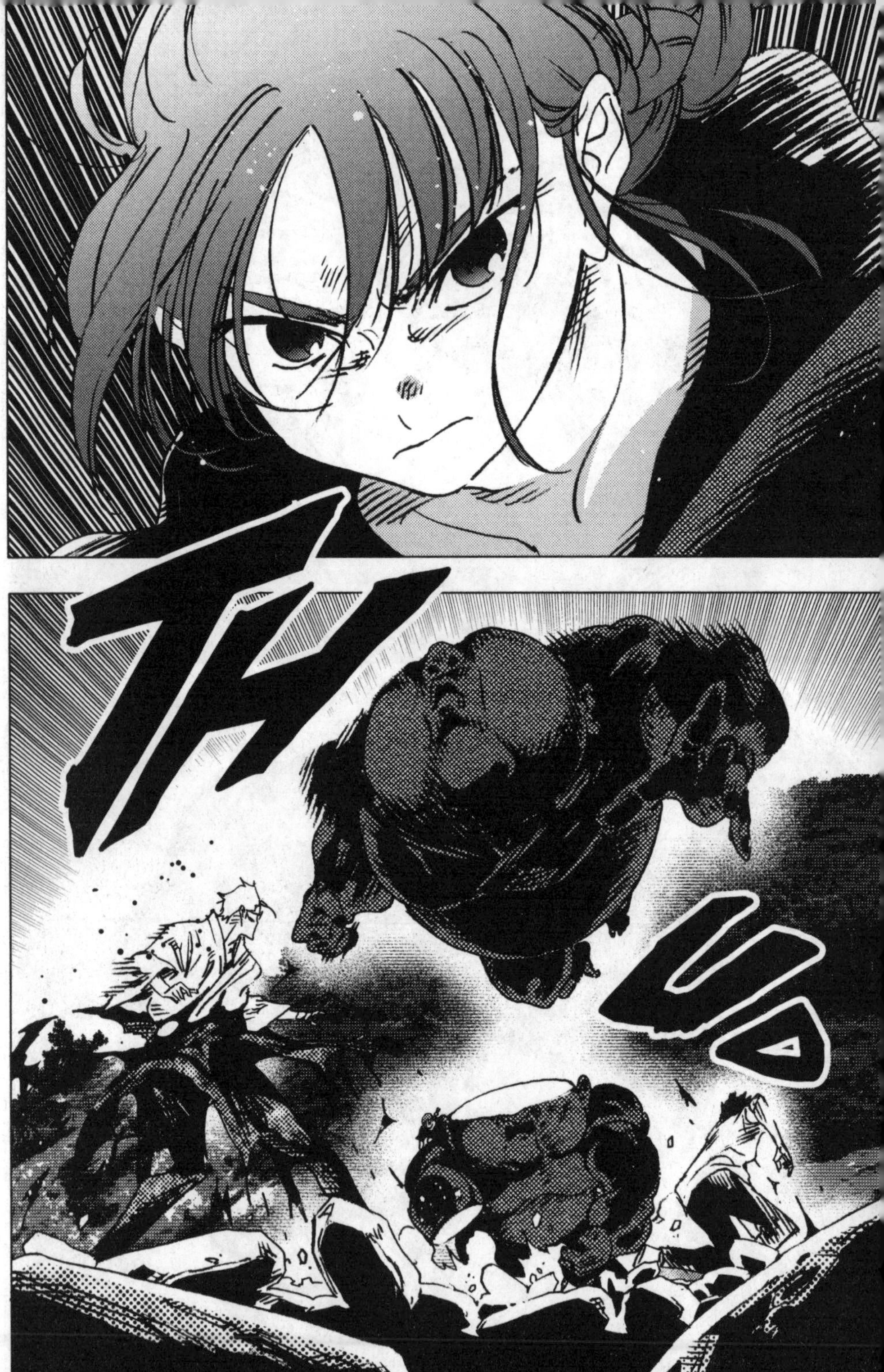

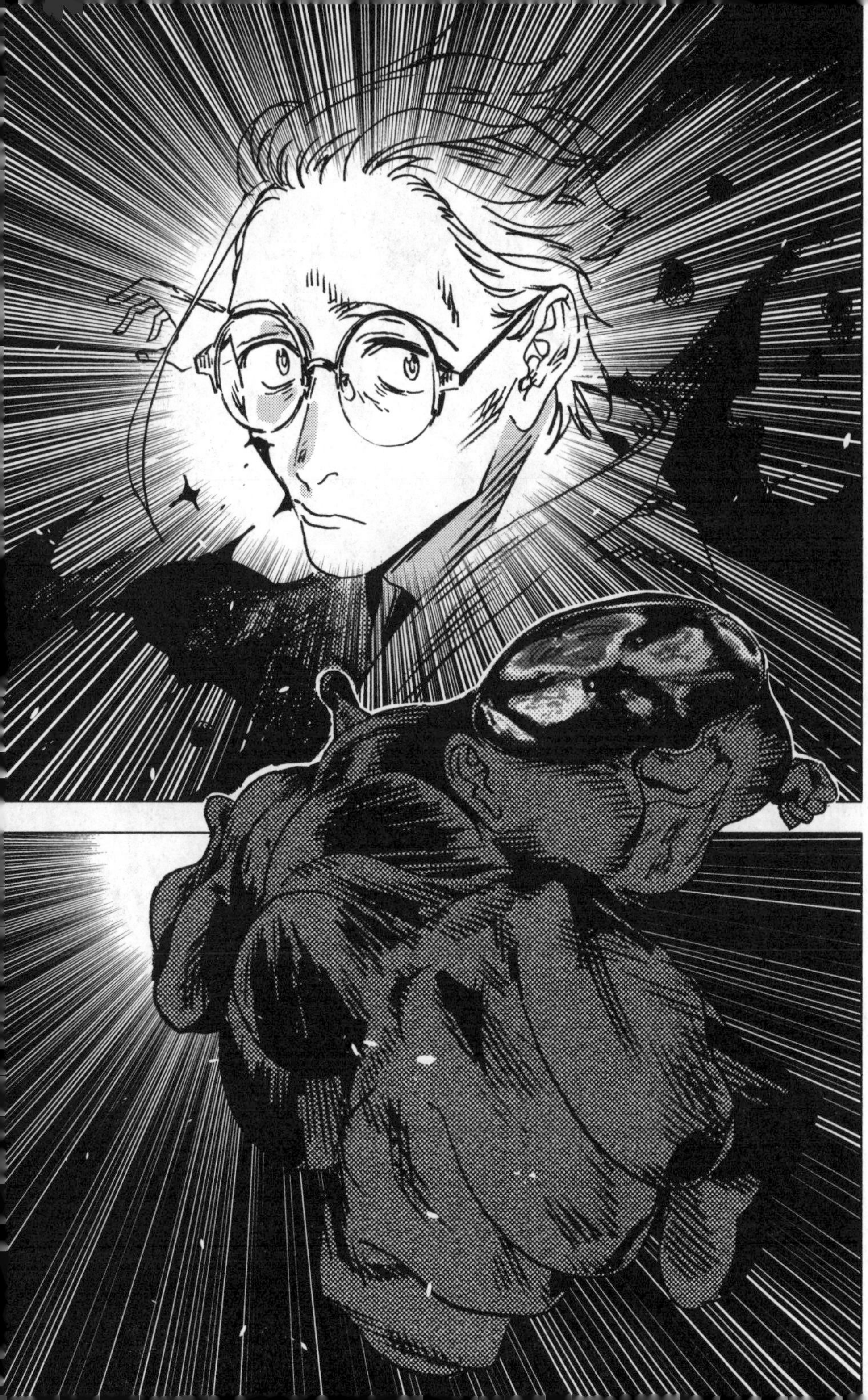

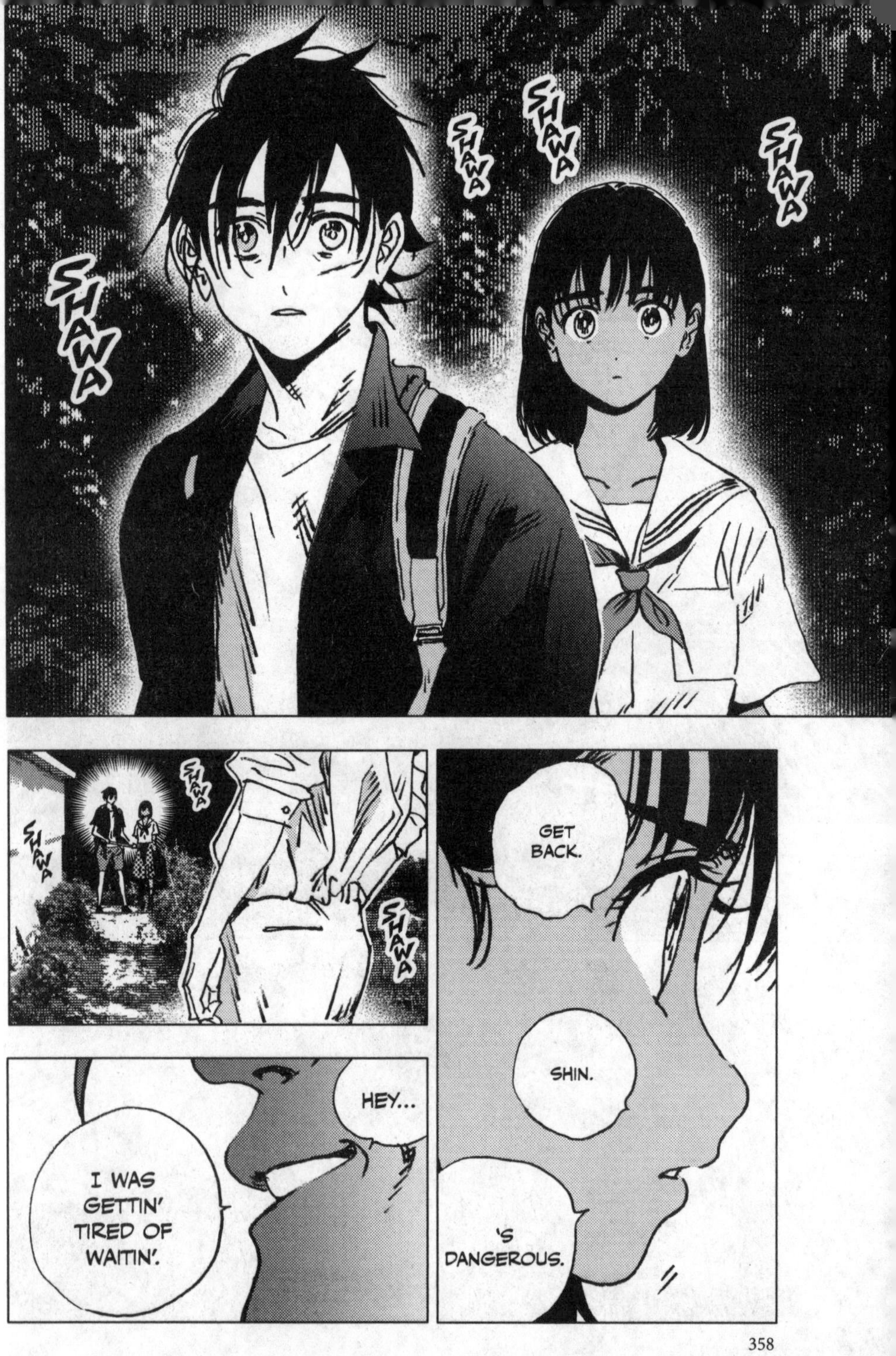
SHAWA
SHAWA
SHAWA
SHAWA
GET BACK.
SHIN.
'S DANGEROUS.
SHAWA
SHAWA
SHAWA
HEY...
I WAS GETTIN' TIRED OF WAITIN'.

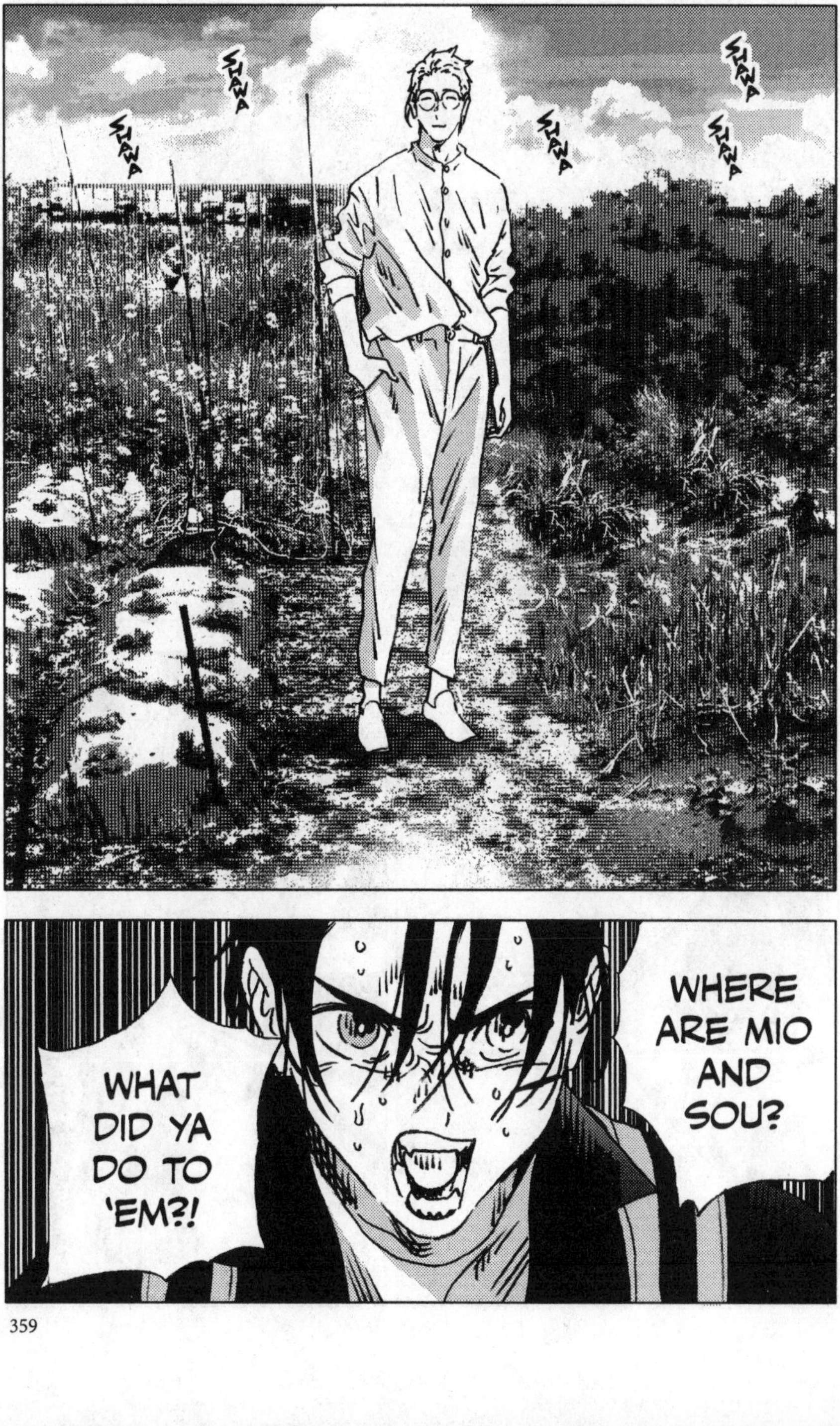
SHAWA
SHAWA
SHAWA
SHAWA
SHAWA
WHERE ARE MIO AND SOU?
WHAT DID YA DO TO 'EM?!

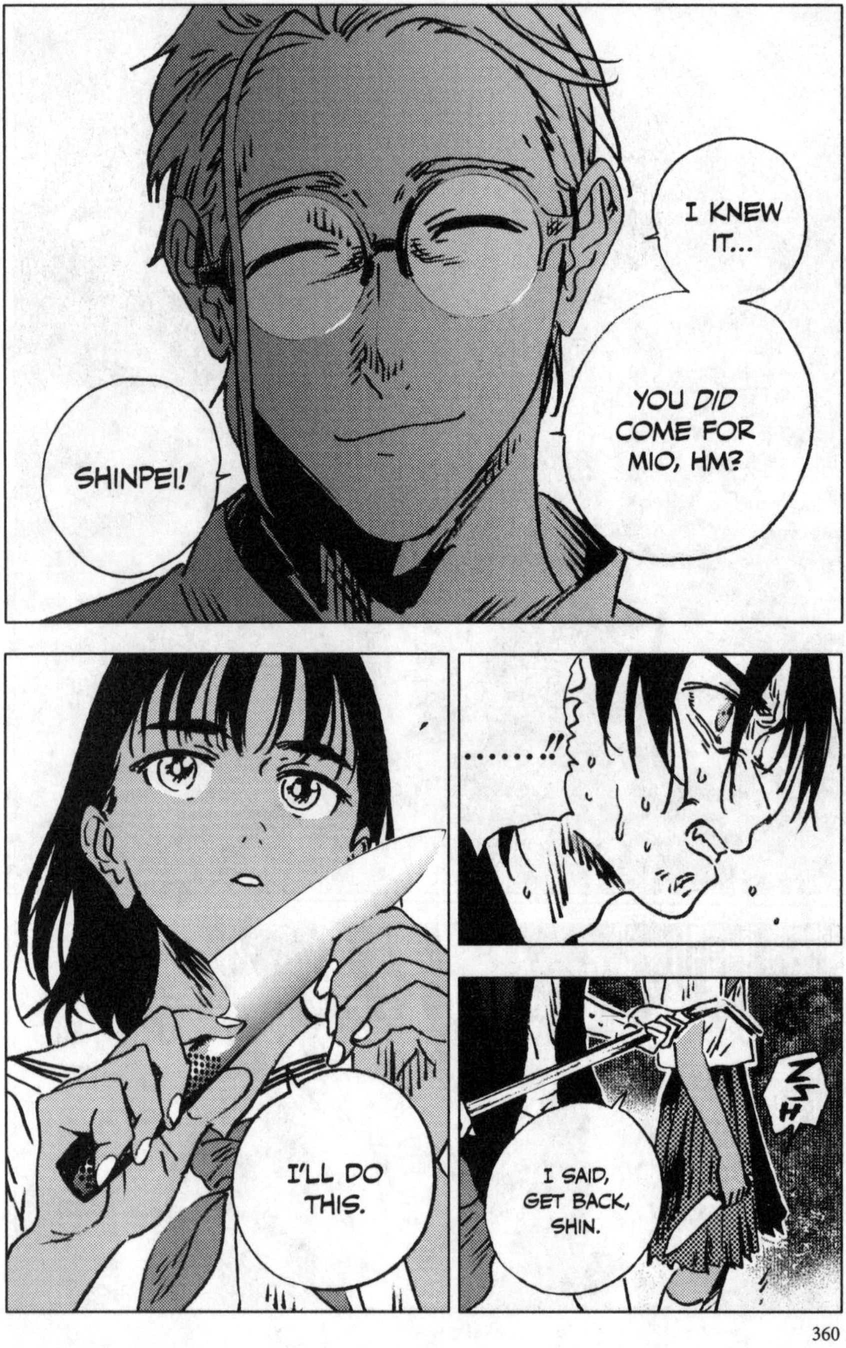
I KNEW IT...
YOU *DID* COME FOR MIO, HM?
SHINPEI!
........!!
I SAID, GET BACK, SHIN.
I'LL DO THIS.

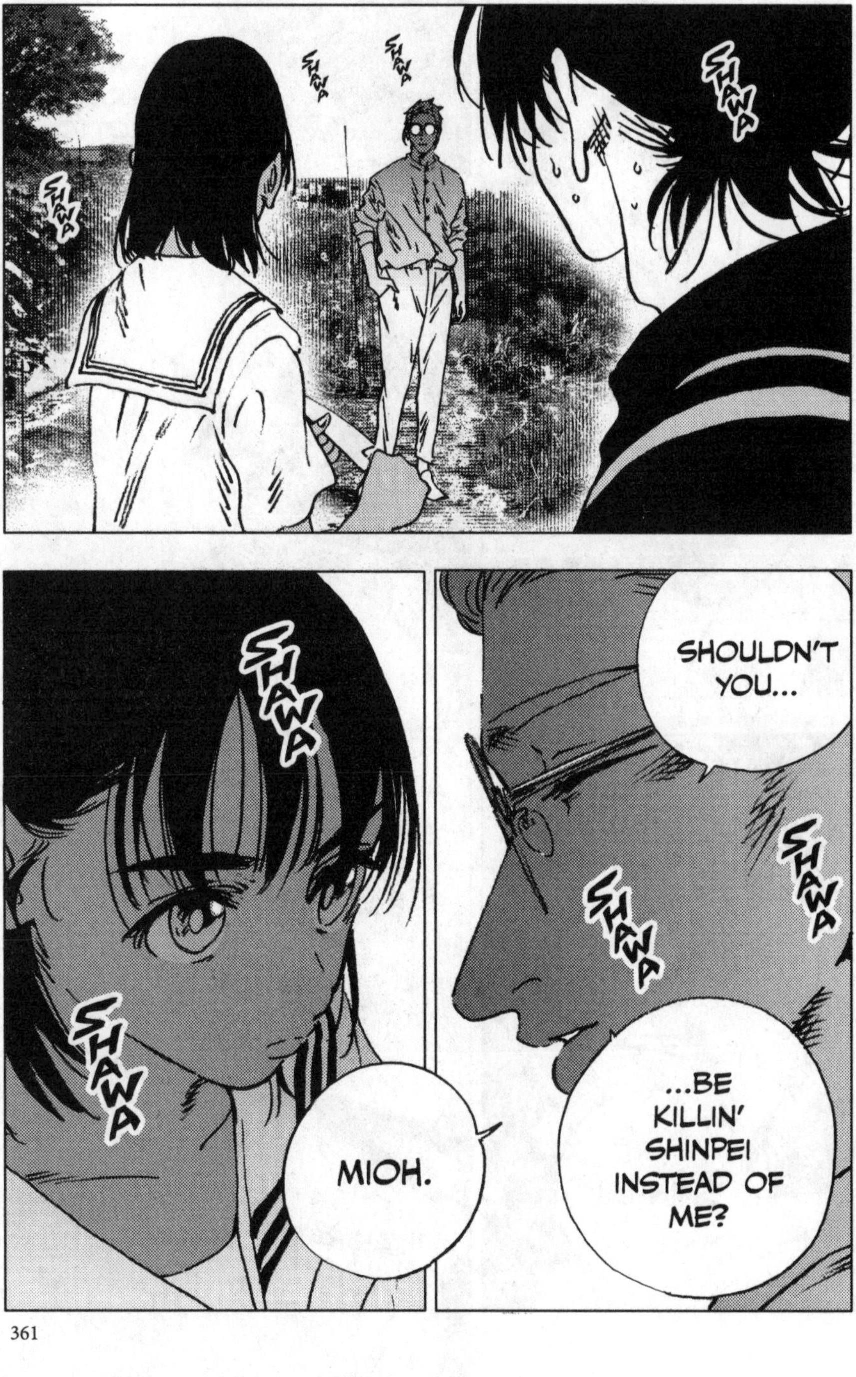
SHAWA
SHAWA
SHAWA
SHAWA
SHOULDN'T YOU...
SHAWA
SHAWA
...BE KILLIN' SHINPEI INSTEAD OF ME?
SHAWA
SHAWA
MIOH.

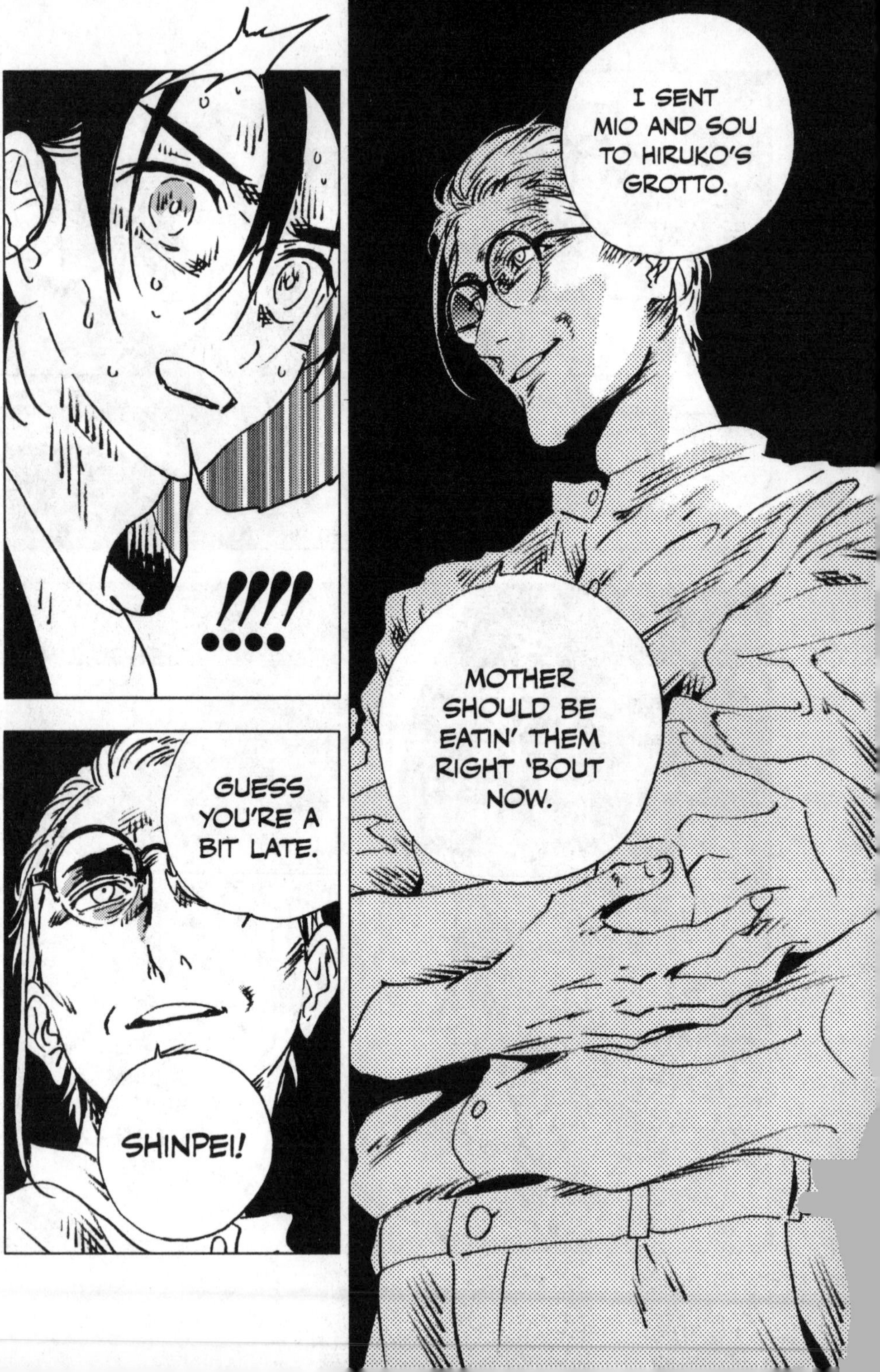
I SENT MIO AND SOU TO HIRUKO'S GROTTO.
MOTHER SHOULD BE EATIN' THEM RIGHT 'BOUT NOW.
!!!!
GUESS YOU'RE A BIT LATE.
SHINPEI!

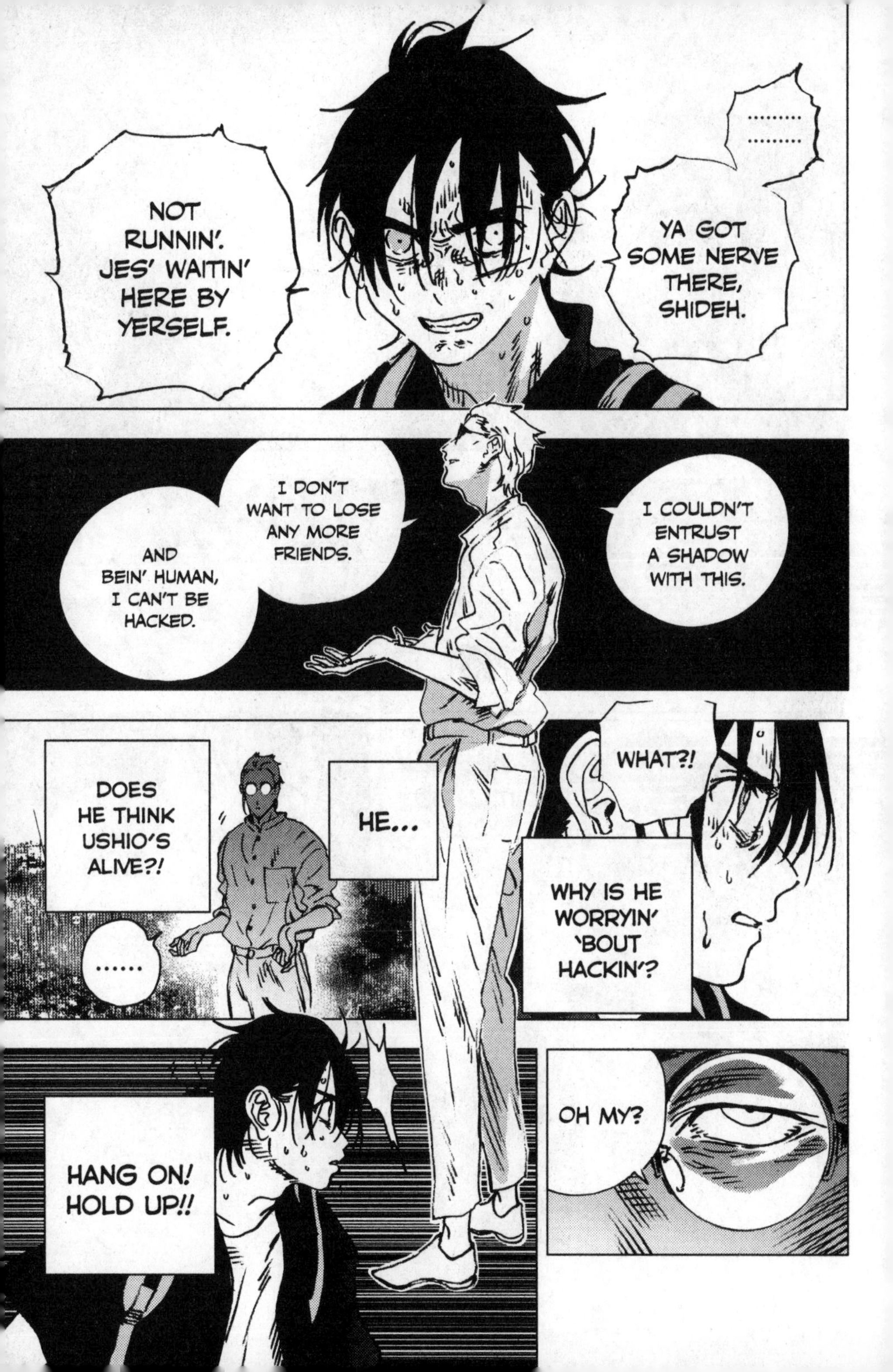
....
YA GOT SOME NERVE THERE, SHIDEH.
NOT RUNNIN'. JES' WAITIN' HERE BY YERSELF.
I COULDN'T ENTRUST A SHADOW WITH THIS.
I DON'T WANT TO LOSE ANY MORE FRIENDS.
AND BEIN' HUMAN, I CAN'T BE HACKED.
WHAT?!
WHY IS HE WORRYIN' 'BOUT HACKIN'?
HE...
DOES HE THINK USHIO'S ALIVE?!
......
OH MY?
HANG ON! HOLD UP!!

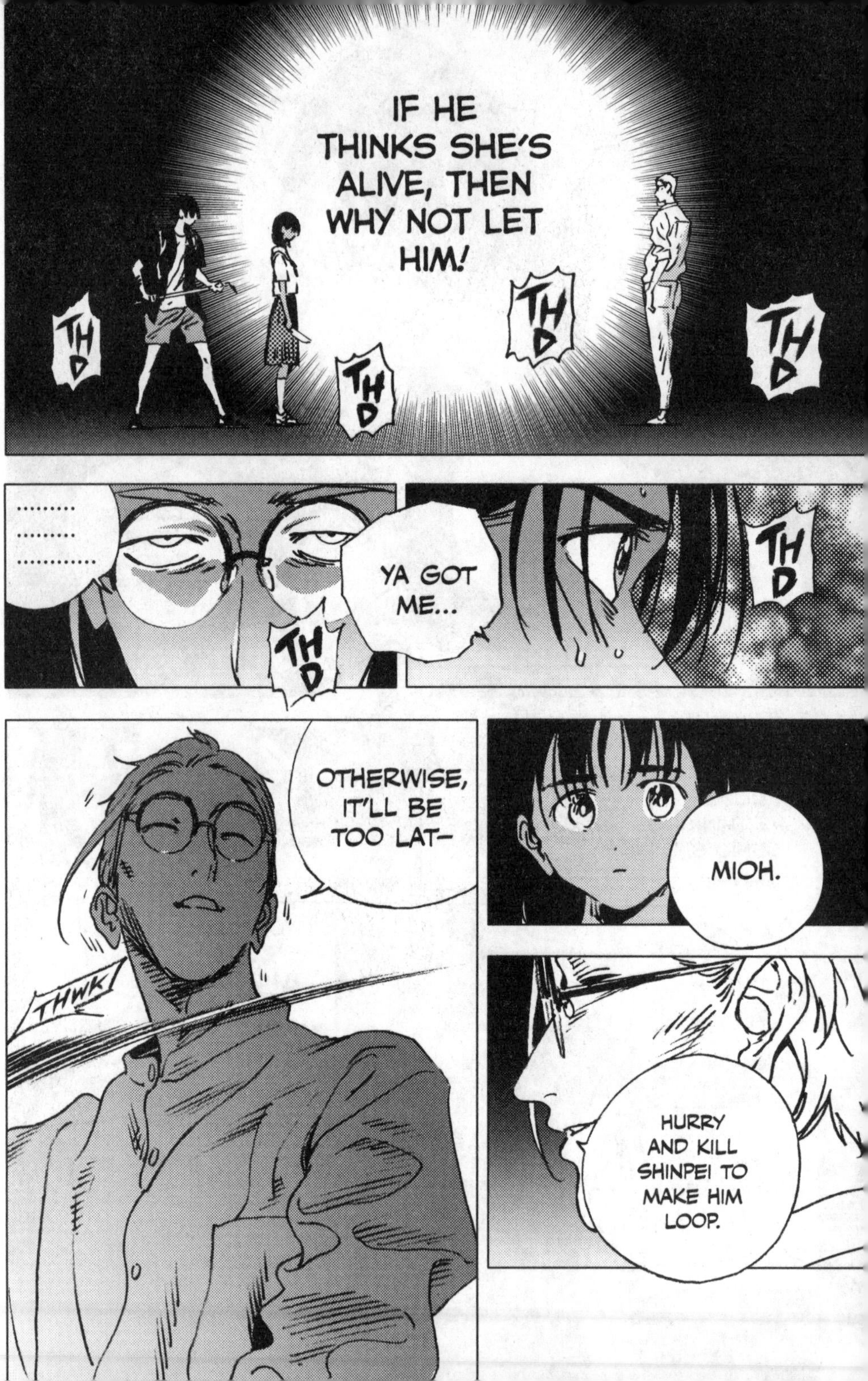
IF HE THINKS SHE'S ALIVE, THEN WHY NOT LET HIM!
THD
THD
THD
THD
THD
YA GOT ME...
....
....
....
THD
MIOH.
HURRY AND KILL SHINPEI TO MAKE HIM LOOP.
OTHERWISE, IT'LL BE TOO LAT—
THWK

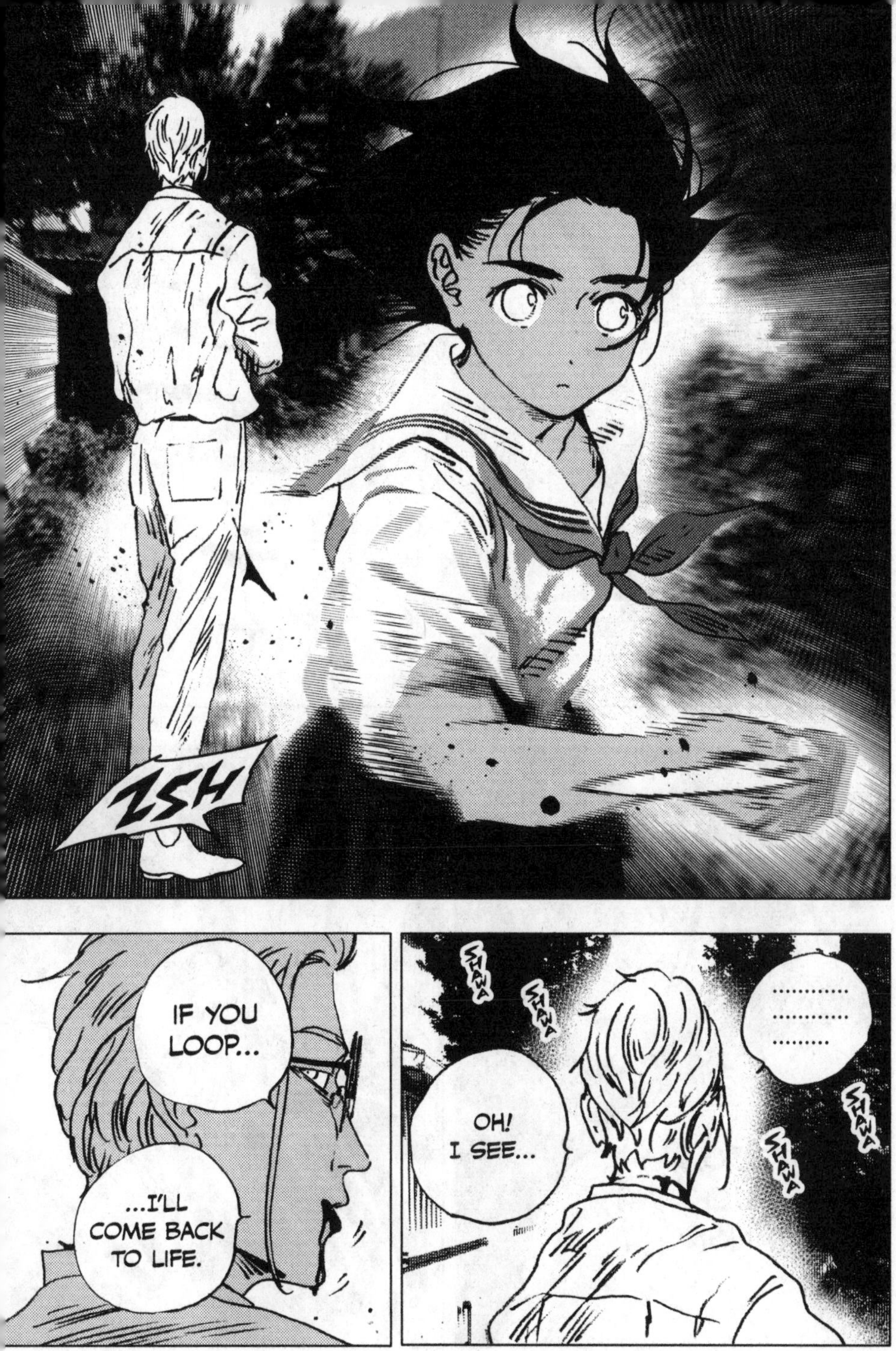
ZSH
....
....
....
SHAWA
SHAWA
SHAWA
SHAWA
OH! I SEE...
IF YOU LOOP...
...I'LL COME BACK TO LIFE.

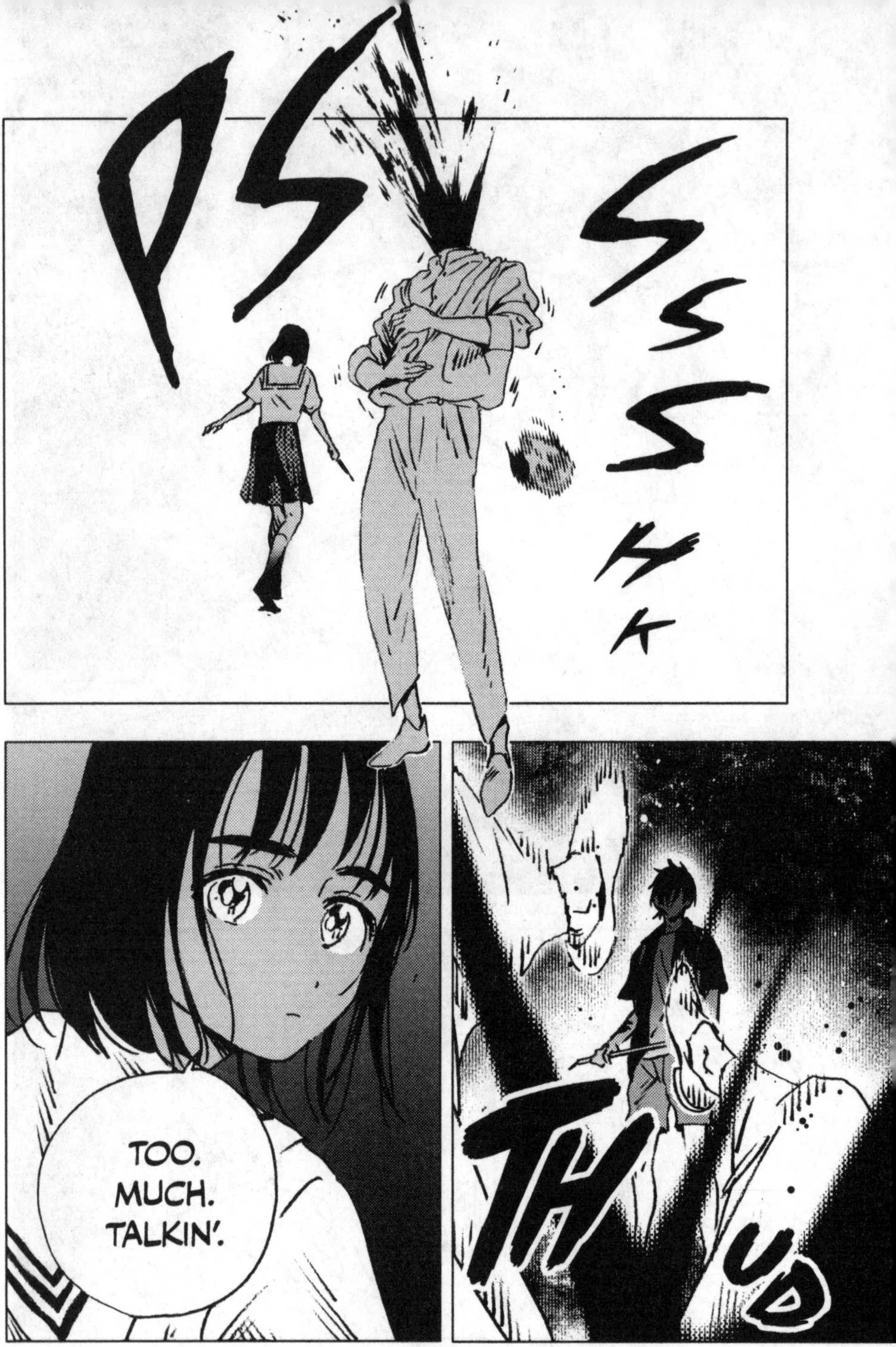
PSSSSHK
THUD
TOO. MUCH. TALKIN'.

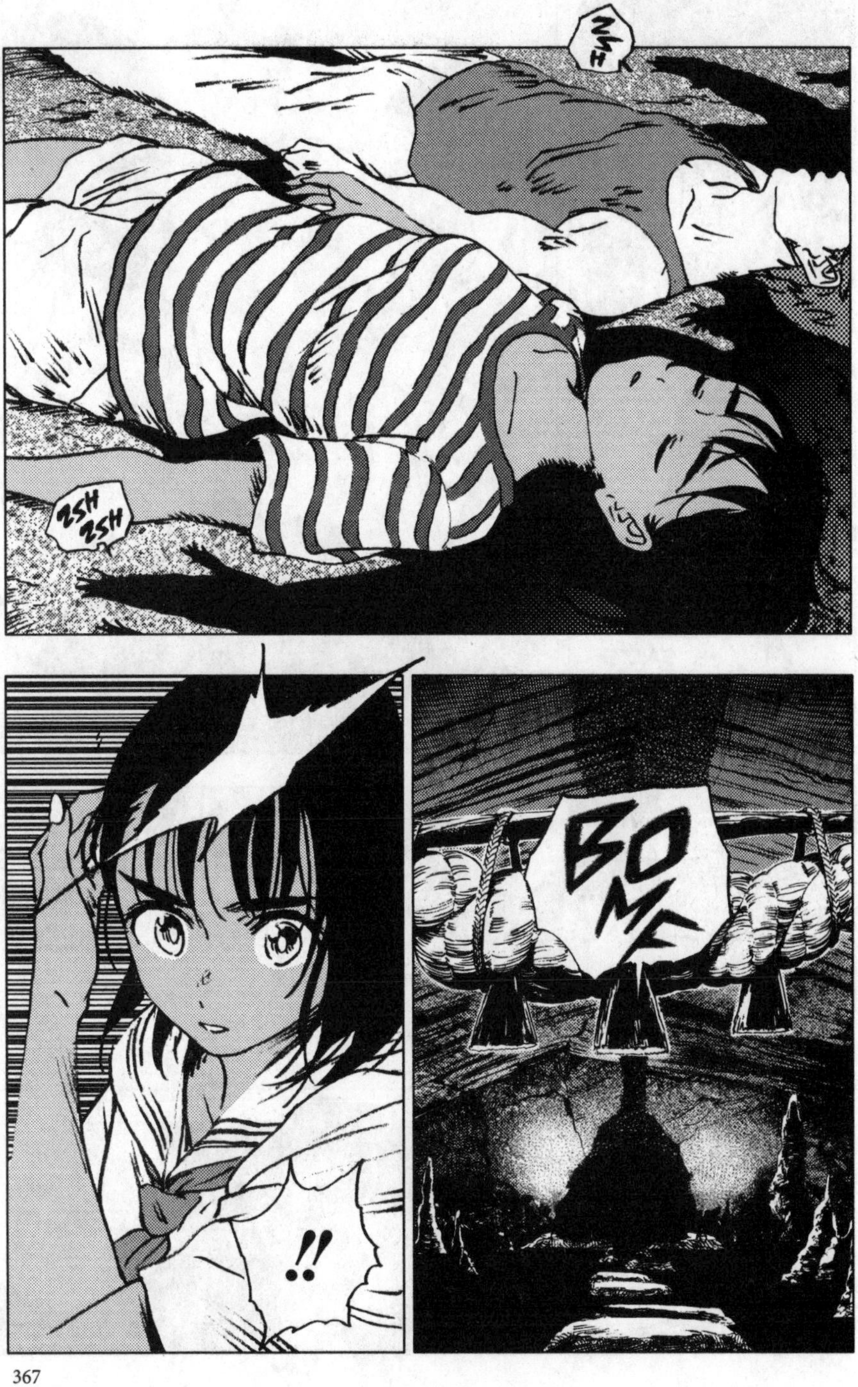
ZSH
ZSH ZSH
BOMF
!!

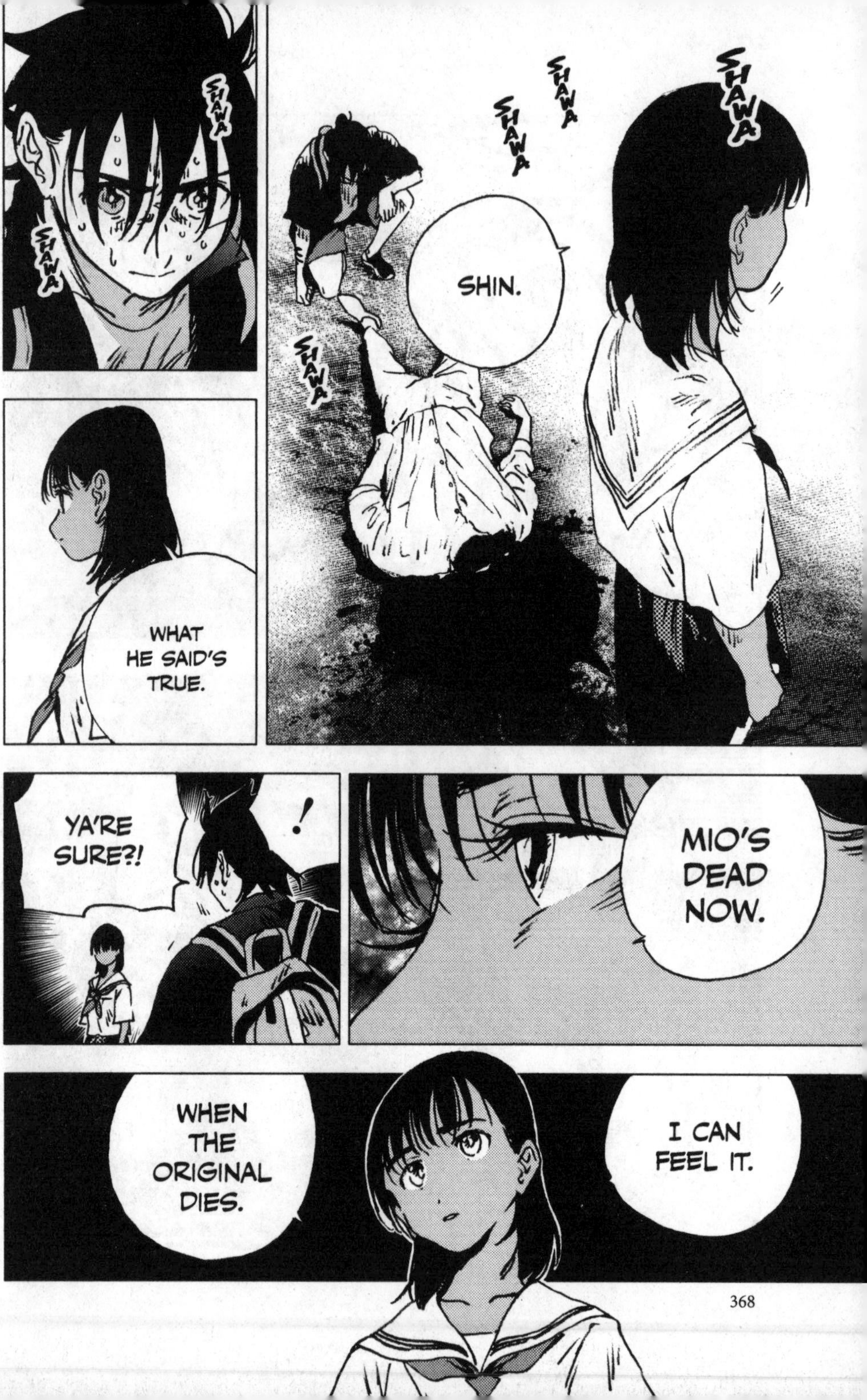
SHAWA
SHAWA
SHAWA
SHIN.
SHAWA
SHAWA
SHAWA
WHAT HE SAID'S TRUE.
MIO'S DEAD NOW.
!
YA'RE SURE?!
I CAN FEEL IT.
WHEN THE ORIGINAL DIES.

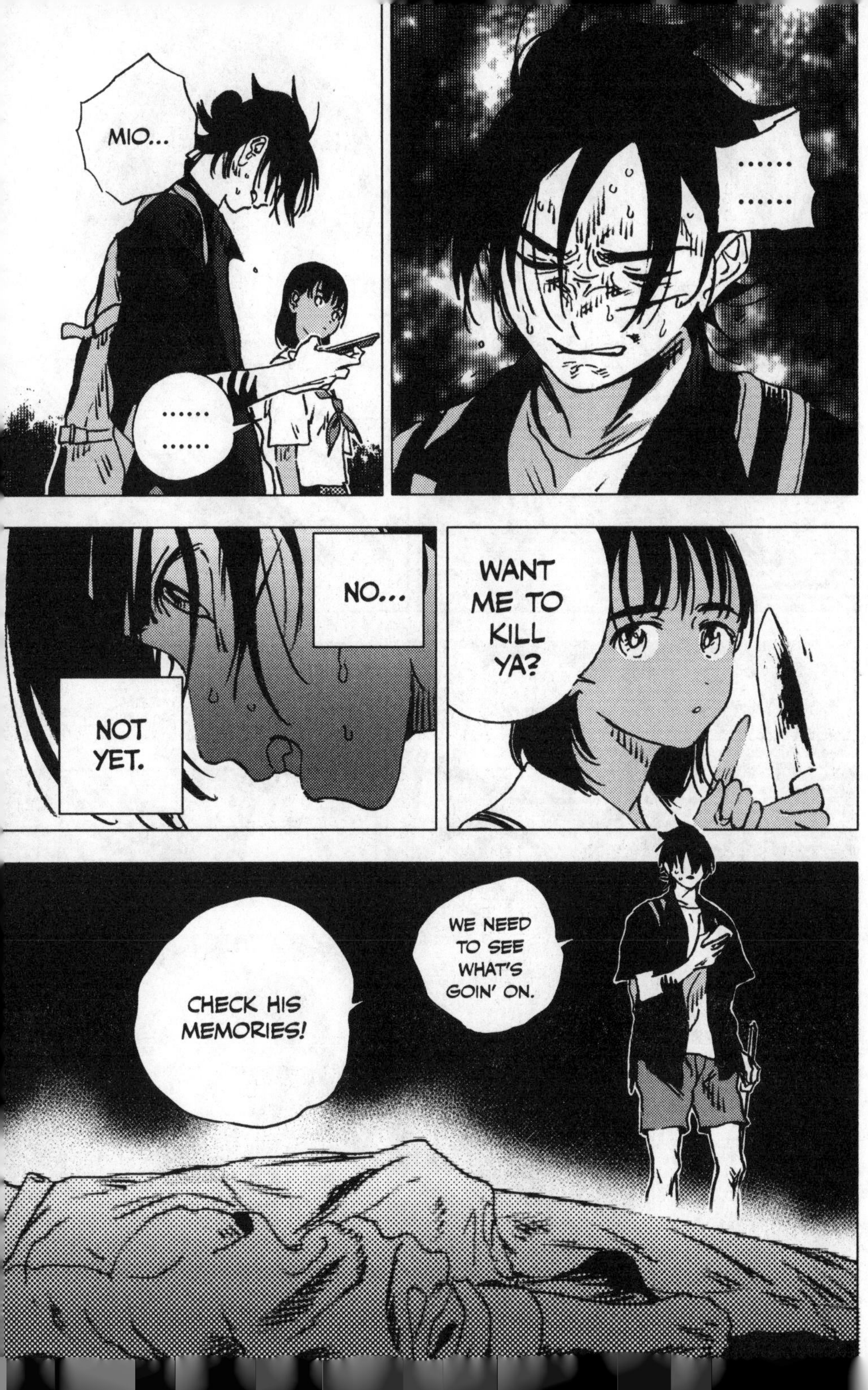
....
MIO...
....
WANT ME TO KILL YA?
NO...
NOT YET.
WE NEED TO SEE WHAT'S GOIN' ON.
CHECK HIS MEMORIES!

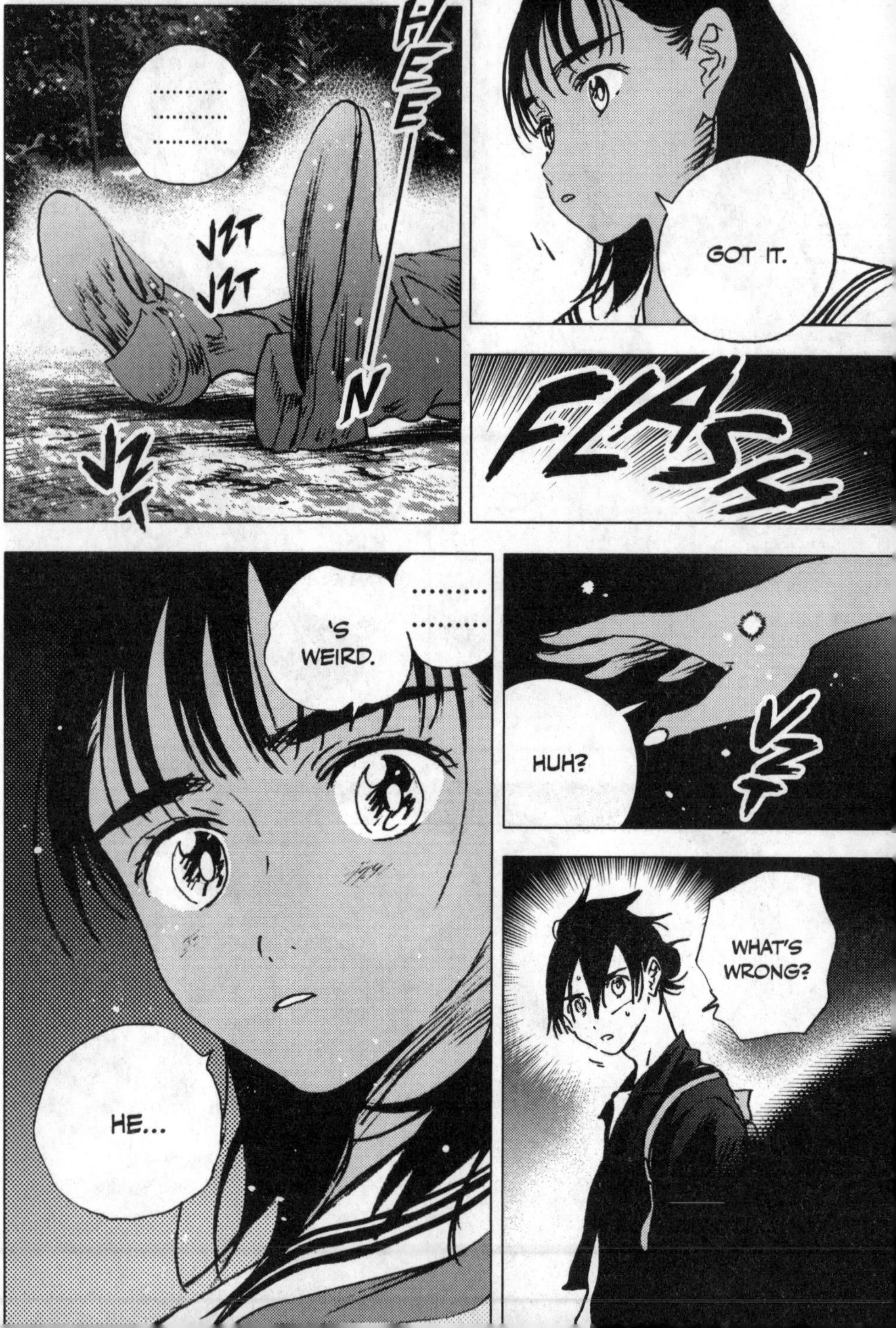
GOT IT.
FLASH
....
....
....
HEEEN
VZT
VZT
VZT
HUH?
VZT
WHAT'S WRONG?
....
....
'S WEIRD.
HE...

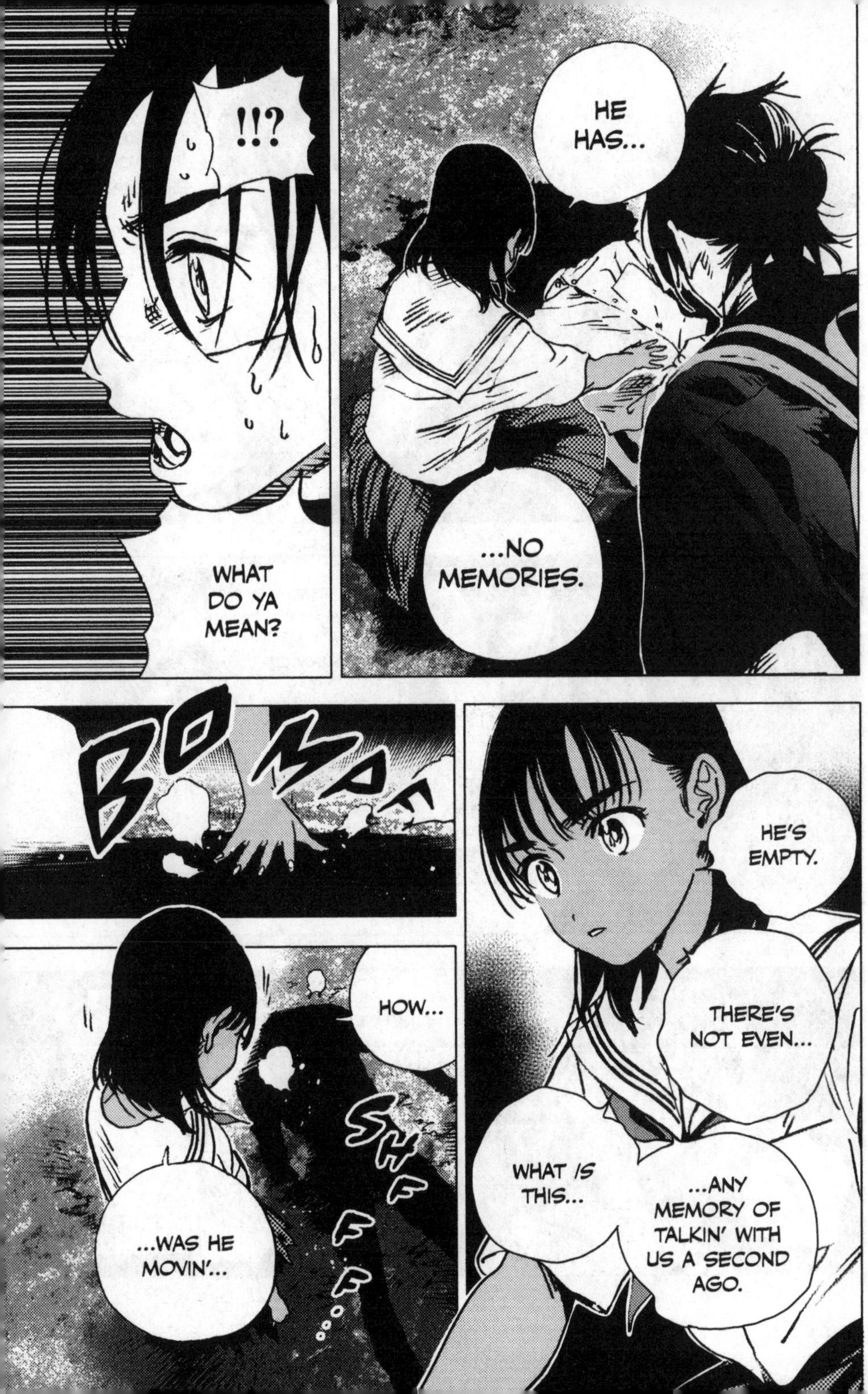
HE HAS...
...NO MEMORIES.
!!?
WHAT DO YA MEAN?
HE'S EMPTY.
THERE'S NOT EVEN...
...ANY MEMORY OF TALKIN' WITH US A SECOND AGO.
WHAT *IS* THIS...
BOMF
HOW...
...WAS HE MOVIN'...
SHFFF

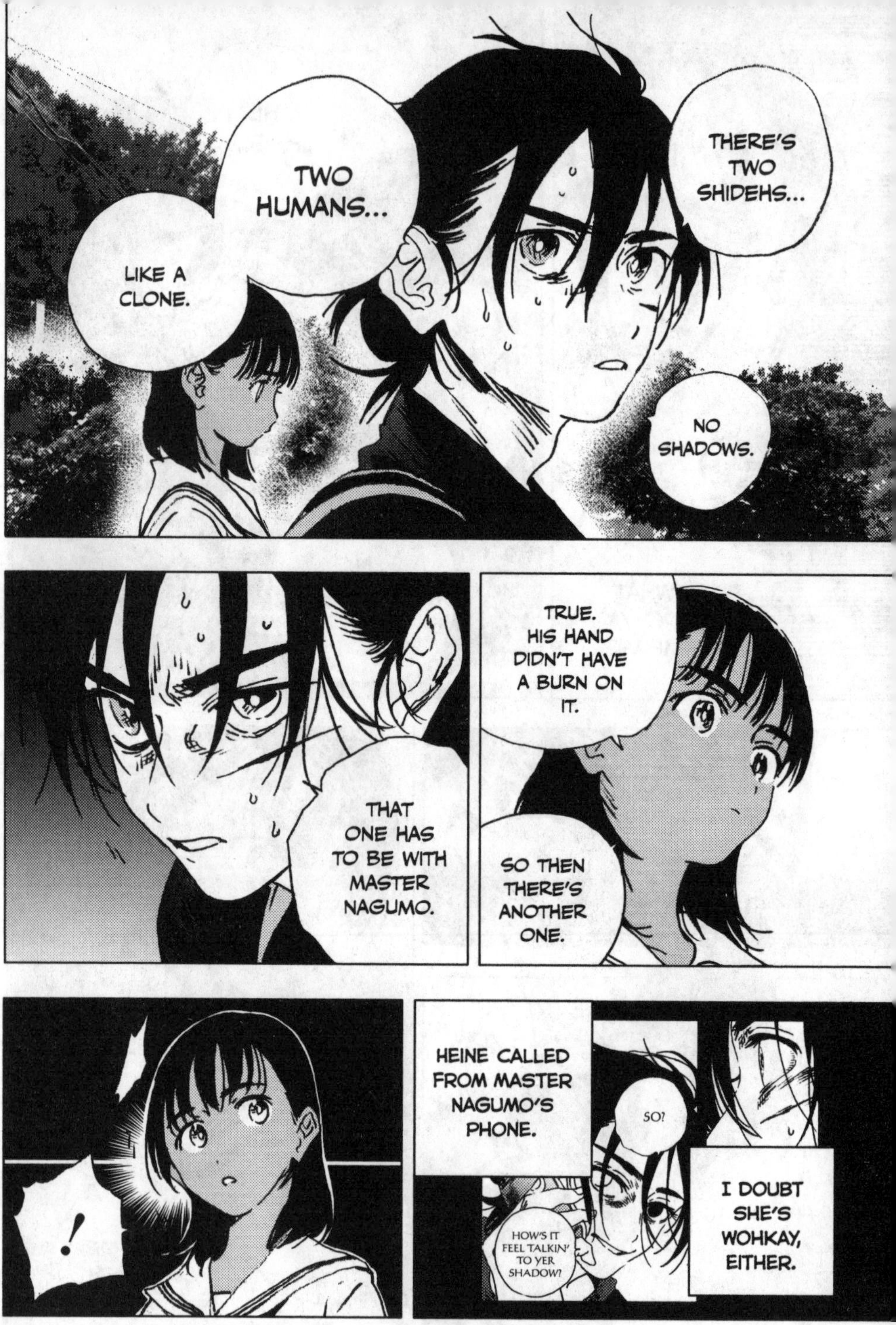
THERE'S TWO SHIDEHS...
TWO HUMANS...
LIKE A CLONE.
NO SHADOWS.
TRUE. HIS HAND DIDN'T HAVE A BURN ON IT.
SO THEN THERE'S ANOTHER ONE.
THAT ONE HAS TO BE WITH MASTER NAGUMO.
HEINE CALLED FROM MASTER NAGUMO'S PHONE.
SO?
I DOUBT SHE'S WOHKAY, EITHER.
HOW'S IT FEEL TALKIN' TO YER SHADOW?
!

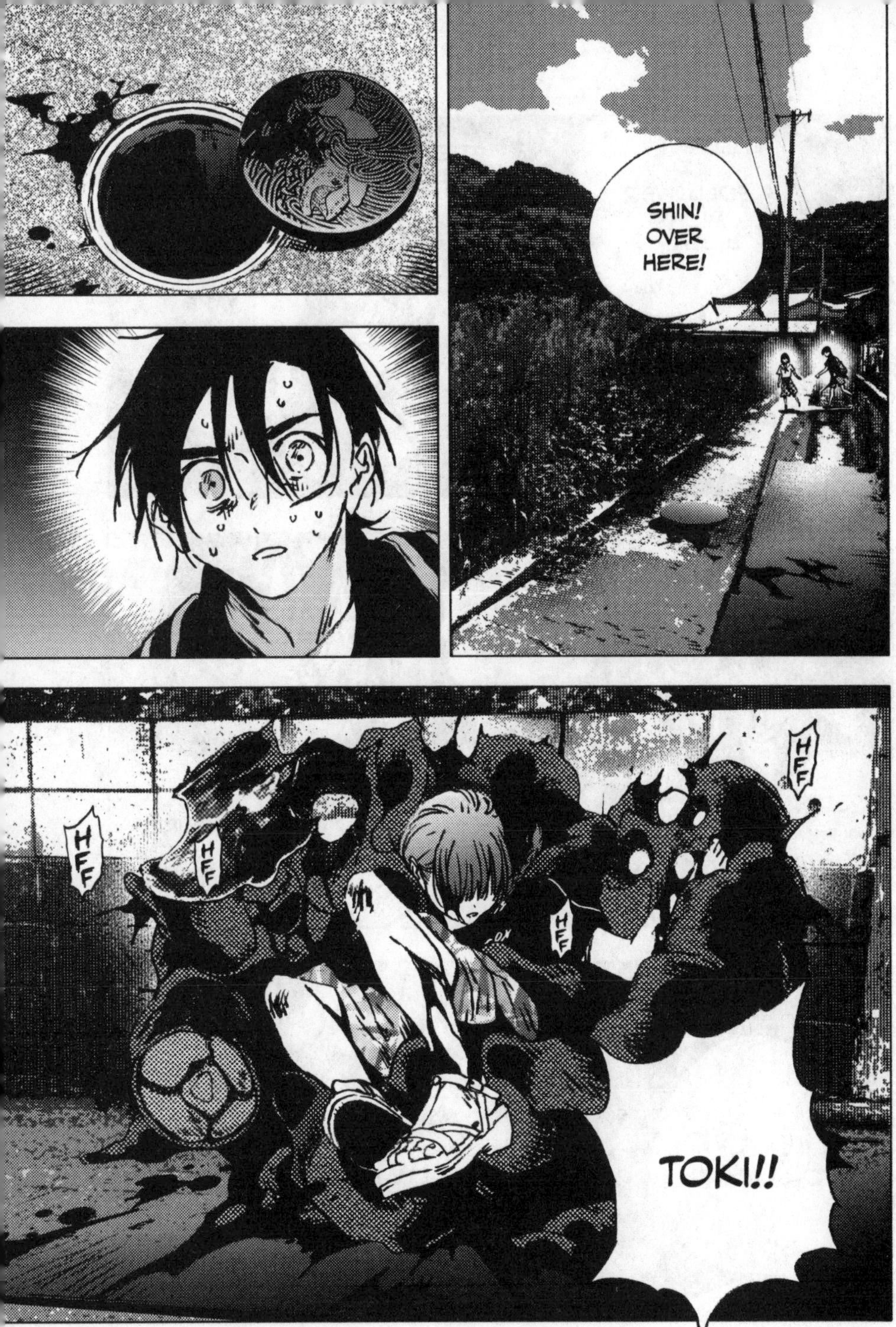
SHIN! OVER HERE!
HFF
HFF
HFF
HFF
TOKI!!

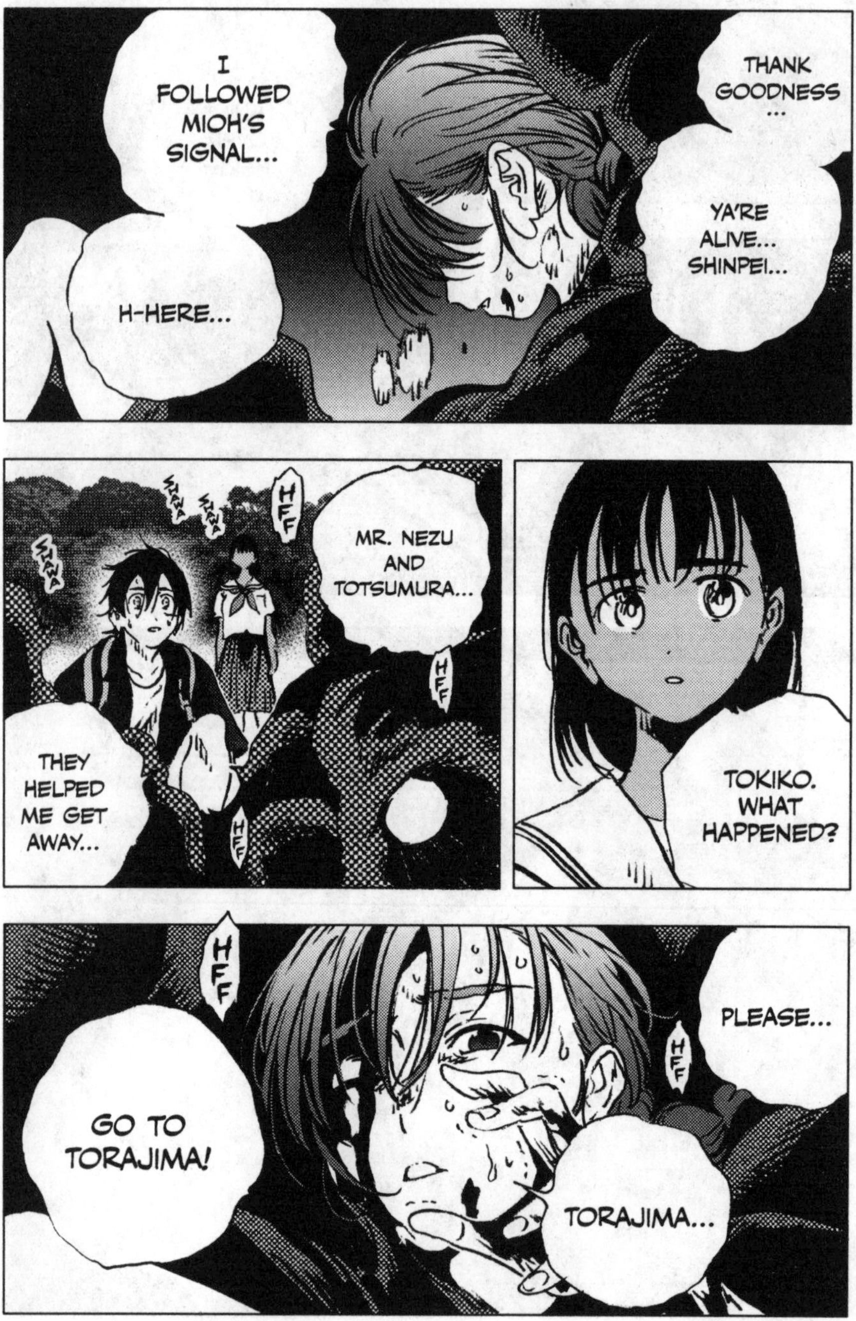
THANK GOODNESS...
YA'RE ALIVE... SHINPEI...
I FOLLOWED MIOH'S SIGNAL...
H-HERE...
TOKIKO. WHAT HAPPENED?
HFF
MR. NEZU AND TOTSUMURA...
SHAWA
SHAWA
SHAWA
HFF
THEY HELPED ME GET AWAY...
HFF
PLEASE...
HFF
HFF
TORAJIMA...
GO TO TORAJIMA!

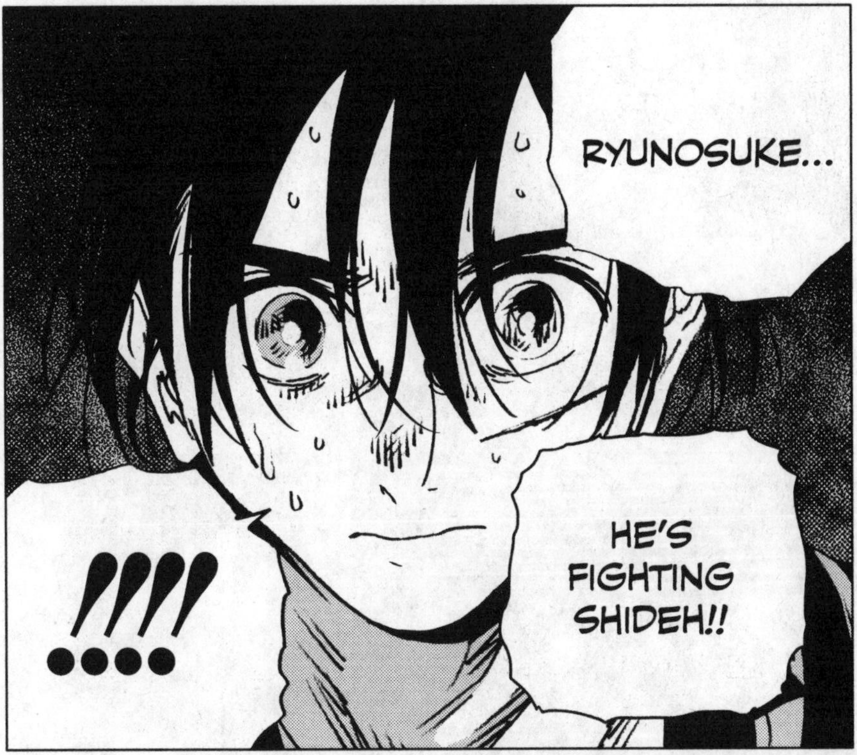
RYUNOSUKE...
HE'S FIGHTING SHIDEH!!
!!!!
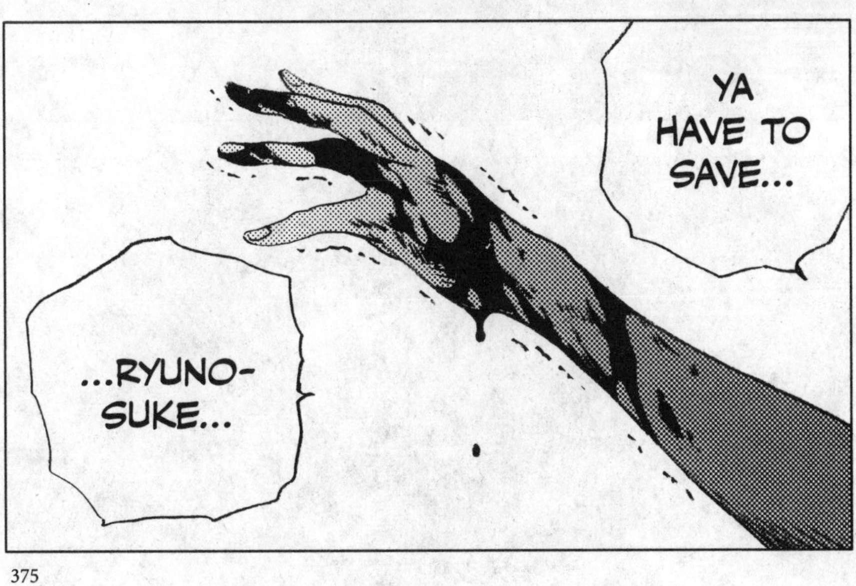
YA HAVE TO SAVE...
...RYUNO-SUKE...

Summertime rendering

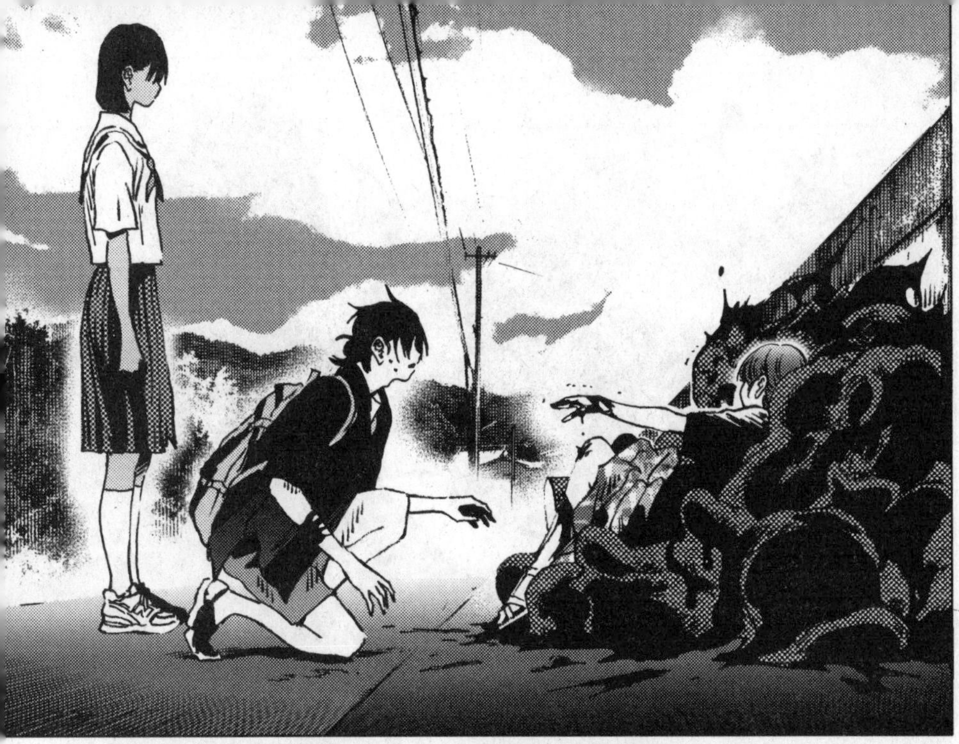

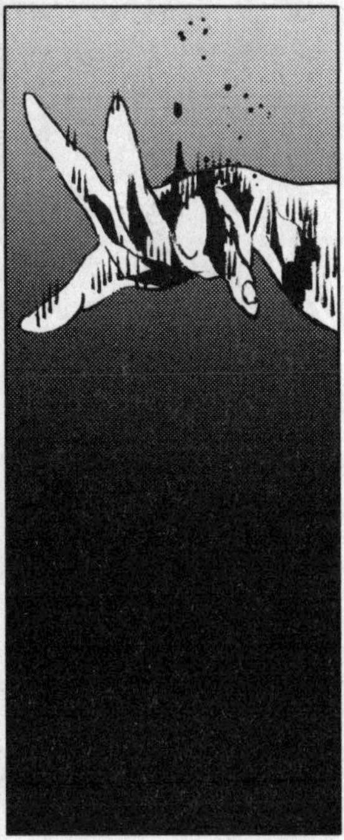

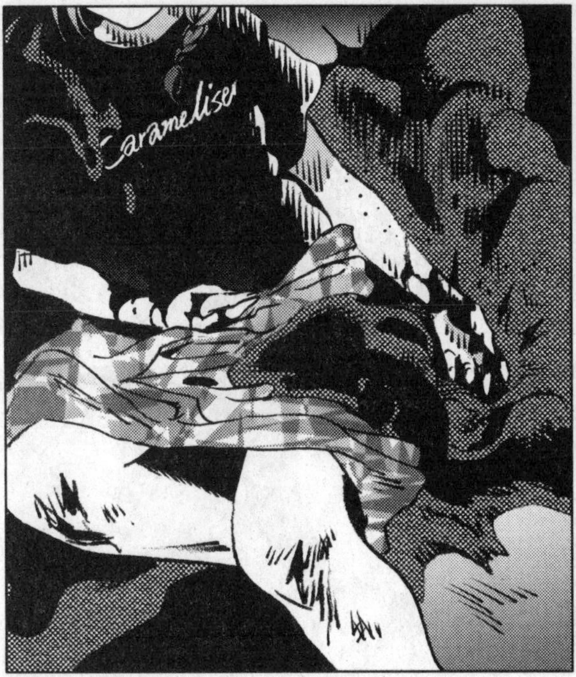
Caramelise

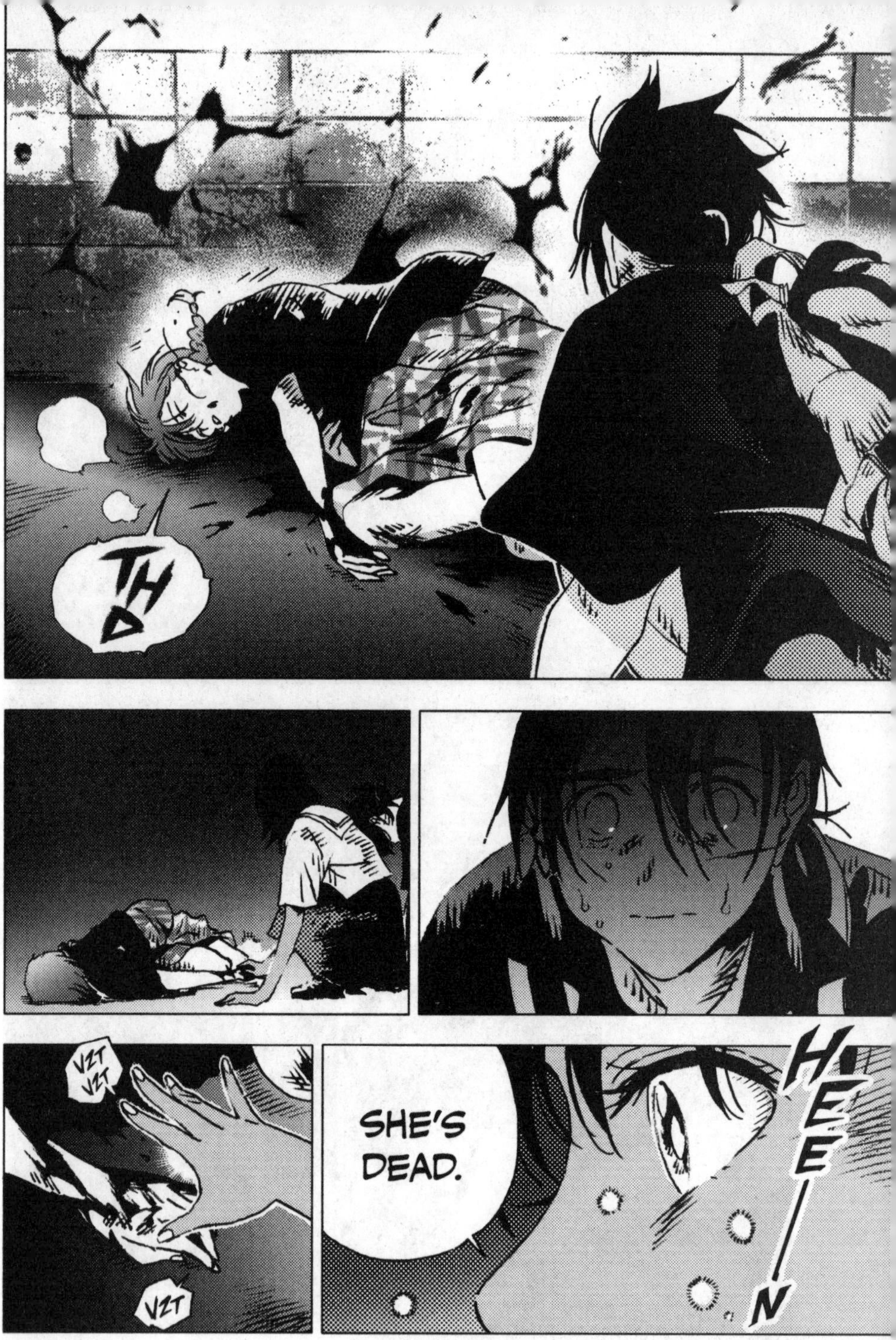
THD
SHE'S DEAD.
HEEE—N
VZT VZT
VZT

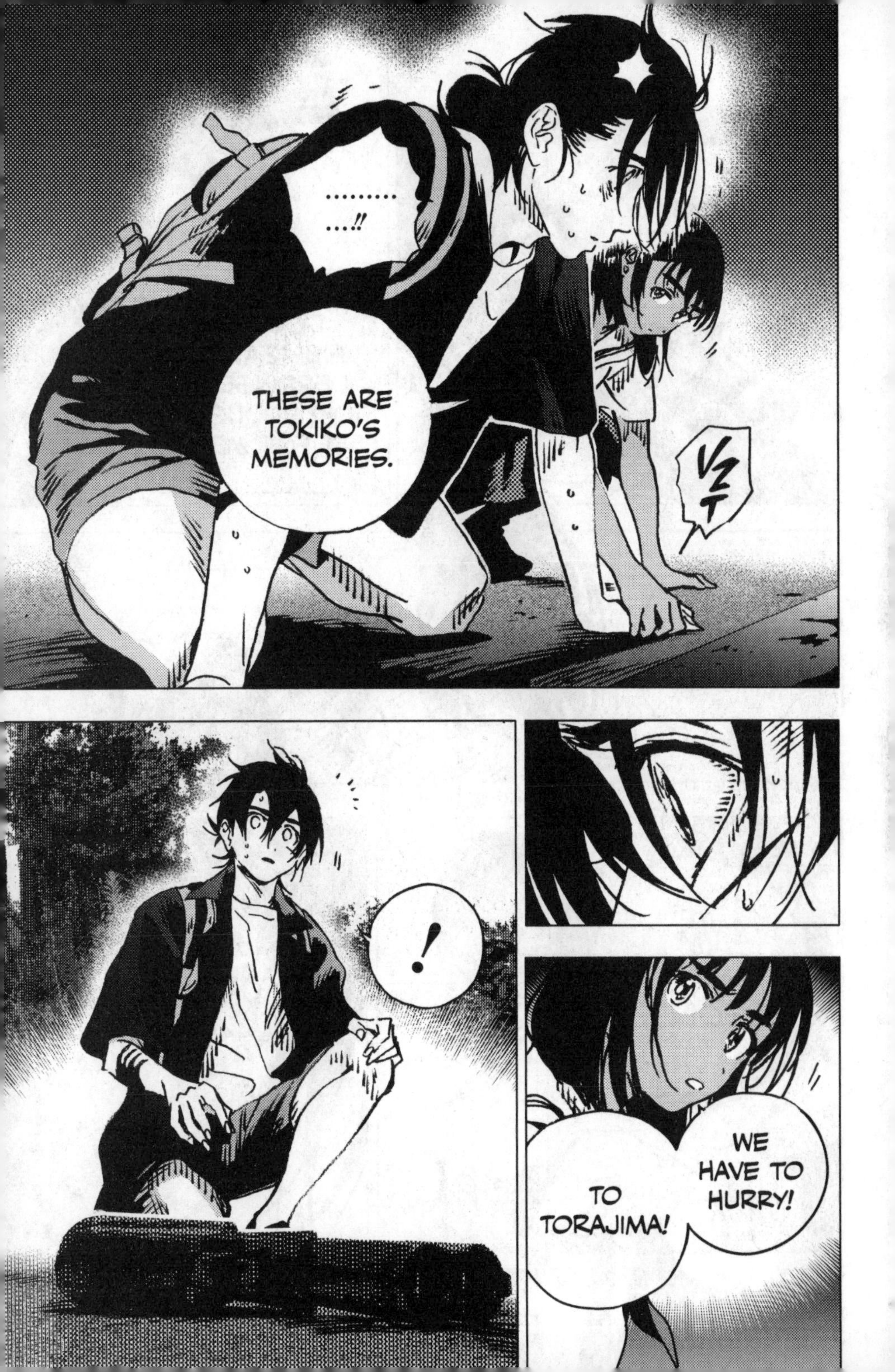
....
...!!
THESE ARE TOKIKO'S MEMORIES.
VZT
WE HAVE TO HURRY!
TO TORAJIMA!
!

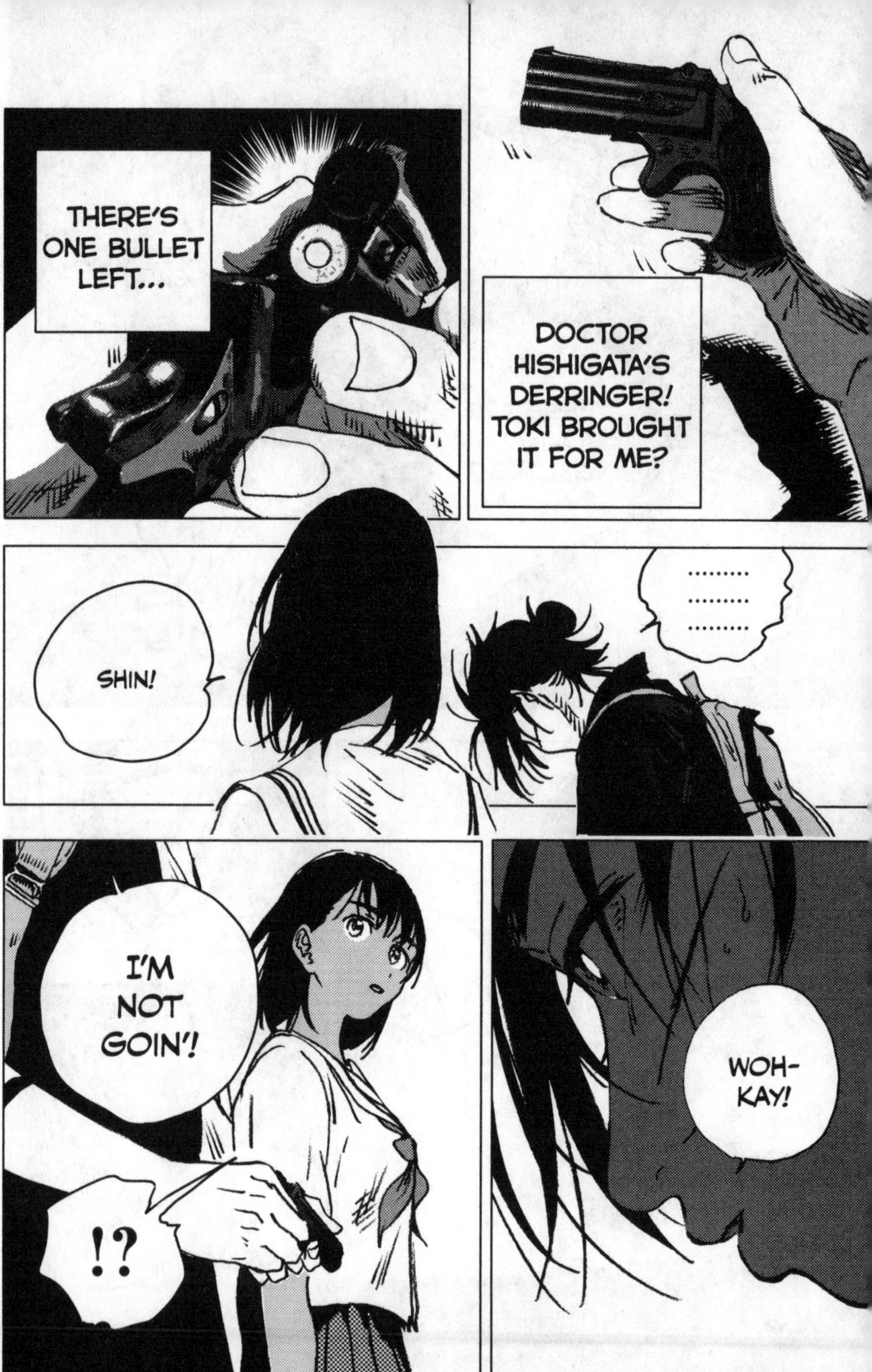
DOCTOR HISHIGATA'S DERRINGER! TOKI BROUGHT IT FOR ME?
THERE'S ONE BULLET LEFT...
....
....
....
SHIN!
WOH-KAY!
I'M NOT GOIN'!
!?

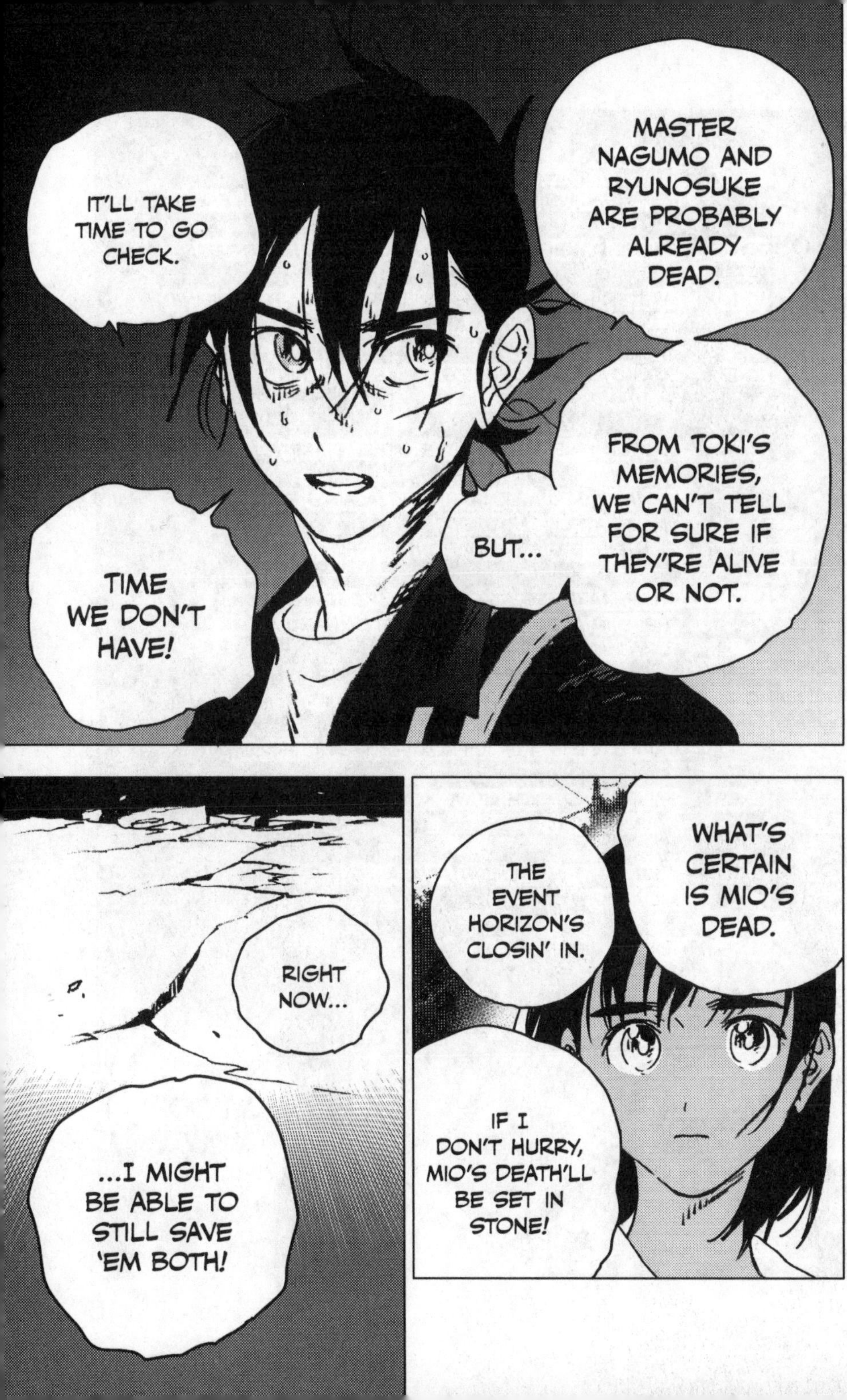
MASTER NAGUMO AND RYUNOSUKE ARE PROBABLY ALREADY DEAD.
FROM TOKI'S MEMORIES, WE CAN'T TELL FOR SURE IF THEY'RE ALIVE OR NOT.
BUT...
IT'LL TAKE TIME TO GO CHECK.
TIME WE DON'T HAVE!
WHAT'S CERTAIN IS MIO'S DEAD.
THE EVENT HORIZON'S CLOSIN' IN.
IF I DON'T HURRY, MIO'S DEATH'LL BE SET IN STONE!
RIGHT NOW...
...I MIGHT BE ABLE TO STILL SAVE 'EM BOTH!

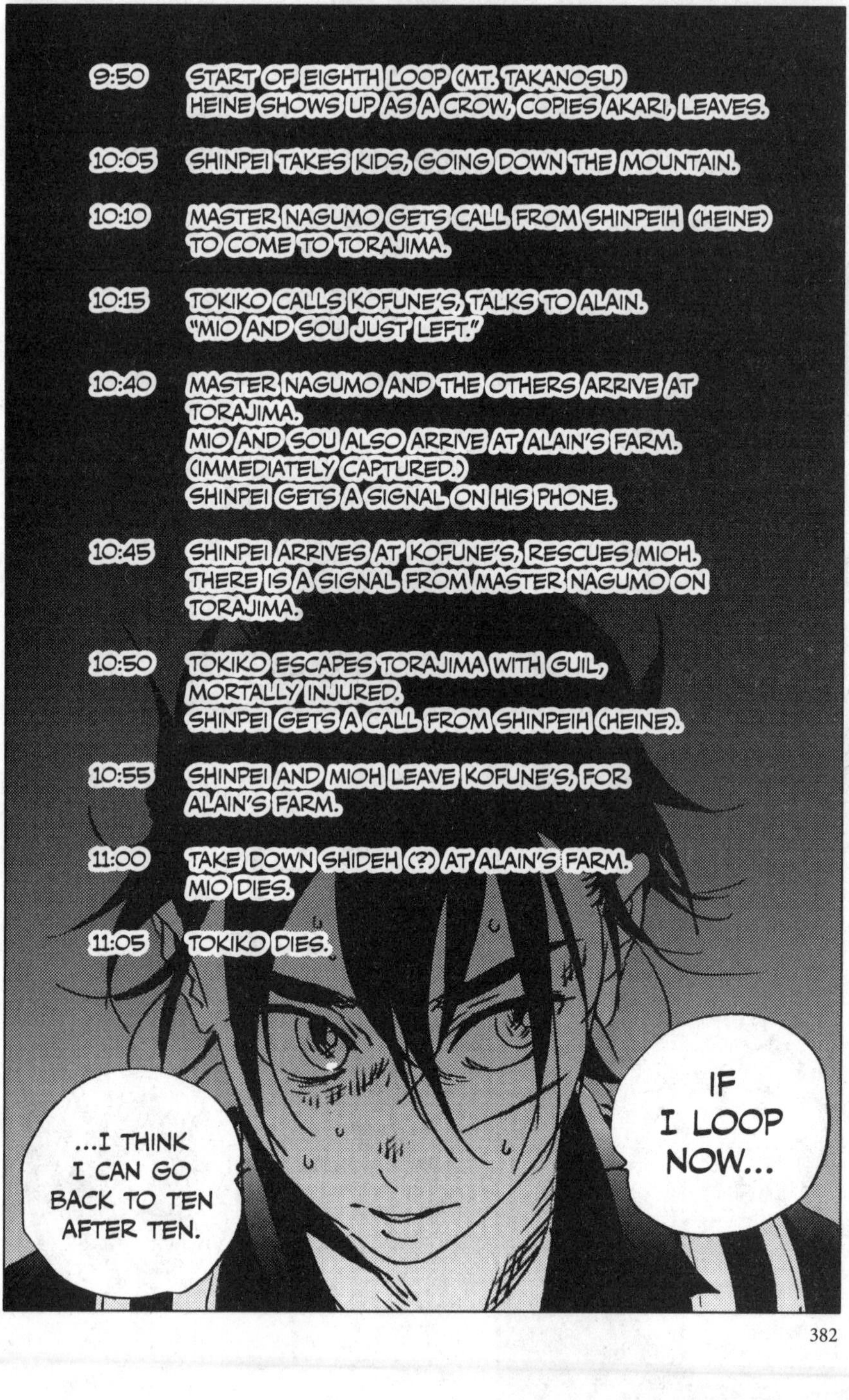
9:50 START OF EIGHTH LOOP (MT. TAKANOSU)
HEINE SHOWS UP AS A CROW, COPIES AKARI, LEAVES.
10:05 SHINPEI TAKES KIDS, GOING DOWN THE MOUNTAIN.
10:10 MASTER NAGUMO GETS CALL FROM SHINPEIH (HEINE) TO COME TO TORAJIMA.
10:15 TOKIKO CALLS KOFUNE'S, TALKS TO ALAIN.
"MIO AND SOU JUST LEFT."
10:40 MASTER NAGUMO AND THE OTHERS ARRIVE AT TORAJIMA.
MIO AND SOU ALSO ARRIVE AT ALAIN'S FARM.
(IMMEDIATELY CAPTURED.)
SHINPEI GETS A SIGNAL ON HIS PHONE.
10:45 SHINPEI ARRIVES AT KOFUNE'S, RESCUES MIOH.
THERE IS A SIGNAL FROM MASTER NAGUMO ON TORAJIMA.
10:50 TOKIKO ESCAPES TORAJIMA WITH GUIL, MORTALLY INJURED.
SHINPEI GETS A CALL FROM SHINPEIH (HEINE).
10:55 SHINPEI AND MIOH LEAVE KOFUNE'S, FOR ALAIN'S FARM.
11:00 TAKE DOWN SHIDEH (?) AT ALAIN'S FARM.
MIO DIES.
11:05 TOKIKO DIES.
IF I LOOP NOW...
...I THINK I CAN GO BACK TO TEN AFTER TEN.

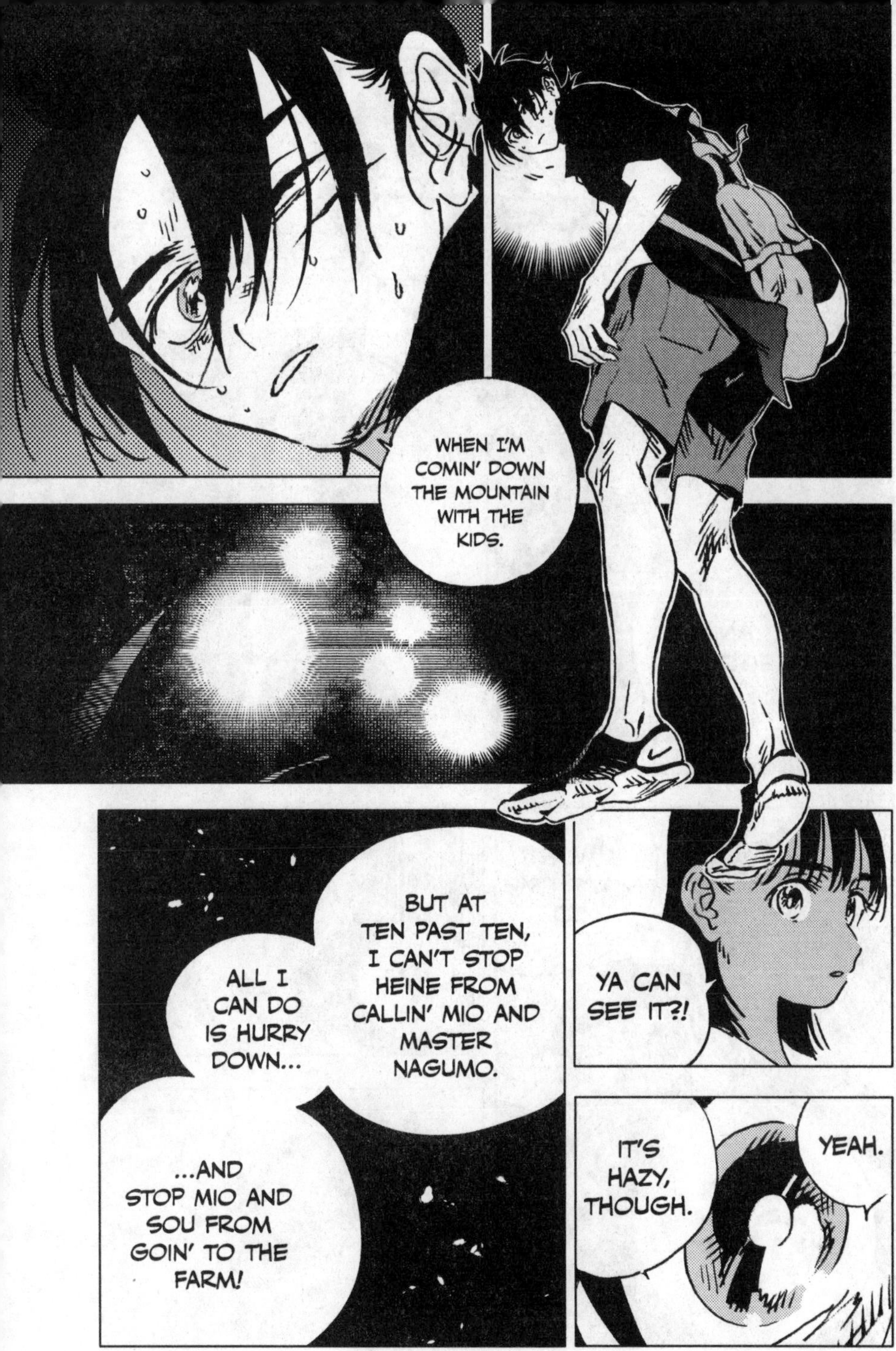
WHEN I'M COMIN' DOWN THE MOUNTAIN WITH THE KIDS.
YA CAN SEE IT?!
YEAH.
IT'S HAZY, THOUGH.
BUT AT TEN PAST TEN, I CAN'T STOP HEINE FROM CALLIN' MIO AND MASTER NAGUMO.
ALL I CAN DO IS HURRY DOWN...
...AND STOP MIO AND SOU FROM GOIN' TO THE FARM!

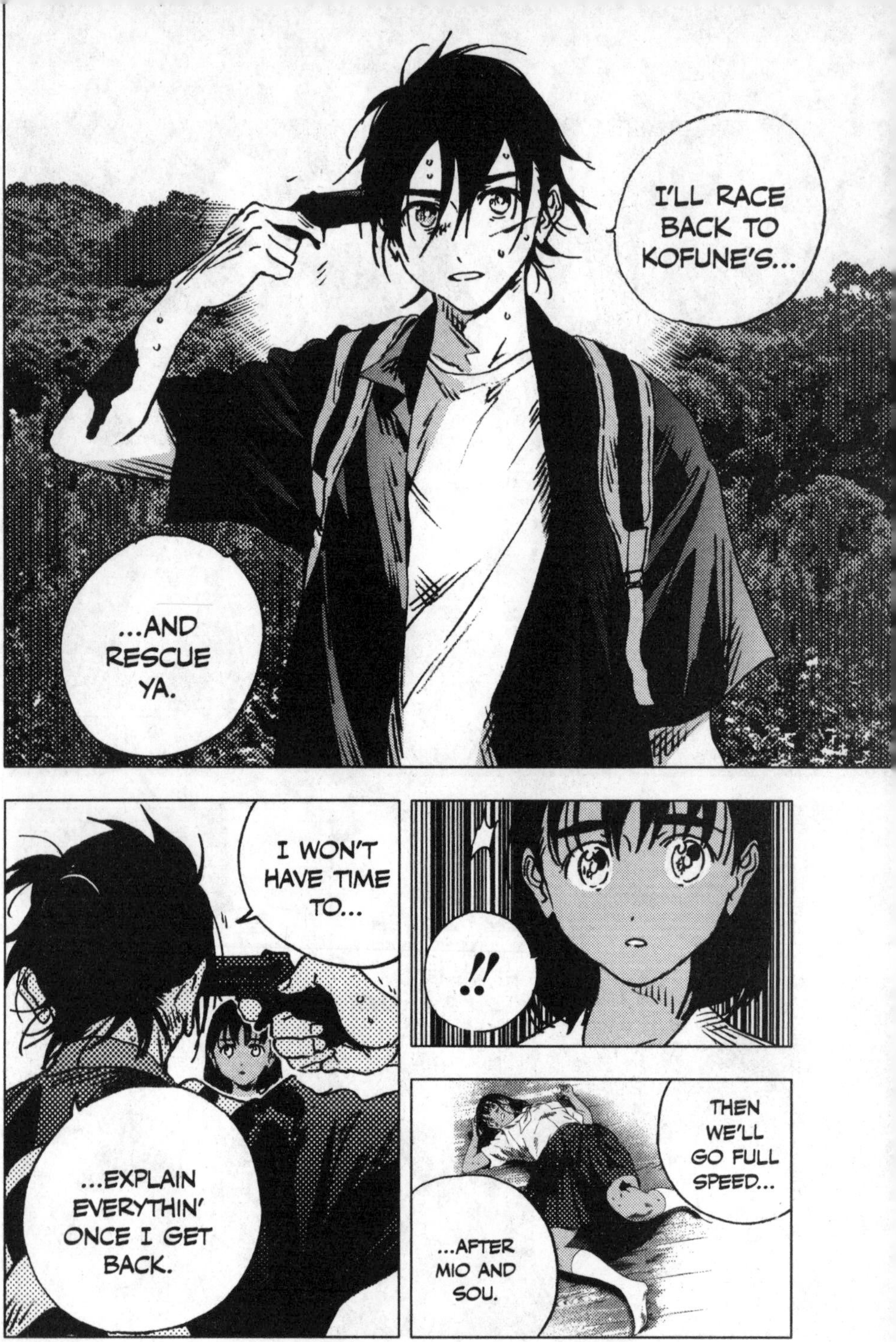
I'LL RACE BACK TO KOFUNE'S...
...AND RESCUE YA.
!!
THEN WE'LL GO FULL SPEED...
...AFTER MIO AND SOU.
I WON'T HAVE TIME TO...
...EXPLAIN EVERYTHIN' ONCE I GET BACK.

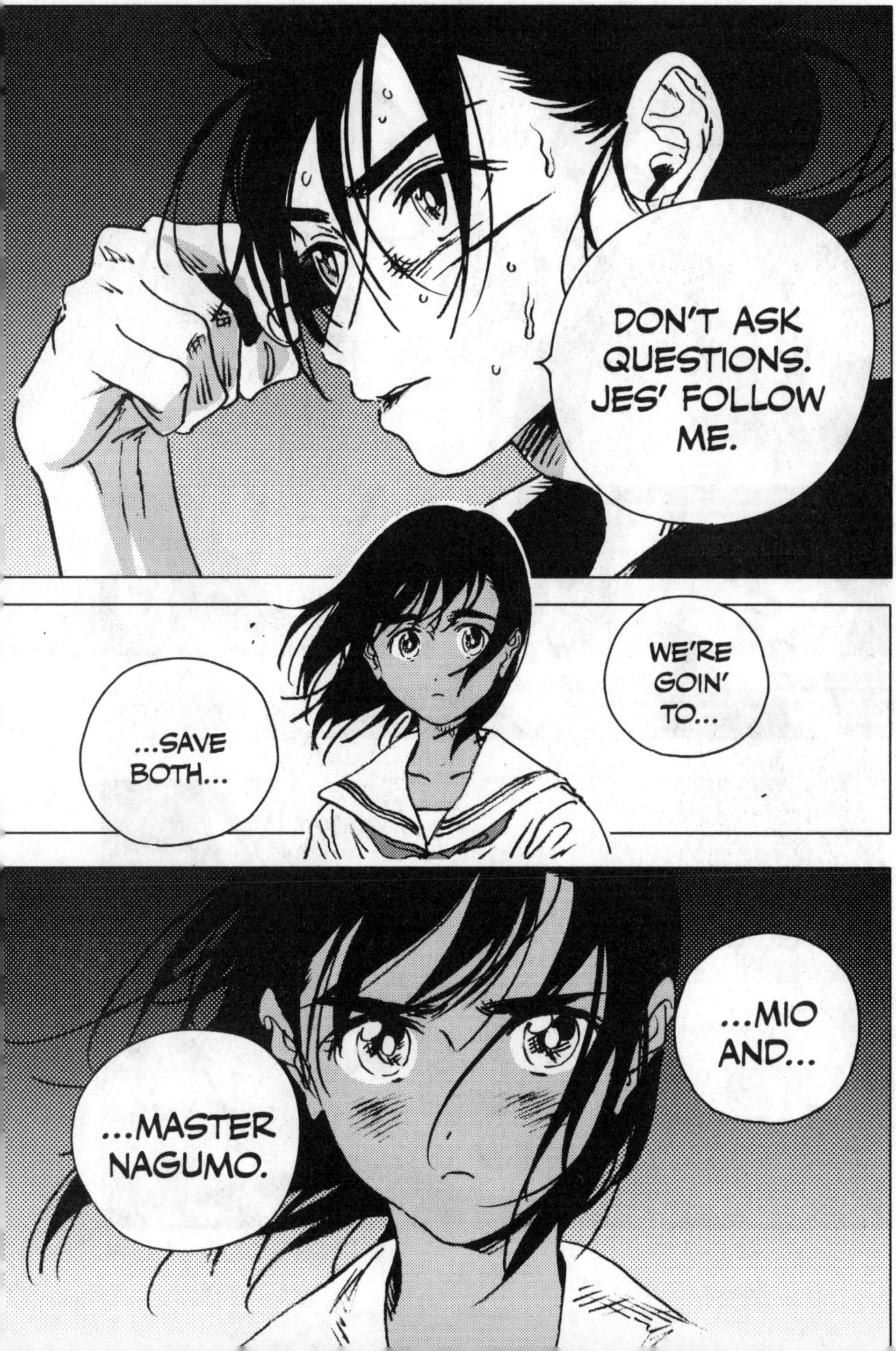
DON'T ASK QUESTIONS. JES' FOLLOW ME.
WE'RE GOIN' TO...
...SAVE BOTH...
...MIO AND...
...MASTER NAGUMO.

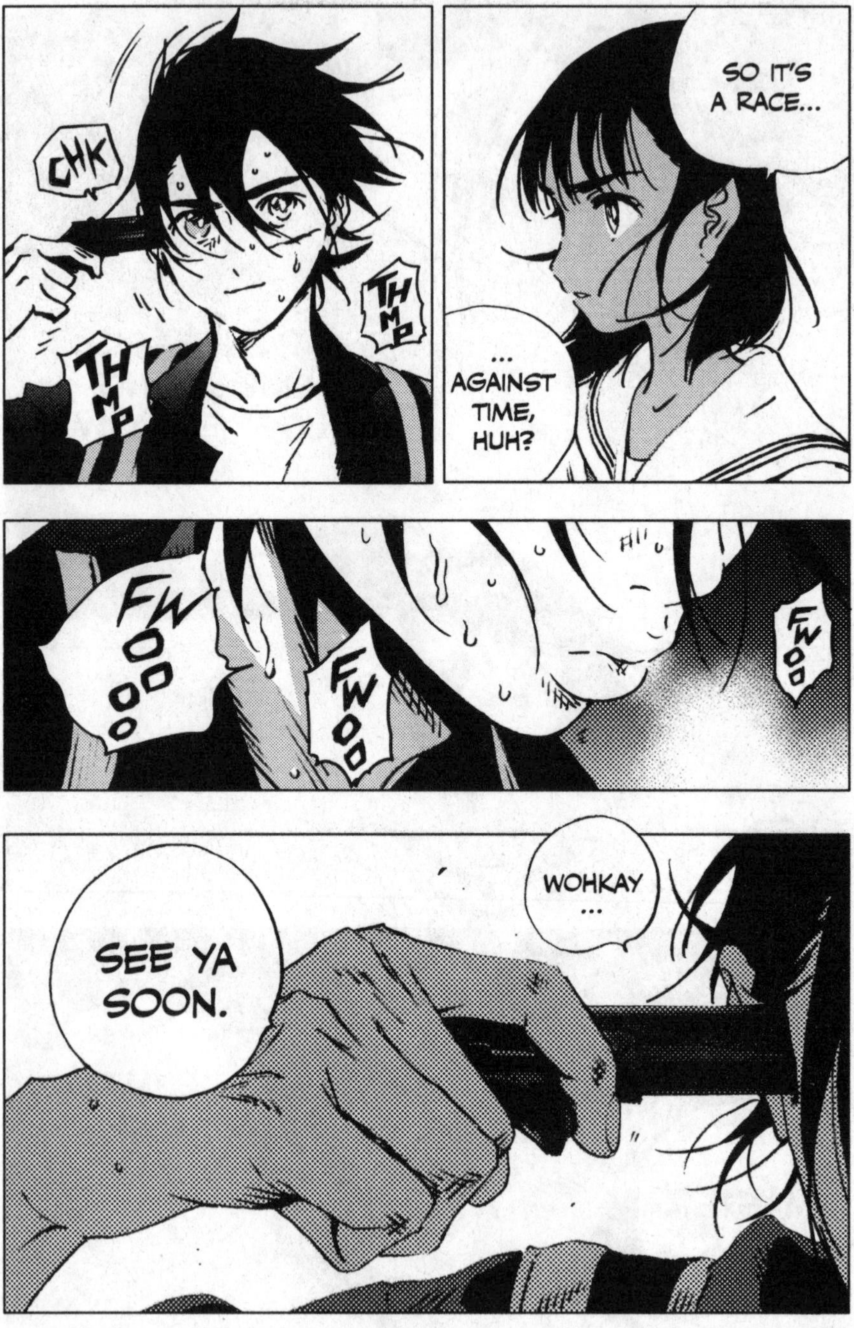
SO IT'S A RACE...
... AGAINST TIME, HUH?
CHK
THMP
THMP
FWOO
FWOO
FWOOOOO
WOHKAY ...
SEE YA SOON.

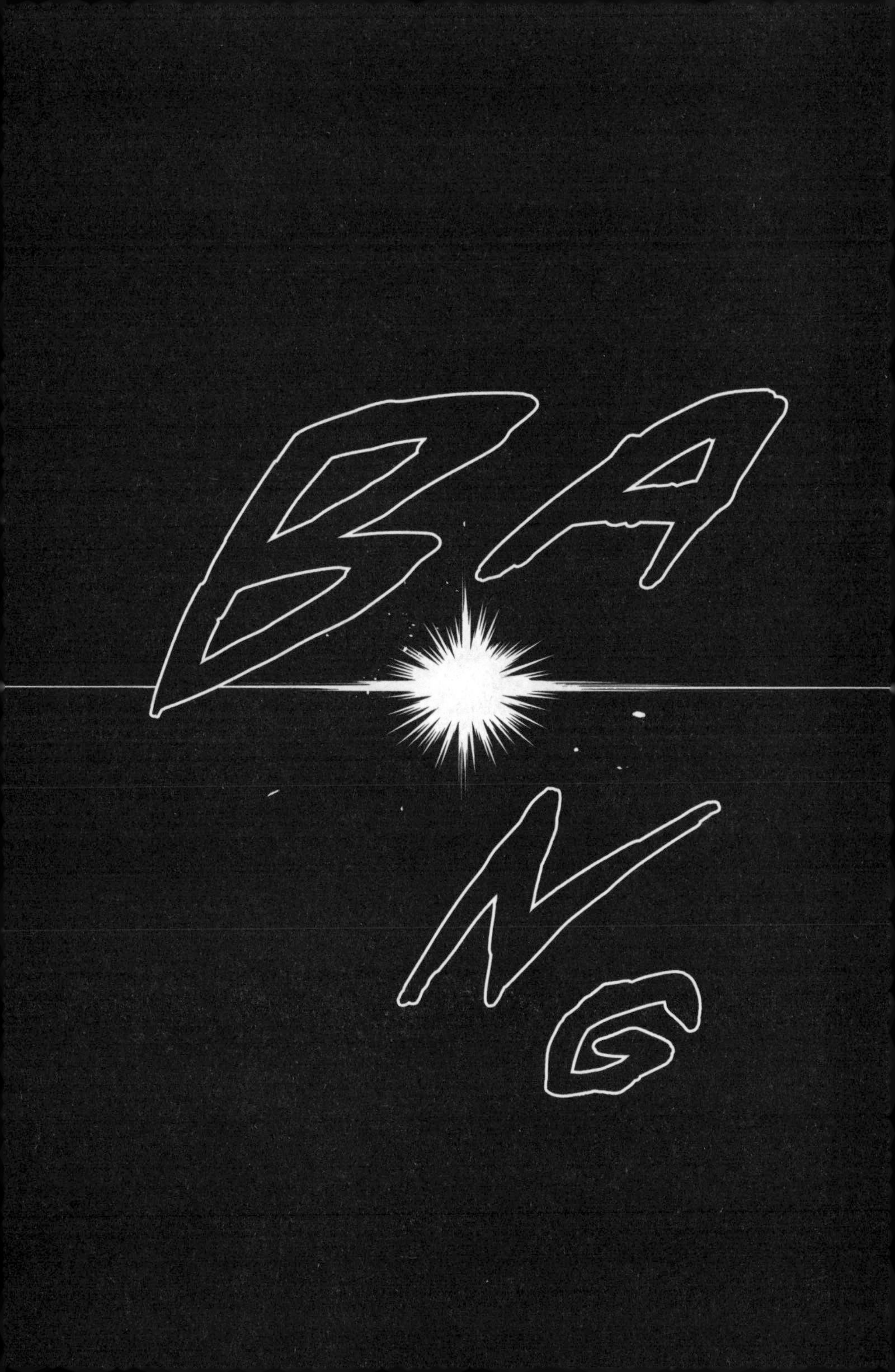
BANG

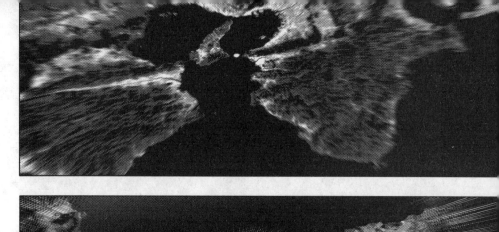

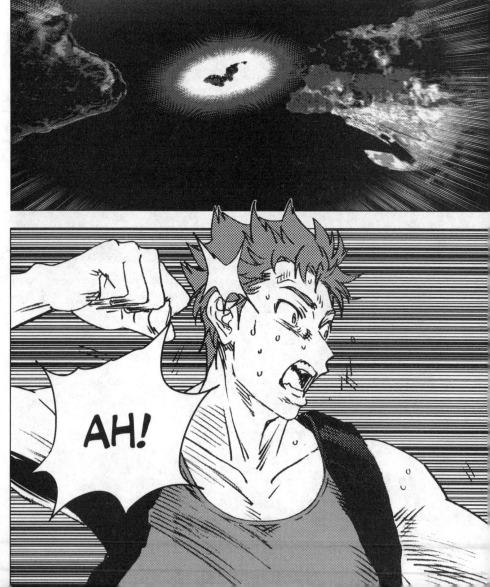

AH!

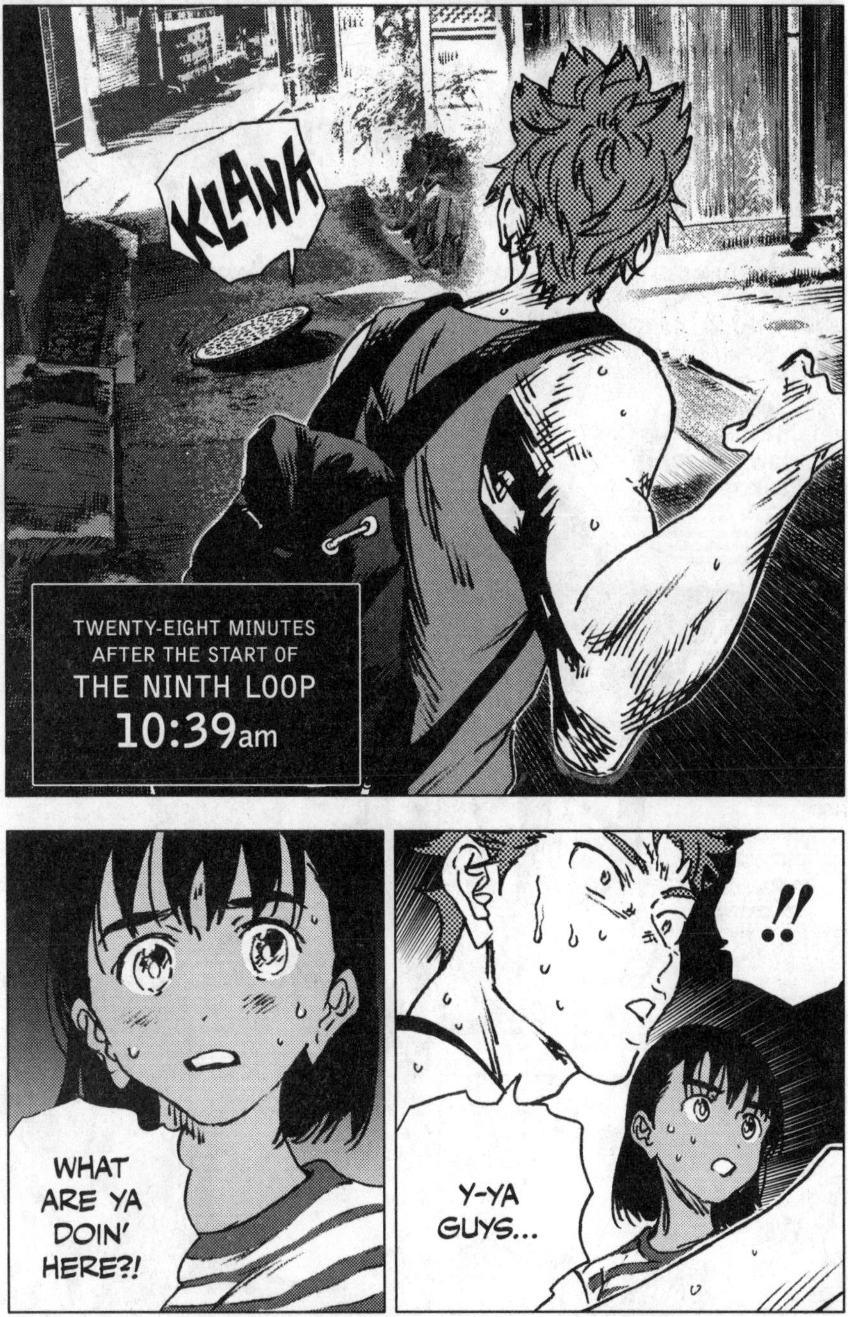
KLANK
TWENTY-EIGHT MINUTES AFTER THE START OF THE NINTH LOOP 10:39am
!!
Y-YA GUYS...
WHAT ARE YA DOIN' HERE?!

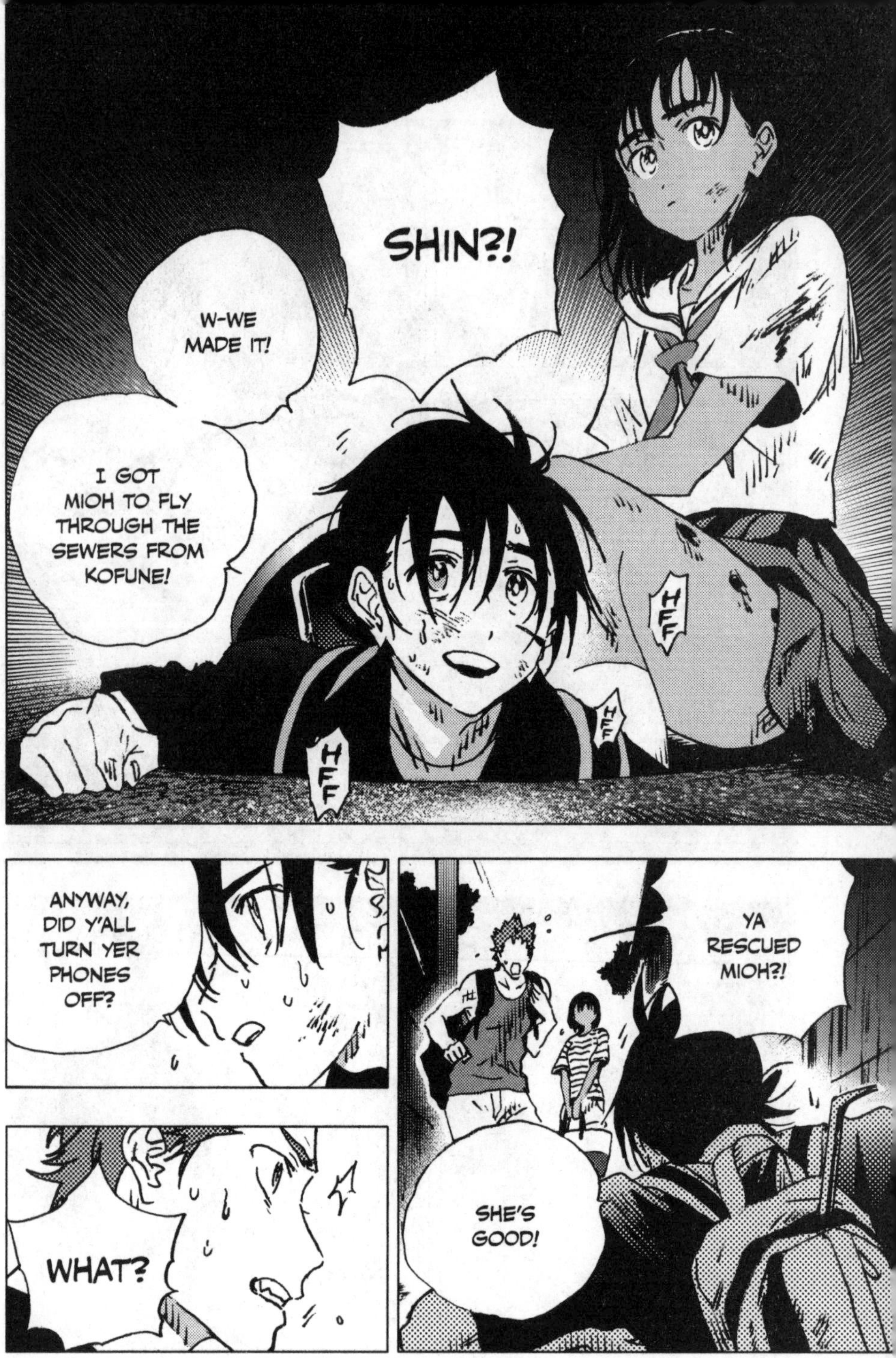
SHIN?!
W-WE MADE IT!
I GOT MIOH TO FLY THROUGH THE SEWERS FROM KOFUNE!
HFF
HFF
HFF
YA RESCUED MIOH?!
SHE'S GOOD!
ANYWAY, DID Y'ALL TURN YER PHONES OFF?
WHAT?

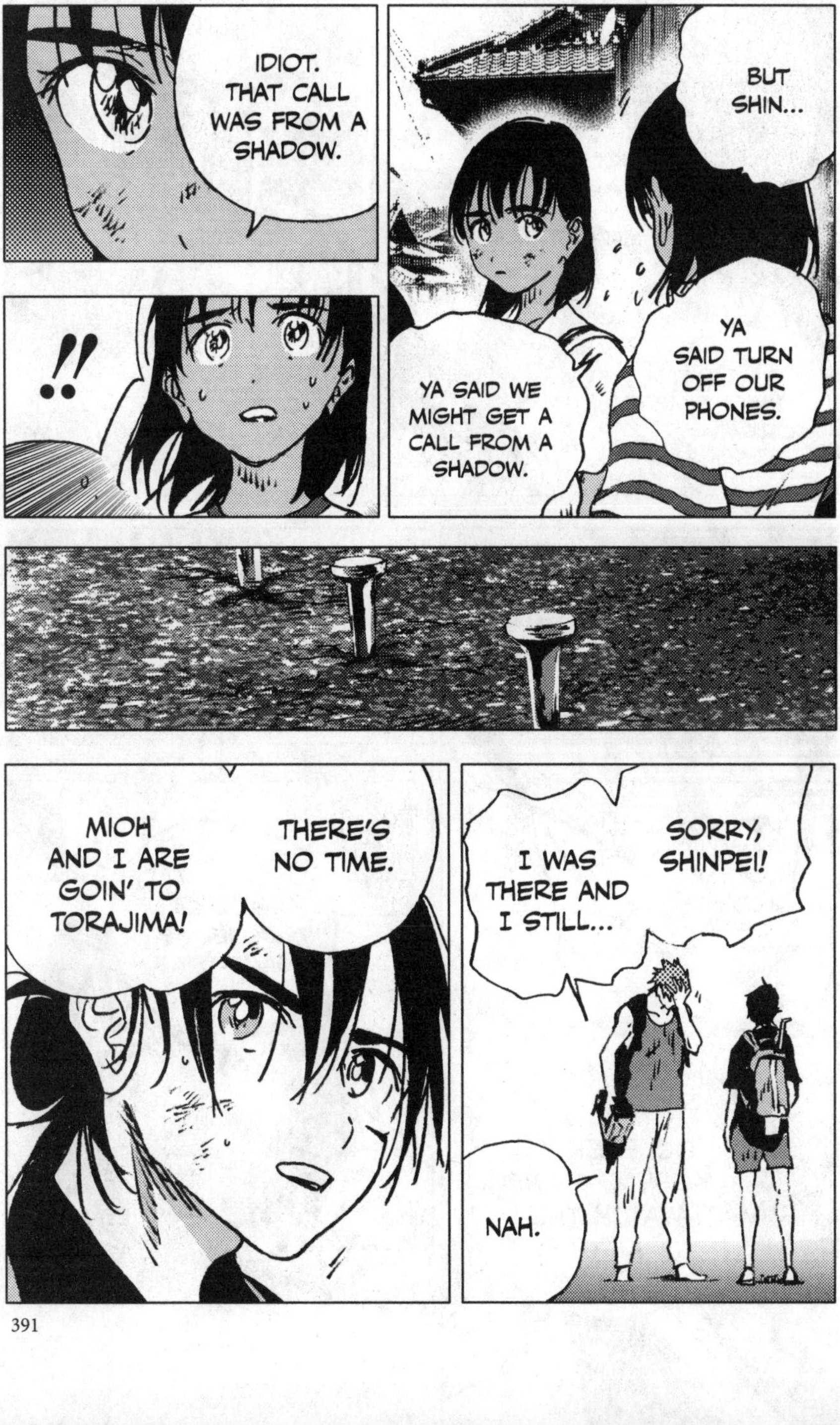
BUT SHIN...
YA SAID TURN OFF OUR PHONES.
YA SAID WE MIGHT GET A CALL FROM A SHADOW.
IDIOT. THAT CALL WAS FROM A SHADOW.
!!
SORRY, SHINPEI!
I WAS THERE AND I STILL...
NAH.
THERE'S NO TIME.
MIOH AND I ARE GOIN' TO TORAJIMA!

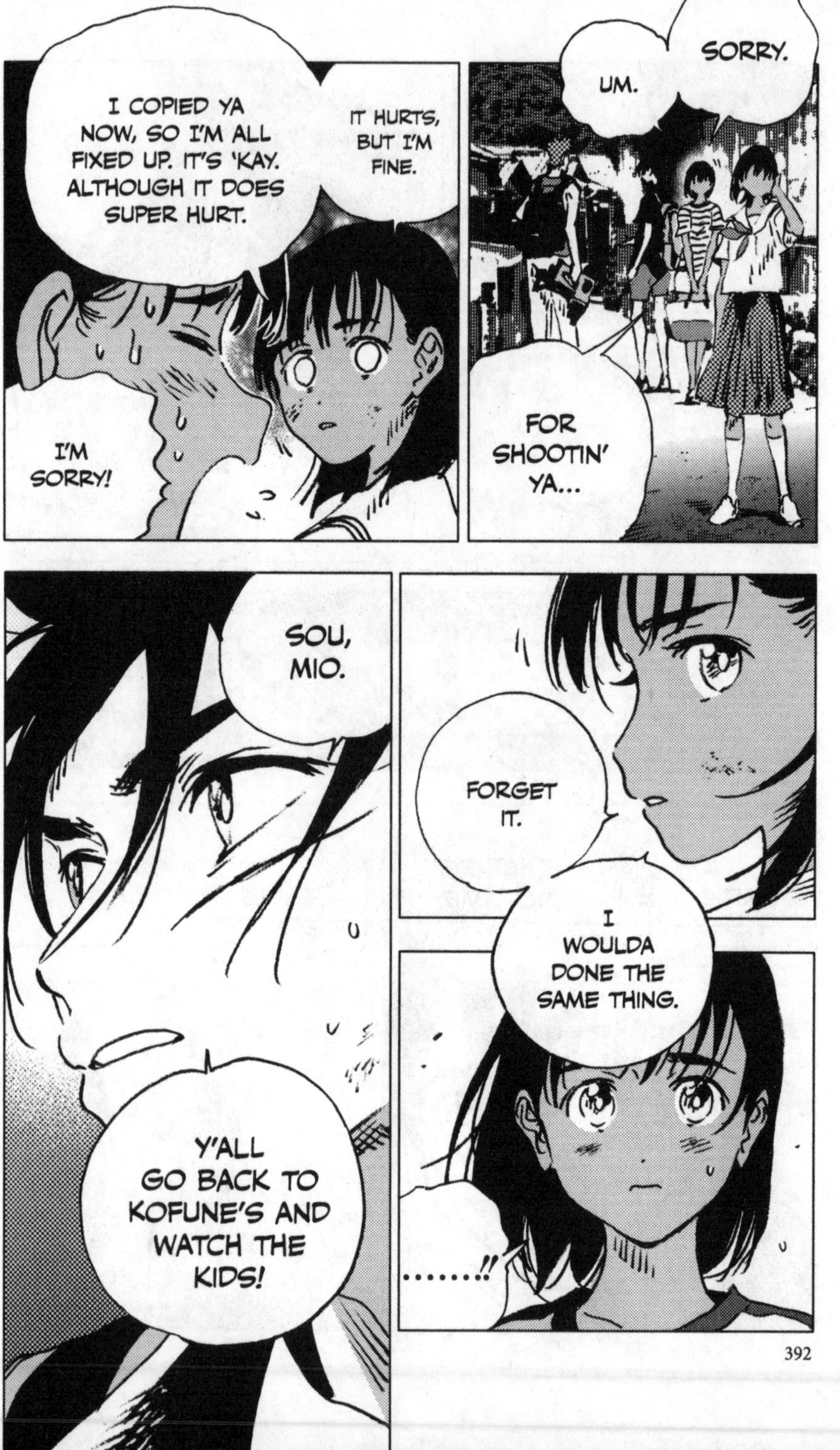
UM. SORRY.
FOR SHOOTIN' YA...
IT HURTS, BUT I'M FINE.
I COPIED YA NOW, SO I'M ALL FIXED UP. IT'S 'KAY. ALTHOUGH IT DOES SUPER HURT.
I'M SORRY!
FORGET IT.
I WOULDA DONE THE SAME THING.
........!!
SOU, MIO.
Y'ALL GO BACK TO KOFUNE'S AND WATCH THE KIDS!

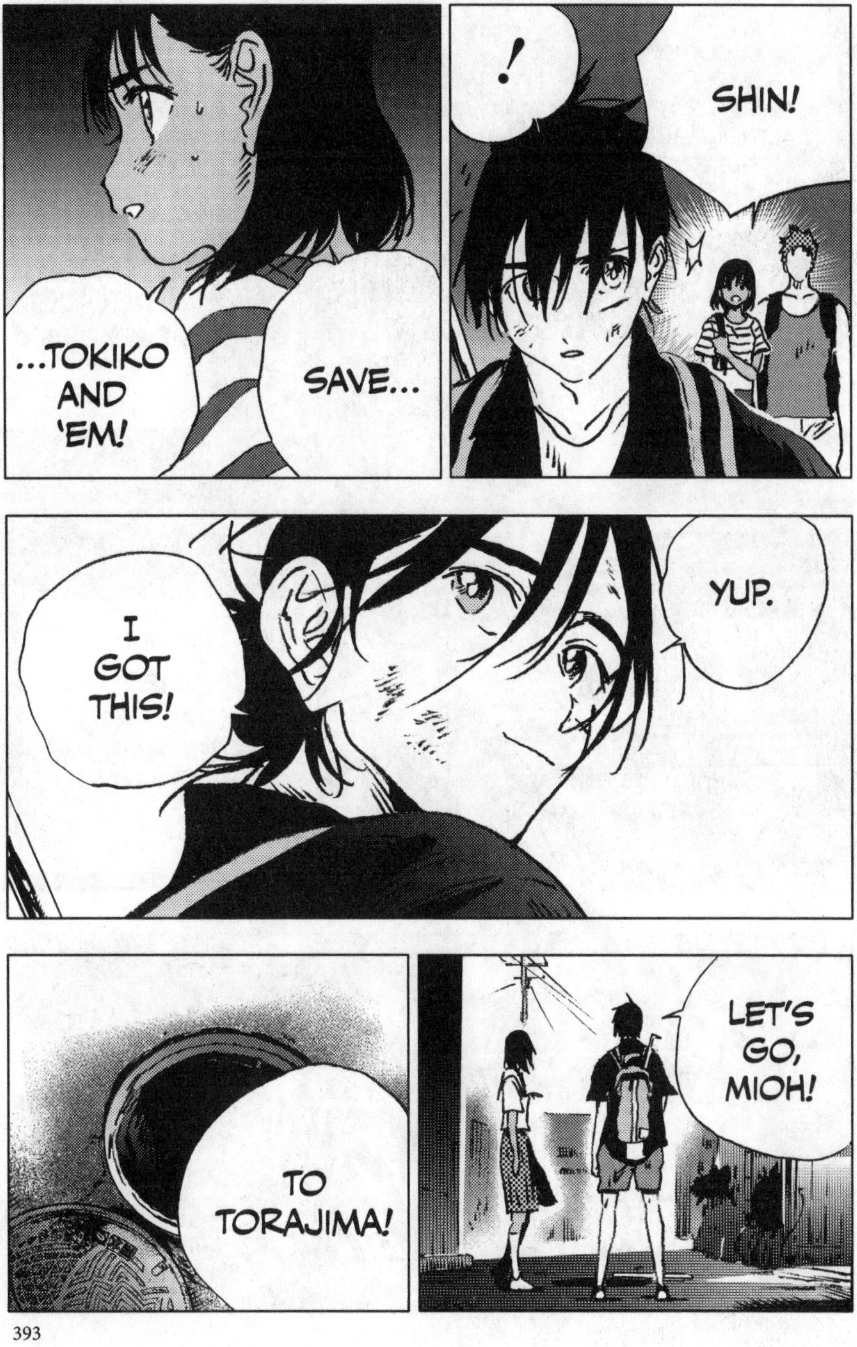
!
SHIN!
SAVE...
...TOKIKO AND 'EM!
YUP.
I GOT THIS!
LET'S GO, MIOH!
TO TORAJIMA!

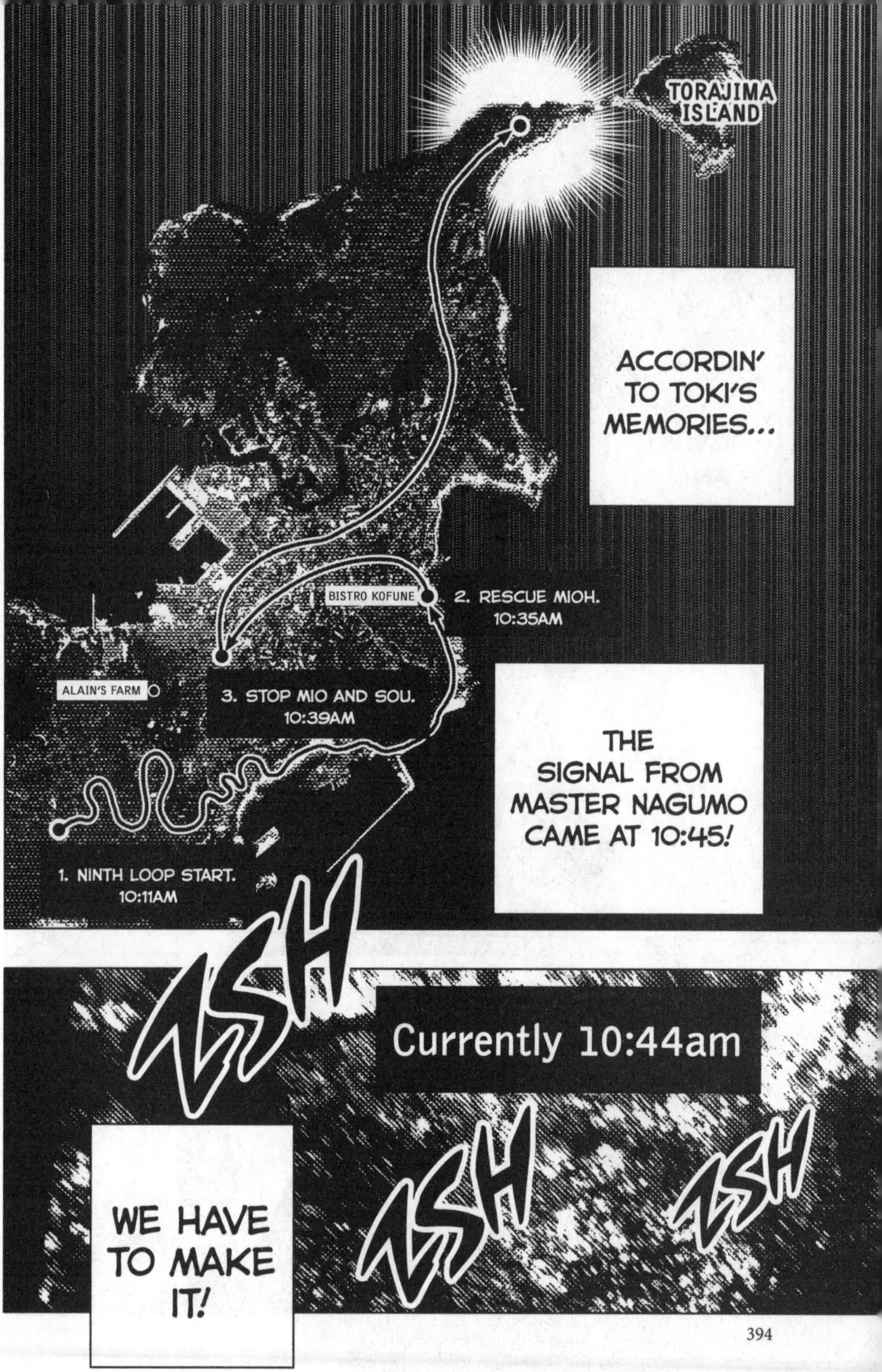
TORAJIMA ISLAND
ACCORDIN' TO TOKI'S MEMORIES...
BISTRO KOFUNE
2. RESCUE MIOH. 10:35AM
3. STOP MIO AND SOU. 10:39AM
ALAIN'S FARM
1. NINTH LOOP START. 10:11AM
THE SIGNAL FROM MASTER NAGUMO CAME AT 10:45!
ZSH
Currently 10:44am
ZSH
ZSH
WE HAVE TO MAKE IT!

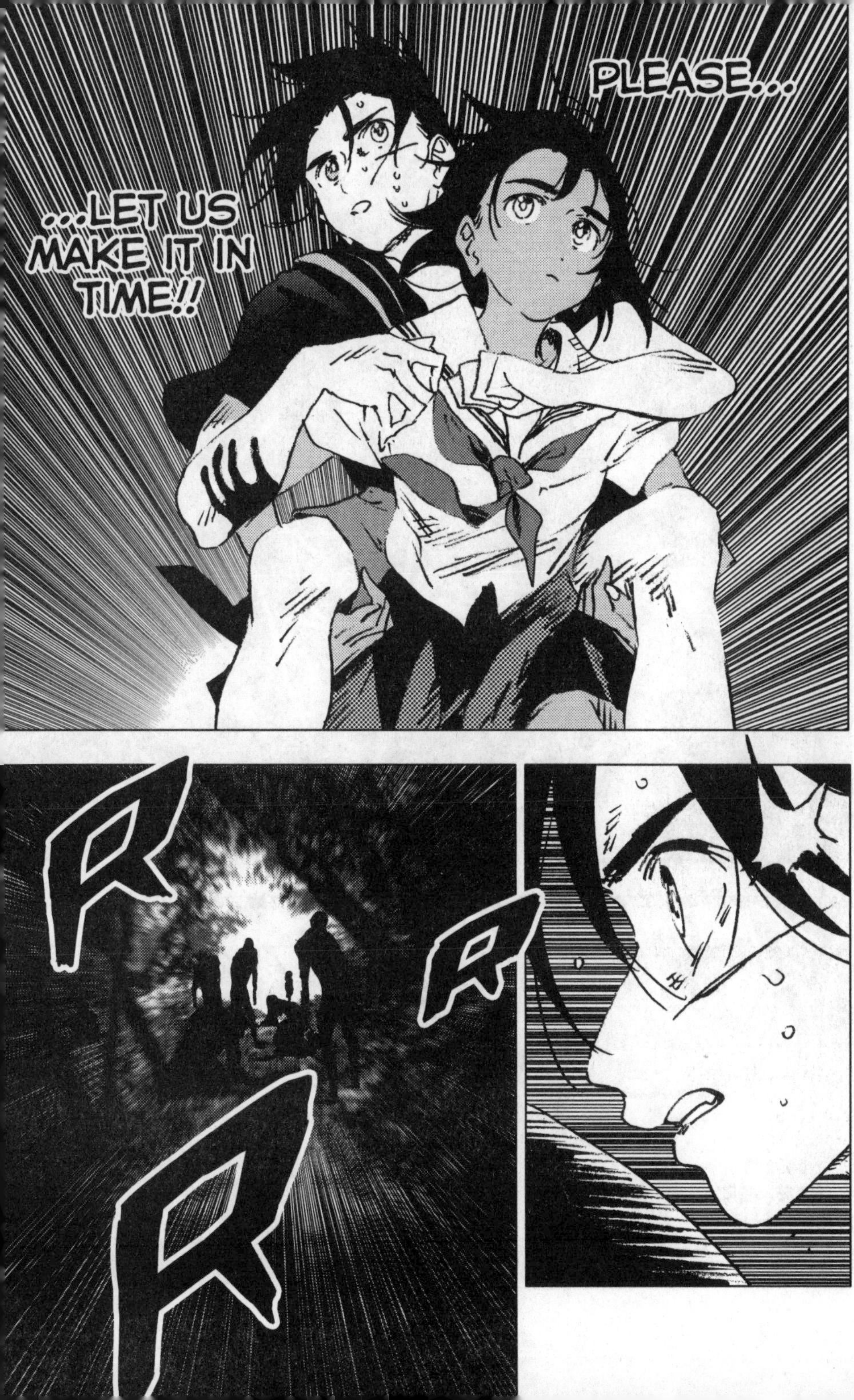
PLEASE...
...LET US MAKE IT IN TIME!!
R R R

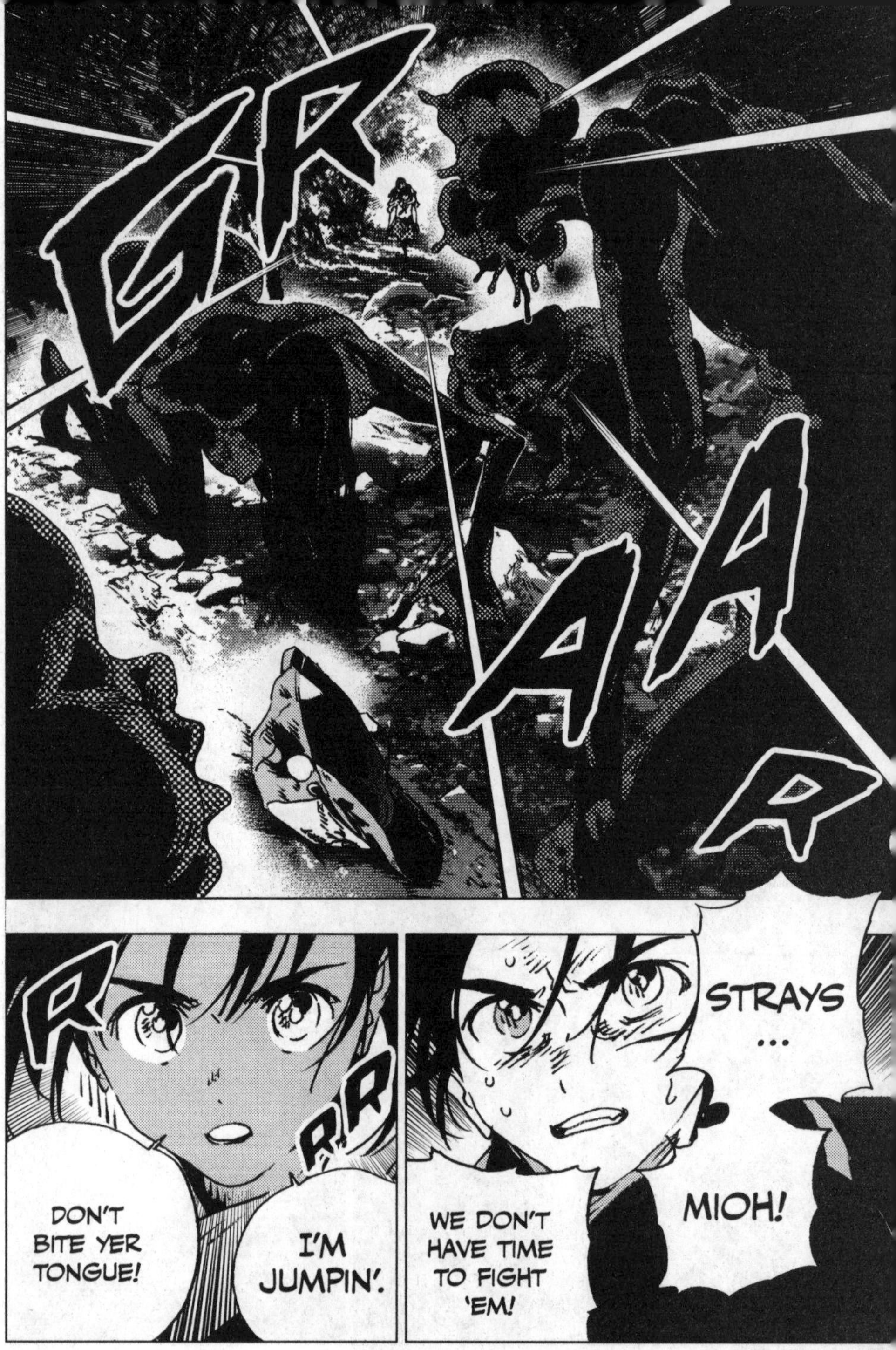
GRAAR
STRAYS ...
MIOH!
WE DON'T HAVE TIME TO FIGHT 'EM!
R RR
I'M JUMPIN'.
DON'T BITE YER TONGUE!

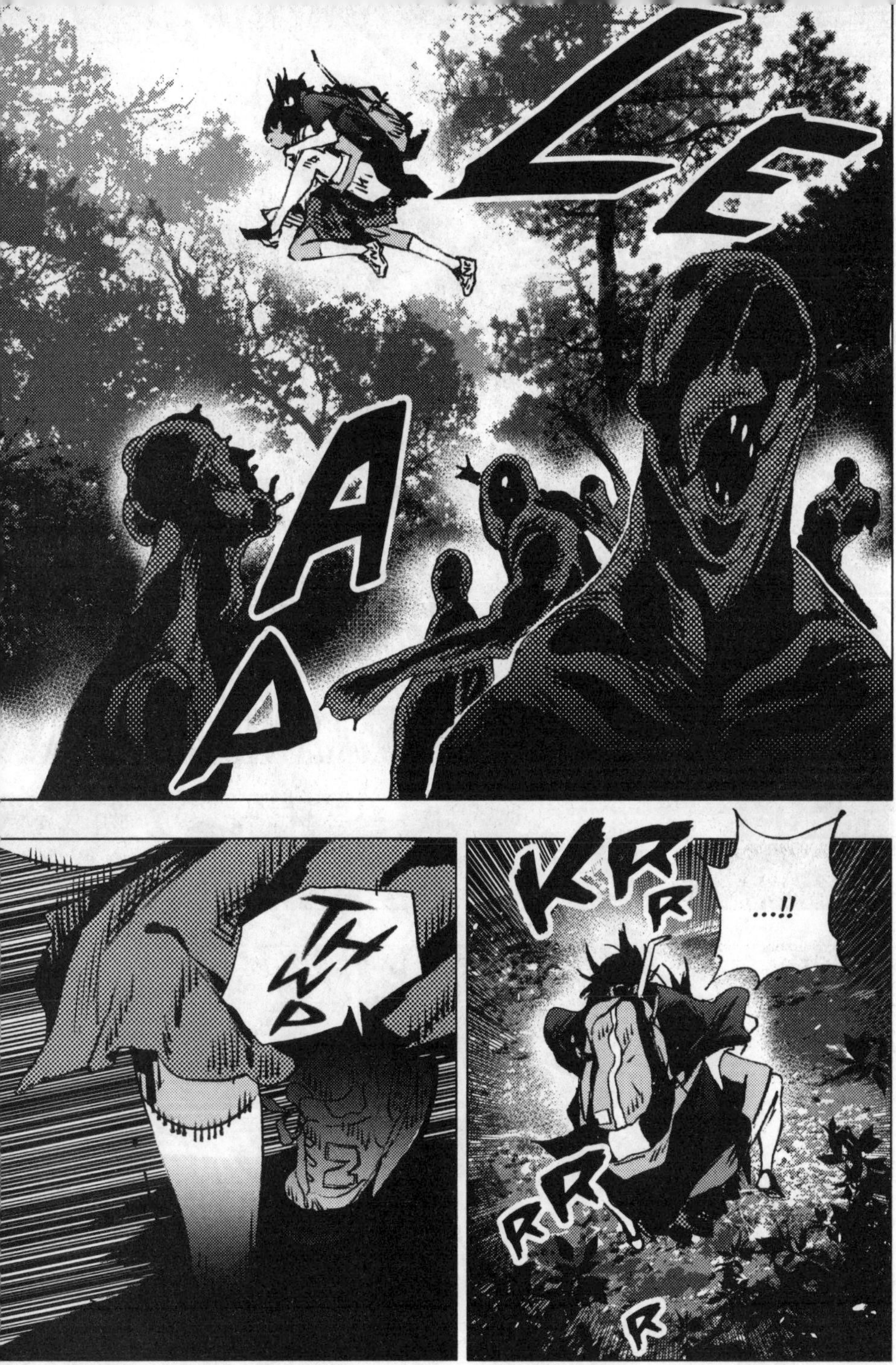

LE
AA
KRR
...!!
RR
R
THWD

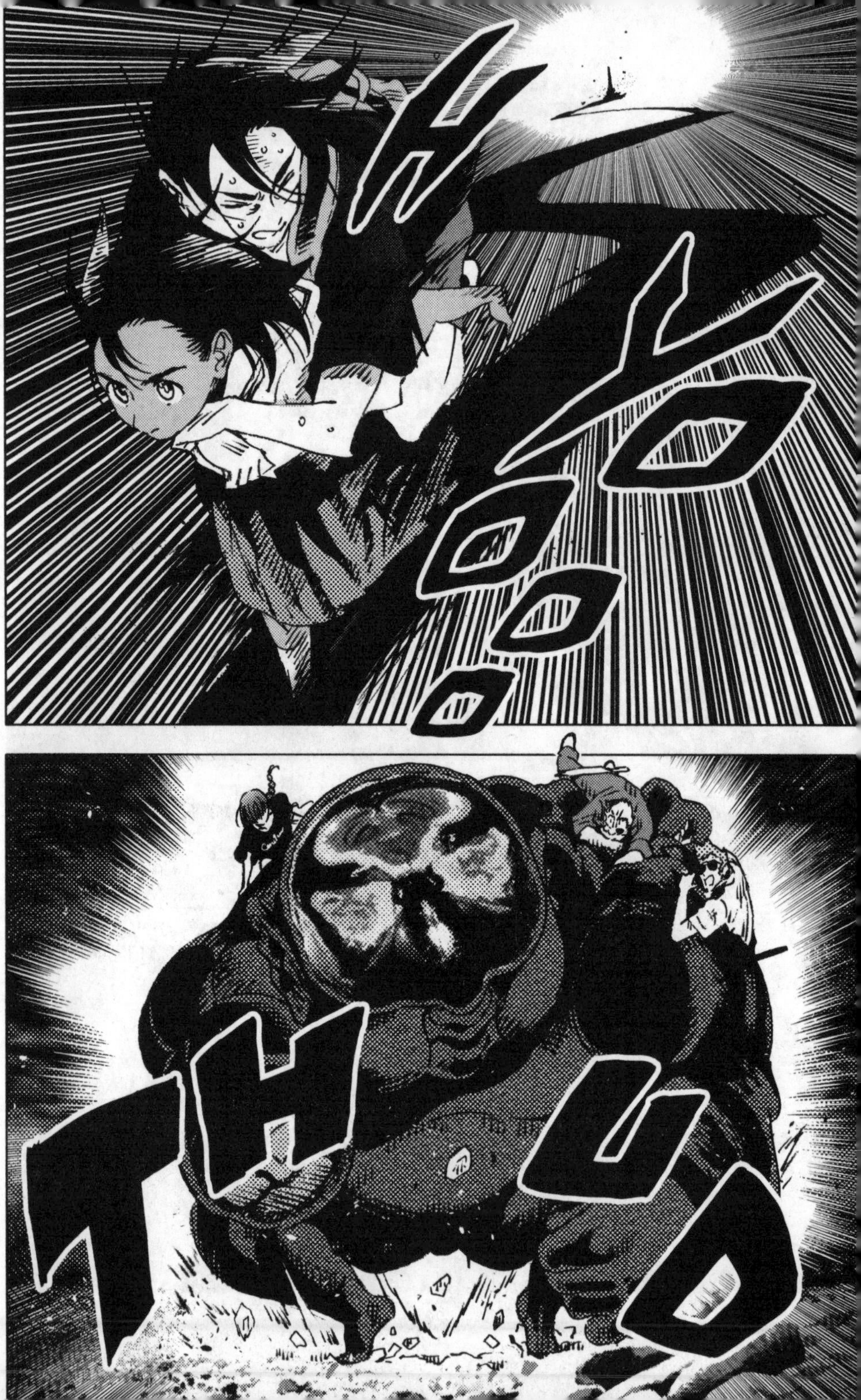
HYOOOO
THUD

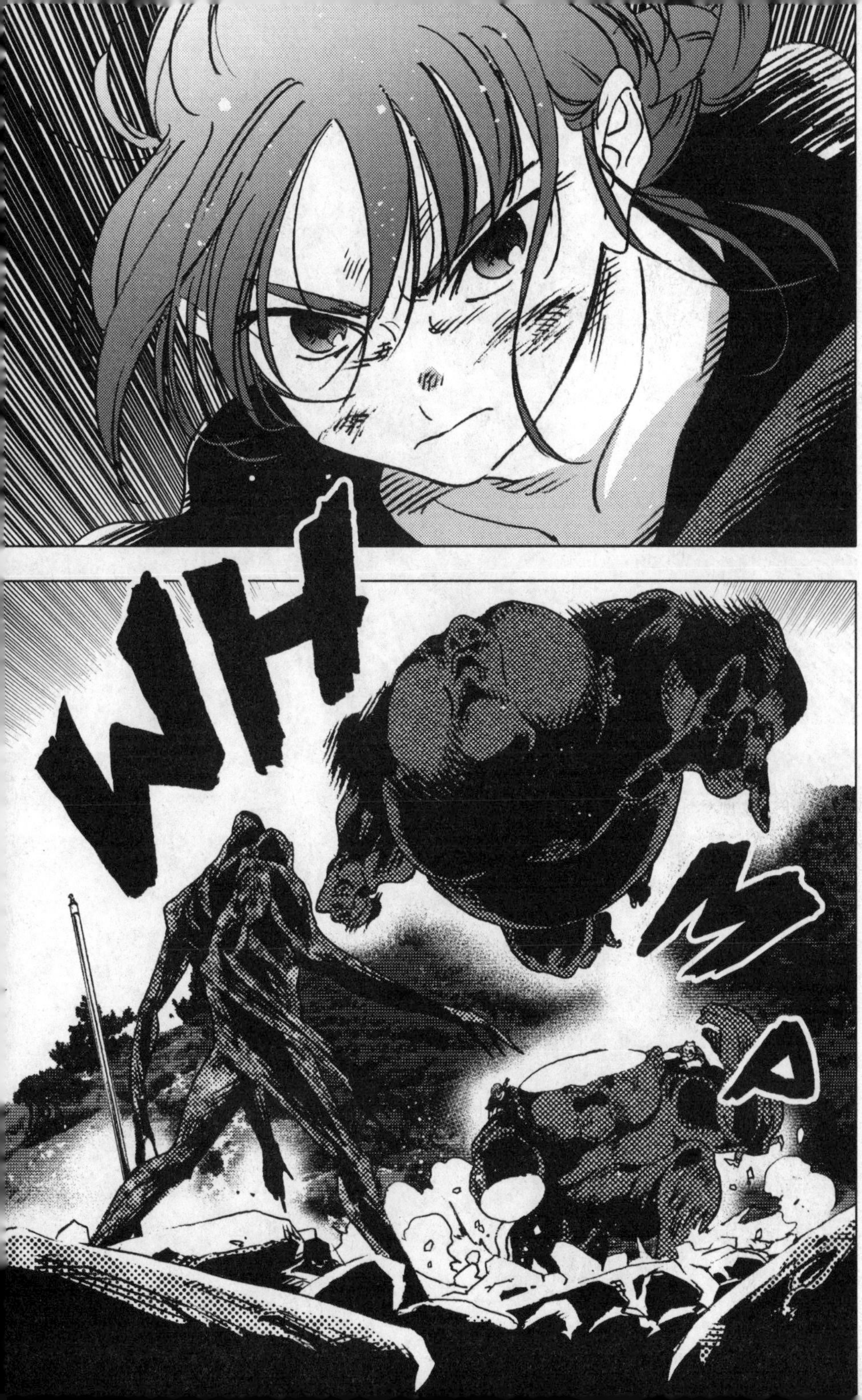
WHMMP

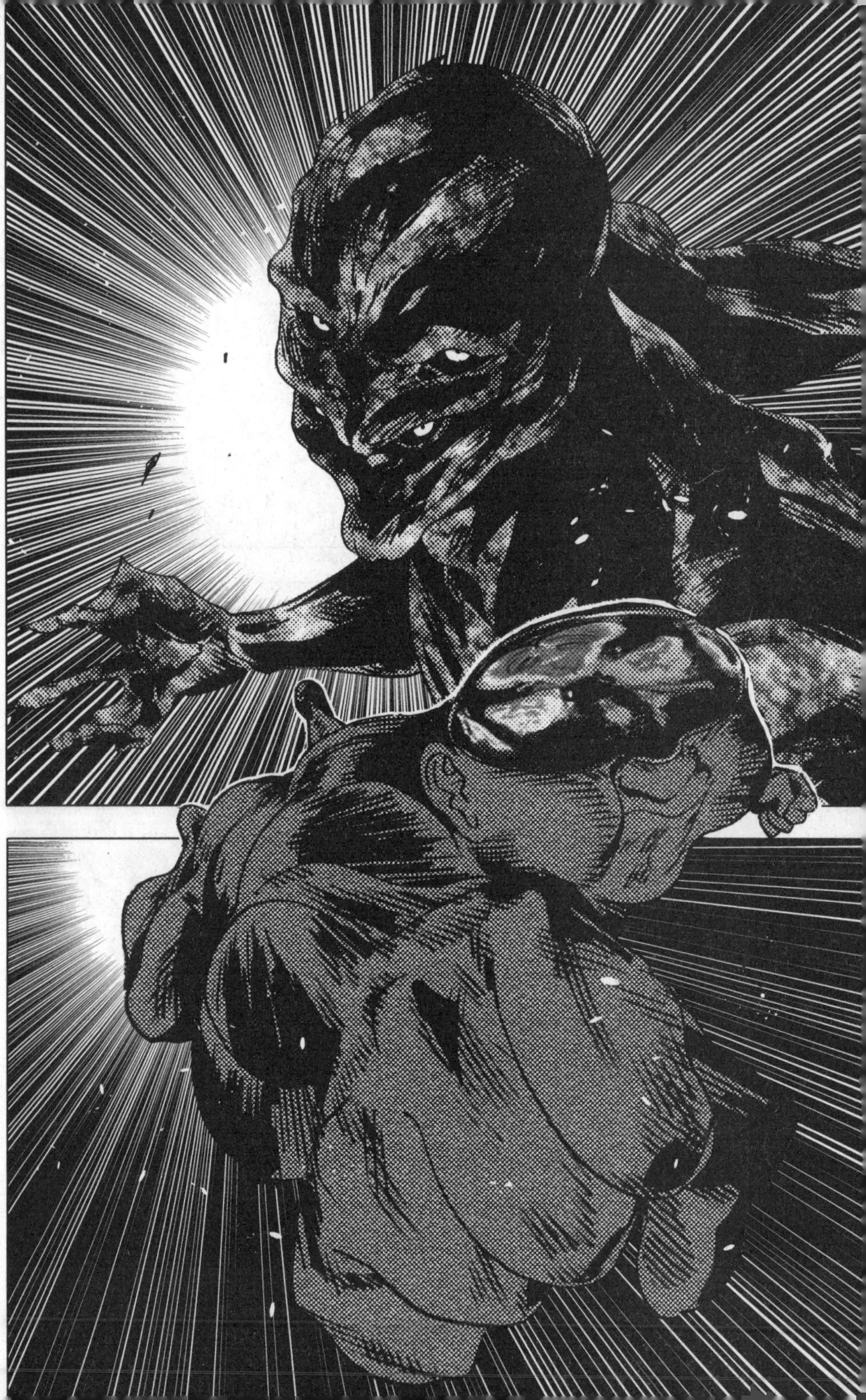

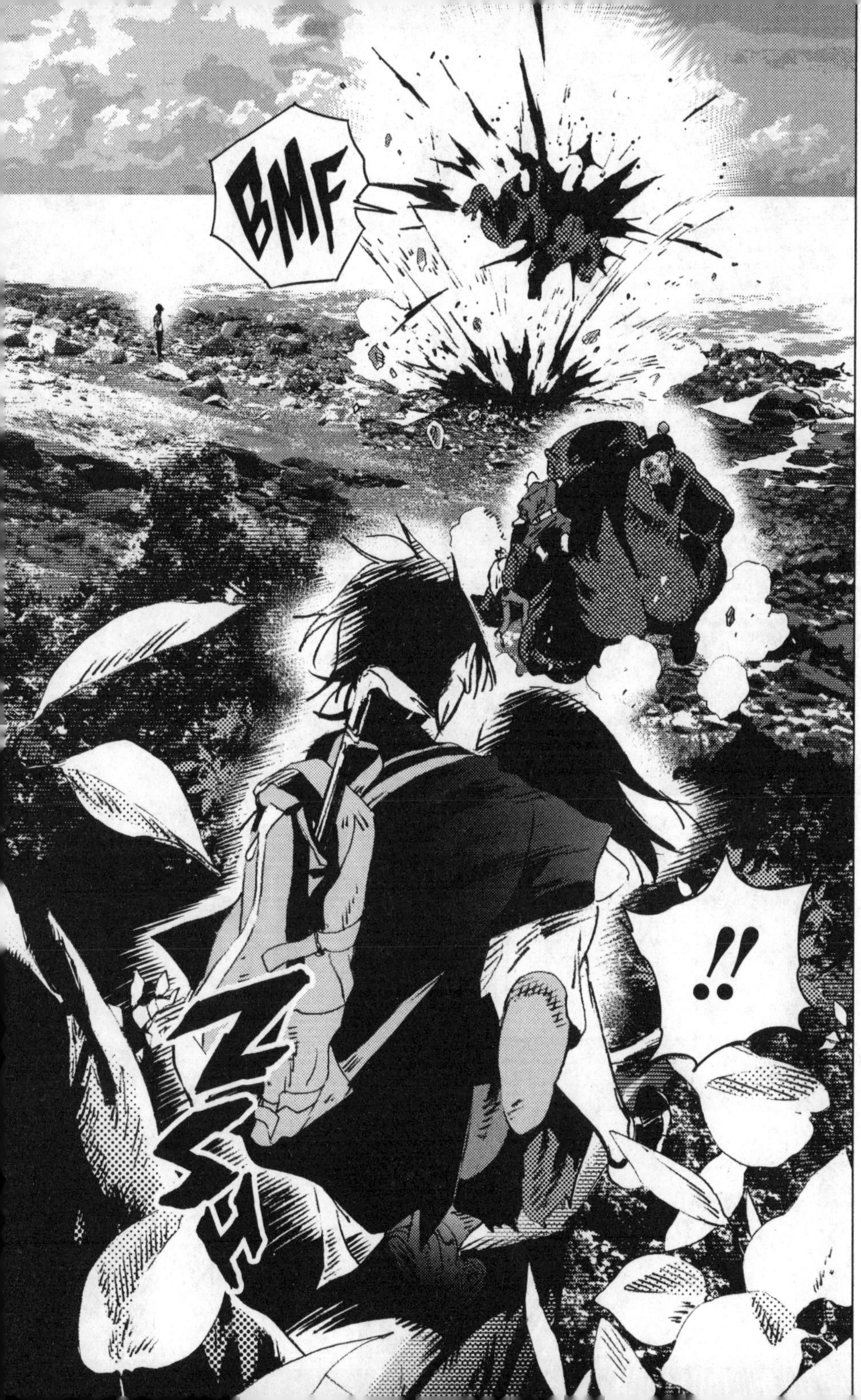
BMF
!!
ZSH

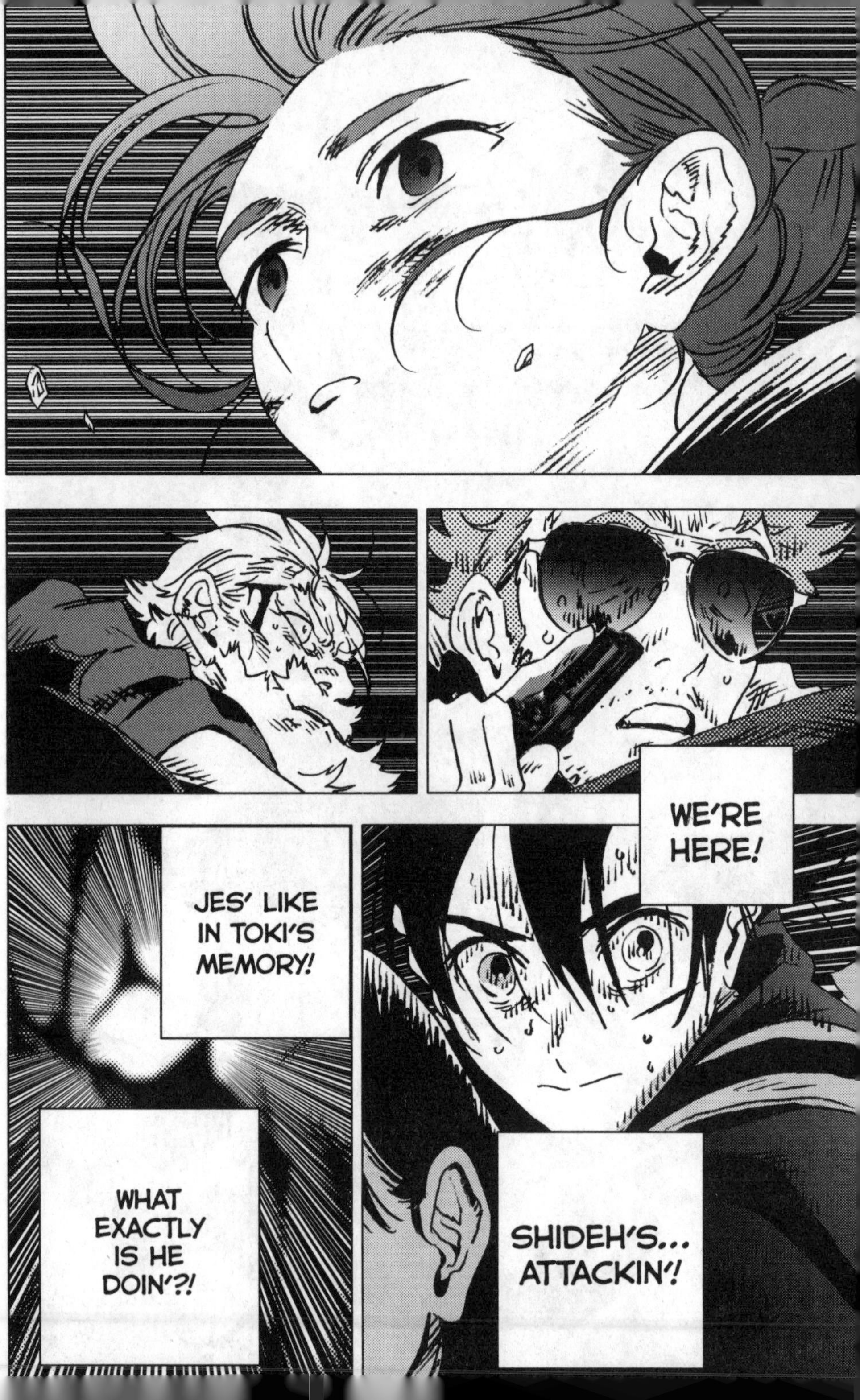
WE'RE HERE!
SHIDEH'S... ATTACKIN'!
JES' LIKE IN TOKI'S MEMORY!
WHAT EXACTLY IS HE DOIN'?!

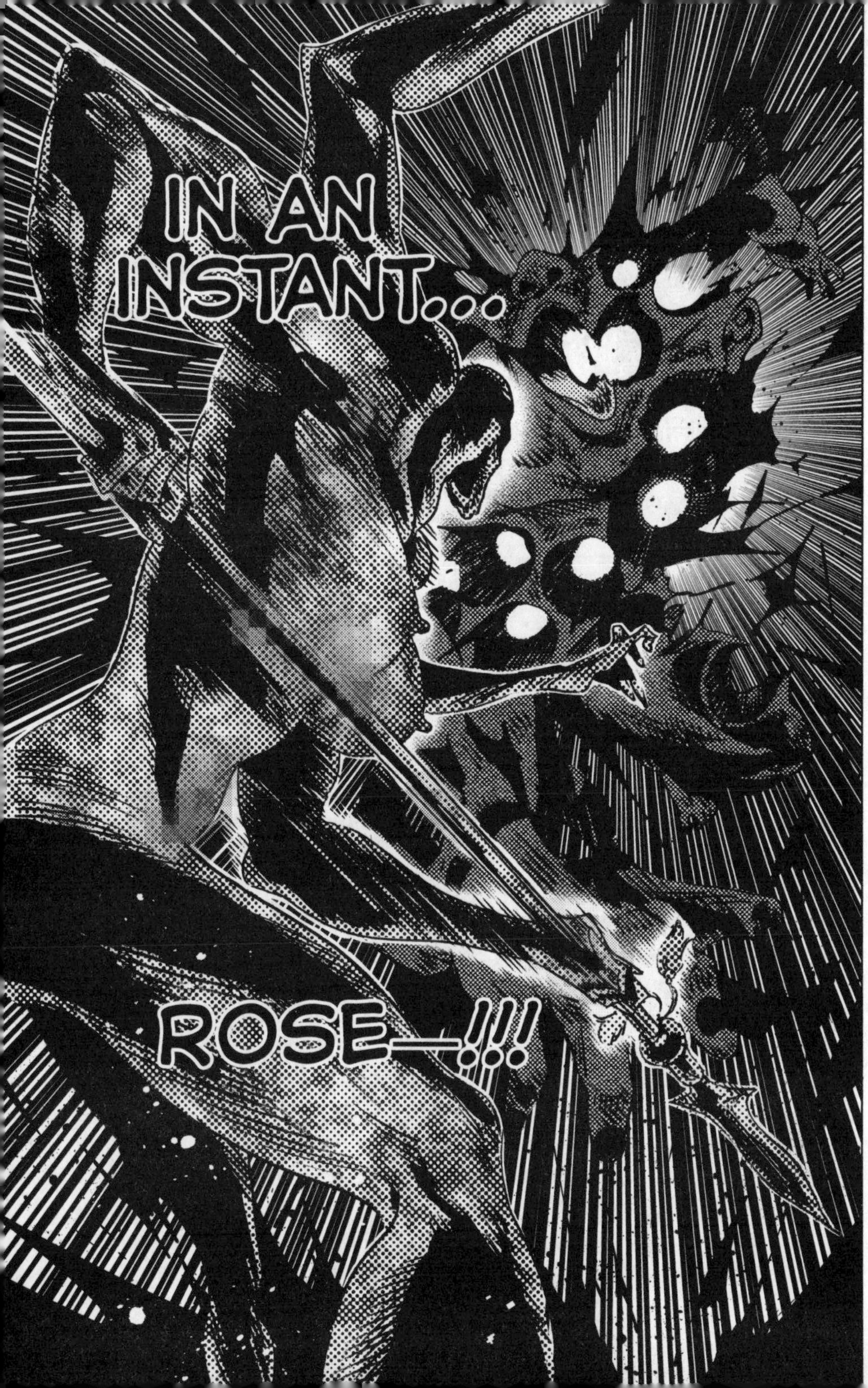
IN AN INSTANT...
ROSE—!!!

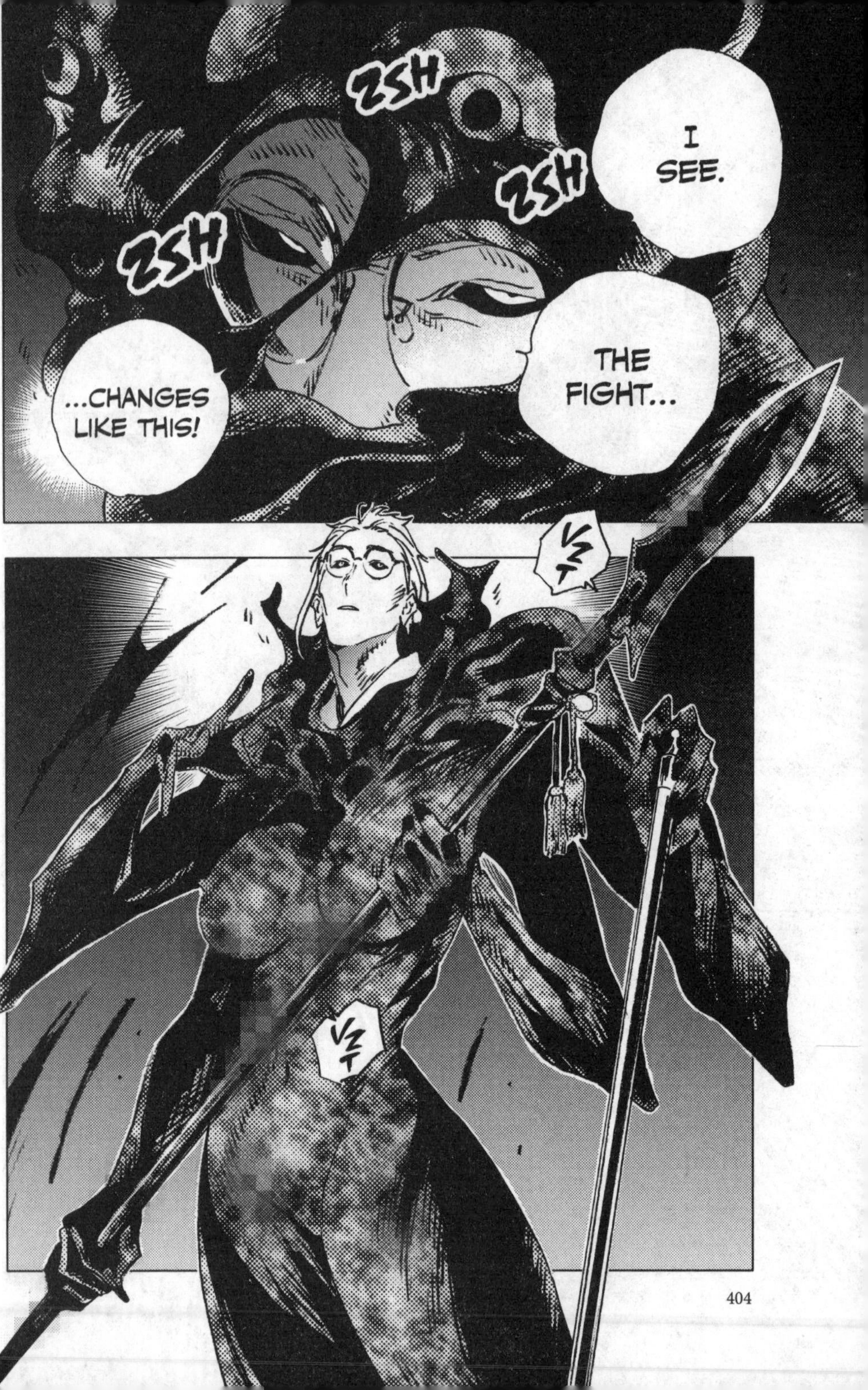
ZSH
I SEE.
ZSH
THE FIGHT...
ZSH
...CHANGES LIKE THIS!
VZT
VZT

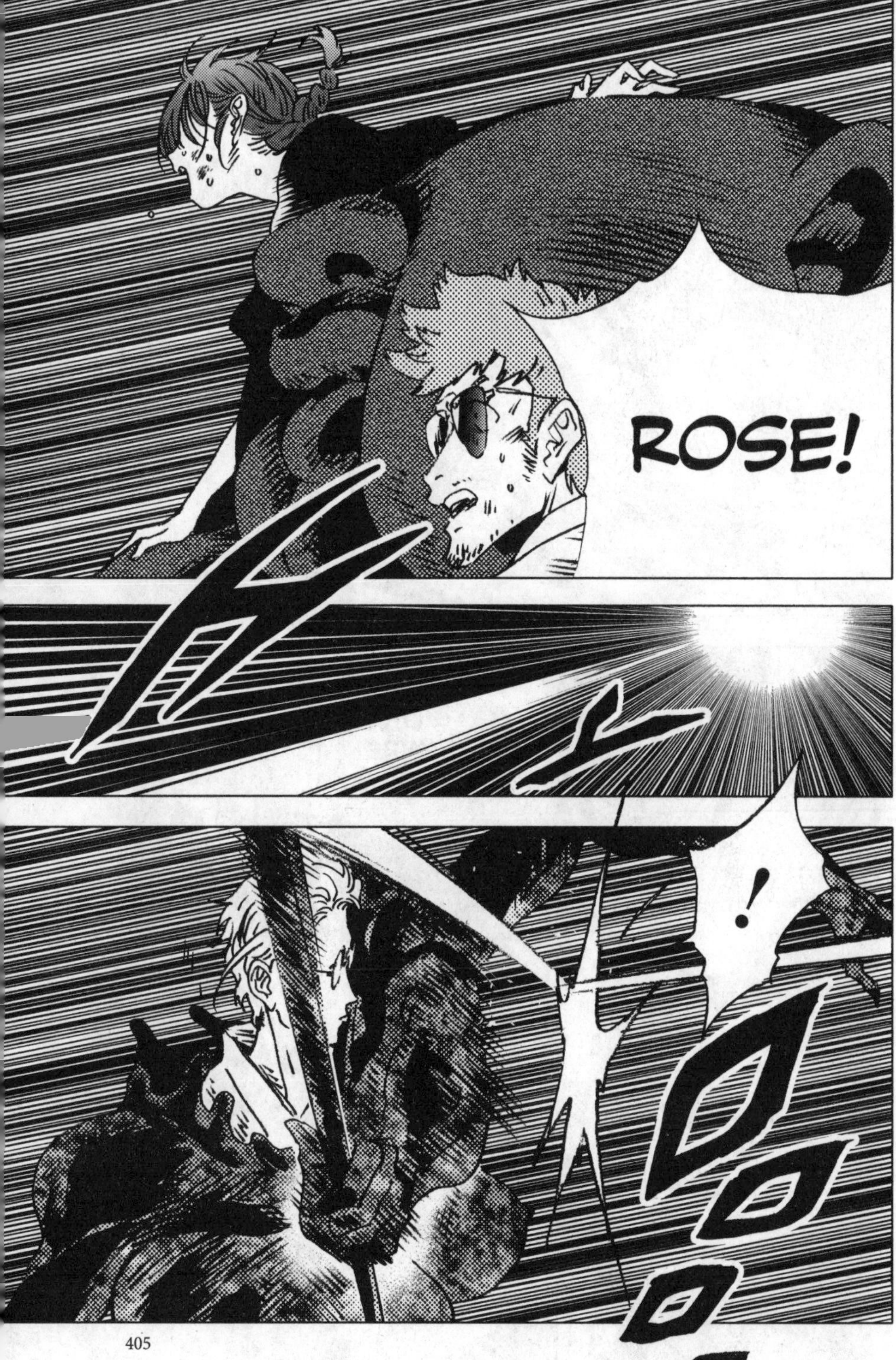
ROSE!
!

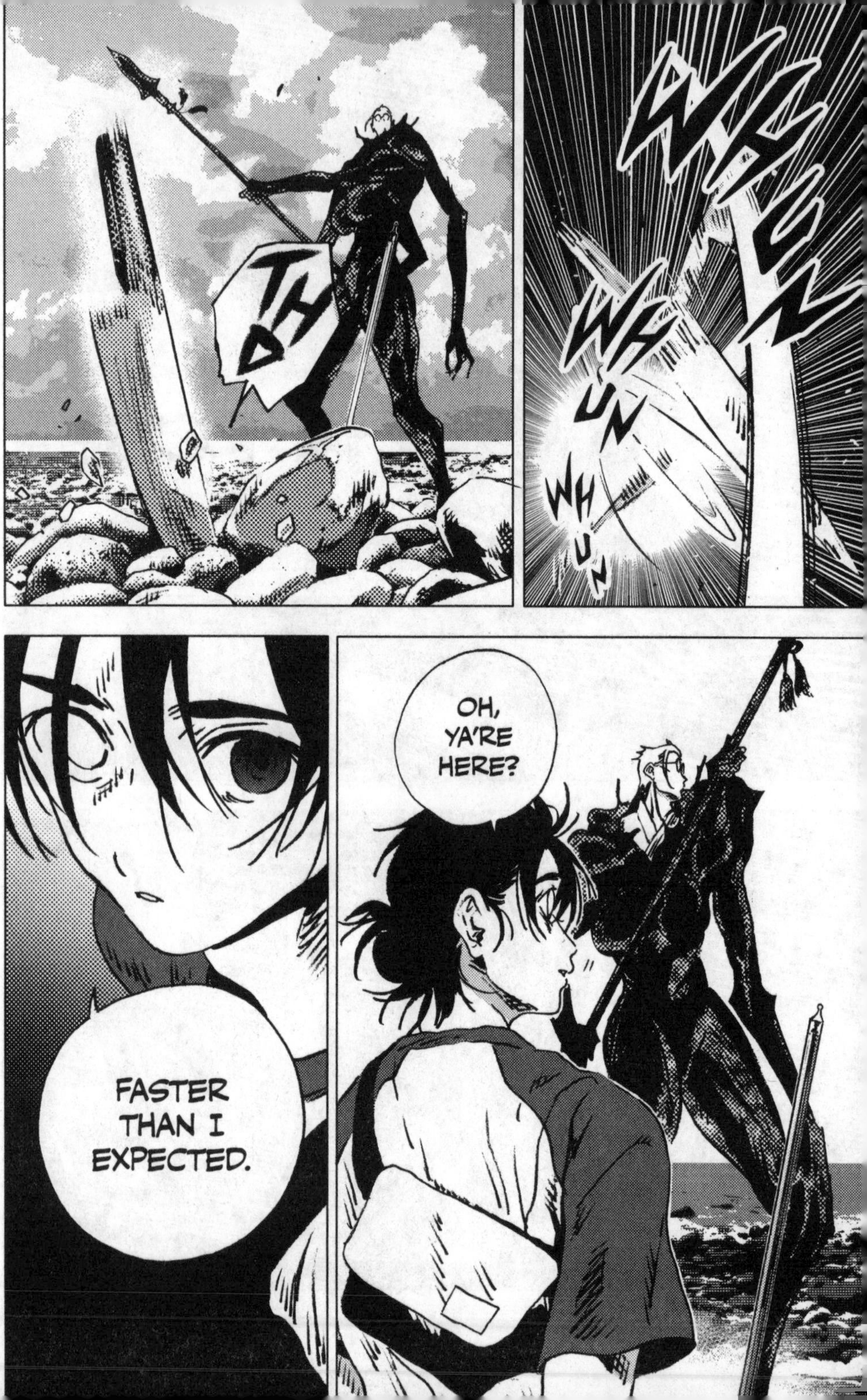
WHOOM
WHUN
WHUN
THD
OH, YA'RE HERE?
FASTER THAN I EXPECTED.

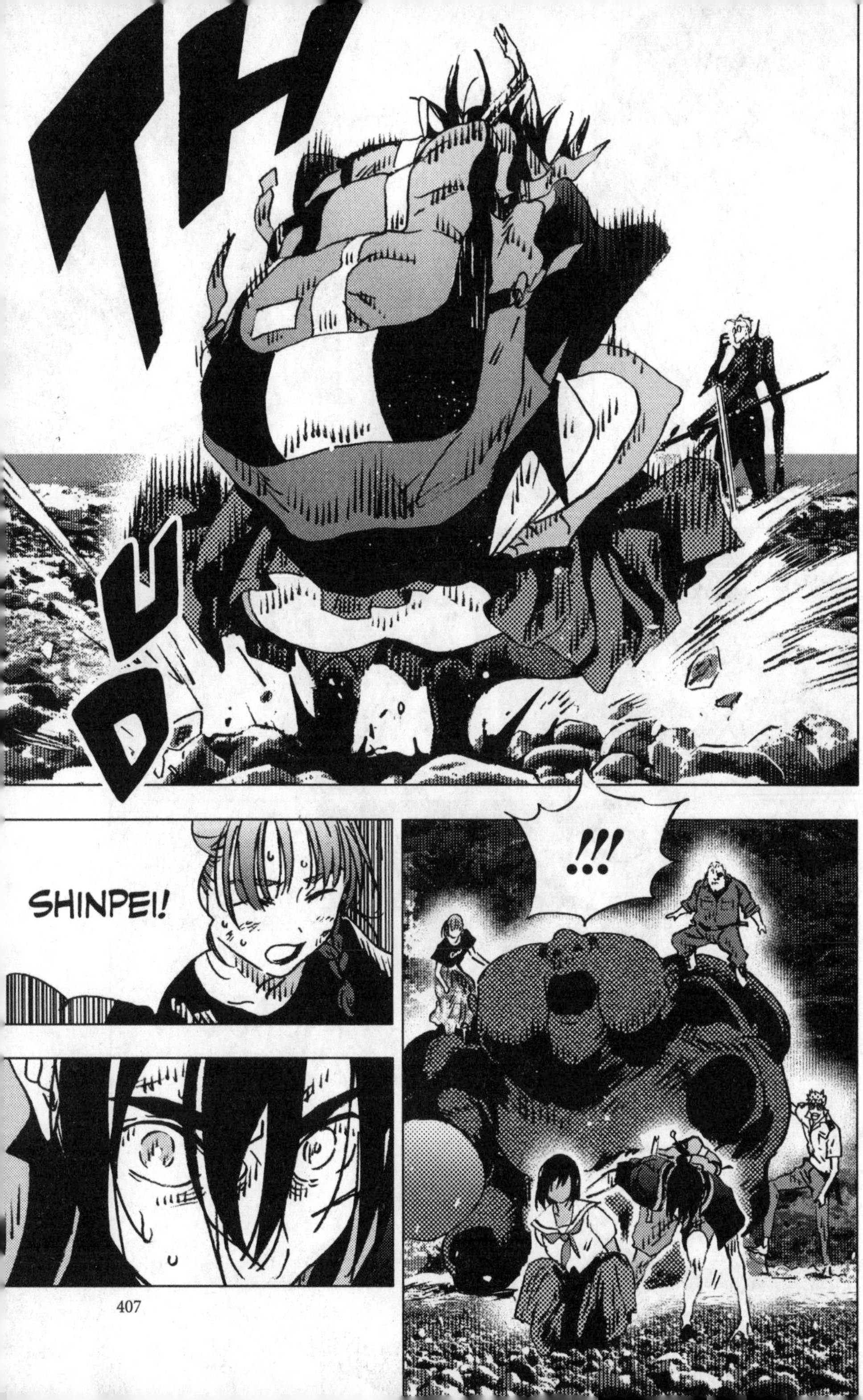
!!!
SHINPEI!

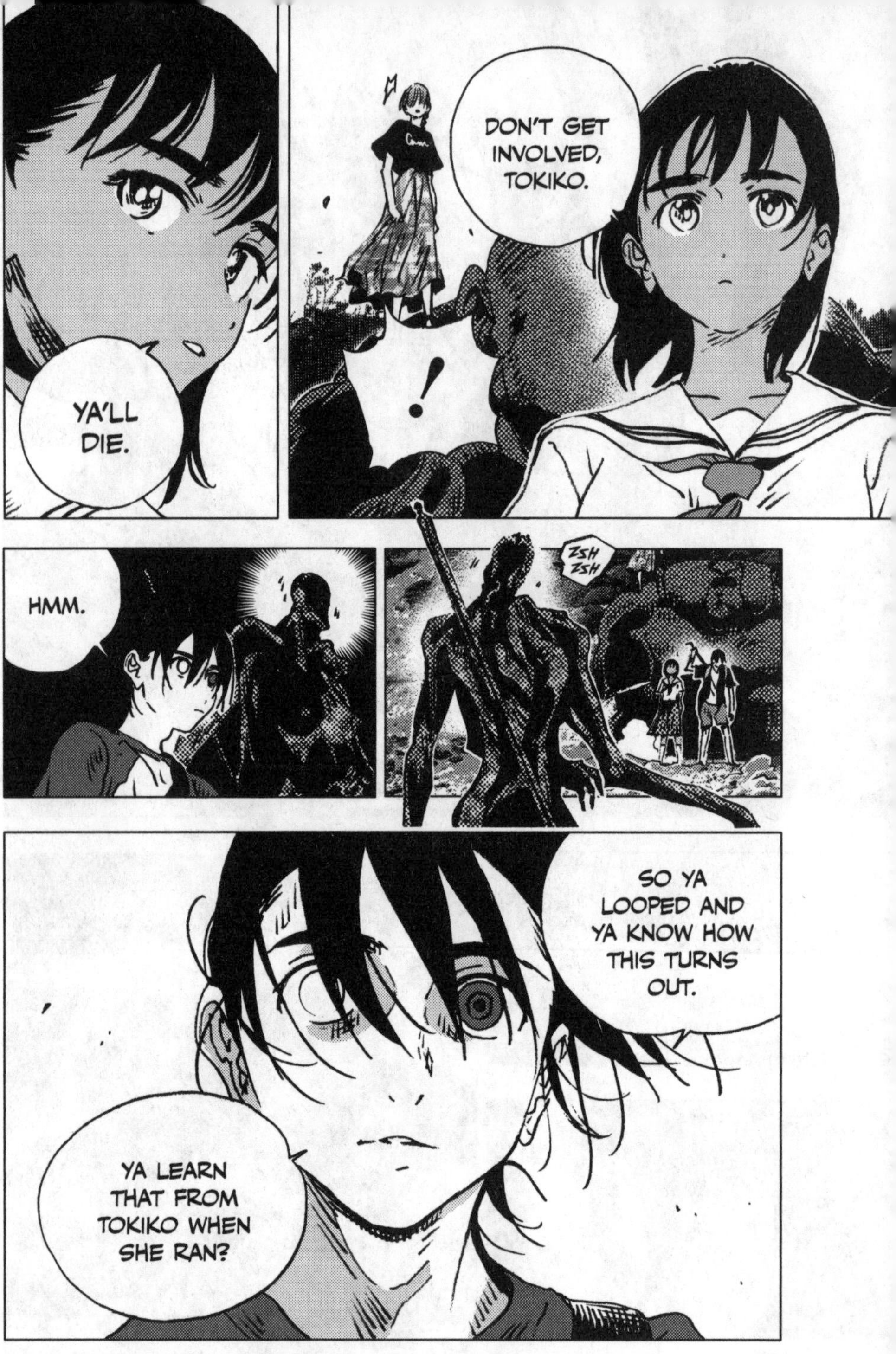
DON'T GET INVOLVED, TOKIKO.
!
YA'LL DIE.
ZSH ZSH
HMM.
SO YA LOOPED AND YA KNOW HOW THIS TURNS OUT.
YA LEARN THAT FROM TOKIKO WHEN SHE RAN?

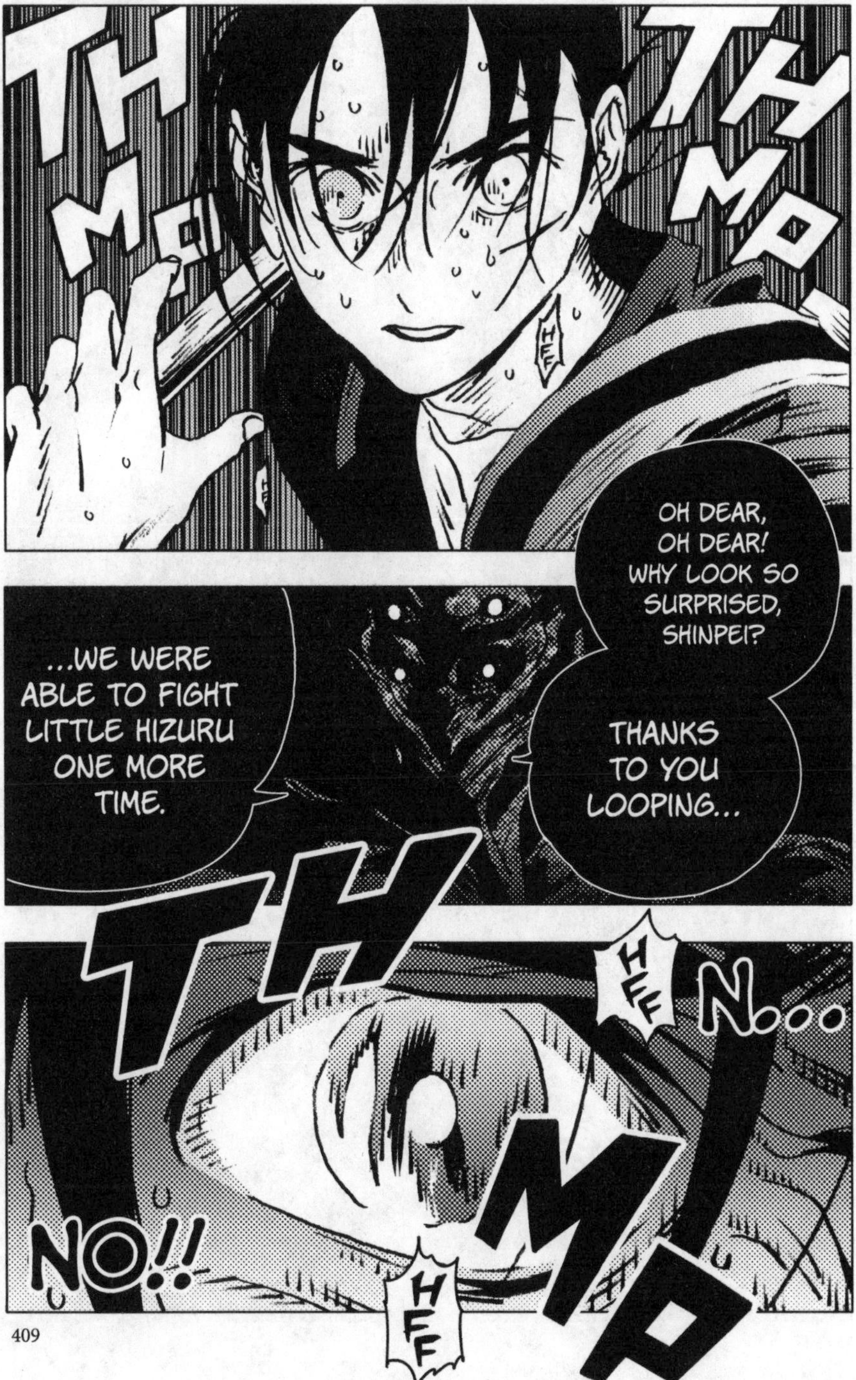
THMP
THMP
HFF
OH DEAR, OH DEAR! WHY LOOK SO SURPRISED, SHINPEI?
THANKS TO YOU LOOPING...
...WE WERE ABLE TO FIGHT LITTLE HIZURU ONE MORE TIME.
THMP
HFF
N...
HFF
NO!!

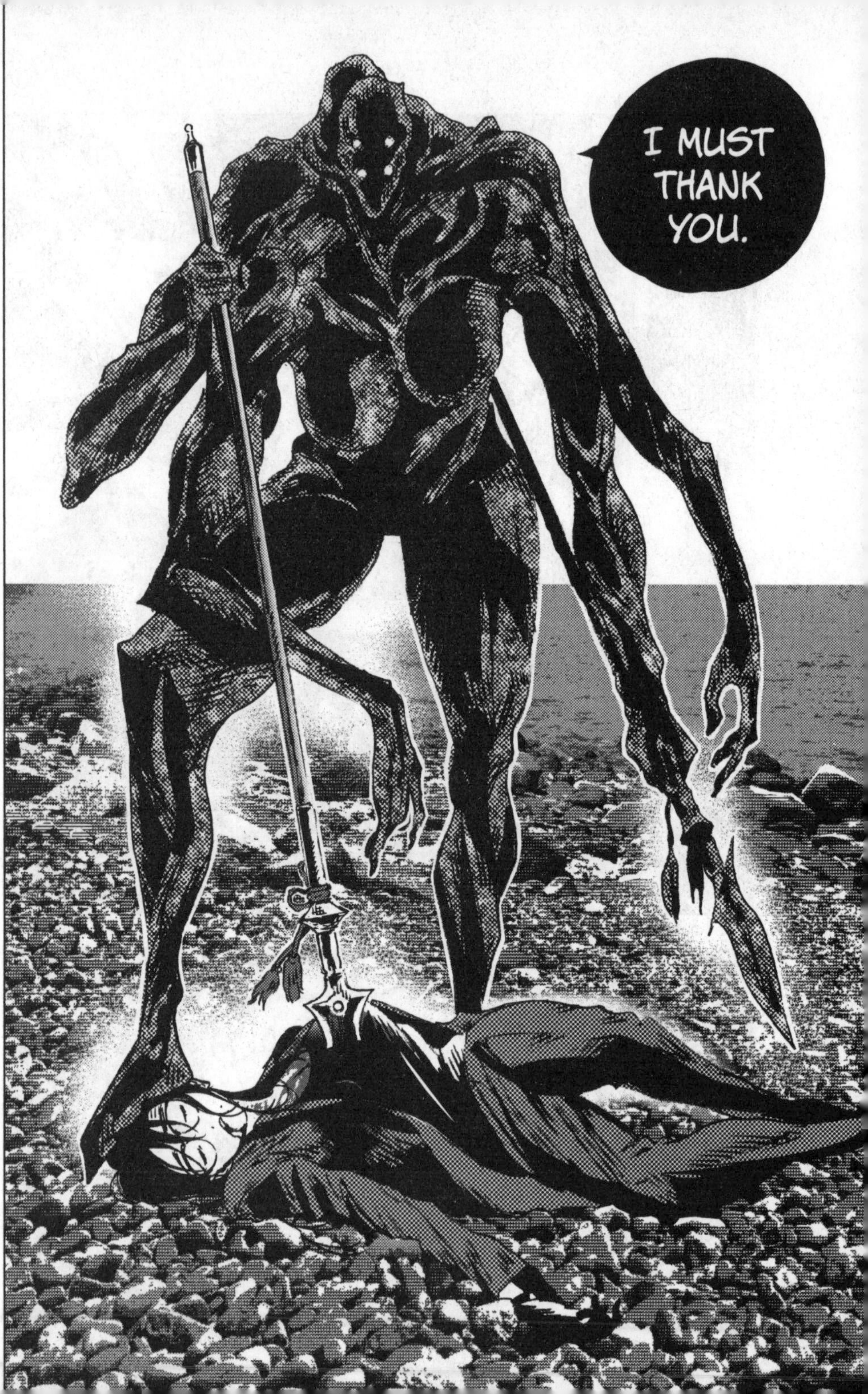
I MUST THANK YOU.

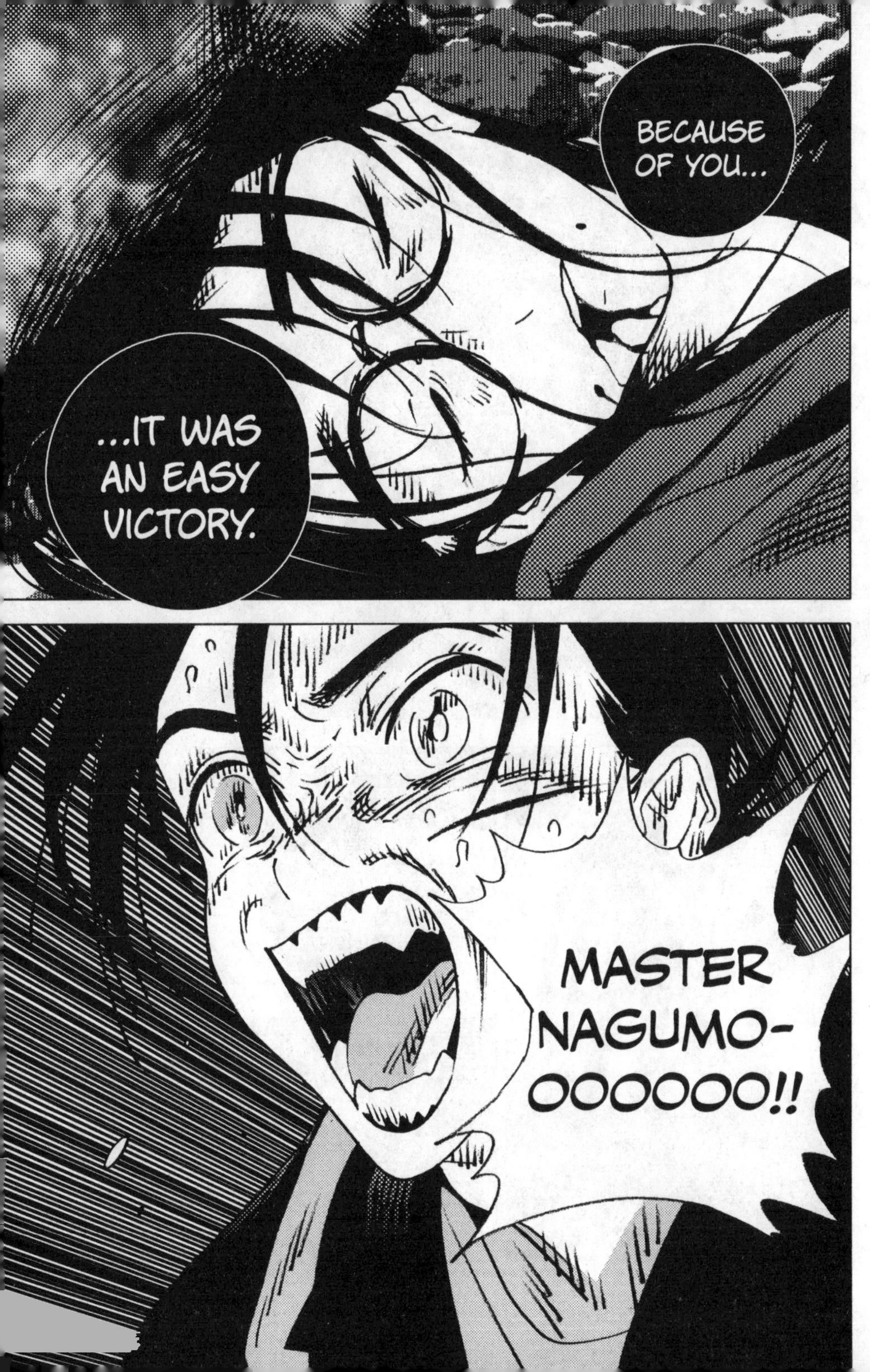
BECAUSE OF YOU...
...IT WAS AN EASY VICTORY.
MASTER NAGUMO-OOOOOO!!

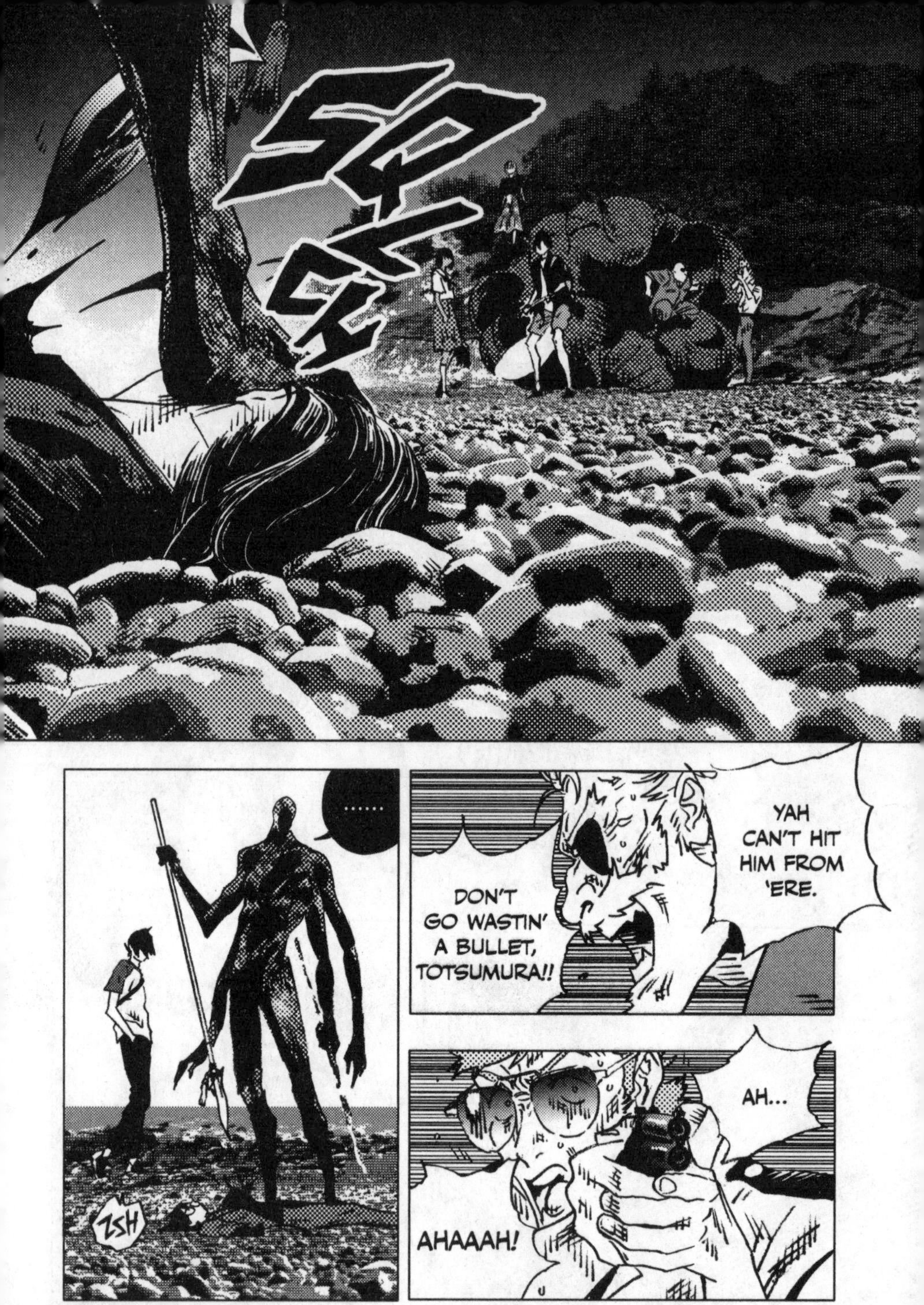
YAH CAN'T HIT HIM FROM 'ERE.
DON'T GO WASTIN' A BULLET, TOTSUMURA!!
AH...
AHAAAH!
......
ZSH

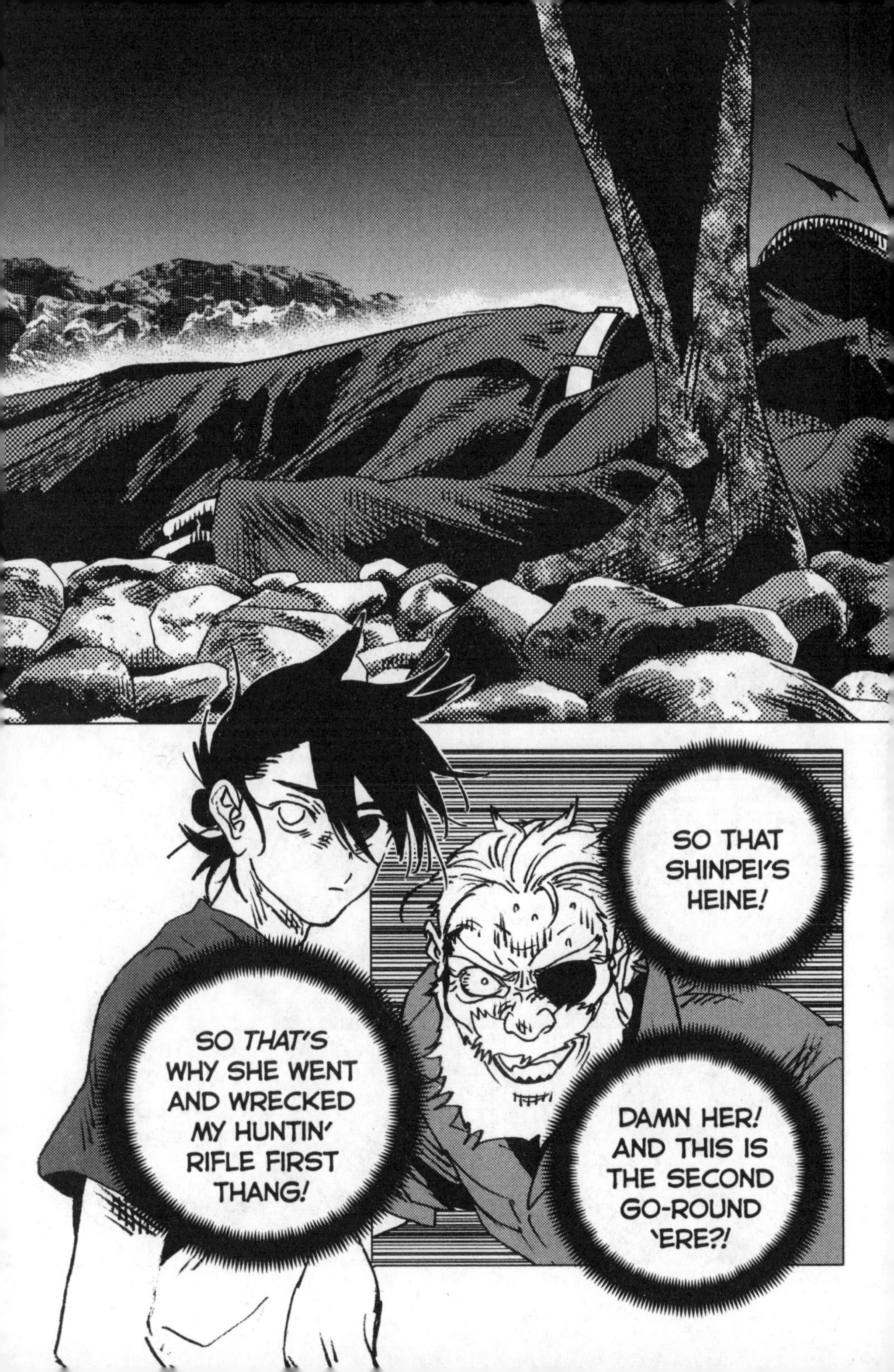
SO THAT SHINPEI'S HEINE!
SO *THAT'S* WHY SHE WENT AND WRECKED MY HUNTIN' RIFLE FIRST THANG!
DAMN HER! AND THIS IS THE SECOND GO-ROUND 'ERE?!

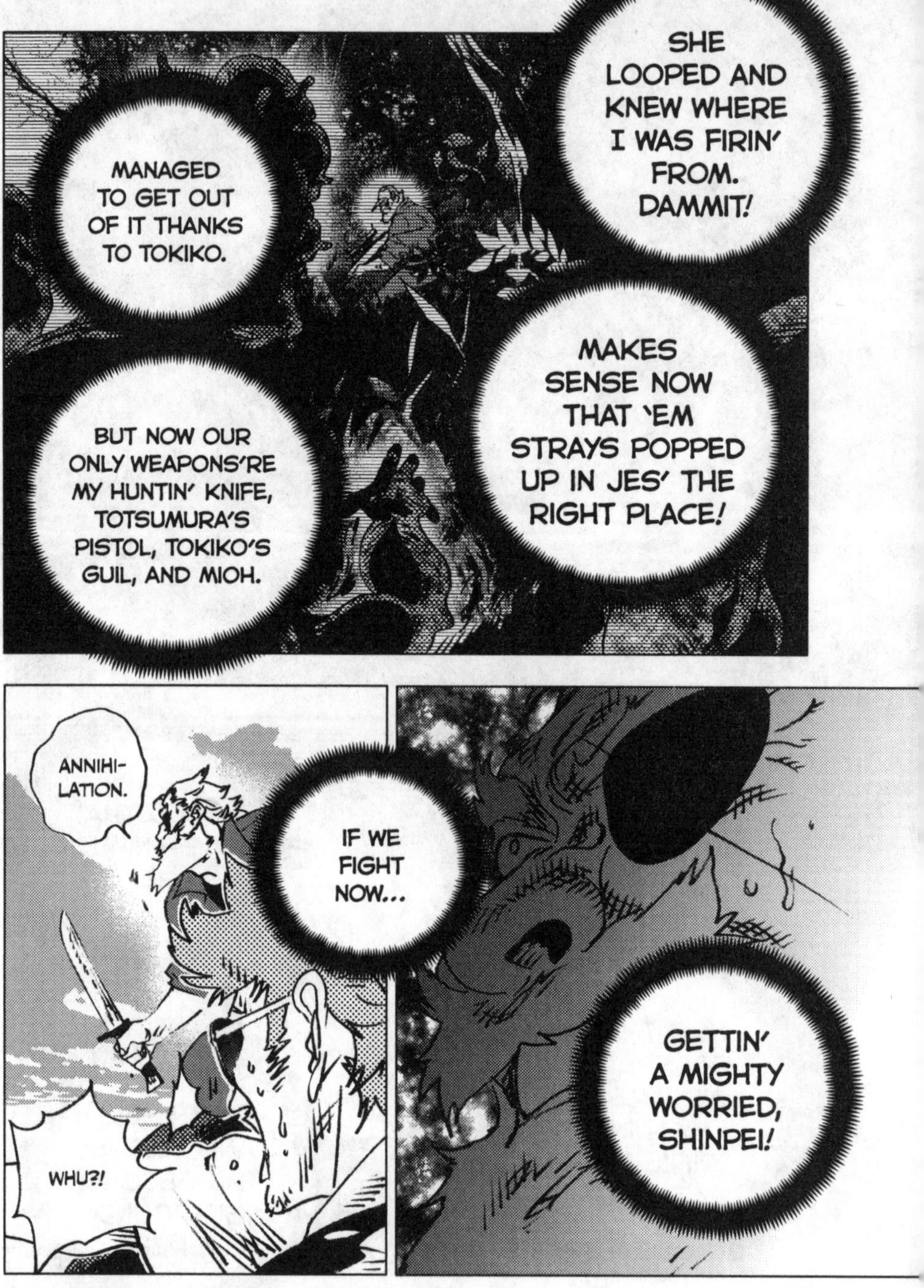
SHE LOOPED AND KNEW WHERE I WAS FIRIN' FROM. DAMMIT!
MAKES SENSE NOW THAT 'EM STRAYS POPPED UP IN JES' THE RIGHT PLACE!
MANAGED TO GET OUT OF IT THANKS TO TOKIKO.
BUT NOW OUR ONLY WEAPONS'RE MY HUNTIN' KNIFE, TOTSUMURA'S PISTOL, TOKIKO'S GUIL, AND MIOH.
IF WE FIGHT NOW...
GETTIN' A MIGHTY WORRIED, SHINPEI!
ANNIHI-LATION.
WHU?!

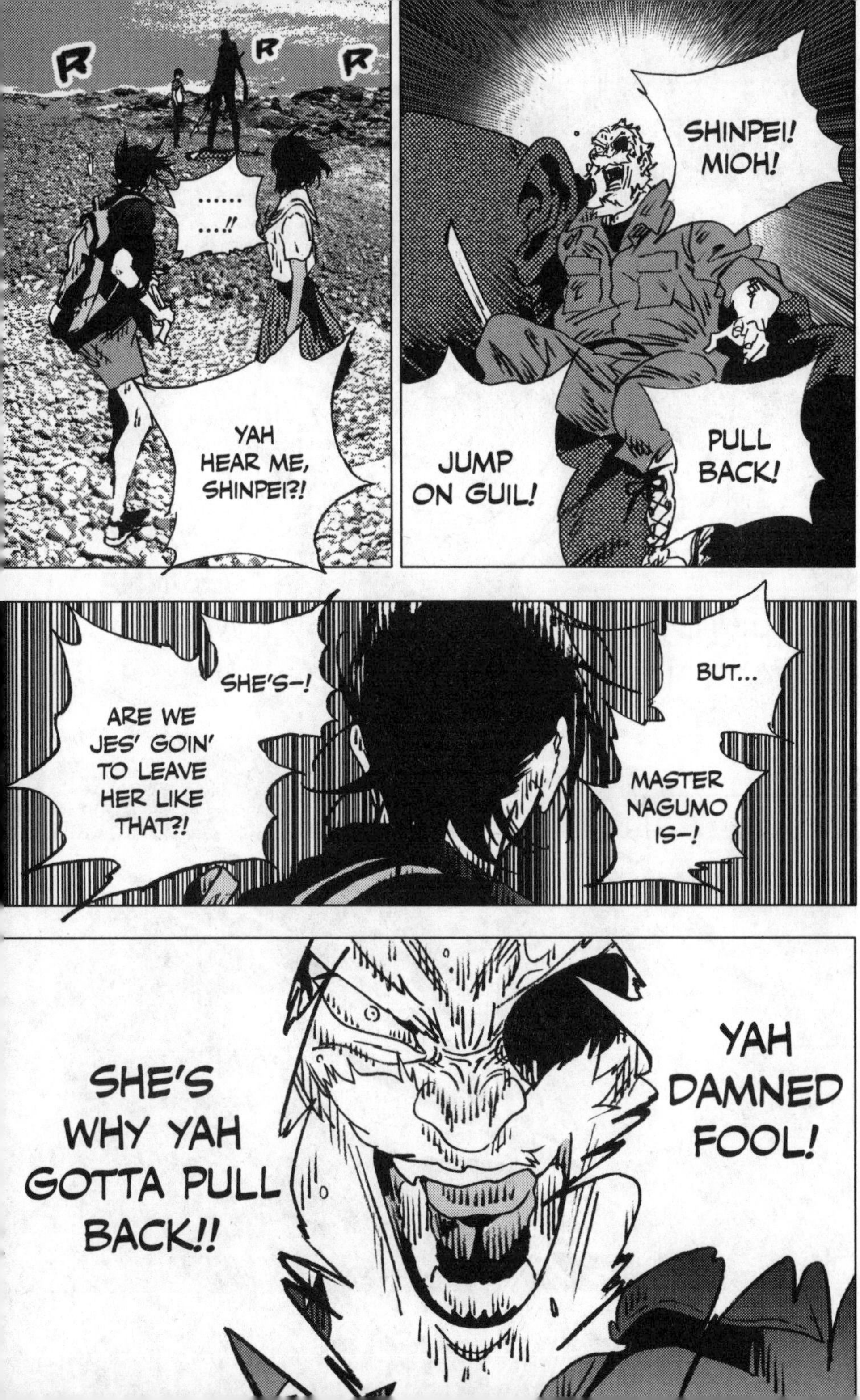
SHINPEI! MIOH!
PULL BACK!
JUMP ON GUIL!
R
R
R
......
...!!
YAH HEAR ME, SHINPEI?!
BUT...
MASTER NAGUMO IS-!
SHE'S-!
ARE WE JES' GOIN' TO LEAVE HER LIKE THAT?!
YAH DAMNED FOOL!
SHE'S WHY YAH GOTTA PULL BACK!!

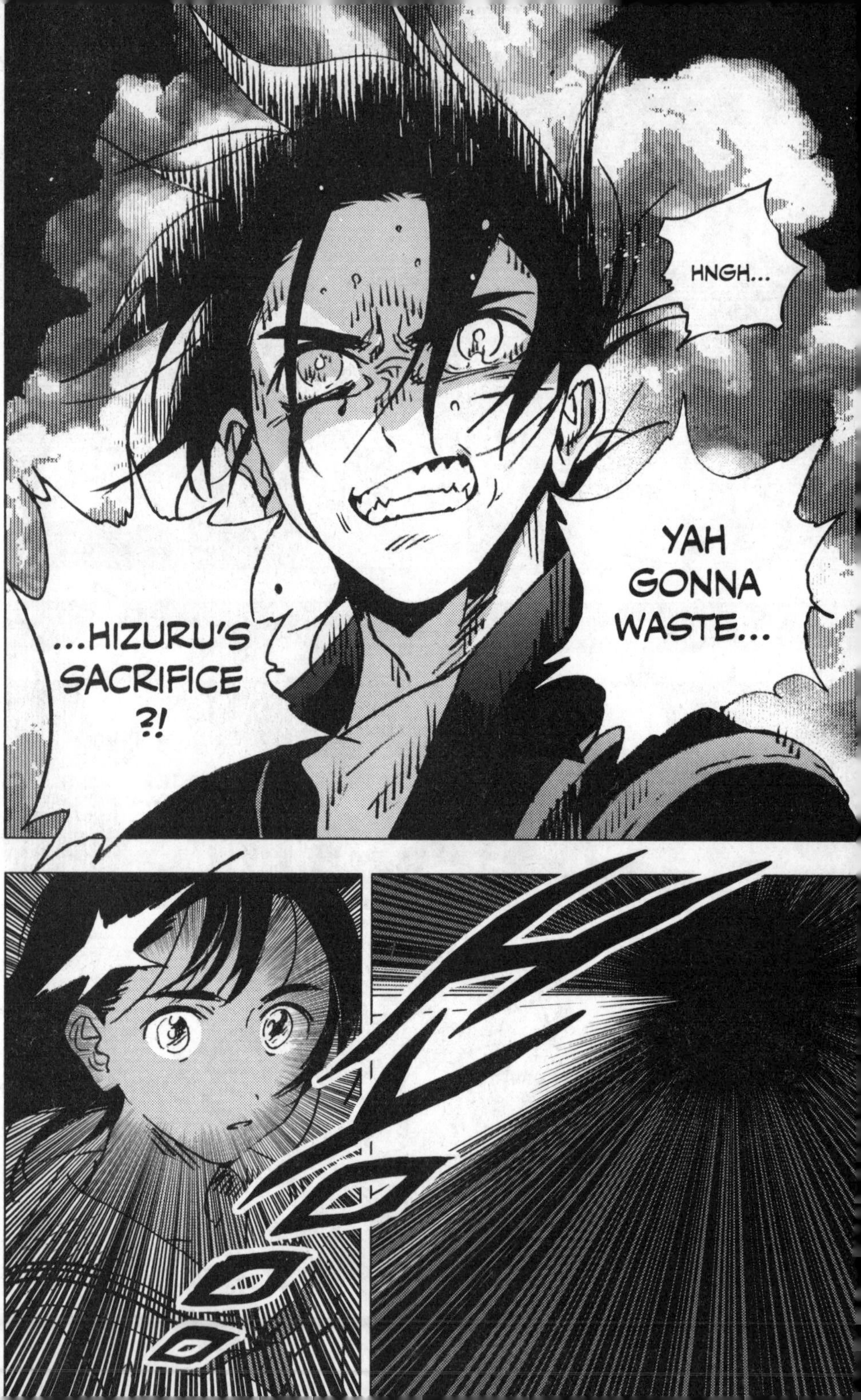
HNGH...
YAH GONNA WASTE...
...HIZURU'S SACRIFICE ?!

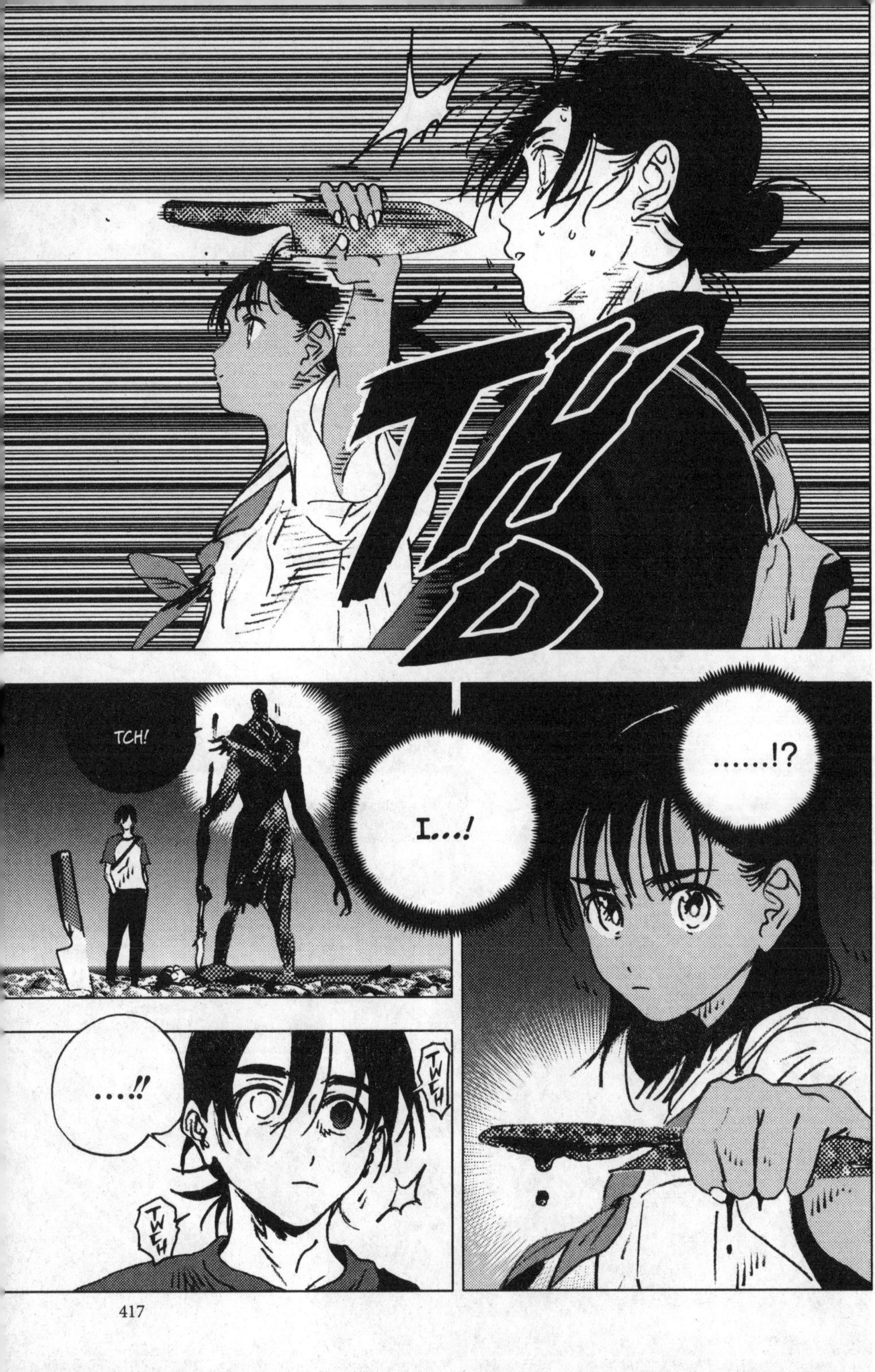
THD
......!?
I...!
TCH!
....!!
TWEH
TWEH

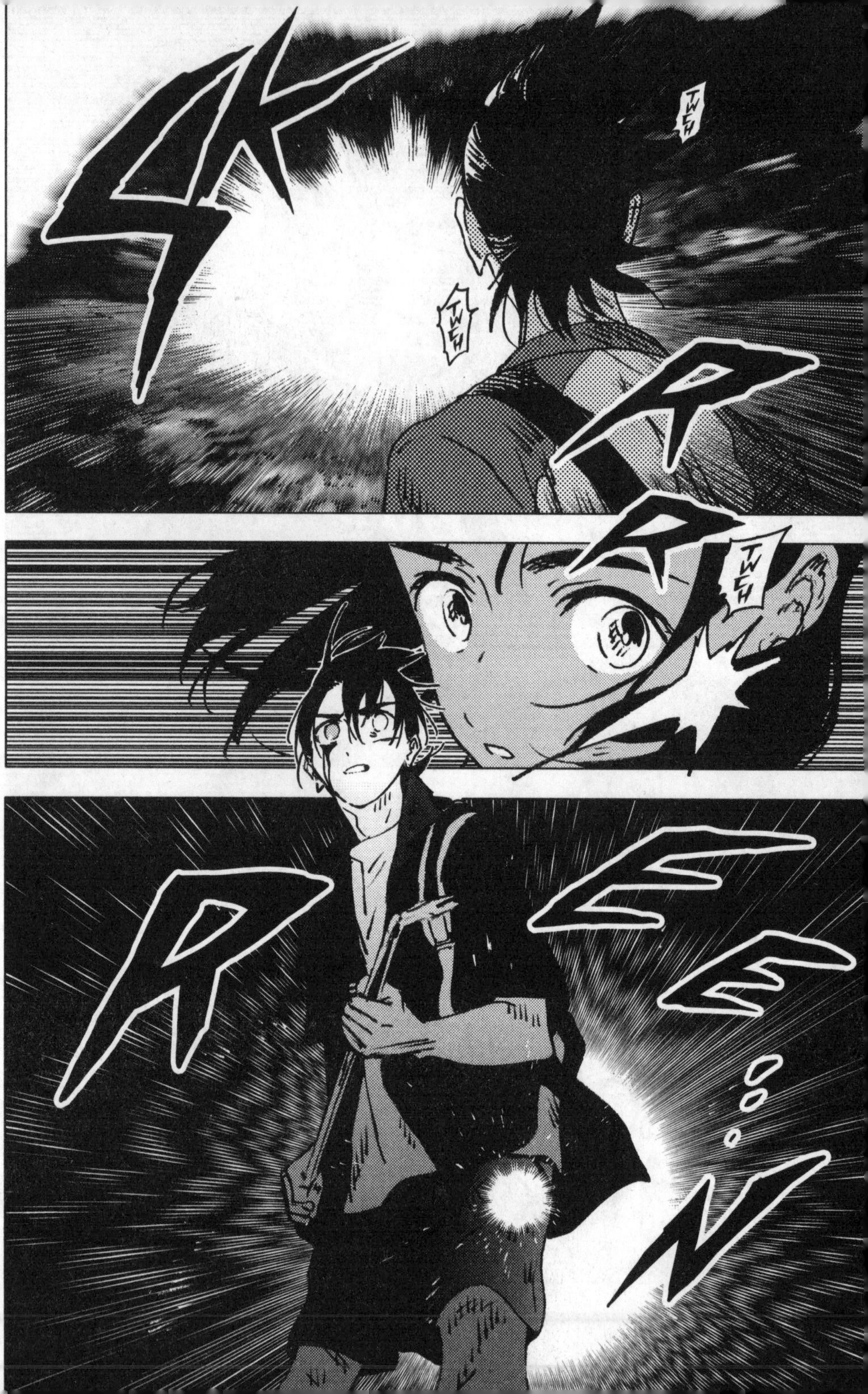

TWCH
SK
TWCH
R
TWCH
R
EEE...N
R

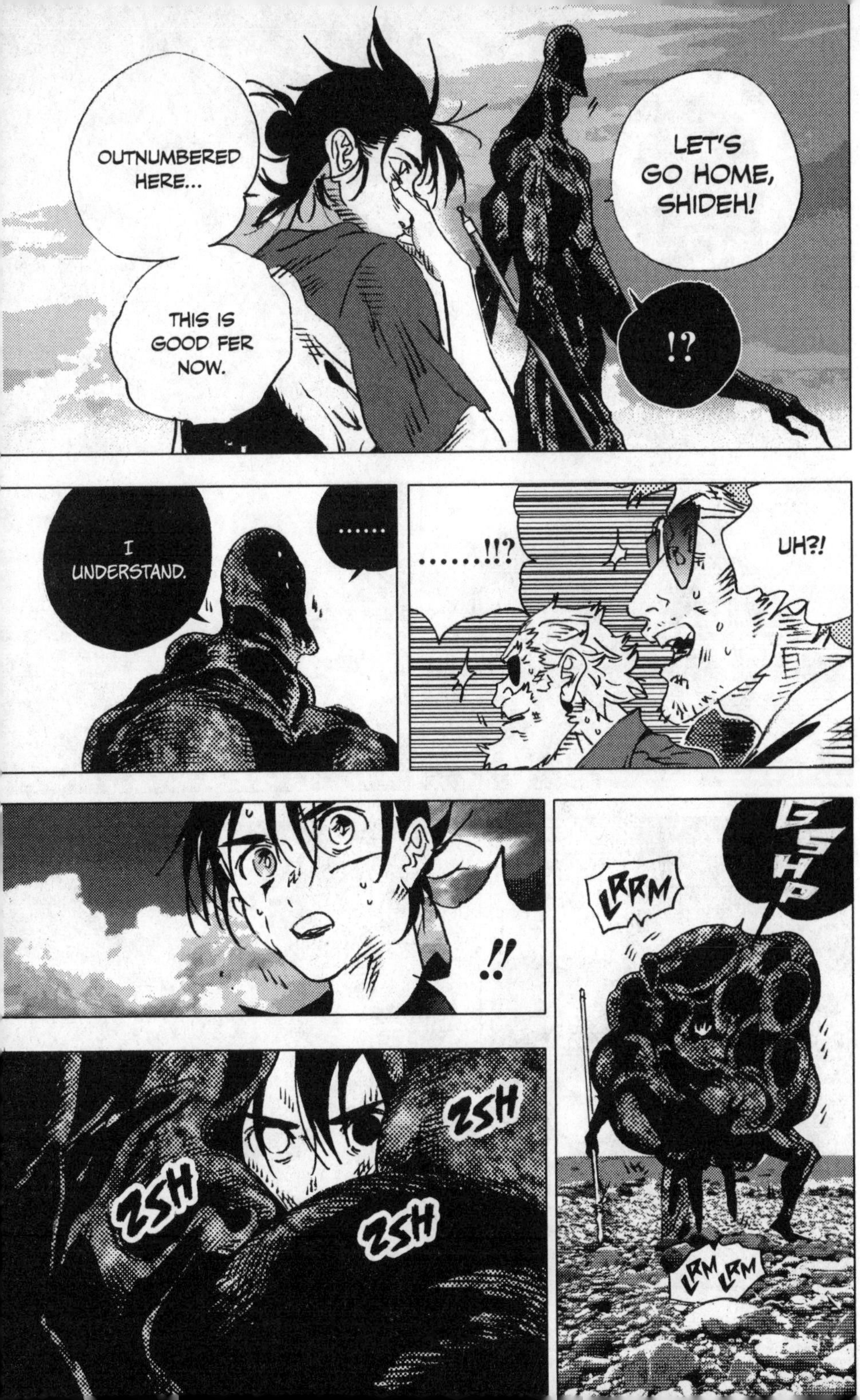
LET'S GO HOME, SHIDEH!
OUTNUMBERED HERE...
THIS IS GOOD FER NOW.
!?
UH?!
.......!!?
....
I UNDERSTAND.
GSHP
LRRM
LRM LRM
!!
ZSH
ZSH
ZSH

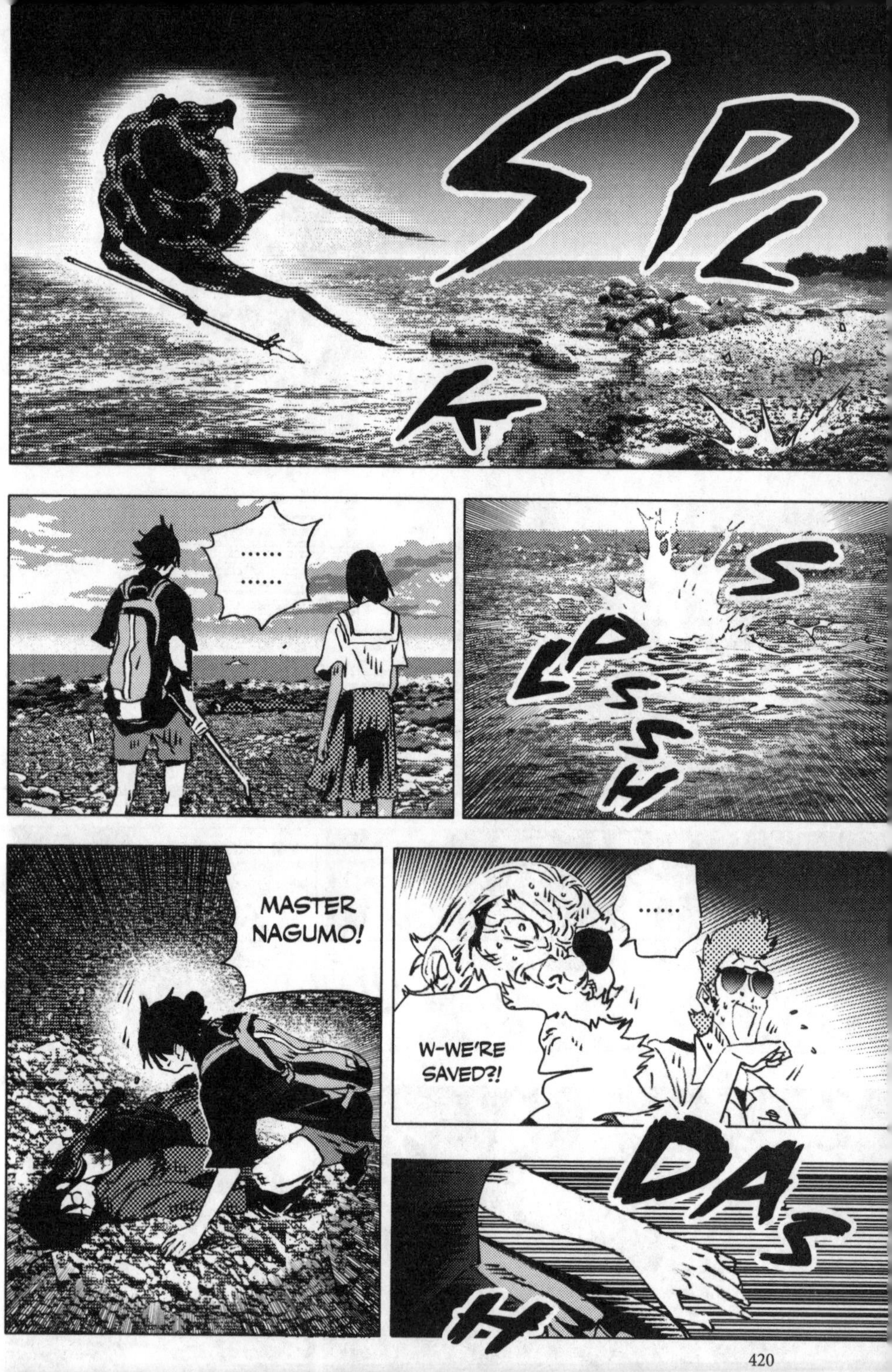

SPLK
SPLSSH
......
......
......
W-WE'RE SAVED?!
DASH
MASTER NAGUMO!

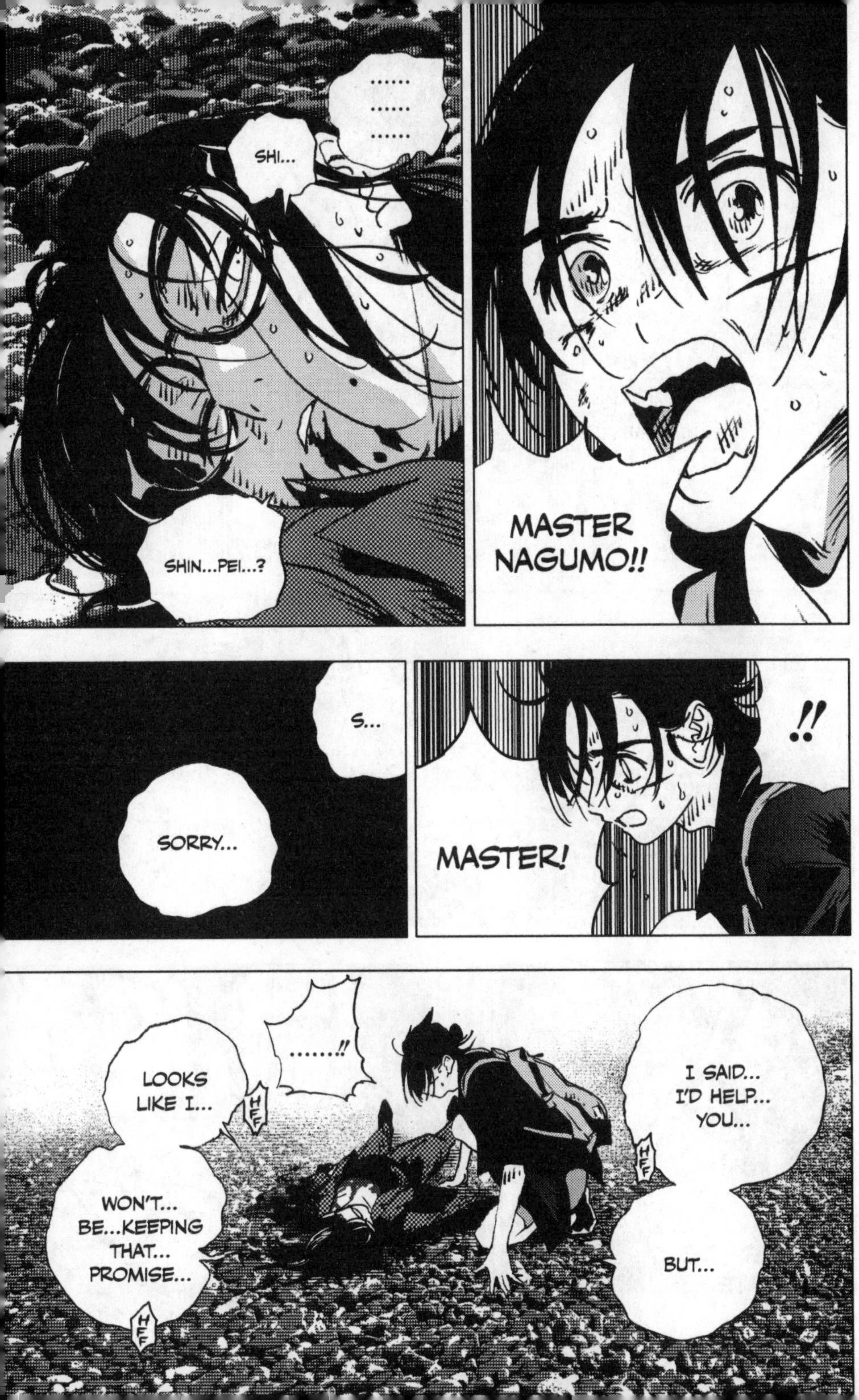
MASTER NAGUMO!!
......
......
......
SHI...
SHIN...PEI...?
!!
MASTER!
S...
SORRY...
I SAID... I'D HELP... YOU...
HFF
BUT...
......!!
LOOKS LIKE I...
HFF
WON'T... BE...KEEPING THAT... PROMISE...
HFF

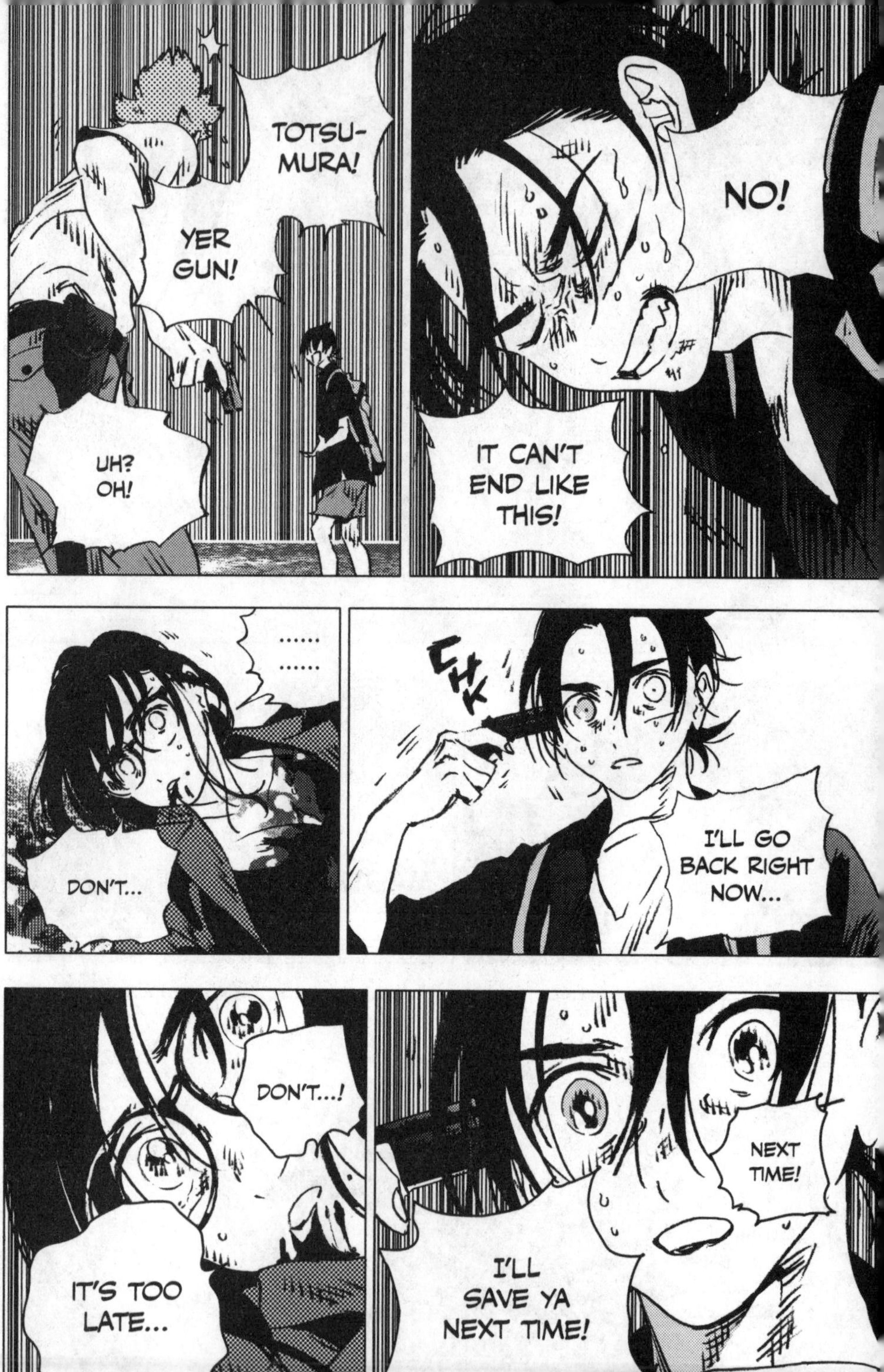
NO!
IT CAN'T END LIKE THIS!
TOTSU-MURA!
YER GUN!
UH? OH!
CHK
I'LL GO BACK RIGHT NOW...
......
......
DON'T...
NEXT TIME!
I'LL SAVE YA NEXT TIME!
DON'T...!
IT'S TOO LATE...

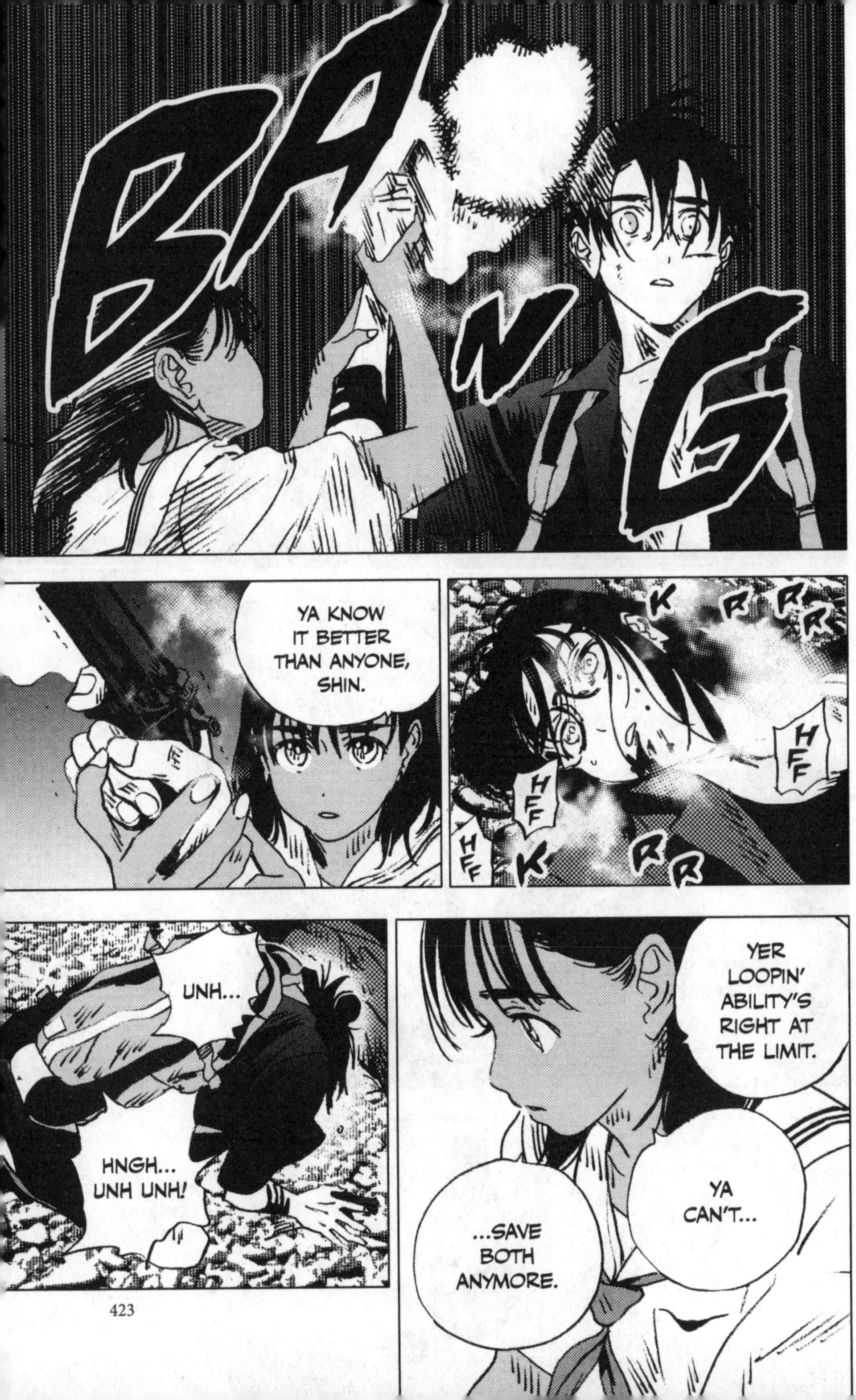
BANG
K RRRR
HFF
HFF
HFF
K RR
YA KNOW IT BETTER THAN ANYONE, SHIN.
YER LOOPIN' ABILITY'S RIGHT AT THE LIMIT.
YA CAN'T...
...SAVE BOTH ANYMORE.
UNH...
HNGH... UNH UNH!

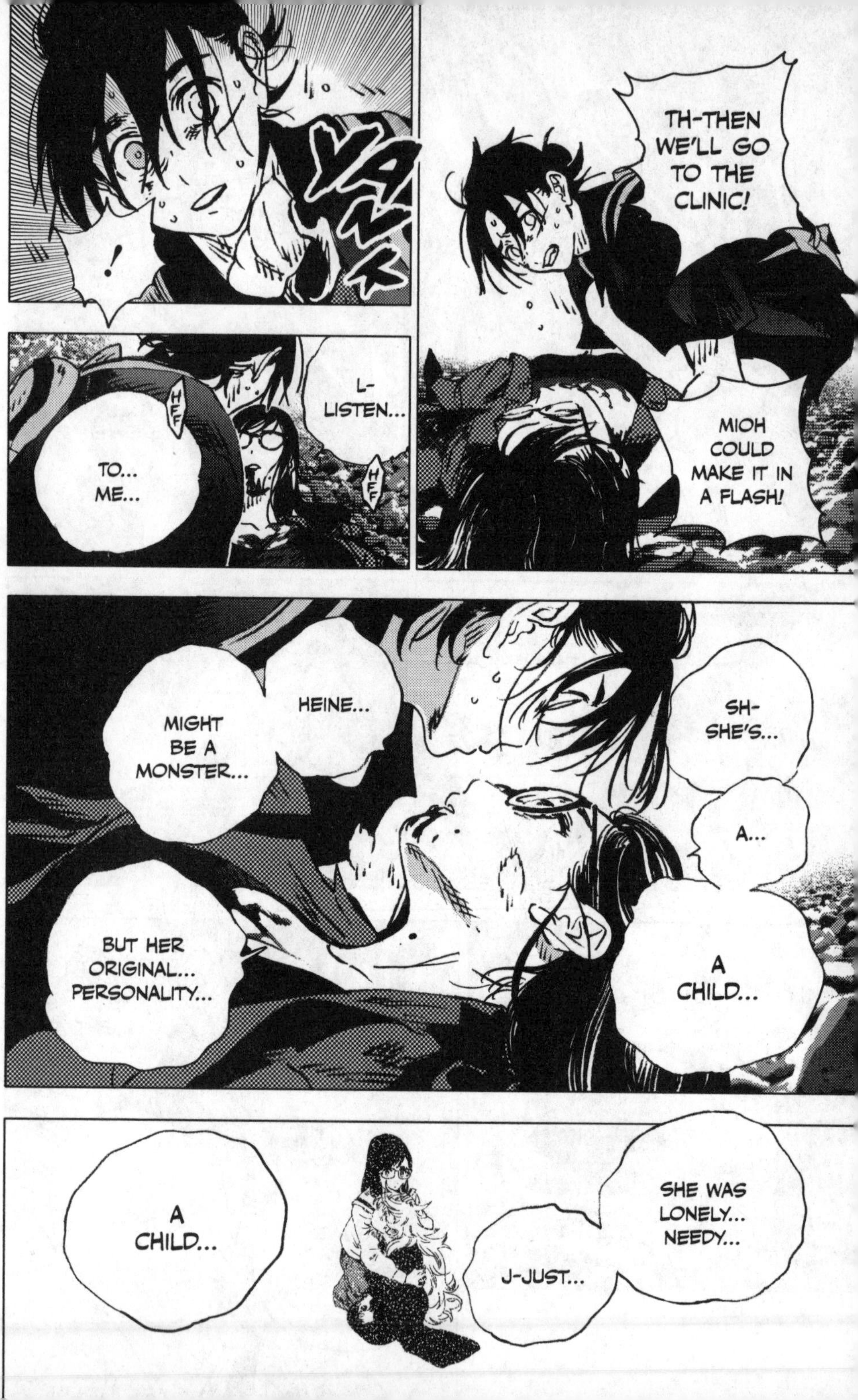
TH-THEN WE'LL GO TO THE CLINIC!
MIOH COULD MAKE IT IN A FLASH!
YANK
!
L- LISTEN...
HFF
TO... ME...
HFF
SH- SHE'S...
HEINE...
MIGHT BE A MONSTER...
A...
A CHILD...
BUT HER ORIGINAL... PERSONALITY...
SHE WAS LONELY... NEEDY...
J-JUST...
A CHILD...

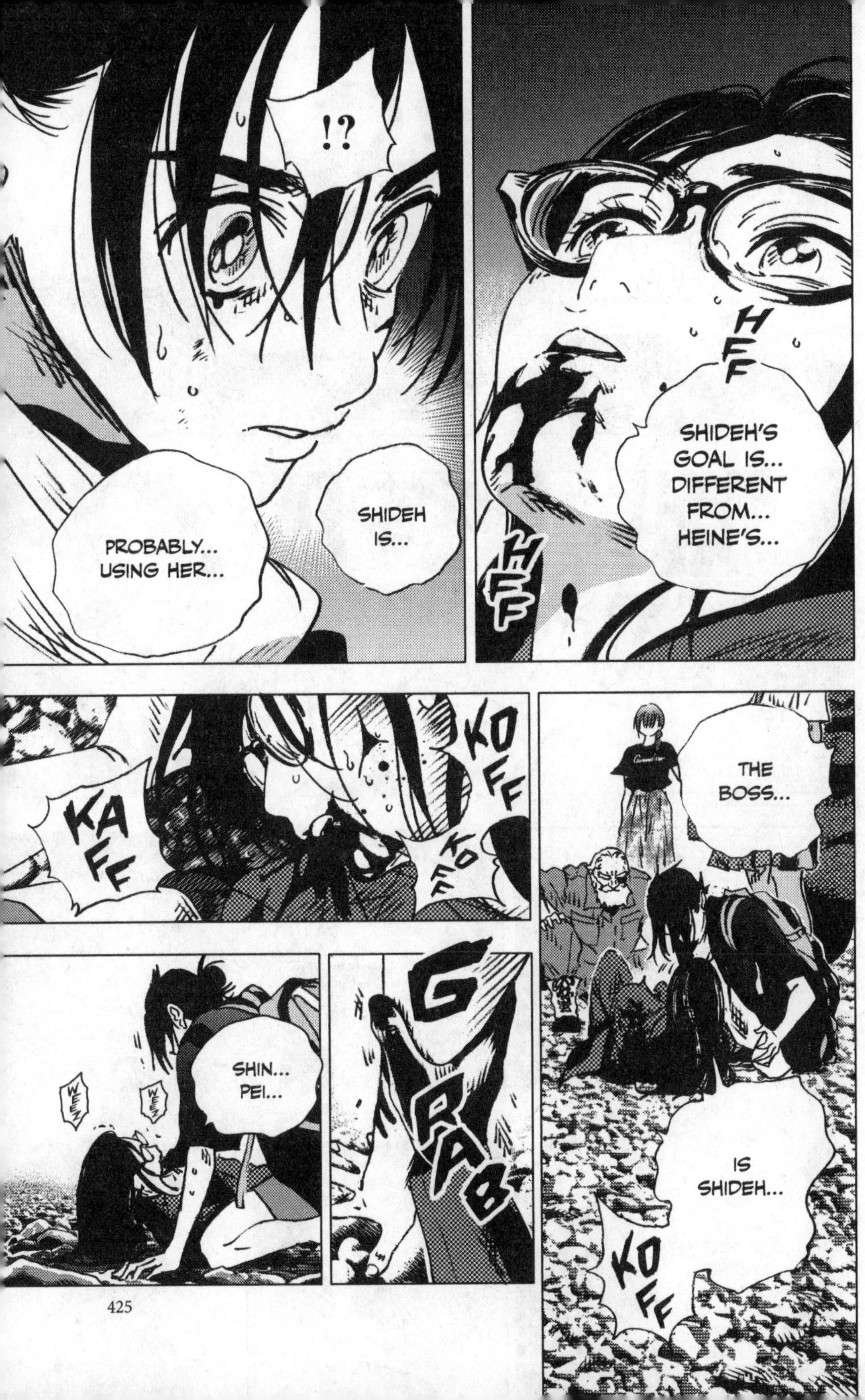
HFF
SHIDEH'S GOAL IS... DIFFERENT FROM... HEINE'S...
HFF
!?
SHIDEH IS...
PROBABLY... USING HER...
THE BOSS...
IS SHIDEH...
KOFF
KOFF
KOFF
KAFF
GRAB
SHIN... PEI...
WEEZ
WEEZ

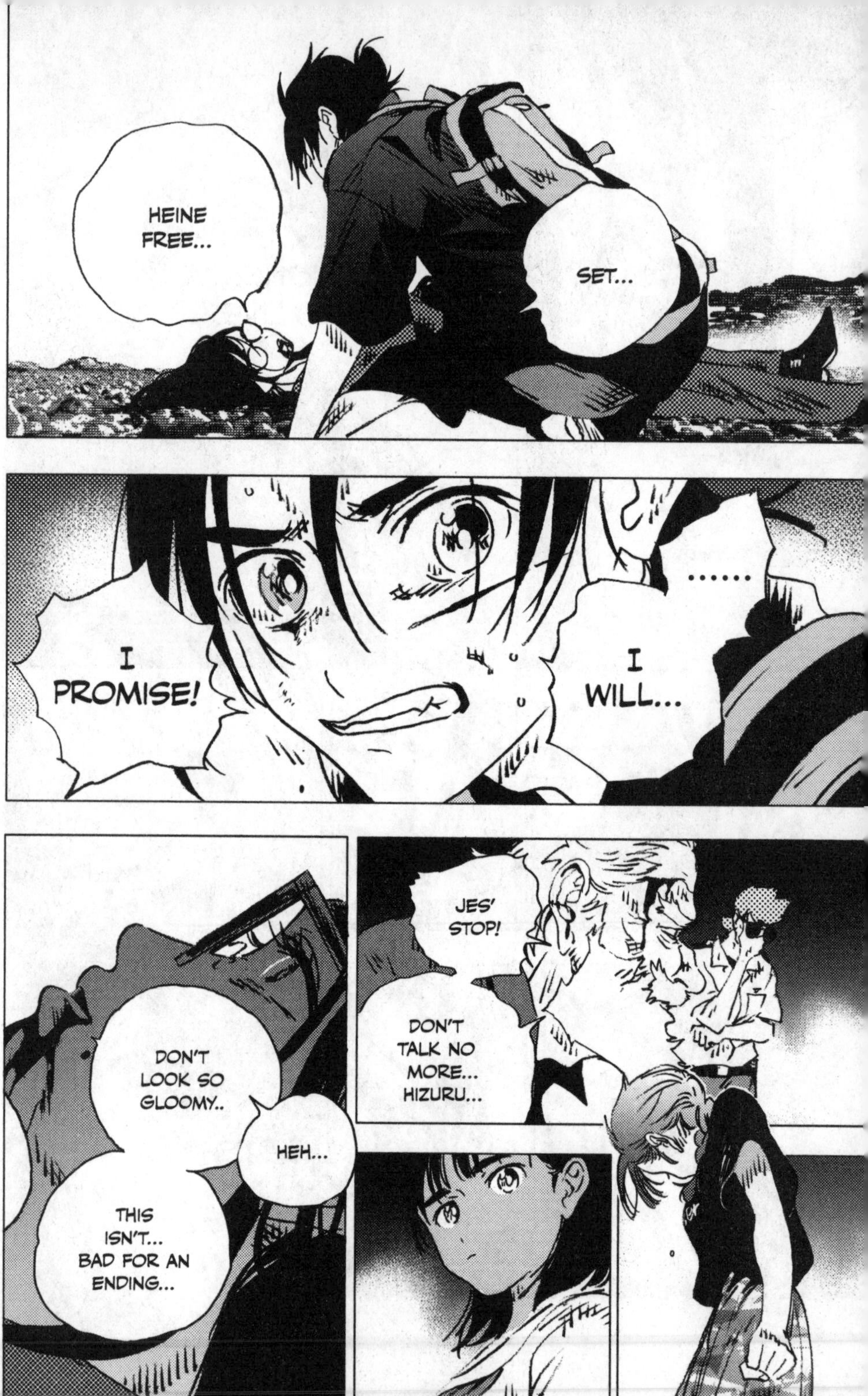
SET...
HEINE FREE...
......
I WILL...
I PROMISE!
JES' STOP!
DON'T TALK NO MORE... HIZURU...
DON'T LOOK SO GLOOMY..
HEH...
THIS ISN'T... BAD FOR AN ENDING...

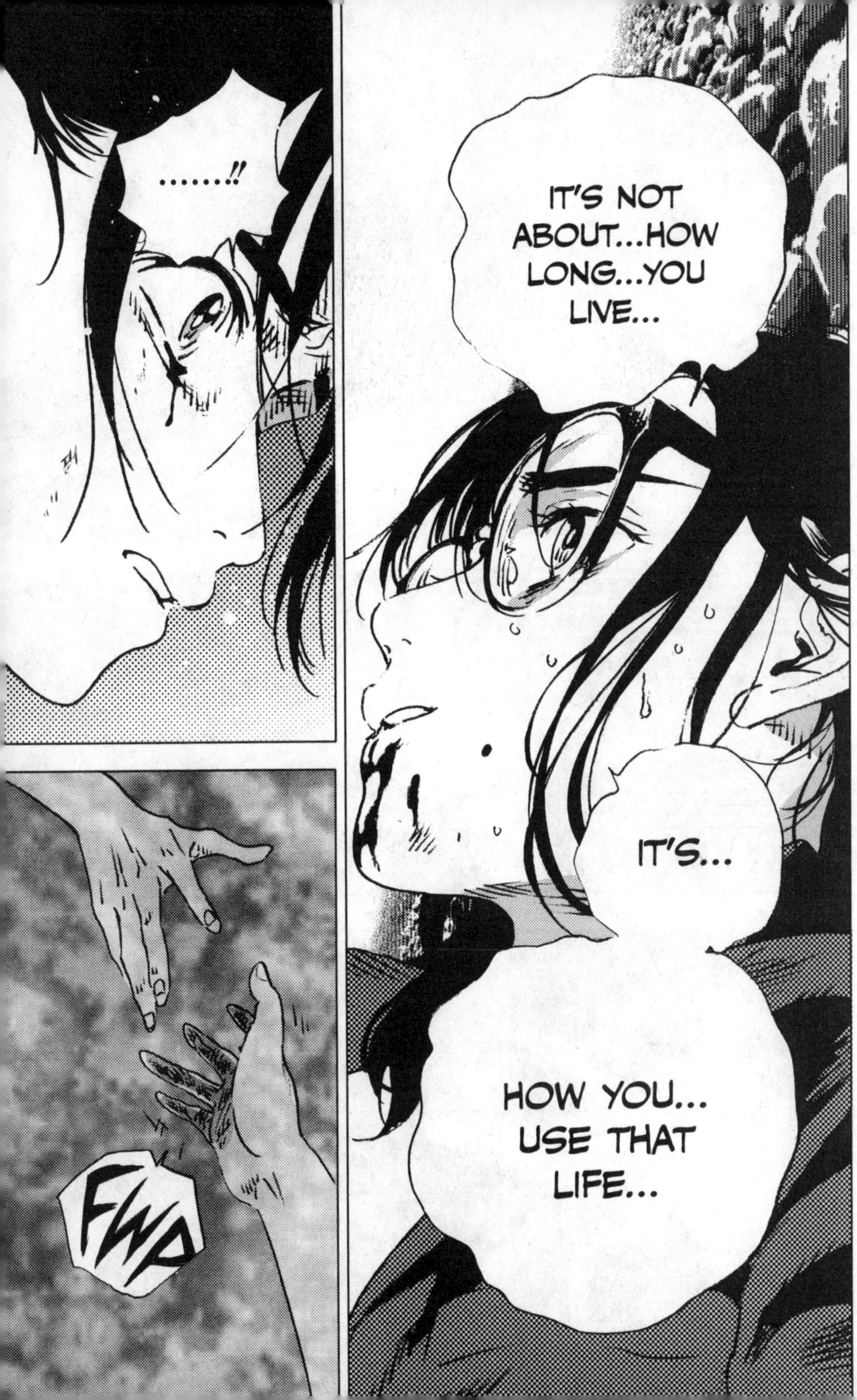
IT'S NOT ABOUT...HOW LONG...YOU LIVE...
IT'S...
HOW YOU... USE THAT LIFE...
......!!
FWP

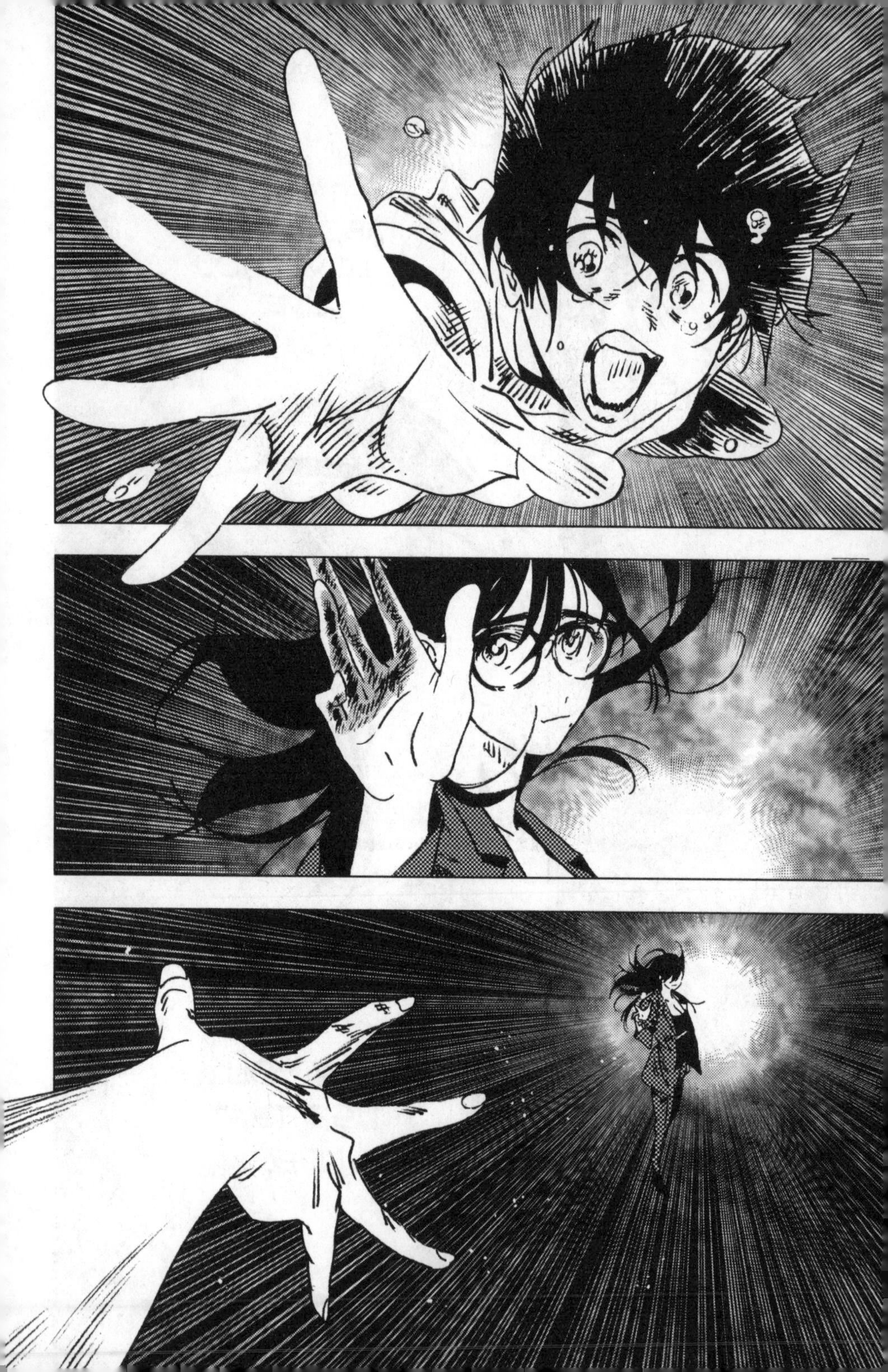

I LEAVE...

RYUNOSUKE... TO YOU...

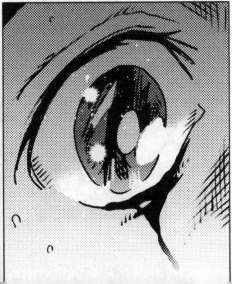

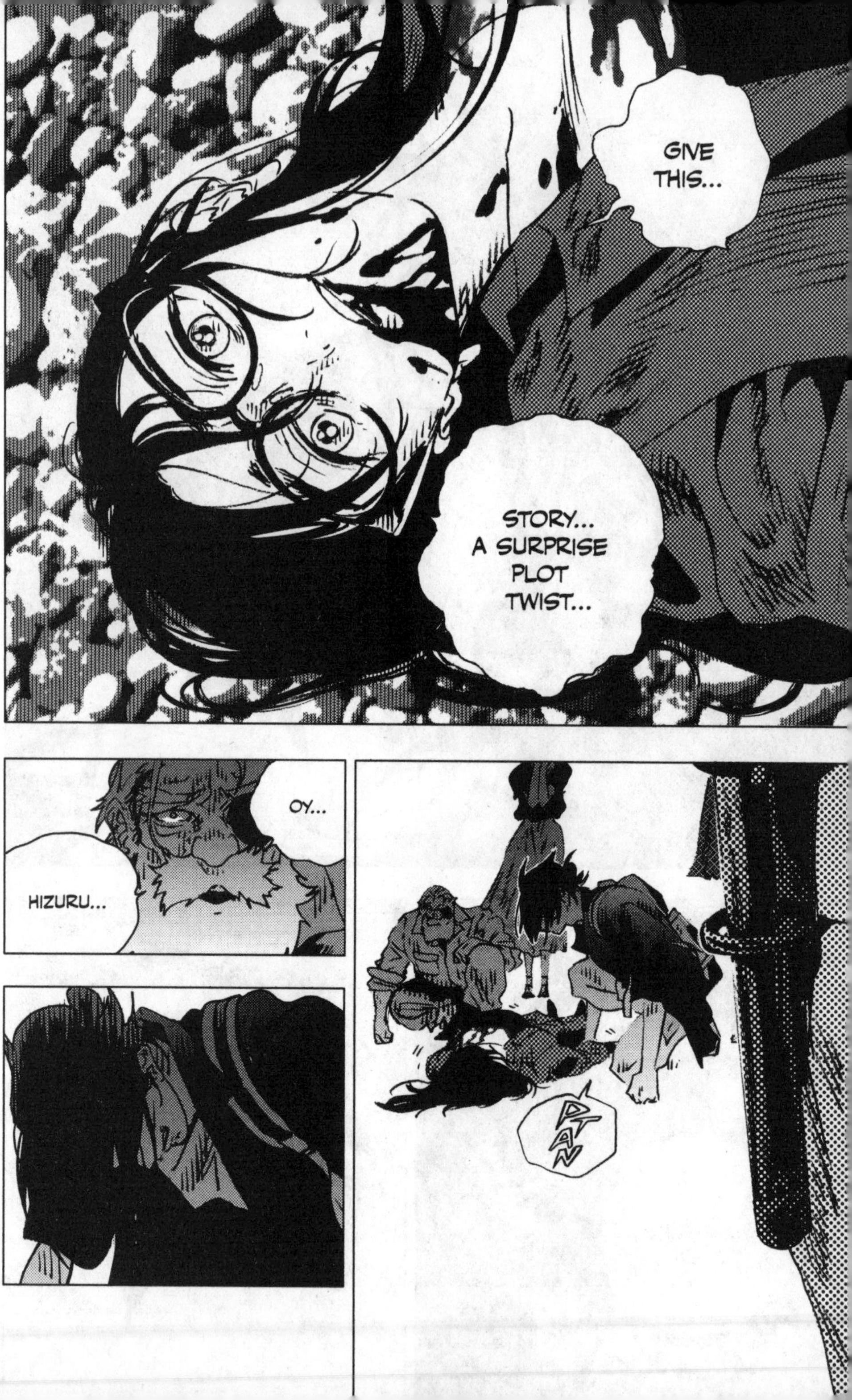
GIVE THIS...
STORY... A SURPRISE PLOT TWIST...
OY...
HIZURU...
PTAN

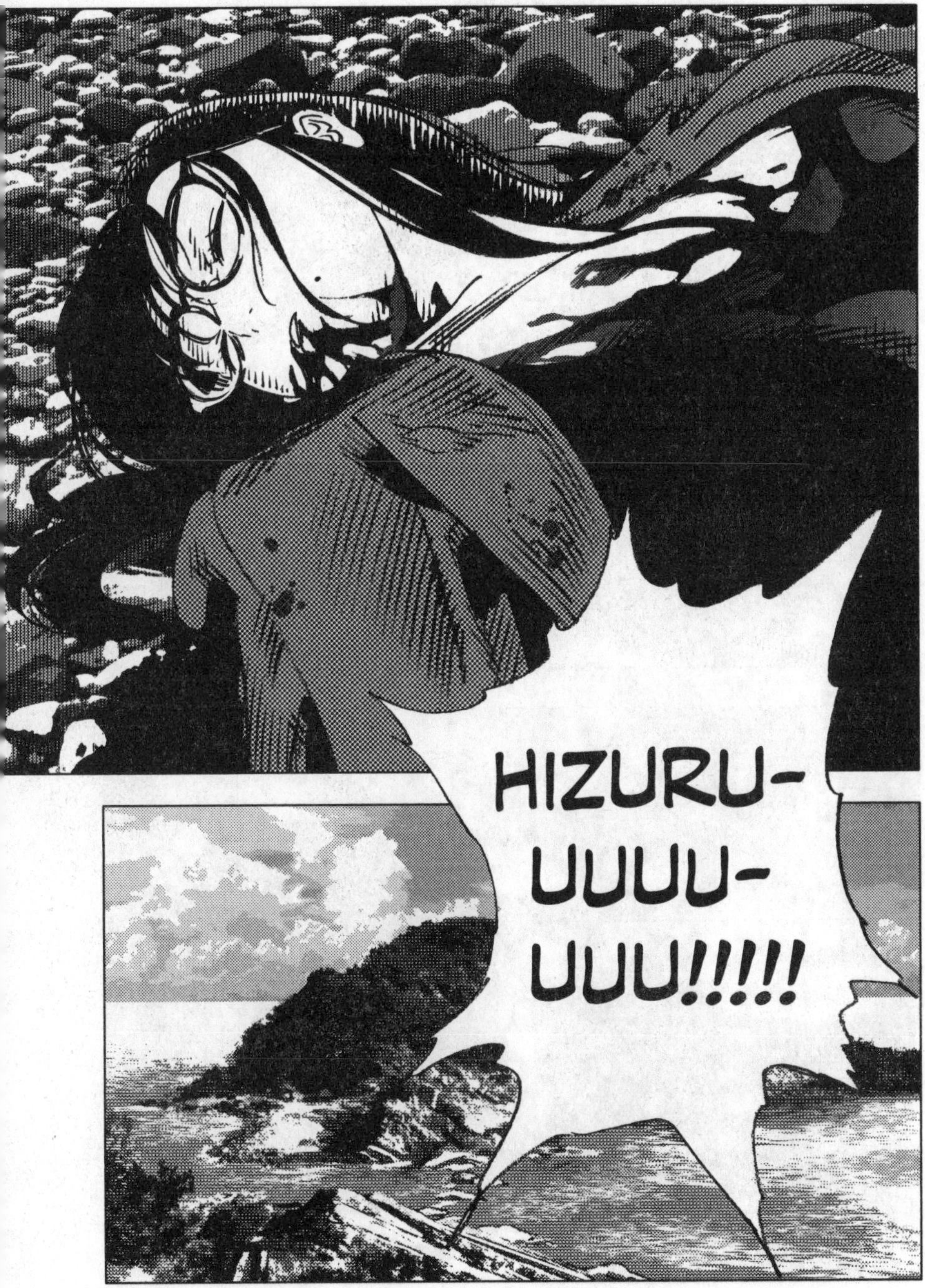
HIZURU-UUUUU-UUU!!!!!

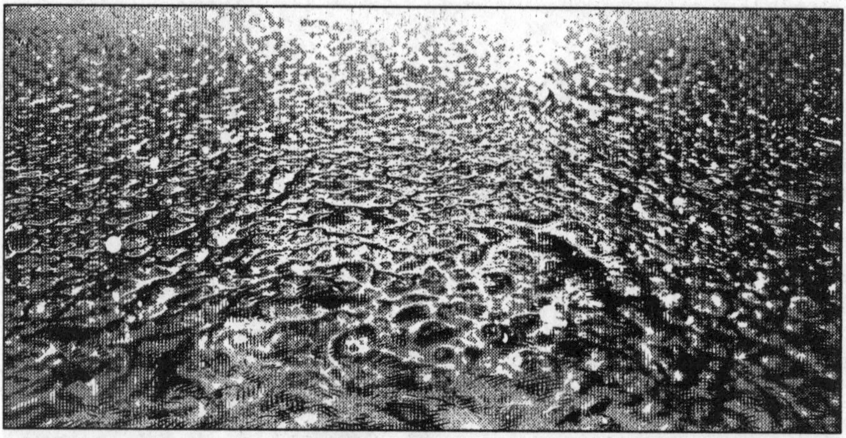

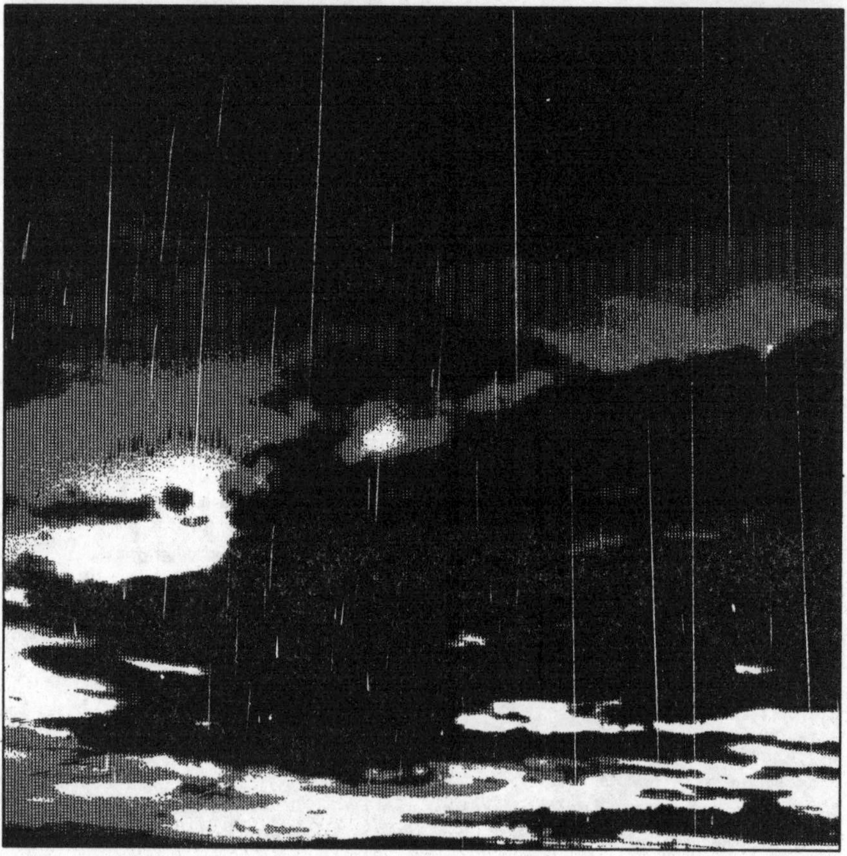

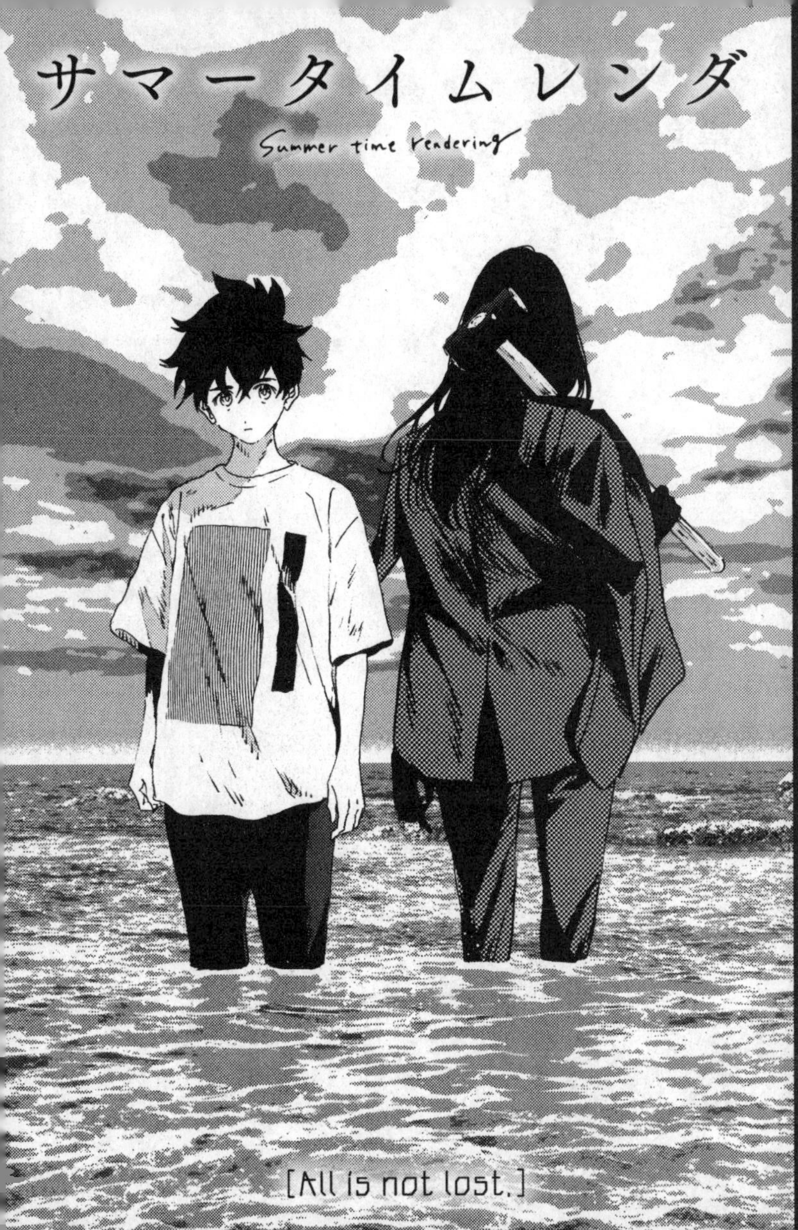
サマータイムレンダ
Summer time rendering
[All is not lost.]

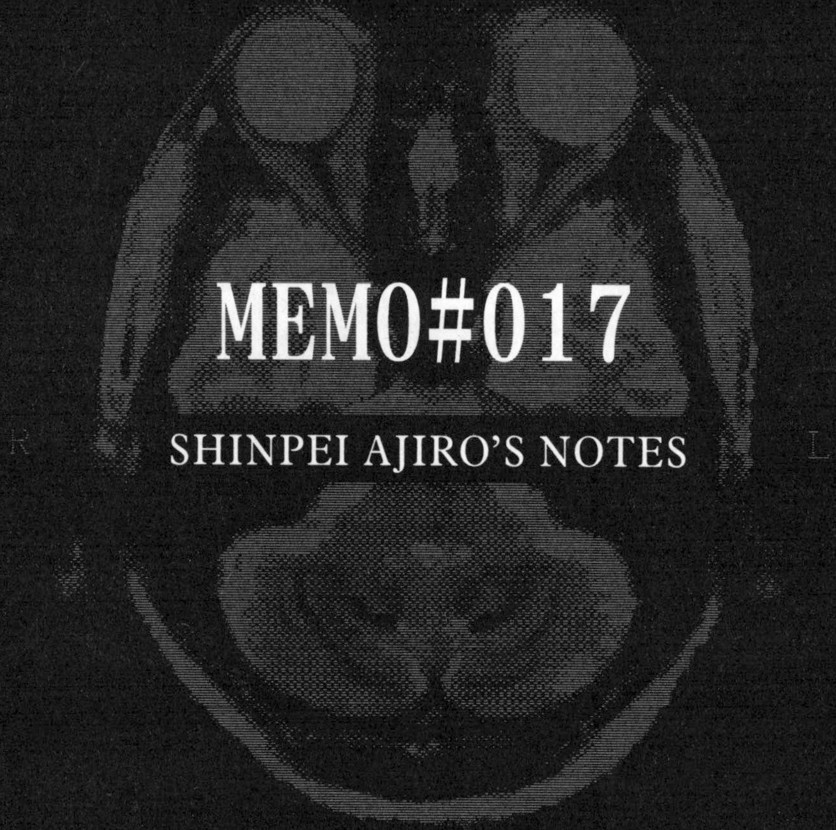
R
L

MEMO#017

SHINPEI AJIRO'S NOTES

THE JULY 22ND OF THE 7TH LOOP, LATE AT NIGHT.

THIS IS AN EXCERPT OF THE NOTES THAT WAS TAKEN DURING THE OPERATION MEETING AT HISHIGATA CLINIC.

[DEALING WITH THE DEVIL]

"THERE'S NO TRUST BETWEEN SEIDO HISHIGATA AND SHIDEH.
HOWEVER, SEIDO GOT HIS HANDS DIRTY AS WELL.
THERE'S NO TURNIN' BACK FOR HIM NOW.
WHEN DID SEIDO REALIZE THE TRUTH 'BOUT SHIDEH?
WE DON'T KNOW IF HE'S GOIN' TO BETRAY US.
IT'S STILL BETTER TO BE CAUTIOUS."

No.

Date   .   .

TESTIMONY OF SEIDO HISHIGATA

July 22nd (7th Loop) about 9:20 pm.

• First floor of the Hishigata house. Seido's in his study. The doorbell rang.

  Door monitor shows it is Nurse Negoro. She said, "I left something here."

• Seido suspiciously opened the door and the scan light suddenly shone.
  (This is when he realized that Shideh had betrayed him.)
    He escaped during the scanning time gap and went to his wife Chitose's room.

• He put Chitose, who had no idea what's happening and was confused,   *Meanwhile, Negoro*
  in a wheelchair, and went through the door to the hospital.   *was trying to erase*
                                                                          all the furniture.

• They were trying to get to the entrance to Hiruko's Grotto at
  the end of the secret passage. (Grotto's connected to the ocean &
                    can escape with diving equipments.)
                                                         Too old to use.
                                                         Dangerous!

• Negoro caught them in front of the elevator's door on the first floor.
  Seido used his gun (a Derringer) in defense, and injured Negoro.

• ~~S~~ Negoro was crying out in pain, as they got on the elevator.
    On their way to the basement Chitose started to act weird.
    She started looking like she was in pain, then she lost it and attacked Seido.

• When they arrived at the basement, Seido ran. Chitose ditched the wheelchair,
  chased down the passage and caught Seido.

  ⎧ Negoro came down to the basement and she collected Ushio's body.
  ⎪ At that point we arrived at the hospital. (9:42 pm.)
  ⎨ Negoro felt the presence of shadows, came out of the corridor, and ran into us.
  ⎩ She then turned back and took Ushio's body and ran to the passage.

• Seido saw Negoro, who was taking Ushio's body, ran into the secret passage.
  Seido got strangled and his heart stopped, but he was saved by Sou's
  resuscitation procedure.

MEMO#018

FLOWERS BLOOMING ON HITOGASHIMA

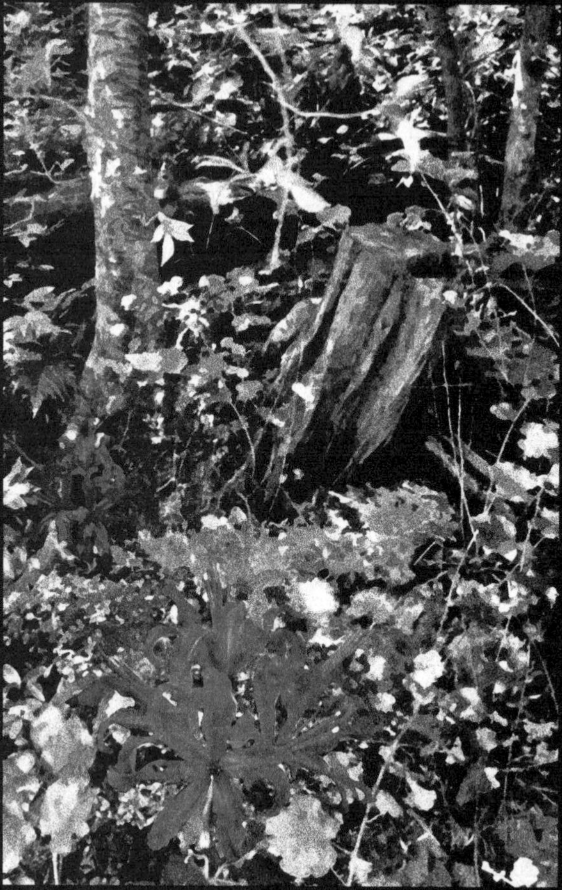

KIKYO (CHINESE BELL FLOWER)

An old flower which was written about in the Manyoshu (Collection of Ten Thousand Leaves). It's also one of the seven spring herbs.

The numbers of the Kikyo have decreased. They have been designated as an endangered species.

Kikyo usually has 5 petals, but the ones you can find on Mt. Takanosu are very rare and they have 4 petals.

NERINE

The flowers native to Africa. They were brought back from Africa in the Taisho era.

They usually bloom from Autumn to Winter, but they are fully in bloom during the whole year on Mt. Takanosu.

They were Ushio's favorite flowers and they were used as parting flowers at her funeral.

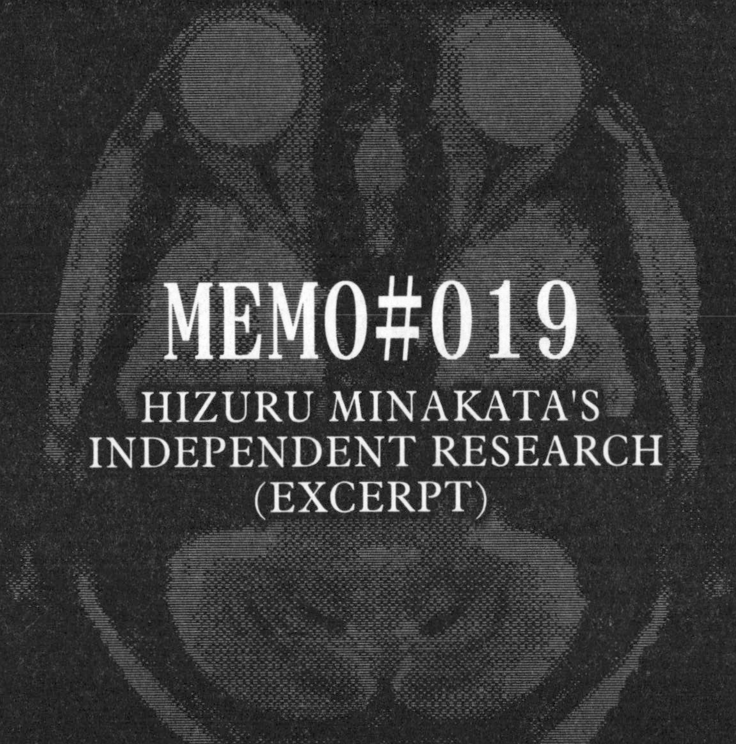
R
L

MEMO#019

HIZURU MINAKATA'S INDEPENDENT RESEARCH (EXCERPT)

THIS IS A REPORT THAT HIZURU MINAKATA DID
WHEN SHE WAS IN 4TH GRADE ABOUT 20 YEARS AGO.

\<CONTENTS\>

Well done, Hizuru!!
You researched quite a lot
and it's so well written that
I was drawn into it!!
Good job!

*SIGNED = BU = BUCCHI

THE REAL IDENTITY OF HIRUKO, GOD OF HITOGASHIMA

Hitogashima Elementary school. Grade 4.
Hizuru Minakata

< Reason for research >

• I read the record of ancient matters and the chronicle of Japan, and I thought the island that the Gods Izanagi and Izanami made could be Hitogashima. So I was interested in the origin of the island.

< Process >

• Go to Hito Shrine and talk to the shrine priest.
The person who told me the story was Mr. Masahito Karikiri, heir to the Hito shrine.

August 10, 1999

• Research at the history museum.

The handle portion was replaced many times and the current handle is made from wood (oak) and was built in the Edo era. Some say the spearhead was made from an iron meteorite and is still as sharp as when it was made without having rusted (there is no scientific foundation to back this up...)

- It wasn't meant for war or battle, and more for ceremonial use. But it's sharp enough to kill something.

In the original publication of Volume 11 of the Japanese edition, there was a mistake that says the person young Hizuru talked to at the Hito Shrine was Iwao Karikiri instead of Masahito Karikiri. This comic panel was published in the correction notice in Volume 12. We have corrected the mistake in our English edition, but wish to include the comic panel here because it is quite funny!

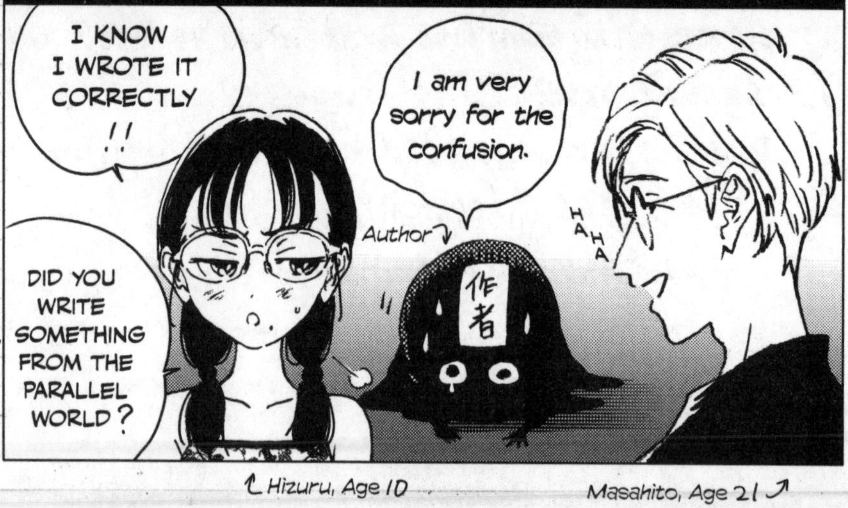
HAHAHA
I am very sorry for the confusion.
Author
作者
I KNOW I WROTE IT CORRECTLY !!
DID YOU WRITE SOMETHING FROM THE PARALLEL WORLD?

Hizuru, Age 10 Masahito, Age 21

4. The Sacred Treasure · Amanonuboko

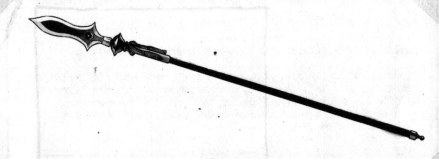

Drawing · Ryunosuke Minakata

- ## Sacred treasure of Hitogashima
  It has the same name as the spear that was used in the mythology of the creation of Japan.
  The Gods Izanagi and Izanami dipped the spear into the ocean brine and churned, and when they lifted the spear up, briny drops from its tip created the first island of Japan, which is called Onogoro Island.

- We don't know when it was given to the Hito Shrine. According to the shrine's history, it was already here several thousand years before people started to live in this island.

AFTERWORDS

ORIGINALLY PUBLISHED IN VOL. 9 OF THE JAPANESE EDITION.

I just wanted to talk about what kind of gamer I am.
For me, a game doesn't mean in-app purchases, leveling up as a task, managing numbers, or interpersonal battles.

So it's almost like I don't know how to play card games, shogi, Othello, or board games. I only learned how to play card games like UNO after I became an adult and I have to look up the rules every time I want to play.

The things I look for in games are:
Game world development > Music > Directing > Story

What I want to do is to walk around the entire world as the main character and "experience" the whole thing. (Of course, I can't ignore things like gameplay design that hinders the experience, or a difficult-to-use UI [user interface], or a main character being handled roughly...)

With that in mind, DEATH STRANDING, which came out on Nov. 8th 2019, was the greatest "experience"!!!!

The only downside was that the UI text was too small to see... and having to skip the identical package-delivery animation over and over again was annoying. (Apparently the UI text will be fixed when they have an update in December!)

The view of the world was overwhelming... moreover, it matched the game design and theme splendidly and made me want to play more. It's definitely addicting.

This game also uses all real actors and it used their actual faces and voices. It starred Norman Reedus, Mads Mikkelsen, and Guillermo del Toro!!! It's just a good thing for me!

Norman was in a movie called THE BOONDOCK SAINTS which I watched when I was in school, and I thought he was the coolest guy and I tried to dress like him and bought a peacoat and a pair of jeans. Mads was in the television drama HANNIBAL and the way he used his fork and knife was so elegant that I tried to eat like him for a while. Del Toro is not usually an actor. Instead, he is a director. I just loved his PAN'S LABYRINTH!!!

Good games leave something in people who played them.

It's not limited to a sense of game achievement or cinematic sympathy.

Most games, whether first-person or third-person, will allow the player to control the protagonist.

In a game, the player gets to have a bird's-eye view. And in the case of a good game, the act of looking down on the world becomes reality for the player and it broadens their horizons.

In other words, my field of view has been expanded to both 3D and 4D and it makes me look at history, life, and the things that are happening in the real world.

And above all, this paradigm shift happens in the game and that is exciting. DEATH STRANDING is just that kind of game!!

While similar games are being produced, such ambitious works are inspiring and I just hope that the next-generation game industry will become richer for it.

I went off-topic... I told you that I have a problem of not remembering the name of characters that I created before... How about the names of characters in games?
Sam; Amelie; Mama; BB-2B; Kainé; Emil; Gwyn, Lord of Cinder; Father Gascoigne; Ebrietas, Daughter of the Cosmos; Kos-or-some-say-Kosm; Toriel; Sans; Zlatko; and Genichirou Ashina!!! I remember them all!!

Noctis Lucis Caelum, Prompto Argentum, Gladiolus Amicitia and Ignis Scientia... I can even remember all the really long FF15 character names without having to look at Wikipedia!! Apparently I can get into games without thinking too much.

Games are the ultimate entertainment for me!!
I am saved only when I am playing games...

SO GAMES FOREVER!!

It's more like a prayer...

2019. 11. 29 田中靖規

I TRIED TO DISCUSS MY GAME THEORY FROM A NEUTRAL STANDPOINT... WHAT DO YOU THINK... MASTER???
...
Geh Geh
YOU NEED TO TELL ME WHAT THE NEUTRAL STANDPOINT IS FIRST!!

MEMO#020　　SHADOW RYUNOSUKE

- The shadow of Hizuru Minakata's twin brother,
  Ryunosuke Minakata (died at the age of 15).

- Hizuru and Ryunosuke are semi-identical twins (two sperms fertilize
  one egg and split into twins) which is rare globally.

- Ryunosuke was killed by Heine when he was 15 and then copied.
  However, he somehow was split into mud and data (Ryunosuke),
  and the mud stole Heine's right eye and went missing.
  The data was printed onto Hizuru's body.

  Because of this, Ryunosuke is 2 seconds ahead of his time
  (thus, Hizuru has experienced fourth-dimensional time travel,
  and she believes in Shinpei's time leaps).

  By the above circumstances, his existence is irregular because
  he doesn't have an actual body.

- Unlike regular shadows, he doesn't have a weakness of a flat shadow
  and he doesn't receive Heine's telepathy.

- He doesn't have ability to copy anyone, but he can mimic
  the behavior of someone he has seen once.

- On the emotional side he has the same personality as Ryunosuke.

- He can feel the presence of other shadows (under the influence of
  Shadow Ryunosuke, Hizuru is able to feel the presence of shadows a
  little bit as well). He has super human reflexes like other shadows, but
  it will be a big burden to Hizuru's body to exhibits his actual abilities.

- Shadow Ryunosuke's presence is controlled by Hizuru.
  His consciousness is awakened when Hizuru ties back her hair.
  Hizuru is the main personality; when Hizuru is awake Ryunosuke is
  unconscious, but when Ryunosuke is awake, Hizuru remains awake.

- They used a voice recorder and memo pad to communicate with each
  other. However, Ryunosuke has only spent a few months awake over
  the past 14 years, so his appearance and mental age remain that of a
  15-year-old boy.

AFTERWORDS

ORIGINALLY PUBLISHED IN VOL. 10 OF THE JAPANESE EDITION.

This comic has made it to Vol. (10)

To those who has bought my manga & supported me - THANK YOU VERY MUCH!!!!!!

When I started this book, I was writing a plot that would end around Vol. 10...

But contrary to my intentions, the characters have started to play active roles as the story is unfolding. So I have decided to up the volumes.

Everyone's doing great jobs... well, I like draw them.

It is like I am doing my own Summertime Rendering.

When I am working on this book, it feels as though I am on Hitogashima Island filming (sketching?) whatever Shinpei, Ushio, Nagumo and the others are doing, like they are moving around on their own.

Every week when I work on my layouts, I am like, "Are they going to do this!?" and "What is he gonna say?" And it surprised every time.

Rather than thinking about the character's feelings, it's more like I'm seeing the character doing things and trying to figure out how they would feel. (Is this okay to do as an creator...)

It's more like I am standing there next to Shinpei and his friends and enjoying the story like I am playing a VR game.

It's a tremendous sense of reality every day. I hope you can enjoy the same sense of reality when you read it as I do when I am drawing.

It would be an unexpected joy if this happiness is conveyed even a little.

See you in Vol. (11)!!

2020. 3. 18 田中靖規

Games I played recently (random order):

- *13 Sentinels: Aegis Rim → it's too fun and it's mortifying!!*
- *Dreams Universe → If only I had more time... I want to make games—!*
- *Celeste → It's difficult, but sooo cute*
- *Control → I just love SCP stuff!*
- *FF7 Remake trial version → It's just great! My expectation is high for the main game.*
- *Nioh 2 → Making characters is too much fun! I can't stop!!*

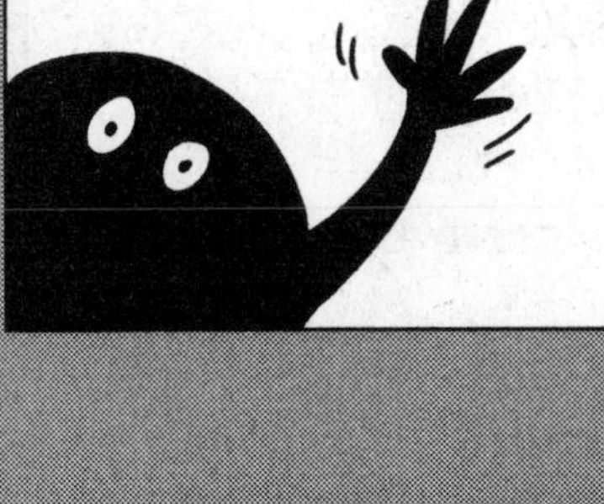

AFTERWORDS

ORIGINALLY PUBLISHED IN VOL. 11 OF THE JAPANESE EDITION.

As with any dialect, the Wakayama dialect is also very complex, and the wording differs depending on the region and generation.

The language is quite different in the northern and southern parts of Wakayama prefecture, and even classmates that lived in the same city had slightly different accents.

In addition, there's an old Wayakama dialect that not only I, a person in their thirties, but also my parents' generation do not speak. (Hitogashima is located in Wakayama city in the northern part of Wakayama prefecture) Among the characters in this manga, Nezu speaks a quite heavy Wakayama dialect, which is modeled on my grandparents' generation.

So, one day, while working on a rough draft, I wrote Nezu's line, 「知るまえ」 "Shiromae", in the sense of 〜かもしれないだろ "Kamo shirenai daro" [It could be ___, right?], but wasn't sure of the nuance so I searched it online.

But nothing came up.

I had heard my grandfather (who would have been in his 90s if he was alive) use that term before, so to make sure, I asked my mother who lives in Wakayama. As I thought, it was surely a term used by my mother's parents' generation. However, this was a term used at times when saying something like 「若いモンは知るまえが」 "Wakaimon ha shiromae ga" [You young people would not know, but...], and was apparently not used in the sense of 「〜かもしれない」 "~kamo shirenai" [It could be ~] (the term is probably a corruption of 『知るまい』 "Shirumai", which uses negative assumption 「〜まい」 "mai" [auxiliary verb]), so I ended up not using this phrase in the line afterall.

However at this point, I realized something.

This dialect expression 「知らすえ」 "Shiromae" is a phrase that will mostly disappeared from this earth when the very few speakers who use it are gone. It surprised me because it was a phrase spoken by a person close to me in the past. In a world that saves all sorts of information, there are phrases that don't even show up on a search engine. And there are phrases that will disappear from this world.

But languages are living things. It's natural they change or perish. So it's not like "Oh, let's save it because it will disappear", or "I'm sad", or "I feel sorry". I just thought "I see", but the emotions I held at that time were none of the feelings of 喜怒哀楽 "Ki Do Ai Raku" (Joy, Anger, Grief, Pleasure).

To my surprise, there were no words in me that could properly express my feelings when I realized that phrases that were familiar to me could gone for good.

There are feelings that are lost when put into words.

With this overwhelming fact right in front of me, emotions, none of which being 喜怒哀楽 (Joy, Anger, Grief, Pleasure), fill my heart again.

2020. 6. 23 田中靖規

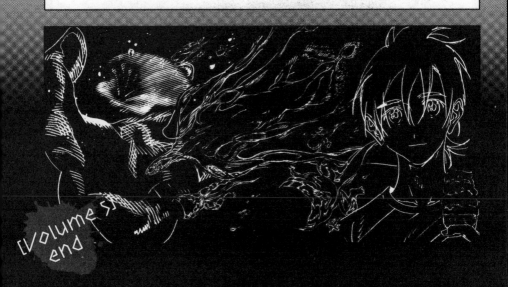

[Volume 5] end

SUMMERTIME RENDERING 5

Story & Illustration by: Yasuki Tanaka

English Edition
Translation: Jocelyne Allen
Additional Translation: Megumi Cummings & Anna Kawashima
Lettering: Janice Leung
Sound Effects & Touch Up: Phil Christie & Jeannie Lee
Copy Editor: Claudia McGivney
Associate Editor: M. Chandler
Graphic & Cover Design: W.T. Francis

UDON Staff
Chief of Operations: Erik Ko
Director of Publishing: Matt Moylan
VP of Business Development: Cory Casoni
Director of Marketing: Megan Maiden
Japanese Liaisons: Steven Cummings & Anna Kawashima

First published in Japan in 2017 by SHUEISHA Inc., Tokyo.
English translation rights arranged by SHUEISHA Inc.
through Tohan Corporation, Tokyo.

This volume contains contents originally published in サマータイムレンダ 9, 10, 11

English language version published by UDON Entertainment Inc.
118 Tower Hill Road, C1, PO Box 20008
RIchmond Hill, Ontario, L4K 0K0, Canada

www.UDONentertainment.com

First printing: July 2022
Hard Cover ISBN: 978-1-772942-42-2
Paperback ISBN: 978-1-772942-36-1

Printed in Canada